Languages in the World

Languages in the World

How History, Culture, and Politics
Shape Language

Julie Tetel Andresen
Phillip M. Carter

WILEY Blackwell

This edition first published 2016
© 2016 John Wiley & Sons, Inc.

Registered Office
John Wiley & Sons Ltd, The Atrium, Southern Gate, Chichester, West Sussex, PO19 8SQ, UK

Editorial Offices
350 Main Street, Malden, MA 02148-5020, USA
9600 Garsington Road, Oxford, OX4 2DQ, UK
The Atrium, Southern Gate, Chichester, West Sussex, PO19 8SQ, UK

For details of our global editorial offices, for customer services, and for information about how to apply for permission to reuse the copyright material in this book please see our website at www.wiley.com/wiley-blackwell.

The right of Julie Tetel Andresen and Phillip M. Carter to be identified as the authors of this work has been asserted in accordance with the UK Copyright, Designs and Patents Act 1988. Claudia Fulshaw Design provided the timelines for Chapters 1, 3, 4, 5, 6, 7, 8, 9, and 10.

Library of Congress Cataloging-in-Publication Data

Andresen, Julie Tetel, 1950– author.
  Languages in the world : how history, culture, and politics shape language / Julie Tetel Andresen and Phillip M. Carter.
    pages cm
  Includes bibliographical references and index.
    ISBN 978-1-118-53125-9 (cloth) – ISBN 978-1-118-53128-0 (pbk.)   1. Language and languages–Globalization.   2. Language and culture–History.   3. Languages in contact.   4. Historical linguistics.   5. Sociolinguistics.   I. Carter, Phillip M. author.   II. Title.
    P130.5.A53 2016
    306.44–dc23
                                                                                            2015019352

A catalogue record for this book is available from the British Library.

Set in 10/12.5pt Galliard by Aptara Inc., New Delhi, India

1   2016

Contents

Map 0.1 World map with language families   xi

Figure 0.1 IPA consonants   xii

Figure 0.2 IPA vowels   xii

About the Website   xiii

List of Maps and Figures   xv

Preface   xvii

Part I   Linguistic Preliminaries: Approach and Theory
Introductory Note: On Language   1

1   All Languages Were Once Spanglish   3
    The Mexican State of Coahuila y Tejas   3
    What Is Language?   4
    How Many Languages Are There?   6
    How and When Did Language Get Started?   9
    The Structure of Spanglish   13
    Final Note: The Encounter of Spanish and English on Television in the
        United States   17
    Exercises   18
    Discussion Questions   20
    Notes   20
    References   21
    Further Reading   21

2   The Language Loop   22
    The Australian Walkabout   22
    Introducing the Language Loop   23
    Language and Cognition   26
    Language, the World, and Culture   28
    Language and Linguistic Structure   31

Language, Discourse, and Ideology 32
On Major and Minor Languages 33
Final Note: The Contingencies of Time, Place, and Biology 35
Exercises 37
Discussion Questions 37
Notes 38
References 38
Further Reading 39

3 Linguistics and Classification 40
The Role of Sanskrit in Philology 40
Of Linguistics, Philology, Linguists, and Grammarians 42
Genetic Classification 46
Areal Classification 48
Typological Classification 51
Functional Classification 55
Final Note: The Role of Sanskrit in India Today 57
Exercises 58
Discussion Questions 59
Notes 60
References 60
Further Reading 61

Part II Effects of Power
Introductory Note: On Power 63

4 Effects of the Nation-State and the Possibility of Kurdistan 65
Lines Are Drawn in the Sand 65
The Status of Language on the Eve of the Nation-State 66
The Epistemology of the Nation-State 69
The French Revolution, German Romanticism, and Print Capitalism 71
Standardization and the Instilling of *Vergonha* 75
Language and Individual Identity 76
What's Race Got to Do with It? 78
The Problematic Race–Nation–Language Triad 79
Final Note: The Kurds Today – Different Places, Different Outcomes 84
Language Profile: Kurdî / کوردی [Kurdish (Indo-European)] 85
Exercises 90
Discussion Questions 91
Notes 91
References 92
Further Reading 93

5 The Development of Writing in the Litmus of Religion and Politics 94
The Story of the Qur'ān 94
Magico-Religious Interpretations of the Origins of Writing 95
Steps Toward the Representation of Speech 97
Types of Writing Systems 100
Religion and the Spread of Writing Systems 105

The Always Already Intervention of Politics 108
Orality and Literacy 111
Final Note: Azerbaijan Achieves Alphabetic Autonomy 114
Language Profile: ﺔ ﻳﺑ ﺮﻋ ﻟا [Arabic (Afro-Asiatic)] 114
Exercises 119
Discussion Questions 122
Notes 123
References 124
Further Reading 124

6 Language Planning and Language Law: Shaping the Right to Speak 125
Melting Snow and Protests at the Top of the World 125
Language Academies: The First Enforcers 127
Another Look at Prescriptivism 129
Making Language Official: A Tale of Three Patterns 131
Language Policy and Education: A Similar Tale of Three Patterns 139
Language Planners and Language Police 144
Final Note: Choosing Death or Life 146
Language Profile: རྡ་ྐྐ [Tibetan (Sino-Tibetan)] 147
Exercises 152
Discussion Questions 153
Notes 154
References 155
Further Reading 156

Part III   Effects of Movement
Introductory Note: On Movement 159

7 A Mobile History: Mapping Language Stocks and Families 161
Austronesian Origin Stories 161
Population Genetics and Links to Language 162
A Possible Polynesian Reconstruction 166
Linguistic Reconstructions Revisited 168
Proto-Indo-European and Its Homeland 173
Other Language Stocks and Their Homelands 176
Models of Spread 183
Lost Tracks 186
Final Note: On Density and Diversity 187
Language Profile: 'Olelo Hawai'i [Hawaiian (Austronesian)] 187
Exercises 194
Discussion Questions 195
Notes 195
References 196
Further Reading 197

8 Colonial Consequences: Language Stocks and Families Remapped 198
Eiffel Towers in Vietnam 198
Time-Depths and Terminology 199
The Middle Kingdom: Government-Encouraged Migrations 201

Linguistic Geography: Residual Zones and Spread Zones   203
Spreading Eurasian Empires: The Persians, Mongols, Slavs, and Romans 206
Religions as First Nations and Missionaries as Colonizers   213
English as an Emergent Language Family   215
Final Note: Creoles and the Case of Kreyòl Ayisyen   218
Language Profile: Tiéng Việt [Vietnamese (Austro-Asiatic)]   219
Exercises   223
Discussion Questions   226
Notes   226
References   228
Further Reading   229

9   Postcolonial Complications: Violent Outcomes   230
Tamil Tigers Create New Terrorist Techniques   230
What's in a Name? Burma/Myanmar   232
Modern Sudan: The Clash of Two Colonialisms   235
The Caucasian Quasi-States: Two Types of Conflict   238
Poland's Shifting Borders   242
Terrorism on the Iberian Peninsula: Basque and the ETA   244
Québécois Consciousness and the Turbulent 1960s   245
The Zapatista Uprising and Indigenous Languages in Chiapas   247
Final Note: The Parsley Massacre in the Dominican Republic   249
Language Profile: Tamil (Dravidian)   250
Exercises   254
Discussion Questions   255
Notes   256
References   257
Further Reading   257

Part IV   Effects of Time
Introductory Note: On Time   259

10 The Remote Past: Language Becomes Embodied   261
Look There!   261
Seeking Linguistic Bedrock   262
The Primate Body and Human Adaptations to Language   263
Evolution in Four Dimensions   269
The Genetic Story   270
Grammatical Categories and Deep-Time Linguistics   275
Complexity and the Arrow of Time   279
Final Note: The Last Stone Age Man in North America   282
Language Profile: !Xóõ [Taa (Khoisan)]   283
Exercises   288
Discussion Questions   288
Notes   289
References   290
Further Reading   291

11 The Recorded Past: 'Catching Up to Conditions' Made Visible 292
    Mongolian Horses 292
    Chapter 3: The Invariable Word in English 294
    Chapter 4: The Shift to Head-Marking in French 295
    Chapter 5: Writing and e-Arabic 299
    Chapter 6: Mongolian Cases 301
    Chapter 7: Reformulating Hawaiian Identity 304
    Chapter 8: Varieties of Chinese – Yesterday and Today 306
    Chapter 9: Juba Arabic Pidgin, Nubi, and Other African Creoles 310
    Final Note: Language Change in Progress 313
    Language Profile: монгол хэл [Mongolian (Mongolic)] 315
    Exercises 320
    Discussion Questions 321
    Notes 322
    References 323
    Further Reading 323

12 The Imagined Future: Globalization and the Fate
    of Endangered Languages 324
    Gold in the Mayan Highlands 324
    Beyond the Nation-State: The Globalized New Economy 325
    Money Talks: What Language Does It Speak? 327
    When the Language Loop Unravels 329
    Language Hotspots 332
    Rethinking Endangerment 334
    Technology to the Rescue 336
    Anishinaabemowin Revitalization in Wisconsin 339
    What Is Choice? 341
    Final Note: Our Advocacies 342
    Language Profile: K'iche' [Quiché (Mayan)] 342
    Exercises 347
    Discussion Questions 349
    Notes 350
    References 350

Glossary 353

Subject Index 359

Language Index 373

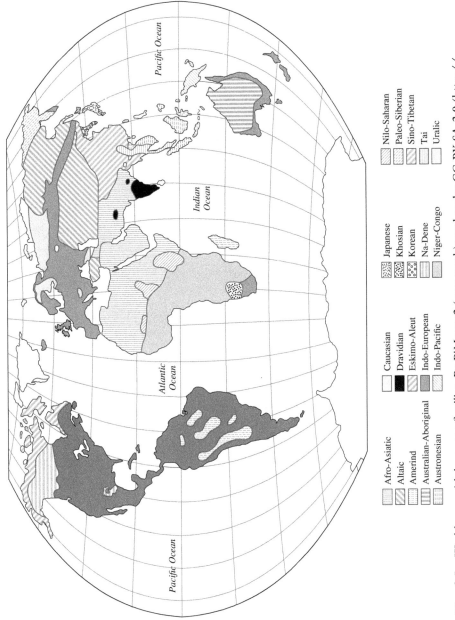

Map 0.1 World map with language families. By PiMaster3 (own work) used under CC-BY-SA-3.0 (http://creativecommons.org/licenses/by-sa/3.0/), via Wikimedia Commons.

Afro-Asiatic	Caucasian	Japanese	Nilo-Saharan
Altaic	Dravidian	Khosian	Paleo-Siberian
Amerind	Eskimo-Aleut	Korean	Sino-Tibetan
Australian-Aboriginal	Indo-European	Na-Dene	Tai
Austronesian	Indo-Pacific	Niger-Congo	Uralic

Pacific Ocean

Indian Ocean

Atlantic Ocean

Pacific Ocean

THE INTERNATIONAL PHONETIC ALPHABET (revised to 2005)

CONSONANTS (PULMONIC)

	Bilabial	Labiodental	Dental	Alveolar	Postalveolar	Retroflex	Palatal	Velar	Uvular	Pharyngeal	Glottal
Plosive	p b			t d		ʈ ɖ	c ɟ	k ɡ	q ɢ		ʔ
Nasal	m	ɱ		n		ɳ	ɲ	ŋ	N		
Trill	ʙ			r					R		
Tap or Flap		ⱱ		ɾ		ɽ					
Fricative	ɸ β	f v	θ ð	s z	ʃ ʒ	ʂ ʐ	ç ʝ	x ɣ	χ ʁ	ħ ʕ	h ɦ
Lateral fricative				ɬ ɮ							
Approximant		ʋ		ɹ		ɻ	j	ɰ			
Lateral approximant				l		ɭ	ʎ	ʟ			

Where symbols appear in pairs, the one to the right represents a voiced consonant. Shaded areas denote articulations judged impossible.

Figure 0.1 IPA consonants.

VOWELS

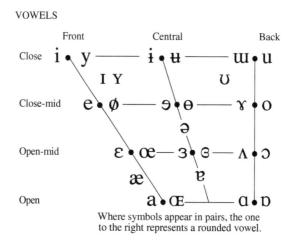

Where symbols appear in pairs, the one
to the right represents a rounded vowel.

Figure 0.2 IPA vowels.

About the Website

Please visit the companion website at www.wiley.com/go/languagesintheworld to view additional content for this title.

- Short follow-up blurbs on one topic from each chapter
- Engaging links and images

List of Maps and Figures

Maps

Map 0.1   World map with language families.   xi
Map 1.1   Map of the states and territories of Mexico as they were from
          November 24, 1824 to 1830.   5
Map 3.1   Early distribution of the Indo-European linguistic groups.   47
Map 4.1   The Middle East before and after World War I settlements,
          1914–1922.   67
Map 5.1   Arabic-speaking countries.   115
Map 6.1   Map of Tibet and China.   126
Map 7.1   Austronesian languages.   169
Map 9.1   Languages of South Asia.   233
Map 10.1 Expansion of human species.   275
Map 11.1 The later Mongol conquests at their greatest extent: 1270.   293
Map 12.1 Native languages of Mesoamerica, approximate distributions at
          European contact, circa 1500.   332

Figures

Figure 0.1   IPA consonants.   xii
Figure 0.2   IPA vowels.   xii
Figure 2.1   Underlying elements in the three frames of reference.   27
Figure 5.1   Genealogy of alphabets.   122
Figure 7.1   The gene.   163
Figure 7.2   Tree model image.   184
Figure 7.3   Wave model image.   185
Figure 10.1 The brain.   264

Preface

To Our Readers

This book began with a simple phone call. In the Fall Semester of 2010, Julie was in Durham, North Carolina, where she is a Professor of Linguistics and Cultural Anthropology at Duke University. Phillip was living in Los Angeles, where he was a Postdoctoral Fellow in the Linguistics Department at the University of Southern California. We were on the phone to speak about the pleasures and challenges of teaching a course called Languages of the World. We found ourselves in familiar conversational territory: lamenting the lack of materials for teaching the course in the interdisciplinary approach developed at Duke. "Well," Phillip said, "we could write our own book." Julie laughed, imagining the amount of work required to pull together a project of the magnitude necessary to capture the dynamics of the pedagogical approach she had helped to create. But the seed had been planted. Only one question remained: Could we do it?

Beginning in the mid-1990s, Julie had been teaching Languages of the World taught at Duke, which was pioneered by Professor Edna Andrews in the Department of Slavic and Eurasian Studies. They wanted their students to have a broad understanding of language. Thus, they balanced the traditional content of such a course – review of the language families of the world, emphasis on linguistic structures, historical reconstruction – with the many rich nonlinguistic contexts in which languages are actually used. So, as students learned about the case and aspectual systems of Russian, for example, they also learned about the history of the Slavic language family, Cyrillic writing, Russian folk songs, and more. This approach required a great deal of work on the part of the instructor, since no materials systematically crossing linguistic structural information with historical, sociocultural, and political contexts existed in one place.

Over time, the course became a resounding success with students, not only among Linguistics Majors, for whom it is a core course requirement, but also with students from across the Arts and Sciences and even Engineering. The students came for what they heard would be a perspective-shifting and challenging experience. In retrospect, it is easy to understand why this course was so compelling to so many of our students.

Our approach does not abstract language away from speakers, but rather situates it around them. It does not abandon experience and affect but makes space to acknowledge that experience and affect are fundamental to understanding why speakers make the choices they make about language. Simply put, students found themselves in the conversations the course made possible.

Once committed to writing our own materials Julie and Phillip agreed to meet in New York City in the Fall Semester 2011 when Julie was teaching the Duke in New York Arts and Media program. We went to work on a book proposal. The next summer, we found ourselves in a part of the world inspiring to both of us: Eastern Europe, with Julie in Romania and Phillip in Poland. We began to outline the book in Krakow, Poland where Phillip was attending Polish Language School, and we began writing the manuscript in Ukraine on a long train ride from Kiev to L'viv. Our research and writing continued nonstop for the next two and a half years, and our project went where we went: Bucharest, Romania; Durham, North Carolina; Los Angeles; Miami; Madrid, Spain; New York City; Saigon, Vietnam; Ulan Baatar, Mongolia.

During these years of writing, we have endeavored to stretch intellectually as far beyond our own experiences as possible. Nevertheless, our personal experiences are clearly reflected in the pages of our book. The most obvious example is that we have written about the languages we know and have studied, which include English, French, German, Mongolian, Polish, Portuguese, Romanian, Spanish, Swahili, and Vietnamese. In addition to being professional linguists, we are committed to language learning, and our knowledge of other languages has given us wide canvases to paint on. For instance, the Language Profiles on Vietnamese in Chapter 8 and Mongolian in Chapter 11 are the direct result of Julie's experience living and studying in Vietnam and Mongolia during the writing of this book.

We are also committed to interdisciplinarity, and our approach to linguistics is informed by a range of disciplines, all of which figure in *Languages in the World*: anthropology and anthropological linguistics, evolutionary theory, historical linguistics, history and philosophy of linguistics, genetics, language variation and change, poststructuralist approaches to critical theory, race and gender studies, and sociolinguistics. Our interdisciplinary commitment is reflected in our diverse intellectual interlocutors. Though you will not find explicit reference to all of the following names in our book, ripples of their thinking are nevertheless evident in our writing: anthropologist Stuart Hall; general scientists Jared Diamond, Charles Darwin, Francisco Varela, William James, and Humberto Maturana; historian Benedict Anderson; linguists (dialectologists, historical linguists, sociolinguists, and psycholinguists) Norman Faircloth, Charles Ferguson, Joshua Fishman, Joseph Greenberg, Jacob Grimm, Roman Jakobson, William Labov, Stephen Levinson, Johanna Nichols, Michael Silverstein, Michael Tomasello, Uriel and Max Weinreich, Walt Wolfram, and William Dwight Whitney; philosophers Judith Butler, Michel Foucault, Antonio Gramsci, Julia Kristéva, and Giyathri Spivak; and sociologists Pierre Bourdieu and Irving Goffman. All of these researchers share a general commitment to understanding the context, *the situatedness*, of humans in their psychosocial and sociopolitical worlds. In an effort to unburden our readers from excessive citations, we have tried to minimize references to these scholars throughout the book and acknowledge our debt to them here.

The familiar questions of a book addressing languages of the world are: What are the language families of the world? and What are the major structural characteristics of the languages in those families? These are, indeed, significant questions. We, too, want to address them here, and we also ask two more questions: Why does the current map of the languages of the world look the way it does? and How did it get to be that way? In order to answer these further questions, we need not only to broaden our perspective but also to create a new organizational framework. First, we acknowledge that the linguistic world goes around on the day-to-day interactions between individuals. Second, we see that the answers to the additional questions we are asking require our approach to focus less on the microdynamics of individual interactions and more on macroconcerns organized by the topics of power, movement, and time. Our extralinguistic attention in this book is thus given to political struggles, population movements both large and small, the spread of religious beliefs, and the ever-present effects of economics.

By organizing our presentation around the topics of power, movement, and time, we are able:

(i)   to put different languages in contact in order to compare and contrast linguistic structures as we go;
(ii)   to offer global reviews on subjects, whether it is the shift of writing systems when a new religion is introduced, the parade of official languages named in the last several hundred years, or the identification of the theorized homelands for the various language stocks;
(iii)   to think critically about language planning and language policy around the world;
(iv)   to acknowledge the importance of language attitudes in shaping language behavior and to factor those attitudes into the stories we tell;
(v)   to introduce the notions of linguistic residual zones and spread zones to help explain why the linguistic map of the world today looks the way it does;
(vi)   to include discussions of basic genetics and evolution in our account of the languages of the world; and
(vii)   to put at issue the very subject we are studying, namely language.

We have written this book with several audiences in mind. To undergraduate linguistics majors and minors, we intend for this book to complement the information presented in your introductory course, where you learned disciplinary metalanguage and reviewed the subdisciplines of linguistics. To undergraduate majors in other social sciences, we want to invite you into the world of language. To graduate students in linguistics who might not have always considered the historical and sociopolitical dynamics of language on a world scale, we hope the information provided here will be new and perhaps eye-opening, just as we hope it will be to graduate students in other disciplines who might not have always been aware of the importance of language in the areas they study. To professional linguists using this book as a teaching resource, we have worked to make a framework generous enough so that you can enrich our chapter discussions and end-of-chapter exercises with your specialties. To professional linguists using this book as a reference, we have endeavored to provide the widest and most diverse archive possible and hope that you find our approach promising. To general readers, we hope to have answered your burning questions about human language. To all of our readers, we have tried to make this sprawling story of the languages of the world as lively as possible.

We acknowledge from the outset that our book will be challenging to many readers in many ways. First, our historical scope is large and extends back at times several hundred thousand years. We have also chosen to tell our story in a nonlinear fashion beginning in the present. To help you manage the weight of this history, we have put a timeline at the beginning of most of our chapters. The part of the timeline with the dates and events in black type is to situate you in the historical time frame that is the main focus of the chapter. The dates and events presented in gray-scale provide relevant background information.

Second, the sheer scope of our subject matter is immense. In order to make sure readers have an in-depth understanding of the kinds of linguistic structure found in traditional Languages of the World textbooks, we offer phonetic, phonological, and grammatical information in every chapter of *Languages in the World*. However, we appreciate that this information will not be enough for all readers to understand how structural phenomena work together. We have therefore also included Language Profiles at the end of Chapters 4–12. The eight languages portrayed are, in order: Kurdish, Arabic, Tibetan, Hawaiian, Vietnamese, Tamil, !Xóõ, Mongolian, and K'iche'. The languages featured in these profiles are furthermore the subjects of the opening stories of their respective chapters, and they often serve as the basis of the chapter's exercises. We hope to make our profiles attractive enough so that readers may be prompted to learn one of these languages or another language in the same family or stock.

We have also included exercises and discussion questions at the end of every chapter. The exercises give hands-on experience with maps, writing systems, linguistic structure, and linguistic methodology. The questions raise language-related issues many people in the world today confront – individual identity, shame, multilingual communities, language rights, language death – and we invite you to consider your own experiences and thoughts with respect to them. There are no right or wrong answers. Our concern is for you to have the occasion to grapple with language questions and conundrums affecting many lives, communities, nations, and beyond.

We hope that all of our readers will be inspired to engage with whatever language issues, however large however small, you confront in the future. In order to help you prepare for that future, we acknowledge the following points to be both true and pertinent:

(i)   we are living in a globalized world;
(ii) the composition of student bodies at both large, public universities and small, private ones reflects this globalization, not only in North America but also in the rest of the world;
(iii) human beings around the world tend to be multilingual; multilingualism is the norm; most people interact with more than one language and/or one speech variety during the course of their lives, and many do so on a daily basis;

(iv) monolingualism is the exception; monolinguals tend to be either speakers of a prestige variety or people in isolated communities; and

(v) the presence of variety does not translate into a hierarchy, where one variant is better or worse than another.

We want to stress at the start of this book that language is not a zero-sum game. Giving room to one language need not take away from another.

In the four years that we have been researching and writing this book, we have profited from many fruitful discussions with friends and colleagues. A small selection of these include: Edna Andrews, Melissa Baralt, Dominika Baran, Tometro Hopkins, Anne Charity-Hudley, Małgorzata Hueckel, Andrew Lynch, Ana Luszczynska, Kim Potowski, Gareth Price, Christine Mallinson, Norma Mendoza-Denton, David Neal, Heather Russell, Ana Sánchez-Muñoz, Kristine Stiles, Ellen Thompson, Priscilla Wald, and Walt Wolfram. We thank them collectively. We are grateful to Margaret Noodin, for providing the poem and narrative in Chapter 12, and to Lydda López, for working on our glossary, bibliography, and language index. We would also like to thank the students in Julie's Mind and Language Focus course at Duke as well as the students in Phillip's Languages and Cultures of the World course at Florida International University for having read the manuscript of *Languages in the World* in the Fall Semester 2014. They were the first student readers of our book, and we are grateful for their impressions, engagement, and feedback. We also thank Danielle Descoteaux at Wiley Blackwell for having so enthusiastically taken on our project and shepherded it through the complex editorial process.

Finally, we would like to remark that we have learned a great deal in writing this book: about the shape of specific languages, about the histories and political dynamics of particular parts of the world, and about the ways in which languages expand and contract over great spaces and great periods of time, to name only a few. However, of all the topics we have confronted in writing this book, one has affected us more than all the rest: the rapidly accelerating loss of the cultures and languages of the world. As professional linguists, we were of course always aware of the problem of language death, but in researching this book, we have come to understand the problem as urgent and entailing devastating consequences. We are so moved by the problem of language endangerment that we here pledge to donate our royalties from the first printing of *Languages in the World* to The Endangered Language Fund.

Part I
Linguistic Preliminaries
Approach and Theory

Introductory Note: On Language

Language is the water humans swim in from the age of five months' gestation, when hearing typically develops in the womb, to the day of death. We are surrounded by, and surround ourselves with, language at nearly every waking moment of our lives and even some nonwaking moments, such as when we dream or talk in our sleep. Only those put in solitary confinement, which is considered punishment, or those who take a vow of silence, such as Trappist monks, are cut off from the normal dynamics of language (but even these monks have developed a form of sign language, and they continue to read). There are also cases of severely handicapped infants who are never able to fully enter the human linguistic world. The rest of the 99.99% of us – that makes seven billion worldwide and counting – are in the never-ceasing flow of language and contributing our parts to the currents.

Because language is as natural as breathing in and out, we tend to take it for granted as we go about our daily business. The goal of *Languages in the World* is to bring the usually invisible workings of language to your attention through a global survey of some of the historical, cultural, and sociopolitical factors that shape language and language behavior. Our account is informed by two very basic observations. The first one is: language is always catching up to conditions. In Chapter 1, we outline some of the historical, cultural, and sociopolitical factors that have brought the particular language variety Spanglish into existence, and we discuss the ways that speakers have woven together the structures of their dual linguistic inheritance of Spanish and English to form a now-emergent language. The story of Spanglish illustrates the way that language is always catching up to the conditions of the movements and interactions of people going about their business.

Languages in the World: How History, Culture, and Politics Shape Language, First Edition.
Julie Tetel Andresen and Phillip M. Carter.
© 2016 John Wiley & Sons, Inc. Published 2016 by John Wiley & Sons, Inc.

The second basic observation guiding the stories we tell in *Languages in the World* is this: speakers' brains are always embodied, and speakers' bodies are always embedded in contexts. In Chapter 2, we introduce you to what we are calling *the language loop* and show how language loops in several directions at once: language links speakers to their fellows' cognitive domains, to their ambient landscapes, and to their cultures as a whole. Language is perspective taking, and particular languages reliably pull their speakers' attentions toward certain psychological understandings, views of the landscape, and social relations, while other languages make other distinctions in these same categories. Importantly, these perspectives are always bound to behaviors.

Chapters 1 and 2 introduce you to some general linguistic terminology, although terminology as such is not the main focus of either of those chapters. In Chapter 3, by way of contrast, a fuller discussion of linguistic terminology is the main event, and our purpose is to review the four main ways linguists have come to categorize the languages of the world. This comparative/contrastive process has led to a rich understanding of languages and their structures. It is in this context of the study of linguistic structure that we place our wider investigation into the historical, cultural, and sociopolitical conditions that have shaped languages since the beginning of the time we can say that language has existed as such.

1

All Languages Were Once Spanglish

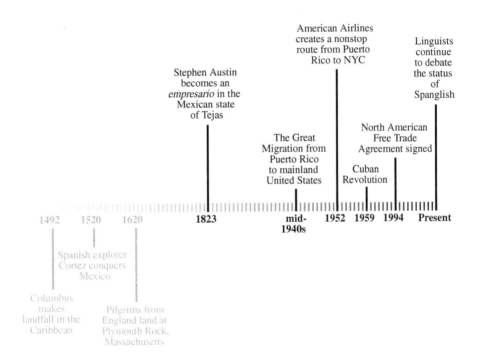

The Mexican State of Coahuila y Tejas

In 1821, Mexico won its independence from Spain and came into control of territory that extended not only over present-day Mexico but also over present-day Central America, as well as large parts of present-day southwest United States. The new

Languages in the World: How History, Culture, and Politics Shape Language, First Edition.
Julie Tetel Andresen and Phillip M. Carter.
© 2016 John Wiley & Sons, Inc. Published 2016 by John Wiley & Sons, Inc.

Mexican government continued the Spanish practice of issuing land grants to stimulate settlement and to consolidate and control the native population.[1] After independence, two rather poor and sparsely populated states, Coahuila and Tejas, were joined together. Since Tejas was the more thinly settled of the two and subject to frequent attacks by Apache and Comanche tribes, the governors of the newly combined state were looking to boost the population there in hopes that incoming settlers could control the Indian raids. The government enacted a system that allowed agents, known as *empresarios*, to promote settlement.

In 1823, the Mexican state of Coahuila y Tejas granted a contract to Stephen Austin, an Anglo farmer, to become one of the *empresarios*, and he brought 300 families to his settlement a few years later. Increasing numbers of Anglos in search of cheap land in the wake of the first depression in the United States eventually led the Mexican government to limit immigration. However, shifts in political sentiments had already begun. In 1836, after many battles with Mexico, Tejas became the independent Republic of Texas, while Coahuila remained part of Mexico. Nine years later, when Texas joined the United States, it brought into the union an English-speaking majority and a significant number of Spanish-speaking *mestizos* who had lived in that territory for several hundred years. The border between Texas and Coahuila thus marks the place where the two main European populations to colonize North and South America drew their definitive political lines (see Map 1.1).[2]

The Tex-Mex border is also the place where English and Spanish met head on and started mixing, like the roiling waters of two oceans encountering one another. Now, 200 years later, the desire of English-speaking American farmers for cheaper land and an immigration law enacted by Spanish-speaking Mexican legislators have produced a *linguistic* result. We may call this result Spanglish, and it is a specific and yet inevitable consequence of how the members of a bilingual community have reformed the grammatical pieces of their dual linguistic inheritance. In order to justify the claim that all languages were once Spanglish, we need first to define language and then to provide an account of the conditions through which languages arise.

What Is Language?

The usual answers to the question go something like this: "Language is a means by which humans communicate their thoughts and feelings through speech, although there are purely gestural languages, such as American Sign Language (ASL) used in the Deaf community." Or: "Language is used to refer to things in the world. The word *book* refers to a particular kind of object." The first description highlights one aspect of language, namely that it is primarily a human activity and primarily a spoken one, which seems apt enough to capture the fact that most humans around the world have tended to spend large parts of their day conducting their business, catching up on gossip, discussing politics, telling stories, flirting, fighting, and making up. The emphasis on the spoken mode is traditional but now somewhat misplaced. Most humans in nonrural parts of the world spend large parts of their day on their phones, surfing and texting. The second description is also useful as a first pass because we do often communicate about objects in our world.

Map 1.1   Map of the states and territories of Mexico as they were from November 24, 1824 to 1830. Source: Golbez [GFDL (http://www.gnu.org/copyleft/fdl.html)], CC-BY-SA-3.0 (http://creativecommons.org/licenses/by-sa/3.0/), via Wikimedia Commons.

In *Languages in the World: How History, Culture, and Politics Shape Language* (hereafter *Languages in the World*), we want to nudge the understanding of language in a direction that will at first feel unfamiliar. Language, as we define it, is an *orienting behavior* that orients the orientee within his or her cognitive-social domain and that arises in **phylogeny**[3] (history of the species) and **ontogeny** (individual development) through recurrent interactions with conspecifics. In plainer terms, we can say that when we speak, we are affecting, influencing, even manipulating – not to shy away from a suspicious-sounding word here – the interest and attention of agents who are similar to ourselves, who belong to our phylogenic **lineage**, that is, who are our fellow human beings. These fellow human beings are also likely to be ones who belong to our particular language group. It is also the case that through our recurrent interactions with our fellow human beings in our particular language groups, we also create ourselves, our identities.

Two points are to be highlighted here. First, one person can only influence the cognitive domain – the thoughts and the coordinated actions – of another to the extent that they share a similar enough history. However, the orienting will never be the same for both parties, because one cannot literally transfer one's thoughts and feelings to another's head. However, with similar enough histories of interactions, the parties will be able to coordinate themselves reliably around a set of signals, be they acoustic (as in speech), gestural (as in sign language), or written (as in texting). The ability to reliably coordinate others and, in turn, be reliably coordinated by others is usually what is taken to mean to be able to speak a particular language.

Second, although language is old enough in the species to be woven into the human genome, the particular ways different communities reliably orient their fellow members and thereby coordinate their activities will necessarily vary. This is because individual groups – communities, societies, cultures – are historical products with their own trajectories. Of course, different groups can and do interact with one another, such as English speakers and Spanish speakers over hundreds of years in Texas, and when they do, they create new trajectories for the ways they orient one another and coordinate their actions. One of these trajectories may be a new language.

How Many Languages Are There?

Another way to approach the question *What is language?* is to ask another: How many languages are there? This question gives us leverage into understanding the way we will be using the term in this book, because it reveals the complexities that the term *language* obscures when used to refer to a seemingly well-known entity such as the English language. Given these complexities, linguists estimate the number of languages in the world today to be somewhere between 4000 and 8000. They often settle on a number between 5000 and 7000. Certainly, there are practical problems in getting an accurate count. The inventory of the languages of the world is necessarily incomplete because linguists are aware of the phenomenon of so-called hidden languages. These are languages spoken, say, in the Amazon or in the highlands of Papua New Guinea, which are obviously known to their speakers but not yet known to linguists, and new languages are somewhat regularly brought to linguists' attention. At the same time, other languages are on the point of extinction. The Celtic language Breton spoken in Brittany, France is only one of many endangered languages in the world today. It is difficult to know whether or not to continue to count it.

While the practical problems do complicate matters, the bulk of the indeterminacy stems from the fact that there are two different, equally valid criteria for determining where one language ends and another begins. Unfortunately, their results do not always coincide and are even sometimes contradictory. The two criteria are:

Criterion no. 1: Mutual Intelligibility. If the term *language* is understood from the point of view of individuals interacting with one another, then the ability of speakers to understand one another should serve as a reliable guide for distinguishing a language from a dialect or, as linguists now prefer to say, language **variety**. The preference among linguists for the term *variety* stems from the fact that the term *dialect* sometimes carries the implication among speakers of a language that a nonstandard variety, that is, a dialect, is inferior. This being said, if speakers of two related speech varieties are able to understand one another, their speech counts as varieties of one language, not as two separate languages. If the two speech varieties are mutually unintelligible, they count as separate languages.

The criterion of mutual intelligibility is notoriously difficult to apply, because it is a scalar notion, a matter of degree. The fuzziness of the criterion is compounded by the fact that it is affected by the amount of contact individuals in the speech varieties have with one another and by the desire of those individuals to understand one another. The phenomenon of **dialect chains** does not make applying the criterion any easier. A dialect chain of A-B-C-D occurs when varieties A and B are mutually intelligible, B and C are mutually intelligible, C and D are mutually intelligible, B and D get along with difficulty, and A and D are incomprehensible. Such a chain extends across hundreds of aboriginal varieties in Australia. Europe alone has several such chains, including the continua of: German, Dutch, and Flemish; the rural varieties of Portuguese, Spanish, Catalan, French, and Italian; as well as Slovak, Czech, Ukrainian, Polish, and Russian.

Criterion no. 2: Group Identity. If the term *language* is understood from the point of view of groups in the context of their social lives, then a language is a language when the group says it is a language. Thus, Swedish, Danish, and Norwegian are respected as separate languages, although there is a potentially high degree of mutual intelligibility among them, as is the case for Czech and Slovak, Dutch and Flemish, Hindi and Urdu, Laotian and Thai, Serbian and Croatian. In other words, groups recognize political and cultural factors in distinguishing themselves from other groups. Taking the political point of view, a language can be seen as a dialect with an army and a navy.[4]

Distinguishing cultural factors may include visible differences, such as different writing systems, which help to confer a separate language status for otherwise mutually intelligible varieties: Hindi is written in the Devanāgari script, while Urdu is written in the Perso-Arabic alphabet; Serbian is written in the Cyrillic alphabet, and Croatian in the Latin alphabet. The use of different scripts often has religious implications and may also line up with geopolitical boundaries. The reverse is also true: mutually unintelligible varieties can be considered as one language. Such is the case for Chinese, which is a cover term for a number of mutually unintelligible speech varieties, where Mandarin, Cantonese, and Taiwanese are among the best known. Nevertheless, it makes political and cultural sense to use the term *Chinese* in certain situations, and the logographic writing system is a powerful unifying factor that can be read by all literate Chinese, independent of their speech variety.

There is yet another factor complicating the matter of determining how many languages there are in the world today, and it is the reverse of the problem of how to count languages that are dying off. It is the problem of how to count languages coming into existence. People from different linguistic backgrounds have always been in contact with one another, and the effects of these contact situations can be found in every language of the world, most often in the form of borrowings. The most obvious kinds of borrowings are lexical. Monolingual speakers of English in the United States are likely to know many words borrowed from Spanish such as *amigo* and *sombrero*, familiar phrases such as *hasta la vista* and *yo quiero*,[5] and even the date *cinco de mayo*.[6] Reciprocally, many varieties of Spanish in the Americas exhibit the influence of English borrowings. The recent use of *man* as a term of address in Colombian Spanish is but one example among many.

Another, more elaborated kind of language mixing is found in bilingual situations all over the world, and it is called *code switching*. Code switching can be defined as the use of two or more languages in the same discourse or the alternation of two languages within a single discourse, sentence, or constituent. There does not seem to be any restriction on the languages mixed, be they Moroccan Arabic and French, Tamil and English, Turkish and Dutch, or Quechua and Spanish. The mixing reflects an individual's and a community's experiences with the languages available to them. It is surely the case that two or more languages meet in the interactions of the community in the marketplace, so to speak. However, it is also the case that languages meet in the cognitive domain of the individual. Sometimes, the two languages will mingle and blend, especially when in the presence of another person who also knows those two languages. Sometimes, the two languages will activate a sense of contrast, such that the speaker feels that he or she has slightly or strongly differing personalities, depending on the language being used and the situation it is used in. Note that we are using the term *cognitive domain* to refer to the joining of the mental (thoughts, feelings) and the physical (actions), because the mental and the physical are in continuous feedback. We are using the term *personality* to refer to a characteristic way of behaving in given circumstances.

Code switching occurs in communities of bilingual individuals who move smoothly and often between languages, thereby interweaving two (or more) languages. A couple, one a native French speaker and the other a native English speaker, both fluent in both languages, may develop their own Franglais. If large numbers of English speakers move into a Spanish-speaking territory or vice versa, the interwoven language may become the norm in a certain place. A speech norm qualifies for the status of a language if it meets one of the two criteria described above. In the case of speech norms in, say, certain Puerto Rican communities in New York City, people who are monolingual either in English or in Spanish would have difficulty understanding a sentence such as: "Why make Carol *sentarse atrás pa'que* (sit in the back so) everybody has to move *pa'que se salga* (for her to get out)?"[7] This form of speech would qualify as a language in that it satisfies criterion no. 1, since it is not mutually intelligible either to English or to Spanish monolinguals. (Presumably bilingual English/Spanish individuals would have no difficulty picking up the speech norms in whatever English/Spanish community they found themselves in.) At some point, these bilingual individuals might be moved to invoke criterion no. 2 and to recognize their variety as something better than just a hodgepodge that is neither so-called good English nor so-called good Spanish. They might decide to give it a name and call it Spanglish. They might be likely to identify any number of varieties of Spanglish in the Western hemisphere.

However, as always in language matters, the case is not clear cut. Accomplished bilinguals are often not aware that they are speaking a new language. They might even deny that they are mixing languages and may identify either English or Spanish as the language (they think) they are speaking, although a linguist might observe otherwise. We might then say that a language is a language when linguists say it is a language, but even here, there is lack of agreement among linguists on the independent grammatical status of mixed forms such as Spanglish. And, of course, linguists have no greater authority than speakers who are apt to say things like: "You [the linguist] say that I am speaking Gullah [a creolized[8] variety of English]. I say that I am speaking English." The opposite also holds: many speakers who mix Spanish and English in the United States believe they speak a language called Spanglish, though some linguists believe this variety to be a variety of Spanish in the United States with many English borrowings. While linguists debate whether or not Spanglish is different from Spanish in the United States, speakers debate whether or not they speak it in the first place. The lack of consensus among linguists and speakers strikes us as completely normal, given that Spanglish – whatever it is – is clearly in its early stages of development.

The identification of a language as a language thus depends on many factors: perceptual, political, ideological, social, and even phenomenological, that is, whether interested observers, for instance, speakers of a particular variety and/or linguists, recognize (and agree) that a language has a separate identity. In this book, the term *language* refers to:

(i)   the means by which one individual more or less reliably orients another's thoughts and actions;
(ii) a culturally determined set of acoustic, gestural, and/or written signals;
(iii) the trans-generational stability of these signals; and
(iv) the functioning of these signals in an environment with artifacts and practices that support the ways the individuals living in that environment are oriented by the language(s) they speak.

This description is circular, and deliberately so. It also is meant to suggest a certain looseness or porosity in the linguistic fabric. History provides ample evidence that languages have enough "give" in them for their speakers to unknit and reknit them in response to their always-changing needs and their always-changing environments. As the linguist, Edward Sapir, once aphorized: "All grammars leak."

Thus, we can say that the number of languages in the world is ultimately indeterminate and that the activity of counting them falls somewhere between an inexact science and a nuanced art.

How and When Did Language Get Started?

The premise of this book is that language is always catching up to conditions. What, then, are these conditions? The example of Spanglish thriving today on the Tex-Mex border opened our discussion to illustrate how normal such mixing is. We can now add the idea that the mixing comes about as a result of decisions taken by people who neither know nor even necessarily care about linguistic causes and effects. The decisions people make are, more often than not, economic.

In the 1940s, the first significant immigration from Puerto Rico to New York City, known as the Great Migration, began as a result of depressed economic conditions in Puerto Rico. Enough Puerto Ricans came that by 1950, East Harlem had become known as Spanish Harlem. Then, in 1952, American Airlines created a nonstop route from San Juan, Puerto Rico to New York City to bring manual labor to the garment industry. All this is to say that when Puerto Ricans moved, and an airline made a decision about flight routes, no one had any reason to think about the linguistic consequences or to imagine the kind of Spanglish now spoken in Spanish Harlem. Nor did the first wave of Cubans, namely the wealthy ones, who came to Miami just before the end of Castro's Revolution in 1959, foresee the mixed language some of their grandchildren would be speaking. (Some may be thinking of it now and lamenting the fact.) Certainly, there have been times and places when people – heads of state, national assemblies, language academies, concerned citizens – have tried to regulate who speaks and how they speak. Many societies have placed legal restrictions on the types of things that can be said and when. In the United States, for instance, we have laws concerning libel (pertaining to print) and slander (pertaining to speech). By and large, however, people do not think about language on a moment-to-moment basis. They just want to have what they want and to get through their day.

The desire to escape an unwanted political regime, the desire for a desirable mate, the desire for better land, the desire for a better job – these desires cause people to move. These are the initial conditions: the need for one group to find a new watering hole or the good berry bushes or the plentiful game, and these needs inevitably bring encounters with other groups engaged in similar searches. For these encounters to have even minimal linguistic consequences, they need to be between groups from a similar or similar enough lineage, first and foremost the primate lineage. Groups belonging to the primate lineage will have both a particular kind of social organization and a particular kind of cognitive organization, ones that include some social gesturing and the ability to make and interpret some lip smacks and grunts. From there, the kinds of encounters producing significant linguistic consequences will be between and among groups who have elaborated these manual and facial gestures, some of which have become reliable indicators of actions to be done, which is to say that the groups have leveraged gestures and sounds to affect, to influence, and to manipulate the thoughts and actions of their conspecifics, the fellow members of their lineage.

Among the important conditions that language is always catching up to are the conditions that language itself makes possible and continually puts into motion. If I promise you that I will meet you at the coffee shop at four o'clock, I have brought a certain state of affairs into existence that could not occur without language, namely one known as 'promising,' and this state constrains my future actions, as well as yours. If I do not show up at the coffee shop at the appointed time, it is not the case that nothing has happened. It is rather that I have now brought into existence a different state of affairs, namely one known as 'breaking a promise,' and this state will also have effects on our future interactions. Our days are filled with such microevents, and the world is filled with similarly structured macroevents, such as December 8, 1941, "The Congress of the United States of America declares war on the Empire of Japan." Events such as promising and declaring war are called *speech acts*, acts that perform the very act by announcing it.

In this book, we advocate what can be called an ecological account of the origin of language. We believe the instantiation and development of language arose from the perceived benefit of one human orienting a fellow human in his or her cognitive domain, the benefit being that the orienting activity was seen to be effective, that is, to affect that person. The phrase "Please pass the salt" makes use of someone else's muscle power. A mother speaking in a soothing voice to her infant relaxes the baby's breathing and heart rate. In an ecological account, any cognitive benefits to the species are deemed to have occurred as a result of the development and maintenance of language. No prior cognitive advances are required to instantiate it. In other words, no cognitive advance is posited here to have bootstrapped humans into language. Theorists who do posit such a prior advance – for instance, God (or some evolutionary event) first endowed humans with the faculty of reason – subscribe to what can be called the rationalist account of the origin of language. Among theorists of all stripes, there is general consensus that human language as we know it was up and running at least 60 kya and probably well before that, easily as far back as 150 kya, if not more. For now, it is enough to point out that the other initial condition to which language is always catching up is that these encounters at the water holes, the berry bushes, or the hunting grounds must be between groups who belong to a particular lineage, namely that of *Homo sapiens sapiens*.

This brief origin sketch also serves the purpose of addressing a fundamental question concerning the origin of the languages of the world that is often cast in terms of a dichotomy: Are the living languages today a result of monogenesis, whereby all languages are descended from one source, or are they a result of polygenesis, whereby they are descended from several sources? The question can be improved upon by pointing out that the dichotomy is a false one and then answered by referring to our definition of language. As long as one human was able to orient another in his or her cognitive domain, that action counts as a linguistic action. It does not matter if they are speaking the same language or a different language. It matters only that the action had an effect and, then, was able to be repeated with generally similar effects. We have no difficulty imagining groups of humans spread out in Africa 100,000 years ago, perhaps somewhat localized in East Africa, encountering one another, and producing over time what would qualify as a dialect chain. There would have been haphazard crossings and recrossings of encounters, such that some of the similarities found in the world's languages today (the fact that all human groups have one, to begin with) are strong enough to suggest some kind of common origin. The differences are sometimes equally striking and point toward different origins. Whatever the initial conditions may have been, enough time has elapsed since humans spread out over the globe for certain groups to have taken what might have originally been maybe more, maybe less common linguistic practices and worked them out on unusual trajectories.

When we say that 'all languages were once Spanglish,' we mean simply to say that all languages – from the first to have arisen in the species some 150,000+ years ago to those taking shape today – arose under a set of conditions. These conditions are necessarily evolutionary (the shape of the vocal tract), cognitive (the ability to parse information and recognize sound sequences), social-psychological (the need to orient conspecifics), and sociohistorical (Spanish and English happen to continually crisscross in parts of North America beginning around 1851). While in the historical world and that of near prehistory the evolutionary, cognitive, and psychological conditions are always given in any instance of language formation, the sociohistorical conditions are not. That is, while the English and Spanish speakers who first encountered one another in Texas were equipped with the evolutionary and cognitive skills to communicate with each other, as well as the social-psychological need to do so, the historical facts leading to their encounter were in effect accidents of history. It is easy to see that Spanglish was not planned or predetermined in any way, but is rather an emergent phenomenon of the conditions under which it is arising. We can say the same of all other languages to have come on the scene since the very beginning of language in the species.

To support this view, we now adopt the perspective of the uniformitarian hypothesis. Uniformitarianism was first formulated at the beginning of the nineteenth century in the field of geology and as a result of interrelated observations: water moving continuously against solid matter alters and, in fact, erodes that matter's form; effects of erosion take place over large stretches of time; and this activity must have been occurring since the beginning of time. In other words, uniformitarianism assumes that the kinds of geological process happening now must have been at work through all time, and this assumption arose in deliberate contrast to catastrophism, the idea that the earth's landforms had been created by short-lived abrupt events and often one-time events. Catastrophism has Biblical overtones and easily accommodates the idea that God created the world in seven days. Uniformitarianism acknowledges that while circumstances are ever changing, the principles involved in explaining those changes are constant.

Later in the nineteenth century, the American linguist, William Dwight Whitney, was perhaps the first to apply the principle of uniformitarianism in the field of linguistics, and he used it to argue against the plentiful and often fanciful accounts of the origin of language produced in response to Darwin's *The Origin of the Species* (Darwin [1859] 1868). Whitney's great Continental rival, Friedrich Max Müller at Oxford, believed that there was a mysterious relationship between sounds and meaning[9] and hypothesized that language began at a time when humans were naturally percussive. That is, upon perceiving an object, a human could feel or ring with the proper word for it. Whitney wondered – rightly, we think – why humans would have had that percussive ability in the deep recesses of time but have lost it now.

In *Languages in the World*, we are following Whitney's suit. We are taking the present as the guide to the past, and we notice that the kinds of encounters humans have today and their linguistic results are likely the kinds of encounters humans have had for all time with similar linguistic results. We humans are a good 100,000 years or more down our linguistic path, and so a lot has happened to make the language dynamics active today somewhat different than those of the remote past. For one, we now have political entities known as nation-states that organize, to some degree, the flow of human movement. For another, we now have ample materials commenting on our languages – dictionaries and grammars, and, in some parts of the world, language academies – that record and sometimes regulate speech. Nevertheless, the complexities of modern life do not alter the fact that we humans have always used the linguistic resources we have at hand, to ignore or to blend as we wish or as the social situation and group practices demand, all the while putting one foot in front of the next.

In yet another way, we are taking a cue from Whitney's lead. He was, among other things, committed to educating the general public about linguistic matters, and this was a commitment that linguists lost, more or less, in the twentieth century. We take up the challenge – alongside many other linguists working today – to use the fruits of the last 150 years of language study to promote greater awareness of language in the general public. We hope the readers of this book will also respond to this challenge. We take as a pertinent model the efforts of sociolinguist, Walt Wolfram, at North Carolina State University who, for the past several decades, has brought language awareness out of the university classroom and into public spaces, including the North Carolina State Fair and the curriculum of North Carolina public schools. In our own efforts to create language awareness in the general public, we the authors are just getting started.

The Structure of Spanglish

Words in a language stand out in a way other features often do not. We can look words up in dictionaries, and we can hear borrowed words if they have an unusual sound or sound sequence. For instance, English speakers recognize Spanish words like *mañana* with its palatal nasal [ɲ] and *yo quiero* with the tapped [r]. If we limited our study of language to lexical items, then we might imagine that Spanglish is spoken when any English speaker or Spanish speaker peppers his or her native language with words from the neighboring language. Indeed, most people in the United States are familiar with the terms *lasso, rodeo, enchilada, fajita,* and *cilantro,* which come into American English from Mexican Spanish. At the same time, Spanish speakers talk about *golf, email, jazz, marketing,* and *música pop.* This of course does make these groups Spanglish speakers. Spanglish speakers obviously make use of the lexicon of both languages – and the degree to which they do this varies – but Spanglish is about more than words. In addition to the lexicon, we also mean to emphasize the variable arrays of linguistic elements speakers use to create a new language variety. These elements are what we call linguistic structure, and they may pertain to the following:

(i) *The sounds of a language, or phonetics.* The sound inventories of all languages are limited to the physical and mechanical possibilities of human anatomy: the length of the vocal tract, the size and shape of the oral and nasal cavities, the range of movement of the tongue, and the location of the articulators. Nevertheless, languages differ with respect to the number and types of sounds they produce. The Austroasiatic language Sedang spoken in Vietnam and Laos is said to have as many as 50 unique vowels, while the Caucasian language Abkhaz, spoken in Georgia and Turkey, is said to have just two. Rotokas, a language of Papua New Guinea, is known for having only six consonants, while the language !Xóõ, spoken in southern Africa, has more than 100. And languages that produce the so-called same consonant may do so in subtly different ways. For example, Spanish and English both produce the sound [d], but while the English version is made by placing the tongue tip on the back of the alveolar ridge, the Spanish version is made by placing the tongue on the back of the teeth.

In the case of Spanglish, speakers may demonstrate pronunciations that are distinctive from those found in monolingual varieties of English and Spanish. Part of what may make Spanglish phonetically distinctive are its patterns of rhythm, stress, and intonation. Monolingual varieties of Spanish and English are characterized by different systems of prosodic rhythm, for example. In Spanish, syllables recur at regular temporal intervals and are of roughly the same duration, whereas in English, syllable durations vary. In the case of Spanglish, these systems may meet somewhere in the middle. Thus, a Spanglish utterance such as "*Llovía bien fuerte,* so *me fui,* I went home" (It was raining really hard, so I left, I went home) may be produced with a Spanish-like rhythm over the differing lexical items, including the words taken from English, with an intermediate pattern, or with two separate systems. This all depends on the speaker and their experiences with both Spanish and English, with some speakers of Spanglish strongly favoring Spanish **prosody**, others favoring English, and others meeting in the middle.

(ii) *The sound system, or phonology.* English does not have the voiced alveolar trill [r] in its sound inventory, and although the tap [ɾ] exists in English, as in the word bu**tt**er, it does not form a minimal pair with another sound and is therefore not used in meaning contrasts. American English speakers may not even be aware they produce the sound, believing instead they are producing [t]. If you produce the word bu**tt**er with [t] or [ɾ], you don't change the standard meaning of the word, only the pronunciation. Similarly, in Spanish, [ð] exists as an allophone of [d] depending on the phonetic environment, or location relative to other sounds. [d] occurs at the beginning of words and after certain consonants, while [ð] occurs after vowels: *diente* with [d], versus *madre* with [ð]. In the case of Spanglish, the phonemic inventory varies from speaker to speaker. While most speakers will use all four **phonemes** – [r], [ɾ], [ð], and [d] – they may use them in ways that differ subtly from so-called monolingual varieties of Spanish and English. For example, a Spanglish speaker may say *mi diente* using the stop [d] rather than the fricative [ð]. Again, this usage is conditioned by the rate of speech, whether the speaker was speaking primarily in English or in Spanish, as well as factors related to the speech event.

(iii) *Word formation patterns, how individual words in a language are structured.* The term *word* is not useful in cross-linguistic descriptions, because the way different languages put their words together varies greatly. Instead, linguists speak of word formation patterns in terms of morphology. While English has relatively little inflectional morphology, Spanish has relatively more. For Spanglish, the weight of inflectional morphology is in favor of Spanish, such that any English verb occurring in a Spanish stretch of an utterance will be conjugated according to the Spanish patterns. For example, the English verb 'to mop' may replace the Spanish verb *trapear,* but will be rendered with Spanish morphology, namely, *mopear* (-*ar* is one of the infinitive marking **morphemes** in Spanish). As often happens when one language starts borrowing a lot of verbs from another language, a default conjugation is chosen. In the case of Spanglish, it tends to be the first conjugation, namely the verbs that end in -*ar,* and the personal pronoun endings from this conjugation are applied. Accordingly, the borrowed verb *janguear* 'to hang out' has the following regular forms:

	Singular	Plural
First person	yo jangue**o**	nosotros jangue**amos**
Second person	tú jangue**as**	
Third person (he/she)	él/ella jangue**a**	ellos/ellas jangue**an**
Formal 'you'	usted jangue**a**	ustedes jangue**an**

In addition, when one language starts borrowing a lot of nouns from another language, and if the borrowing language has a gender system, a default gender is often chosen for the borrowed words. However, in Spanglish, English nouns are assigned gender sometimes by the phonetic form of the word, for instance, *the block* becomes *el bloque*, another word for 'neighborhood'. Sometimes, the gender transfers from the Spanish equivalent. Because *la nariz* 'the nose' is feminine in Spanish, one can speak of *una runny nose* in Spanglish (*una* is the feminine indefinite article 'a'), though at this stage no one would bat an eye if a speaker said *un runny nose* instead. English does not mark plurality on definite articles, but Spanglish does. Thus, 'the munchies' might be rendered *los munchies* in Spanglish. Gender for Spanish nouns is routinely assigned, but the particular assignments are not necessarily stable across Spanglish speakers or speech communities.

High-profile inflectional morphemes from both Spanish and English find their way into Spanglish. The present progressive suffix *-ing* is widespread in English. The Spanish counterparts *-ando* and *-iendo* are also common. However, as flexible as Spanglish grammar is, speakers are unlikely to put a Spanish suffix on an English verb, or vice versa. The English verb *to run* cannot by itself take the Spanish suffix *-ando* just as the Spanish verb *corer* 'to run' cannot take the English suffix *-ing*. However, sometimes Spanglish speakers incorporate English verbs into Spanish phonology, as we saw with *janguear*.

Similarly, reflexive verbs are common in Spanish and nearly absent in English to express activities such as 'going to bed,' which in Spanish is *acostarse*. The *-se* suffix is the reflexive and refers to the person doing the action, and *acostar* means something like 'lying down.' Thus, 'going to bed' in Spanish is the idea of 'laying oneself down.' This word turned up as a deverbal noun in the phrase *al acostarse* 'at the time of going to bed' in a medicine prescription issued by a Walgreens in Miami, which came with the following instructions: *Aplicar* a thin layer to scalp *y* forehead *cada noche al acostarse por 2* weeks. (Apply a thin layer to scalp and forehead every night upon going to bed for two weeks.) An example of Spanglish earlier in this chapter included two reflexive verbs: "Why make Carol *sentarse atrás pa'que* (sit in the back so) everybody has to move *pa'que se salga* (for her to get out)?" Here the speaker nicely balances out the grammatical possibilities of the two languages, making the two Spanish utterances parallel through the use of the reflexive in both. Similarly, the speaker of the utterance: "*Apaga la televisión*. (Turn off the television.) Don't make me say it again! *¡Ponla* off!" is able to double the force of the command by marshaling two different verb constructions for the same action.

(iv) *The restructuring of the lexicon.* In the utterance, "Man, *vamos a la marqueta pa' comprar* doughnuts" (Man, let's go the market to buy doughnuts), the speaker has replaced the Spanish word *tienda* and imported the English word 'market,' which is exactly what one expects when two languages mix. Because English has borrowed so many words from French, it so happens that Spanish and English share many cognates, given the common Latinate origin of French and Spanish. In the title of the Spanglish album *El Talento Del Bloque* by Farruko, a Puerto Rican reggaeton singer, the word *talento* is a cognate and is transparent across the Spanish divide. Sometimes, a cognate in Spanglish will adopt a meaning from English not present in Spanish. Such a cognate is *actualmente*, which in Spanish means 'right now.' In the Spanglish utterance: "*Fue al súper a las dos. No, actualmente fue a las tres*" (S/he went to the supermarket at two o'clock. No, actually, she went at three o'clock), *actualmente* has the English meaning of 'actually, in fact.' Such an utterance makes no sense in varieties of Spanish outside of the United States.

The lexicon can also be restructured by means of **calques**. A calque is a loan translation, where the idea is borrowed but not the words. The Spanglish verb for 'to call (someone) back' is *llamar pa'tras*, possibly a translation of the English way to express this idea. The Spanish verb is *devolver la llamada* 'return the call.' *Llamar pa'tras* is widespread in the Spanglishes spoken in California, Texas, and Miami, and it is particularly reviled by monolingual speakers of Spanish as an example of the way Spanglish degrades Spanish. From a linguistic point of view, however, these types of lexical phenomena are completely normal.

(v) *Larger phrasal and sentential patterns, also known as syntax.* Because English and Spanish have the same basic word-order pattern: Subject–Verb–Object, there is not much pressure on the word order in Spanglish. However, we find that Spanglish speakers tend not to switch languages at locations where the grammars of the two languages do not line up. An important difference between English and Spanish is that in English, adjectives precede nouns, while the opposite is true in Spanish. Thus, Spanglish speakers are unlikely to make switches between nouns and adjectives. 'Un coche blue' is as unlikely 'an azul car.'

(vi) *Other phenomena, generally classed as cultural, such as endearments and terms of address.* Clearly, the 'man' in an utterance above is borrowed from an English terms of address. In the utterance: "Don't worry *mi'jo, te voy a cuidar*" (Don't worry my son, I'm going to take care of you), the term *mi'jo* is a term of endearment from *mi hijo* 'my son.' The familiar/formal *tú/usted* distinction in the second singular 'you' forms of address in Spanish may be disappearing in Spanglish, such that speakers primarily only use *tú*. The Spanish plural *vosotros* 'you' is gone completely, just as it has in varieties of Spanish in Latin America. However, respectful terms of address such as *don, doña, Señor*, and *Señora* may be used by Spanglish speakers to be polite, even while speaking mostly English.

In his book *Pardon My Spanglish*, humorist Bill Santiago quips that Spanglish has "twice the vocabulary and half the grammar" (Santiago 2008). In reality, as the above examples are intended to show, the most competent speakers of Spanglish have the best command of both languages. They make their switches from one language to the other at the point where the words on both sides of the switch are grammatical with respect to both languages. Although we can say that Spanglish is grammatically flexible, the belief that Spanglish is simply a hodgepodge of words with no grammar is a misunderstanding borne out of popular beliefs about what language is or should be.

We have begun our structural review of the languages of the world with examples from Spanish, English, and Spanglish because we imagine that many of our readers are familiar with these languages. Although English and Spanish have their grammatical and vocabulary differences, they also share quite a lot due to the vagaries of history. For instance, it is a coincidence that both languages form the plural of nouns with a final -*s*; the Western Romance languages, French, Spanish, and Portuguese, share this feature, while the Eastern Romance languages, Italian and Romanian, do not. English is a Germanic language, and 1000 years ago only 35% of Old English nouns had the plural ending with a final -*s*, namely the masculine nouns. About 700 years ago, these *-s* plurals started to spread to all nouns and stabilized about 500 years ago, leaving irregulars such as tooth/teeth, ox/oxen, deer/deer, etc. The fact that Spanish and English could both generalize *-s* plurals in the first place is because they belong to the language stock known as Indo-European. This means both have inherited a cast of structural characters particular to this stock, and the depth of these structural similarities no doubt facilitates the ease of the Spanglish mix.

Some of these Indo-European structural tendencies are exceptions to the ways most languages of the world go about their grammatical business, and so we end our review of Spanglish by describing one such exception. In English and in Spanish, the **marking** of the syntactic relation of possession is put on what is called the **dependent** noun: in the phrase *the man's house* and *la casa del hombre* the possessive morpheme *-s* is bound to the word *man*, and the possessive form *del* is determined by the gender of *hombre*. In a language like Hungarian, which belongs to the Uralic language stock, the possessive relationship is marked on what is called the **head** noun: *az ember haza*, where *az* is 'the,' *ember* is 'man,' and *haz* is 'house.' The final *-a* on *haz* 'house' marks the possession:

Dependent (Possessor) Marking	Head (Thing Possessed) Marking
the man+s house	az ember haz+a
the man+possesses house	the man house+belongs to man
la casa del hombre	the house possessed+by man

In other words, in Hungarian the thing possessed bears the grammatical mark of possession, not the possessor, and it turns out that the Hungarian pattern is the more common one among the languages of the world. To speakers of Indo-European languages this grammatical preference might seem strange. It might also seem to be relatively insignificant. However, marking preferences are structural features, as we will see in later chapters, with large implications.

Final Note: The Encounter of Spanish and English on Television in the United States

From the earliest days of television in the United States, Spanish was heard in American living rooms through the character of Ricky Ricardo on *I Love Lucy*. He was played by Desi Arnaz, the real-life husband of Lucille Ball, who was the star of the show. Ricky/Desi was a bandleader of Cuban origin whose catchphrase was, "Lucy, you got some 'splainin' to do!"[10] Indeed, Lucy's antics would regularly exasperate him enough to send him off into a rant in Spanish. The sight of a handsome Latin man losing his temper with his wife while spouting a stream of incomprehensible speech always played for laughs. The comedy arising from the Spanish–English language gap is in evidence 50 years later on *Modern Family* whose character, Gloria Pritchett, played by Colombian bombshell, Sofia Vergara, regularly mangles English pronunciation to comic effect.

If Spanish is treated as an object of amused incomprehension on English-language American sitcoms, how is English portrayed on Spanish-language American programs? On the Telemundo channel, owned by NBC Universal and broadcast throughout the United States, one popular *telenovela, Marido en Alquiler*,[11] has a character named Doña Teresa Cristina Palmer de Ibarra with *la nariz respingada* 'nose in the air.' She is apt to say things like, "Good morning, *disculpen pero no me gusta decir buenos días en español.*" (Good morning, excuse me but I don't like to say 'good morning' in Spanish.) 'Good morning' and *buenos días* are on the one hand equivalent salutations that perform the same social function, namely, a morning greeting. But Doña Teresa Cristina's use of the English 'Good morning' while otherwise speaking Spanish indicates that in the United States, the languages are not equal in terms of social status. While many Spanish speakers in the United States feel proud to speak Spanish, many nevertheless feel that English conveys a higher social status.

The actors who play the lead protagonists on this *telenovela* also embody a European physical preference. They have light skin and light eyes, and they come from Venezuela, Colombia, and Argentina, although they do not speak their regional varieties on the show. Rather, they use a nonspecific variety with an occasional mix of Mexican slang so that their speech will appeal to the broadest segment of the viewing audience, namely the Spanish-speaking Mexicans who comprise over 65% of the overall Latino population in the United States. The question is: Why are the Mexicans now the largest overall Latino population in the United States? The answer is: the signing of the North American Free Trade Agreement (NAFTA) in 1994, which had a negative effect on small farmers south of the border, thereby sending them north to find jobs.

Throughout this chapter, we have seen the persistent effects of economic pressures on human movement. Here at the end, we perceive the sometimes-subtle, always-present workings of one of the most powerful forces in language dynamics: attitudes about language in response to prestige.

Exercises

Exercise 1 – map making

Chicanos in the United States have an expression: "I didn't cross the border, the border crossed me." This is a theme we explore throughout this text, not only here in Chapter 1. Sketch a map of Mexico in 1821. Use annotations and/or different colored pencils to illustrate the events of 1836 and 1845. What does your map show about the history of Spanglish in North America? What does it show about the historical presence of Spanish speakers in the United States and English speakers in Mexico?

Exercise 2 – code switching

Part of the beauty of Spanglish is that it is grammatically flexible. Speakers can say many things in many different ways, but it is not the case that anything goes. In an experiment, sociolinguist Jacqueline Almeida Toribio gave the following fairy tales written in Spanglish to native Spanish/English bilinguals. One of the stories was easy for most participants to comprehend and read aloud fluently. The other was more tricky, and participants stumbled as they read aloud in many parts of the text. If you are able to read Spanish, perform the experiment on yourself – read both passages aloud and decide which is the well-formed Spanglish fairy tale and which is ill-formed. If you are not able to read the Spanish words, analyze the texts and make your best guess. Is there a difference in the type of code-mixing you can observe? What patterns can you discern?

"Snow White and the Seven Dwarfs/BLANCANIEVES Y LOS SIETE ENANITOS" ÉRASE UNA VEZ UNA LINDA PRINCESITA BLANCA COMOLA NIEVE. SU MADRASTRA, LA REINA, TENÍA UN MÁGICO mirror on the wall. The queen often asked, "Who is the MÁS HERMOSA DEL VALLE?" Y UN DÍA EL mirror answered, "Snow White is the fairest one of all!" Very envious and evil, the REINA MANDÓ A UN CRIADO QUE MATARA A LA PRINCESA. EL CRIADO LA LLEVÓ AL BOSQUE Y out of compassion abandoned LA ALLÍ. A squirrel took pity on the princess and led her to a PEQUEÑA CABINA EN EL MONTE. EN LA CABINA, VIVÍAN SIETE ENANITOS QUE returned to find Snow White asleep in their beds. Back at the palace, the stepmother again asked the ESPEJO: "Y AHORA, QUIÉN ES LA MÁS BELLA?" EL ESPEJO OTRA VEZ LE answered, without hesitation, "Snow White!" The queen was very angry and set out to find the CASITA DE LOS ENANITOS. DISFRAZADA DE VIEJA, LA REINA LE OFRECIÓ A BLAN-CANIEVES UNA MANZANA QUE HABÍA laced with poison. When Snow White bit into the apple, she CALLÓ DESVANECIDA AL SUELO. POR LA NOCHE, LOS ENANITOS LA found, seemingly dead …

"The Beggar Prince/EL PRÍNCIPE PORDIOSERO" EL REY ARNULFO TENÍA UNA HIJA MUY HERMOSA QUESE LLAMABA GRACIELA. AL CUMPLIR ELLA LOS VEINTE AÑOS, EL REY INVITÓ many neighboring princes to a party. Since she was unmarried, he wanted her to choose UN BUEN ESPOSO. Princess Grace was sweet Y CARIÑOSA CON TODOS. TENÍA SOLAMENTE UN DEFECTO: she was indecisive. Surrounded by twelve suitors, she could not decide and the king SE ENOJÓ. GRITÓ, "JURO POR DIOS QUE TE CASARÉ CON EL PRIMER HOMBRE that enters this room!" At that exact moment, a beggar, who had evaded A LOS PORTEROS, ENTRÓ EN LA SALA.EXCLAMÓ, ".ACABO DE OÍR LO QUE DIJO USTED! JURÓ POR DIOS! The princess is mine!" There was no going back on such a solemn oath Y EL PORDIOSERO SE PREPARÓ PARA LA BODA. Everyone was surprised to see LO BIEN QUE SE VEÍA in his borrowed clothes. DESPUÉS DE ALGUNAS SEMANAS, the beggar made an announcement to the princess. EL NUEVO ESPOSO LE DIJO A LA PRINCESA that the time had come to leave the palace. They had to return to his meager work and a house QUE ERA MUY HUMILDE …

Discussion Questions

1 After reading this introductory chapter, has your understanding of language changed in any way? Have your beliefs about language been nudged in any particular way? How so?

2 Code switching is an important part of Spanglish, but it is also an important way for many bilinguals the world over to express themselves. Do you code-switch with the languages you speak? If so, in what social circumstances? If not, why not? If you are a monolingual, when have you observed others to engage in code switching? What do you make of it?

3 Why do you suppose linguists, speakers, and laypeople are so interested in determining whether or not Spanglish counts as a so-called separate language from Spanish? What does it say about popular views of language that the indeterminate status of Spanglish is so anxiety-producing for so many people?

4 Many people have strong attitudes about Spanglish and other bilingual mixed languages. Do you have any insight on the origin of these attitudes? What do the attitudes do for the person who holds them? What do they do for the Spanglish speaker who hears them articulated?

5 The title of this preliminary chapter is deliberately provocative. What does it mean to say that "all languages were once Spanglish?" In what sense is this true? How does that statement square with popular attitudes about Spanglish and other bilingual mixed languages?

Notes

1 Large land grants were called *ranchos.*

2 Not without a war, of course, namely the Mexican–American War of 1846–1848.

3 Terms shown in bold appear in the Glossary.

4 The linguist Max Weinreich is usually credited with bringing this formulation to the American linguistic community in the mid-twentieth century. Earlier in the century, the French socialist leader, Jean Jaurès, is known to have said: "One names *patois* (=dialect) the language of a defeated nation."

5 The late 1990s ad for the fast-food restaurant chain Taco Bell, owned by Pepsico, used this phrase with the confidence that most Americans would be able to infer its meaning.

6 This date is not associated with Mexico's Independence Day, which is September 16, but rather commemorates the Mexico's victory over the French in the Battle of Puebla. Mexican–Americans also celebrated the day as a way to honor Mexican culture in the United States.

7 This example comes from Shana Poplack's ([1979] 1980) article "Sometimes I'll start a sentence in Spanish *y termino en español.*"

8 For a discussion of creoles, see Final Note to Chapter Eight. For a definition, please see the Glossary.

9 We would now call this *sound symbolism.* If an English speaker were asked: "Which is bigger, a frip or a frope?" they would likely answer "Frope" without knowing what either thing was. That is because there is some correlation between high front vowels and small things (itsy bitsy, teeny weenie) and back vowels and big things (*drop* as opposed to *drip*). Note, however, that the word *small* has a back vowel, and *big* has a high front vowel.

10 This phase from the 1950s has entered American English. On the November 14, 2013 episode of *The Daily Show*, host Jon Stewart admonished the image of the crack-smoking mayor of Toronto, Rob Ford: "You got some 'splainin' to do!"

11 A *telenovela* is a kind of soap opera invented in Latin America and popular around the world. *Telenovelas*, as opposed to soap operas lasting for years and years, are of limited duration. The phrase *marido en alquiler* means literally 'husband for hire' and figuratively 'my dear handyman.'

References

Darwin, Charles (1859) 1968. *Origin of the Species by Means of Natural Selection or the Preservation of Favoured Races in the Struggle for Life, Edited and with an Introduction by J.W. Burrow*. London: Penguin Books.

Poplack, Shana (1979) 1980. Sometimes I'll start a sentence in Spanish *y termino en español*. *Linguistics* 18: 581–618.

Santiago, Bill (2008) *Pardon My Spanglish: One Man's Guide to Speaking the Habla*. Philadelphia: Quirk Books.

Further Reading

Lyovin, Anatole (1997) *An Introduction to the Languages of the World*. Oxford: Oxford University Press.

Pereltsvaig, Aysa (2012) *Languages of the World: An Introduction*. Cambridge: Cambridge University Press.

Veltman, Calvin (1983) *Language Shift in the United States*. Berlin: Mouton De Gruyter.

2

The Language Loop

The Australian Walkabout

Aboriginal Australian cultures have a rite of passage known as the Walkabout. Adolescent males spend up to six months on foot tracing paths established by their ancestors. These journeys can be as long as 1000 miles, and the young men are expected to complete them without a compass. Although adolescent girls do not traditionally take part in this rite of passage, the 2002 movie *Rabbit-Proof Fence* tells the story, based on historical events of the 1930s, of two Aboriginal girls who, after being taken from their family under Australia's so-called half-caste reeducation program, undertake a journey on foot of more than 1000 miles and eventually arrive home. Their journey does not count as a Walkabout as such. However, it does suggest that the girls were able to undertake the challenge because they did not think it impossible to walk many miles across a barren landscape. The girls were, in effect, observing a cultural norm.

The practice of the 1000-mile Walkabout reveals something significant about the intertwined relationship between language, culture, and cognition. In this case, the noteworthy phenomenon is the relationship between an ability known as *dead reckoning* and what are called absolute spatial frames of reference common in Aboriginal Australian languages, such as Guugu Yimithirr. Dead reckoning refers to an ability to navigate a large space by taking an areal perspective on the terrain to be covered. Absolute spatial frames of reference are organized around what English speakers might call the cardinal directions of north, south, east, and west. English, by way of contrast, organizes the horizontal spatial plane in terms of either relative or intrinsic frames of reference, and English speakers organize significant parts of their lives around these frames. For now, the point is that language, culture, and cognition are thoroughly intertwined and shape one another.

Languages in the World: How History, Culture, and Politics Shape Language, First Edition.
Julie Tetel Andresen and Phillip M. Carter.
© 2016 John Wiley & Sons, Inc. Published 2016 by John Wiley & Sons, Inc.

This chapter is devoted to exploring some of the dimensions of this mutual shaping, which issues forth from the basic fact that languages are always embodied in individuals who are embedded in contexts. We undertake this exploration by examining the various dimensions – the cognitive, the cultural, the structural, and the ideological – of what we are calling *the language loop*.

Introducing the Language Loop

In Chapter 1, we defined language as an orienting behavior that orients the orientee within his or her cognitive domain. We pointed out that this behavior arises both in the phylogenic development of the species *Homo sapiens sapiens* and in the ontogenic development of nearly all individuals (but not every single one, alas) born into the species. We also pointed out that this behavior takes place through recurrent interactions with fellow human beings. In phylogenic terms, those recurrent interactions may well have taken two million years to develop into a behavior modern humans would say qualifies as a human language as such. In ontogenic terms, a human baby – unless something goes awry – is born into a linguistic bath, so to speak, surrounded by language, and is involved in recurrent interactions with conspecifics for the rest of his or her life.

We furthermore defined the word *cognition* in terms of the integrated effects of the mental and the physical. The preliminary discussion of the phrase *orienting the orientee within his or her cognitive domain* was, however, necessarily incomplete. Given the use of the term *cognition* in this book, one could argue that if I push you, I am orienting you in your cognitive domain by requiring you to reorganize your bodily disposition with respect to the space we are both occupying. This event, however, does not count as a linguistic event, and so our definition requires a first expansion: the orienting must be achieved by means that are independent of the orienting interactions themselves. If I say, "Please move," and you kindly step aside, then I have brought about a change in your position (where you are standing) by means that are independent of the orienting interactions themselves (through the use of language).

Notice that the members of all social species are able to more or less reliably orient their conspecifics within their cognitive domains by similar means. The dance of a bee is able to orient fellow bees' behavior by indicating the direction, distance, and quality of certain resources, such as fields of flowers, water, and new places to build hives. Wolves howl, among other reasons, to mark their territory by "informing" other wolves of their location. When this howling orients nonconspecifics in their cognitive domains, it doubles as a type of interspecies communication. For instance, humans who cohabit territory with wolves are likely to attend to such howls and behave accordingly. Humans are particularly good at reliably coordinating themselves through recurrent interactions with their cats, dogs, and horses. However, the domains of interactions of the two organisms or of the two groups have to be to some extent comparable, that is, they have to share both a close lineage in phylogeny and a history of interactions in ontogeny, in order for their ability to orient one another to be fully relevant for both organisms and/or groups. In other words, although you have a history of interactions with your dog, you and your dog do not share a close phylogenetic lineage, only an ancient common mammalian ancestor. Thus, while the two of you can successfully coordinate certain types of actions, the range of those actions is necessarily limited.

Bee dances, wolf howls, primate calls, whale and bird songs, and so forth, qualify, broadly speaking, for the label *communication*, as much as do human languages. If we step back and survey the array of modes by which organisms communicate, we could say that it does not matter whether the mode is sight (bee dancing, ASL), sound (howling, singing, whistling, spoken English), chemical signals (insect pheromones), smell (deer marking territory with urine), or even touch (if a deaf signer goes blind, they can hold the hands of the person they are speaking with to feel the shapes of the signs). We can say that the choice of mode is arbitrary, that is, the particular mode is not in itself important, only the fact that it succeeds in reliably coordinating behavior matters. However, from the point of view of the specific organism or group of organisms, of course, the mode put to use is hardly arbitrary in the sense of being random and has everything to do with the physiology of the organism, for instance, whether or not the organism has hands.

The principle of the arbitrariness of the sign is well known in linguistics and refers to the relationship between the form (phonetic shape, sound) and content (meaning) of a word. Except for onomatopoeia, words that imitate the sound of a thing or action they refer to (*tick-tock* goes the clock), the relationship between the way a word is pronounced and its meaning is arbitrary. The sun, moon, and stars do not now nor ever did emit audible vibrations, and humans do not now nor ever did have the percussive power to ring at celestial frequencies and thereby to bring forth the names for bright things in the sky. The first day in any foreign language class illustrates this principle of arbitrariness: the English word *water* is not universal. In order to refer to water, the student of German must learn the word *Wasser* and remember that it is neuter, and the student of Polish must learn the word *woda* and remember that it is feminine, while the student of Vietnamese must learn the word *nước* and remember that it has a rising tone. The student of Vietnamese will also be learning new associations for the word, because *nước* also means 'country.'

We have yet to distinguish the ways we humans orient our fellow humans in our respective cognitive domains from other forms of communication found in other species. Humans can and do refer to objects in a way that other species cannot, and this ability is known as the referential function of language. However, despite the fact that languages have many names for many objects, human language does not function as an inventory of names for things, nor did language come into being through the process of naming. Individual words are byproducts of the dynamics of the recurrent interactions through which humans induce their fellow humans to take a perspective on a situation for the purpose of effective coordinated action. Human language is perspective taking. When we speak (sign, write), we ask our fellow humans to turn their attention this way or that. The coordinated action that results may be only that of the mental state of understanding, but this is already a lot, because understanding is effective for keeping open the possibility of further interaction. We could also call these turnings *tunings*, such that learning a language and growing up to be a competent member of a community means becoming tuned to certain features of the social and physical environments of that community, knowing how to attend to what feature when and knowing what behaviors are called for in response to that attention.

In the last half century, much scientific study has been devoted to nonhuman primates and their cognitive domains, with a significant part of this research devoted to testing various nonhuman primates' linguistic abilities and limits. Of relevance to the present discussion, this research shows that:

(i)   vervet monkeys can reliably coordinate their actions around specific calls; one member of the troop, upon spying a snake on the ground, will utter a particular call, and the other members will scramble up the nearest tree; another member of the troop, upon spying a hawk flying overhead, will utter a different call, and this one will send the others diving into the bushes for cover;

(ii) nonhuman primates in general are good at social cognition, and members of a troop know their place in the hierarchy and behave accordingly, which includes sometimes challenging that place and striving for a higher one; the many words found in human languages distinguishing among social ranks – *king, queen, lord, lady, sir, madam* – reflect the human version of this social fact of primate life;

(iii) bonobos can learn human language to a degree not imagined only a few decades ago, the most famous bonobo being Kanzi, who happened to learn language while his mother was being unsuccessfully trained and is now able to make (some of) his thoughts and desires known to his human caretakers.

In other words, we can detect human-like language behaviors in our closest phylogenic relatives and primate-like behaviors in humans. The point here relates to the ecological account of the origin of language mentioned in Chapter 1: human language emerged out of primate cognition and is continuous with it. It is a natural product rather than a special case of some kind and is as much a part of the human niche as water is for fish.

Yet, what vervet monkeys do when responding to a call cannot be called taking a perspective on a situation, and there are features of human languages that *induce* certain kinds of cognition that would not be there otherwise, spatial frames of reference being an excellent example. Navigation is a particularly important skill for any species, and the way that human groups have differentially worked out how to coordinate their actions with respect to space on the horizontal plane attests to the crucial way language structures (some of) human cognition. As for Kanzi, we could call him genetically bonobo and epigenetically human, just as humans raised by wolves could be called genetically human and epigenetically wolf. Kanzi, no matter how much linguistic training, cannot be transformed into a human with the full range of language behaviors and cognitive repertoires.

The members of all social species are able to coordinate the cognitive domains of their conspecifics; we humans distinguish ourselves by coordinating each other through language, now defined as *coordinations of coordinations*. This is not the usual way language is talked about, and it is not at first easy to understand and requires more language to work the idea out. We coordinate our interactions with one another by giving our actions an extra encircling tug, by creating mental reins, whereby we send each other's thoughts and actions sometimes in unexpected directions, sometimes down well-worn paths. My saying "Hi, how are you?" does nothing more than pull your attention momentarily in my direction and may prompt you to return my greeting. When confronted with the phrase *coordinations of coordinations*, you may have briefly frowned and looked away from the page in order to think about it. As a start, you could think of language as elaborated cognitive loops, complex braids of mental–physical routines, beautiful lace tatted throughout our neurons with tendrils extending down through the larynx to the diaphragm, organizing and coordinating not only breathing rates but also muscle patterns as we act and interact with one another throughout our days and lives.

Language loops in several directions at once. We examine each way in turn.

Language and Cognition

As has just been said, language loops one human's cognitive domain with all others who speak that same (or similar enough) language, making language constitutive of the kind of cognition often called 'cultural thinking.' Language is thus not a personal possession, as some theorists have claimed over the centuries, but rather an intersubjective phenomenon. Just as we can and do get in one another's faces and under one another's skin, so we can and do get into one another's heads through our recurrent interactions. Those recurrent interactions, in turn, create ever-new conditions, both big and small, to which language in the broadest terms – a repertoire of tonal and intonational patterns, lexical resources, syntactic particularities, implicational and inferential expectations, mental–behavioral routines providing stability in change – is always catching up.

Let us return to the varying frames of spatial reference we brought up at the beginning of this chapter. We mentioned that Aboriginal Australian languages favored the **absolute** frame of reference.[1] When referring to the location of objects in space with respect to one another on the horizontal plane, individuals speaking the Aboriginal language Guugu Yimithirr will say, for instance, "The man is north of the house." An English speaker, if standing next to the Aboriginal, will describe the same scene either in terms of a viewer-based **relative** frame of reference, "The man is to the left of the house," or in terms of an **intrinsic**, object-centered frame of reference, "The man is in front of the house." As you have been reading these sentences, it is likely that you have had to make some mental shifts to imagine where the English speaker and the Guugu Yimithirr speaker are standing with respect to the man and the house in order for the three different descriptions of the same scene to line up. For more help, see Figure 2.1. The point is, for the Guugu Yimithirr speaker, mastery of the cardinal directions is an integral part of learning to speak the language, just as learning left from right is integral to knowing English; and this mastery cannot be appreciated without also noticing that: the Walkabout turns an Aboriginal boy into a man, in part by demonstrating his command of dead reckoning; and the names of the cardinal directions in these languages often derive from specific landmarks in the local geography and so do not really correspond to what, in English, qualify as cardinal directions.

Frames of reference

INTRINSIC

"He's in front of the house."

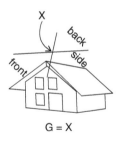

G = X

F

RELATIVE

"He's to the left of the house."

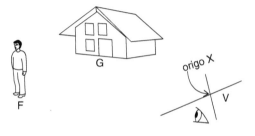

G

origo X

V

F

ABSOLUTE

"He's north of the house."

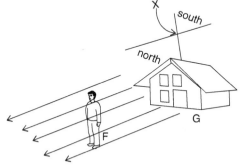

south

north

G

F

Figure 2.1 Underlying elements in the three frames of reference. Source: Levinson (2003). Reprinted with permission of Cambridge University Press.

If you are an English speaker, and you are asked to give directions, you are likely to activate a mental strip map of the route to take and trace it out in your head: the first right, the second left, then go straight, and so forth. As you issue your directions, you are likely to gesture left, right, and straight. When you sit down at a table, you expect the knife and spoon to be to the right of your plate and the fork to the left. When you learned left from right, you may have done so by identifying which hand you write with, perhaps moving your fingers as if holding a pencil just to be sure. Even as an adult, you may still have to pause on occasion to sort out left from right, and you might even get them wrong. When your friend tells you to turn right, and you turn left, your friend may correct you with the jocular comment, "No, your *other* right." When you are in a complicated yoga pose, it may take quite a lot of thought to identify which leg your instructor asks you to move.

If you are a speaker of an absolute frame of reference language, when asked to give directions, you will likely activate a mental areal map and give directions in terms of the cardinal points relevant in your particular landscape. You are likely to point with amazing accuracy in the direction of your home, even if you are 50 miles away. You are also likely to remember how the action of a scene unfolded in terms of cardinal directions, and, if asked to replay it, all your actions will be oriented in the same directions as those of the original scene. You will know in the dark which faucet is the northward one of the sink in a kitchen you have never been in before. You will understand the meaning of the saying in your culture that: "To not know where north is, is to be crazy."

Language organizes significant portions of our world of thought and perceptions, illustrated by the varying frames of reference through which humans orient themselves with respect to the horizontal plane.

Language, the World, and Culture

Language loops into the so-called real world. Humans are good observers, and one of the reasons to preserve endangered languages is that they represent what we might call *the first science*, and their speakers possess vast stores of knowledge, built up over time, about the dynamics of the ecosystems they inhabit along with the local plants and animals with which they share that ecosystem. The Yupik, who live in the Arctic, are experts on ice, snow, and wind conditions there. The Tuvan in western Mongolia know everything there is to know about yaks, and their language and culture treasure that information. Aboriginal Australians understand their geography like no one else. Because languages are always embodied in individuals who are embedded in places, languages and landscapes are connected.

Speakers are also always embedded in cultural contexts. Different languages might include grammatical information about social status. For instance, both Japanese and Korean have an array of suffixes, known as honorifics, that one puts on verbs depending on with whom one is speaking. The social complexities might also involve word choice and a requirement to end a sentence with a particular particle, as a show of respect. Japanese has three levels of speech: casual, polite, and honorific/humble.

These levels will require different vocabulary items and verbal endings. The honorific/ humble category shows two ways to show respect to another person by elevating that person and/or humbling yourself.

Languages also differ in the ways they express common behavioral routines, both single, customary events and multifaceted, complex events. These expressions depend on the cultural conventions. Nick Enfield's (2002) *Ethnosyntax* provides examples. When it comes to representing a single, ordinary event such as *going to the bathroom*, English speakers cover the whole event with the general verb *to go*. Speakers of Lao, which is spoken in Laos, use a construction for the same event, which is equivalent to *enter room-water* (Enfield 2002:230). Thus, in Lao, the whole event is identified by a more punctual activity. How complex events are described also depends on the customariness of two or more activities occurring together in a particular culture. In Hmong, which is also spoken in Laos as well as neighboring countries, the events of *dancing (while) playing the pipes* as opposed to *dancing (while) listening to a song* will be perceived and, then, spoken of differently. In the first case, dancing and playing the pipes are a customary unitary event in the culture and is therefore considered so syntactically; the idea is expressed by the equivalent of the English *he dances blows bamboo pipes*. Dancing and listening to a song, however, are not considered unitary, and so mention of the two activities together requires a connective, roughly the equivalent of *he dances **and** listens to music* (Enfield 2002:241). Without the *and*, this latter sentence is ungrammatical. As Enfield puts it in the opening sentence to his book, "Grammar is thick with cultural meaning."

The thickness of this **ethnosyntax** is, indeed, rich. Even the humble English word *dozen* is infused with it. This word was borrowed from French *douzaine* meaning 'a group of 12' (*douze* = 12) and is first found in the written record of English during the fourteenth century.[2] French uses the *-aine* suffix productively: *dizaine* 'group of 10', *quinzaine* 'group of 15', *vingtaine* 'group of 20', and so forth. English has no similar productive number-grouping suffix of its own; and when English speakers had the chance, they did not borrow the French suffix for producing number-groups, but borrowed only the lone exemplar *dozen*.[3] This word now appears in common expressions. When describing a situation when two items are equivalent and the choice does not matter, one calls it *six of one, a half-dozen of the other*. It is also used either hyperbolically or for a moderately large number of things, for example, *The chemist spent dozens of years working on his formula* and *There are dozens of books piled up on the table*. When an item is relatively plentiful, it is described as being *a dime a dozen*.

The point is that this word does not have currency only in linguistic expressions, because the specific quantity 12 has effects in the real world of English speakers. Over the centuries, the word *dozen* has established a stable cultural relationship with egg packaging, the listed prices of certain bakery goods like bagels and donuts, the preferred number of roses in a bouquet, and the number of bottles in a traditional case of wine. The word is looped into the material lives of English-speaking bakers, florists, wine merchants, and people who make certain kinds of packaging. It plays a part in their behavior in terms of, among other things, pricing policies and the ways they arrange their products. It affects the ordering practices of their customers.

The word *douzaine* was borrowed into Romanian, however only relatively recently, and it is not commonly used, although there is a phrase *de duzină* meaning 'mediocre.' It is found in the phrase *un om de duzină*, which means basically 'a worthless person.' Otherwise, the word is not found in any sayings, nor is it ever used as a number-group for things. It furthermore has no cultural relationship with the prices of bakery goods or with eggs, which in Romania come in cartons of either four or 10. As for the number of flowers one offers to a girlfriend or as a hostess gift, the number must always be odd, the reason being that in Romania even-numbered bouquets are only for the dead.[4] The point here is that the 'same' words *dozen/duzină* are not at all equivalent in different cultural contexts.

Speaking of numbers, the Hispanic custom of the *quinceañera* – the birthday celebrated when a girl turns 15, involving a mass, a special dress, and a party – is quite a bit more culturally salient in the communities where it is practiced than is the somewhat parallel North American notion of *sweet 16*, which finds cultural currency mostly in songs or allusive use, such as in the movie title *Sixteen Candles*, and has no religious connection, such as including a church service. It could have been that 15 was chosen as the watershed year for North American girls, which might have produced the phrase *fine 15* or *fair 15*, but it wasn't. In any case, the key thing for English speakers is for the phrase to alliterate. The strong preference for alliteration in English can be traced back to poetic practices in Old English and is found in clichés and coupled words: *busy as a bee, cool as a cucumber, hell in a handbasket, right as rain, wild and wooly, wrack and ruin*. It even seems to be at work in the choice speakers make to use the shortened form of *because*: "I put my coat on, 'cuz it's cold." The phrase also sounds better that way, and speakers do like what they say to sound right. The idea here is that different cultures weave similar practices – here, a girl's coming of age – differently into cultural practices, just as linguistic differences may shape certain cultural notions.

Cultural practices emerge and develop in particular settings, just as linguistic structures both support and are supported by cultural practices. In Australia, children in certain Aboriginal cultures play dead reckoning games they are not expected to solve correctly until age eight or so. In the English-speaking world, children aged four and five play the circle game Hokey-Pokey, where "You put your right hand in. You put your right hand out...". As the children successively put in their left hand, right leg, left leg, and so on – with all the ensuing confusions and giggling – they are learning right from left. And, as the song says: "That's what it's all about." The respective interactions of dead reckoning and right/left distinctions with regard to cultural practices illustrate the ways that language, culture, and cognition complement and shape one another.

In this section, we have been speaking of contexts, specifically cultural contexts in microcorners of the English-speaking world versus Romania as well as Latin America versus North America. The study of how contexts influence the interpretations of meaning is called **pragmatics**. In a specific cultural context, one can study how variables such as time, place, social relationships, and a speaker's assumptions about the hearer's beliefs come into play. The moment one leaves the dynamics of one cultural context and moves to another is the moment one discovers how different can be words, phrases, syntactic possibilities, social relationships, and even the kinds of assumptions speakers make in relationship to cultural practices. Ethnosyntax might therefore also be called *cross-cultural pragmatics* or *comparative pragmatics*.

Language and Linguistic Structure

Language loops in and around itself. The final *-s* in the third person singular present-tense English verbs, for example, *she eats*, does not refer to the extralinguistic world and can only be understood on its own terms. Quite a bit of the linguistic structure discussed in Chapter 1 forms the ways language loops around itself. This means that not all of language coincides with all of the culture in and through which it is looped, nor even do grammatical features necessarily align with any objective reality. To live in and through a particular language is to take the perspectives one's predecessors have worked out in their recurrent interactions.

The speakers of some languages, like English, split their perspectives on the way they conceive of all objects in the universe and make a distinction between nouns they can count and nouns they conceive of in terms of mass. Count nouns are concrete things like *books* and *chairs*, and abstract things like *jobs* and *governments* that get pluralized when there is more than one. Mass nouns are concrete things such as *water, snow*, and *salt* or abstract things such as *damage* and *hope*. English speakers can refer to five books and three chairs, and talk about holding down two jobs or the way one government follows another. When it comes to *water, snow*, and *salt*, however, English speakers do not refer to two waters (unless they are waiting tables and using short hand for how many glasses of water they need to get to their customers) or one snow (unless they are referring to snow collectively, as in 'the first snow of the season') or one damage. Mass nouns require a way to be talked about, a way to be construed: a drop of water, a flake of snow, a grain of salt, a pat of butter, a dollop of cream, and so forth. When you're estimating relative sizes of count nouns, and the question arises: How many books are there? The answer could be either: very many or very few. When you're estimating relative sizes of mass nouns, the question becomes: How much hope is there? And the answer is now either: very much or very little.

Speakers of other languages make no distinction between count nouns and mass nouns, and view all objects in the universe as mass nouns. In Vietnamese, when a noun is particularized by being counted or used with a demonstrative, such as *this* and *that*, a numeral classifier (CL) is grammatically necessary. Examples include:

- *một cái áo*
- 'one' (CL) 'shirt'
- 'one shirt'
- *hai quyển sách*
- 'two' (CL) 'book'
- 'two books.'

Note that the nouns *shirt* and *book* require no plural morpheme, and be aware that without the numeral classifier, it is difficult for a Vietnamese person to understand what you are talking about. When learning a language with numeral classifiers, Chinese for instance, your teacher may tell you that if you don't know the proper classifier or have forgotten it, it is better to insert the most common classifier *gè* into whatever you are counting than nothing at all in order to be understood. In addition to Vietnamese and Chinese, other numeral classifier languages include, among others, Japanese, Korean, and Malay. These languages tend to have between 20 and 200 classifiers, and they almost always involve the size and/or shapes of the noun particularized.

Here, we note that English has an incipient classifier system, with *piece of* as the default classifier that particularizes many mass nouns such as *luggage, gum, gossip, news, furniture,* and *pie*.[5] An example of an obligatory classifier in English exists for the restricted set of mass nouns *golf, applause, violence, government measures* (e.g., *taxes, funding cuts,* etc.), and *drinks* (in the sense of group participation). When particularized by a number, the indefinite article *a,* or the adjective *another,* these nouns require the classifier *round of* to be used. In other words no one says *play two golfs or *play another golf. Games in general in English are viewed as mass nouns. We either play a game of tennis or play tennis but we do not *play a tennis. In other European languages, Romanian for instance, it is possible to say, colloquially, *joc un tenis* 'I am playing a [game of] tennis.'

The point is that language is perspective-taking. This perspective-taking varies from language to language and therefore gets structured differently from language to language. Linguistic structure is language looping around itself and then pulling the speaker's attention toward one perspective or another.

Language, Discourse, and Ideology

Language loops into ever-greater stretches of cultural and cognitive practices. These are called **discourses,** and they are characteristic ways of talking about and understanding certain ideas, attitudes, thoughts, and beliefs, all of which affect behaviors. For example, in the United States, we can identify a deeply ingrained *discourse of opportunity* that reflects and animates a set of beliefs, practices, and policies, and which intersects with another time-honored discourse, that of *equality,* as in "we hold these truths to be self-evident, that all men are created equal." These discourses have shaped one another over the centuries, such that what is in play today is not necessarily the idea that "all men" are equal in terms of talent. Nor is it the idea that everyone is equal in deserving their fair share. Rather, it is that everyone is deserving of their fair shake. Now, we have the *discourse of equal opportunity,* and equality of opportunity is supposed to be a guarantee of United States citizenship. Discourses express accepted sets of beliefs, which, like everything else in the world, have consequences. For example, if you believe that every American citizen has equal opportunity, you may believe those with the highest status earned their status through hard work, while those with the lowest status did not work hard enough. This attitude may affect who you become friends with, who you marry, who you apply to work with, who you hire, and so forth.

Discourses also express ideologies, which are sometimes conscious, sometimes unconscious ideas about the way things work. When it comes to popular concepts of the relationship between language and dialect, correct and incorrect language, we see the working of a language **ideology** that is a set of beliefs and attitudes, loaded with moral and political interests, that speakers either impose on other speakers or assume for themselves when adopting a speaking style. Language ideologies always privilege some speakers and stigmatize others. The workings of language ideology are most powerful and effective when they are invisible, operating like the Wizard of Oz. When Toto (in this case, the linguist) draws the curtain back to reveal that eighteenth-century **grammarians** manipulated the dials a long time ago, students are sometimes surprised to discover that the attitudes and rules they have acquired through schooling and living in a particular culture do not reflect universal truths but are as contingent as everything else affecting language. Students are then sometimes moved to think differently and then act differently toward people who speak nonstandard versions of a language or a mixed language like Spanglish.

In sum, language, culture, and cognition shape one another in small and large ways that can and do change over time: culture informs language and cognition; language informs cognition and culture; cognition informs culture and language. These terms are, however, not neatly coincident. Good dead reckoners can be found in communities where an absolute frame of reference is absent, and the use of the relative spatial frame of reference is the norm. The use of knives, forks, and spoons is common across Western cultures with their many different languages, just as the use of chopsticks is common across Eastern cultures with their many different languages. Language ideologies exist everywhere in the world, and people variously accept or reject them. These examples point to only some of the complexities involved in unknotting the extended feedback system involving language–culture–cognition that we identify as the language loop.

On Major and Minor Languages

A major language could be said to be one that has a large number of speakers, widespread use over an extended geographic area, and/or a long and important literary tradition. A minor language could be said to be one that has relatively few speakers who might also be isolated from neighboring groups and/or who might have a non-technological culture, which might be transmitted only orally. In other words, the terms *major* and *minor* have nothing to do with the richness or worthiness of the language loop characterizing a language classed as either major or minor. The terms are social designations, not linguistic ones.

Because *Languages in the World* is organized around the three themes of power, movement, and time, it is the case that major languages have more presence in the following pages than minor ones. Speakers of major languages are the ones who have typically been long involved in power dynamics, or have been constantly on the move, and/or have produced written records that give historical linguists material objects to study. We, the authors, have tried, when possible, to bring minor languages into our discussions, but we are aware that we emphasize the languages of Eurasia, Africa, Oceania, and, to some extent, Australia at the expense of languages spoken, say, in Papua New Guinea and the Americas. We trust that instructors using this book will supplement our materials to give coverage to the languages we do not have space to properly outline.

The value of the study of minor languages should not be underestimated. Indeed, we opened this chapter with the phenomenon of dead reckoning in the Australian language Guugu Yimithirr to underscore the importance of the contribution of absolute frames of reference to the understanding of how humans around the world have variously worked out spatial cognition on the horizontal plane. Absolute frames of reference are found in about one third of the world's languages. It must be said, however, that these languages are among the lesser known and spoken. So, it is not the case that one third of the world's people speak languages with absolute frames of reference. What is the case is that such languages are found from Australia to New Guinea to Nepal to Mesoamerica and in all types of environments from open desert to closed jungle, meaning that no simple ecological determinism can explain the development of such systems (Levinson 2003:48). Without the knowledge that so many different peoples and cultures have converged on a particular way to cognize, talk about, and navigate horizontal space – all the while working out this type of system with great variety – we would be missing a significant piece of an important feature of the language loop.

Similarly, human beings the world over have found a wide variety of ways to exploit the vocal tract to produce contrastive sounds. The voiceless velar stop [k] in English is produced when the back of the tongue comes up against the velum to form full closure of the vocal tract and is then released to produce the sound. There is another type of [k] with a different quality of sound. It occurs when the glottis is closed at the same time as the velum is closed off, and this double closure compresses the air in the pharynx. The compressed air is released when the back of the tongue is lowered while the glottal stop is maintained, and shortly thereafter the glottal stop is released. Stops made with a glottalic mechanism are called **ejectives**, and the diacritic indicating an ejective is [']. You will read more about them in the Language Profile of K'iche' in Chapter 12. The point at present is this: there is nothing odd or peculiar about ejectives. The human vocal tract easily accommodates them. However, they happen to be widely found in Native American languages and languages spoken in the Caucasus, and their relatively high occurrence in so-called minor languages is a coincidence. Major languages also have them, such as ones found in Africa, for example, Hausa, which has 34 million first-language speakers and up to 18 million second-language speakers.

Sometimes, certain syntactic features have a higher incidence in minor languages than they do in what we are calling major languages, but – once again – the terms *major* and *minor* refer to social weight and are not ways of evaluating syntactic constructions. Speakers around the world have worked out different ways to conceive of the relationship between transitive and intransitive verbs, which also entails ways of treating them different syntactically. Readers of this book are necessarily familiar with what is called **accusative alignment**, where subjects of both transitive and intransitive verbs are in the nominative case, while objects of transitive verbs are in the accusative case. Consider the following sentences:

I	see	him
subj.	verb	obj.

I	walk
subj.	verb

He	walks
subj.	verb

The object of the transitive verb 'to see' is *him*, and it is in the accusative case. In the case of the intransitive verb 'to walk,' the subjects *I* and *he* are in the nominative case, just as they are for transitive verbs.

In contrast, many readers of this book may not be familiar with what is called **ergative alignment**, where there is one case, namely the ergative case, that marks the subject of transitive verbs, while there is another case, namely the absolutive case, that marks the subject of intransitive verbs and the object of transitive verbs. Now, consider this pair of sentences from Basque:

Martin ethorri da
'Martin came'

Martinek haurra igorri du
Martin child sent
'Martin sent the child'

The subject of the transitive sentence, namely *Martinek*, has the -ek ergative ending. The subject of the intransitive verb, namely *Martin*, and the object of the transitive verb *haurra* 'child' have no ending, which, in the case of Basque, marks them for absolutive (Comrie 1987:13). The point here is yet again the fact that ergative alignment is widespread in minor languages, such as those original to Australia, and this distribution is coincidental. We will see more examples of ergativity in the Language Profiles for Kurdish, Tibetan, and K'iche', in Chapters 4, 6, and 12, respectively.

In other words, lesser-known and lesser-studied languages (except by linguists) are rich with the ways humans have looped their communicative interactions into their interior and exterior landscapes and into their lives.

Final Note: The Contingencies of Time, Place, and Biology

We began Chapter 1 with the story of the emergence of Spanglish as a result of Spanish speakers and English speakers meeting on the Tex-Mex border. We end Chapter 2 with a review of the linguistic effects of the encounters of these Spanish and English speakers with the very different groups of people they met in the New World, namely the Native Americans.

When the Spanish and the English began their extensive post-Columbian explorations of North and South America, they arrived on the new shores with certain similarities. They came from a similar gene pool. They came speaking languages from the same language stock. They came with similar motivations, namely in search of riches, whether it was gold or farmland or pelts or tobacco. They brought with them similar technologies: ships, navigational instruments, cartographic skills, and firearms. They both brought the all-important horse. Although they might not have brought the whole of the material culture available in their home countries – the full range of clothing, cooking utensils, furniture, musical instruments, literature, reference books, and so forth – they came with similar experiences and understandings of this extensive material culture. The Spanish were Catholic, and the English were Anglican; the Spanish were willing to fight the English to bring them back into the Catholic fold and lost what is known as the Spanish Armada in 1588. Nevertheless, the English and the Spanish both counted themselves Christian. They held very similar cultural attitudes and beliefs concerning the Native Americans they were encountering, including ideologies about the languages these indigenous people spoke. They both knew the other was on the hunt and kept track of one another's movements. The encounter of the Spanish and English explorers in the New World was certainly dramatic, but it also occurred on a fairly level playing field.[6]

The same cannot be said for the encounters of the Spanish and the English with the Native Americans, the latter having had no way to know what was coming, and these encounters illustrate the notion of contingency: an unforeseen circumstance that comes into play when one group going about its business meets another group's current state of affairs, and this unforeseen circumstance then plays out with retrospective necessity. A contingent event marks the moment when being in the right (or wrong) place at the right (or wrong) time produces its unintended consequences for the groups of people involved in the event, and these consequences then become the preconditions for the next set of unforeseen circumstances to occur, making the history of the world one long, intertwined series of contingencies.

The first and most crucial contingency in the case of the encounter of the Europeans with the Native Americans was their respective biologies. Along with everything else the Europeans brought, they also came with smallpox, influenza, and measles, and these were diseases for which the indigenous populations, who had been alone on the two continents for at least 15,000 years, had no appropriate antibodies. There has long been dispute about the population size of Native Americans in pre-Columbian times and the percentage loss of that population after the arrival of the Europeans. However, recent genetic studies estimate a decline of 50%, which fits with the historical records telling of a drastic population loss. For the year 1900, the number of Native Americans north of Mexico is agreed to be around 500,000. Today, the number is around 3,000,000, a clear rebound. Nevertheless, the linguistic effects of European contact were immediate: lose the speakers, lose the languages.

In North America, if your tribe had settled on the east coast, you were in an unfortunate location and in the first line of groups to be killed, absorbed, or displaced. *The Last of the Mohicans* tells part of that story. If you had settled on good farmland, your situation was no better, as in the case of the Cherokee in North Carolina who were removed to Oklahoma in the infamous Trail of Tears of the 1830s. If you were in

South America, and your tribe was powerful and rich, which meant that you had a lot of gold, you were definitely in the crosshairs. You fared better if you were isolated in the dense rain forest of the Amazon, owned few valuables, and had access to few natural resources. If you survived all of this and long enough, then it is possible that your language could find some protection as an official language, as Guaraní is today in Paraguay. Or perhaps, like the Navajo in the southwestern United States, you occupied land whose resources of uranium, natural gas, and coal were not considered useful until the early part of the twentieth century, and by that time you had acquired civil rights and knew how to negotiate with the federal government. In Chapter 12, we explore the varying fates of Native American languages along with other endangered languages and speculate on the future of our globalized linguistic world.

In sum, *Languages in the World* undertakes to sketch the broad outlines of the historical and sociopolitical contingencies that have shaped and continue to shape linguistic structures and language use today.

Exercises

Exercise 1 – the language loop

A recent study of infant cognition found that French infants were unable to discriminate between sentences read in Dutch and English, but were able to discriminate between sentences read in Japanese and English. The researchers believe that this is due to the fact that Dutch and English have similar systems of rhythm, while Japanese and English do not. The babies were using cues in the rhythmic properties of the languages to recognize their mother tongue, which the researchers measured with pacifier suckling rate. Researchers have also found that elephants can tell certain human languages apart and even determine human gender and relative age from listening to people speak. In the study, elephants were played samples of two local languages over a loudspeaker. One of the languages (Maasai) was associated with poaching practices, while the other (Kamba) was not. While the elephants remained calm when listening to Kamba, they retreated when hearing Maasai.

First, individually or in teams, describe what the studies show about the ways in which the language loop involves human cognition and coordinated action. Then, construct a visual representation of the language loop that illustrates these points. Your visual can take any material form you choose, so long as you are able to depict the major points. For an extra challenge, try and present your points using little or no text. Present your visual representations of the language loop to the class (Nazzi *et al.* 1998).

Discussion Questions

1   Does the discussion of the language loop in the first part of this chapter alter your views of human language? How so? What was the most surprising, interesting, or useful thing you read in this section?

2 What does it mean when the authors write "human language emerged out of primate cognition and is continuous with it?" Have you heard this type of argument before?

3 What does it mean to say that language is an intersubjective phenomenon? How does the intersubjectivity of language operate in your life, both in terms of the ways you acquired your language(s) and in terms of the ways in which you use your language(s)?

4 Unless you live in Australia or have studied linguistics or cognitive science previously, chances are you have never heard of the language discussed in this chapter, Guugu Yimithirr. Why do you suppose you have not?

5 In this chapter, we introduce the notion of language ideology. There are many ideologies about language; one of them is known as standard language ideology – a set of beliefs about what language is or should be. First, how do you observe standard language ideology to operate around you in your own speech community? Second, how has reading this chapter challenged your own ideological beliefs about language?

Notes

1 Much of the information concerning spatial frames of reference in the present discussion comes from Stephen Levinson's (2003) *Space in Language and Cognition: Explorations in Cognitive Diversity.*

2 In 1066, William the Conqueror successfully defeated English troops at the Battle of Hastings, an event known in history as the Norman Conquest. Thereafter, French words started to be borrowed into English.

3 English has other number-grouping words such a *pair*, *couple*, and *score*. The only reason anyone would know the last one today is because of the first two words of the Gettysburg Address.

4 To round out our story, in France eggs tend to come in dozens or half dozens, as do oysters. Bouquets must contain an odd number of flowers.

5 Pie can be viewed as a count noun (two pies are cooling on the counter) or as a mass noun (piece of pie).

6 Differences certainly exist in the ways that North and South America were settled. The Puritans came to New England for religious freedom and had no desire to mix with the locals (except for a Thanksgiving feast, perhaps). The Portuguese imported into Brazil five to six times as many African slaves as did the United States. The Spanish actively pursued a policy of European intermarriage with local populations, all the while retaining a ruling class that was 100% Castilian.

References

Comrie, Bernard (ed.) (1987) *The World's Major Languages.* Abingdon, UK: Taylor & Francis.

Enfield, Nick (2002) *Ethnosyntax: Explorations in Grammar and Culture.* Oxford: Oxford University Press.

Levinson, Stephen (2003) *Space in Language and Cognition: Explorations in Cognitive Diversity*. New York: Cambridge University Press.

Nazzi, T., J. Bertoncini, and J. Mehler (1998) Language discrimination by newborns: Toward an understanding of the role of rhythm. *Journal of Experimental Psychology* 24:756–766.

Further Reading

Andresen, Julie Tetel (2013) *Linguistics and Evolution: A Developmental Approach*. Cambridge: Cambridge University Press.

Foucault, Michel (1971) The discourse on language. *Social Science Information* 10: 7–30.

Foucault, Michel (1994) *Ethics. Subjectivity and Truth. Essential Works of Foucault 1954–1984, Volume I*, edited by Paul Rabinow, translated by Robert Hurley and others. New York: New Press.

Hall, Stuart (1997) *Representation: Cultural Representations and Signifying Practices*. London: SAGE.

James, William (1981b [1907]) *Pragmatism*. Indianapolis: Hackett Publishing.

Milroy, James (2005) Some effects of purist ideologies on historical descriptions of English. In Nils Langer and Winifred V. Davies (eds.), *Linguistic Purism in the Germanic Languages*. Berlin: Walter de Gruyter, 324–342.

Tomasello, Michael (1999) *The Cultural Origins of Human Cognition*. Cambridge, MA: Harvard University Press.

Tomasello, Michael (2003) *Constructing a Language: A Usage-Based Theory of Language Acquisition*. Cambridge, MA: Harvard University Press.

Wexler, Paul (1974) *Purism and Language*. New York: Indiana University Press.

Whitney, William Dwight (1875) *The Life and Growth of Language: An Outline of Linguistic Science*. New York: D. Appleton.

Wolfram, Walt and Natalie Schilling-Estes (2007) *American English: Dialects and Variation*. 2nd edition. Malden, MA: Blackwell.

3

Linguistics and Classification

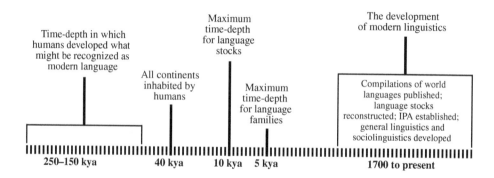

The Role of Sanskrit in Philology

In 1778, William Jones, a lawyer in London with a taste for politics, heard the news that one of four Supreme Court judge positions in India was open. The judges were all appointed in England, because by that time, the Persian Mughal Empire in India had come under the military and administrative rule of the British East India Company. Jones knew he wanted the judgeship. No one else in England – or Europe, even – was better versed in the Orient than he was. He knew Persian fluently, a key skill for someone working for the Company, because Persian was the language used by native

Languages in the World: How History, Culture, and Politics Shape Language, First Edition.
Julie Tetel Andresen and Phillip M. Carter.
© 2016 John Wiley & Sons, Inc. Published 2016 by John Wiley & Sons, Inc.

princes in their letters to the Company. Jones also knew Mohammadan law, another key skill because the former rulers of the territory the Company had encroached upon were Muslim. Jones wanted the post mostly for the salary. The judgeship paid £6000 a year. He figured he could save £20,000 in five years, return to England, and go into parliament (Cannon 1964:55).

Five years later, he finally made it to Kolkata (Calcutta) in the Indian state of Bengal.[1] He had a life-long passion for social justice and quickly discovered major injustices in the court system toward Indians. He determined that if there were a good system of laws and a just administration of them, there would be long-term peace, not to mention prosperity for Great Britain. He immediately encountered one large problem: he did not know Sanskrit. When hearing a case, a lawyer might cite a point, no matter how illogical, and claim it to be part of Hindu code. Jones had no alternative but to accept it. Knowing well the pitfalls of translations, he was wary of depending on Persian versions of Hindu laws, and he was unimpressed with the single English translation that existed of an original Sanskrit law code. So, he set out to learn Sanskrit, whereupon he encountered another large problem: no Brahman would take him on as a student, and this caste was the keeper and preserver of the sacred language and its manuscripts. Even when he assured the Brahmans he would not defile the religion by asking to read the Vedas, no one would help. Eventually, he found a *vaidya*, a medical practitioner, who knew Sanskrit but who himself was prohibited from reading certain texts, to teach him. Over the next few years, Jones applied himself to learning this important language.

Having been well educated at Harrow and University College, Oxford, Jones also knew Greek. It did not take him long to see that the Greek word for such a common verb as 'I give,' namely *dídōmi*, was very similar to the Sanskrit word for 'I give,' namely *dádāmi*. In fact, he found the verbal paradigms of the two languages to be remarkably coincident, along with great stretches of vocabulary. In 1786, in his Third Anniversary Discourse to the Royal Asiatic Society of Bengal (a society he himself established), he had determined that ancient Sanskrit and classical Greek and Latin bore "a stronger affinity," as he put it, "both in the roots of verbs and in the forms of grammar, than could possibly have been produced by accident; so strong indeed, that no philologer could examine all three, without believing them to have sprung from some common source." He went on to suggest that Germanic and Celtic as well as Old Persian were also likely related. This discourse was the first and clearest expression of the possibility that Sanskrit, Greek, and Latin, and perhaps others, were divergent later forms of some single prehistoric language.

Although Jones's works on Hindu law did form the basis for much of Indian jurisprudence for the next hundred years or more, he was never able to see through his list of judicial reforms. Neither did he ever return to England, for he died in Kolkata at the age of 48. He did, however, make a lasting contribution to language studies for pointing scholars to the right path for working out the historical relationships among the languages of Europe and South Asia. It is the focus of this chapter to summarize the major kinds of classifications of the world's languages – historical, areal, typological, and functional – that linguists have developed in the more than two centuries since Jones's Third Anniversary Discourse.

Of Linguistics, Philology, Linguists, and Grammarians

In Chapters 1 and 2, our effort was to discuss the dynamics of the language loop in terms of the historical, cultural, and cognitive dimensions in which it is instantiated, developed, and maintained. Another way of saying this is: individuals – no matter what linguistic activity they are engaged in, be it speaking, signing, listening, reading, or writing – are always in one context or another. They have been so since the beginning of the time we identify humans as such; they are so from the moment they are born. However, there are important traditions of study that take languages out of context in order to compare and contrast them, and to see what kinds of understandings fall out from comparative process. In this book, we call the practice of taking language out of context in order to study it **philology**.

The modern use of the classical term *philology* was created in Germany toward the end of the eighteenth century. A student named Friedrich August Wolf refused to register in any of the four faculties that then constituted the entire university curriculum at Göttingen University: philosophy, medicine, law, and theology. Wolf wanted to study the ancient Greeks, and so he was advised to register in the theology division, because Greek was part of the training it offered. Wolf insisted that he did not wish to study Greek in order to read the New Testament; he wanted to learn Greek in order to study Homer. He was finally enrolled as *studiosus philologiae*. During the course of the nineteenth century, a distinction came to be made between literary and linguistic scholarship, and the term *philology* came to settle on the study of language, which meant the comparative study of the Indo-European languages for the purpose of reconstructing their history.

In the early nineteenth century, the term *linguistic* was reserved to refer to the databases of the world's languages that had been expanding since Columbus and that had reached global proportions by the early-to-mid nineteenth century. Since the seventeenth century onward, the term *linguist* had been uniformly equivalent to *polyglot*, that is, 'someone who speaks many languages.' The early comparative philologists, the most prominent being Franz Bopp and Jacob Grimm, did not refer to their own work as linguistics. By the way, Jacob Grimm is one of the Grimms of fairy tale fame. In order to write his *Deutsche Grammatik* of 1819 (Grimm 1819), he and his brother were inspired to collect fairy tales told in varieties that might have preserved some of the oldest forms of the language. He and his brother were also motivated by the belief that in popular culture could be found national identity, which was the possession of *das Volk*, or the (common) people. The early work in comparative philology was also tinged with beliefs about German national identity and, in fact, helped create that identity. When Grimm formulated The First Germanic Sound Shift, also known as Grimm's Law, it was his belief that the cause of the shift was the independent spirit of the Germanic people. We will explore the relationship between language and nation more explicitly in Chapter 4.

In the early decades of the twentieth century, the term *linguistics* came to mean 'the science of language,' and comparative philology was retroactively dubbed comparative linguistics. Linguists are now students or practitioners of linguistics, and they may or may not speak many languages, although popularly and in certain contexts, the term *linguist* can still mean 'polyglot' and/or 'translator.' Linguists are furthermore devoted to discovering the descriptive rules of a language, that is, how people *do* speak. Linguists thus distinguish themselves from grammarians, who design prescriptive rules for how people *should* speak. Prescriptive grammar arose in the eighteenth century, and the English-language grammarians Robert Lowth and Thomas Sheridan, for instance, laid down rules still taught in American high schools and style manuals today: don't split an infinitive; don't end a sentence with a preposition; when speaking of two items, the word *between* is to be used, and when more than two are at issue, *among* is to be used; don't use a double negative; don't use a double modal; don't use the word *ain't*, and so forth.

Linguists, by way of contrast, believe that what native speakers say is by definition correct, and they are therefore interested to observe and understand what people do say. Many speakers of any number of varieties of English use double negatives: *I don't got none* or *I ain't got none*, while speakers in the parts of the American South may combine modal verbs such as *might*, *should*, *could*, and *would* in an utterance such as *I might should do my homework*. Some of these variations are regional, while some correlate with the socioeconomic status of the speaker. From a linguistic point of view, they are all correct.

We have rehearsed the brief history of the terms *linguistics*, *philology*, *linguist*, and *grammarian* here in order:

(i)   to note that the judgments grammarians make about language and those that linguists make are quite different;

(ii) to reintroduce the term *philology* and to define it as 'the study of language for its own sake,' that is, 'the study of language when taken out of context'; and

(iii) to recognize the effort of this book in terms of the original meaning of the word *linguistics*, that is, as a contribution to the amassed knowledge of the living languages of the world.

Our effort is now to ally this body of knowledge to work in the social and biological sciences. We are dedicated to a linguistics that provides thick descriptions of the various dimensions of the dynamics of the language loop, here only outlined.

Bopp and Grimm were comparative philologists. They, among many others, took the ball Sir William Jones got rolling and engaged in the grand nineteenth-century project of reconstructing the Indo-European languages. Scholars in Europe had suspected since the Middle Ages that the languages spoken in Europe came from some source and perhaps from a single source, the most likely candidate being Hebrew. However, efforts to connect European languages to Hebrew were unsuccessful. In the sixteenth century, a Scythian hypothesis was first proposed to account for the unity of European languages, the Scyths being an equestrian people who inhabited the Eurasian steppe in antiquity and who were known to the Greeks and Romans. This hypothesis received some attention over the next few centuries, but the proposal remained vague. Then came Jones and his startling hypothesis.

It was left to succeeding generations of philologists to work out the details of the relationships among the Indo-European languages through the process of **linguistic reconstruction**, and comparative philology became known for its methodological rigor. The reconstructive process is necessarily a retrospective activity, a jigsaw puzzle put together from present-day pieces and historical records to make a picture of a source language. The name Indo-European is geographic and indicates the eastern and western historical (pre-Columbian) boundaries where the languages are spoken. The name given to the reconstructed language itself is Proto-Indo-European (PIE). A reconstructed **protolanguage** is a common ancestor language that spawned at least one descendant. For instance, Proto-Romance is the term given to what is popularly called Vulgar Latin, which gave rise to French, Italian, Spanish, Portuguese, and Romanian. Many of the protolanguages we will be referring to in this book are prehistoric, and these are pictures of source languages as they might have existed before written records.[2] Thus, languages such as Sanskrit, Greek, and Latin are prized among the Indo-European languages, because they have the oldest written records and therefore bear evidence of forms that might be closest to what could be hypothesized as the original.

Latin, in particular, was valued because the Romans produced two things of linguistic relevance: an empire whose legacy lives on in the many daughter languages of Latin, known as the Romance language **family**,[3] and a rich classical literature. In addition, this culture of writing extended to the earliest stages of the various Romance languages. Because of these factors, the Romance branch of Indo-European was used to test reconstructive methods. When a word or a grammatical construction is found in a written record, it is attested. If a form is reconstructed, and there is no written record to show evidence of it existing in exactly that form, it is unattested and marked with a *, exemplified here with the reconstructed PIE root *$b^h er$- 'to bear, carry.' This root comes attested into English as *bear*, into Latin as the root *fer-*, into Greek as the root *pher-*, and so on. Romance philologists wisely did not use the rich inventory of Latin manuscripts proactively. Rather, they used them retroactively. If the philologists were able to reconstruct a historical source word from the modern Romance languages or from the historical records of these languages, and if they were able to find that word exactly attested in a Latin manuscript, then their reconstructive methods were confirmed. The Latin database served as a strong methodological backstop.

One of the most important reconstructive principles is that of the regularity of sound change. We see this regularity when we compare varieties of a language, say, American English. Northerners pronounce the first person pronoun 'I' with the double vowel, or diphthong, [ai]. Southerners pronounce it with the single vowel, or monophthong, [aː], which in this case is long. The fact is, this sound correspondence [ai]~[aː] is regular. It holds across all instances of the Northern and Southern pronunciations of this vowel. We also see this regularity when we compare cognates from related languages, such as the English, Greek, and Latin cognates for the PIE root *bher- that all have a meaning similar 'to carry.' The differences in their pronunciations will be accounted for, below. Another example would be English *wagon* and German *Wagen* 'car' pronounced with an initial [v], with both forms meaning something like 'a wheeled conveyance.' The sound correspondence [w]~[v] also holds between English and German in many pairs of cognates, such as: *white~weiss, week~Woche, while~weil, wonderful~wunderbar*, and so forth. These are stable correspondences. English speakers do not slip up and on occasion say "Oh, that's vonderful." They regularly pronounce a [w] where the Germans pronounce [v].

Grimm introduced the principle of the regularity of sound change in 1822 when he proposed the following set of sound correspondences, here simplified:

PIE: *p   *t   *k   *b   *d   *g   *b^h *d^h *g^h
           ↓   ↓   ↓   ↓   ↓   ↓   ↓   ↓   ↓
Germanic: *f   *θ   *h   *p   *t   *k   *b   *d   *g

Note: the superscript [^{h}] stands for an aspirated consonant, one that includes a little puff of air.

Expanding these correspondences to include Latin and Greek, we have the series, again simplified, of attested sounds:

Latin: p   t   k   b   d   g   f   f   k
Greek: p   t   k   b   d   g   p^h t^h k^h

Grimm's Law captures one of the major differences between the Germanic branch of the Indo-European languages and, say, Greek and Latin, which retained most of the original sounds inherited from PIE. So, all instances of PIE *p became *f in Germanic, all instances of PIE *t became *θ in Germanic, and so forth. English perfectly exemplifies Grimm's Law because it is a Germanic language with so many Latin borrowings through French. Thus, finding pairs of words showing the correspondences is easy. For instance, when seeking the identity of the **f**ather of a baby, a **p**aternity test might need to be administered. When you want the car to go faster, you put your **f**oot on the **p**edal. In the zodiac, the sign of the **f**ish is **P**isces. A person who likes to play with **f**ire is called a **p**yromaniac. These pairs are extremely robust in English for all of the correspondences. As for the case of the PIE *[b^h], the expanded form of Grimm's Law shows that this sound regularly became the fricative [f] in Latin and the devoiced aspirated stop [p^h] in Greek, thus explaining the pronunciation of the cognates for *b^{h}er- 'to carry' in those languages, mentioned above.

It is of interest to note that Indo-European was not the first language **stock**[4] to have been accurately proposed. This honor goes to Uralic, also known as Finno-Ugric, whose identification dates to 1770.[5] This language stock includes Hungarian, Finnish, Estonian, and Samoyed spoken in Siberia. It is the only other multilanguage stock found in Europe. There is the case of Basque, a non-Indo-European language spoken in northern Spain. However, Basque is considered to be a language **isolate**, which is equivalent to saying it is its own stock. At some point in the distant past, it had to have been related to other languages. However, those languages are now gone. Some linguists consider such well-known and well-studied languages as Korean and Japanese to be isolates, as well. Some linguists class one or the other or both in the Altaic language **phylum**.[6] The language stocks of the world will be discussed in Chapter 7.

The significant point to make here is that reconstructive practices take languages out of their contexts in order to compare and contrast their vocabularies and grammars with those of other related languages. The practice is fairly straightforward. Romance philologists, for instance, line up words on a page and try to construct the original phonetic material that the present-day words came from. Here is an example of a set of cognates meaning 'night':

Italian	French	Spanish	Portuguese	Romanian
notte	nuit	noche	noite	noapte
[nɔttə]	[nyi]	[notʃe]	[noitə]	[noaptə]

Through establishing the regular sound changes that occurred as Latin and then Vulgar Latin developed into the various daughter languages, philologists reconstruct Latin *noctem*. They try again with a set of cognates meaning 'eight':

Italian	French	Spanish	Portuguese	Romanian
otto	huit	ocho	oito	opt
[ɔttɔ]	[yit]	[otʃo]	[oitɔ]	[opt]

They are encouraged to reconstruct Latin *octem*.

Sure enough, *noctem* and *octem* can be found in Latin manuscripts; they are therefore attested, and the asterisk is removed. Across a long list of cognates, the Latin medial consonant cluster -ct- can be seen regularly to turn into a geminate (double) consonant in Italian, be lost entirely in French, and become palatalized in Spanish, unclustered in Portuguese, and dissimilated in Romanian. The phonetic processes of gemination (Italian), palatalization (Spanish), and dissimilation (Romanian), as well as full (French) or partial (Portuguese) consonant loss, are likely the very same ones that affect other consonant clusters in the respective languages as they evolved. In all cases, modern French is the language the most phonetically distant from Latin, since it lost many final vowels and consonants. Its spelling is conservative, however, and in many cases retains final segments no longer pronounced, as in the word *nuit* 'night,' which is written with a final -t# but pronounced without it. The structural details of the development of Latin into the Romance languages will be taken up in Chapter 8. A more in-depth look at language change is the topic of Chapter 11.

The process of decontextualizing languages so that they may be compared and contrasted has led to four principal ways to classify languages.

Genetic Classification

A genetic classification is necessarily historical, and the story of these languages is one of divergence over time and space. The hypothesis is that families of languages classed in a stock descend from a common source, known as the protolanguage. All protolanguages are prehistoric, and there are no documents written in those languages. The people speaking the protolanguage are thought to have lived together for an extended period of time, perhaps even thousands of years, and then at some point they start to spread out and move away from one another, with different groups going in different directions. The movement of people and time are major organizing themes in this book, and we will be taking them up in Parts III and IV, respectively.

In the past several hundred years and more, philologists have worked out the general language stocks of the world. In some cases, the evidence is equivocal and leads to disagreements, such as the case of the classification for Korean and Japanese. In some cases, disagreements about where to divide between stocks are due more to cognitive taste, depending on whether one is a so-called lumper or a so-called splitter. In this book, we:

(i)   accept for Africa, Eurasia, and parts of Oceania a classification of 13 different language stocks, with their major branches; we accept perhaps seven phyla, three of which cover the languages of Australia (Aboriginal Australian), New Guinea (Indo-Pacific), and an old lineage in Africa (Khoisan); these are listed in the front matter of this book;

(ii) recognize that North and South America have dozens of language stocks;

(iii) acknowledge the possibility that some stocks and phyla may be areal classifications, sometimes called *wastebaskets* rather than genetic classifications; and

(iv) want to acknowledge furthermore that genetic classifications for the world's sign languages do not yet exist.

Sign languages do not all derive from one source, and their lineages do not necessarily line up with the spoken languages around them. The language family for ASL, for instance, includes French, because ASL is a combination of Martha's Vineyard Sign and French Sign. It is not historically related to British Sign Language. There are over 130 documented sign languages in the world, and certainly others undocumented, in addition to countless so-called village sign languages, developed away from urban centers, and even idiosyncratic forms of home signs that arise in the context of individual families who are not connected to larger deaf communities.

The oldest reconstructable language stock is Caucasian whose time-depth goes back to 8 kya. The Indo-European stock (see Map 3.1) is reconstructable to 6 kya, meaning

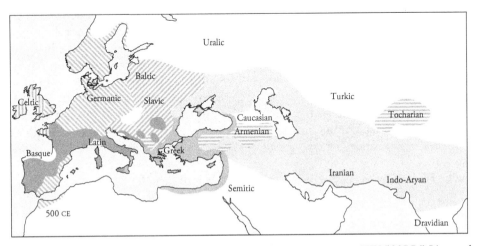

Map 3.1   Early distribution of the Indo-European linguistic groups. "IE1500BP." Licensed under CC BY-SA 3.0 via Wikimedia Commons (http://commons.wikimedia.org/wiki/File: IE1500BP.png#mediaviewer/File:IE1500BP.png).

that it has taken that many years to produce languages as different as Hindi and Welsh, Polish and Tajik. For the sake of consistency in dating stocks and families, time-depth is determined by the time of the hypothesized break-up of the population of speakers. Because human language as we know it may well be 150,000 years old, there is an enormous time gap between those beginnings and the glimpse we get of language from their relatively modern reconstructions. We take up the challenge of filling that gap in Chapter 10.

Areal Classification

An areal classification is by definition geographic, and the story of these languages is one of convergence in time and space. Whereas genetic classifications are based on hypothesized reconstructions of languages long dead, areal classifications arise from known circumstances and give linguists rich understandings of the kinds of context-induced changes that can happen when speakers from different languages inhabit a defined geographic area for a long period of time.

Many linguistic areas exist around the globe. One is mainland Southeast Asia (Vietnam, Cambodia, Laos, Thailand, Peninsular Malaysia, parts of northeast India, and southern and southwestern China) where languages from three different language stocks have been in contact for millennia, namely Austric, Hmong-Mien, and Sino-Tibetan. Another is South Asia, where centuries of contact between Indo-European (Urdu, Marathi) and Dravidian (Kannad'a) languages have induced structural and semantic similarities, even without many borrowed words. The Americas provide any number of examples, the Vaupés River Basin in Brazil and Columbia being but one, where unrelated Native American languages have converged on certain phonetic and grammatical features in a way unique to that region. Mesoamerica is another.

Some linguists argue that Africa is a convergence zone all its own, because, among other things, some unusual phonetic features are found only in African languages. However, even within Africa, there are further convergence zones, such as the Kalahari Basin in southern Africa, where speakers of Khoisan languages and at least one Bantu language have been in contact for an extended period of time. Some linguists have suggested Europe as a convergence zone. In the 1930s, linguistic anthropologist, Benjamin Lee Whorf, proposed a notion of Standard Average European to capture broad grammatical similarities shared by the languages spoken in Western Europe. He focused in particular on the ways speakers of these languages conceive of time as a smooth-flowing continuum and how they express this conception by means of past, present, and future tenses. Not all languages organize their temporal distinctions this way.

The kinds of influences found in areal classifications include:

Phonetic influences

As was noted in Chapter 1, lexical items get traded rather easily when speakers and their languages are in contact. It is not uncommon for phonemes to be traded, as well. Take the high front round vowel [y]: there is a continuous area of Europe where [y] is found, beginning in France and extending up along the northern coast of Europe including not only Belgium, the Netherlands, northern Germany, Denmark, Sweden, and Norway, whose citizens speak an Indo-European language, but also Finland, where Finnish is a Uralic language. Now notice that French has this sound, whereas the other Romances languages, namely, Italian, Spanish, Portuguese, and Romanian, do not. German has this sound, whereas English does not, though both are West Germanic languages. We know in the case of English that Old English had this sound but later lost it, so the [y] in German may well be an inheritance from Common Germanic. However, the presence of the sound in French cannot be explained by the history of the Romance languages. Only geographical proximity to speakers who do have this vowel can explain it.

Another strong areal feature involving sound can be found in Asia. Many of the languages of East Asia – Lao, Thai, Vietnamese, all varieties of Chinese, and some varieties of Tibetan – are **tone languages**. In tone languages, word meaning is distinguished by the pitch or 'tone' put on individual words. The kind of tones found in languages in Asia tend to be **contour tones**. To pronounce individual words the voice may rise, fall, fall–rise, stay flat, break in the middle of a word, or make some other kind of gliding movement. In Vietnamese, the following words are in contrast:

giấy	*giày*	*giay*
rising tone	falling tone	flat tone
'paper'	'shoe'	'second' (as part of a minute)

If you say the syllable *giay* as if you were asking a question (in English), you are saying 'paper.' If you say the syllable as if it were at the end of a sentence (in English), you are saying 'shoe.' If you say the syllable with no fluctuation of your voice, you are saying 'second.' Change the tone, and you change the meaning of the word. The number of tones varies in number from language to language. Mandarin has four. Thai has five. Vietnamese has six. Cantonese has nine or 12, depending on how one counts. Burmese, Japanese, and Korean have a simpler tone system, often called *register* or *pitch*, where the tones can be described in terms of points within a pitch range. Register tone languages are found widely in Africa. To round out the picture in Asia, some languages have no tone: Malay (Austronesian), Khmer (Austroasiatic), and the Philippine languages Tagalog and Ilocano.

English and Indo-European languages in general are **intonation languages**. English speakers, for instance, change the contour of whole sentences in order to make a statement a question, for instance, or to emphasize what is most important. Note the difference in the tone you use when saying: "This is *really* interesting!" as opposed to saying, in astonishment: "*Really?*" You are not changing the meaning of the word; you are indicating a different emotional relationship to it. Although Indo-European languages in general, and the Germanic languages in particular, are not known for having tone, it is the case that Norwegian and Swedish, two North Germanic languages, are classed as tone languages and have a binary tone contrast.

What is amazing to consider for our current discussion is the fact that Vietnamese began as a nontone language, though under the influence of the surrounding languages, it has acquired contour tone. The presence of tone in Vietnamese is not a genetic feature inherited from Proto-Austroasiatic, its source language, but rather an areal feature, acquired through sustained contact over time with tonal languages.

Syntactic influences

Grammatical constructions can also spread across an area. The term *Sprachbund* 'language league' was originally coined to capture the linguistic situation in the Balkans. Here, a variety of languages – all Indo-European, but from different branches – have met and mingled for centuries: Romanian (Romance), Albanian (Albanian), Greek (Hellenic), Roma (Indo-Iranian),[7] and the South Slavic languages Bulgarian, Croatian, Macedonian, and Serbian. In some cases, the varieties of Turkish, a Turkic language, spoken in the Balkans as well as Hungarian, a Uralic language, show Balkan features. Certainly, there are many Slavic and Hungarian words in Romanian and, conversely, many Romance words in the South Slavic languages, as well as Turkish words in Romanian and South Slavic.[8] Of note is the fact that the word *balkan* is the Turkish word for 'mountain.'

More to the point, and to repeat what was said about Spanglish, mixing languages means more than sprinklings of lexical borrowings. Rather, the mixing occurs on fundamental structural levels. In the languages of the Balkans, there has been a remarkable convergence of grammatical features. We mention only four here and exemplify them by Romanian:

(i)   All have replaced the infinitive with an analytic subjunctive. Instead of saying 'I want to go,' the preferred pattern is *vreau să merg*, 'I want that I go,' where *să* is the conjunction 'that'; the verb endings show the person, meaning that personal pronouns are not always necessary.

(ii) Bulgarian, Macedonian, Romanian, and Albanian have postposed definite articles. Instead of saying 'the boulevard,' which is the preferred pattern in Greek, they say *bulevardul*, 'boulevard the,' where *-ul* is the definite singular article for masculine and neuter nouns.[9]

(iii) They make use of resumptive **clitic** pronouns of the type *am văzut-o pe Maria*, 'I saw/have seen-her Mary,' that is, 'I saw Mary' where the pronoun *-o* is cliticized to the past participle of the verb 'to see,' and the preposition *pe* picks Mary out.

(iv) They mark the future with a verb or participle from the verb 'to want' rather than 'to be' and/or 'to have,' which is common in other Western Indo-European languages; so the *vom* of *vom vedea* 'we'll see' is etymologically related to *vrem* 'we want.'

These grammatical convergences are evidence of multilingualism existing in this area for centuries and perhaps even millennia.

Sociolinguistic influences

Affecting areal classifications are several sociolinguistic factors. One of these – prestige – travels well across linguistic and cultural borders, and relative prestige indexes who the lenders are and who the borrowers. We, the authors, have an expression: Chinese is the Arabic of the East, Arabic is the Greek of the Middle, and Greek is the Chinese of the West. That is to say that Chinese (Mandarin), Arabic, and Greek (plus Latin) have had enormous influence on the languages and cultures in their respective regions, which we will be seeing throughout this book. Prestige creates asymmetric effects of one language on another.

The plain root *$b^h er$*- illustrates the story for the West. It comes into English, as mentioned above, in the word *bear* as in 'to bear a child' or 'to bear a burden.' It is recognizable in the word for 'child' in Scottish *bairn* and Danish *barn*. Reflexes of this root have come into English by way of the plentiful Latin words borrowed mostly through French with the root *-fer*, as in *confer, defer, infer, prefer, refer, transfer,* and so forth. We should count those with *-late*, as well, because the verb 'to carry' in Latin is suppletive, which means that its subparts do not match, and its subparts are: *fero* (present tense) *tuli* (past tense) *latus* (past participle).[10] The past participle gives us further borrowings of the type *relate* and *translate*. Finally, there are the Greeks with their root *phor-/pher-*, which have given English words such as *metaphor* and *paraphernalia*, the latter literally 'that which you carry around with you.' Now note that *transfer, translate,* and *metaphor* (meta = trans) are translations of one another. The point is that the Western European Indo-European languages have acted as a kind of recycling mill for Indo-European roots for the last 2000 years, with Greek and Latin supplying most of the grist.

A second sociolinguistic factor affecting languages in contact concerns speakers' attitudes and cultural norms. We got a glimpse of speakers' attitudes already at the end of Chapter 1 with respect to English and Spanish. All over the world, some groups are more open, and some groups less open, to borrowings and contact-induced changes. If two groups are in economic or political conflict, they are less likely to be open to linguistic tradeoffs. There may even be cultural prescriptions, for instance, against lexical borrowings, such as in the Vaupés area in the Amazon, mentioned earlier, although this restriction did not stop grammatical restructuring. In North America, differing cultural attitudes among the Iroquoian languages resulted in different impacts from the encounter with French and English. The conservative Ononadaga resisted linguistic change due to contact, while the Mohawk, with a different attitude toward outsiders, accepted it (Mithun 1992).

Typological Classification

In contrast to genetic, which is historic, and areal classification, which is geographic, typological classifications are both ahistoric and ageographic. This kind of classification captures similarities between and among languages not genetically related and which may have never come into contact. Several types of typological classifications exist:

Morphological

Speakers of modern English currently show a preference for what we will call *the invariable word*. Other Indo-European languages have quite a bit of inflectional morphology inherited from PIE. Modern English does not. Modern English no longer has gender classes for nouns, and it has only one case left, the genitive *'s*, which is sometimes restricted in use for animate things: *the dog's collar* or *the boy's book* versus *the windows of the building*. This is to say that modern English speakers no longer have, nor like, a lot of variation in the forms of individual words. One of the last places left where there is morphological variation is the English pronoun system, and pronoun usage is currently in flux. Even speakers interested in prescriptive norms say things like "between you and I" as opposed to the so-called correct form *between you and me*. Children will say things like: "Him and me are going to the store." Adults may respond to the question: "Who went to the store?" by answering: "Me and him." We make our pronouns into nouns without a blink. A baby is born, and a friend asks, "Is it a he or a she?" In many nonstandard or vernacular varieties of English throughout the English-speaking world, these forms are subject to variation, in most cases by leveling the morphological variants. *That's **Mary** hat*, with the invariable form *Mary*, is a possible utterance in African American English. The point is that English speakers have been shedding their verbal morphology for about a thousand years, and the process continues into the present.

This preference for the invariable word is shared by a language such as Chinese, which has no historical relationship to English and no sustained contact with English until relatively recently. This preference is a typological possibility, and it is called **analytic morphology** or, formulaically: one morpheme, one meaning. Analytic typologies come in two variants, either all morphemes are free (separate words) or morphemes are strung together in one word, and the latter is called **agglutinative morphology**. Chinese keeps to the one morpheme, one meaning formula, and all words are separate: the word 'three' is *san*, the word 'ten' is *shí*, the word 'thirteen' is *shí san*, and the word 'thirty' is *san shí*.

An example of agglutinative word formation in English is *goodness*. It is composed of the free morpheme *good* meaning 'good' and the bound morpheme *-ness* meaning 'abstract noun.' The preference for agglutination is shared by many speakers and languages, such as Turkish (Turkic) and Swahili (Niger–Congo), to name another two historically and geographically unrelated languages. Turkish agglutinates using only suffixes, the oft-cited example being *evlerinizden*:

ev-	*-ler-*	*- iniz-*	*-den*
'house'	'plural'	'you' (plural)	'from'
'from your (plural) houses'			

In contrast, Swahili agglutinates using primarily prefixes. The verbal morphemes include *a-* simple present; *na-* present progressive, *li-* simple past; *me-* present perfective; *ta-* future, and so forth. The pronoun 'he/she' is *a-*. With the noun *m-toto*, 'the child' and the verb *soma* 'to read' various utterances can be constructed such as:

*mtoto **a**soma*	*mtoto **na**soma*	*mtoto **li**soma*	*mtoto **ta**soma*
'the child reads'	'the child is reading'	'the child read'	'the child will read'

Without a specific noun, the word ***a**soma* will be interpreted as 'he/she reads,' ***ana**soma* as 'he/she is reading,' etc. The point is, in Turkish and Swahili, the morphemes have one meaning apiece and they agglutinate, that is, they stick to the root to form words.

In contrast to analytic morphology is **fusional morphology** or: one morpheme, many meanings. Verb endings in Polish exemplify synthetic word formation morphology. The ending *-iła* on the word *mówiła* 'she speaks' puts four ideas into one morpheme: third person, singular, past tense, and feminine. The terms *analytic* and *fusional* refer to the morpheme-to-meaning correspondence.

When speaking of the morpheme-to-word correspondence, languages might be **isolating**, that is one morpheme–one word. A good example is Chinese. Or they might be synthetic/polysynthetic, that is, many morphemes–one word, and whether the term **synthetic** or **polysynthetic** is applied depends on who is doing the counting. The latter is also sometimes called *incorporating* morphology. In this type, it is difficult to separate the subjects from the predicates, since all parts of an utterance are incorporated into either a verbal or nominal expression of an action/idea. The vaguest sense of polysynthesis can be found in the verb *to babysit*, where the object of the action is incorporated into the verb, but polysynthesis is not a characteristic of English. A good example from Nootka, a Native American language found in British Columbia, would be the verb *inikihlminihisita*, which breaks down into the morphemes:

inik-	-ihl-	-minih-	-is-	-it-	-a
'fire'	'in house'	'plural'	'small'	'past'	'ongoing'

'several small fires were burning in the house'

Elaborate polysynthesis is commonly found in the languages of the American Northwest.

Word order

In addition to word-formation typologies, word-order typologies tell us a lot about speaker preferences. In the late 1950s, historical and comparative linguist, Joseph Greenberg, started investigating word-order patterns in a wide variety of languages, and the first thing he noticed was that speakers the world over have a strong preference for putting the subject before the object. Word-order typologies compare the basic word-order patterns in the world's languages with respect to the arrangements of the principle parts of a sentence, namely the subject (S), verb (V), and object (O). A basic word-order pattern is defined to be the most numerous type and/or the one with the least number of presuppositions. For instance, the German utterance *Die Mutter küsst die Tochter* could be either 'the mother kisses/is kissing the daughter' or 'the daughter kisses/is kissing the mother' because the definite feminine article *die* is the same in both the nominative (subject) and accusative (object) case. However, the first interpretation is the more basic, because it would be the answer to the question 'What is the mother doing?,' which contains no presuppositions about that activity. The second interpretation would require a question presupposing that the daughter is doing something to someone, namely kissing, and we don't yet know whom she is kissing. In order to secure the effect of the second interpretation, *Mutter* is likely to be stressed.

There are six possibilities for a basic word order: SVO, SOV, VSO / / OVS, OSV, VOS. The first three are commonly found around the world, which suggests that speakers have a general preference for subjects before objects. The patterns OVS and OSV are not common but do occur, and VOS might be nonexistent. PIE and Old English were SOV languages, as are Japanese, Korean, Cherokee, Tibetan, Mongolian, and Georgian, just to name a few of this most prevalent worldwide pattern. Modern English and the standard Romance languages are SVO languages along with Vietnamese and Hausa, which is spoken in Nigeria and Niger. Arabic is a VSO language, along with Hawaiian, Welsh, and Squamish, another language spoken in British Columbia. The Amazonian language Urarina is OVS. Other languages of the Amazonian Basin are OSV, such as Jamamadi. ASL might well qualify as an OSV language. There is debate whether any true VOS languages exist. One candidate is regularly put forth, namely Malagasy (Austronesian), spoken on Madagascar.

What is most interesting about word-order typologies is how the basic word-order pattern of a language harmonizes with other word-order patterns in the language. One could categorize languages along any number of criteria, but these criteria may or may not reveal anything else interesting. For instance, one could make a list of all the tone languages in the world and all the intonation languages in the world, but those lists will not yield any further insight into the workings of those languages. A basic word-order pattern, however, predicts that when the object precedes the verb (SOV, OVS, OSV):

  (i)   the indirect object precedes the object;
  (ii) the auxiliary comes after the verb;
  (iii) the relative clause precedes the object of the clause;
  (iv) adjectives precede nouns; and
  (v)   genitives precede nouns.

Conversely, when the verb precedes the object (SVO, VSO, VOS):

  (i)   the indirect object follows the object;
  (ii) the auxiliary comes before the verb;
  (iii) the relative clause follows the object of the clause;
  (iv) adjectives follow nouns; and
  (v)   genitives follow nouns.

In other words, SVO/VSO and SOV are mirror images of one another. The phrase 'I give the red book to the boy' in French is:

je	*donne*	*le*	*livre*	*rouge*	*au*	*garçon*
'I'	'give'	'the'	'book'	'red'	'to the'	'boy'

The direct object 'the book' is next to the verb, thus making it literally direct, while the indirect object (to) 'the boy' is farther away from the verb (S–V–D.O.–I.O.), thus making it literally indirect. Furthermore, the adjective 'red' follows the noun. The same order of elements is the case for the phrase 'I give the red book to Taro' in Japanese, only in reverse:

watashi-wa	*taroo-ni*	*akai*	*hon-wo*		*agemasu*
'I' 'subject'	'Taro' 'to'	'red'	'book'	'object'	'give'

Note that with the verb at the end, the direct object is still next to the verb, while the indirect object now precedes the direct object (S–I.O.–D.O.–V), making it farther away from the verb. Finally, the adjective 'red' precedes the verb. Note further that English – always hedging its bets – does not type perfectly. Although it is now a very staid SVO language, adjectives precede nouns, as do genitives (of animate objects, *the woman's purse*). German is an interesting case because it, too, hedges its bets only in a different way: in main clauses, the order is SVO, and the auxiliary precedes the verb, while in dependent clauses, the order is SOV, and the auxiliary dutifully follows the verb.

Head/dependent

A third typological classification exists, and this concerns where grammars (and presumably their speakers) choose to put what morphological information, of the kind we saw at the end of Chapter 1. In a nutshell: on the phrasal level, the marking of, for instance, possession can go either on the possessors (dependents) or on the things possessed (heads); at the clausal level, the marking of, for instance, grammatical relations can go either on the nouns (dependents) with case markers or on the verbs (heads) with what is called agreements with arguments.

The immediate point to make here is that typological classifications are possible in the first place because humans have found only a couple of ways of keeping track of what is going on in an utterance, which is a rapidly fading signal that necessarily unfolds in a linear fashion over time. Some of us have worked it out by attaching grammatical relations – who's doing what to whom/with whom/for whom – on the verb. Some of us have worked it out by distributing the information in elements surrounding the verb.

Functional Classification

This classification is not about the grammatical properties of a language but rather its use. Linguists and language specialists have noticed that certain advantages accrue to languages and, then, necessarily to their speakers, that have some kind of official status as the language of:

(i)   classroom instruction;
(ii)   parliamentary procedures;
(iii) a broadcast medium; and/or
(iv)   an important body of writing, be it literary, religious, or legal.

Sometimes, all three bodies of writing are in one document, as is the case of the Qur'ān. The importance of writing is the topic of Chapter 5, and the effects of language policy and laws are taken up in Chapter 6.

Written languages with official status along with literary, legal, and/or religious force are known as power languages or H, for High (status). We note, first, that power is one of the organizing themes of this book and the subject of Part II and, second, that power languages are languages nonspeakers want to learn. Speakers of other languages, ones without official status and/or an important body of writing, sometimes suffer the consequences of those lacks. Nevertheless, they may enjoy an in-group feeling from speaking these languages, and they are known as solidarity languages or L, for Low (status). These are languages nonspeakers have little desire to learn, and it may be the case that if a foreigner does try to learn that language, the speakers may have a variety of reactions. They may be surprised and flattered by the attention. They will likely be completely puzzled by the effort. It is also possible they may not wholly appreciate the intrusion. The distinction between H and L expands our earlier discussion of major and minor languages – but only in a way. While it is highly likely the case that all major languages are H, it is not necessarily the case that all minor languages are L in the terms described at the end of Chapter 2.

When power and solidarity languages exist side by side and are two forms of the same (or similar enough) language, the situation is called **diglossia**, and the two forms serve two different functions in the community. H may be used in school, on television, and in any and all formal settings. L may be used in the family, on the street, and in any and all casual settings. H is always written. L is usually unwritten or is used in limited written situations, say, the conversation bubble of a cartoon. However, the advent of social networking has led to an increase in various Ls now being written. Diglossic situations are found in all corners of the globe: across the Arab world, Modern Standard Arabic is the H version, while a wide variety of local Ls exist. In Switzerland, Hochdeutsch (High German) is H, and Switzerdeutsch (Swiss German) is L. In India, highly Sanskritized Hindi is H, while vernacularized Hindi is L. In the Caribbean, the metropolitan varieties of English, French, and Dutch are H, as opposed to English-, French-, and Dutch-based creoles, which are L, as in Haiti, where French is H, and Kreyòl is L. It is important to note that H and L may be varieties of the same language, or they may be completely unrelated languages, as is the case with Spanish and Guaraní in modern-day Paraguay.

The dynamics of H and L have surely existed for all time. In the time of Alexander the Great, Attic Greek would have been H, and all other varieties of Greek or other local languages would have been L. The Greeks had a word for the nonspeakers of Greek: *barbari*. This word comes through Latin and eventually into English as 'the barbarians,' which definitely has a negative connotation, although it might not have had one in ancient Greek. In Medieval Europe, Latin was H, while Italian, French, and Spanish were L. Following the Norman Conquest in England, French was H, and English was L. In older traditions of historical linguistics, the terms *substratum* (L) and *superstratum* (H) were used to describe the effects of contact between languages with differential power.

An important point can easily be made here. Over the course of human history, it has usually been the case that several or more languages, often with asymmetrical indices of prestige, have been in contact with one another, often for extended periods of time. This means that most humans have lived, and now live, their lives through two or more language varieties or two or more separate languages. Only speakers of a prestige variety and people living in isolated places tend to be monolinguals. If you are surprised by the observation that most humans commonly speak more than one language or language variety, then you have assumed the language ideology of the nation-state, to be taken up in Chapter 4. The fact is, in the world today and likely for all time, multilingualism is the more common linguistic condition than is monolingualism.

In writing this book, we have been inspired by the valuable findings provided by these types of classifications, and we know there is further work to be done in all areas. *The World Atlas of Language Structures* (Maddieson 2011), first published in 2005, is a great resource for further philological work. We, the authors, contribute our part by recontextualizing the world's languages. We want students of language to appreciate some of the dynamics that produced the features that have been classified, and we want students of political science, cultural anthropology, and/or sociology interested in different parts of the world to become aware of the importance of the often-overlooked lynchpins, namely the languages that make our social and political worlds go round.

Final Note: The Role of Sanskrit in India Today

In the pages to come, many topics will recur, but one in particular stands out: the relationship between language and religion. We saw it already in the obstacle religion created in Sir William Jones's quest to learn Sanskrit. We will further see it woven through Chapter 5, which discusses the development and importance of writing systems, as well as Chapter 8, which discusses colonialism. Sacred languages tend to carry a lot of cultural importance, and any efforts to alter them and/or teach them to non-believers are going to be met with strong resistance.

The effects of their sacred nature can also be long lasting. Latin has not been spoken for several thousand years, but it is still considered a prestigious language, worth being taught in high schools and colleges in many places. In part, its prestige derives from the cultural and political importance of the Roman Empire. Another part of its prestige comes from its long place in the Christian Church and its status of the language of the Bible in Western Europe. In the fourth century CE, Eusebius Hieronymus, known today as St. Jerome, translated a number of Hebrew and Greek manuscripts to create a *versio vulgata*, or Latin Vulgate Bible. This version became the official one used by the Church, as was Latin the official language of all Christians until the Protestant Reformation in the sixteenth century. Even into the eighteenth century, Latin had currency as a language of administration, for instance in the Austro-Hungarian Empire, and in scientific discourse. All learned men at the time were expected to read and write Latin.

Such is the continuing place of Sanskrit in India today. In the August 10, 2014 edition of *The Hindu*, an English-language newspaper in India, appears the article "Where are the Sanskrit speakers?" (Sreevatsan 2014). In it, Professor Ganesh Devy of the People's Linguistic Survey of India acknowledges that no one speaks Sanskrit today, with Hindu priests using it only during ceremonies. Nevertheless, because of the continuing high prestige of this language, 14,000 people in this country of over one billion claimed it as their mother tongue in the 2011 census. (Census 2011 language figures have not yet been released.) Devy calls Sanskrit a language with influence but no presence, placing it nowhere and everywhere. He says that Sanskrit is an idea with a strong hold on the Indian imagination. People like to think that somewhere in India, it is still spoken.

In October 2014, the Central Board of Secondary Education instituted a Sanskrit Week for schools, where students engage in activities such as learning and singing a Sanskrit hymn and practicing Vedic Mathematics, which dates back thousands of years when Sanskrit was the main language used by scholars. Like learning Latin as the basis for knowing Spanish, French, and Italian, the argument for Sanskrit Week is based on the idea that knowing something about Sanskrit helps understanding of Hindi, Bengali, and Marathi. However, like everything concerning language in a multilingual state, speakers of languages with no historical relationship to Sanskrit are not necessarily in favor of celebrating this language. In the state of Tamil Nadu, for instance, where Tamil, a Dravidian language, is spoken, certain inhabitants called for a Classical Language Week, where each state could focus on its own linguistic heritage. The point is that the inauguration of a Sanskrit Week is now infused with political overtones and effects. The language–religion–politics intersection is yet another one we will see often enough in the following chapters.

Exercises

Exercise 1 – Grimm's Law

Using the sound correspondences found in the text, match the native English word with the fancier borrowed Latin word with the same Indo-European root:

English (Germanic)	Latin borrowing
father	pedal (<pes, ped- 'foot')
fish	paucity (<paucus 'few')
few	paternal (<pater 'father')
foot	pisces (<piscis 'fish')
thirst	trio (<tres 'three')
three	tumescent (<tumere 'swell')
thumb	torrid (<torrere 'dry')
hundred	capital (<caput 'head')
heart	cornucopia (<cornu 'horn')
hall, hell	cellar (<cellarium)
horn	century (<centum 'hundred')
head	cordial, cardiac (<cor/car 'heart')
hound	canine (<canis 'dog')
puff	labiodental (<labium 'lip')
lip	buccal (<bucca 'inflated cheek')
teach	dentist (<dens 'tooth')

ten   dictate (<dicere 'say')
tooth   decade (<decem 'ten')

corn   grackle (<graculus 'jackdaw')
cool   glacial (<glacies 'ice')
crow   genuflect (<genu 'knee')
kin   grain (<granum 'grain')
knee   genus, generate (<genus 'race, kind')

Exercise 2 – arbitrariness of the sign

Using the principle of the arbitrariness of the sign, make linguistic groups (and sub-groups, where possible) based on the following comparative vocabulary of languages spoken in Europe.

	one	two	three	head	eye	ear	nose	mouth	tooth
1.	bat	bi	hiryr	byry	begi	belair	sydyr	aho	orts
2.	edin	dva	tri	glava	oko	uxo	nos	usta	zeb
3.	ēn	tvē	drī	hōft	ōx	ōr	nōs	mont	tant
4.	wen	tuw	θrij	hed	aj	ijr	nowz	mawθ	tuwθ
5.	yks	kaks	kolm	pea	silm	korv	nina	sū	hamas
6.	yksi	kaksi	kolme	pæ	silmæ	korva	nenæ	sū	hamas
7.	œn	do	tRwa	tet	œj	oRej	ne	buš	dā
8.	aijns	tsvaj	draj	kopf	auge	ōr	nāze	munt	tsān
9.	uno	due	tre	testa	okjo	orekjo	naso	boka	dente
10.	jeden	dva	tši	glova	oko	uxo	nos	usta	zōp
11.	un	doj	trej	kap	okj	ureke	nas	gura	dinte
12.	adin	dva	tri	galava	oko	uxo	nos	rot	zup
13.	uno	dos	tres	kabesa	oxo	orexa	naso	boka	djente
14.	en	tvo	tre	hyvud	oga	ora	næsa	mun	tand

Three language stocks with representative language are: Basque: Basque; Uralic: Estonian and Finnish; and Indo-European: Bulgarian, Dutch, English, French, German, Italian, Polish, Romanian, Russian, Spanish, and Swedish.

Note that in no. 11 the word *gura* and in no. 12 the word *rot* stand out; in no. 13 the word *kabesa* might give you pause. However, base your grouping on the strength of the similarities of the other eight words with the group you think these language belong in.

Discussion Questions

1 How does the distinction between descriptive rules and prescriptive rules alter your view of language? Are you what linguists call a "prescriptivist?" From what sources did you inherit your prescriptivist beliefs – what do they do for you?

2 Is this the first time you have encountered a conversation about historical linguistics and the historical reconstructive method? Why do you suppose it has not been a part of your education until now?

3   Hopefully, you have appreciated from reading this chapter that attitudes about languages almost never have anything to do with the languages themselves but rather are attitudes about speakers. If this is the case, where do attitudes about language come from? What kinds of storylines did you hear as a child about the language varieties in your community and beyond?

4   What are the power and solidarity language varieties spoken in your community? How do you suppose those particular language varieties achieved those particular statuses? Can you imagine that the power language variety could ever become the solidarity language variety and vice versa? If so, what kinds of conditions (social, political, economic, etc.) would need to be in place for that reversal to happen?

5   A key word in this text is contingency. What does it mean to describe something as contingent? What does it mean to describe language, or a specific language variety, as contingent? Contingent on what?

Notes

1   He was knighted upon his arrival in India and is known in history as Sir William Jones.

2   A protolanguage is a common ancestor language, which has produced at least one descendant. It is not by definition one without written records. It simply happens to be the case that the protolanguages reconstructed for the major language stocks of the world antedate written records.

3   The term *family* refers to a group of languages that are related at a time-depth of 2500–4000 years.

4   The term *stock* refers to a group of languages that are related at a time-depth of 5000–10,000 years ago.

5   The Austronesian stock was recognized as early as 1706 but not fully worked out.

6   The term *phylum* refers to a group of languages that may have more or less evidence of being related at a time-depth greater than 10,000 years.

7   Roma is the language spoken by the Roma people, erroneously called Gypsies because it was once believed they came from Egypt. DNA studies confirm the linguistic evidence linking Roma to other Indo-Iranian languages, in that three genetic markers found in a study of Roma groups in Bulgaria show the same chromosomal background as Indian and Pakistani subjects (Kalaydjieva et al. 2005).

8   Hungarian has many Iranian borrowings, but that is a story for Chapter 8.

9   For a linguistic area to be a linguistic, we do not want to admit languages with similarities that are from geographically distant places. Postposted definite articles are found in Norwegian and certain northern varieties of Russian.

10 The modern English verb *to go* is also suppletive. Its present tense comes from the Old English verb *gān*, and its past tense *went* comes from a different Old English verb, namely *wendan* 'to go.' One can still say, "Look, the woman over there, wending her way through the marketplace, is my sister." The past tense of this verb is now *wended*.

References

Cannon, Garland (1964) *Oriental Jones: A Biography of Sir William Jones (1746–1794)*. Bombay: Asia Publishing House.

Grimm, Jacob (1819) *Deutsche Grammatik*. Göttingen: Dieterischen Buchhandlung.

Kalaydjieva, Luba, Bharti Morar, Raphaelle Chaix, and Hua Tang (2005) A newly discovered founder population the Roma/Gypsies. *Bio Essays* 27: 1084–1094.

Maddieson, Ian (2011, September 24) Consonant inventories. In Matthew S. Dryer and Martin Haspelmath (eds.), *The World Atlas of Language Structures Online*. Retrieved from Max Planck Digital Library. http://wals.info/chapter/1.

Mithun, Marianne (1992) External triggers and internal guidance in syntactic development: coordinating conjunction. In M. Gerritsen and G. Stein (eds.), *Internal and External Factors in Syntactic Change*. Berlin: Mouton de Gruyter, 89–129.

Sreevatsan, Ajai (2014) Where are the Sanskrit speakers? *The Hindu* August 10.

Further Reading

Andresen, Julie Tetel (1990) *Linguistics in America: 1776–1924: A Critical History*. London: Routledge.

Aikhenvald, Alexandra and R.M.W. Dixon (eds.) (2001) *Areal Diffusion and Genetic Inheritance: Problems in Comparative Linguistics*. Oxford: Oxford University Press.

Aikhenvald, Alexandra and R.M.W. Dixon (eds.) (2006) *Grammars in Contact: A Cross-Linguistic Typology*. Oxford: Oxford University Press.

Bloomfield, Leonard (1933) *Language*. Chicago: University of Chicago Press.

Campbell, Lyle (2004) *Historical Linguistics: An Introduction*. 2nd edition. Cambridge, MA: The MIT Press.

Jakobson, Roman (1990) *On Language*. Cambridge, MA: Harvard University Press.

Whitney, William Dwight (1867) *Language and the Study of Language. Twelve Lectures on the Principles of Linguistic Science*. London: Trübner.

Part II
Effects of Power

Introductory Note: On Power

Power is often associated with money and muscle. Indeed, power and money do attract one another, and there is no doubt that the richer you are and the bigger and stronger you are, the more often you get your way. However, in matters of language, power has qualities more like wind or water or *chi* in that it is ever present and relentless, and circulates in the spaces, both large and small, where it can. We begin our examination of the macrodynamics of the language loop through the prism of power in Part II by noting that:

(i)   Power is bound to freedom and flows through fields of possibilities. Although actions taken by individuals are not predetermined, they are nevertheless always bound by the constraints of a given time and a given place. The rebellious teen who freely chooses to go Goth has, first of all, not invented the category *Goth* and must, second of all, live with the consequences of this identity choice. When, in the twentieth century, ethnic Croats decided to become independent, they did not imagine their liberation in terms of a feudal state, a city-state, or a monarchy; they wanted a nation-state, just like all their neighbors had. Turning to the relationship between language and the nation-state, as we will do in Chapter 4, it was a necessary part of the Croats' independence that Croatian would be understood to be a separate and distinct language from Serbian.

(ii) Power is productive; it brings states of affairs into existence. Once the contingencies of science and politics have created the category *insane*, the nation-state can produce and then mobilize an apparatus affecting the behavior of those identified as insane. Similarly, once the contingencies of science and politics have produced the domain of sexuality as a field of knowing, then certain identities come into being: homosexual, heterosexual, bisexual, asexual, and so forth.

Languages in the World: How History, Culture, and Politics Shape Language, First Edition.
Julie Tetel Andresen and Phillip M. Carter.
© 2016 John Wiley & Sons, Inc. Published 2016 by John Wiley & Sons, Inc.

These identities then organize the social worlds of those hailed into those categories and can determine, for instance, the legal rights pertaining to whether two people can be married. In Chapter 5, we will trace how the domain of writing came into existence and then explore the consequences of this invention. The power of the written word is well known, and those who know how to read and write are able to produce such things as sacred texts, Declarations of Independence, laws, writs, literature, blogs, op-ed pieces, and textbooks (the list is endless), which represent the beliefs/demands/rights/views of those who have access to this kind of power.

(iii) Power is not held absolutely; it is diffused. This is to say that one need not be in the position of power in order to exert power. A female phone sex worker, fulfilling the fantasies of men she would find offensive and subjugating in her private life, makes more money the longer she can draw out her clients' fantasies. A prisoner may go on a hunger strike as a way to assert control over his life and actions. When it comes to matters of language, as we will see in Chapter 6, power plays are found everywhere and often lead to violence. However, as long as one has a voice, one can use it, if one dares. In 2010, Cantonese speakers took to the streets of Guangzhou (historically, Canton) to protest a local politician's proposal that a local television station stop broadcasting in Cantonese and replace it with Mandarin.

We humans are far enough down our sociohistorical language road to have produced well-defined institutions – religious, economic, political, legal, educational – through which power moves and by which systems of differentiation are created. In the eighteenth century, grammarians wrote their prescriptive rules in order to distinguish between those who knew how to speak correctly and those who did not, with the former enjoying privilege and prestige and all the benefits that come with position. Several centuries earlier, Africans had been captured and taken as slaves to both North and South America. In the United States, the conditions under which these people lost their African languages and adopted English produced a variety known today as African-American English, which is often stigmatized, just as its speakers sometimes are.

In the chapters that follow, we are concerned with putting under global review the ways speakers and their languages are advantaged and disadvantaged by the effects of power, for example, whether their language is seen as a national language or is deemed a dialect, whether their historical records are preserved in libraries or are set in flames, and whether their language is declared official or is banned.

4

Effects of the Nation-State and the Possibility of Kurdistan

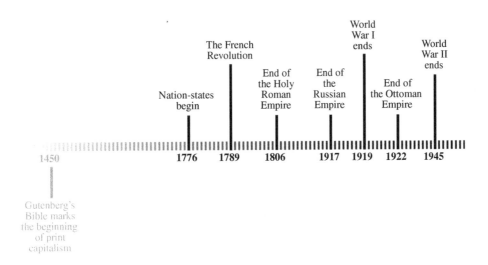

Lines Are Drawn in the Sand

In 1915 and 1916, while World War I was ravaging Europe, an English diplomat, Sir Mark Sykes, and his French counterpart, François Georges-Picot, met in a series of negotiations. The result of these meetings was the Sykes–Picot agreement that would determine the zones of influence in the Middle East for Britain and France. Arab cities such as Baghdad (present-day Iraq) and Kuwait City (present-day Kuwait) were placed under British rule, while Beirut (present-day Lebanon) and Damascus (present-day Syria) fell under French rule. Their negotiations seem to have been an exercise in cartographic whim. Sykes is reported to have said, "I should like to draw a line from the *e* in Acre to the last *k* in Kirkuk."

Languages in the World: How History, Culture, and Politics Shape Language, First Edition.
Julie Tetel Andresen and Phillip M. Carter.
© 2016 John Wiley & Sons, Inc. Published 2016 by John Wiley & Sons, Inc.

Sykes almost got his wish. The present-day Iraqi border with Syria and Jordan begins in the west not far from the Lebanese city of Acre and extends in nearly a straight line north and east toward Kirkuk in Iraq before jogging north to Turkey. The borders of Iraq were drawn when the League of Nations was created in 1919 soon after the end of World War I. That is to say, the nation-state of Iraq was a twentieth-century invention, and it was created by cobbling together the three separate provinces of Mosul, Baghdad, and Basra that had been under Ottoman rule. Indeed, the entire Middle East is a product of lines drawn primarily to serve British civilian and military ambitions. T. E. Lawrence, the famous Lawrence of Arabia, is rumored to have bragged that he and Winston Churchill had designed the modern Middle East over dinner. Whatever the truth of the boast, by 1922 the deed was done (see Map 4.1).

The end of World War I coincided, more or less, with the end of the Ottoman Empire. With its partitioning among the Allied Powers of Europe, some consideration was given to creating an independent state for the Kurds, who speak Kurdish, an Indo-European language, which makes them one of the largest non-Arabic-speaking populations in the region. However, no proposal was agreed upon, no separate state was created, and a significant Kurdish population found itself drawn inside the lines of northern Iraq. Seventy years later, in 1990, another conflict involving the West erupted in the region, and the Persian Gulf War began with Iraq's invasion of Kuwait. At the end of the conflict, United States President George H. W. Bush went on Voice of America Radio and encouraged Iraqis to "take matters into their own hands." The Kurds, perceiving weakness in the government, saw their opportunity to take control of their fate, but Saddam Hussein managed to quell all popular uprisings. The result was the mass departure of nearly two million Kurds, who left Iraq mostly on foot. The problem was, given the historical contingencies, the Kurds had no particular place to go.

In this chapter, we trace the rise of the nation-state in Western Europe and seek to illustrate how it came to be solidified during the course of the eighteenth century. As we will see, nation-states came to cohere around the one nation, one language ideology, which created at the same time a new association between a particular language and a particular place – and a particular place to go was exactly what the Kurds were lacking when they walked out of Iraq. The disenfranchised Kurds leverage our understanding of nation-states as human creations, not timeless and universal realities, and give us a wedge into exploring the various ways language and place-based political identity have been put to strategic use in order to construct and maintain states and to contain and constrain the speakers within those states. We end the chapter by looking at some of the bedeviling effects of a sometimes hidden third term standing alongside of one nation, one language ideology, and that is *race*.

The Status of Language on the Eve of the Nation-State

Language has not always been central in the organization of political structure and identity, nor have languages always been delimited by precise boundaries. The rulers of the monarchies and empires antedating the modern European nation-states did

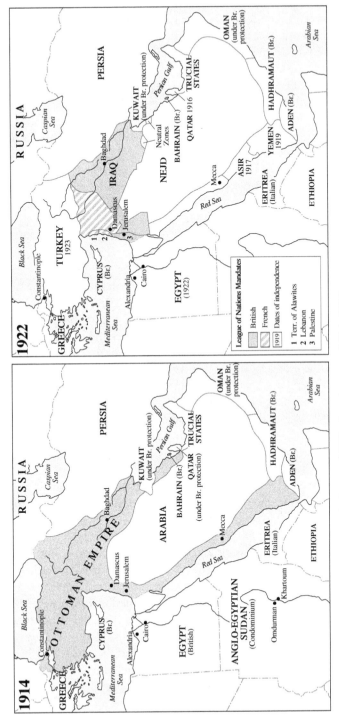

Map 4.1   The Middle East before and after World War I settlements, 1914–1922.

not concern themselves with the languages their subjects spoke, nor did they perceive the boundaries of their realms as fixed, since they waxed and waned with wars and marriages. In pre-eighteenth-century Europe, dynastic power was concentrated in centers and radiated out over large expanses to somewhat fluid borders. Dynastic legitimacy was secured by divine right, and identity cohered around religion. For many centuries, religious diversity was perceived as a threat, while linguistic diversity was simply a fact of life. However, during the eighteenth century, attitudes surrounding language began to shift in concert with the reorganization of political power. The ruling powers sometimes did and sometimes did not take heed of the winds of change. In either case, still today many places across the landmass Eurasia are dealing with the linguistic fallout of the dissolutions of the Holy Roman Empire (962–1806), the Russian Empire (1721–1917), and the Ottoman Empire (1453–1922).

At the end of the eighteenth century, the Holy Roman Emperor Joseph II,[1] House of Habsburg and leader of the Austro-Hungarian Empire, ruled over speakers of a wide variety of languages, including Hungarian (aka Magyar), which is Uralic, as well as Croatian, Slovakian, Ukrainian, Italian, and Austro-German, all of which are Indo-European. In the 1780s, he made the decision to change the administrative language of the empire from Latin to German because he deemed the mediaeval Latin of the nobility unsuitable to carry out the needs of the masses. (Perhaps he caught the whiff of a populist scent coming from the Americas.) He chose German not because he felt a special allegiance to the German language, culture, or people as such, and he was certainly aware that many of his own relatives did not speak this language. Rather, he made his choice based on the fact that of all the languages in the empire, German had the most developed cultural and literary tradition, as well as the fact that there were significant numbers of German speakers in all parts of the empire. The emperor's choice was pragmatic.[2] In retrospect, it also looks natural. In the context of the Austro-Hungarian Empire, it was unremarkable that many members of the House of Habsburg did not speak German. However, in the context of twenty-first-century nationalisms, it is difficult to imagine a member of the German Bundestag (Parliament) not being able to speak German.

Similarly, it would be difficult to imagine any president of Russia not being able to speak Russian. However, the Tsarist Romanovs spoke French at their court in St. Petersburg in the eighteenth century, while much of provincial nobility spoke German. It took 20 years after Napoleon's 1812 siege of Moscow for a sense of Russian nationalism to begin to circulate in the Russian court, but it was not until Alexander III (1881–1894) that Russification became official dynastic policy. Before the nineteenth century, however, the Romanovs, like many Habsburgs with respect to German, had no affinity for the language of the people in whose midst they lived, namely the Russians. They had no need for such affinity, because they did not interact with people outside their own circles. The Romanovs ruled over speakers of a wide range of languages, representing at least three language stocks: Finnish, a Uralic language; German, Armenian, Russian, and Latvian, all Indo-European languages; and finally a variety of Central Asian Turkic languages, such as Tatar,[3] which were brought into the empire by Ivan the Terrible in the sixteenth century. Although administrators in Tsarist Russia were not particularly interested in making language policy and could be thought of as having been asleep at the wheel around the time of the Russian

Revolution, the Bolsheviks who came in the wake of 1917 were keenly interested in matters of language, since they were determined to create a modern state.

As for the Ottomans, Ottoman Turkish, a Turkic language, was the imperial language of the Ottoman Empire and was required for official correspondence with the government. It was a lingua franca, a unifying language bridging across groups of people who speak different languages – just as Latin was an administrative lingua franca of the Holy Roman Empire, and French was the lingua franca of the cultural elites, that is, the aristocrats in Europe. Especially influential within the Ottoman Empire were both Arabic, an Afro-Asiatic language, and Persian, an Indo-European language. Beyond that, the great linguistic diversity within the Ottoman Empire was not considered a threat to imperial power, and the many languages spoken in the realm belonged to equally diverse language stocks: Georgian, a Caucasian language; Berber and Somali, Afro-Asiatic languages like Arabic; Hungarian, once again, Uralic; Greek, Kurdish, Romanian, and Ukrainian, all Indo-European languages. No one could have guessed that when the Ottoman Empire came to an end, nation-states called Georgia, Somalia, Hungary, Greece, Romania, and Ukraine, all articulated around national languages bearing their name, would have come into existence but not a state called Kurdistan.

When these empires fell, and new political units organized themselves around the idea of the nation, one resource that had previously been mostly unremarkable to the political elite – namely language – found a central place in this reorganization. Nation-states came into being at the same time their titular national languages came to be recognized as such. To say it another way, when the state reorganized itself along linguistic lines, the nation came into being.

The Epistemology of the Nation-State

Despite being a relatively recent form of political organization, nations, with their cultural, political, and military apparatuses and their corresponding ideologies of nationalism, are driving forces in world politics today. Indeed, much of the conflict of the world is over the resources, spaces, and identities thought to be owned or contained within certain nations. Among the resources nations try to harness and control are the languages spoken within their boundaries; and nations, with their laws, services, and schools, are invested in controlling them by classifying them, for example, Variety A counts as a language, while Variety B counts as a dialect. In the political ideology of nationalism, language and the nation-state are one, while dialects are inconvenient residues to be marginalized, swept under the rug, or erased altogether. The one nation, one language ideology is the reason we have insisted on understanding *language* and *dialect* as sociopolitical terms in this book. It is also the reason linguists, who wish to step outside these classifications in order to get a perspective on them, choose to speak in terms of language *varieties*, a politically and historically neutral term.

When the empirical realities about place and language change, thereby engendering new forms of identity and citizenship and civic life, so also do the ways people think about these new realities change. We call this transformation *epistemological*. We define an epistemological framework to be a set of presuppositions, stakes, temperamental positions, preferences, and/or stylistic attitudes taken with respect to large-scale questions. It is a set of assumptions, concepts, definitions, and distinctions through which questions get raised and answered, and by which what is deemed a fact is both made possible and constrained. An epistemological framework is an interpretive repertoire, a systematically related set of terms, often used with stylistic and grammatical coherence, and often organized around one or more central metaphors. These frameworks can be seen to be composed of interlocking discourses and ideologies, and although they are systematic, they are not always self-consistent, since humans are not famous for being strictly logical. These frameworks make up important parts of the common sense of a culture, although some may be specific to certain institutional domains, disciplines, or subcultures. Another way to understand an epistemological framework is to say that it is a way of knowing.

Epistemological frameworks can refer to historical periods such as Enlightenment versus Romanticism. Enlightenment ways of knowing typically include: a theory of progress in which the future is always better; an emphasis on reason, order, and precision; and a foundationalist and universalist understanding of human nature. As for language, it is seen as a man-made construction, a social reality susceptible to reform and so-called improvements based on reason. We can call this the *political conception of language*. Recall from Chapter 3 that prescriptive grammar was a product of the eighteenth century. The Enlightenment is furthermore closely associated with eighteenth-century France.

By way of contrast, Romanticist ways of knowing typically include: the notion that things were better in the past; an emphasis on emotional punch; and the relativist recognition that people and cultures are different one from the others. As for language, the life and growth and even death of language are solely in the province of *das Volk*, the nameless, faceless masses; no one person or group can intervene in the process of language change. We can call this *the organic conception of language*. Recall from Chapter 3 that Bopp and Grimm were devoted to historical reconstruction. Their goal was to uncover the original language, or *Ursprache*, the one before time has withered it, corrupted it. Recall again that Grimm thought the sound correspondences he identified were the unconscious work of the independent spirit of the German people. Romanticism is closely associated with nineteenth-century Germany.

The most important take-away from this discussion of epistemological frameworks is the idea that in the absence of a competing way of knowing, the one prevailing in a group, a community, a nation, and/or the world is called *reality*. We find the reality of nations inscribed on maps with well-defined borders, which at times are physically instantiated in walls and fences separating one nation from the next. Although language does not fit neatly within these national borders, it has been successfully mobilized since the eighteenth century as one among the symbolic resources recruited to construct nations. Other well-known symbolic resources include flags, pledges, great seals, national anthems, and certainly money. We have tangible evidence of our identities in our driver's licenses, our social security cards, and our passports, and we all have relationships with the Department of Motor Vehicles, the Internal Revenue Service, and border guards. There is a convergence between the immaterial (linguistic) and the material resources, in that the material resources consistently use one variety of a language, the standard variety. The convergence is so complete that many times a nation and its primary national language are synonymous, such that it is now seemingly self-evidently true to say: "In France, they speak French. In Spain, they speak Spanish." These statements, however, assume that languages such as French and Spanish are things existing in clearly defined forms differentiated from other languages. They assume that France and Spain are timeless places with clearly defined borders and homogeneous ethnic populations, namely the French and the Spanish. Even in an immigrant, ethnically diverse nation such as the United States, it is a truism to say that Americans speak English.

The French Revolution, German Romanticism, and Print Capitalism

The question can now be asked: What were the contingencies that made the ideology of the linguistically homogeneous nation possible and, with it, the creation of nation-states with clearly defined borders?

The creation of national consciousness in Western Europe was the product of a long process that began with the Renaissance. It gained momentum throughout the course of the eighteenth century as prior religious and dynastic frameworks lost favor in Europe. In the seventeenth century, Louis XIV could confidently declare: *L'état c'est moi* ('I am the state').[4] In the eighteenth century, with Enlightenment rationalism and the political conception of language, a new conception of the state came into being, and with it came a new formulation: *une langue, une nation* ('one language, one nation'), first coined by the French grammarian Nicolas Beauzée.[5] The heretofore separate realms of language and political entity are now clearly harnessed.

It is relatively easy for Americans to understand Enlightenment epistemology, because the United States itself is a partial by-product of eighteenth-century French political thought. The idea that the future will be better is in the rhetoric of all American presidents up through Obama, who still encourages Americans to strive for "a more perfect union." Thomas Jefferson, well versed in Enlightenment thought, was deeply invested in matters of language. He devoted some of his wide-ranging interests to the recording of Native American languages, particularly those in Virginia, such as Powhatan (Algonquin) and Cherokee (Iroquois).[6] He was also a linguistic liberal, arguing successfully against naming English, or any other language, as the official language of the United States.

North and South American colonists were among the first to assert their nationhoods, well before most of Europe. The United States was founded in 1776, Haiti in 1804, Paraguay in 1811, and Mexico, Peru, and Venezuela in 1821. The colonial revolutionaries were the cultural elites and shared the language of the ruling classes of the governments they were separating from. On equal linguistic ground with their sovereigns, they were determined to establish equal and necessarily independent political ground. About that (literal) ground, the consciousness of their place in the world – their physical space – was high. To become President of the United States, one must be born in the United States or a place outside the United States considered American soil, such as an army base or an embassy. In a monarchic or a dynastic state, the place of birth of the ruler is irrelevant, and so is his or her so-called national background, as the succession of non-English monarchs on Britain's throne for the last thousand years attests.

The political achievements of the colonial revolutionaries certainly caught the interests of political thinkers and political activists in Europe. Now we can identify three intertwined strands – an historical event, an intellectual movement, and an economic development – that, when woven together, solidified the one nation, one language ideology begun in pre-Revolutionary France and made it exportable to the rest of the world.

Historical event: the French Revolution

In Europe, the French Revolution, whose symbolic beginning is July 14, 1789, was a galvanizing event in the development of nationalisms. With the abolition of the French monarchy, the new Republic was organized around the democratic principles of *liberté*, *égalité*, and *fraternité*. Of these, the emphasis on *égalité* ('equality') is especially noteworthy for the present discussion, because the revolutionaries determined that one of the first inequalities was language. Before the Revolution and even well into the nineteenth century, no more than 10% of the population spoke what we would think of today as French. Rather, people living in what is now present-day France spoke languages such as: Breton, a Celtic language; Alsatian and Flemish, both Germanic languages; Catalan, Corsican, and Occitan, all three Romance languages; as well as Basque. In addition, innumerable, often mutually unintelligible varieties of a loosely defined French were spoken. Although these languages are still spoken in France today, they have all experienced significant decline since the Revolution.

The Revolution had a profound impact on language in France for at least two reasons. First, the revolutionaries believed that linguistic difference was a potential cause of inequality, which would violate the revolutionary principle *égalité* and undermine the success of the new Republic. Thus, Standard French was promoted as one of the foundations of the nation-state. An important figure in universalizing Standard French was Abbé Grégoire. In 1794, he presented his *Report on the necessity and means to annihilate the patois and to universalize the use of the French language* (Abbé Grégoire, 1794) to the National Convention. It is of note that today Abbé Grégoire is called a man ahead of his time for the stance he took against racism and slavery, and for his support for universal suffrage. His stance on abolishing dialects goes unnoticed and is less admirable than the stance he took on abolishing slavery. Such are the workings of language ideology: they work best when they are invisible.

Second, as a part of the effort to centralize the state through the French language, a strong national education system was developed, and the education system moved French further and further into the non-French-speaking regions. The so-called grammarian patriot, Urbain Domergue, had begun publishing a biweekly publication, *Journal de la langue françoise* before the Revolution, and so after the Revolution, his journal disseminated the linguistic norms to be taught in what would be known as *normal schools*. The norms, or standards, taught in these schools were based on a variety of French spoken in Paris, known as *Île de la Cité* French, after the name of an island in the Seine, considered the very center of the capital. This variety was promoted as the perfect language and was selected as the language of the state and the language of the new, central education system. The selection of Parisian French, actually the French of the court, as the national standard was understood as an egalitarian move in keeping with the priorities of the Republic, making what was once the province of the elite, the shared patrimony of all the citizens.

Thus perhaps for the first time in history was language recruited alongside other symbolic resources to help *construct* the identity of a nation-state through emblematic associations. Standard French was understood in pragmatic terms and as the answer to the question: Which language variety would be used in national institutions? However, it was also understood in symbolic terms, as language standing for and representing the state. In the long term, however, the imposition of Standard French created rather than eradicated inequality, in the sense that it sparked the association of non-standard varieties of French and regional non-French languages with feudalism and the lower classes. The French Revolution marked perhaps the first occassion in which the *symbolic value* of language was so profound that people could experience personal shame for the way they spoke. The Occitans in the south of France call this experience *la vergonha*. If shame is the fear of not being worthy of connection, *vergonha* is the fear you feel when you perceive a need or pressure to disconnect from your mother tongue.

The intellectual movement: German Romanticism

Around the time of the French Revolution, German romantic philosophers such as Johann Gottfried Herder and Wilhelm von Humbolt, in an era of monarchies and dynasties, began to theorize the nation as a revolutionary concept. Herder was especially influential in this regard, and his ideas were influential in the development of nationalisms across Europe. His thinking on nationalism focused on the concept of *das Volk*, those masses understood to be the core of the nation. He articulated a view of national patriotism rooted in folk practices, including folk tales.

The Grimm brothers, Jacob and Wilhelm, mentioned in Chapter 3, used Herder's work as their inspiration to collect and record German-language folk tales, which were understood to reflect the true German character. Herder believed these cultural traditions were the basis for national character, *Volkgeist*, and were crucial for nation-building efforts. Language, above all other cultural resources, was understood as the direct manifestation of an identity that was not merely cultural, but also national in nature. In other words, language was the precise distillation of all culture, which stood as the symbolic center of the nation. Herder's view on language and national identity is summarized in his phrase: *Denn jedes Volk ist Volk; es hat seine National-Bildung wie seine Sprache* ('Since every people is a People, it has its own national culture through its own language.') In Herder's philosophy, the German concept of *Bildung*, or self-growth, is extrapolated to the level of the nation, where it literally comes to mean 'nation building,' in the sense of creating a national identity.

The nationalism and state formation based on the political and conceptual groundwork laid by late-eighteenth-century political thinkers expanded rapidly in the nineteenth century. Herder in Germany and the revolutionaries in France set the terms of the debate. Their theories of language differed: the French held a mechanical conception of language, while the Germans held an organic conception of language; the French thought language was a tool that could be tinkered with and improved; the Germans took a hands-off policy toward language change. The French and the Germans nevertheless coincided in their belief in the relationship between nation and language: they converged on the ideology of the monolingual nation-state.

The economic development: print capitalism[7]

In his landmark book *Imagined Communities*, Benedict Anderson theorizes the **nation** as a new kind of community, and he attributes the new-found ability of people to imagine such a political entity to two forms of writing that flowered in the eighteenth century: novels and newspapers (Anderson [1983] 2006:24–25).[8] Readers of novels and newspapers receive a sense of historical, clocked time in which characters who might not know one another and events that might seem otherwise unrelated are gathered in one space to create a sense of an interacting world that is beyond the reader's experience but fully within the grasp of her imagination. In order to have a consciousness of a nation, one must be able to imagine one's fellow Americans, Haitians, Mexicans, Paraguayans, Peruvians, or Venezuelans – the vast majority of whom one will never meet – linked in real space and time. One must have a sense that the group of one's fellows is acting together with unknown effects on one another like characters in a novel, and that these actions occur simultaneously, such as events reported upon each day in the newspaper. This consciousness is different than a person imagining himself to be a subject of, or a believer in, a higher power, such King George III or Mohammad. A national consciousness has horizontal range linking fellows with no higher authority and comes with rights and responsibilities.

Jefferson recognized the preeminent importance of newspapers when he said, "If I had to choose between government without newspapers and newspapers without government, I would not hesitate to choose the latter." He was stressing the importance of an informed populace, for only an informed populace can make good choices concerning their governance. However, in an Anderson-style argument, Jefferson's quotation serves to suggest that a newspaper-reading public, one that shares the common knowledge of what is going on around them, becomes a community, the community of newspaper-readers. This community is imagined, but not imaginary.[9] The nation's reality is insured by the operation of the **state** – the particular set of bureaucracies, laws, police, military, educational system, etc. Any group making a claim to being a nation can now also make a claim to deserving a state. The identification of the Palestinian nation brings with it the possibility of a two-state solution with Israel.

One of the Founding Fathers of the United States was a printer: Benjamin Franklin. Printers get to print what they want, and they stay in business as long as they sell what they print. It is perhaps unfortunate for Franklin's printing legacy that he was not the printer in January, 1776 of Thomas Paine's *Common Sense* (Paine 1776), the American bestseller of all times in terms of sales in proportion to the size of the population.[10] This pamphlet created an immediate sensation in the colonies, and

George Washington made sure it was read to all his troops as they surrounded the British in Boston. This work was furthermore translated into French, and Paine was received as a political Prometheus when he arrived in Paris in 1787.

Beyond the novel, the newspaper, and the rabble-rousing pamphlet, print capitalism was a driver in the rise of national consciousness in three ways. First, it democratized reading, since the public was interested in reading materials printed not in Latin, the literary language of the educated elite, but in languages they could understand. A language leveled of strong vernacular features made it possible for speakers of the many disparate and sometimes unintelligible varieties of French or Spanish, for example, to understand one another through the written word. Second, the printed word provided the illusion of the permanence of language, which gave speakers who had not previously imagined being related to other speakers beyond their families or villages a sense of material connection to a broader community. Finally, and most importantly, print capitalism elevated certain languages to positions of power at the same time as other languages and language varieties were demoted.

Print capitalism also made possible the publication of monolingual dictionaries, which were ideologically congruent with the idea that languages were contained by national borders. That is, it was now possible to imagine not only that each state could have its own language, neatly contained within its own borders, but also that all the words of that language could be neatly contained within one book. In addition, dictionaries are crucial in establishing literary varieties, rather than colloquial ones, as the national standards. The dictionary that attended the rise of monolingual nation-states reinforced the idea that words could be literally separated from their usage in context, an idea that has increased in currency until today. We can thus conclude that the standard language ideology still operating in much of the West is a consequence of the epistemology of monolingual national standards developed in the eighteenth and nineteenth centuries in Europe, of which the dictionary is an important symbol. It remains an emblem of authority today.

In sum, the rise of nationalisms across Europe, spurred by and through the rise of print capitalism, created the fuel for the ideological development of the monolingual nation-state.

Standardization and the Instilling of *Vergonha*

Nations are imagined to be culturally and linguistically homogeneous, and so too must the standard national languages appear to be culturally neutral. While the nation is imagined but not imaginary, the standard language is an illusion of neutrality because it is always necessarily constructed out of one or more regional varieties. The quintessential example is Standard Italian, which is based on the Tuscan dialect that gained political and cultural cachet as early as the thirteenth century when it was used in the literature of authors such as Dante and Petrarch. Before the process of standardization, language in Italy could best be thought of as a long dialect chain running from south to north. To this day, some Italian dialects, such as the variety spoken in Sicily, are thought of as separate languages, given their low mutual intelligibility with Standard Italian.

The standardization of national languages took place in the context of state formation across Europe. For example, during the development of Hungarian state formation in the nineteenth century, Standard Hungarian was constructed based on the varieties of Northeast Hungary, and language planners were careful to avoid borrowings from other languages, including Latin, but especially German.[11] Throughout the eighteenth, nineteenth, and twentieth centuries, European nations constructed national standards as a part of their nation-building efforts. When standardizing a language, the first questions to ask are: Which variety will be the basis? and Which language variety will symbolize the whole? In other words, standardized varieties of languages in most cases attended, not preceded, the rise of nation-states in Europe. This is to say that whether or not Czech is a separate language from Slovak has not always been a relevant question. The rise of nationalism, though, required that Czech and Slovak be contrasted as much as possible in order to justify separate nations, and this effort required that some variety of Czech and some variety of Slovak be selected as *the* national language.

We will now give a point we have made several times final emphasis: many people assume dialects are derived, or degenerated, from a core, underlying, or somehow correct language. As a matter of historical fact, however, it is often the other way around, as the above examples illustrate. In the case of Hungarian, the standardized national language derived from a local variety. In the case of French, it derived from the group who once had the most social power. Here you can see how the notion of one nation, one language and then even one people works in tandem with the standard language ideology. Once French was articulated as the one and only language of the French Republic, standardized French, based on the speech of the elite classes in Paris, could be promoted as the so-called best French. We can now see that *la vergonha* is not only the shame of the need to disconnect from your native language but also the shame that you cannot fully connect to the standard language. Now even native French speakers who do not speak Parisian French can experience *la vergonha*.

Language and Individual Identity

In France, where there was once an unbroken dialect chain running from the *langue d'oc* in the south to the *langue d'oïl* in the north,[12] today there is only French, with vestiges of the old dialect chain still present in the rural areas. As successful as the project of consolidating France through the French language has been – both as an idea and as a set of policies – French speakers nevertheless still sound differently from one to the next. The differences are due in part to the fact that different regional varieties are spoken in cities such as Lille, Lyon, and Toulouse. But even within a city such as Paris, linguistic difference moves outward from center to periphery, such that residents in the city center sound differently from the residents in the *banlieue*, or suburbs. These differences in speech – from neighborhood to neighborhood and person to person – owe largely to a corresponding set of differences, namely, those having to do with the group and individual identities of the speakers themselves.

In this book, we understand speaker identity to be the result of the always incomplete interplay between a speaker's choice, what we call *agency*, and the limitations on those choices, what we call *identity constraints*. No identity is fully chosen by the individual, just as no identity is fully determined by forces external to the individual. This endless interplay between constraint and choice means that identities are necessarily dynamic, emergent, and contextual rather than static, predetermined, and immutable.

Speakers' identities are first always constrained by the speech communities into which they are born. A baby born into the *banlieue* surrounding Paris will by the contingency of birth end up speaking a noticeably different variety of French from the baby born into *le 16e arrondissement*, an area of Paris associated with great wealth. If the baby is born a girl, she will likely be socialized with other girls, thus reinforcing gendered language practices, and perhaps may even be instructed from a young age to speak in a way that adheres to cultural prescriptions for normative gendered behavior. If the child is born a boy, he will likely be socialized differently and coached in the ways of sounding like a boy.[13] Should the child be born into the *banlieue*, there is a good chance she will be of Moroccan, Algerian, or Libyan descent, which means that in the French national context, she may be understood to be *Magrébine*, or French North African.[14] She may also be born into a French Arabic bilingual household. We call these dimensions of her identity – gender, ethnicity, socioeconomic class, and home language group – *assigned identities*, in the sense that they come with birth and are not chosen. Assigned identities are not fully deterministic of a speaker's linguistic behavior, but they nevertheless shape the contours of what is possible.

Although the speaker born in the Parisian *banlieue* is tied to categories such as *female* and *North African*, and although she alone does not determine the social meanings of those categories, she can nevertheless exercise some degree of choice concerning her identity and corresponding language behavior. As she matures, she will inhabit various communities that will likely shape her use of language. As a teenager, she may enjoy listening to Arabic French hip-hop, and she may therefore link up with others who share that interest. Together they may develop a style of speech characterized by the sound patterns and grammatical structures associated with vernacular varieties of French, Arabic French code switching, and even the occasional expression associated with hip-hop culture in the English-speaking world. She may alternatively become involved in a young women's group at a local mosque, identify strongly as Muslim, and over time become well versed in Qur'ānic Arabic.

Her social-psychological experiences will also affect her language and identity decisions. For example, she may have experiences as a child that made her feel shame for being poor, an immigrant's child, or knowing Arabic, and may develop an uncomfortable or even hostile posture to her parents' language. She may try and contain her shame by consciously giving up Arabic and attempting to speak the variety of French she hears on the evening news. However, these very same experiences could make her feel immense pride for being North African, and she may therefore prefer to share the company of other Arabic French bilinguals.

The ability of an individual to actively highlight or dampen an ethnic identity may be constrained by the perceptions in the ambient society and stereotypes projected upon them. Certain ethnic groups have more or less freedom in making these identity choices than other groups. A third-generation Polish American living in Chicago may identify strongly as an ethnic Pole and may highlight her ethnic Polishness by living in a Polish neighborhood, by introducing herself as Małgorzata rather than Maggie, and by celebrating her *imieniny*, or name day. Her younger brother may have no interest in being ethnically Polish and so does not engage in these practices, may just want to be American, and may find himself easily identified as such. In contrast, a third-generation Korean American from Los Angeles may feel American and have no interest in identifying as ethnically Korean. It may well be the case that it is more difficult for him to make the identity choices he would prefer on account of others who assign him to the category *Asian*.

Children develop a sense of their own identities at the same time as they develop language. Language is thus tied to identity from the first words uttered. This mutual development – learning how to speak and learning how to *be* – is called language socialization, and it necessarily occurs in local communities. While local communities are at the crux of the relationship between language and identity, for most of the world's speakers, the interplay between identity choice and identity constraint now also takes place within national contexts. National language policies and ideologies linking certain languages to certain nations influence who speakers are and how they speak.

What's Race Got to Do with It?

Everything. And, in the end, nothing.

Scholars, such as sociologists and anthropologists, among others, who study race often remark that "Race isn't rocket science – it's harder!" The difficulty arises from the fact that the term **race** is not a biologically coherent category. Population geneticist, Luigi Cavalli-Sforza, notes that the measurable genetic distance between two populations generally increases in direct correlation with the geographic distance separating them. However, regardless of type of genetic marker used – and these can be selected from a very wide range – the variation between two individuals chosen at random from within any population is 85% as large as that between two individual selected at random from the world's population (Cavalli-Sforza 2000:29). We will return to the biological problems with this nonbiological category in Chapter 10.

The difficulty surrounding the term *race* is compounded by the fact that it swirls through so many popular discourses and that it seems somehow important as a way to classify people. In this book, we understand race to be a socially constructed category, rather than a biological reality, and since it is one that has structured and continues to structure our society, it has had and continues to have consequences. Many members of a society in which the term *race* has traction have tended to think of it as real, and some of these people not only organize their own identities around the category but also organize the identities of others.

For much of the history of the United States, a person was classified as *Negro* under the so-called one-drop rule if it could be determined that they had a drop – whatever that meant – of African blood. Yet, many people who fit that classification could pass as White, and, indeed, many people who never thought twice about being White technically fit the definition of Negro. In the 1820s, freed, English-speaking slaves from the United States established the West African nation of Liberia. Although these slaves were assigned the racial identity Negro or Black in the context of the United States and although they were the direct descendants of Africans, they were considered by their new African neighbors to belong to a different ethnic group on the basis of ostensible differences in language, dress, and experience. They were called Americo-Liberians.

We now define an **ethnogroup** as a group identifiable by an assemblage of markers, including dress, diet, belief systems, rites and rituals, kinship organization, and of course language. In this book, if we need to identify a group, we will do so by the term *ethnogroup*. We use the term *race* in the next subsection only to show the incoherent nature of its use, after which we eliminate it.

The Problematic Race–Nation–Language Triad

A third term has been lurking at the edges of the nation-language intersection, and it is *race*. The link between race, nation, and language is problematic because it is both historically variable and geographically variable. For example, when Irish Catholics first immigrated to the United States en masse in the midnineteenth century, they were considered racially different from White Protestants, in part because of their association with African Americans in the labor sector. Today in the United States, no one would consider John F. Kennedy, an Irish Catholic, any race other than White. In the 100 years separating the height of Irish immigration in the 1860s and the election of Kennedy as the President of the United States in 1960, the identification of the racial identity of the Irish had changed. It is difficult to know if this change could have happened so easily had the Irish maintained rather than lost Irish Gaelic during those years. However, it is not difficult to imagine that Kennedy would not have been elected if his first or primary language was Irish rather than English.

Just as race is not historically stable, neither is it geographically stable. Immigrants are often surprised to discover that their race has changed overnight as they move from one country to another. This is the case with Latino/as in the United States. A man moving from Buenos Aires to Miami may find he went from being White in Argentina to Latino in the United States. Similarly, a woman moving from Santo Domingo to New York City may have thought herself to be *india clara* 'light Indian' in the Dominican Republic but may be assumed to be Black in the United States. Her racial identity may change again if she were overheard speaking Spanish, in which case she may then be considered to be Latina.

As unstable and ever changing as the race–nation–language triad is, it has been central in the development of the European nationalisms. When Herder imagined *one nation, one language, one people*, the people he had in mind belonged to the race *German*, defined by the biology of blood. Until 1999, German citizenship was predicated on the principle of *jus sanguinis* 'right of blood,' in contrast to *jus soli* 'right of soil,' which meant German citizenship was available to anyone able to prove German descent but not to immigrants and their children born in Germany. This definition of citizenship created problems for the *Gastarbeiter* 'guest workers,' mostly Turks, who lived in Germany, who learned German and took jobs considered undesirable for German citizens, yet until 1999 could not enjoy the benefits of full German citizenship.

The problematic race–nation–language nexus plays itself out in different ways in different nations and places. We review the story of this nexus in Japan, Brazil, and North Carolina.

No. 1: Japan, asserting itself as ethnically homogeneous

Some nationalist ideologies rely more heavily on explicit notions of race than others. In Japan, ideas about national identity exist within an ideology of racial homogeneity in which the Japanese are constructed in opposition to the other known as *uchi*. In popular discourses, Japanese national identity is seen as comprising an extended family of citizens related by blood. As such, racial others can be discursively excluded from national identity by being constructed as unrelated to the national family. The nationalist ideology of racial homogeneity is linked to language in the sense that the Japanese language is considered the first language of the Japanese, and therefore languages other than Japanese spoken in Japan are taken as signs of ethnic otherness, or they are said not to exist in Japan in the first place.

In 1894, prominent Japanese linguist Ueda Kazutoshi is said to have proclaimed his gratitude for the fact that Japan was not a multilingual nation, which meant that there was no need to deal with minority languages that would detract from creating national cohesion through Japanese. This was the heyday of the German university, and Kazutoshi had just returned from a year-long postdoctoral study program in Germany, one of the incubators of the one nation, one language, one people ideology. The denial of racial, ethnic, and linguistic diversity within Japan remained publically evident nearly a century later, when Prime Minister Nakasone Yasuhiro declared Japan to be a *tan'itsu minzoku*, or 'mono-ethnic nation' (Gottlieb 2006:74–75).

In empirical reality, Japan is not an ethnically homogeneous nation, although the presence of minority populations is denied in popular discourses. In addition to a sizable Korean immigrant population, several large indigenous groups reside within Japan, including the Okinawans and the Ainu. The Okinawans are one of several groups of ethnic Ryukyuan people who inhabit the Ryukyu Islands in Okinawa Prefecture. Ryukyu languages, including Okinawan, in the Japonic family, were thriving until the end of the nineteenth century when the Ryukyu Kingdom was abolished by the Japanese government and incorporated into the Japanese state. The number of Okinawan speakers has severely declined throughout the twentieth century. Today, most Okinawans speak a local variety of Japanese.

When it comes to the Ainu, they are constructed as extinct or already assimilated into Japanese society and therefore do not contradict national ideology of racial homogeneity. The Ainu were not even recognized officially by the Japanese government as a legitimate indigenous group with a language and culture distinct from that of mainstream Japanese until 2008. Over a century of denying the existence of the Ainu people has had devastating effects on the Ainu language, a language isolate, which today is extremely endangered and is spoken as a first language by only a handful of elderly speakers on the northern island of Hokkaidō. As in Europe, the process of state formation in Japan resulted in the consolidation of ethnolinguistic difference, which had the effect of reducing the overall visibility of ethnic groups and setting in motion the loss of minority indigenous languages. These losses took place through a specific form of nationalism that imagined ethnic Japanese as an extended family who shared the same blood and the same language.

An interesting challenge to the race–nation–language triad in the Japanese context are the *Nikkeijin*, ethnic Japanese living abroad who have returned to Japan. Of the 2.6 million ethnic Japanese residing outside of Japan, the largest population is by far in Brazil (1.5 million). At the end of the nineteenth century, when the feudal system was waning, and Japan was consolidating itself as a nation-state, Brazil was transitioning from an empire into a constitutional republic and in 1888 finally outlawed the slave trade.[15] The abolition of slavery in Brazil resulted in labor shortages in its booming coffee industry. As a result, the Brazilian government sought nonslave labor from other parts of the world, and Japanese migrants went to Brazil en masse to work on coffee plantations. When Japan's economy soared in the 1980s, the Japanese government provided visas to ethnic Japanese in South America, the descendants of those who had left Japan, so that they could return to Japan to work in factories.

How did the return migration fit within Japan's self-image of racial homogeneity? The Nikkeijin are Japanese by lineage, but in most cases they are Portuguese speakers rather than speakers of Japanese. On account of this difference, they are seen as not fully Japanese and have experienced discrimination in Japan, despite the importance placed on racial homogeneity in the narrative of Japanese national identity. The situation of return migration to Japan illustrates the constructed and unstable relationship among race, nation, and language. If Japanese citizenship and national identity were truly predicated on biology, as the national narrative suggests, Japanese born elsewhere would not be seen as others. However, race is a cultural construct, not a biological one, and therefore questions of language, place of birth, and cultural orientation bear upon determinations of group membership. By 2009, the Japanese economy had sunk into a prolonged recession, and the Japanese government offered unemployed Nikkeijin from Brazil and other countries in South America a stipend for repatriation to their home countries.

No. 2: Brazil, asserting itself as a linguistically homogeneous racial democracy

While Japan's national identity developed around the myth of racial homogeneity, Brazil's national identity developed, in contrast, around discourses of racial democracy. The term *mestiçagem* in Portuguese refers to the high degree of ethnic mixing that resulted from the history of colonialism, slavery, and immigration, and it is this high degree of mixing that is supposed to make Brazilians tolerant of racial difference. National narratives suggesting that Brazil is a racial utopia without racial conflict obscure the sociological realities of social stratification and inequality based on difference in contemporary Brazilian society. Brazilians of African heritage experience racial discrimination, income inequality, and fewer and more negative media depictions than Brazilians of European heritage.

Once again, the ideology of racial democracy is interwoven with differences in language. While differences in race are acknowledged and supposedly celebrated, differences in language are denied in popular discourses, including in popular media (Massani-Cagliari 2004:19). This supposed linguistic homogeneity denies both variation within Brazilian Portuguese and the existence of languages other than Portuguese, both immigrant and indigenous. While denial of linguistic difference supports the Brazilian ideology of a racially diverse monolingual nation, the reality is that Portuguese has many regional varieties. The speech of the Paulistas in São Paulo differs from that of the Cariocas in Rio de Janeiro and the Gaúcha variety in Rio Grande do Sul. The variety of Portuguese spoken in Bahia is replete with borrowings from African languages such as Yoruba (Byrd 2012) and Bantu languages such as Kimbundu and Kikongo (Castro 2002:198). To the extent that regional varieties in Brazil reflect differences in immigration and contact, they can be said to be racialized. However, as linguist Massani-Cagliari notes, "Differences between Brazilians who speak differently and who mark their different identity precisely in the way they speak are simply erased" (Massani-Cagliari 2004:15). And the differences among Brazilian Portuguese varieties are dwarfed in comparison with 170 indigenous languages spoken by about 345,000 people, mostly in the Amazon.[16]

In Japan, a discourse of racial homogeneity downplaying ethnic difference occults the empirical reality of Japan's ethnolinguistic minority groups. In Brazil, an opposing discourse of racial democracy highlighting the country's ethnic diversity erases linguistic difference. In both cases, popular discourses weave ideas about race through ideas about language in the production of an identity that is *national* in nature.

No. 3: the Lumbee, struggling with self-assertion in North Carolina

In the United States, the legacy of one Native American group, the Lumbee Indians of North Carolina, provides a noteworthy counterpoint to the race–nation–language triad in Japan and Brazil. With a population of around 50,000, the Lumbee are the largest Native American group in the United States east of the Mississippi River, although chances are you have never heard of them unless you happen to live in or around Robeson County, North Carolina. How could it be that the ninth largest Native American tribe in the United States could be both so absent from American awareness and, furthermore, ineligible for the benefits full federal recognition bestows?

The answer issues forth from the answer to a prior question: What does it mean to be Native American? The answer involves, as you might guess, race, nation, and language. While the Lumbee are themselves unambiguous in their self-identification as Native Americans, outsiders ranging from nonnative community members to governmental agencies have been reluctant to accept Lumbee identity claims. This reluctance has resulted in over 200 years of changing racial classifications of this group. Although the Lumbee were once considered to be White, they were grouped with African Americans as Free Persons of Color in revisions made to North Carolina's Constitution in 1835. Exactly 50 years later, their status changed again, when the state government passed legislation recognizing them as Indians. The instability in racial classification is evidenced by the long list of labels used to name the group: Croatan Indians, Indians of Robeson County, Cherokee Indians of Robeson County, Siouan Indians of the Lumber River, and, since 1953, Lumbee Indians. Each of the names situated the Lumbee differently with respect to other Native American groups, popular understandings of race, and government policy.

The Cherokee of Western North Carolina objected to the adoption of the name Cherokee Indians of Robeson County, fearing a reduction in their own tribal benefits should the federal government recognize the Lumbee as Cherokee and then split the allocated funds between the two groups. As the Lumbee shifted through ethnic categories (White, Black, Indian) and tribal names (Croatan, Cherokee, Sioux, Lumbee), scientists representing the state sought to define the Lumbee in terms of physical characteristics thought to index so-called authentic Indian-ness. In the 1930s, physical anthropologists were hired by the federal government to scientifically investigate physical features of the Lumbee. Blood samples were taken to ascertain if the Lumbee had Indian blood, or enough of it, cranial measurements were recorded, and Lumbee hair was even subjected to a thinness test, as thin hair was thought to be a physical trait of Native Americans. This test worked by inserting a pencil into a test subject's hair. If the pencil stayed in place after vigorous hair shaking, the hair was deemed too thick to be authentically Indian; if it fell, the opposite was true. In certain cases, this test placed siblings into separate categories, Indian and non-Indian.

In the twentieth century, the state of North Carolina recognized the Lumbee as Lumbee Indians in 1953. However, when a congressional act was passed in 1956 to officially recognize the Lumbee at the federal level, it stipulated that "nothing in this Act shall make such Indians eligible for any services performed by the United States for Indians because of their status as Indians." Thus, federal recognition not only as Indians but also as a specific tribe, Lumbee, was still not enough to earn tribal benefits. As ever, the question of authentic ethnicity is related to language. If the Lumbee still spoke a Native American language, their argument for full federal recognition would have been settled in their favor long ago.[17]

The Lumbee can, however, lay claim to linguistic distinctiveness. The Lumbee speak a variety of English, which shares features in common with the contiguous White and African American communities but which is also characterized by unique lexical, phonological, and grammatical features. Two examples of grammatical structures that distinguish Lumbee English from contiguous varieties are the use of perfective *I'm* ("I'm been there before") and finite *bes* ("That's how it bes sometimes"). These structures combine with features shared by other local language varieties, including the regularized past tense use of *weren't* in negative constructions ("I weren't there/she weren't there") and unique phonological patterns (*hit* for *it* and *hain't* for *ain't*) to create a variety that sets the Lumbees apart from other language groups in the region. The presence of a distinctive variety of English, however, has not proven to be convincing evidence of Lumbee nationhood first to North Carolina state officials and then to federal officials who subscribe – consciously or not – to the ideology in which so-called dialects are deemed to be illegitimate derivatives of real languages.

The situation with the Lumbee underscores how questions of language and ethnic identification have political and economic consequences. In the Lumbee case, local, state, and federal governments have great stakes in the outcome. Are the Lumbee eligible for tribal sovereignty? Are they eligible for federal assistance? The language of the Lumbee today is a unique variety of English, which developed like all language varieties, through the historical conditions of its speakers, and in this respect is no different from a hypothetical tribal language the Lumbee may have once spoken. Because of this linguistic distinctiveness, we, the authors, believe the Lumbee deserve the same state and federal rights enjoyed by other recognized Native American ethnogroups.

It is fairly easy to see how contemporary Lumbee identity has been shaped out of its relationship with the state, which has explicitly involved questions of race and more implicitly involved questions of language. We would like to suggest that all group identities are defined at least in part through some relationship with the states they inhabit, and in turn, these groups shape the social meanings of national identity. Language is often the crux of the interplay between the state and the groups. It is on linguistic terrain that certain groups make claims to statehood, and language is a valuable tool with which already-formed states maintain social control, as we will see in Chapter 6.

In this section, we have seen that the workings of the race–nation–language triad vary from place to place. In Japan, national identity was imagined in terms of racial homogeneity, but when for economic reasons Japanese from South America were repatriated in the 1980s and did not speak Japanese, they soon became unwelcome when the economy faltered. In contrast, Brazilian nationalism is imagined to be a racially heterogeneous democracy through *mestiçagem* (mixing), but the unity comes at the cost of denying all linguistic difference. In the United States, the Lumbee have experienced and continue to experience double jeopardy. First, they were denied recognition as Native Americans in the absence of a tribal language. Now they have been given recognition as Native Americans, but their distinctive variety of English is denied. In all three cases, the issue of language is key.

A final point to make is this: the above examples illustrate how the term *race* carries the self-important claim of a relationship to reality, since it figures so prominently in certain political discourses. However, since the term has never been and cannot be applied in any consistent way, it has no more descriptive utility to the perspective taken on language in this book than the term *dialect* does to sociolinguistics, and we eliminate it from further discussion.

Final Note: The Kurds Today – Different Places, Different Outcomes

So, where does all of this leave the Kurds, who were left off the map at the end of World War I? Today, Kurdistan refers to a geocultural region where ethnic Kurds form a numerical majority of the population, speak Kurdish, and share a cultural heritage. This region includes portions of Syria, eastern Turkey, and northern Iraq. In Syria, after decades of oppression of the Kurdish language, things seem to be letting up. As President Bashar Assad's government loses ground in Kurdish areas, the Kurdish language is being taught there for the first time in years. The Kurds in Turkey have also seen gains. In 1928, a law was passed officially banning the letters X, W, and Q, which do not exist in the Turkish alphabet but which are common in Kurdish names. As recently as 2005, Kurds in Turkey were fined for displaying signs at a New Year's Eve festival containing the letters Q and W. Finally, in 2013, the letter-ban law was overturned, and it is now possible for the Kurds in Turkey to spell Kurdish without the fear of legal retribution.

It is in Iraq – the country from which the Kurds were forced to flee on foot in 1990 – where the Kurds have made the greatest political gains. In Iraqi Kurdistan, an autonomous region governed by the Kurds in Northern Iraq, the people are now able to talk about the issues they would have debated had Kurdistan made it onto the map sometimes in the 1920s. That is, they are now engaged in addressing the question about the official language: Should it be a variety known as Sorani, written in the Perso-Arabic script and spoken by some five million Kurds, or Kurmanji, written with the Latin alphabet and spoken on both sides of the Iraqi–Turkish border by about one million Kurds? The issue of the Kurdish language has also fared well on the national stage. The ratification of the Iraqi Constitution in 2005 made Kurdish a co-official language of the nation, alongside Arabic. In 2014, an amendment calling for the use of Kurdish in official government correspondence, national passports, and Iraqi currency was passed in the Iraqi National Assembly. In the same amendment, Turkmen, Syriac, and Asuri languages were also recognized as co-official languages, although they do not have the full status of Arabic and Kurdish.

The politics of the region change as quickly as the sands blow in the deserts of Western Iraq. In 2014, large swaths of Iraq and Syria fell under control of the so-called Islamic State of Iraq and Syria (aka ISIS). Aside from stirring tensions in an already-fragile region, the fact that ISIS is not invested in a unified Iraq means that the country is closer to disintegration than ever. At the same time, Turkey, who long sought to block an independent Kurdistan, seems to have softened on the idea of an independent Kurdish state. This is likely due to the ever-present and increasingly important dynamic of global economics: over 1000 Turkish companies operate in Iraqi Kurdistan, while Iraqi Kurds operate a new oil pipeline that terminates in Turkey. Though the future of the Kurds in Iraq and elsewhere remains uncertain, it appears that a sovereign Kurdistan is more of a possibility than at any time since the end of World War I.

Language Profile: Kurdî / کوردی
[Kurdish (Indo-European)]

Functional overview

Kurdish belongs to the Indo-Iranian branch of the Indo-European language family. Speakers of Kurdish, who number approximately 30 million, are primarily dispersed across four modern nations: Iran, Iraq, Syria, and Turkey. Approximately seven million Kurds live in Iran, where they are the largest ethnic minority group. In Iraq, about four million Kurds – a majority in that country – live in the autonomous northern region known as Iraqi Kurdistan. The Kurdish cultural capital of Iraqi Kurdistan is the contested city of Kirkuk, which at the time of the writing of this book had just come under the political control of the Kurds. Outside of the autonomous region, Kurdish speakers can also be found in Iraq's other major cities, including some 300,000 in Baghdad and some 50,000 in Mosul. In Syria, Kurds comprise about 9% of the population and are again the largest ethnic group. The Kurdish presence is numerically largest in Turkey, where approximately 50% of the overall Kurdish population live and where Kurds make up 15–20% of the Turkish population. The heavily Kurdish southeastern region of Turkey is unofficially known as Turkish Kurdistan.

The two main varieties of Kurdish are Kurmanji, spoken predominantly in Turkish Kurdistan, and Sorani, spoken further to the south in Iran and Iraq. Not only are these dialects the basis for the two main literary traditions in Kurdish, but also they are written in different scripts, Kurmanji in the Roman alphabet, Sorani in the Perso-Arabic script. These varieties are for the most part mutually intelligible, though they demonstrate a number of grammatical differences. First, the Kurdish varieties spoken in the north of the region mark nouns for gender, while the dialects in the south do not. In contrast, the varieties spoken in the south mark subjects for plural number and use definite articles, while the varieties in the north do not. The most striking difference between northern and southern varieties of Kurdish, however, has to do with the arrangement and grammatical marking of syntactic elements in a sentence. Southern varieties are characterized by accusative alignment, while northern varieties are characterized by ergative alignment. We describe ergativity in the following section on structural characteristics.

Prominent structural characteristics

Ergativity   The grammar of most Indo-European languages contrasts grammatical subjects with grammatical objects. If the language has morphological case, subjects appear in the unmarked nominative case, and objects appear in the morphologically marked accusative case. Thus, the word for 'dog' in Polish takes the unmarked form *pies* if it is a subject and *psa* if it is an object. *Pies* is the form found in the dictionary and will always be the form of the subject, no matter if the verb is transitive, that is, it takes an object, or intransitive, that is, it takes no object. This configuration of subjects and objects characterizes accusative alignment systems.

The grammar of the northern varieties of Kurdish is characterized by a different configuration in which the object of a transitive verb – 'the ball' in 'the girl threw *the ball*' – is grouped with the subject of an intransitive verb – 'the boy' in '*the boy* slept' – and appears as unmarked in the nominative case (NOM, below). This is contrasted with the subject of a transitive verb ('the girl' in '*the girl* threw the ball'), which is marked in the oblique case (OBL, below). This configuration is known as an ergative alignment system, and is widespread in languages of the Himalayas, the Caucasus, Australia, and beyond. Within the Indo-European language family, all of the languages demonstrating ergativity, including Kurdish, are in the Indo-Iranian branch. The following examples (Karimi 2012) illustrate the way ergativity works in the northern varieties of Kurdish.

(1) *tu*   *be*   *pilíkān čuy-í*
     you.NOM   with stairs   went-2.SG
     'You went down the stairs.'

(2) *min*   *tu*   *dít-í*
     I.OBL   you.NOM   saw-2.SG
     'I saw you.'

(3) *te*   *ez*   *dít-im*
     you.OBL   I.NOM   saw-1.SG
     'You saw me.'

In the first example, the subject of the intransitive verb *tu* appears in the nominative. This is the same case used to inflect the objects of the transitive verb in examples (2) and (3). Note that we see the same form *tu* when 'you' is used as the subject of the intransitive verb in (1) and the object of the transitive verb in (2). In contrast, 'you' is marked in the oblique case as *te* when it is the subject of the transitive sentence, as shown in (3). Speakers of languages such as English are generally not aware of the differences between verbs such as 'to sleep' (intransitive) and 'to throw' (transitive) unless they take a course in grammar. Because of the ergative nature of Kurdish grammar, speakers must be aware of differences in transitivity.

Subjunctive mood   We have already seen that verbs can be inflected for grammatical categories such as person, number, tense, and aspect. Inflectional endings can also be used to allow speakers to take particular stances toward the ideas they express. This grammatical stance-taking is known as mood, and it may be expressed with or without special morphology. English speakers sometimes give advice using a construction that begins with the subordinate clause "If I were you," as in "If I were you, I would exercise more." When they do this, they take a hypothetical stance on their utterance, and they use the subjunctive mood to do so. Subjunctive is one of several moods known together as *irrealis*, which indicate that the expressed action may not have happened or may be incorrect. Irrealis moods are also used to express doubt, fear, hope, and other emotions.

Mood is characteristic of the Indo-European languages, in which up to four mood distinctions can be made. Some languages in the Samoyedic branch of the Uralic family make more than 10 mood distinctions. In modern Kurdish, three mood distinctions are made, and unlike in modern English, unique morphological prefixes and suffixes are used on verbs to distinguish among them. The *indicative* mood indicates that an utterance is taken to be true, the *imperative* mood indicates a command, and the *subjunctive*, as we have seen, indicates that an utterance is hypothetical or as yet unrealized.

The indicative is the default, unmarked mood in Kurdish, which means that no special morphology is needed. To form the subjuctive in the present tense, the prefix *bí* is attached to a conjugated verb. For example, the verb *chûn* 'to go' appears as follows in the subjunctive: *bíchim* 'I (may) go,' *bíchi* 'you (may) go,' and so on. If the utterance is negative rather than affirmative, *bí* is replaced by the negative subjunctive prefix *ná*, as in *náchim, nachi*, and so on. The present subjunctive is used in the following types of constructions (Thackston 2006):

(1) Deliberatives
Dargâ bíkaynawa?   'Should we open the door?'

(2) Cohortatives
Bâ bíroyn   'Come on, let's go!'

(3) Complement to verbs of wanting
Amawe bíchimà mâɫe   'I want to go home'

As we have said before, all grammars leak (Sapir 1921), and in Kurdish, the subjunctive morphology is used with certain conjuctions such as *bar l' awaí* 'before' and *ba be awaí* 'without,' which do not necessarily express subjunctive mood.

Clitics   In Chapter 3, we saw that in Romanian, pronouns may attach to inflected verbs in constructions such as *am văzut-o pe Maria*, 'I saw/have seen-her Mary.' Linguists call this type of construction a clitic, a structure that resembles a bound morpheme but has word-like characteristics and is phonologically dependent on the word to which it attaches. Clitics can attach to different parts of the host word and are named accordingly. Thus, *proclitics* attach to the beginning of the word, *mesoclitics* between the stem and another affix, and *enclitics* at the end of the word. In the French expression *je t'aime* ('I love you'), the object pronoun *te* attaches as a proclitic to a conjugated form of the verb *aimer*.

Kurdish allows several types of enclitics, including possessive pronouns and other pronominal structures. In addition, speakers of Kurdish cliticize a special structure known as *ísh*, which serves an important discourse function of expressing agreement and generally means 'too,' 'also,' or 'even.' It can attach to single nouns or pronouns, as well as to noun phrases containing an adjective. The following examples illustrate the way the enclitic functions grammatically (Thackston 2006):

min I/me   *mínísh* I/me too

If the word to which the enclitic attaches ends in a vowel, the initial vowel *i* is lost:

ema we/us   *ema'sh* we/us too

If the word to which the enclitic attaches already has an attached pronominal enclitic, the *ish* enclitic attaches between the noun and the pronoun. The following examples illustrate how enclitics concatenate in Kurdish:

bâwkí his father	*bâwkíshí* his father too
pârakáyân their money	*pâraká'shyân* their money too
rafíqakânim my friends	*rafíqakânishim* even my friends

A salient cultural characteristic: loanwords from near and far

Kurdish-speaking peoples have been living under the sphere of influence of three linguistic, cultural, and political superpowers for centuries. First, Kurdish and Persian (Farsi) have intermingled since antiquity. The influence of Persian on Kurdish literature is particularly noteworthy. Second, the relationship between Kurdish and Arabic is particularly close, given the prominent role of Arabic in Islam and the prominent role of Islam in Kurdish culture. The fact that the Sorani variety is written in the Perso-Arabic script makes this relationship especially clear. Finally, Kurdish entered a close relationship of language contact with Turkish when Kurdistan was annexed by the Ottoman Empire in the early sixteenth century. The close historical links between Kurdish and its more powerful neighbor languages is also evidenced in the number and type of lexical borrowings from these languages.

The presence of loanwords from Arabic, Persian, and Turkish is not perceived as unproblematic, and here again we are able to observe the ever-present dynamic of language and politics come into play. In the early part of the twentieth century, as much as half of Kurdish lexical stock comprised loanwords, mostly from Arabic. As Kurds struggled with their subordinate place in the emerging post-War Mideast, concerns about language, especially about word origins, took on great political importance. In the 1920s, a movement known as *Kurdí Petí* (Pure Kurdish) gained popularity with Kurds across the Kurdish regions who were interested in restoring some historical Kurdish terms that had been replaced by loanwords, mostly from Arabic.

Efforts to "purify" the Kurdish lexicon were largely successful. Today 10–15% of the Kurdish lexicon comprises loanwords. Compared with modern English – whose lexicon is less than 30% Germanic in origin – this figure is very low and represents a great reduction in non-Kurdish lexical stock since the 1920s. Of the loanwords that remain, the vast majority – about 10% – come from Arabic. Words from Persian, Turkish, and European languages each comprise about 1% of the current Kurdish lexicon.

Purification efforts have continued into the present, although the shape that they take depends on the geopolitics of the region. In Iraq, Kurds are interested in de-Arabicizing the lexicon and often replace Arabic-origin words with Persian-origin words. The Arabic words *iqtidar* 'power,' *serwet* 'wealth,' and *dinya* 'world' have been replaced with Persian words *twana, saman,* and *geti.* Kurds in Turkey have also turned to Persian for loanwords to replace Turkish borrowings. The use of

Persian terms is seen as justifiable on the grounds that Kurdish and Persian are both Indo-European languages. Meanwhile, the Kurds in Iran are interested in de-Persianing the lexicon and often replace Persian-origin words with Arabic-origin words. Because Arabic and Kurdish are unrelated, no appeals to common genetic heritage are possible.

Kurdish culture is tied to Arabic through the dynamic of religion, and many speakers are bilingual, both in liturgical settings and beyond. The Arabic vocabulary will likely continue to influence Kurdish in the future.

Exercises

Exercise 1 – map making

Individually or in teams, sketch maps of the Holy Roman Empire, the Russian Empire, and the Ottoman Empire at the time of their collapse. Use a separate sheet of paper for each map. With a different-colored pencil, sketch an overlay of the current nations constructed within the former imperial boundaries. How have the changing borders affected language?

1 The *une langue, une nation* ideology associated with the French Revolution has had a tremendous effect on the linguistic situation of France. Make a bar graph depicting the number of speakers of Basque, Breton, Corsican, and Occitan in the place now called France in 1800, 1900, and 2000. If needed, use alternative dates based on the data you find.

2 The one nation, one language ideology has been effective in convincing people not only that nations should be monolingual, but that they actually already are. That is, many people are uninformed about the linguistic diversity in the communities and nations where they live, despite the empirical reality of multilingualism around them. Distribute a questionnaire to 20–30 people in which you ask them which languages are spoken in the following countries: Australia, Brazil, China, France, Russia, Spain, South Africa, and United States. Add any other places that you think may elicit an interesting response. Tabulate your data and present your findings in a visually interesting way. What do your data suggest about people's understandings of language and nation?

Exercise 2 – you decide

Imagine that you have been hired as a special representative to the United Nations. Your expertise is language, and your charge is to advise on the question of Kurdish statehood. Write a well-informed position statement that argues for or against statehood, focusing on the language issues at play. Your statement should be as specific as possible and should take into consideration (a) the broader linguistic and cultural situation of the region and (b) the perspectives on language and nation raised in this chapter.

Discussion Questions

1 What do the authors mean by *historical contingency*? Describe the contingent relationship between language and place described in this chapter. Can you think of other contingencies that are involved in the production of language in the place where you live?

2 What does it mean to suggest that the terms *language* and *dialect* are sociopolitical rather than technical? Is there a way to speak about languages and dialects without referring to them as such?

3 The authors identify two epistemological frameworks and their corresponding views of language. What are they? Do you think these frameworks affect the way people see language in the place where you live?

4 The authors write that language ideologies work best when they are invisible. First, describe what this means in the context of the chapter. Then, think critically about what kinds of invisible ideologies about language may be at work in the place where you live. What are they? Why do people invest in and perpetuate them? In whose interests do these beliefs about language work?

5 How does shame operate in concert with the one language, one nation ideology? Have you personally ever felt shame about the language varieties you speak? Can you trace the origins of that shame to broader beliefs about language in your community or nation?

6 In the English-speaking world, a common answer to the question "Is that a real word?" is "Is it in the dictionary?" The question and the answer presume that there is a single authority on language. What other kinds of texts, people, or institutions are invoked as authorities on language?

7 The relationship between language and identity involves both identity *assignments* and identity *choices*. How does this operate with respect to your own use of language?

8 This chapter shows how language is involved in the social construction of race. Describe how this operates using the examples of the Lumbee, Japan, and Brazil.

Notes

1 His sister was Marie Antoinette, the ill-fated Queen of France.

2 Joseph's successor, Leopold II, was less pragmatic and reinstated Latin in response to Hungarian hostility and rage (Anderson [1983] 2006:73, 73 n. 18, 102).

3 The name *Tatar* is a Mongolic ethnonym. The Turkic, Mongolic, and even the Tungusic stocks have been in intense contact over a very long time and share many diffused words.

4 No proof exists that he actually said this. However, the possibility that he could have said it and meant it is clear.

5 Among other things, Beauzée contributed the article *Langue* to the masterful French *Encyclopédie* where he defines language as the "ensemble of usages belonging to a nation in order to express their thoughts by voice."

6 Other early Americans, such as John Pickering in Boston, were interested in recording the native languages, since those on the east coast were rapidly disappearing. Powhatan died

out in the 1790s. The shift to English had begun. Cherokee is still spoken today but is endangered.

7   Print capitalism is set into motion by Gutenberg in the midfifteenth century.
8   The following discussion condenses, but does not do justice to, Anderson's account of the development of nation-states, nationalism, and national consciousness.
9   Two hundred years later, after the invention of a new collective information-sharing medium, namely television, and after the entrenchment of nationalisms around the globe, comedian Stephen Colbert usurped the ideology and created his own political imaginary, The Colbert Nation. During the time he hosted *The Colbert Report*, he frequently addressed his audience, "Nation, you won't believe what just happened …".
10   Franklin's printing legacy for linguistics lies in his popularization of the graph [ŋ] pronounced 'engma' for the phonetic spelling of English. For the record, Paine's printer was Robert Bell.
11   See note 2, this chapter.
12   The historic names of the regions come from the opposing way they say *yes*: *oc* in the south and *oïl* in the north. The south is still sometimes referred to as the *Languedoc*. The northern pronunciation has, over time, changed to *oui* [wi]. The final *-l* has vocalized.
13   The primary difference between male voices and female voices is pitch, which is determined primarily by the length of the vocal tract above the larynx. Adult men have a vocal tract length that is on average a few centimeters longer than the average adult female vocal tract. The longer the vocal tract, the deeper the pitch. However, boys and girls do not have such a difference. Linguistic anthropologists have shown that boys in some Western societies learn to lower their larynx in order to achieve a longer vocal tract and thus a deeper-pitched voice.
14   The name *Maghreb* to refer to North Africa mostly west of Egypt comes from the Arabic word for 'west.'
15   Brazil was the last country in the West to outlaw slavery.
16   Severo and Makoni (2014) note that during the Brazilian colonial era, there was a great deal of interest in the indigenous languages of region. Understanding these languages was seen as an important way to spread Christianity and the Portuguese language. See also Chapter 8, section "Religions as First-Nations and Missionaries as Colonizers."
17   Wolfram and Reaser (2014:233). Most of the information about the Lumbee and in particular, their particular variety of English comes from Wolfram and Sellers (1999) and Wolfram and Reaser (2014).

References

Anderson, Benedict (1983) 2006 *Imagined Communities: Reflections on the Origin and Spread of Nationalism*. London: Verso.
Byrd, Steven (2012) *Calunga and the Legacy of African Language in Brazil*. Albuquerque: University of New Mexico Press.
Castro, Yeda Pesso de (2002) *A língua mina-jeje no Brasil: Um falar africano em Ouro Preto do século XVIII*. Belo Horizonte, Brazil: Fundação João Pinheiro/ Secretaria de Estado da Cultura.
Cavalli-Sforza, Luigi (2000) *Genes, Peoples, and Languages*. New York: North Point Press.
Gottlieb, Nanette (2006) *Linguistic Stereotyping and Minority Groups in Japan*. New York: Routledge.

Grégoire, Abbé (1794). *Report on the Necessity and Means to Annihilate the Patois and to Universalize the Use of the French Language*. Report presented at French National Convention.

Karimi, Yadgar (2012) The evolution of ergativity in Iranian languages. *Acta Linguistica Asiatica* 2: 23–43.

Massani-Cagliari, Gladis (2004) Language policy in Brazil: Monolingualism and linguistic prejudice. *Language Policy* 3.1: 3–23.

Paine, Thomas (1776) *Common Sense*. Philadelphia: W. and T. Bradford.

Sapir, Edward (1921) *Language*. New York: Harcourt, Brace & World.

Severo, Cristine Gorski and Sinfree Makoni (2014) Discourses of language in colonial and postcolonial Brazil. *Language and Communication* 34: 95–104.

Thackston, W.M. (2006) Sonari Kurdish: A reference grammar with selected readings. http://www.fas.harvard.edu/~iranian/Sorani/sorani_1_grammar.pdf.

Wolfram, Walt and Jason Sellers (1999) Ethnolinguistic marking of past tense be in Lumbee vernacular English. *Journal of English Linguistics* 27: 94–114.

Wolfram, Walt and Jeffrey Reaser (2014) *It's Talkin' Tar Heel: Voices of North Carolina*. Chapel Hill: University of North Carolina Press.

Further Reading

Barbour, Stephen and Cathie Carmichael (2000) *Language and Nationalism in Europe*. Oxford: Oxford University Press.

Bourdieu, Pierre (1991) *Language and Symbolic Power*. Cambridge, MA: Harvard University Press.

Butler, Judith (1990) *Gender Trouble*. New York: Routledge.

Bynon, Theodora (1979) The ergative construction in Kurdish. *Bulletin of the School of Oriental and African Studies* 42: 211–224.

Carter, Phillip M. (2014) National narratives, institutional ideologies and local talk: The discursive formation of Spanish in a "new" U.S. Latino community. *Language in Society* 43: 209–240.

Duany, Jorge (1998) Reconstructing racial identity: Ethnicity, color, and class among Dominicans in the United States and Puerto Rico. *Latin American Perspectives* 25.3: 147–172.

Faircloth, Norman (1989) *Language and Power*. Routledge: New York.

Hassanpour, Amir (1992) *Nationalism and Language in Kurdistan, 1918–1985*. San Francisco: Mellon Research University Press.

Heller, Monica (2011) *Paths to Post-Nationalism: A Critical Ethnography of Language and Identity*. Oxford: Oxford University Press.

Kristéva, Julia (1993) *Nations without Nationalism*. New York: Columbia University Press.

Snyder, Timothy (2003) *The Reconstruction of Nations: Poland, Ukraine, Lithuania, Belarus, 1569–1999*. New Haven, CT: Yale University Press.

Twine, France Winddance (1998) *Racism in a Racial Democracy: The Maintenance of White Supremacy in Brazil*. New Brunswick, NJ: Rutgers University Press.

Weiner, Michael (ed.) (1997) *Japan's Minorities: The Illusion of Homogeneity*. New York: Routledge.

Zhou, Minglang (2012) Historical review of the PRC's minority/indigenous language policy and practice: Nation-state building and identity construction. In Gulbahar H. Beckett and Gerard A. Postiglione (eds.), *China's Assimilationist Language Policy*. New York: Routledge, 18–30.

5

The Development of Writing in the Litmus of Religion and Politics

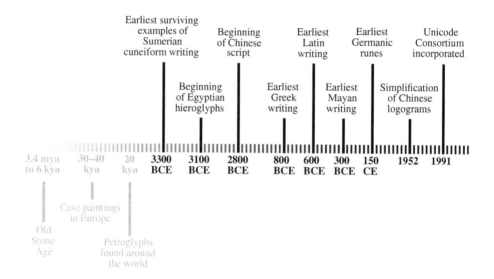

The Story of the Qur'ān

According to Islamic tradition, the Qur'ān is a book of God revealed to the Prophet Muhammad. It did not come to him in the form of a complete book but rather in parts over a period of several decades. The first part was revealed in 610 at *Jabal an-Nur* 'The Mountain of Light' near Mecca when the Prophet was 40 years old. A few years later, he began his public preaching. Thereafter, different parts continued to be revealed to him until his death in 632. Before the time when the Qur'ān was revealed, the Egyptians had already invented a good writing material made from the

Languages in the World: How History, Culture, and Politics Shape Language, First Edition.
Julie Tetel Andresen and Phillip M. Carter.
© 2016 John Wiley & Sons, Inc. Published 2016 by John Wiley & Sons, Inc.

papyrus plant. Whenever any part of the Qur'ān was revealed, scribes wrote it down on papyrus or *qirṭas* in Arabic. During this process, people also committed the verses to memory so that they could recite them during prayer.[1] Thus, the Qur'ān continued to be simultaneously memorized and written down, and this method of preservation continued throughout the lifetime of the Prophet.

The most important part of this story, from the point of view of the present chapter, is the fact that the Prophet is said to have been illiterate. The belief in Mohammad's illiteracy secures the belief in the Qur'ān as the word of God in two ways. First, Muhammad's illiteracy underscores his simplicity, making him an appropriate conduit through which the word of God could be revealed. Second, Muhammad's illiteracy preemptively removes doubt that these words could come from a source other than God, because an illiterate man could not have created a work of such beauty and complexity as the Qur'ān. History tells us that Muhammad was a successful merchant before his call as a messenger prophet, so he must have known how to count. During his time, letters were used to represent numbers in Arabic, as they were in all Semitic languages, including Hebrew.[2] So, it is possible that Muhammad knew how to write and record a transaction. Our purpose here is not to offer an opinion on the state of Muhammad's literacy; it is rather to emphasize the fact that, despite potential evidence to the contrary, the belief in Muhammad's illiteracy is bound to the conception of the Qur'ān as the direct word of God. The further implication is that once the divine word has passed through the human agent, the writing down of those words can be regarded as a sacred act. It is but a small step to make the inference that writing itself is a divine creation.

The story of the Qur'ān serves three purposes for this chapter. First, it illustrates the intertwined relationship between religion and the written word. Second, it suggests the power of the written word, and this power, as we have just seen in Chapter 4, circulated forcefully enough throughout the eighteenth century in the form of print capitalism to reinforce a new political entity known as the nation-state. In this chapter, we will see that the power of the written word as the word of God often goes hand in hand with political power. Third, the story of the Qur'ān brings attention to the dynamics of orality and literacy in that the development of religious tradition drives not only particular linguistic practices (prayers, chants, etc.) but also the very scripts used to represent languages.

Magico-Religious Interpretations of the Origins of Writing[3]

The multifaceted relationship between religion and writing is wrapped in layers of legend and mystery. The oldest known writing system was created in Mesopotamia, that of the cuneiform (Latin *cuneus* means 'wedge') script of the Sumerians whose cultural and linguistic origins are not well known. When the Akkadians migrated into the area in the fourth millennium BCE, they adapted the cuneiform script of Akkadian, a Semitic language, and revered Sumerian as the sacred language of the priests. At about that same time, the Egyptians had gone beyond decorating pottery with pictures of animals, birds, and symbols of deities, and were carving onto their temples and tombs interpretable narratives in a pictorial word-script. The Egyptian god Thoth was one of the most important of the deities, and the Egyptians believed him to be responsible for inventing, among other things, religion and the alphabet. In the second century CE, the Greeks gave the Egyptian pictorial word-script a lofty name: hieroglyphs (*hiero* 'sacred' *glyph* 'carvings'). The Greeks believed hieroglyphs to be mysterious symbols that could only be interpreted mystically, since the priests who once wrote and read them were long gone. It was not until the twentieth century that these symbols were successfully deciphered.

Halfway around the world, the two great civilizations of Mesoamerica, the Aztecs in central Mexico, who spoke Nahuatl, and the Maya on the Yucatan Peninsula, who spoke Mayan, produced separate scripts that post-Columbian scholars both called *hieroglyphs*. When the first Spanish expeditions arrived in the early sixteenth century, the Aztecs were already in possession of an abundant literature. Surviving manuscripts, written on deerskin or a kind of paper made from the bark of fig trees or from agave fibers, are mostly historical–mythological or calendrical–astrological in content. The custodians and experts of this writing were the priests. With respect to the civilization of the Mayan people, who also created both a type of paper and a complicated picture script, religion once again plays a role, albeit an unhappy one. The Franciscan Bishop of Mérida, Diego de Landa, took enough interest in the Mayan hieroglyphs to attempt to relate them to the letters of the Spanish alphabet – a method of decipherment that proved unsuccessful. Unfortunately, de Landa's interest in the script did not extend to a desire to preserve it. In 1562, he ordered the burning of many Mayan religious symbols and writings, such that today only four manuscripts remain of the dozens that were produced. The Aztec treasures had fared no better. Following the earlier conquest of Mexico by Cortez, the Spaniards burned their books, as well.

Examples of a belief in the religious or mysterious origins of scripts abound. In India, the curly cued script known as *Devanāgari* means 'the script of the City of the Gods' (*deva* 'God'; *nāgari* 'city') and is used for writing Hindi, Marathi, Nepali, and so forth.[4] In Eastern Europe, the name of the Cyrillic alphabet comes from one of the two ninth-century Christian apostles, the brothers Constantine (later called Cyril) and Methodius, who adapted the Greek alphabet for a language known as Old Church Slavonic, so called in reference to the literature recorded in it. In reference to its genetic classification, this language is known as Old Bulgarian. The Cyrillic alphabet was later adopted for use by many Slavic languages, including modern-day Bulgarian, Macedonian, Russian, and Ukrainian, and some non-Slavic languages, such as Mongolian. In Africa, the Nsibidi script is used to write Igbo and Efik, both spoken in Nigeria and both Niger–Congo languages, and those who use this script believe it to be a means of magic. Although the meaning of the name of this script is disputed, some suggest that *sibidi* means both 'to play' and 'to bewitch' (Jensen 1969:217).

A sense of mystery and magic of the written word can be found in English, as well, in the word *spell* that refers not only to how words are written but also to a set of words with supernatural powers. The Germanic languages were originally written in an alphabet known as runes. In Old English, the word *rune* meant 'mystery' or 'secret.' In one variety of Norwegian the noun *runa* means 'a secret formula,' while the verb form means 'to cast a spell.' In modern German, *raunen* means 'to whisper' and in Irish, a Celtic language, the word *rúnda* is translated as 'a secret.'

Although the Sumerians' cuneiform is considered to be the oldest established writing system, the Chinese script can claim the distinction of being the oldest writing system still in use today. It is at least 3000 years old. In one Chinese tradition, the invention of the script is attributed to Ts'ang-Chieh and Chu-Sung, two secretaries in the court of the Yellow Emperor or Huangdi in the third millennium BCE, to whom divine honors were later accorded as *tzi shen* 'dieties of writing.' According to legend, the secretaries gazed high in the sky to the constellations and low into the ground to the traces left by animals and the patterns found on tortoise shells. Out of the beauty of these curves came writing. When the first writing was composed, so the legend goes, the ghosts wept because the spirits could no longer hide their shapes from humans.

Divination is the practice of 'reading the signs of the universe' in an attempt to interpret God's plan. In China, archeological discoveries of bones and tortoise shells give evidence that divination was practiced from the earliest times. Upon these bones and shells were etched questions concerning weather or crops or military operations. Heat was then applied until the bones or shells cracked, and the people who knew how to read the cracks, namely the priests, were asked to interpret them. In early Germanic times of several thousand years ago or more, priests cast onto the ground *staben* 'sticks/staffs' from the *buch* 'beech' tree and then interpreted the meaning of the pattern of the sticks as the priests gathered them up. The modern German lexicon bears traces of this magical practice: the word *buch* means 'book,' *Buchstabe* means 'letter (of the alphabet),' and *lesen* means both 'to gather' and 'to read.'

Thus, from the earliest times, writing – certainly a human invention – was associated with the divine or the magical, and this association invested the written word with a power that was to be guarded by a restricted inner circle of the initiated, that is, by the diviners or the priests.

Steps Toward the Representation of Speech

Object writing

People from language groups and cultures all over the world have devised ways to communicate with one another through objects. An X scratched into the ground can mark the spot one human either wants to remember or wants another human to notice. A pile of stones can serve as a landmark or monument, and, indeed, man-made stacks of stones are found all over the world. Stones on a grave – put there for whatever reason – over time came to be interpreted as a 'memory'-al – whose original meaning is now often forgotten in the word *memorial*, which takes the form of an engraved headstone today. To mark paths, hunters and migratory people often scatter grass or leaves or set up sticks.

Different types of objects serve communicative purposes. A notched stick, or tally (cognate with English *till* and German *zählen* 'to count'), can be used to record lines of ancestry or commercial transactions involving debts and credits.[5] A messenger stick calls dispersed peoples to meetings. Woven objects serve varied purposes. Among the speakers of Iroquois and Algonquin in North America, belts were made up of four or more strings; on each string were rows of shells bored through the middle. These came to be called wampum belts after the Iroquois name for the shells, namely *wampum*. Depending on the design of the shells, war or peace or a truce could be declared. Another type of woven object, the knotted cords of the quippu of the Incan empire of western (Andean) South America, had enough importance to have been read only by special officials, the *quippu camayocuna*.[6] Although the exact use of the *quippu* has been lost, scholars have suggested that they might have recorded chronicles, legal codes, literature, and inventories, or even made astronomical predictions. Turning once again to China, Lao Tzu noted the use of knotted cords in his *Tao-te-ching* of the sixth century BCE. Such cords were in use even into the twentieth century of our era on the Ryukyu Islands in the East China Sea southwest of the Japanese island of Kyushu. Other objects, such as badges of ranks and symbols of professions, count as object writing, with the red-and-white-striped pole of the barber being but one example.

Although all cultural groups have devised what can be called object writing, not all cultural groups have created a system to represent a specific sequence of sounds, what can be called writing proper. Objects such as stones, sticks, tallies, belts, cords, and badges have never been transformed into representations of acoustic signals. However, acts such as painting, scratching, and scoring have historically provided the first steps toward writing, and the terms themselves in Indo-European languages tell the story. The English word *write* is cognate with Old Norse *rīta* 'to scratch (runes).' Latin *scribere* 'to write' is also etymologically 'to scratch, to score,' as is the original meaning of the Greek word 'to write,' namely *graphein*, which in turn is cognate with German *kerben* 'to notch' and English *carve*. The Gothic word *mēljan* 'to write' corresponds to German *malen* 'to paint'; the relationship between painting and writing is again found in the Russian word *pisat'* 'to write' and the Polish word *pisać* 'to write,' and these are cognate to Latin *pingere* 'to paint' from which the English word *paint* comes.

Similar associations can be found outside of the Indo-European languages. In Chinese, the word for 'script-sign' *wen¹* (文) means at the same time 'ornament.' Similarly, *kirja* means 'book' in Finnish but also 'an embellishment, bright colors.' In Fijian, the word *tusi* denotes 'striped, colorful material,' while in Samoan, the same word means 'writing.' In the Semitic languages, one finds the Assyrian root *š- ṭ -r* 'to write' cognate with Arabic *sāṭūr* 'a big knife,' while the original meaning of the Semitic triliteral root *k-t-b* 'to write' is preserved in the Syrian word *maktəbā* 'an awl.' Note, first, that the Syrian word has the prefix *ma-*, which is used to form a word for an instrument, in this case a cutting instrument; and note, second, that the vowels only modify the main meaning of the word, which is expressed by the three consonants *k*, *t*, and *b*.

Pictographs

The act of drawing – painting, scoring, scratching, etching – to create pictures for communicative purposes is the first step toward writing, but it is not yet what linguists consider to be writing. Humans have been drawing with great sophistication for many millennia. In 1940, cave paintings at Lascaux, France were discovered and date back to 16 kya, while those at Chauvet, France date back to 33 kya. In Cantabria, Spain, the El Castillo cave is even older, going back to 40 kya. In 2014, seven limestone caves on the Indonesian island of Sulawesi were discovered to have wall art, and scientists date these paintings to be likely as old as the earliest European cave art. In the caves at Lascaux, for instance, the scenes are of the hunt, and they are drawn with grace and keenly observed images of galloping horses. Although no one today knows who drew these images or what purpose they served, they certainly had a limited audience because, in order to draw them and to see them at Lascaux, it was necessary to go down a shaft on a 20-foot rope with a lamp. Some art historians speculate that these drawings were created by a priestly class of artist-shamans. Whatever their purpose, they were certainly meaningful to those who drew them and saw them.

Rock drawings (petroglyphs when carved, petrograms when painted) have been found on all continents, the oldest in Europe dating back to the late Paleolithic (Old Stone Age) period, 20–10 kya. Their meanings are lost to us today. Other kinds of drawings with specific meanings include proprietary marks, such as brands for livestock and clan or house marks, as well as so-called skin-writing, also known as tattooing. Not incidentally, tattooing as a religious practice is a kind of branding, where one displays the propriety mark of one's god on one's body. Today, tattoos still often signal adherence to a specific group, be it a gang, a cult, or a military unit. In India, women wear henna tattoos in their role of bride.

The point here is that within language groups and cultures, certain pictures – whether they are drawn on cave walls, rocks, houses, pottery, or skin – can take on conventional meanings over time to become stable word-pictures of things and actions, and even abstract ideas. Two things tend to happen next. First, the number of word-pictures often increases. Second, the growing stock of word-pictures creates the need to simplify individual ones, that is, to stylize them, to abbreviate them. These abbreviations then also come to be conventionalized, such that quite a lot of technical skill is required to understand them and to reproduce them. This reproduction, furthermore, must be done faithfully, if one is going to use them to record something important, like the history of dynastic succession or religious doctrine. History shows that the people with this technical skill will always be the diviners, that is, the priestly class.

The crucial step

It was the ancient Egyptians who, with their complex and long-enduring civilization and with their papyrus, took the final steps toward writing.[7] The development of the Egyptian word picture-script followed the above scenario with the added twist: the distance between the original word-picture and its stylization eventually became so great that the visual association between the stylized word-picture and its meaning weakened, and the sound associated with the stylized word-picture strengthened. This transition is called *phoneticization*. The great advantage of this transition was that now an even greater number of things and concepts could be represented, since unconnected ideas or concepts, if they were homophones, could be represented with one and the same picture. These phoneticized pictures could even take on entirely new meanings when linked with other pictures. The process at issue here is known as rebus or word play. Children's primers sometimes make use of the process as an aid to reading: a stylized bee next to a 4 can be read as 'before.' Texters make use of the process when they choose to spell the word *great* as gr8. In sum, the key moment in the shift from the representation of things and actions and ideas to writing proper is the shift from the optical value of a picture to its acoustic value.

This process of transition can also be described as a shift from **ideograms** to **logograms**. Ideograms are culturally conventional word-pictures of things, actions, and concepts rather than specific sequences of sounds. Logograms are no longer pictures but rather abstract symbols uniformly interpreted as particular sequences of sounds. For instance, a thumbs-up sign is an ideogram. It conveys an idea, and this idea can be expressed any number of ways in English: "Good job." "Way to go." "Excellent." By way of contrast, an example of a logogram in English would be the ampersand &, which is pronounced as the fixed sound sequence [ænd]. Depending on the context, the dollar sign can function as an ideogram: the sequence $$$ could be expressed adjectivally as "expensive," "pricey," or "costing a lot of money," or could stand for the nouns *money* or *wealth*. The dollar sign functions more or less as a stable logogram when it is used in a price, such as $10, where it represents the fixed sound sequence [dalɪz], although this sound sequence can take on any number of phonetic substitutions such as *bucks, clams, smackeroos,* etc.

With the Egyptians, then, come the first word-pictures to have phonetic value only. Even from the earliest surviving writing on vessels dating from the First Dynasty, around the middle of the fourth millennium BCE, there is evidence that the script had added to its stock of word-pictures both syllable signs and single consonant signs (alphabetic letters). Because ancient Egyptian was a Semitic language,[8] there are a considerable number of words that could be considered homonyms, at least from the point of view of the consonants, because, as was said above, the consonants in these languages form the fixed, basic elements of the words, while the vowels modify the meanings. A syllable sign is one consisting of two consonants and derives from a word-picture that had become phoneticized. This syllable sign could be used to write any word with that sequence of consonants. Not every two-consonant word-picture turned into a syllable sign, but enough of them did to have had a goodly number in the Egyptian script. As for alphabetic letters, 24 consonant signs were created. There were no vowel signs. The Egyptian script remains extremely complicated because it carried with it over the millennia all the stages of development that had presumably come before. It is thus a composite script and far from purely phonetic.

This discussion of the Egyptian script contains two significant lessons. First, the steps toward phoneticization are the same for all writing systems in the world; and, second, the phonological and morphological characteristics of the language undergoing phoneticization affect the way the language will come to be written, as we will see in the next section.

Types of Writing Systems

The shift from the optical value of a picture to its acoustic value resulted in four major categories of writing systems: logograms, abjads, alphabets, and syllabaries. We review each one in turn.

Logograms

With respect to the first lesson to be learned from the discussion of the Egyptian script, the development of logograms (hanzi, that is, 'Han character') in China is parallel to the Egyptian case in that written Chinese emerged through the rebus process and advanced through the stylization of the earliest logograms. In the days before writing in China when a person of rank or importance who had been banished was forgiven, that person would receive a ring as an invitation to return. The word *huan²* meant 'closed ring' as well as 'to come back.' Still today, the logogram 回 – evidently the picture of a closed ring and now pronounced *hui²* – means 'to come back.' This symbolism could only arise because of the phonetic identity of the two words. At first, writing consisted only of ideograms, which indicated the sense, but not the sound, of the word concerned. Over time, the ideograms gave way to logograms based on the rebus, or punning, principle. At some point, a series of semantic markers was developed to sort out the amount of punning that can be done with those logograms, especially in a tone language like Chinese, and these new types of logograms were created in abundance in the time of the Han Dynasty (206 BCE to 221 CE). The well-known case of the word *ma* illustrates how semantic markers operate. The logogram for *ma³* 'horse' is 馬, and perhaps you can just make out the stylized image of a horse running. The logogram for *ma¹* 'mother' is 女馬. The basic phonetic information is indicated with the sign for 'horse,' and the semantic marker, or **radical**, that precedes it, namely 女, is the sign for 'woman.' The logogram for *ma⁴* 'scold' is 口馬. Again, you see the sign for 'horse,' which gives the phonetic information, and now it is preceded by the radical 口, which is the sign for 'mouth.'

This phonetic–semantic process can be further understood through a hypothetical example from English: the syllable pronounced [ai] could represent the word *eye*, *I*, or *aye*. Now, imagine a word-picture for an eye that looks something like 👁 and stabilizes as a logogram. In order to disambiguate which [ai] is at stake, the logogram with no radical is to be read 'eye.' The logogram 亻👁 means 'I,' here borrowing the radical 亻 from the logogram 人 'person,' while 口👁 means 'aye,' since it contains the mouth radical. The logographic writing system in China today has several hundred semantic markers. These markers are a part of the logogram whose purpose is to disambiguate meaning.

Again, like the Egyptian case, the earliest pictograms, which developed into logograms in Chinese, were attempts to represent things, actions, or concepts by recognizable pictures. Some pictures are still recognizable today: 木 'tree' shows the branches above and roots below; 門 'gate, door' depicts two leaves of a door; 心 'heart' is seen in terms of its muscles; 手 'hand' shows a forearm with five fingers; 田 'field' is seen from above divided into parcel; 言 'word, to speak' shows a mouth with breath coming out; the logogram 貝 is for 'treasure, wealth' and depicts a cowrie shell. Some of the early logograms took on abstract meanings such as 中 depicting a target with an arrow to mean 'middle.' It is the symbol of China still today, since China was historically considered The Middle Kingdom. Over time, however, the logograms became stylized, and the visual association was broken. The logogram for 'woman' is 女, as we have just seen, and derives from the picture of a woman seated cross-legged. In the case of Chinese, not all stylizations led to more simplicity. In fact, many logograms in traditional Chinese writing are very complex and require many brush strokes. In the 1950s, Chairman Mao Zedong ordered the simplification of the script in order to increase literacy. The logogram for 'horse' in simplified script now has four brush strokes: 马, instead of the 10 of 馬.[9] We will return to the topic of literacy later on in the chapter.

The evolution of writing materials is a story in itself. The earliest Chinese writing was done on stone, metal, wood, bone, and bamboo. A revolution in writing technique occurred in the second century BCE with the invention of the bristle brush and a soft writing material made from silk waste. In the first century CE, it was discovered that a cheaper writing material composed of bark, hemp, rags, and plant fibers could be made, and this was the first paper in the world. This product was introduced in the Near East in the eighth century but did not make it to Europe until the eleventh and twelfth centuries, when paper arrived in Spain and Sicily as an import. Thereafter, Europeans set up their own paper mills, and thus there was a ready supply of a smooth plane surface ideal for mass reproductions of texts and pictures, just in time for the upsurge of print capitalism in the eighteenth century. A further innovation in paper manufacturing occurred in the nineteenth century when a very inexpensive form of paper began to be made of wood pulp, which gave rise to the expression *pulp fiction* referring to the dime novels printed on this cheap paper. Today, of course, the goal of most classrooms and offices is to go paperless. Our most recent and most important writing material is electricity.

The discussion of the Egyptian script also shows how the phonological and grammatical characteristics of the languages being phoneticized affect the production and development of the writing system. Chinese is monosyllabic. It furthermore has very little inflectional morphology.[10] The example of 'horse,' above, furthermore shows how changes in the tone of a syllable changes meaning, the syllables thus lending themselves to plentiful punning. The logographic system is one that has proved useful for transcribing a monosyllabic tone language such as Chinese. It has certainly been enduring.

Abjad

Abjad used to be called consonant writing, and we have already seen an example of the earliest type of this writing in the ancient Egyptian script, which produced 24 consonant signs but no vowel signs. The term *abjad* may come from the first four letters found in all Semitic languages a-b-ǧ-d, and it is an apt name for the writing system of a Semitic language such as Modern Standard Arabic, where the consonants and vowel length are indicated, leaving the reader to supply the short vowels based on what makes sense in context. The earliest manuscripts of the Qur'ān lacked vowels, as did Biblical Hebrew. In Modern Hebrew, the trend is to indicate the vowels.

Alphabet

The term *alphabet* comes from the first two letters of the Greek alphabet, appropriately so, since it was the Greeks who first brought a fully alphabetic script into being. Not only does the Greek alphabet have offshoots in the Roman and Cyrillic alphabets, which have provided scripts for the whole of Europe and now parts of the rest of the world, but also it has served as the model for other scripts developed for non-European languages, both of Indo-European origin and not.

The need to have letters for vowel sounds has everything to do with the phonological structure of Indo-European languages, which have, in comparison with Semitic languages, large numbers of consonant clusters and therefore large numbers of syllabic possibilities. Words and then sentences lacking vowels are intolerably ambiguous for speakers – that is, readers – of Indo-European languages, s ths cls ndcts ('as this clause indicates'). Around the eleventh to tenth centuries BCE, through trade in the Mediterranean, the Greeks probably first encountered the script of the Phoenicians inherited from the Egyptians and began to develop it for their own use, with the earliest extant inscriptions in Greek dating from the end of the eighth century BCE. Because Greek, an Indo-European language, and Phoenician, a Semitic language, are unrelated, the Greeks were able to easily shift the phonetic values of some of the Phoenician letters to serve as Greek vowels. On the whole, however, the order of the letters of the Greek alphabet closely follows the order of the Phoenician consonants, and the letter names are also similar.

What is interesting to consider is the direction of the writing and the letters. The first letter of the Old Phoenician script is 'lef' or 'ox head' stylized as α 'alpha' in Greek. In the Roman alphabet, this first letter rotated 90 degrees to the right to become 'A.' Semitic languages have stabilized writing in a right-to-left direction, while Western languages have stabilized writing in a left-to-right direction. However, the earliest writing did not have a set direction, and the ancient Greeks even developed a bi-directional type of writing known as *boustrophedon*, from the Greek 'as the ox ploughs.' In other words, one line would be written right-to-left and the next left-to-right, causing the inscriber to flip the direction of the letters. This kind of writing was common on stone. From these variations in direction have come the differing orientations of the letters in the Greek and Roman alphabets.

The type of material used to write upon also affects how the script looks. The script known as Devanāgari, used to write both Indo-European and Dravidian languages in South Asia, was described as curly cued, above. The curls of the letters were developed because the script was originally written on palm leaves, and the lines of the writing needed to adapt to the challenge of writing on curves. The Germanic runes, also mentioned above, have a contrasting and markedly angular style, one avoiding all curves. Because runes were probably written on wood, their shape was determined by the need to avoid splitting the wood, which any curve or horizontal stroke might have done. Given the impermanence of wood, most runes have survived as stone inscriptions, and they are found throughout all Germanic countries. They were written in a left-to-right direction and likely predate the fourth century CE.

Syllabary

Semitic word formation facilitated the advent of consonant writing. The complex syllable structure of Greek dictated a need for vowels. When a language has a simple syllable structure, however, another type of writing system can develop, one known as a syllabary, which means a system of sound-complexes indicating single syllables. This is a suitable system for writing a language with few syllable patterns. Japanese, for instance, has only three syllabic possibilities: (i) a vowel (V); (ii) a consonant plus a vowel (CV); and (iii) consonant, vowel, plus the nasal [n] (CVN). The Japanese words borrowed into English show this pattern: *bansai, bonzei, dojo, Fuji, futon, geisha, ikebana, judo, kimono, kirin, mitsubishi* ('ts' is phonemic in Japanese and not two separate letters, and the syllable is *tsu*), *sensei, sumo, Tokyo*, etc. These examples furthermore indicate that Japanese words are polysyllabic. It also has morphology indicating subjects and objects, and indirect objects and the like. In addition, as mentioned in Chapter 1, Japanese is a nontone, or limited tone, language.

In other words, Japanese is quite different in structure from Chinese. When, possibly as early as the fifth century CE, Chinese writing made its way into Japan, the demands of writing Japanese in terms of the Chinese system compelled adjustments. The major adjustment involved the development in Japanese of two *kana* (syllabaries), the hiragana and the katakana, each with 47 signs. Hiragana is used to write the grammatical elements of Japanese. Katakana is used to transcribe foreign words, which of course have to conform to the syllable structure of Japanese, as is the case of the Japanese word *besubaru* borrowed from the English *baseball*. Similar to the Greeks, who were not necessarily bound by the phonetic values of the Phoenician letters, the Japanese could adapt Chinese logograms to serve syllabic purposes. However, in a few cases, the pronunciation of the syllable-sign is taken from the Japanese word for the Chinese concept. For instance, the katakana sign ミ that arose from the Chinese logogram 三 'three' *san¹* has the phonetic value [mi] because the Japanese word for 'three' is [mi]. Similarly, the katakana sign メ that arose from the Chinese logogram for 'woman' 女 has the phonetic value [me] because the Japanese word for 'woman' is [me].

Both Japanese syllabaries evolved over a long period of time, as Chinese logograms were simplified and then fixed in their acoustic syllabic values. The importation of the Chinese logograms for the nongrammatical elements of Japanese – the so-called material words – was relatively unproblematic because logograms themselves have no phonetic components. Thus, the Chinese logogram 山 *shan¹* 'mountain' could be easily used for the Japanese word for mountain, which happens to be pronounced [jama]. The nouns, verbs, and adjectives in Japanese, that is, the vocabulary written in borrowed Chinese logograms, is known as *kanji*. The Japanese did not stop their borrowing practices there. Over the last century, Japanese has been transliterated into the Roman alphabet, and this transcription is known as *rōmāji*. This script is sometimes used to help foreigners who do not know how to read the kanji and the kanas, and rōmāji might be found in guidebooks or on street signs or on the packaging of foreign products in Japan. Rōmāji is also used as the input to computers to write Japanese, just as pinyin, the system for transcribing Chinese into the Roman alphabet, is used as the input to computers to write Chinese. Speakers of Chinese and Japanese who constantly use romanized inputs to type on their computers sometimes complain that they forget how to write the logograms correctly by hand, just as English speakers develop a dependence on spell check.

Another well-known syllabary is the one invented by Se-quo-ya (also written: Sequoyah) in the early nineteenth century for the Cherokee language spoken in western North Carolina and Oklahoma.[11] The story told by the Cherokee was that

Se-quo-ya saw White men reading their newspapers and that he, unlike other Cherokee, did not believe that these so-called talking leaves were either a product of sorcery
or a special gift. He single-handedly created a syllabary of some 77 signs. At first,
Se-quo-ya's signs bore little resemblance to known alphabets. Recognizing the need
for additional symbols, Se-quo-ya took inspiration from shapes he saw in European
Bibles. Having more Roman-like symbols also made it easier to create new fonts for
printing purposes in early America.

The development of a particular writing system and the way it looks is influenced:
(i) by the structure of the language being written; (ii) by the writing materials at hand,
be they soft, hard, flat, or curved; and (iii) by the presence of a preexisting cultural
force, whether prestigious or practical: the existence of hieroglyphs available to be
abbreviated and stylized into consonantal letters by the Egyptians; the presence of
the Phoenician consonantal alphabet to serve as the model for Greek letters which,
in turn, influenced the Roman and Cyrillic alphabets; the range and sophistication of
Chinese logograms to be transformed into the Japanese kanas and borrowed as kanji;
the need for the Cherokee syllabary to adapt to the fonts available at early American
printing presses.

Cultural influences on writing systems continue. In a commencement address given
at Stanford University in 2005, Steven Jobs, CEO of Apple at the time, mentioned
how, after he had dropped out of college, he dropped in on a course on calligraphy
(Greek for 'beautiful writing') at Reed College. He explained how what he learned in
that course about typography influenced the typefaces and letter and line spacing pro-
grammed into the Mac. While Apple might have set the typographic aesthetics for the
way writing systems look on computers, it is the Unicode Consortium incorporated
in 1991 in California that decides which scripts can be written on computers, because
this body governs the character coding system used worldwide to process and display
the scripts of the diverse languages and technical disciplines.

Religion and the Spread of Writing Systems

Thus far, we have examined the relationship between religion and the origin of writing, and we have attempted to explain how writing systems are established and how
they develop. Now we offer an overview of their spread. The prime motivator for the
adoption or abandonment of a writing system is, once again, religion, and examples
abound.

When the Germanic tribes were Christianized throughout the first millennium CE,
they stopped writing in runes and began writing in the Roman alphabet. The Great
Schism of 1054 in Christendom resulted in a split not only between Rome and Con-
stantinople but also in the alphabets used to write Slavic languages. East Slavic languages, such as Belarusian, Russian, and Ukrainian, are written in Cyrillic and follow
the Orthodox East as Eastern Orthodox. West Slavic languages, such as Czech, Polish,
and Slovak, are written in the Roman alphabet and follow the Latin West as Catholics.
As for the south Slavic languages, Bulgarian and Serbian are written in Cyrillic, while
Croatian and Slovenian are written in the Latin alphabet, and the religious affiliations

of their speakers vary accordingly. The result is that Serbian and Croatian look very different in written form, despite the fact that they are mutually intelligible. Similarly, Hindi and Urdu are very close linguistically, and yet Hindi speakers tend to be Hindu and write their language in Devanāgari, while Urdu speakers tend to be Muslim and write their language in an adapted Arabic script. Buddhism brought Chinese writing into Korea and Japan. Returning to Europe, Yiddish is a West Germanic language spoken by many Eastern European Jews before World War II. However, Yiddish is written not in the Roman but rather the Hebrew alphabet. The vowels are marked, except for Hebrew borrowings for which vowels are unmarked.

The spread of Catholicism around the world has meant the spread of the Latin script. Sometimes, a population being converted already has a writing system, but it is displaced, as we saw in the case of Bishop Diego de Landa and his notorious destruction of the Mayan script in New Spain Mexico. De Landa then set out to rewrite the history of the Mayans, with the result that much of what we know of it today exists only in Spanish, and furthermore modern Mayan languages are now written in the Roman alphabet. When Portuguese missionaries went to Vietnam in the early sixteenth century, they encountered a language that was written mostly in borrowed Chinese logograms. These missionaries created romanized phonetic script for Vietnamese known as *quốc ngữ*. A century later, the French Jesuit missionary, Alexandre de Rhodes, further regularized the spelling conventions for Vietnamese that the Portuguese had begun. However, the prestige of the Chinese writing system was great enough to have been maintained in use until the twentieth century. Now, Vietnamese is written exclusively in the Roman alphabet, and it is one of the very few languages in all of South Asia and East Asia to be written in that alphabet.[12] Not surprisingly, many Vietnamese, particularly South Vietnamese, are Christian.

Similarly, the spread of Islam around the world has meant the spread of the Arabic script. After the Prophet Mohammad's death, Islam spread in three directions: east along the Silk Road and then as far as Indonesia, which is the most populous Islamic country in the world today, west across North Africa, and south to sub-Saharan Africa. To the east, the indigenous Persian script was abolished following the Islamization of Persia after 638. Today, speakers in the Iranian branch of the Indo-European languages who are Muslim, such as the Tajiki and the Iranians, write their languages, Tajik and Farsi (Persian), in an adapted Arabic script. As Islam moved west, it encountered, among others, speakers of Berber, descendants of pre-Arab inhabitants of North Africa, who had their own script, which was eventually replaced by the Arabic alphabet. Swahili, a Niger–Congo language spoken on the East Coast of Africa in modern-day states such as Kenya and Tanzania, was an unwritten language until its speakers adopted Islam beginning in the ninth century. By the eleventh century, Swahili was written in Kiarabu, as the Swahili–Arabic script is called in Swahili.

Throughout the centuries, and on a global scale since the sixteenth century, missionaries have largely been the ones responsible for replacing scripts for the purpose of erasing reference and access to old gods; they have also been almost exclusively responsible for creating writing systems for previously unwritten languages. While Spanish missionaries were busy in New Spain (Mexico), French missionaries were working in

New France (Quebec). Gabriel Sagard-Théodat, for example, lived among the Wyandot for many decades in the seventeenth century so that he could learn the language in order to write a version of the Bible in that language.[13] He also wrote the first descriptions of the language along with a dictionary. What is known about this language, which is now extinct, largely comes from Sagard-Théodat's work, which was expanded upon later in the century by other commentators. It must be said that this French missionary describes the language accurately. He correctly identifies the sounds of the language and the basic grammatical processes. However, his emphasis is not on what the Wyandot language has, but rather what it *lacks*: labial letters, for instance, and words such as *Trinity* and *Holy Ghost*. It was not until the early nineteenth century that linguists and language theorists began to entertain the possibility that languages are not all adjusting to one reality and that the absence of a concept or a grammatical process is not a sign of cultural or intellectual underdevelopment.

Missionaries today are just as active as they have always been. An organization formerly known as the Summer Institute of Linguistics and now known as SIL International formed in the United States in the 1930s to train missionaries in linguistic theory and translation practice. The purpose of this training is to make Bible translations. SIL International has offices all over the world, and they operate the website called Ethnologue, which is a valuable resource for linguistic information of the world's languages. They also determine exactly how many languages there are in the world. At present count, there are 7105, which is the number of languages calculated to need a separate Bible translation. For professional linguists, by way of contrast, the number of languages in the world is believed to be, in principle, indeterminate (see Chapter 1). Other religious organizations involved in worldwide missionary and translation/conversion efforts include Wycliffe International and The Church of Jesus Christ of the Latter Day Saints.

Speaking of the Bible, the remarkable revival of Hebrew as a modern spoken language can be credited, in large part, to the fact that the Hebrew Bible remained an integral part of Jewish culture during the approximately 1750 years when Hebrew as a spoken language could be considered clinically dead. The ancient version of the language dates back to approximately the fourteenth century BCE, and its symbolic end is dated to the second century CE, with the failed Bar-Kokhba Revolt against the Romans in Judea in 132–135 CE. Before this particular event, however, the language had already been in decline. It is possible that the decision taken around 200 CE by Rabbi Judah haNasi and his collaborators to write down the oral tradition – what is called the Mishnah or the Oral Torah – was inspired by a perception that soon there would no speakers of Hebrew left, thus prompting the need to create a written record to preserve the religion. Centuries later, in the nineteenth century, pogroms (from the Russian 'to destroy' 'to destruct') started against the Jews in Eastern Europe, in response to which arose Zionism, a movement dedicated to the repatriation of Jews to the Land of Israel. The successful revival of Hebrew as a spoken language in modern Israel cannot be understood without recognizing that Hebrew as a written language had always remained alive in religious practice and study. In the case of the origins of modern Hebrew, the usual relationship between the spoken and the written – where the written follows the spoken – is inverted.

The case of the revival of the Hebrew language and the establishment of the Jewish state of Israel in 1948 explicitly opens our discussion onto politics.

The Always Already Intervention of Politics

The cultural organization created by a religious structure is, except in a very few instances, hierarchical, which means that power is differentially distributed throughout the system. The religious organization of a group cannot always be neatly separated from the corresponding political organization of a group. In ancient Egypt, religious and political control went hand in hand. It would be impossible to write the history of Western Europe without reference to the fall of the political force of Rome in the fifth century CE and the rise of the religious force of Rome thereafter. Henry VIII's decision to create an Anglican Church in 1534, autonomous from Rome, and to make himself head of the church was but one attempt to negotiate the relationship between these two powers, the religious and the political. Another was the First Amendment to the United States Constitution formally declaring a separation between Church and State.

There are at least two types of political power: the so-called hard power of the military and the so-called soft power of a compelling culture. Religion, as we have seen, can be very compelling; so can a well-developed literature or a well-developed movie industry. All types of power are strengthened further by the existence of a writing system, to which accrues prestige. The power of prestige can be seen in the case of Chinese logograms, which were borrowed at one time or another by peoples in neighboring countries whose languages are not related to Sino-Tibetan, namely Korean (language family unknown), Japanese (language family unknown), Vietnamese (Austric), and Mongolian (Mongolic).

The act of writing is a powerful extension of the spoken language and goes in two directions: in space and across time. Before the advent of modern media, a written message extended much farther in space than did a spoken one. It would be difficult to conceive of ancient empires such as that of Alexander the Great or the Persians existing without some kind of writing system to maintain unity by means of military orders and a judicial system. For this reason alone, it must be the case that the knotted-cord quippus of the Inca served specific communicative purposes, given that the Incan empire extended over thousands of miles. Likewise, ancient Mayan hieroglyphics served as a written lingua franca uniting the various languages of the empire.

Throughout this chapter, we have been referring to a language called Chinese, but there is no single such language, as we have pointed out before. The political entity of mainland China has, depending on how one counts, at least 10 varieties of the language – Mandarin and Cantonese being the most well known – but it nevertheless does make sense to speak of a unified so-called Chinese because the link of the common logographic writing system *literally* held the country together for millennia. The visual unity of Islam is found not only in the Arabic script of the Qur'ān but also in the great variety of languages spoken by Muslims written in that script. The Arabic alphabet is a strong sign of Islamic unity. On that note, Turkey, a Muslim nation, might not have been inducted into NATO in 1952 if Turkish had not by that time been written in the Roman alphabet. The Roman alphabet puts Turkey's foot into European culture more forcefully than does the northwest bit of the country fanning out on European soil.

Before modern media, written language extended much farther over time than did the spoken language. Extension in time allows for the creation of the accumulation of cultural goods, now often called cultural capital. Writing safeguards achievements, stabilizes ethical and religious and civic values, sets legal precedent, and establishes historical truths, which are then often subject to rewriting, depending on the winners of the next war. A sense of the unity of a people comes out of their writing, identifying the We as opposed to the They. Of course, peoples whose languages were or still are unwritten – although these are fewer and fewer – have their own oral traditions and practices that establish unity. However, the point here is that writing makes a *material link* to group consciousness or what we now call identity.

Although the task of creating or changing a writing system has been largely left to the religious caste, certain political leaders have recognized the importance of writing and nationhood. In the thirteenth century, the Mongol ruler Genghis Khan got rid of Chinese characters and had a Mongolian script created as a way to consolidate the Mongolian state. Two centuries later, King Sejong of Korea made a similar intervention by presiding over the creation of Hangul, the alphabet for writing for Korean. However, the Korean logograms borrowed from Chinese (hanja) were not so easily banished. Just as the Latin alphabet was slowly adopted for Vietnamese, so using Hangul to write Korean did not come into universal practice until the twentieth century. Nevertheless, King Sejong's effort was nationalist in purpose, as was Se-quo-ya's, since the latter could have transcribed Cherokee in the Roman alphabet.

The most dramatic case of a writing reform is that of Mustafa Kemal Atatürk, the first President of Turkey, who decreed in 1928 that Turkish would no longer be written in the Arabic alphabet but rather would be written in the Roman alphabet. Up until that point, Turkish had been written in an adapted form of the Arabic alphabet for a thousand years. Atatürk's motive was to disrupt Turkey's relationship with Islam, to make Turkey a modern, secular state. Today, some Turks believe that this alphabetic change cut them off too abruptly from their past and their ability to appreciate that past. The sense of being cut off from one's past happens any time a writing system changes for whatever reason. If the Soviet Union had taken over the United States in the 1950s and decreed that henceforth English would be written in Cyrillic, everything from the Constitution to inscriptions on historic buildings would now look alien to Americans. Severing visual ties to a culture's past is one way of creating a new identity.

Genghis Khan, King Sejong, and Se-quo-ya all attempted to foster a sense of ownership or nationhood for their people by establishing what can be called a writing system of their own. After the Cherokee Trail of Tears in 1830s, Se-quo-ya dreamed that his already-invented syllabary would reunite the dispersed tribes. King Sejong could have left Chinese logograms in place and adapted them better to the grammatical structure of Korean, as did the Japanese. Now, however much the Chinese writing system was not well suited to a language like Korean, the hanja were prestigious, as we have said. So prestigious, in fact, that when Hangul was invented, it was decided the letters would be stacked into syllables to spell words, so that the writing system would have the visual complexity of logograms, even though Hangul was an alphabet. As for the Japanese, they maintain a sense of identity by having a syllabary for writing foreign words, the katakana, and thus make visible the distinction between the native (even if originally borrowed from Chinese) and the foreign stock of the vocabulary. The Polish population in the nineteenth century successfully resisted the efforts of Tsar Nicholas I to change the alphabet of Polish from Latin to Cyrillic. The attempt to reform the Polish language was abandoned when it became clear that the Russification of the Polish script would have led to revolt and insurrection. The Latin alphabet was the Polish population's badge of national pride at a time when they lacked both political independence and state organization.

In the past four centuries, Western European Empires – the Portuguese, the Spanish, the Dutch, the French, and the British – reformed the world enough so that we can now say that the sun never sets on the Latin alphabet. When the Portuguese colonized Goa on the west coast of India and Macau, not far from Hong Kong, they immediately set up printing presses. The Dutch colonized the East Indies, now Indonesia, and replaced Arabic with the Latin alphabet to write the Bahasa language. Still today, Bahasa is written in the Latin alphabet (called Rumi), although Indonesia remains a predominately Muslim nation. The British in Africa transliterated Swahili from Arabic to Roman.

During the nineteenth century, worldwide nationalist movements came into being, Zionism being only one. The first rumblings in favor of the nation-state of Turkey, for instance, began in the late nineteenth century as the Ottoman Empire was in decline, and came to fruition when Atatürk came to power and enacted his alphabet revolution. In Eastern Europe, the country of Romania was consolidating itself as an independent nation-state in the midnineteenth century. As a result of their location, Romanians are Eastern Orthodox. Given their linguistic heritage, they are speakers of a Romance language. In the period 1860–1862, Romanians looked West and made the switch from writing in Cyrillic to Roman, and efforts were made to relexify the language by replacing Slavic roots borrowed long since with Latin and French words.[14] There was also a long period of orthographic instability that continued even after the fall of communism in 1989. After that moment, there arose the battle between the *î from i* and the *î from a*, the former appearing Slavic and being privileged during the period of communism, the latter appearing in Latin and pro-Western and favored nowadays. For instance, before the 1989 revolution, the word 'bread' was spelled *pîine*. Afterwards, it became *pâine*, and indeed this latter spelling looks more like its Romance counterparts: *pain* (French), *panne* (Italian), *pan* (Spanish), and *pão* (Portuguese), from Latin *panem*.

When the Bolsheviks came to power as a result of the Russian Revolution in 1917, they wanted to replace Cyrillic with the Latin alphabet. The issue of Latinizing the writing system was not new in Soviet Russia, since it had at least a 200-year history through a long line of Russian intellectuals who desired a relationship with the West. However, with the arrival of the Bolsheviks, new motives for alphabet reform arose:

(i)   The Cyrillic alphabet suddenly looked bourgeois because it was visually continuous with the Tsarist past.

(ii)   The Bolsheviks believed their movement was international in scope, and the Latin alphabet was to be the tool for extending the socialism to the whole world. They had identified Western Europe as the place where the next proletarian revolution was going to take place, and their goal was to unite the world through the Latin script. This unification was to include Korea and China, and official commissions, which were created to Latinize Russian, started the process of Latinizing Korean and Chinese, as well.

(iii) The Bolsheviks inherited from the vast Tsarist Empire a lot of territory in Central Asia inhabited by Muslims who were mostly speakers of Turkic languages written in the Arabic script. The decreed shift from the Arabic alphabet to the Latin was calculated to isolate these people from the Islamic world and religion. The early Soviet leaders were, furthermore, encouraged by Atatürk's success at alphabet reform for Turkish.

(iv)   The Cyrillic alphabet was deemed too complicated, and the Latin alphabet was valued for being simpler and more elegant. Therefore, according to the demands of Marxist pedagogy, the Latin alphabet was to be preferred, since it would erase illiteracy. The Yeni Alif, The New Alphabet Committee, was created in 1928 to begin work on this enormous Latinization project.

By the time the reforms were ready to be put into place for Russian, namely in 1930, Stalin rejected the Latinizing plan, and the Cyrillic alphabet survived. However, the issue of Latinizing in the Russian Federation has not completely disappeared. In 1999, the Russian Republic of Tatarstan put forth a proposal to shift its alphabet from Cyrillic to Latin. The argument was to bring Tatar, a Turkic language, into the modern world of the Internet. The proposal was opposed by many Tatars, both inside and outside the country, who protested that the shift would threaten Tatar national culture and the people's ties to their past. The Russian Duma (elected legislative body) formally rejected the proposal. In 2002, Vladimir Putin, then president of Russia, had a law enacted that made the Cyrillic alphabet mandatory for all languages in the autonomous republics within Russia. Of the case of Tatar, Putin said that the shift from Cyrillic to Latin was a threat to unity of the Russian Federation. No greater statement about the importance of a script to the integrity of a political organization can be made.

Orality and Literacy

High rates of literacy foster a group's sense of unity. Marxist pedagogy explicitly promoted literacy, just as democratic regimes strive for literate populaces to participate in civic life. Indeed, communist states have historically produced populations with high rates of literacy. These include present-day Cuba and Vietnam. As noted earlier, Mao Zedong organized a commission to simplify Chinese logograms in 1952. Some 400 little-used and complicated logograms were discarded, and another 800 had their number of strokes drastically reduced. The simplification seems to have helped literacy rates in China because now they are near full literacy. The ability to read a newspaper requires knowing around 2000 logograms. Educated people know about 4000.

Upwards toward 55,000 are said to exist. The reform of Chinese is thus an ongoing process and has furthermore an ongoing relationship with romanization. Many attempts at romanization have occurred in the past hundred years or more, the official one, pinyin, having been created in 1958.

We began this chapter with the story of the Prophet Mohammed, his alleged illiteracy, and the dual preservation of the revelation of the Qur'ān through individuals who memorized the texts and through scribes who wrote them down. Before widespread literacy began after the sixteenth century in Europe and in the past 100 years in the rest of the world, individuals responsible for a store of information relied on their memories. The Sanskrit grammarian, Pāṇini, of the fourth century BCE, is known for having created his 3959 rules of Sanskrit grammar. What is debated is whether he wrote them down as he composed them or whether he composed the whole from memory. What is known is that he had disciples who committed the work to memory, just as there were, and still are, those who commit the Qur'ān to memory. In the Middle Ages, it was commonplace for bards to memorize the epics their audiences expected to hear. The Old English masterpiece *Beowulf* has 3182 lines. It would have been sung on three successive nights, like a miniseries, with the performance of a little over a thousand lines a night. The first reference to a manuscript of this work comes in the eighth century, but there is evidence to suggest that the story came over in purely oral form with the Angles and the Saxons when they left their Continental homeland and began arriving in Britain in 449 CE.

The point here is, first, in oral cultures memory is prized, and second, memory is affected by literacy. Humans have always had sources of what is called transactive memory, or so-called external memory. In a family or work environment, different people remember different things. Your roommate or your significant other may remember the date of a dear friend's birthday, while you may remember the best route to your family's favorite restaurant. The experience of transactive memory is completely familiar to everyone. However, with the advent of the Internet, we now have access to information in an unprecedented way, and this unlimited access seems to be having an effect on how people remember things. Most significantly, it seems that we tend to forget what we know to be available externally, and now we are more likely to remember where an item has been stored rather than the identity of the item itself. The result is that we are in as much of a transactive memory relationship with our digital devices now as we are with other human beings. This reliance has become normalized. Losing one's phone is equivalent to losing touch with the universe.

These remarks about orality, memory, and literacy were introduced primarily to lead to the subject of access to the Internet, which has now become less of a luxury and more of a basic need – one that not yet everyone in the world has. The problem of access is an old one, since the invention of writing as such when the priests had exclusive purchase on its power. When the grip on that power relaxes, the cultivation of literacy often serves the purposes of extending the reach of religion, with the original choice of script dictated by religion, as we have seen. Henry VIII, who severed religious ties with Rome, was the first English monarch to allow the translation of the Bible into English, thereby making his Anglicism more available to his subjects.[15] Before the American Civil War, when African-American slaves were taught to read, the purpose was always so that they would be able to read the Bible. One of the stated goals of SIL International today is to promote literacy in less literate societies, and their text of choice remains the Bible. In the twentieth century, the communists officially banned the practice of religion and promoted literacy so that comrades would have access to another kind of literature and become good Marxists.

Restrictions to access come in different forms. Women, at many times in history and in many places around the world, have been denied access to basic education and literacy. Because of this lack of access, women in the Hunan province of China invented in the thirteenth and fourteenth centuries a script known as Nüshu. This is a syllabic script whose symbols are based on simplified versions of logograms. It reached its height in the seventeenth century and is no longer used. Today, as we have just said, China has near full literacy, with the percentages equal between the sexes. In Japan, one of the kanas was feminized, namely the hiragana, which was developed and used originally by women, while men used the more prestigious kanji and katakana.

Who has access to what kinds of writing and what form the writing takes can bring into play such varied power dynamics as the one between the sexes, the dominant versus subordinate languages in a multilingual country such as Russia, or even the status of bilingual education in an immigrant country such as the United States. Since the beginning of the United States, politicians, school boards, and voters whose ranks also include naturalized citizens have had to work through whether and how to provide children from successive groups of immigrants the means for becoming literate in the language of the home. Many immigrant groups take the educational burden upon themselves and set up Saturday and Sunday schools where their children learn to read and write the heritage language.

In *Grassroots Literacy: Writing, Identity and Voice in Central Africa*, Jan Blommaert undertakes an examination of certain writing practices in places where "literacy skills are generally rare and access to advanced and sophisticated forms of literacy is severely restricted" (2008:3). Blommaert's study highlights the fact that the phrase *ability to write* can mean very different things in different places. In Central Africa, which has a colonial history and where many regions have been destabilized by violence, it might mean practices where the writer knows the graphic symbols to use but has spelling difficulties, erratic punctuation, and nonstandard uses of upper- and lower-case letters, and may include drawings to illustrate whatever document the writer is producing. Blommaert is aware that these skills are not the same as those involved in writing, say, a college-level term paper. Blommaert also studies the effects of globalization on different cultures around the world (see Chapter 12). We, the authors, now tell our students that an elite type of literacy means something more today than it might have even 50 years ago. For instance, it is now necessary for citizens of the world to be able to handle more than one alphabet, leaving the meaning of *to handle* undefined here, and perhaps even to know a basic number of Chinese logograms, again leaving the basic number indeterminate. Whatever elite norms of literacy may arise in the future, we applaud all the efforts people make in adding literacy to their skills so that they have a wedge into the circulation of information and ideas in this age of globalization.

Final Note: Azerbaijan Achieves Alphabetic Autonomy

Azerbaijan is an ex-Soviet state of slightly more than nine million people in an area slightly smaller than the US state of Indiana. It borders the Caspian Sea and is nestled between Russia to the north, Georgia to the north and west, Armenia to the west, and Iran to the south. The titular language of the country, Azerbaijani, is Turkic. The majority of the people who speak it are Muslim. Like five other currently independent states in Central Asia – Uzbekistan, Kazakhstan, Krygyzstan, Turkmenistan, and Tajikistan[16] – Azerbaijan was decolonized by default after the break-up of the Soviet Union in 1991. At that moment, the new Azerbaijan government faced the problem of securing their sense of nationhood, which they did in part through the well-established practice of consolidating their national language.

Of interest here is the issue of the alphabet. In the last 100 years, this population has endured three alphabet changes, and these changes help us summarize several lessons of this chapter. First, Azerbaijani was originally written in the Arabic script when the population converted to Islam, thus underscoring how the original choice of script stems from religion. Then came the intervention of politics with the Russian Revolution and the Bolsheviks who failed to Latinize Russian but who nevertheless succeeded in Latinizing the Turkic languages spoken in the territories inherited from the Tsars. This alphabet change was for the purpose of disrupting the visible relationship to Islam. Later, namely in 1939, Stalin rescinded the Latinizing policy and replaced it with a Russifying policy. Thus, Azerbaijani was transliterated into the Cyrillic alphabet, and this further shift illustrates the importance of a script as a symbol of political unity. After 1991, the Azerbaijani government had a decision to make. They chose de-Russification and embraced the Latin alphabet.

The adoption of the Latin alphabet was facilitated by the fact that a Latin version suited for the particular phonetic needs of Azerbaijani had already been produced in the 1920s. The Azerbaijanis also successfully rejected the attempt by Turkey to promote their version of the Common Turkish Alphabet. The adoption of a new alphabet is no small matter and requires the effort and expense of changing all public signage, transliterating all existing legal documents and literature, and creating anew all instructional materials. It also automatically disenfranchises a generation of adults who, in the case of Azerbaijan, were literate in Cyrillic. Two factors in particular have helped the successful transition to the Latin alphabet in Azerbaijan. First, the Azerbaijani Latin alphabet was standardized in Unicode, making its use available on computers worldwide; and second, UNESCO supported the creation of an Azerbaijani database of full texts of Azerbaijani writings called *Treasures of the Azerbaijani Language* (Kellner-Heinkele and Landau 2012:33)

Language Profile: اللعربية [Arabic (Afro-Asiatic)]

Functional overview

Arabic is the only multicountry language profiled in *Languages in the World*. Of the others profiled, Vietnamese and Mongolian are one-country languages. Kurdish is a no-country language, as was discussed in Chapter 4. Tamil also has no titular country associated with it, although it does have official language status in Sri Lanka along with Sinhala. The political status of Tibetan changed when Tibet became an autonomous region of China and now has speakers in that region as well as in exile. Hawaiian is the language of one state of the United States. And !Xóõ distinguishes itself by being spoken by people who preserve the hunter-gathering way of life, while the others arose in the wake of the spread of agriculture. Arabic, like Tibetan and its relationship to Tibetan Buddhism, has prestige because of its identification with Islam. However, in contrast with Tibetan, Arabic spreads across 28 countries, either as the primary language of the country or as one widely spoken in it. Thus, its social and political dynamics are necessarily different than those affecting the other languages we profile.

In Africa, Arabic is spoken in Algeria, Chad, Comoros, Djibouti, Egypt, Eritrea, Libya, Mauritania, Morocco, Sudan, Tunisia, Tanzania, Somaliland, and Western Sahara. In the Middle East, Arabic is spoken in Bahrain, Iraq, Israel, Jordan, Kuwait, Lebanon, Oman, Palestinian territories, Qatar, Saudia Arabia, Syria, United Arab Emirates, and Yemen. It is difficult to make an accurate assessment of the numbers of speakers of Arabic because it is difficult to pin down where the borders of the language start and stop over such a large geographic area, with so many opportunities for language varieties to blend. A conservative estimate is that well over 200 million people speak Arabic (see Map 5.1). At the same time, it is easy to think that probably upwards toward 400 million people speak some kind of Arabic.

The Arabic-speaking world is distinguished by the prominent language politics surrounding the high status (H) of Modern Standard Arabic (MSA), which is the language of education, media, government, and all official occasions, and the low status

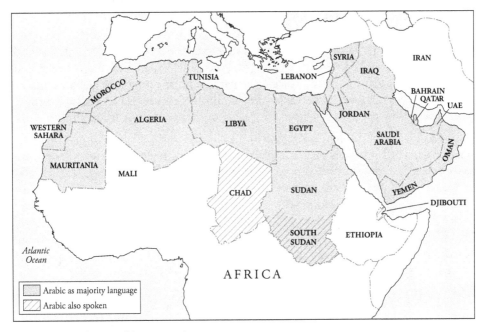

Map 5.1   Arabic-speaking countries.

(L) of the local varieties of Arabic. The L varieties are not necessarily mutually intelligible and are sometimes referred to as *darija* 'everyday language.' MSA is, for all
intents and purposes, Classical Arabic, which has remained unchanged since the seventh century, although given the linguistic dynamics prevailing at all times, certain
local varieties of MSA can be said to exist. For the most part, however, it is a stable
and uniform language. MSA is no one's native language; it is taught in schools, which
means that every educated speaker of Arabic deals with at least two varieties of the
same language (historically speaking, at least) throughout their lives and likely on a
daily basis.

Prominent structural characteristics

The language of the ḍād (ض)   Speech sounds are created when air comes up from the
lungs and passes in different ways through the vocal tract.[17] Vowels are created when
there is a modification of an open vocal tract with no buildup of pressure above the
glottis. Consonants are created by complete or partial closure of the vocal tract, and
they are identified by the ways the air leaves the vocal tract:

(i)   Oral/nasal – if the velum is lowered, the air goes through the nose to produce
      a nasal; nasals in English include [m], [n], and [ŋ]; all other consonants in
      English are oral.
(ii) Voiced/voiceless – when the vocal folds vibrate during a consonant constriction,
      a voiced consonant is produced such as [d]; if they cease vibration, a voiceless
      consonant is produced such as [t].
(iii) **Place of articulation** – consonants vary by the place where the full or partial
      constriction of the vocal tract occurs, and these places include, among others,
      the larynx, pharynx, glottis, velum, hard palate, alveolar ridge, teeth, and lips.
(iv) **Manner of articulation** – if there is full constriction of the vocal tract, a stop
      sound is produced such as [d] and [t], both of which are oral and alveolar, and
      vary by the feature voiced/voiceless; if partial constriction of the airflow is made,
      a fricative is produced, such as [v] and [f], both of which are oral and labiodental,
      and vary by the feature voiced/voiceless; other manners of articulation exist.

MSA and many L varieties exploit a place on the vocal tract that English does not:
the pharynx. There is a series of four consonants – [ḍ] (ض), [ṣ] (ص), [ṭ] (ط), and
[ẓ] (ظ) – sometimes called *emphatics*, which are produced with the tongue on or
around the alveolar ridge along with a constriction of the pharynx and which vary
by the features voiced/voiceless and manner stop/fricative. They are so distinctive
that Arabic is self-described as the *lugat aḍ ḍād* 'language of the ḍād.' Please note
that the transliterations have a dot below what corresponds to the Latin equivalent
(more or less) of the sound. These dots will help you sort out Exercise 1 in this
chapter.
   In addition, MSA has glottal stop [ʔ] called *hamza* and written (ء). It is distinguished from the voiced pharyngeal fricative with a similar-looking phonetic symbol [ʕ] but written distinctively in Arabic (ع). Its unvoiced counterpart is [ħ] (ح).

Controversy swirls around the exact descriptions of these sounds, and they certainly vary in their pronunciations over the vast Arabic-speaking area.

The triliteral root The Germanic languages once had a productive morphological process organizing the verbal system and some associated nouns and adjectives, exemplified here by the two series: *sing–sang–sung–song* and *wring–wrung–wrung–wrong*. In English, internal vowel changes to distinguish singular from plural are few, for instance *man* versus *men, mouse* versus *mice,* the most unusual being *woman* versus *women,* whose distinction is seen in writing in the second syllable but is heard in pronunciation in the first syllable: [wɪmn] versus [wʊmn]. In German, by way of contrast, internal vowel change to distinguish singular from plural is robust. These regular vowel variations are called *Ablaut,* a term coined by Jakob Grimm.

Arabic is also organized around internal vowel changes but in a different way than the process operates/operated in Indo-European languages. You saw examples in this chapter and now in Exercise 1 of the triliteral roots, which can sometimes be biliteral and even quadriliteral. These roots can only be consonants or long vowels. They function as the fundamental lexical units around which vowels are inserted and to which prefixes and suffixes may be added to form the many pattern-templates that produce the verbal and nominal possibilities in the language. In order to look up a word in a dictionary, you have to be able to identify the root, because the 'spin-offs' from the pattern-templates are listed under the root and not in strict alphabetical order. The word *maktaba* 'library' will not be found in the words beginning with letter 'm' but under those with 'k' because the root is: k-t-b 'to write.' This entry will furthermore appear very near the beginning of the 'k's because 't' (ت) is the third letter of the Arabic alphabet.

Arabic is one of the languages of the world with a long history of study and discussion, and it is because of Islam. In the East, commentary on language can be found in the sixth century BCE and the work of Lao Tsu. In the West, it starts in the fourth century BCE and Plato's *Cratylus.* In the Middle East, the first work on Arabic grammar comes in the eighth century CE and the grammarian Sībawayh's great *al-Kitab.* Sībawayh was not an Arab; rather he was Persian, and his observations on Arabic have stood the test of time. He is the one who first noted the pattern-templates of Arabic and started the tradition of representing them thusly:

CaCaCa or
C1aC2aC3a

This is the pattern-template for creating the past tense (masculine). If we plug in the triliteral root for 'to write,' we get *kataba* 'he wrote.'

If we use the template:

maCCaC

we can produce words that mean something like 'place where,' such as *maktab* 'office,' *madras* 'school' from d-r-s 'to study, learn,' *matbax* 'kitchen' from t-b-x 'to prepare food, cook,' *maghreb* 'North Africa' from ʀ-r-b 'to depart, withdraw' and, by extension, 'stranger' and 'west' (presumably someone coming from the west).

Broken plurals   Arabic has a regular process of forming plurals with suffix *-ūn* for masculine nouns and *-āt* for feminine nouns: *muʔallim* 'teacher (male)' versus *muʔallimūn* 'teachers (male)' and *maktabah* 'library' and *maktabāt* 'libraries.' However, there is another process known as *broken plurals* that is both distinctive in Arabic and widespread. It is found in other Semitic languages but is in the most evidence in Arabic, and it is found in other languages that have borrowed heavily from Arabic through Islamicization, namely Azerbaijani, Kurdish, Pashto, Persian, Turkish, and Urdu.

The pattern-templates are many and nearly unpredictable:

Singular form	Plural form	Example	
CiCaC		*kitāb* 'book'	*kutub* 'books'
CaCīCa	CuCuC	*safina* 'ship'	*sufun* 'ships'
CaCīC		*sabīl* 'path'	*subul* 'paths'
maCCaC	maCāCiC	*maktab* 'office'	*makātib* 'offices'
maCCiC		*masjid* 'mosque'	*masājid* 'mosques'

(Can you guess what the triliteral root s-j-d means?)

CāCiC	CuC$_2$C$_2$āC	*kātib* 'writer'	*kuttāb* 'writers'
		ṭālib 'student'	*ṭullāb* 'students'
miCCāC	maCāCīC	*miftāh* 'key'	*mafātīh* 'keys'
maCCūC		*maktūb* 'message'	*makātīb* 'messages'

These examples are only a taste of the variety of the so-called broken plurals in Arabic. They give the language part of the complexity for which it is justly famous and often revered.

Salient cultural characteristic: diglossia

We said in Chapter 3 that the H/L linguistic situation in the Arabic-speaking world is known by the term *diglossia* and that it is a common enough occurrence throughout the world. To take but one example, in Haiti the L Kreyòl Ayisyen (see Final Note, Chapter 8) is opposed to the H Standard French.

In the Arabic-speaking world, diglossia is particularly complex because of the size of that world. On the one hand, the L varieties share common deviations from the Classical norm, from general trends such as the loss of case endings and the loss of the dual in the verbs and the pronouns to specific similarities such as the replacement of Classical *raʔā* with *šāf* 'to see' (Versteegh 1984:17). Perhaps the most salient difference between H and L is the fact that H MSA is VSO, while the L varieties are SVO.

On the other hand, the L varieties also differ from one another phonologically and grammatically, as well as lexically. The lexical differences are due to the languages with which the L varieties have come into contact over the centuries. In North Africa, for instance, L varieties have borrowings from French. Of the L varieties, Egyptian is the most widely understood not only because it is in the geographic center of the Arabic-speaking world but also because the products of its television and film industry are popular.

How and why did this diglossic situation arise? The short answer lies in the linguistic effects of the spread of Islam following the death of the prophet in 632. The next question is: What was the linguistic situation in the Arabic-speaking world *before* the spread of Islam? The pre-Islamic period is known as the *Jahiliyyah*, or Period of Ignorance. The word comes from the root j-h-l 'to be ignorant, act stupidly' and produces, among other words, *jahl* 'ignorance' and *jahaalah* 'foolishness.' In the Jahiliyyah, it is believed that the tribes on the Arabian peninsula spoke different varieties of Arabic. Although no one knows the precise extent of the differences among the varieties, these differences do not seem to be great. There was an intertribal variety often referred to as a *poetic koine* that was used for poetry and prophecies and the like. The existence of this variety, however, does not offer evidence that it was used as a separate level, or register, of language. In other words, before Islam there was no diglossia.

In the first centuries after the spread of Islam, Arabic underwent a rapid change when the language of the nomadic Bedouin (*al-'Arab*) spread far and wide and into cities with their diverse populations and languages. It is the thesis of Arabic scholar Kees Versteegh (1984) that the features of this New Arabic, the basis of today's L varieties, show effects of creolization as converts to Islam – and therefore to the Arabic language – began to change the language. For the point being made here, what is important to note is that commentators and grammarians in the early centuries of the Islamic period became alarmed by the ways these new converts were changing the language, and these changes necessarily threatened to affect the recitation of the Qur'ān. Thus, the establishment of a Classical norm was necessary. Well over 1000 years later, that norm is generally referred to as MSA. In other words, before Islam there was no diglossia, because there was no need for it. The need was created by the success of the Islamic conquest.

Exercises

Exercise 1 – Arabic roots you already know

Determine which Arabic word in Part ii Meanings, below, is the source for the following words. You may write in either the number of the Arabic root or the Arabic letters themselves:

i. Alphabetic according to the Roman alphabet	*Trilateral root transliterated*	*Arabic root*
1. Abdul	ʕ – b – d	
2. (al)cohol	k – ħ – l	
3. (Al) Jazeera	ʤ – z – r	

i. Alphabetic according to the Roman alphabet	*Trilateral root transliterated*	*Arabic root*
4. (Al) Ham(b)ra	ħ – m – r	
5. Arab/Arabic	ʕ – r – b	
6. baraka (French slang for 'good luck')	b – r – k	
7. blède (French slang for 'podunk')	b – l – d	
8. caliph	x – l – f	
9. cipher (also French *chiffre* 'number')	ṣ – f – r	
10. cube	k – ʕ – b	
11. Fatima (a woman's name)	f – ṭ – m	
12. fatwah	f – t – w	
13. Hamas	ħ – m – s	
14. hazard	z – h – r	
15. hijab (look it up, if you don't know)	ħ – ʤ – b	
16. Intifada	n – f – ḍ	
17. Islam	s – l – m	
18. Jamil (a man's name)	ʤ – m – l	
19. jihad	ʤ – h – d	
20. Kaaba (the sacred shrine)	k – ʕ – b	
21. Kareem	k – r – m	
22. kitap (Turkish for 'book'); kitabu (Swahili for 'book')	k – t – b	
23. Madrassa (religious school)	d – r – s	
24. Maghreb (look it up, if you don't know)	ʀ – r – b	
25. maktaba (Arabic for 'library')	k – t – b	
26. matador (borrowed from Spanish)	m – ʔ – t	
27. mate (as in 'check mate')	m – ʔ – t	
28. Melek ('king' as in Melek Rik=Richard the Lionheart)	m – l – k	
29. Mujahedin	ʤ – h – d	
30. Muslim	s – l – m	
31. nisba (a linguistic term – does anyone know it?)	n – s – b	
32. (al)Qaeda	q – ʕ – d	
33. Qur'an	q – r – ʔ	
34. Sahara	ṣ – ħ – a	
35. Safari	s – f – r	
36. Salaam	s – l – m	
37. sharia (look it up, if you don't know)	ʃ – r – ʕ	
38. Sudan	s – w – d	
39. Sultan	s – l – ṭ – n	
40. Swahili	s – ħ – l	
41. Taliban	ṭ – l – b	
42. toubib (French slang for 'doctor')	ṭ – b – b	
43. zero (same as 'cipher')	ṣ – f – r	

ii. Meanings

	Meaning	Root
1.	blessing, benediction	ب – ر – ك
2.	town, city	ب – ل – د
3.	island	ج – ز – ر
4.	beautiful, handsome	ج – م – ل
5.	struggle, endeavor, strive	ج – ه – د
6.	cover	ح – ج – ب
7.	to redden, to color or dye red	ح – م – ر
8.	enthusiasm	ح – م – س
9.	succeed, follow, come after	خ – ل – ف
10.	study, learn	د – ر – س
11.	die (one of two dice)	ز – ه – ر
12.	coast	س – ح – ل
13.	to unveil, to send on a journey, to send away	س – ف – ر
14.	rule, control, command	س – ل – ط – ن
15.	peace, well-being, safety	س – ل – م
16.	black	س – و – د
17.	legislate	ش – ر – ع
18.	desolate, bleak, desert	ص – ح – ر
19.	be empty	ص – ف – ر
20.	treat medically	ط – ب – ب
21.	seek (as in knowledge)	ط – ل – ب
22.	servant; worship	ع – ب – د
23.	Bedouin (also 'to conjugate')	ع – ر – ب
24.	west, stranger (presumably someone from the west)	غ – ر – ب
25.	decree, give a legal opinion	ف – ت – و
26.	wean	ف – ط – م
27.	read	ق – ر – ا
28.	sit; base	ق – ع – د
29.	write	ك – ت – ب
30.	spirits	ك – ح – ل
31.	generous, gracious	ك – ر – م
32.	make cubic	ك – ع – ب
33.	die, perish	م – ا – ت
34.	own	م – ل – ك
35.	descent, origin, relationship, affinity, kinship	ن – س – ب
36.	come suddenly awake; to break through	ن – ف – ض

Figure 5.1   Genealogy of alphabets.

Exercise 2 – handwriting versus typing

A recent study in the journal *Psychological Science* (Mueller and Oppenheimer 2014) shows that writing the old fashioned way – with pen and paper – boosts memory and the ability to retain concepts more than typing with a laptop. First, read the article. Then, consider the findings in light of what you read about the language loop in Chapter 2 and about writing in this chapter. Write a paragraph describing what the role of writing in the language loop may be, as it pertains to human cognition.

Exercise 3 – monogenesis of the alphabet

Examine Figure 5.1, depicting the development of the modern Latin alphabet from the first Phoenician alphabet. In what ways did the Greeks adapt the Phoenician script for their own language? What is Etruscan and where was it spoken? What types of adaptations did they make for their language? Finally, what types of adaptations did the Romans make when adapting Greek to Latin?

Exercise 4 – Latin alphabet adaptations

The Latin alphabet is the single most used alphabet used to write the languages of the world today. Many languages have adapted it to suit the needs of their unique phonetic inventories. Sometimes, this involves deleting or adding letters, while other times, it involves adding diacritic marks to existing letters. Make a table of 10 languages that have adapted the Latin alphabet in at least one way, and give examples of the adaptations. What are the adaptations intended to accommodate?

Discussion Questions

1   If you practice a particular religion, what is the relationship between your faith and writing? Does your religion insist that texts be recorded in a particular language, or instead does it hope that holy works will be written in as many languages as

possible? Is the written word more or less important than the spoken word in your religious tradition?

2 Describe the steps through which writing systems become phoneticized. What is interesting or surprising to you about this process?

3 In 2014, the Unicode Consortium announced that it would be releasing 250 new emoji characters. Emojis are essentially ideograms and pictographs. When texting with conventional orthography is so easy, why do you think emojis are so popular? What kinds of meanings do they convey? How are they used in conjunction with conventional text?

4 In what ways can religion's influence on language also be understood as political influence? What ethical issues are involved in the intertwining of religion and politics as far as language is concerned?

5 How has access to literacy been limited by social power relations? Can you think of additional examples from your own community? What personal, social, and political problems might the lack of access to literacy and lack of access to the Internet engender?

6 What do the Azerbaijani alphabet changes illustrate about the relationship between written language, national identity, religion, and politics? Were you aware of this relationship before now?

7 There have been numerous attempts to romanize Chinese logographic writing, including the creation of the successful pinyin phonetic system. What are the advantages and disadvantages of continuing the logographic writing system for Chinese languages, Chinese people, and the nation-state of China?

Notes

1 The word *qur'ān* means 'recitation' from the Arabic root *qr'* 'to read aloud.'

2 The use of letters for numbers in the Semitic languages is similar to the way some Roman numerals came from the Roman alphabet, for instance C from the first letter of *centum*, which means 'hundred,' a root found in the word *century*, and M stands for *millennium* 'a thousand.' Incidentally, what we call Arabic numerals were developed in India around 600. They were introduced into the Arabic-speaking world in the middle of the eighth century.

3 This subsection and the next, Steps Toward the Representation of Speech, are enriched by the work of Jensen (1969).

4 Devanāgari was adapted throughout South Asia to languages beyond Indo-European, and now the Dravidian languages Telugu, Kannad'a, and Malayālam are written in a script derived from Devanāgari.

5 It is of interest to note that the Chinese logogram for 'contract' *ch'i⁴* includes the image of a notched stick (丰) and the sign (刀), which means 'knife.' The oldest object believed to be a tally has been found in the Blombos Cave in South Africa and is dated back to 75–80 kya.

6 The modern language spoken by the ancient Incan empire is known as Quechua in modern-day Peru.

7 The Mesoamericans independently took the same steps. The Egyptians are the prime movers in the story here for geographic reasons: their writing advances ultimately influenced the Mediterranean culture to the west and the Semitic cultures to the east.

8   Ancient Egyptian is a different language than the Egyptian spoken today in Egypt. Ancient Egyptian belongs to the Semitic branch of the Afro-Asiatic languages, as does modern-day Arabic, of which modern Egyptian is a variety, but ancient Egyptian is believed to have diverged from the Semitic branch at an early date. A form of ancient Egyptian, known as Coptic, was spoken until the seventeenth century of our era.

9   Richard Sears, aka Uncle Hanzi, has a website tracing the origins of 6552 of the most common modern Chinese logograms. This site has been a big hit in China since 2011. Sears predicts that, over time and despite the simplification of the script, the use of logograms will eventually disappear, and people will write pinyin.

10   For instance, *-men* is a pluralizer, but it is restricted to multisyllabic human nouns.

11   The Cherokee do not call themselves Cherokee. They call themselves Ki-tu-wah.

12   Most Hmong speakers, who can be found native to China, Vietnam, Laos, and Thailand, now use a romanized alphabet for writing. Also, Hinglish (Hindi/English) is written in the Roman alphabet with the Hindi bits in romanized transliteration and the English bits in standard British orthography.

13   The Jesuit missionaries called the Wyandot by the name *Huron* from the French word *huré*, which means 'bristly, unkempt, shaggy' – clearly a pejorative designation.

14   These relexification efforts had some success. The Slavic term *a blagoslavi* 'to bless' has been crowded out by *a binecuvânta* < Latin *bene conventus* 'good meeting.' Similar back-to-the-roots efforts occurred for English in the second half of the nineteenth century. The Anglo-Saxon compound *foreword* was created at that time but did not succeed in eliminating *preface*. Rather, the two words coexist.

15   Several centuries earlier, John Wycliffe was not authorized to translate the Bible into English, but he dared to do so anyway. After his death, he was declared a heretic. His body was dug up and burned, as were his translations.

16   In this group, only Tajikistan uses a language that does not belong to the Turkic language group. Tajik is closely related to Persian (Indo-European).

17   However, see the discussion on clicks and ejectives in the Language Profile !Xóõ.

References

Blommaert, Jan (2008) *Grassroots Literacy: Writing, Identity, and Voice in Central Africa*. New York: Routledge.

Jensen, Hans (1969) *Sign, Symbol, and Script: An Account of Man's Efforts to Write*. New York: Putnam.

Kellner-Heinkele, Barbara and Jacob M. Landau (2012) *Language Politics in Contemporary Central Asia: National and Ethnic Identity and the Soviet Legacy*. London: I.B. Taurus.

Mueller, Pam A. and Daniel M. Oppenheimer (2014) The pen is mightier than the keyboard: Advantages of longhand over laptop note taking. *Psychological Science* 25: 1159–1168.

Versteegh, Kees (1984) *Pidginization and Creolization: The Case of Arabic*. Amsterdam: John Benjamins.

Further Reading

Versteegh, Kees (1997) *The Arabic Language*. New York: Columbia University Press.

6

Language Planning and Language Law

Shaping the Right to Speak

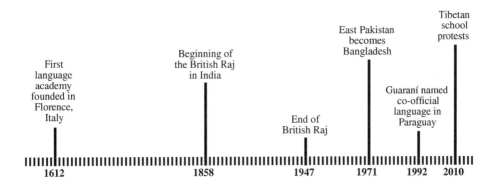

Melting Snow and Protests at the Top of the World

In 2010, government officials in Quinhai Province in western China detained 20 people for participating in protests that consumed the region for several days. The detained were not professional activists, radicals, or members of a well-funded political organization. They were students, some in middle school, some in high school, and others in college. They had joined thousands of other demonstrators, mostly other students in the Autonomous Region of Tibet. They were protesting a decision by the central government to change the medium of instruction in schools in the Chinese-controlled Tibetan-speaking regions from Tibetan to Putonghua, the standardized variety of Mandarin Chinese promoted by the central government in Beijing. Under the proposed policy, the Tibetan language could only be used in Tibetan-language class. As a form of protest, some of the students chanted "Equality of People, Freedom of Language." Their prospects for equality and freedom have not improved. In

Languages in the World: How History, Culture, and Politics Shape Language, First Edition.
Julie Tetel Andresen and Phillip M. Carter.
© 2016 John Wiley & Sons, Inc. Published 2016 by John Wiley & Sons, Inc.

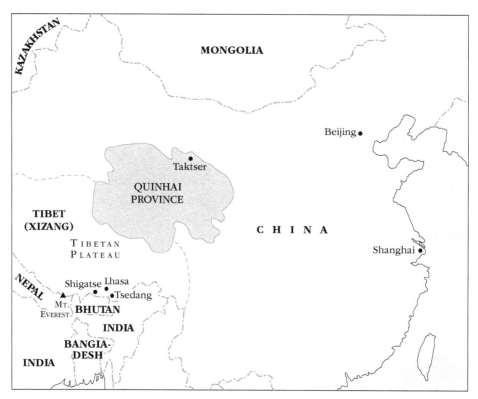

Map 6.1   Map of Tibet and China.

2015, the possibility that a Tibetan child will be educated in Tibetan through the course of his/her education are even bleaker than in 2010. The central government has continued its monitoring and crackdown on Tibetan schools.

Quinhai Province was once a part of eastern Tibet called Amdo. In 1928, China absorbed it and renamed it. In 1935, a baby was born in the town of Taktser in Quinhai/Amdo who would soon be identified as the fourteenth Dalai Lama. The intertwined relationship of language with religion and politics outlined in the previous chapter is at work in Tibet (see Map 6.1). A popular belief among Tibetans is that the 13th Dalai Lama chose to be reborn in historic Amdo in order for the people of that region to have a closer feeling to Tibet, as a way to reclaim Amdo as part of Tibet. We offer no opinion here on reincarnation; however, we can affirm that when a language ceases to be a medium of instruction and becomes an object of instruction, its days as a living language are numbered. The breath of the Chinese dragon (Mandarin) has been blowing ever closer to the remote, snow-capped Tibetan language for the last 3000 years, and now the dragon is breathing fire down the neck of the Tibetan language. The Tibetans revere their language, their script, and their scripture, and fear the impending loss of all three. As the Tibetan lama, Arjia Rinpoche (2010:vii),[1] puts it, Tibet's "language, its religion, its culture, and its native people are disappearing faster than its glacial ice."

On the one hand, China protects minority languages in its constitution by allowing the Autonomous Regions, such as Tibet, to set language policy. On the other hand, China is pestered by the ideology of the monolingual nation-state discussed in Chapter 4. However, China is hardly alone in trying to square the circle of its multilingual reality, since societal multilingualism is the norm the world over. In fact, of the world's current 10 most populous nations – in descending order, China, India, United States, Indonesia, Brazil, Pakistan, Nigeria, Bangladesh, Russia, and Japan – only Japan could be thought of as solidly monolingual by the numbers. However, as discussed in Chapter 4, the presence of indigenous languages such as Okinawan and Ainu trouble Japan's purported monolingualism, to say nothing of English, Korean, and Chinese, which are also highly influential.

We now turn our attention to the ways that nation-states, once constructed, bring language planning and language law to bear on the language behavior of their citizenry in the halls of government, in classrooms, and sometimes even in the streets and marketplaces. None of the regulation and planning of language by the state can be carried forth without a well-developed bureaucracy and the resources of an ample and controlled print culture.

Language Academies: The First Enforcers

The crystallization of the one nation, one language ideology was a long time in the making and was supported by prior efforts to regulate language in the newly forming countries in Western Europe as they emerged from the Renaissance. The first language academy was the Italian *Accademia della Crusca* (The Academy of Bran) founded in 1582 by a group of intellectuals, and it is still in operation today. The emblem of the academy is a sieve, the idea being that the academy's job is to separate the wheat from the chaff. The academy is located outside of Florence, which means that the so-called chaff would be the features of Italian – pronunciations, words, and/or grammatical structures – not found in the Tuscan variety of Florentine speech. Clearly, the original purpose of this academy – and of many academies – was purism: the cleansing of anything not deemed good and proper Italian. Their next job was to create Standard Italian, and one of the ways they did so was to produce a prescriptive dictionary, *Vocabolario della lingua italiana*, in 1612.

Other European language academies followed Italy's example. The French Academy was established in Paris in 1635. The Spanish Academy was founded in Madrid in 1713. The Scientific Academic of Lisbon was created in Portugal in 1779. The Russian Academy, founded by Catherine the Great on the model of the French Academy, came along in 1783 (and was reconfigured in the Soviet era in 1944). At first, these academies, like the Italian model, were devoted to making, say, *Île de la Cité* French or Castilian Spanish pure of the perceived taint of surrounding varieties or they were interested in compiling the language and/or getting a sense of a unified whole. The Russian Academy, for instance, produced a six-volume Russian dictionary. However, over time and with the threat of globalization, the French Academy, in particular, turned its focus on sanitizing French of the English borrowings flooding into the language. One high-profile example is the word *email* for which the Academy offered the properly French *courriel*. This does not mean, of course, that all French speakers use it, but surely they have heard it. As for the Spanish Academy, its mission has shifted to one of keeping the Spanish world linguistically intact, and it currently has affiliates with language academies in 21 other Hispanophone countries, including the United States, whose *Academia Norteamericana de la Lengua Española* was founded in 1973.[2]

Notably absent from the very long international list of national language academies are entries for Anglophone countries such as Australia, Great Britain, and the United States. After Italy and France had established their academies, and Spain was founding hers, discussion took place in Great Britain about the need for such a language-planning body. In 1712, Jonathan Swift published his *Proposal for Correcting, Improving and Ascertaining the English Tongue*. By 1750, the proposal for an academy was dead, with the great lexicographer Samuel Johnson railing against such prescriptive bodies as striking a blow to English liberty. Later in the century, on the other side of the English-speaking Atlantic, Thomas Jefferson and John Adams debated the issue. Adams was in favor of an academy whose main job, he argued, was to be the regularizing of English spelling. The purpose of that effort was to create a reasonably spelled language for export, since the Founding Fathers were clear both in their mission to promote democracy on the world stage as the best form of government and in their idea that the English language was the best vehicle to carry this democracy around the world. Jefferson countered that it was not the government's business to regulate the speech of its citizens. He believed that each person had the right to speak in accordance with whatever group's speaking norms the citizen wanted. Jefferson's arguments carried the day.

Many academies understand their main purpose to be spelling reform, such as Adams envisioned for American English, and they may also set educational standards. A common undertaking involves increasing a language's lexical stock through neologism or borrowing, or through altering the meanings of existing words. In the twentieth century, the following academies, among many others worldwide, were established: in 1918, the Basques created the Group Keepers of the Basque Language as a bulwark against the surrounding languages; the Language Commission in Turkey was established in 1928 and did much more than simply switch from Arabic script to Latin script. In Atatürk's desire to make Turkey a modern state, he charged the Commission with purging Turkish of its Arabic loans – some of great antiquity, on the order of the presence of French borrowings in English – and had them replaced with native coinages; the Academy of the Arabic Language came into being in 1934 and united 10 Arabic-speaking countries. It is concerned with preserving Classical Arabic as well as with developing scientific and technical terminology; the Azerbaijan National Academy of Science was created in 1945 and was conveniently on hand when, after 1991, the Azerbaijanis faced another alphabet decision; the Academy of the Hebrew Language came about in 1953 and coined new words. Biblical Hebrew, which formed the basis for the modern language revival and which had not been spoken for nearly 2000 years at the time of the revival, was not fully up to the task of working in the modern world; finally, the People's Republic of China's State Language and Letters Committee was started under Mao Tse-tung in 1954 for the purpose of creating simplified characters to improve literacy rates. The Polish Language Council is one of the more newly formed bodies, having been established in 1996.

The force of these academies is ultimately limited because speakers will for the most part speak the way they want to speak. Although academies tend to have only the power of suggestion, they can nevertheless create what we, the authors, think of as mischief. Languages are sociohistorical products. As such, a given ethnogroup's traditions, which contribute to the identity of the group, are built up over long periods of time and layered into their language. When an academy cuts people off from their history, linguistic and otherwise, it is always traumatic. It is also traumatic when an academy operates with a zero-sum attitude and the intent to erase what they perceive as the competition. A standard language is a good and even necessary thing for an ethnogroup/nation/world to have. However, it is not the only linguistic thing to have, and nonstandard varieties as well as different languages are sure to enrich the places and cultures in which they are spoken.

Another Look at Prescriptivism

A bossy older sister smugly corrects her younger brother, "Everybody knows you're supposed to say *brought* not *bringed*, Nathan." The press skewers President George W. Bush for saying in a speech that "some have misunderestimated the compassion of the United States," and Vice Presidential candidate Sarah Palin is mercilessly mocked when the word *refudiate* slips out of her mouth. People prefer not to be corrected and mocked. In midseventeenth-century France, provincial nobles consulted language guides in order to avoid ridicule when they went to Versailles. These were not prescriptive grammars as such. Rather the royal courtiers themselves were aware of some of the distinguishing features of their language and leveraged them as marks of status. One scholar, Claude Favre de Vaugelas,[3] was alert enough to collect the courtiers' usages and to sell them to the rustics who were going to sit as close as they could to the cool kids' lunch table at court. In other words, prescriptivism comes in many forms and has likely always been a semiconscious and sometimes even conscious fact of life, with or without language academies, proper usage books, and language laws. This is true in societies in which asymmetrical power relations among social groups are reflected in sociolinguistic terms. In contrast, prescriptivism simply does not exist in small tribal communities where there is instead only the notion of "how we talk."

Conscious prescriptivism in Western Europe was a slow development in the centuries leading up to the eighteenth century. As linguistic historiographer Douglas Kibbee so pithily put it, "The French have always been poster children for linguistic prescriptivism" (2011:1). So we will take France as our example and look first to law. Language and law have a long and intertwined history, and what unites them is the concept of *usage*. Just as the legal practices of a community over time produce common law (the usages out of which formal law is codified), so the linguistic practices of a community over time produce common vocabulary, phrases, and structures (the usages out of which prescriptive grammar is codified). Changes in legal practice in France over the centuries effected changes in linguistic practice. The significant event was the eventual successful attempt by French kings to replace trial by ordeal with trial by inquest. In trial by ordeal, God determines who is right. In trial by inquest, the court takes accounts of two witnesses and necessarily needs a common language in order to compare them. The king's usage was law, and thus is a legal standard born.

Turning to language matters in England, although the English rejected the establishment of a language academy, they were not averse to establishing language standards. The prescriptive grammarians mentioned in Chapter 3 set themselves the task of what they called *ascertainment*: their job, given the various pronunciations and grammatical structures in eighteenth-century England, was to determine the one and only correct pronunciation for a particular word and the one and only correct grammatical structure for a particular expression. Once determined, that is, ascertained, the standards were then supposed to be set for all time. However, the grammarians reckoned without the most basic fact of linguistic life: language is constantly catching up to the conditions in which speakers find themselves.

An effect of the grammarian's work on ascertainment was the development of the idea the English language could be good or bad. The search for the best English thus ensued. In 1700, the writer John Dryden determined Chaucer to be the high-watermark of the purity of the English tongue. By midcentury, the idea of language purity was taken to mean that the language had declined in value. Lexicographer Samuel Johnson, who wrote a monumental English dictionary, was the first to include quotes from authorities concerning the usage of the word being defined. He chose writers from before the Restoration, namely 1660, whose language was supposedly pure and undefiled. The assessment that English had been defiled created the urgent need for grammarians to fix what had gone wrong and return English to an earlier, more pure state. Modern language attitudes were born, and as a result speakers were subjected to judgments about their adherence to, or defection from, the new grammar rules.

An important belief to emerge from this period was the notion that the best English was spoken by the Queen. In 1712, writer/grammarian Jonathan Swift chose the reign of Queen Elizabeth as the time when the English language received its most improvement. Since Swift's time, the phrase *the Queen's English* has remained popular. The question can now be asked: Does the Queen of England speak the Queen's English? In a study of Queen Elizabeth II and her yearly Christmas message broadcast by the BBC since 1952, Harrington et al. (2000:927–928) found that the Queen's vowels had drifted over the decades from the standard accent known as *received pronunciation* to a southern British accent more typically associated with speakers who are younger and lower in the social hierarchy. It has long been known that the younger generation drives changes in pronunciation. The question behind the study of the Queen's English was to determine to what extent older members adapt to the changes around them. The answer is: older members are as enmeshed as everyone else in the dynamics of the language loop.

Language creates, and is created by, human bonds that lasso us in and keep us within the human circle. In this particular context of prescriptivism, one of the many distinguishing features of the language loop stands out: its unavoidability. You can (and perhaps should) avoid talking about certain topics with business associates and in-laws; religion and politics come to mind. However, when talking about whatever topic, you cannot avoid the use of one variety of speech or another, which also necessarily privileges one variety over another. We, the authors, are aware that we participate at all times in the unavoidability of language. For instance, we have written this book in Standard American English, and the Queen of England herself does not escape the semiprescriptive dynamics of the language loop. After all, she is only human.

Because our primary interest in this book is not on the microdynamics of individual and face-to-face interactions, we turn our attention toward the macrodynamics of social and political language planning and control, which are explicit forms of language control exercised by nation-states. We note that those responsible for language planning are rarely linguists or language experts and almost always politicians or government officials. Of course, these individuals, acting on behalf of a state, likely believe their language-planning efforts are for the good of the majority. This is surely the case in China, where state language planners see the promotion of Putonghua in regions such as Tibet as a means of recruiting minority populations into China's developing economy, which is overwhelmingly oriented around this official version of Mandarin. In 2013, the state announced that 400 million Chinese citizens could not speak Putonghua and identified this inability as a stumbling block for the country's economic advancement. In contrast, many Tibetans see the legal imposition of Putonghua into Tibetan regions of China as a form of cultural imperialism and even religious intolerance, given the important role of the Tibetan language in Buddhist culture.

Making Language Official: A Tale of Three Patterns

A language variety is made an *official language* when it is declared as such in a legal document, say, in a constitution or charter, which then gives this language the power of status to be used for administrative purposes. The specifics – whether the language must be used as a medium of instruction in state schools, for example – depends on the way a particular constitution or charter is written. A *national language* may or may not be recognized by the government and is usually the first language of the majority of the population. For example, in the West African country of Burkina Faso, French is the sole official language, which means it is the main language of administrative and judicial institutions and the medium of instruction in schools. The Niger–Congo languages Moore, Fula, and Dyula are considered national languages, which means they are the languages of large ethnic groups and are seen as important in Burkina Faso's national identity. In the United States, no language is specified in the Constitution as the official language of government; English is thus technically a national, rather than official, language.

The ways language academies and/or other national committees determine which language(s), if any, are to be named official fall into three patterns worldwide:

(i) the *compromise pattern*, in which powerful and less powerful language groups agree either to a language policy in which both languages are officially recognized or to a plan to incorporate elements from both languages into the official language;

(ii)   the *neutral language pattern*, in which the most powerful group recognizes the need for an official language that is neutral, namely one not related to their own native language; and

(iii) the *dominant language pattern*, in which might makes right. The most powerful group simply names their own language as the official language, even if gestures are made to make it look like this language is somehow neutral.

The following discussion on official language policy is further categorized into two types of multilingual situations: first, European nations not subject to colonial language influence and second, postcolonial situations outside of Europe in which decisions must be made not only about precolonial multilingualism but also about the colonial language. When it comes to the status of the colonial language in postcolonial times, the most usual case is that one of the languages named official will be the one spoken by the colonizers. When it comes to the way an official language is chosen, the most frequent way around the world is the dominant language pattern.

Multilingual European states

Although we credit Europe with exporting to the rest of the world the idea of the monolingual nation-state, we note that in the twentieth century, official multilingual policy took shape in several European nations. We look first at Belgium then at Switzerland.

The modern country of Belgium was created through a disagreement over language policy, namely whether Dutch would be made an official language in regions where French was also widely spoken, and this disagreement sparked the Belgian Revolution in 1830. The result of the revolution was the separation of the Dutch- and French-speaking Kingdom of Belgium from the Dutch-speaking Kingdom of the Netherlands. With the political separation, the language Dutch was now dubbed Flemish. The linguistic problems did not, however, end with the creation of a new nation-state. Following independence the Belgian Constitution stipulated freedom of languages, which meant that government officials could use the language they saw fit with citizens, but not necessarily the other way around. Because French was the language of the elite, French gradually became the language of administration and instruction in schools. Among the Dutch-speaking Flemish, tensions mounted until the dawn of the twentieth century, when the Law on Equality named Flemish and French as official languages. In practical terms, this meant that Flemish and French were equally valid in legal texts and that bilingual signage would become mandatory in certain cities, such as Flemish-speaking Flanders. In 1970, the Constitution was changed to acknowledge Belgium's four linguistic regions: Flemish, French, German, and the Flemish/French bilingual city of Brussels. Because Brussels is the de facto capital of the European Union, the 24 official languages of the union can also be heard across the city among the diplomats and government officials of the member states.

Switzerland's official language policy is reflective of its geographic location, boxed in as it is by France to the west, Germany to the north, Austria to the east, and Italy to the south. The Federal Constitution written in 1999 establishes four official languages: German (mostly Swiss German), French, Italian, and Romansch, a Romance language spoken mostly in the Swiss canton of Graubünden. The Swiss constitution stipulates that the government is required to communicate in the official languages, and parliamentary proceedings are simultaneously translated in three of them: German, French, and Italian. These provisions are remarkable in that some 85% of the Swiss citizenry speak either German (65%) or French (20%), while Italian is spoken as a first language by only 5% of the population, and Romansch by less than 1%. In actual practice, the government only provides some of its printed materials in Romansch, but it is required to communicate directly with Romansch speakers in Romansch if the speaker so desires. The constitution also stipulates that students should learn a national language other than their mother tongue, which means high levels of functional bilingualism are the norm in Switzerland.

Postcolonial multilingualism and the compromise pattern

The compromise pattern is best illustrated by the language policy in Paraguay where the indigenous language Guaraní and the colonial language Spanish share co-official status. Paraguay is a landlocked country the size of California, flanked by South America's two economic powerhouses: Portuguese-speaking Brazil to the east and Spanish-speaking Argentina to the south and west. Paraguay also shares a border with Bolivia to the north. In countries of Andean South America, indigenous languages are widely spoken in large communities, and they are usually considered socially inferior to Spanish, which is spoken by a majority of the population, including by social and political elites, making Spanish the language of prestige. In Bolivia and Peru, for example, Quechua (25% in Bolivia, 16% in Peru) and Aymara (17% in Bolivia, 3% in Peru) are spoken by sizable populations, but these languages are considered socially inferior, even where they have co-official status with Spanish, as is the case in Bolivia. In Bolivia and Peru, indigenous languages tend to be spoken only by indigenous people and not by political elites who tend to be of European or mixed ancestry. Many indigenous speakers are also bilingual in Spanish.

The case of Guaraní offers a remarkable contrast. The move to designate it as a co-official language in the Paraguayan Constitution of 1992 was uncontroversial not only because Guaraní had already been considered a symbol of national identity for some time but also because it is a national language with widespread use among nonnative speakers. More than 90% of Paraguayans speak Guaraní, including many in the middle and upper classes and people of European and mixed ancestry. This degree of fluency is remarkable considering the fact that the overall indigenous population in Paraguay is just 5%. Paraguay is the only country in the Americas to have successfully promoted a pre-Columbian indigenous language as a national and official language with such a high degree of functional use. Needless to say, Guaraní is no more or less worthy of preservation than any other native language, and we would like to emphasize that the *lack* of controversy around the promotion of an indigenous language by a nation-state in late modernity is, as ever, the result of particular contingencies, and its success was ensured through a series of historical events through which Guaraní and its speakers gained status.

In the sixteenth century, Jesuit missionaries translated books into Guaraní, thereby giving the language material presence. Following Paraguay's independence from Spain in 1811, an unusual ally to the Guaraní rose to power. José Gaspar Rodríguez de Francia, known as *El Supremo*, was both a fan of the ideals of the French Revolution and an opponent of the Spanish class system. He was therefore interested in creating a centralized nation but did not want to do so by promoting the Spanish elite, whom he banned from marrying one another. Spaniards could only legally marry people of African descent, indigenous people, or people of mixed ethnicity, with the goal of weakening European power in the country. At the same time, Francia spoke Guaraní, which won him support with native Guaraní speakers, and thereby integrated Guaraní into mainstream society. Thus, by the time Paraguay became a Constitutional Republic at the end of the twentieth century, Guaraní had already been established as a natural choice for being declared one of the official languages.

Elsewhere in South and Central America when indigenous languages have been given official status, the designation is mostly symbolic. This is certainly the case for present-day Mexico, where, in the early sixteenth century, some 150 indigenous languages were spoken vibrantly. In the early nineteenth century, when Mexican officials established an independent nation-state, the language they were most interested in was Spanish, particularly a variety of Spanish they could identify as totally legitimate and uniquely Mexican. They chose to promote the one nation, one language ideology with and through this variety.[4] The documentation of indigenous languages was an important part of the efforts to create a sense of national identity and a common national past, even though no efforts were made to promote the use and maintenance of indigenous languages as such. In the nineteenth and twentieth centuries, the development of the Mexican economy and the growth of major cities, both of which were oriented toward Spanish, had further alienating effects on indigenous communities and their languages. Participation in the new market required Spanish, even though Spanish had not been a hard and fast requirement for indigenous subjects under the Spanish crown in the preindependence period.

The Mexican Constitution of 1917 stops short of designating any official languages of the state, including Spanish, which is today a de facto official language, although it does recognize the right of Mexico's indigenous communities to preserve their languages, including through bilingual education programs. The indigenous languages won more protection in 2003 with the passage of a law to preserve the linguistic rights of indigenous peoples, which designates indigenous languages as national languages and ensures the rights of indigenous communities to use their languages in any government dealings. The Mexican government now officially recognizes 68 indigenous languages, including the Uto-Aztecan language Nahuatl, which is the only indigenous language of Mexico with more than one million speakers, along with Maya, Mixtec, Tzeltal Maya, Yucatec, and Zapotec.

The protection for indigenous languages in Mexican language policy, however, comes at a time in which over 90% of the population speaks Spanish as the first language, and only about 6% of the total Mexican population speaks a pre-Columbian language. This stands in stark contrast to the time of the first Mexican Constitution in 1812 in which only about 35% of the total population spoke Spanish. In other words, recognition and protection for pre-Columbian languages come after 200 years of language policy effectively eradicating the power of the indigenous communities, which was preceded by about 300 years of Spanish colonial rule.

Postcolonial multilingualism and the neutral language pattern

The neutral language pattern is most clear in Indonesia, where postcolonial language planning efforts naming Bahasa Indonesian (BI) as the official language were conflict free. The ease of this decision is especially remarkable in light of the fact that many ethnic groups and some 500 languages are spread across some 17,000 islands. BI, which is essentially the same language as Malay and which is spoken in Malaysia and elsewhere in the region, was originally selected as the national language in 1928 while Indonesia was still under Dutch colonial rule. The choice of Malay at that time is remarkable for several reasons: (i) many of the young Indonesian nationalists who advocated for Malay were actually more proficient speakers of Dutch, the colonial language; (ii) Malay was mostly relegated to the status of lingua franca in the Indonesian archipelago, with few native speakers relative to other groups; and (iii) some more widely spoken languages, such as Javanese, already had long literary traditions. Yet when Indonesia achieved its independence from the Netherlands in 1945, Malay was renamed BI and became the only official language in the Indonesian Constitution. The largest ethnogroup, the Javanese, accepted this choice without controversy.

The lack of controversy likely stems from the fact that the Constitution acknowledges the right to use the regional languages coupled with the value that Indonesian society puts on linguistic diversity. As a result, bilingualism is high, and people learn BI for formal interaction yet maintain ethnic languages such as Javanese, Balinese, and Sundanese for their personal interactions. A language academy was set up to oversee the promotion of BI as the national language and was charged with spelling reform and the expansion of BI vocabulary. Although Javanese has helped to flesh out BI lexical stock, BI has continued to face the problem of a lack of vocabulary in the areas of technology and business. For lexical items in these domains, it has relied on English and to such an extent that the government has tried to ban the practice, but with little success (Dardjowidjojo 1998).

When Pakistan first achieved independence from Britain in 1947, the selection of Urdu as the official language was not exactly a neutral selection, but it was nevertheless selected in favor of two much larger languages, Punjabi and Bengali. Pakistan was one of the first modern states, like Israel, to be set up primarily on the basis of religion. On the Indian subcontinent, two Muslim-majority regions formed the original Pakistan and were physically separated by the Hindu majority in India in the middle. This physical separation was known as The Partition, the nickname for this new state composed of two geographical regions, East and West Pakistan, separated by 1000 miles of Indian territory.

The problem for the new, partitioned state of Pakistan was the fact that the same languages were not spoken in the eastern and western portions of the country. Bengali, spoken by about half the population of Pakistan, was the most widely spoken mother tongue overall, but it was nevertheless *not* a clear frontrunner for official status, since its speakers were concentrated in East Pakistan. There, about 98% of the population spoke Bengali, but 1000 miles to the west, only an extreme minority did so. In contrast, some

70% of the population in West Pakistan spoke Punjabi, which was spoken only by a tiny minority in the East. Another contender for official language status was Urdu. It was spoken by a small minority but had the advantage of being spoken by roughly equal numbers of speakers in the East and the West. Moreover, Urdu was written with the Perso-Arabic script, which has symbolic associations with Islam as we saw in Chapter 5.

Advocates of Bengali emphasized the majority-rule dimension of democracy, while advocates of Urdu emphasized its Islamic connection. When Urdu was selected as the sole official language of Pakistan, two controversies followed. First, opponents of Urdu noted that it is essentially the same language as Hindi, which had been named an official language of India, and was therefore undesirable. However, proponents argued that the two languages are differentiated not only by script (Hindi uses Devanāgari, while Urdu uses Perso-Arabic) but also by vocabulary (Hindi relies on Sanskrit, while Urdu draws on Arabic). These arguments did not satisfy everyone. Second, the Bengali speakers as the majority in East Pakistan were angered that Urdu was chosen as the only official language, and they pointed out the success of states such as Canada and Switzerland with official multilingual language policies. After years of oftentimes violent protests, Bengali was named an official language of Pakistan in 1956. However, a new controversy ensued when the decision was taken to replace the Bengali script with the Perso-Arabic script used to write Urdu.

The vision of a unified Muslim state with a divided geography fell apart when East Pakistan separated from West Pakistan in 1971 and formed the modern state of Bangladesh. Bengali was designated the official language in the constitution. Disagreement about language policy, specifically whether Bengali would be granted co-official status with Urdu, resulted in the dissolution of biregional Pakistan. Thus, the unifying force of religion, in this case Islam, was superseded by questions about official language status and script choice.

Postcolonial multilingualism and the dominant language pattern

The dominant language pattern is by far the most common. As we have just seen, the dissolution of the British Empire in the Indian subcontinent engendered enough language controversies in Pakistan to result in a new country, Bangladesh. In India, the language problems were especially prickly, given that India has roughly 400 languages spoken by a population of over one billion. These languages fall into four language stocks: Indo-European, Dravidian, Afro-Asiatic, and Sino-Tibetan. The largest of these in terms of overall number of speakers is the Indo-European stock, which in India includes languages such as Bengali, Gujarati, Hindi, Marathi, Oriya, and Punjabi.

During the period known as the British Raj, which began in 1858, English was the elite language of education and government administration. Heated debate about the linguistic future of India ensued for several decades leading up to India's independence in 1947. Fearing that India would disintegrate at the conclusion of the Raj, Mahatma Gandhi advocated for a single language to be used as a lingua franca to unite the subcontinent's diverse regions and, further, that this language should be an Indian language, which meant not English. Hindi, already spoken widely in the north, was the frontrunner and was championed by Mahatma Gandhi.

In the postindependence period, the central government took steps to promote Hindi as an English replacement, including providing language training to government workers. As support for Hindi gained momentum in the north, opposition to it solidified in the Dravidian south, particularly among Tamil speakers who favored the continued use of English. The Tamils in the south associated Hindi with the Brahmin caste who, they felt, oppressed Tamil language and culture. The argument was advanced that Hindi was as much a foreign language for Dravidian speakers as English. In response, India's first Prime Minister, Jawaharlal Nehru, proposed allowing the continued use of English in government. However, this conciliatory gesture was not enough. Violence in the south erupted and lasted for several years. To quell the protests, Indira Gandhi, Nehru's daughter and the third Prime Minister of India, advocated codifying English as an official language in the Indian constitution. In 1963, the law passed designating English Associate Official Language and thereby cementing the role of English in Indian society. In addition to Hindi and English, the Indian Constitution designates 22 additional Eighth Schedule Languages, so named for the part of the constitution that deals with language. Many of these form the basis of India's states.

When the Philippines gained independence from the United States in 1946, the government had to decide which of the estimated 150 languages would be named the official language. The government passed a law to create a National Language Institute, charged with national language policy, including designating an official language. The choice came down to three languages: Tagalog, Ilocano, and Visayan. The committee chose Tagalog based on the fact that: (i) it was the language of Manila, the political, cultural, and economic capital of Philippines; (ii) it had the longest literary tradition; and (iii) it had the largest number of speakers. This choice angered speakers of other ethnic groups, who complained that the decision favored ethnic Tagalogs who were already the political elites in Manila. In order to mitigate the controversy, a decision was made to name the new official language Pilipino as a way of distancing it from the Tagalog ethnogroup. Throughout the second half of the twentieth century, the government continued to deal with the fallout of this decision and twice more took up the issue of official language. First, the government changed the name from Pilipino to Filipino and made decisive efforts to promote the language throughout the country. This cosmetic and aggressive move did nothing but further anger ethnic groups who felt left out of language policy. Finally, the government changed the constitution to indicate that Filipino would eventually be shaped by regional languages other than Tagalog.

Today, it is understood that Filipino is essentially the same language as the variety of Tagalog spoken in Manila, with little lexical or structural influence from other languages, as had been planned. Filipino is now the co-official language of the Philippines, along with English, which was introduced during the period of United States imperialism from 1899 to 1946. The colonial language prior to English was Spanish and has no official status, nor is it recognized as one of the eight regional languages, which include Cebuano, Ilokano, Pampango, and Tagalog. Thus, the result of language planning in the Philippines, which began with egalitarian aims, is that the official languages – English and Filipino – reflect the linguistic interests of the elite.

About 1600 miles south of Manila lies the tiny country of Timor-Leste, known in English as East Timor. Moored between the Banda Sea to the north and the Timor Sea to the south, Timor-Leste finds itself at anchor between two national giants: Indonesia to the north and west, and Australia to the south. Timor-Leste has also been continually buffeted between ruling powers: the Portuguese were in charge from the sixteenth century until 1975, after which the Indonesians took over. Since declaring independence from Indonesia in 2002, Timor-Leste has been divided over language policy. Two languages were selected to be official languages of government: Tetum, an Austronesian language spoken widely throughout the island, and Portuguese, the colonial language, spoken among elites who make up about 5% of the population. The selection of Portuguese was met with hostility by many, who contended that Portuguese favors the elites, is no longer the international language of prestige it was in the sixteenth century, and is no longer a language of Asia, as it has not been maintained in the former Portuguese colonies of Goa, India and Macau, China. Many Timorese would have preferred that English or BI, already a widespread lingua franca, be named co-official language with Tetum. As an indication of their dissatisfaction with the government's decision to promote Portuguese, the national university in the capital city of Dili has decided not to offer courses in Portuguese, making them available instead in Tetum, BI, or English.

Africa is a story in and of itself. The independent states, which began to emerge out of the imperial map in Africa at the end of the European colonial period, were faced with many difficult decisions about language policy, especially regarding the status of the former colonial language. The Portuguese established colonies in present-day Angola and Mozambique. The French took over:

(i)   most of the Maghreb, that is, Morocco, Tunisia, and Algeria;
(ii) much of West Africa, including the Ivory Coast, Senegal, and Burkina Faso; and
(iii) Central Africa, which comprises Cameroon, Chad, and Democratic Republic of the Congo.

The British colonized:

(i)   much of sub-Saharan Africa, namely South Africa, Botswana, and Zimbabwe;
(ii) West Africa with Nigeria;
(iii) East Africa, with Kenya and Tanzania; and
(iv) northeast Africa, with Sudan and Egypt.

The Italians took much of the Horn of Africa, including present-day Eritrea, Somalia, and parts of Ethiopia, in addition to Libya. The Belgians had the Congo. When the Europeans began to leave Africa in the twentieth century, they left behind their languages, which took hold in certain places but not in others. They also left behind an extremely complicated set of language politics.

The status of colonial languages in Africa today depends in part on how much the various colonial powers succeeded in – or even cared about – imposing their language on their colonies. The Italians were not particularly successful in promoting the Italian language in Africa, and therefore none of the modern states emerging from the Italian Empire, namely Libya, Eritrea, Somalia, and Ethiopia, have given Italian official status. For example, when Somalia declared its independence in 1960 after many years of Italian and British influence, Somali was named the official language of the state. This decision was easy in light of the fact that 95% of the population speaks Somali. In contrast, Portuguese was named the only official language of Angola when it declared independence from Portugal in 1975, likely due to the fact that schooling had been established in Portuguese in the cities during colonial rule.

In the rest of Africa, the situation has rarely been as simple as in Somalia and Angola. The problem of official language in South Africa illustrates this point. Before the end of apartheid in 1994, there were two official languages in multilingual South Africa: Afrikaans and English. This fact reflects the colonial influence of the Dutch[5] and the British, and made linguistically concrete the political, social, and cultural privilege of Whites in the country at the time. The South African Constitution of 1994, however, attempts to reverse the problem by recognizing 11 official languages: Afrikaans, English, Ndebele, Northern Sotho, Sotho, Swazi, Tswana, Tsonga, Venda, Xhosa, and Zulu. The postapartheid government led by Nelson Mandela recognized the need for linguistic parity in the creation of a stable multiracial nation in Africa.[6] It is noteworthy that Mandela's vision of national unity was predicated on the notion of a multilingual state rather than a monolingual one.

In sum, colonial languages have almost always achieved official status in the former colonies we have discussed here: (i) Spanish in Mexico and Paraguay; (ii) English in South Africa and India; and (iii) Portuguese in East Timor and Angola. The absences of Dutch in Indonesia and Italian in Somalia are exceptions, although we also acknowledge that these languages hold less international sway than larger colonial languages such as English and Spanish.

Language Policy and Education: A Similar Tale of Three Patterns

Official language status is related to language and education, because it affects what language or languages are used in schools as the medium of instruction. The choices are usually based more on political factors than on sound education research. In fact, those charged with making decisions about language and education oftentimes actively *ignore* research from linguists and educators. The asymmetrical relationships among more and less powerful ethnolinguistic groups in a society are usually reflected in language and educational policy. One way to consider these arrangements is to ask the question: Who must be educated in another group's language? In South Africa, Black children tend to be educated in English and Afrikaans, the languages spoken primarily by South Africans of European descent, but Anglo White children are rarely educated in widely spoken precolonial languages such as Xhosa or Zulu (Webb 1996:152). This is true even though there are far more first-language speakers of Xhosa and Zulu than English or Afrikaans.

Because the major driving forces in educational policy pertaining to language are politics and language ideology, here again three patterns can be identified:

(i)   the minority language is promoted, while the majority language is demoted in order to protect the minority;

(ii) minority languages are supported alongside majority languages through bilingual education programs; and

(iii) majority language are promoted, while minority languages are ignored or actively marginalized.

Unsurprisingly, the third pattern is the most common. We will end this section by considering one aspect of language education in the more or less monolingual state of Mongolia, where policy makers are concerned about the threat to Mongolian as a minority language in the context of Central Asia.

Minority languages promoted

In nation-states where ethnolinguistic minority groups have been given a degree of autonomy over language and education policy in particular regions, the minority language may be made the primary language of instruction in that region. This has been the case in Spain's Catalonia, where Catalan is the primary medium of instruction. When democracy returned to Spain in 1978 after the end of the dictatorship of General Franco, regional governments were guaranteed autonomy to set educational policy. In Catalonia, the Catalan government implemented so-called linguistic normalization policies in order to ensure the future of Catalan in the region; the primary normalization mechanism has been Catalan-medium education.

Because Spanish is a prominent international language and the primary language of Spain, value is placed on bilingualism, and Spanish is offered as a subject course. The large numbers of Spanish-speaking immigrants from Latin America to Catalonia receive Catalan language support in what are called *reception classes* provided by the government upon arrival. Today, Catalan proficiency is high throughout the region on account of the regional government's efforts to promote Catalan in schools. The success of Catalan in education owes to the unique provisions in the postdictatorship Spanish Constitution, the strength of the Catalonian economy, and the tenacious efforts of the regional government over many years of promoting the regional language.

Minority languages supported

Language planners in India have understood that if Hindi were the only language of instruction throughout the country, students in the parts of the north where Hindi is the first language, such as Delhi, would be given an unfair scholastic advance. Therefore, language planners set forth in 1968 what became known as India's Three Language Formula. This formula requires that, in any given Indian state:

(i)   the first language to be studied will be the mother tongue or a regional language;

(ii)   the second language in (a) Hindi-speaking states, will be some other modern Indian language or English, and in (b) non-Hindi-speaking states, the second language will be Hindi or English; and

(iii)   the third language in (a) Hindi-speaking states will be English or a modern Indian language not studied as the second language, and in (b) non-Hindi-speaking states, the third language will be English or a modern Indian language not studied as the second language.

The intention of the Three Language Formula was for school children across India to become proficient in three languages, including their own mother tongue and the national language, Hindi, by the end of their secondary education while at the same time strengthening cultural integration across diverse linguistic regions.

In practice, the formula has been implemented inconsistently across the states. First, some states, particularly in the so-called Hindi-belt, have neglected to teach the mother tongue first, under the assumption that Hindi is the mother tongue for most children. This means that Hindi is taught as the first language rather than as the second or third, as the formula suggests. English can be taught as the second language, and some states have opted to teach Sanskrit, the Classical parent of Hindi, as a second or third language rather than offer a state or regional language at all. The result is that many students in Hindi-speaking regions do not receive primary education in the mother tongue, or in a major language of India other than Hindi. Dravidian languages are customarily not taught in the Hindi-speaking states. Thus, one of the major goals of the formula – specifically, cultural integration – has not been met. Likewise, in the Dravidian-speaking south, the Three Language Formula has become in certain places a two-language formula, in which the state language, for example, Tamil, is taught alongside English, and Hindi is not taught at all. In short, politics, especially that rooted in ethnolinguistic and regional conflict, has been a major force shaping decisions about language and education in India.

Majority language promoted

The power of the English language is unprecedented in global and historical terms, and data show that children educated in the United States will learn English, irrespective of their home language. Nevertheless, the educational system in the United States remains, for the most part, indifferent or hostile to multilingualism. A combination of formal policies and informal pressures against languages other than English maintain English as the sole medium of instruction in most schools in the United Station. For example, in California in 1998, a law called English for the Children, known as Proposition 227, was approved by 61% of voters, effectively dismantling bilingual education in one of the most linguistically diverse parts of the United States. The law does allow parents to sign petitions to start bilingual education programs and request waivers from the law, but such efforts are difficult to arrange in practice, especially in immigrant communities where parents may demonstrate deference to the school system.

Although the law is concerned with language and educational policy, it was written neither by professional linguists nor by educators but by a software entrepreneur with political aspirations by the name of Ron Unz. As linguist Wong-Fillmore (2004:354) points out, this was the first time in the history of the United States that a pedagogical approach was put forth for popular vote. The law passed in spite of the ongoing success of many bilingual education programs in California because the political arguments[7] put forth to frame the law positively made common sense in terms of the one nation, one language ideology. In other words, voters were swayed by ideological beliefs about language and its relationship to the state, not by linguistic, sociological, or educational realities. Today, through the concerted efforts of parents and educators, there are many successful two-way immersion bilingual education programs in California in languages such as Korean, Japanese, Mandarin, Cantonese, and Spanish. The success of these programs exists in spite of legislation that sought to implement statewide English-only policies. In 2000, a similar English-only education measure was passed in Arizona, namely Proposition 203, but without the possibility for parental petition. Bilingual education is thus banned in another one of the most bilingual states in the United States.

In most states, official bans on bilingual education are not necessary, since the overwhelming majority of schools operate English monolingual programs as a matter of course and no matter what the home languages of the student body. Linguistic anthropologist Otto Santa Ana notes that, oddly, the educational system has arrived at a moment in which the ideology of monolingualism – the belief that the full rights and benefits of United States citizenship come with being a monolingual English speaker – is so potent that functional bilingualism actually ranks as less than English monolingualism. He writes that when it comes to contemporary public discourse on education, "speaking a language in addition to English is effectively taken to be as much an educational barrier as non-English-monolingualism" (Santa Ana 2002:228).

Instead of bilingual education programs, English-as-a-Second-Language courses (ESL) are commonly offered throughout the United States. Many school systems simply assume that children will learn their heritage language in the home from parents. However, this perspective ignores two realities: first, although children may learn oral comprehension and speaking skills in the family language at home, literacy skills are most commonly acquired through dedicated instruction in schools and may be difficult for parents to teach. Second, myriad *informal* pressures against immigrant languages may block successful acquisition of the home language. Consider a child whose first language is Spanish. This student, who only heard Spanish at home until age five, will be placed in ESL on the first day of first grade, and may be discouraged from speaking, reading, or even hearing Spanish while at school. Many children learn that this means that their home language is not valuable and develop a sense of shame for their heritage language. This same student may never hear another word of Spanish at school again until he or she signs up for Elementary Spanish in high school, only to learn that this class is taught less as a serious opportunity to (re)learn the language he/she has mostly likely lost and more of an occasion for a trivialized in-school *fiesta*.

Sociolinguist Joshua Fishman (1974) points out an oddity of an educational system that it goes out of its way to turn multilingual immigrant children into monolingual English speakers, only to later reteach what was taken away now as a foreign language. Sociolinguist Ana Celia Zentella (1997:283) notes that the value placed on bilingualism in the United States has class implications. She asks, "Why is the bilingualism of the well-to-do a source of linguistic security and a sought after advantage while the bilingualism of the poor is a source of insecurity and a disadvantage? How do we explain the fact that bilingual education is looked down upon as remedial program while many mainstream adults pursue second language studies?" In other words, the multilingualism of poor and immigrant children in the United States can be understood as an impediment to educational success at the same time that adult students and students from more affluent families pursue foreign language education.

In the contemporary United States, language policies are limited not only to multilingual or foreign languages but also to the varieties of English spoken by native English speakers as their first language. For example, in 1996, the school board of the Oakland Unified School District in Oakland, California, passed a measure that recognized African American Vernacular English (AAVE), which they referred to as Ebonics, as the primary language of African American children, who comprised a numerical majority in their district. They further proposed using AAVE transitionally in the Language Arts classroom to help their students master Standard English. The proposal resulted in national controversy. Reporters from respectable media outlets across the country reported on Oakland's decision to "teach slang" to African American students, and eventually a special hearing was called by the United States Senate. Prominent, well-respected linguists voiced support for the proposal during the Senate hearing. The chairman of the Senate subcommittee in charge of the hearing tried and failed to find an African American linguist to testify against the proposal. He did, however, find a preacher and a popular columnist willing to come forth and speak against it. However, neither had any credentials in linguistics. This incident illustrates one of the major points of this section: educational policies about language are more frequently about ideology and politics than they are informed by linguistic theory and practice.

The overall educational goals of a nation-state are to produce citizens who can function appropriately in that nation-state. Our review of language and educational policy has focused on large, multilingual nation-states. However, for a smaller state such as Mongolia, with no burning minority language issues, a further goal of education is now to maintain and strengthen a sense of national identity. On news programs, in the newspapers, even in pop-culture music lyrics, Mongolians express their awareness of their population size relative to that of China: less than three million Mongolians as opposed to well over one billion Chinese. One response to this sense of threat has been for Mongolian policy makers to foreground something unique to their culture, namely its traditional writing system.

The socialist era came to an end in Mongolia in 1990. In 1992, the first democratic constitution was written, and it included a provision that all middle school children, aged 12–16, would learn what is called Old Script, the script devised for Mongolian in the thirteenth century. At the same time, lessons began on television to teach Old Script to the population. Beginning in 2000, legislators began to debate whether to expand the teaching of Old Script in the schools, and in 2008 it began to be introduced in primary school, to children aged 6–11. Today, the Mongolian government has legislated a full 12 years of instruction in Old Script, for all aged 6–18. Mongolian is still written in Cyrillic, but the teaching of Old Script is surely one way the educational system is keeping a sense of national uniqueness and identity alive.

Language Planners and Language Police

Although nation-states may be imagined to be monolingual, very few actually are, and this is where language planning and the legal apparatus of the state come into play. Language planning refers to the policies, laws, and programs designed to change the language behavior of people in a given language community and/or the language itself. Language-planning efforts often fall under the aegis of language academies, discussed above. All language-planning efforts, whether or not they come from official language academies or are inscribed officially in law, are ultimately about social control. Examples of one group controlling and/or curtailing the language rights of another group abound the world over. Some efforts are in response to old grievances. In Slovakia, a law was passed in 2009 prohibiting the use of Hungarian by state officials and in state institutions. Slovakia was once subjugated under the Austro-Hungarian Empire, and the recent ban reflects ongoing tensions between Slovaks and Hungarians, and conflict over national sovereignty and national identity.

In certain of these cases, language inspectors actually monitor how language laws are enacted and enforced. Two examples will suffice. The first concerns the small Baltic nations of Latvia and Estonia, which have struggled since the post-Soviet era to balance competing realities: on the one hand, the need to promote their own national languages, Latvian and Estonian, which were subjugated under Soviet rule; and on the other hand, the sociodemographic reality in which Russian speakers make up a large percentage of the overall population. In Latvia, where about one third of the population speaks Russian as a first language, ethnic Russians have claimed linguistic discrimination, while ethnic Latvians have claimed their language needs strict protections after centuries of marginalization by Russian in Tsarist and Soviet Russia. A proposal to make Russian an official language was put to popular vote in 2012 and was overwhelmingly rejected by voters.

A similar sociodemographic situation with a different political solution is found to the north, in Estonia. About one third of the Estonian population speaks Russian as a first language, and most of these speakers are concentrated in parts of the country where Russian is the main language. At the same time, Estonians are interested in preserving the Estonian language, a Finno-Ugric language spoken by barely more than one million people and which nearly disappears in comparison with Russian, which has about 150 million native speakers worldwide, and nearly as many more second-language speakers. Estonia has handled the situation by establishing a National Language Inspectorate, a government agency charged with monitoring the use of Estonian by government employees, including teachers, who can be reprimanded, fined, or fired for not speaking Estonian.

The second situation concerns Quebec. There, language inspectors are also at work, acting to uphold the provisions set in a law requiring children in Quebec to attend French-medium schools. Until recently, the law was understood to apply only to the classroom setting, with no particular provision for the hallways, cafeterias, and playgrounds. However, in 2011, the School Commission of Montreal proposed an extension of a bill known as *Loi 101* now requiring French to be spoken throughout the school grounds, including the playgrounds. The chairperson of the commission explained to the local press how the law would be enforced, namely by monitors who would gently tap children on the shoulder, and not on the head, to remind them to speak French. The tap is a nonverbal way to say, "Remember, we speak French. It's good for you."

Language inspectors in Quebec have moved into the realm of linguistic purism, which we, the authors, often think leads to ultimately unproductive activities. An often-cited definition of linguistic purism is provided by linguist George Thomas who describes it as "the manifestation of a desire on the part of a speech community (or some section of it) to preserve a language form, or to rid it of, putative foreign elements or other elements held to be undesirable. Above all, purism is an aspect of the codification, cultivation, and planning of standard languages" (Thomas 1991:12). The language inspectors in Quebec are concerned not only that people are speaking, reading, and hearing French but also that all of the words they speak, see, and hear are French. They ensure that international corporations conform to local expectations for the use of French. For example, a large United States clothing store could be fined for running an English language ad campaign that would pour English words through Quebec stores. The inspectors also monitor language on a much smaller scale. Controversy broke out when the Quebecois Office of the French Language sent a letter to the owner of an Italian restaurant informing him that he had broken the law by including too many non-French words on his menu, including *pasta* and *bottiglia,* rather than the French *pâtes* (pasta) and *bouteille* (bottle). Clearly, the language inspectors in Quebec are reacting to a perception of threat as if it were coming from all quarters and not just from the main competitor, English.

Efforts to purify a language of foreign elements are, of course, not simply about language but also about cultural identity and power, and, mostly specifically, asymmetries in power relations. In the Indian state of Tamil Nadu, throughout the twentieth century the Pure Tamil movement has sought to cleanse Tamil of words derived from Sanskrit. Today, the Tamils' concern is with words borrowed from English (Ramaswamy 1997). In North and South Korea, efforts have been taken by language planners to restrict the use of words of Japanese origin, which were thought to have flooded Korean during the Japanese occupation from 1910 to 1945 (Park 1989). Today, concerns about language purity are directed, once again, toward borrowings from English. Taiwan has been open to borrowings from English, Japanese, and other languages, while the People's Republic of China has a strict policy of limiting borrowings into Mainland Chinese. It allows only those words approved by the national Xinhua News Agency (Li 2004).

The control of language behavior around sensitive topics comes in many forms and from various sources. In Israel, the Arabic word for the 1948 creation of the state of Israel is *nakba* 'catastrophe.' This word has been officially removed from Arabic language textbooks. In New South Wales, Australia, the state health department has informally banned the use of the words *darling, sweetheart, honey,* and *mate* in interactions with patients. These particular words were seen as too informal. In 2003, the United States Congress changed the name *French fries* to *Freedom fries* in all congressional restaurants as a form of protest against the French who did not back the United States-led war in Iraq. While so-called Freedom fries will likely go the way of the term *liberty cabbage,* given to sauerkraut during the World War I era of anti-German anxiety, the point holds: proposals to modify language, as ephemeral as they may be, reflect the political and cultural sensitivities of a society, and constitute a form of social control.

The case of Persian, also known as Farsi, in Iran shows how investments in language purism change with political winds. Prior to the Islamic Revolution in 1979, efforts were made to purify Farsi of foreign elements, especially borrowings from Turkish and Arabic. This involved the creation of new words using Farsi morphology as well as the revival of historical Farsi words long replaced by Arabic borrowings. After the Islamic Revolution, the orientation toward Arabic shifted from one of hostility to one of reverence, and anxieties about Arabic influence correspondingly dissipated. What was once considered corrosive to the language was now considered among its purest elements. The situation in Iran illustrates that attitudes about what constitutes the so-called pure form of a language are ideological in nature and depend on the political, social, and cultural conditions present in a given time at a given place.

Government agencies do not always react in negative and limiting ways toward changing global conditions that result in new multilingual situations. When it comes not to the language police but to the real police in the United Kingdom, they have started to learn basic phrases in important immigrant languages. As travel among European Union member states has become easier, new patterns of immigration have resulted in new situations of language contact. In the town of Bedfordshire, England, Polish has emerged as an important immigrant language, and police officers are able to sign up for 10-week-long courses to learn basic Polish phrases such as *Jak Pan ma na imię?* 'What's your name?' and *Czy Pan mówi po angielsko?* 'Do you speak English?' The decision to offer Polish courses to British police officers was pragmatic, in the sense that the police need to have a way to communicate effectively with the Polish immigrant community. It was also symbolic, in showing that effort was made to accommodate a new immigrant group and to break down barriers between the English-speaking and Polish-speaking communities.

Similarly, in Los Angeles County, the Department of Motor Vehicles has decided to offer exams in 31 languages including American Sign Language, Arabic, Armenian, Turkish, and Welsh. California law requires only that state materials be translated into languages spoken by 5% or more of the population, which means that only translations into Spanish are technically required. The Los Angeles County Department of Motor Vehicles has decided to be accommodating to increase the efficiency of its operation. The DMV saves money and time by accommodating linguistic diversity rather than insisting on monolingual language policy. It is clearly possible for governmental agencies to demonstrate great flexibility in accommodating the multilingual populations they serve. We, the authors, applaud both the pragmatism and the symbolism of this embrace of linguistic diversity.

Final Note: Choosing Death or Life

The situation in Tibet raises important questions about language laws, language rights, and linguistic diversity. What role, if any, should states play in promoting national languages? To what extent, if any, should ethnolinguistic minority languages be supported with legal protection and governmental policy? Who gets to decide what language or languages will be used in education? What is the effect of language laws – both those that promote certain languages and those that limit or even outlaw others – on the world's linguistic diversity? These are big, overarching questions, ones for which we, the authors, do not have definitive answers for every case in the world.

However, the situation in Tibet does allow us to answer the more punctual question about what happens to speakers who are negatively impacted by language planning and language laws. The headquarters for the Government of Tibet in Exile is currently in Dharamshala,[8] India. The fourteenth Dalai Lama, the one who was born in Quinhai/Amdo, fled the Tibetan capital, Lhasa, in 1959 when the Chinese cracked down on their occupation, and he has been in exile ever since. Fifty years later, in the Tibet Autonomous Region under Chinese control, Tibetans are feeling enough loss of control and despair that since 2009, over 100 young Tibetans – some monks, some not – have engaged in a form of protest that is difficult for many people to imagine: self-immolation.

There is another way. In Dharamshala, young Tibetans who have fled Chinese Tibet have chosen life over death, and they have established a new way of protesting. Now there is the Lhakar Movement, *lhakar* meaning 'white Wednesday,' which is the Dalai Lama's "soul day." Every Wednesday, Tibetans in exile celebrate Tibetan culture by watching Tibetan movies and listening to Tibetan music. Most importantly, they protest by speaking Tibetan and only Tibetan, with no switching to Mandarin, Hindi, or English. Recall from Chapter 4 that in eighteenth-century France, Abbé Grégoire advocated annihilating language differences in the service of creating the nation-state France. Over 200 years later, in most nations, language policy with respect to ethnolinguistic minority groups has continued along the path of annihilation of the minority languages and the promotion of the sole standard. We, the authors, think the Lhakar Movement – in choosing life over death – is wholly to be supported. Mostly, however, we would like to live in a linguistic world where such a choice was not necessary in the first place.

Language Profile: བོད་སྐད [Tibetan (Sino-Tibetan)]

Functional overview

The Tibetan peoples live across the Tibetan Plateau, a wide area of eastern Central Asia, and parts of South Asia. They speak about 25 Tibetan languages, all derived from Classical Tibetan. The language variety known in the West as Tibetan is spoken by about 5 million people in the Tibet Autonomous Region, which has been a part of the People's Republic of China since its annexation in 1951. Some 200,000 speakers of Tibetan reside in exile outside of Tibet in Bhutan, Nepal, and especially India, where the exile government is headquartered. Tibetic languages, including Standard Tibetan, are in the Tibeto-Burman branch of the Sino-Tibetan language family.

A Tibetan proverb says, "Every valley has a river and every village has a dialect" Reynolds (2012:1). The proverb reflects the fact that the Tibetan landscape – mountain peaks, valleys, vast rivers, and plateaus – has kept different groups of speakers separate from one another, and this separation has facilitated the rise of great linguistic diversity in spoken Tibetan. Standard Tibetan is based on the prestige variety spoken in Lhasa, the administrative capital of Tibet. Dozens of other varieties are more or less intelligible with Standard Tibetan, and differ from one another in terms of grammar, phonetics, and lexicon. The Golok variety spoken in the extreme northeast of Tibet is representative of so-called conservative varieties that are thought to have changed little from Classical Tibetan, relative to the Lhasa variety, which is considered innovative. The Golok variety is completely nontonal and pronounces all nasal-initial consonant clusters as [m]. It distinguishes between present- and past-tense pronunciations of verbs, such that the present/past pair of the verb 'to look at' is *lta* (present) and *bltas* (past), which are rendered as [hrt] and [ft]. The Lhasa variety, in contrast, makes tonal distinctions, has undergone a process of nasal place assimilation with following consonants, for example, [nth], [nd], and [mph], and makes no distinction between present and past pronunciations.

Prominent structural characteristics

Tone   While all spoken human languages vary pitch in some way or another, only certain languages use conventionalized pitches, known as tones, to create meaning contrasts. This means that the meaning of a single phonological form (a word) can vary depending on the tone that accompanies it. In Standard Tibetan, there are two contrastive tones – high and low – that distinguish words such as [màh] (low tone) 'mother' and [máh] (high tone) 'low.' Other varieties of Tibetan have up to four tones. As a point of comparison, Vietnamese makes contrasts with six distinctive tones, as we will see in the profile in Chapter 8.

The term *tonogenesis* refers to the development of tone in a language that previously did not have it. Tone can be borrowed from one neighboring language to another, as is the case with some Chadic (Afro-Asiatic) languages that have taken tone from Niger–Congo. Tone may also arise as an epiphenomenon of phonological changes otherwise taking place to a language. In nontone languages, vowels following voiced consonants are characteristically produced with a lower pitch. If voicing contrasts are lost in a language over time, these differences in tone may concretize, become identifiable, and themselves serve for lexical and grammatical contrasts. In this case, tone is 'left over' from an earlier phonology, and some linguists have therefore termed this process *Cheshirization*, after the Cheshire Cat in *Alice in Wonderland*, whose beguiling grin remains even when the cat disappears. Between 1000 and 1500 CE, the prevocalic voicing distinction of consonants in historical Tibetan was lost in the Lhasa dialect, and to take its place, preexisting tonal differences in pronunciation settled into indentifiable contrastive tones.

Optional ergativity   In the profile from Chapter 4 on Kurdish, we saw that not all languages arrange subjects and objects in the same way. In accusative alignment languages, all subjects are treated in one way and all objects another, irrespective of whether or not the verb is transitive or intransitive. In ergative alignment languages, the subject of an intransitive verb and the object of a transitive verb are grouped together and contrasted with the subject of a transitive verb, which is marked with the ergative case. Thus, in the Tibetan sentence 'he prepares the meals,' the subject 'he' is case-marked in the ergative (ERG) and the verb in the imperfective (IMP).

khong-ki'	khala	so-kiyore'
he-ERG	food	make-IMP

In a nonergative case-marking language, the object *khala* 'food' would be the marked form, rather than the subject of the transitive verb 'make.' What makes ergativity different in Tibetan from other ergative languages such as Kurdish is that the ergative morphological case marker is optional. That is, it can be present or absent from the noun phrase without changing the interpretation of the action. The same sentence could therefore be rendered with no case marking as:

khong'	*khala*	*so-kiyore'*
he	food	make-IMP

A third possibility includes the case marker and a change in word order:

khala	*khong-ki'*	*so-kiyore'*
food	he-ERG	make-IMP

These are not simply three ways of saying the same thing. The use of the ergative in the first contrasts the individual actor with someone else, such as the person who makes the drinks or serves the food. The second utterance with no case marking is likely a response to the question "What does he do?," while the final utterance may be translated as 'he is the one who prepares the meals,' contrasting 'he' with others who may prepare meals (Tournadre 1995:264). Optional ergative languages such as Tibetan use case morphology and word order for information structure, that is, to focus a topic and to foreground or background new and given information.

Copula verbs Copula verbs are characteristically described as 'to be' verbs that link grammatical subjects to nouns and adjectives in the predicate. Copula verbs function differently in different languages. In Russian, the copula is optional in the present tense, while Portuguese makes use of two copula verbs, one for temporary conditions, *estar*, and another for permanent conditions, *ser*. Tibetan is similar to Portuguese in that it makes use of different verbal forms depending on the nature of the attribute expressed in the predicate, but is unique in that it also distinguishes between attributes of subject known to the speaker through experience and attributes known only through outside sources.

The first distinction Tibetan copula verbs make is similar to that of Portuguese; that is, between those forms that express an inherent quality of the noun, known as essential copulas, and those that express a temporary characteristic of the noun or an evaluation of the speaker, known as existential copulas. This difference is illustrated in the following examples that show the two forms of 'I am':

Nga	*Tashi*	*yin* (essential, first person)
I	Tashi	am

'I am Tashi'

Nga	*Pö*	*la*	*yö* (existential, first person)
I	Tibet	in	am

'I am in Tibet'

The essential form *yin* is used for inherent qualities, such as a person's name, while the existential form *yö* is used for temporary conditions, such as a person's location.

The second distinction Tibetan copula verbs make has to do with the type of assertion given. If the speaker has firsthand knowledge of the assertion being made, the form *du* is used. This is known as a testimonial copula. If the speaker only knows of a situation through secondhand information, the form *yod-red* is used. This form is known as the assertive copula. Thus, whereas an English speaker would say, 'there are yaks in Tibet,' a speaker of Tibetan will need to choose the appropriate copula form according to his/her knowledge of the situation:

Pö la yag du (Speaker has seen yaks in Tibet.)
Tibet in yaks are.
'In Tibet there are yaks.'

Pö la yag yod-red (Speaker has heard or read that there are yaks in Tibet.)
Tibet in yaks are.
'In Tibet there are yaks.'

Tibetan does not inflect the copula verbs for tense, since time is surmised from context. Nor is a morphological distinction made between singular and plural forms. However, unique forms appear for negative and interrogative constructions. In negative constructions, the essential form *yin* becomes *min*, and the existential form *yö* becomes *me*. No additional negative marker is needed, as these forms are only used in negative constructions. For example:

nga	*Lahasa*	*la*	*me*
I	Lahasa	in	am-not

'I am not in Lahasa.'

Volitional verbs   In English, perceptual verbs such as smell, taste, see, and hear are considered to be nonvolitional; that is, the action is not directed by the subject. In the sentence *I taste the salt*, the verb 'taste' is involuntary and can be contrasted with a volitional verb such as 'eat' in the sentence *I eat dinner late*. The subject does not control the sensation of tasting but makes decisions about whether and what to eat. English does have a limited number of volitional pairs, such as see/watch and hear/listen. One therefore 'sees an accident' but 'watches a TV show' and 'hears a noise' but 'listens to music.' In Tibetan, this distinction is widespread, and verbs generally fall into one of two verb classes according to volition.

Volition in Tibetan is morphologically marked, with volitional and nonvolitional verbs receiving a separate set of inflectional suffixes in each of the tenses: past, present, and future. Inflected verbs are formed by adding a verbal particle, for example, *gi*, and a tense/volitional marker to a stem. The verbs *sa-ua* 'to eat' (volitional) and *dro-go-to-pa* 'to be hungry' (nonvolitional) fall into different verb classes, and therefore receive different inflections. The inflections mark tense and volitionality.

nga yak-sha sa-gi-yö (volitional)
I yak meat eat+VERBAL+PRES/VL
'I eat yak meat.'

nga dhro-go-to-gi-du (nonvolitional)
I (to be) hungry+VERBAL+PRES/NON-VL
'I am hungry.'

The morphology marking volitional and nonvolitional verb classes changes according to the tense in which the verb is inflected. While *yö* and *du* mark volitional and nonvolitional in the present tense, the past tense is marked with *pa-yin* and *song* for first person and *pa-re* and *song* for second and third person. Again, Tibetan does not inflect for number.

Nga chu thung-pa-yin
I water drink+VERBAL+PAST/VOL
'I drank water.'

Nga je-song (nonvolitional)
I forget+PAST/NON-VL
'I forgot.'

A salient cultural characteristic: the language of Tibetan Buddhism

Another Tibetan proverb says, "every valley has its dialect and every lama has his religion" (Reynolds 2012:1). In Tibetan Buddhism, a lama is a teacher of *dharma*, or the cosmic order of the universe. The proverb illustrates the diversity of spoken Tibetan and the importance of religion in Tibetan culture. Indeed, the two are inseparable; Tibetan is the medium through which Buddhist scripture is transmitted, and it is therefore considered to be a holy language.

Tibetan Buddhism emphasizes orality, and spoken language is at the center of Tibetan religious practice. Spoken mantras, or prayers, are said aloud or repeated quietly to oneself. The chanting of a mantra as a form of meditation is thought to evoke enlightenment. The most basic Tibetan mantra is *Om mani padme hum*. Recitation of these six syllables is thought to invoke compassion, and every Tibetan learns this mantra as a child. Mantras are chanted in daily life – sometimes thousands of times – and constitute an important part of Temple practice and prayer walks, known as *kora*, which are pilgrimages to or around holy sites.

Despite the importance of spoken language in Tibetan Buddhism, written language is also highly valued, and for this reason, Tibetan script is also considered sacred. For example, the act of seeing a mantra written is thought to have the same spiritual effect on a reader as an oral recitation has on a speaker. The Tibetan alphabet was devised in the seventh century when a group of boys was sent to India to learn the art of writing. Only one of them is said to have returned to Tibet. His name was Thonmi Sambhota, and he introduced the ancient Indic script he learned abroad to the Tibetan King, who is credited with adapting it to the Tibetan language. Important Buddhist texts were immediately translated, and translation and recording of holy works continued for the next five centuries. These works are now known as the Tibetan Buddhist Canon and are the central texts in Tibetan religious and cultural practice. We can conclude that not only have writing and Tibetan Buddhism been inextricably bound to one another since the seventh century, but contemporary Tibetan culture would not be possible without the development of writing.

Tibetan script is written by combining consonant radicals with vowel diacritics to create stacked syllables. Vowel diacritics are written above or below consonants. For example, the vowel ཨི (/i/) combines with the consonant མ (/m/) to form the mono-syllabic word མི /mi/ ('person'), ཨོ (/o/) combines with the consonant པ (/p/) to form the word པོ /po/ ('male'), and the vowel ཨུ (/u/) combines with ས (/s/) to form the word སུ /su/ (who). Although the syllable structure of spoken Tibetan has undergone significant change since the recording of the Tibetan Buddhist Canon, spelling reform is unlikely, given the centrality of the texts to Tibetan identity.

The popularization of Tibetan Buddhism and the spread of meditation in the West means that the elegant script can now be seen in yoga studios, bookshops, temples, and private homes around the world. Colorful Tibetan prayer flags, which bear mantras written in Tibetan script, are flown not only in Lhasa and Kathmandu but also in cities from London to Los Angeles, where English-speaking practitioners of yoga and meditation chant the Tibetan mantras, starting with *Om mani padme hum.*

Exercises

Exercise 1 – you decide

You have once again been appointed special commissioner to the United Nations, this time to find a workable solution to the language problem in Tibet highlighted in this chapter. On the one hand, the Chinese government is interested in promoting Putonghua as a vehicle for economic development and national unity. On the other hand, the Tibetans are interested in preserving their language and cultural traditions. Your job is to write a coherent policy solution. No matter what you decide, your report should address the interests of the government and of Tibetans. Your policy decision must be an informed one, so make sure you are familiar with language policy in China.

Exercise 2 – map making

As we have described in this chapter, the continent of Africa was divided up among the European colonial powers, whose languages left legacies both small and large.

Sketch a map of Africa. Use a different-colored pencil to indicate regions influenced by: (a) Dutch, (b) English, (c) French, (d) German, (e) Italian, (f) Portuguese, and (g) Spanish.

Exercise 3 – national versus official languages

Official languages and national languages do not always correspond with one another, as we have seen in this chapter. Make a table with four columns: National language(s), Official language(s), Prominent Minority Language(s), Notes. The notes column is a space for you to list any other information about the language scene you find interesting. Provide this information for each of the following 15 countries, which will constitute the rows in your table. Add as many additional rows as you would like.

Angola
Australia
Brazil
Cameroon
Central Africa Republic
Democratic Republic of Congo
Haiti
Iran
Kenya
Morocco
Nepal
Republic of Ireland
Sierra Leone
Turkey
Uzbekistan

Discussion Questions

1 In 2012, the *Real Academia Española* announced that it would add the word *espanglish* 'Spanglish' to the 2014 edition of their official dictionary, which is considered the most prestigious in the Spanish-speaking world. The decision was met with controversy, even among some of the most fervent supporters of the Academy. Why do you suppose the decision was a controversial one for those who believe in the authority of language academies?

2 Have you encountered the notion of "the Queen's English" in your own life? In what contexts? How does the Harrington study about the Queen's pronunciations challenge the trope of the Queen's English?

3 Although there is no language academy for the English language as such, speakers sometimes take it upon themselves to regulate the speech of others. That is, prescriptive ideas about 'good' and 'bad' English nevertheless abound. Where do those ideas come from? How do they circulate? What are their effects?

4 What are the advantages and disadvantages of adopting the language of a previous colonial power in postcolonial context? Think about this in the context of individuals, groups, and institutions, as well as the nation in general.

5 What was the role of Mahatma Gandhi, Jawaharlal Nehru, and Indira Gandhi in setting language policy in India? What were the advantages and disadvantages of their policy interventions?

6 What kinds of social, political, economic, and ideological factors influence policy decisions about language in education? Think critically about the language of instruction in the place where you received your primary education. How did the selection of this language benefit or harm you? How did the selection of this language benefit or harm others in your school with different linguistic backgrounds? What changes would you make to the language and education policy in your community?

7 India's Three Language Policy has not been implemented in the way in which it was envisioned by its authors. What does this say about the workings of power in public policy and educational policy as they pertain to language?

8 When multilingualism is so prized in many parts of the world, what factors have supported the steadfast monolingualism of most schools in the United States, despite the undeniably multilingual population? That is, how do you think English monolingualism has come to be seen as superior to multilingualism in many educational contexts in the United States?

9 Why do you suppose the Oakland School Board decision to use a nonstandard dialect of English as a medium of instruction for teaching the standard variety was met with so much misunderstanding and controversy? What does the controversy say about the way language is understood by the public in the United States? How can sound language policy decisions be made in educational contexts when publics are so frequently misinformed about basic language issues?

10 What effect do you think the teaching of Mongolian Script will have in Mongolia? Will it be effective in engendering national identity?

11 The linguistic situation in Latvia and Estonia involving Russian makes visible the tension between the right for all speakers to speak their native language and the need for small languages, often spoken in small states, to preserve their linguistic heritage. How can the state strike a balance between these competing interests? What other tensions are at play here – for speakers of Estonian and for Russian speakers living within Estonia?

Notes

1 The term *Rinpoche* is an honorific given to revered teachers and incarnated lamas; it means 'precious one.'

2 With 37 million speakers who use Spanish as their primary language at home, the United States is the fifth most populous Spanish-speaking country in the world, behind Mexico, Spain, Colombia, and Argentina. When speakers who use Spanish as the secondary language of the home as well as Spanish learners are included, the United States is the second most populous Spanish-speaking country, behind only Mexico.

3   Not incidentally, Vaugelas was one of the first members of the French Academy and the first editor of its dictionary project.

4   In the 1820s, before Texas achieved independence from Mexico, Anglo immigrants claimed a right to communicate with the Mexican government in English. Stephen Austin explained the importance of translating the laws for persons who did not speak Spanish and won for all Texans the right of access to government in a "known tongue." Thus, bilingual services in Texas today are not the invention of modern government but rather a right English speakers secured 200 years ago; see Juárez, Jr. (1995).

5   Afrikaans is a Germanic language that developed independently in the eighteenth century based on the language of Dutch settlers in modern-day South Africa.

6   Mandela's original first name was Rolihlahla, which in Xhosa means 'tugging a tree branch.' He was given the Christian name Nelson on his first day at a missionary school near his rural village of Mveso in Transkei, South Africa.

7   Backers of Prop 227 talked about the value of knowing English, which was a red-herring argument. Learning English was never at stake – students in English-only and bilingual education programs learn English. What was actually at stake was whether students would acquire only one language (English) or two. The rhetorical strategies ("English for the Children") nevertheless successfully framed bilingual education as taking English away from immigrant students.

8   Dharamshala is the capital of the Tibetan government in exile and should not be confused with the Indian town of similar spelling, Dharmasala, which is located in a different state.

References

Arjia Rinpoche (2010) *Surviving the Dragon: A Tibetan Lama's Account of 40 Years under Chinese Rule*. New York: Rodale.

Dardjowidjojo, Soenjono (1998) Strategies for a successful national language policy: The Indonesian case. *International Journal of the Sociology of Language* 130: 35–47.

Fishman, Joshua (ed.) (1974) *Advances in Language Planning*. Berlin: Walter de Gruyter.

Harrington, Jonathan, Sallyanne Palenthorpe, and Catherine Watson (2000) Does the Queen speak the Queen's English? *Nature* 408: 927–928.

Juárez, José Roberto, Jr. (1995) The American tradition of language rights: The forgotten right to government in a "known tongue." *Law and Inequality* 13: 443.

Kibbee, Douglas (2011) Rethinking Prescriptivism. Berkeley Language Center, Public Lecture, October 21.

Li, Chris Wen-Chao (2004) Conflicting notions of language purity: The interplay of archaizing, ethnographic, reformist, elitist, and xenophobic purism in the perception of standard Chinese. *Language and Communication* 24: 97–133.

Park, Nahm-Sheik (1989) Language purism in Korea today. In Bjorn H. Jernudd and Michael J. Shapiro (eds.), *The Politics of Language Purism*. Paris: Mouton de Gruyter.

Ramaswamy, Sumathi (1997) *Passions of the Tongue: Language Devotion in Tamil India 1891–1970*. Los Angeles: University of California Press.

Reynolds, Jermay J. (2012) Language variation and change in an Amdo Tibetan Village: The case of bilabial nasal coda /m/. Doctoral dissertation, Georgetown University.

Santa Ana, Otto (2002) *Brown Tide Rising: Metaphors of Latinos in Contemporary American Public Discourse*. Austin: University of Texas Press.

Thomas, George (1991) *Linguistic Purism*. London: Longman.

Tournadre, Nicolas (1995) Tibetan ergativity and the trajectory model: New horizons in Tibeto-Burman morphosyntax. *Senri Ethnological Studies* 41: 261–276.

Webb, Vic (1996) Language planning and politics in South Africa. *International Journal of the Sociology of Language* 118: 139–162.

Wong-Fillmore, Lily (2004) Language in Education. In Edward Finegan and John Rickford (eds.), *Language in the USA: Themes for the Twenty-First Century*. Cambridge: Cambridge University Press, 339–360.

Zentella, Ana Celia (1997) *Growing Up Bilingual: Puerto Rican Children in New York*. Malden, MA: Blackwell.

Further Reading

Alisjahbana, S. Takdir (1974) Language policy, language engineering and literacy in Indonesia and Malaysia. In Joshua Fishman (ed.), *Advances in Language Planning*. Paris: Mouton De Gruyter, 391–416.

Altoma, Salih J. (1974) Language education in Arab countries. In Joshua Fishman (ed.), *Advances in Language Planning*. Paris: Mouton De Gruyter, 279–313.

Amritavalli R. and K.A. Jayaseelan (2007) India. In Andrew Simpson (ed.), *Language and National Identity in Asia*. Oxford: Oxford University Press, 55–83.

Beckett, Gulbahar H. and Gerard A. Postiglione (2012) China's language policy for indigenous and minority education. In Gulbahar H. Beckett and Gerard A. Postiglione (eds.), *China's Assimilationist Language Policy: The Impact on Indigenous/Minority Literacy and Social Harmony (Comparative Development and Policy in Asia)*. New York: Routledge.

Benedikter, Thomas (2009) *Language Policy and Linguistic Minorities in India*. Berlin: LIT Verlag.

Bhatt, Rakesh M. and Ahmar Mahboob (2008) Minority languages and their status. In Braj B. Kachru, Yamuna Kachru, and S.N. Sridhar (eds.), *Language in South Asia*. Cambridge: Cambridge University Press, 132–152.

Bradley, David (2005) Language policy and language endangerment in China. *International Journal of the Sociology of Language* 173: 1–21.

Cifuentes, Barbara (1992) Language policy in Mexico. *International Journal of Sociology of Language* 96: 9–17.

Dixon, Robert M.W. (1994) *Ergativity*. Cambridge: Cambridge University Press.

Edwards, Viv (2004) *Multilingualism in the English-Speaking World*. Malden, MA: Blackwell.

Heath, Shirley Brice (1972) *Telling Tongues: Language Policy in Mexico, from Colony to Nation*. New York: Teachers College Press.

Hidalgo, Margarita Guadalupe (2006) *Mexican Indigenous Languages at the Dawn of the 21st Century*. Berlin: Mouton de Gruyter.

Jhingran, Dhir (2009) Hundreds of home languages in the country and many in most classrooms: Coping with diversity in primary education in India. In Tove Skutnabb-Kangas, Robert Phillipson, Ajit K. Mohanty, and Minati Panda (eds.), *Social Justice through Multilingual Education*. Bristol, UK: Multilingual Matters, 263–282.

Kaplan Robert (ed.) (2000) *Language Planning in Nepal, Taiwan, and Sweden*. New York: Multilingual Matters, 60–106.

McCabe, Allyssa and Catherine S. Tamis-LeMonda (2013) Multilingual children: Beyond myths and toward best practices. *Social Policy Report* 27.4: 1–21.

Musa, Monsur (1996) Politics of language planning in Pakistan and the birth of a new state. *International Journal of the Sociology of Language* 118: 63–80.

Newman, Michael, Adriana Patiño-Santos, and Mireia Trenchs-Parera (2013) Linguistic reception of Latin American students in Catalonia and their responses to educational language policies. *International Journal of Bilingual Education and Bilingualism* 16.2: 195–209.

Samuelson, Beth Lewis and Sarah Warshauer Freedman (2010) Language policy, multilingual education, and power in Rwanda. *Language Policy* 9: 191–215.

Shackle, Christopher (2007) *Pakistan*. In Andrew Simpson (ed.), *Language and National Identity in Asia*. Oxford: Oxford University Press, 100–115.

Sheorey, Ravi (2006) *Learning and Teaching English in India*. London: Sage.

Siguan, Miquel (1993) *Multilingual Spain*. Amsterdam: Swets & Zeitlinger B.V.

Tsao, Feng-fu (2000) The language planning situation in Taiwan. In Richard Baldauf and Robert Kaplan (eds.), *Language Planning in Nepal, Taiwan, and Sweden*. New York: Multilingual Matters, 60–106.

Part III
Effects of Movement

Introductory Note: On Movement

Humans have been on the move since the beginning of time, and they have always taken with them their material cultures, their technologies, and their languages. In Part II, we surveyed some of the ways power circulates to organize and reorganize the social and political realities of various groups of people with respect to their languages, and we put emphasis on events in the last several centuries. In Part III, we now extend our purview to include the last 10,000 years and trace the paths of human movements around the world in near-prehistory. We then look at the consequences of the more recent crossings and recrossings of the globe through the last 3000 years of colonization. We address the effects of movement in terms of the kinds of things that can move:

(i) People move. In Chapter 1, we suggested why people move: in search of the more plentiful berry bushes, the less crowded watering hole, the better mates. How they move also has effects. The humans who first left East Africa some 60 kya were hunter-gatherers. They went on foot and began to domesticate wolves, breeding them into dogs 18–12 kya. More recently, namely 1000 years ago, the Inuit were able to move eastward across the Canadian Arctic with their dog sleds and kayaks. In Chapter 7, we indicate some of the technological advances that made certain demic expansions possible, the domestication of large animals and agriculture being of prime importance. We return to the topic of historical reconstruction and introduce the philological principles behind the reconstruction of protolanguages. We then identify the homelands for the various language stocks along with their major structural characteristics. We end by reviewing models for representing how daughter languages diversify from the protolanguage.

Languages in the World: How History, Culture, and Politics Shape Language, First Edition.
Julie Tetel Andresen and Phillip M. Carter.
© 2016 John Wiley & Sons, Inc. Published 2016 by John Wiley & Sons, Inc.

(ii)   Languages move. When the British first entered India in 1612, the merchants of the British East India Company set up shop in English. When the Raj ended in 1947, the British left behind their language deeply engrained in Indian daily life. Today, India is the call center for the world, because there are so many Indians who speak English either natively or near-natively. The idea here is that when colonization first takes place, the colonizers naturally have a physical presence; however, once colonization is under way or has even ended, the physical presence of the colonizers is not necessary in order to continue linguistic effects. In Chapter 8, we look at the way languages move around the world through colonialism with its administrative structures, military order, system of trade, laws, and cultural prestige. We end by considering the possibility that English is at the beginning of a process of becoming its own language family.

(iii)   Weapons and money move, and with them borders. If you had been born in 1910 and lived your entire life in a town now called Uzhgorod, you would have begun life as a subject of the Austro-Hungarian Empire and become, in succession, a citizen of the Republic of Czechoslovakia (1919), of Hungary (1938), and finally of Ukraine (1944). The language dynamics governing your social life would have been no less unsettling than those governing your political life. Chapter 9 takes up what happens to speakers and their languages as a result of geopolitical power struggles that create conflict and war, and new political realities. In modern times, many of these struggles have occurred when a colonial power decamps, and a postcolonial nation-state suddenly confronts its precolonial multilingual reality, with a minority group making a claim to a new border. Other times, namely during political or economic warfare, ethnogroups may find themselves moved by a government or displaced by an advancing army. At all times, these conflicts create not only physical pain and suffering but also psychosocial pain and suffering when an ethnogroup fails to create a new border, is inscribed by a new border, or is forced across a border. Geopolitical conflicts typically result in one group or another losing their social and political leverage, their language, their identity, or all three.

The movements of people and languages along with the fluctuations of geopolitics have created our modern world, for better or worse. These movements are at every moment implicated in the accompanying circulation of goods and services, and mediums of exchange. To put it another way, we can say that language, money, and markets constitute extended traditions, whose interlacing, once stabilized in time and place, can become recognized as a culture. The movement of people in and out of Europe provided Italian cooks with the ingredients for their quintessential dish *pasta pomodoro*, which is a happy combination of the tomato from North America and pasta from North Africa. Less happy circumstances occur, and unwanted disruptions to these extended traditions can cause trauma. Desired disruptions create new cultural forms. Students from around the world converge every August on the campus of Duke University. They come with their own sense of style, which is remade and displayed by the end of the first semester by means of Duke-labeled sweatpants, hoodies, and T-shirts. College campuses are furthermore hot houses of slang and the latest speak, which their mobile student bodies take and text out into the world.

7

A Mobile History
Mapping Language Stocks and Families

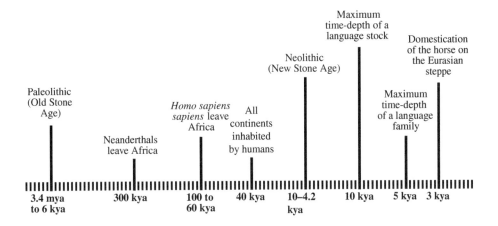

Paleolithic (Old Stone Age)

Neanderthals leave Africa

Homo sapiens sapiens leave Africa

All continents inhabited by humans

Neolithic (New Stone Age)

Maximum time-depth of a language stock

Domestication of the horse on the Eurasian steppe

Maximum time-depth of a language family

3.4 mya to 6 kya   300 kya   100 to 60 kya   40 kya   10–4.2 kya   10 kya   5 kya   3 kya

Austronesian Origin Stories[1]

The precolonial Polynesians revered a supreme deity who, according to the story, huddled in an egg-shaped shell for countless ages in endless space. After an infinite period of impenetrable darkness, the god hatched himself. Upon beholding a void, he was inspired to create the heavens and the earth, and all the other gods. This deity also brought forth the seas and the islands. Once land was formed, the creator of the universe sent a vine to earth, and from the worms clinging to this vine, humans developed. The Samoans called this god Tagaloa, the Tongans called him Tangaloa, the Māori of New Zealand called him Tangaroa, the Tahitians called him Ta'aroa, and the Hawaiians called him Kanaloa. What is most interesting about this story from a linguistic

Languages in the World: How History, Culture, and Politics Shape Language, First Edition.
Julie Tetel Andresen and Phillip M. Carter.
© 2016 John Wiley & Sons, Inc. Published 2016 by John Wiley & Sons, Inc.

point of view is that the name for this god could well serve comparative philologists in telling another origin story, that of the Austronesian languages. The various names for the supreme deity in these five Pacific languages – Samoan, Tongan, Māori, Tahitian, and Hawaiian – can start the process of reconstructing Proto-Austronesian.

In this chapter, we explore in more depth the methods of comparative philology (historical linguistics) mentioned in Chapter 3, and we summarize the fruits of this philological labor that has established the major language stocks, identified the diverse homelands where the protolanguages were likely spoken, and catalogued their major structural features. We also engage with another group of scientists interested in origin stories, namely population geneticists who seek to establish the genetic relationships among the world's populations. Whereas comparative philology has been around for well over 200 years, population genetics is hardly more than 50 years old. However, the latter has made great progress, especially since the Human Genome Project finished mapping the complete human genome in 2003.[2] It is exciting to discover the places where the results of these two independent disciplines – comparative philology and population genetics – coincide to indicate places where the genetic make-up of certain populations and the languages they speak separate and diverge. These places of coincidence are the topic of this chapter, for they tell us the story of the spread of the peoples and their languages across the globe during the last 10,000 years.

Population Genetics and Links to Language

The contemporary student of linguistics – the contemporary student of almost any field – needs at least a passing knowledge of both genetics and evolution. We will take up the topic of evolution in Chapter 10. Here, we sketch the basics of genetics and its relationship to the discipline of linguistics.

A **gene** (Figure 7.1)[3] is defined as a basic unit of molecular inheritance. Physically, a gene is a particular sequence of a combination of four organic molecules called nucleotides – A (adenine), C (cytosine), G (guanine), and T (thymine) – that form base pairs, such as G–C and A–T, and these pairs are the building blocks of DNA. Functionally, a gene is a unit that codes for a particular protein. The entirety of an organism's basic physical hereditary material is called a **genome**. The human genome has between 20,000 and 25,000 protein-coding genes, a good 50 times fewer than the genome of the organism with the largest known genome, the rare *Paris japonica*, a flower native to Japan, and a whopping 1300 times larger than the genome of the organism with the smallest known genome, *Encephalitozoon intestinalis*, a parasite of humans and other mammals. Some genes are famous. In 2013, Hollywood actress Angelina Jolie's preemptive double mastectomy brought a spotlight on *BRCA* (pronounced 'brocka') whose mutated variants correlate highly with breast cancer of the kind that killed Jolie's mother at a relatively early age.

A gene is found on a **chromosome**, which is an organized structure of DNA found in cells, mostly in the nucleus. In humans, the genes are spread across 23 pairs of chromosomes, thus giving humans 46 chromosomes per cell. The chromosome pairs cross in a way to create a high-waisted X and thereby create two long arms and two

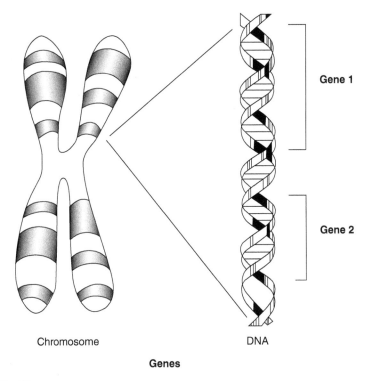

Gene 1

Gene 2

Chromosome   DNA

Genes

Figure 7.1   The gene.

short arms for each pair. Perhaps the most well-known pair of chromosomes is chromosome 23, which determines sex: XY for male and XX for female. Genetic mutations can occur in many places, including on the sex chromosomes, and there is a condition known as *Fragile X* that results from mutations in one or more genes on the X chromosome causing a range of nontypical development in both boys and girls. Chromosomal abnormalities can occur, as well, such as Trisomy 21 or Down Syndrome, which results when all or part of chromosome 21 has a third copy.

An **allele** (Greek *allo* 'other') is an alternate form of a gene or a group of genes in close proximity on a chromosome, and these variants account for the individual **phenotype** of an organism, its particular set of characteristics, many of which are observable. Once a group of organisms has been classed into a species, that is, once it is determined that the members of this group share a **genotype**, the next thing to notice is that the members of this group are all different one from the other – physically, biochemically, behaviorally – which is to say they all have different phenotypes. One of the reasons for these phenotypic differences is genetic variation. Variations in hair, eye, and skin color are commonly observable differences among humans, and these variations are attributable to specific alleles. Susceptibility to certain diseases, as has just been noted, can also be due to specific alleles. The genes *BRCA 1* and *2*, which are found on the long arms of chromosomes 17 and 13, are not breast cancer genes in and of themselves. Only their mutated alleles are associated with the manifestation of the disease.

By comparing and contrasting genetic variations, population geneticists can distinguish among groups and subgroups of populations, just as philologists compare and contrast cognate sets in order to identify language families (groups) and branches (subgroups). A **haplogroup** (Greek *haplo* 'single, simple') is a group of similar **haplotypes** that share a common ancestor having the same single nucleotide – A, C, G, or T – variation in all haplotypes. For instance, in comparing stretches of DNA samples of different groups, if Strand 1 has the sequence C–G T–A A–T at the very location where Strand 2 has the sequence T–A T–A A–T, this then qualifies as a SNP (pronounced 'snip'), a single nucleotide polymorphism (variation) with two alleles, C–G and T–A. These two haplotypes belong to the same haplogroup. There is a parallel here, once again, with the philologists' sound correspondences, which help determine where the branching points are in the groups and subgroups of languages.[4] Haplogrouping is often called *deep ancestry* and can be used to trace lineages much farther back in time than can philologists' linguistic reconstructions, which do not apply at a time-depth much greater than 10,000 years.

The haplogroups studied in human populations often involve the Y-chromosome (**Y-DNA**), which is passed along solely in the patrilineal line from father to son, and mitochondrial DNA (**mtDNA**), which is passed from the mother to all offspring. Unlike nuclear DNA, which is found in the nucleus of a cell, mtDNA is found outside the nucleus in a cellular organelle called the mitochondrion. MtDNA does not recombine; there is no shuffling of genes from one generation to the next, as there is with nuclear genes. For this reason, and because the rate of mutation of mtDNA was thought to be statistically regular, mtDNA was once considered to function as a molecular clock and used to date divergences in populations. However, this chronological reliability has proven to be an oversimplification. Nevertheless, it seems to be the case that all men today belong to one of 18 main Y-DNA haplogroups on their paternal line and one of 26 main mtDNA haplogroups on their maternal line.

Into the story of human dispersal now comes a 100-year-old lock of hair. It came from an aboriginal man living in a remote corner of southwestern Australia. He gave it to Alfred Cort Hadden, a British anthropologist who traveled the world in the early twentieth century, seeking samples of hair, among other exotica.[5] The hair sample lay in a museum drawer until 2011 when an international team of geneticists mapped it and identified 2,782,401 SNPs, of which 449,115 were considered high-confidence. The age of the sample is important because the man was born before aboriginals mixed with Europeans, and indeed the team found no genetic evidence of European mixture. These results were then compared with other major SNP studies of African, European, and Asian populations in order to help to sort out the details of the human dispersal from Africa. The leading model had once been that all Asians arose from a single migration of modern humans. Now, it has become clear(er) that there were two dispersals, a first one ~62–75 kya that led to Australia ~50 kya and a second one separating East Asians from Europeans ~25–38 kya, after which came the Asian split with Native American ancestors ~15–30 kya.

When the species *Homo sapiens sapiens* left Africa and began to roam the globe in what can be called Globalization 1.0, they were sure to encounter at least two sets of now-extinct cousins, the Neanderthals[6] and the Denisovians, a subspecies of *Homo sapiens*. The Neanderthals left Africa for Eurasia perhaps as long ago as 300 kya. The

Denisovians of West Asia, a newly discovered sister species to the Neanderthal, might have left not long thereafter. We modern humans – ever curious about such things – have long wondered whether our ancestors interbred with other ancient populations. Recent genomic comparisons say they did, with estimates suggesting that the Neanderthal contributed 1–4% to modern Eurasian genomes and the Denisovians 4–6% to modern Oceanic (Melanesian and aboriginal Australian) genomes. These analyses are the results of comparing a particular human leukocyte antigen (HLA) – vital in immune defense and reproduction and therefore critical for human survival – with that found in the Neanderthal and the Denisovian genome with their archaic HLA haplotypes carrying particular alleles. One of these ancient alleles was acquired by humans as they traveled through West Asia, likely around 50 kya. Whatever the impetus for the interbreeding, the result was a good one for humans: there was an advantage for these small migrating groups to mix and mingle with folk whose immune systems were better adapted to local pathogens.

We are now prepared to refine our story of the Austronesians. First, we follow a second dispersal of humans who make their way out of Africa and arrive over the millennia in what is now China. Then we identify a particular group – let's call them the *pre-Proto-Austronesians* – who settle for a time, perhaps to the south of Hangzhou Bay on the East China Sea, not far from modern-day Shanghai. Their culture is Neolithic (New Stone Age). Around 6 kya, all or part of this population sails south to an island now known as Taiwan where they encounter a culture that is Paleolithic (Old Stone Age) and replace it. The period of the development of the language of these people on their homeland of Taiwan would be considered to be Proto-Austronesian. At this point, the comparative philologist draws a line separating this group of Austronesian speakers from other groups in the region. The breakup of this new language family begins around 4 kya when Austronesian speakers begin colonizing the northern Philippines.

The next step is to determine what languages can properly be classed under the family heading Austronesian. Or, rather, it is the case that the heading *Austronesian* is a post-hoc label the philologist attaches to a group of languages whose protolanguage can be reconstructed with confidence. The first branching of Austronesian is between Formosan[7] and Malayo-Polynesian. Formosan languages are spoken in Taiwan and a few surrounding islands, and are presently in the minority in Taiwan where the majority languages are Taiwanese Mandarin and Mandarin. The Malayo-Polynesian languages are all the rest, and these stretch across a geographic range second in vastness only to that of the current range of the Indo-European languages. In the case of the Malayo-Polynesian languages, however, most of the area is covered by water. Malayo-Polynesian languages can be found, on the far western (Malayo-) end, on Madagascar in the Indian Ocean off the east coast of Africa and, on the far eastern (Polynesian) end, on Easter Island in the Pacific Ocean whose nearest continental point is Chile in South America. One of the major languages in this branch is Malay (Bahasa Indonesian), and it is spoken in Malaysia, Indonesia, Singapore, Brunei, and Thailand.

The Polynesians were the first human inhabitants of the far-flung mid-Pacific islands and the most daring deep-sea voyagers and explorers the world has ever known. In double-hulled ships fashioned from stone tools, they settled every habitable island in the vast expanse between Hawaii on the north, New Zealand on the south, Easter Island on the east, and Tonga and Samoa on the west. It is likely they even made it all the way to the coast of Peru. When Spanish sailors first visited the islands in the sixteenth century, they discovered that the Polynesians had the sweet potato. This vegetable is apparently native only to the Western Hemisphere, and it was an important food crop in Peru when the Spanish conquered the Incas. No Native Americans had seagoing ships capable of a voyage to Polynesia. Thus, the sweet potato in Polynesia must have been obtained from Peru, and there is linguistic evidence to that effect: the Peruvians call the plant *kumar*, while the universal Polynesian name is *kumara* (Wexler 1943:35). In exchange, the Polynesians gave the South Americans chickens.

As for the western settlements of the skilled seafaring Austronesians, there is some disagreement whether they spread their language by primarily inhabiting empty spaces or whether they mixed with local populations who absorbed their forms of speech. However, if the Austronesians did encounter local populations in their western settlements of Island Southeast Asia, it is likely that these were Paleolithic, like the indigenous population the Austronesians encountered in Taiwan. As for the branch of the languages of the eastern settlements, sometimes called Oceanic or Polynesian, it is clear: the islands were previously uninhabited, with Samoa and Tonga settled around 1500 BCE, New Zealand around 1200 CE, and Tahiti and the Hawaiian Islands around 500 CE.

What route ancient populations took out of Africa and which populations they absorbed (or did not absorb) along their way is a question to be answered by population genetics. Determining the relationship among the languages these dispersing people spoke is the job of comparative philology. Among nonmigrating traditional peoples and cultures, such as some of those found in southern Africa, a relatively stable degree of coincidence between genetic group and linguistic group is expected.[8] The Austronesians form a middle ground: in the east, there is a coincidence of genetic group and linguistic group because they populated previously uninhabited islands; in the west, there might be less coincidence. For modern mobile populations, the situation is completely different, and the coincidence of the genetic group and the linguistic group is likely to be small. Large numbers of modern speakers of English worldwide, for instance, have little or no direct genetic connection to the West Germanic tribes of the Angles and the Saxons who settled England in the fifth century. Similarly, speakers of Romance languages worldwide need have no genetic connection to the ancestral Celts and Dacians who were in Western Europe before the Roman Empire, just as the Celts and Dacians had little genetic connection to the Romans whose language they adopted.

A Possible Polynesian Reconstruction

We said in the introduction to this chapter that the small set of cognate words for the supreme deity offered a start to reconstructing Proto-Austronesian, beginning with a set of cognates in the Polynesian branch. To remind you what was said in Chapter 3, the reconstructive process starts by establishing sound correspondences, and the

names for this god – Tagaloa, Tangaloa, Tangaroa, Ta'aroa, and Kanaloa – offer four
promising possibilities:

(i) the first syllables have the initial consonant alternations:
   #t ~ #t ~ #t ~ #t ~#k;
(ii) the second syllables have the consonant cluster alternations:
   -g- ~ -ng- ~ -ng- ~ ʔ ~ -n-;
(iii) the third syllables have the consonant alternations:
   -l- ~ -l- ~ -r- ~ -r- ~ -l-; and
(iv) the vowels are stable.

Why would comparative philologists find the alternations in this small set of cognates so promising? The answer is because they apply a version of the uniformitarian
hypothesis to the reconstructive enterprise, which is a way of saying that once philologists have a sense of the types of phonetic processes at work in one or more language
families, they are reassured when they see the same (or similar enough) processes at
work in other data sets. To remind you again what was said in Chapter 3, a typological classification captures similarities among languages regardless of their historical and geographic connection. Typological classifications give linguists information
about the kinds of things speakers do with their languages as they physically disperse,
and their languages develop along different trajectories. Typological information thus
sometimes functions as a plausibility check.

Let us take a look at the Polynesian data set, phonetic segment by phonetic segment:

(i) the initial consonants [t] and [k] belong to a **natural class** of sounds because
   they share the phonetic features [+stop] and [-voice]. They differ only in their
   place of articulation, [t] being [+dental] and [k] being [+velar], so the possibility of their correspondence is easy to imagine;
(ii) it is also easy to reconstruct *-ng- for the second syllable, and then posit that
   Samoan regularly lost the *-n-, and Hawaiian regularly lost the *-g-, while Tahitian turned the cluster into [ʔ] a glottal stop;
(iii) alternations of [l] and [r] are widespread in families of languages that have one
   or the other or both phonemes, and so this alternation raises no eyebrows, for
   example, the French and Spanish cognates for 'purse' *bourse* and *bolsa*, respectively; and
(iv) the stable vowels in word final position can be considered a gift to the philologist.

The tentative reconstruction for the name of the god would thus be something like
*tangaLoa, where the L signals a midpoint between an [l] and an [r] whose resolution
would depend on further information.

As a note of caution, we have said that religion can be a compelling cultural influence, and so it is possible that one or the other of these cultures may have borrowed
the religious beliefs, along with the name for the god, and adapted the pronunciation
into the sound system of their language. So, the next task for comparative philologists is to find as many sets of cognates showing these correspondences as possible.

The question arises: Is there any evidence of regular sound correspondences across the Polynesian languages and the thousands of miles of water? The answer is: Yes.

For instance, in Samoan, Tongan, Māori, Tahitian, and Hawaiian, the cognate set for 'one' confirms the initial consonant [t] ~ [k] correspondence:

tasi ~ taha ~ tahi ~ tahi ~ kahi

The cognate set for 'person' shows that the consonant correspondence is not restricted to initial position but is found throughout the word, as the third syllables demonstrate:

tagata ~ tangata ~ tamata ~ taʔata ~ kanaka

A quick check of a Hawaiian grammar, furthermore, shows that [t] is not in the phonetic inventory of this language. Thus, it is safe to say that all *[t] became [k] in Hawaiian. As for the consonants in the medial syllable of the Māori word *tamata* 'person,' further investigation is needed to account for why there is an -m- instead of the expected -ng-. Furthermore, the cognate set for 'one' shows another consonant alternation, namely -s- ~ -h- ~ -h- ~ -h- ~ -h-, along with some vocalic differences, which set the philologist down a new path of investigation. On the whole, however, with just these few examples, it looks like it is possible to imagine a Polynesian language family. However, in order to confirm the possibility, grammatical similarities also must be found. Upon investigation of the grammars of these languages, a Polynesian language family can be posited, and it furthermore looks possible to draw a line to attach it to a larger Austronesian stock (Map 7.1).

The precise terminology here matters. We are using the term *family* to refer to a group of languages whose clear, historical relatedness has a time-depth of 2500–4000 years. We are using the term *stock* to refer to a group of languages whose (hopefully clear) historical relatedness has a time-depth of 5000–10,000 years. Of further importance is the fact that the techniques of reconstruction do not apply at a time-depth much greater than 10,000 years. To round out our temporal terminology, we use the term *phylum* to refer a group of languages with a possible relationship that dates back 15,000–40,000 years or more. Finally, the term *lineage* is used as a cover term for a language grouping of any age.

Linguistic Reconstructions Revisited

In Chapter 3, we introduced the idea of linguistic reconstruction. We can now boil the whole of the reconstructive enterprise down to one sentence: it is based on one fact, one hypothesis, and one principle. The fact is that massive lexical and grammatical similarities hold among certain groups of languages. The hypothesis is that these similarities must have descended from a common source. The principle is that of the regularity of sound change. Another way of stating this principle is to turn it around and to say that a shared irregularity is the mark of common descent. All Germanic languages share the so-called irregularity of having #f- where Latin and Greek have #p-. Thus, the Germanic languages make their own branch. The PIE word for 'rain' can

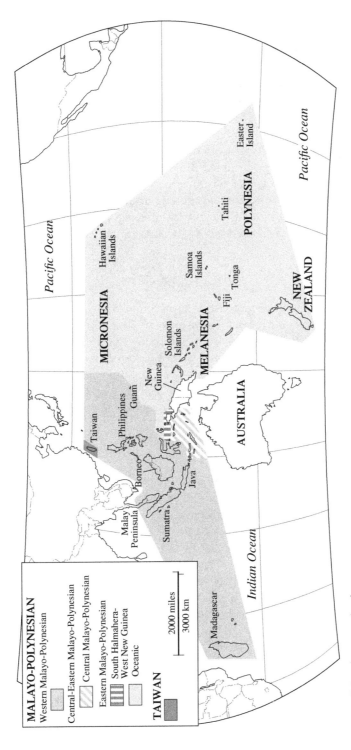

Map 7.1 Austronesian languages.

be reconstructed as *plewō and shows up, for instance, in Latin as *pluor* 'rain.'[9] The Proto-Altaic word for 'rain' can be reconstructed as *agà. The languages that descend from these two protolanguages will share the irregularity of those original forms. The difference between *plewō and *agà is not usually called an irregularity. Rather, the difference is attributed to the arbitrariness of the sign. Since the word for 'rain' could be anything, those languages having a similar phonetic form for this thing/concept are likely to have inherited it, and the languages that share some form of *plewō are therefore likely to be related, just as those that share some form of *agà are likely to be related. Arbitrariness can be called *the original irregularity*. The dramatic difference between *plewō and *agà is one of the multitude of differences that distinguishes the Indo-European languages from the Altaic languages.

The moment the philologist begins the reconstructive effort, however, intriguing problems immediately arise to trouble the fine principle of the regularity of sound change and its inverse of shared irregularity marking common descent. These are described in the following subsections.

Borrowings

Philologists need to know where to look in the vocabularies and structures of the languages in order to begin the reconstructive process. They want highly stable words and constructions presumably inherited from an imagined protolanguage, not words and constructions borrowed through contact with speakers of languages from a different family. Likely categories of stable vocabulary include the names for: family members and relationships, body parts, features of the natural world (sun, moon, sky, etc.), numbers one through 10 at least, and common animals and plants indigenous to the homeland.

Likely categories of stable structural features include:

(i) The sound system and syllable structures: in Chapter 5, we noted that the Greeks needed to turn some of the Phoenician symbols into vowels because Indo-European languages characteristically have syllables with a large number of consonant clusters. They also have midsized phonemic inventories. By way of contrast, Austronesian languages avoid consonant clusters and have relatively small phonemic inventories.

(ii) The pronoun system and what kinds of distinctions are made: singular, dual, plural, etc., as well as the words for the pronouns themselves. Hawaiian, for instance, has we-inclusive *kakou* 'all of us including you' and we-exclusive *makou* 'all of us excluding you,' and this distinction seems to have been a feature of Proto-Austronesian, since it is found throughout the Austronesian-speaking world from Hawaiian in the east to Malagasy in the west and important points in between, including Indonesian and Tagalog.

(iii) Word-formation preferences: Swahili favors agglutinative morphology by prefixing, while Turkish favors agglutinate morphology by suffixing, as mentioned in Chapter 3. A widespread characteristic of Austronesian languages is their use of infixing, which involves inserting a personal pronoun morpheme and/or a tense morpheme into the word itself. Tagalog has borrowed the English word *graduate*. To say the past tense 'I graduated,' the infix *-um-* is inserted near the beginning of the word *grumaduate*.

(iv)   Word-order patterns: many, but not all, Austronesian languages have verb-initial word order. Language stocks and families tend to have preferred word orders, but one of the many structural features that can change over time in a language is dominant word order. Nevertheless, widespread preferences for word order in a family and stock are common. The Dravidian languages, for instance, all tend to be SOV. It is not surprising that Austronesian languages all show a preferred VSO order.

Instabilities in some of these more-or-less stable categories can always be found. Although pronouns are not likely candidates for replacement, speakers of English gave up their West Germanic third person pronouns along with the plural forms for the verb 'to be,' and they borrowed *they, them, their,* and *are* from Old Norse. Numbers can be revealing. When a language has two ways to refer to numbers, this is often a sign of long domination by another language. The English ordinal *second* is not based on the English cardinal *two* but is borrowed from French. The Vietnamese numbers begin: *một, hai, ba, bốn* ... , and the days of the week begin: *thứ hai* meaning 'day two,' namely Monday, and *thứ ba* meaning 'day three,' namely Tuesday. However, the word for Wednesday is *thứ tư* meaning 'day four' (instead of *thứ bốn*), after which the names for the days of the week revert to compounds with the Vietnamese cardinal numbers. Additionally, in Vietnamese the word for an intersection of two streets is *ngã tư*, meaning 'crossroads/corners four.' The word *tư* 'four' is a Chinese borrowing.

Apart from these minor observations, we can say that the *borrowing* patterns we see today are probably those that have existed for all time, and when we eliminate those, we get down to the stable vocabulary. In English, we easily spot borrowings in categories such as food (*sushi, taco, wurst*), clothing (*kimono, serape, dirndl*) and specialized domains such as opera, which gives us Italian words such as *soprano, alto, vibrato*, and so forth, along with the word *opera* itself.

Analogy

The Old English plural of 'cow' was *kine*. The Modern English plural is *cows*. No plausible regular sound change can be invented to account for this change. Only from the reformation of the noun classes during the Middle English period, when the -s# plural that was on 35% of Old English nouns began to generalize, can the change from *kine* to *cows* be explained. The plural *cows* was reformed by analogy to the many other nouns adopting the *-s* plural at that time. Analogy can also be called *pressure of the system*. When children learning English say "she bringed me a cookie," they are forming the past tense by analogy to the many other past tenses they know that form a system. Eventually they adjust to the normative and irregular form *brought*.

The example of *bringed–brought* demonstrates how the principle of shared irregularity as a mark of common descent and the workings of analogy lock into one another. In Modern German, 'to bring' is *bringen*, and the past tense 'I brought' is *ich brachte*. In Modern German, 'to think' is *denken*, and the past tense 'I thought' is *ich dachte*. Despite the fact that English and German have verbs like *ring–rang–rung/ringen–rang–gerungen* and *drink–drank–drunk/trinken–trank–getrunken*, the verbs 'to bring' and 'to think' in both languages share closely related irregular past tenses. They must have inherited these irregularities rather than independently inventing them in just those words. This shared irregularity is thus (one of) the mark(s) of the common descent of English and German as West Germanic languages. At the same time, the philologist has to be on the lookout for forms that speakers have analogized, that is, regularized over time, and be willing to invoke the working of analogy to override the principle of the regularity of sound change. The principle of shared irregularity marking common descent and the working of analogy help the philologist understand the contours of the jigsaw puzzle pieces used to reconstruct the protolanguage.

The reconstructed PIE word for 'daughter-in-law' *snusós* makes an interesting example.[10] The -*ós* is of interest because it is a masculine ending reconstructed for a clearly feminine entity. The reason for the choice of the ending comes from the forms for the attested words in Latin *nurus* and Greek *nuos*, which both have masculine endings. All other Indo-European cognates have a feminine ending. So, Greek and Latin must have inherited the shared irregularity of a feminine entity carrying a masculine ending. All other languages must have analogized the ending to make it conform to other feminine nouns, because there is no sound change that will account for why the other languages changed an -os# to an -a#. This reasoning makes more sense than imagining that Greek and Latin inherited an originally feminine ending and both independently and for no apparent reason decided to give it a masculine ending.

Taboo deformations

Long before there were language academies and language police, societies as a whole placed restrictions on words. Today, the words for certain body parts and body functions tend to come under taboo, as well as do so-called four-letter words. No sound laws will account for the phonetic shape of the nearly endless string of euphemisms in English for words under taboo: *dang, darn, durnit, fooey, fudge, gee, gee whiz, gee willikers, golly, gosh, heck, jeez, sam hill, shoot, shucks,* ... the list is long. The only way to account for how they sound is by how well they deform the word under taboo, thereby diminishing its strength, while still keeping some part of it audible.

The names for things to be feared and respected also need to be altered, so that one does not draw the power and the wrath of the thing named. (Don't take the Lord's name in vain!) Medical researchers may refer to cancer as The Big C. The M-word is uttered at a confirmed bachelor's peril. The L-word has a variety of interpretations. Sometimes, whole words are replaced. In modern Judaism, the word *Adonai* refers to the Lord because the name *Yahweh* is not to be pronounced. Some times, the words are not uttered in the first place. "I'm hoping for a good outcome for my grant application, but I don't want to tell you to which funding agency I submitted it, so as not to jinx it." We don't really and truly believe in the magical power of words (do we?), but sometimes we behave as if we do.

The Germanic, Baltic, and Slavic branches of Indo-European presented philologists with a puzzle concerning the question of whether or not the Proto-Indo-Europeans knew about bears. It seemed that they lived in an area that had bears, and enough IE branches had words for bears that made the reconstruction *arkth- possible for 'bear.' However, the northern tribes – the ones presumably encountering bears fairly regularly – had words for this animal such that no amount of sound correspondences could lead back to *arkth-*. The problem was resolved by appealing to the notion of taboo replacement. Each language found a way to refer to bears without invoking them, and they did this by nicknames. The Germanic peoples called them some form of 'bruins,' that is, a 'brown one,' making *bear* and *brown* cognates. The Baltic people referred to them as a 'shaggy one,' *lācis*, while the Russians called them a 'honey-eater,' *medved*, which is also a Russian family name. The Bear itself is the symbol of Russia.

We have spoken of population genetics and linguistic reconstruction, but thus far we have conjured without the help of cultural anthropology or archeology. Part of the interest of philology is that reconstructed languages give glimpses into the cultural and intellectual conditions of the speakers in a way that the archeological evidence provided by burial mounds or pottery shards cannot. What words can and cannot be reconstructed for a protolanguage reveal much about the local conditions in which the speakers of that language lived, the material culture they possessed, and even some of the abstract and/or religious and political ideas they held. At the same time, cultural information can and at times must be imported into the reconstructive enterprise. Albanian *nu* means 'bride.' It was used to help reconstruct PIE *snusós*, despite its phonetic divergence from the original form, because there is ample evidence that Indo-European culture was highly patriarchal, and a bride would leave her family home and move in with the husband's family, thus becoming at the same time a daughter-in-law. Thus, *nu* is deemed an appropriate cognate. For certain Native American reconstructions, the words for 'hair' and 'feather' might be legitimate cognates.

Philologists bring long-lost human worlds into existence by organizing available facts by means of tested principles and feats of logic. Historical and comparative philology is a sometimes frustrating, often challenging, and always fascinating exercise in ingenious inference.

Some of this ingenuity is mobilized for the purposes of determining the historical homelands of the speakers of the various protolanguages. Archeologists have long worked in tandem with cultural anthropologists and linguists, and more recently with population geneticists to determine the most likely locations for these homelands. It is generally agreed that Formosa/Taiwan was the incubator for Proto-Austronesian. However, in the case of the homeland of the pre-Proto-Austronesians, the possibility of their settlement around Hangzhou Bay before arriving in Formosa/Taiwan is cast in some doubt by the cultural fact that in this area of China, the agricultural staple is rice, while the Formosan's is millet, and the Formosan culture has an agricultural rite the heart of which is millet. On the other hand, a word for 'rice' can be reconstructed for Proto-Austronesian. Lining up what can be imagined for the past with what is known in the present is a tricky business.

Proto-Indo-European and Its Homeland

No homeland has received more attention than that of the Proto-Indo-Europeans. Early philologists based their hypotheses solely on linguistic evidence, in the kinds of flora and fauna that could be reconstructed to belong to the source language as a way to narrow down the geographic range. The Proto-Indo-Europeans knew bears, for instance. They also knew wolves, rabbits, beavers, mice, weasels, deer, geese, ducks, snakes, sheep, goats, pigs, dogs, and horses, among other animals; as for plants, they encountered oak, beech, pine, birch, and willow trees. In addition, the kinds of animals and plants they did not encounter are also significant: no anciently common Indo-European words can be reconstructed for elephant, camel, lion, tiger, monkey, crocodile, rice, bamboo, or palm. Because there are common words for snow and freezing cold, more or less widely spread over the Indo-European territory, the conclusion is that the homeland had to be in a place that was fairly cold.

An early group of philologists put special consideration on two words, in particular: *bee* and *beech*. The ability to reconstruct a PIE word for 'bee' is of interest because the honeybee is native to Europe but not to the locations in Asia ever considered as possible PIE homelands; and the honeybee is relevant because PIE also has a reconstructed word for 'honey.' The beech tree was at one time considered a particularly promising way to pinpoint the homeland because the range of the common beech is relatively limited: it is more or less confined to central Europe and is not native east of Poland and the Ukraine. Unfortunately, no one can be sure the PIE word that developed in various IE languages and came into English as *beech* referred to the tree we know as the beech tree. The word and the thing correspond in Latin and the Germanic languages. However, the word means 'oak' in Greek, and in other languages it came to designate 'elder' and 'elm.' There is the further problem of determining whether the current native range of the beech tree is the same as its range 6 kya.

The point here is that the lexical testimony for the homeland is obviously important, but it also leaves wriggle room. In addition, evidence from two now-extinct branches of the Indo-European stock, Hittite and Tocharian, can and should come into play, even if there are not enough records of them to weigh in on the bee/beech issue. The Hittites had an empire about 1600 years ago on the Anatolian plateau of what is present-day Turkey. The Tocharians lived around 2000 years ago in Xinjiang, the northernmost and westernmost province of China. Clearly, these two branches expand the scope of the geographic search.

At present, there are at least seven competing hypotheses for the PIE homeland, among which we will consider only three:

Kurgan theory

The first is archeologically based, and it is the Kurgan theory. It was first proposed in the 1970s by Lithuanian-American archeologist Marjia Gimbutas, who placed the PIE homeland in the Russian steppes, perhaps present-day Ukraine, north and a bit east of the Black Sea, around the fifth millennium BCE. The name *kurgan* comes from a Turkic loanword in Russian for the type of burial mounds that are found at archeological sites in the region. The story here revolves around the reconstructed words for 'horse,' 'wheel,' and 'axle,' and the question of whether or not the Indo-Europeans had domesticated the horse and had wheeled conveyances; and these technological innovations are seen as the cause of the Indo-European expansion. In a further effort to harmonize our terminology with our time-depths, we reserve the term *expansion* to refer to the movements of proto-speakers away from a homeland, that is, movements that have taken place in near prehistory. In the older version of the PIE expansion, the Proto-Indo-Europeans were represented as proud horsemen, noble warriors absorbing or eliminating the pastoralists/peasants they encountered as they moved into new territories. Gimbutas reinterpreted this earlier representation in a more violent light and argued that these later PIE warrior-like Indo-Europeans replaced an earlier more peaceful, female-centered society.

Anatolian steppes

The second hypothesized site for the PIE homeland is the Anatolian steppes of present-day Turkey around the seventh millennium BCE. The Anatolian hypothesis was first promoted by British archeologist Colin Renfrew, and it is based on a larger hypothesis that in the past 10,000 years, most of the language families that now exist derive from populations who developed or acquired systematic forms of food production. When these populations took up agriculture and/or animal husbandry, they dispersed and displaced the hunter-gatherers into whose territories the farmers expanded. Population densities of farmers are 10–100 times higher than those of hunter-gatherers, within the same environment. This is because farmers, with their livestock, grains, vegetables, and orchards, have much more food available to them. Hunter-gatherers, in contrast, have to spread out over large areas to hunt the game and to find the edible wild plants.[11]

Major agricultural-origin regions include China, Mesoamerica, sub-Saharan Africa, as well as Southeast Asia, and these regions are hypothesized to be the homelands of many of the major language stocks of today, as we will see below. The Middle East is also such a region, and so a population moving from there into the Anatolian plains is not difficult to imagine. The acquisition of agricultural practices not only supported larger populations than those of the hunter-gatherers[12] but also prompted language dispersal. Thus, archeologist Peter Bellwood believes that Indo-European languages spread not by language shift on the part of populations the Indo-Europeans encountered – in his opinion, not necessarily sedentary hunter-gatherers – but by the movement of a significant number of Indo-European speakers themselves (2001:33).

East of the Caspian Sea

The third candidate for the PIE homeland is farther east, in fact east of the Caspian Sea, specifically in the vicinity of Bactria-Sogdiana, which is around the present-day Tajikistan–Uzbekistan border. The homeland is proposed at a time-depth of 6–7 kya. This is Johanna Nichols's position (Nichols 1999). She has long maintained that while many historical linguists assume that Indo-European is a normative language family, it is in fact the odd man out. For one thing, the usual amount of branches language families around the world show at this time-depth is up to three; Indo-European has a dozen or more. In addition, PIE shows a typological diversity that, say, the Austronesian, Turkic, and Mongolic families do not. Third, even before PIE broke up, an internal phonetic division can be identified, and it split along geographic lines.[13] From what is known from archeological and textual evidence of a mythology and a poetic tradition, along with what can be reconstructed socially, culturally, archeologically, linguistically, and even ecologically, only a very particular homeland could produce a language stock with such unique characteristics.

Nichols identifies Bactria-Sogdiana as the most likely epicenter from which the Indo-Europeans spread, since this location puts them at the frontier of Near Eastern civilization and gives them access to the Eurasian steppe across which they would eventually fan out. This particular locus reconciles the conflicting lexical evidence about the PIE homeland, which suggests both urbanized and nomadic practices as well as knowledge of both dry grasslands and forests. As opposed to Gimbutas, Nichols sees the Proto-Indo-Europeans on the move not as warriors but rather as nomadic pastoralists and herders who introduced their language to the nonmoving populations they encountered in their expansion and induced language shift in those populations.

We, the authors, have not brought forth the arguments of these three accounts in order to decide among them. Rather, we mention them to point out that even for an extremely well-studied language stock, not all researchers agree about how the available evidence for the homeland lines up or even about what the available evidence is or should be. We also note that population genetics, once again, may eventually help decide the issue. Already in the 1970s, there were genetic clues that the first farmers living in Europe had links to ancient farming cultures in the Near East. More recently, several large-scale studies of bones show that:

(i)   only 30% of modern Europeans show genetic linkages to the earliest farmers coming into Europe about 8500 years ago;
(ii) hunter-gatherers and farmers lived side by side for a very long time in Europe;
(iii) groups moved around quite a bit; that is, it is not the case that when a group settled in a particular place in Europe 8, 6, or even 4 kya, they necessarily stayed there;
(iv) the Neolithic transition from Paleolithic hunting and gathering to farming was prolonged and nonlinear, with successive waves of farmers coming into Europe who learned to coexist with the populations already there (Balter 2013a, 2013b, Brandt et al. 2013).

Our tentative conclusion is that the very first farmers entering Europe from the Anatolian plain were not speaking a language from the Indo-European stock.

Other Language Stocks and Their Homelands

With the exception of the Aboriginal Australians and perhaps the Melanesians of Papua New Guinea and the Khoisan of southwest Africa, the settlements of the homelands of the various established families have occurred in relatively recent times, namely within the last 10,000 years or so. These settlements coincide with the shift from the Old Stone Age to the New Stone Age, along with the introduction of agriculture and metalworking. In terms of geological epochs, these settlements occurred during the shift from the Pleistocene, which extends back 2,588,000 years and covers the period of the earth's glaciations, to the Holocene, which began 11,700 years ago at the end of the last Ice Age and is associated with warmer periods.[14]

As we have just seen, the identification of the homeland for a well-studied stock such as Indo-European is far from settled. Quite a number of other issues in historical linguistics also remain unsettled, beginning with the terminology. Historical linguist Lyle Campbell distinguishes between the terms *family* and *stock* on the basis of evidence. For Campbell (1998:187), a family is a grouping whose evidence of relationship is strong, while a stock is a grouping whose evidence of relationship is weak. Indeed, Campbell even cautions against using terms such as *stock, phylum,* and *macrofamily* because they cause confusion. However, in Chapter 3, we introduced Johanna Nichols's definitions, which are based not on evidence but on time. For her, a family has a time-depth of 2500–4000 years and a stock a time-depth of 5000–10,000 years, while a phylum refers to a group of languages that may have more or less evidence of being related at a time-depth greater than 10,000 years. We continue to follow Nichols's usages here.

Going beyond Indo-European, we offer a historical and geographic overview for the rest of the stocks (with representative families and/or languages noted in parentheses) in the following subsections.

Sub-Saharan Africa

Khoisan (Khoi, San)   The San may have been one of the first populations to differentiate from the East Africans who eventually peopled the world, given that the San Y-haplogroup suggests a separation at least 60 kya. Instead of migrating north and east as did the East Africans, the ancestors of the Khoisan migrated south. Because the time-depth puts us well out of the range of 10,000 years that we are saying is the norm to confidently propose a stock, Khoisan may be only a convenient geographical cover term.

Niger–Congo (Bantu; well-known Bantu languages include Swahili and Zulu)   The homeland is in West Africa. Although the Sahara Desert is now one of the driest places on earth, between 11 and 5 kya it was a green region containing savannah grasslands and humid tropical forests. The increasingly arid conditions began in the west 5 kya. A Bantu expansion began, propelled by agricultural practices, about 3 kya in modern Cameroon and eastern Nigeria such that now the lower half of Africa is dominated by speakers from this branch, called Niger–Congo B. Western sub-Saharan Africa is peopled by speakers of Niger–Congo A, such as Wolof, spoken primarily in Senegal, and Yoruba, spoken throughout West Africa. These languages are known for vowel harmony, tone systems of three or more levels, vowel nasalization, SOV word order, and a comparative using 'exceed' as the comparative marker.

Nilo-Saharan (Chadic)   The eastern Sudan is the hypothesized homeland for Nilo-Saharan probably 8 kya. Languages in this stock are dotted all over Eastern, Central, and West Africa, lacing among Afro-Asiatic languages to the north and Niger–Congo languages to the south. The structural features of the languages are variable. Some are tone languages, and some not. Most have SVO word order, but there are those with SOV as well as some with VSO order. Their speakers are equally mixed in lifestyle, with some seminomadic pastoralists and others who are agriculturalists. The ethnogroup known as Fur were thrust onto the world stage in 2003, when they were caught in the midst of a geopolitical conflict known as the War in Darfur, which will be discussed in Chapter 9.

Europe

Europe was home to human habitation well before the Indo-Europeans arrived beginning about 4 kya. We know this from the cave paintings in France and Spain, some of which date back to 30 and 40 kya, and from the peat bogs in Northern Europe, whose excavations show that people lived there as long ago as 10 kya. Two language isolates in Europe, Basque, and now-extinct Etruscan, are a puzzle. Not enough is known about Etruscan, which was spoken on the Italian peninsula before the arrival of the Indo-Europeans, to speculate about its origins. Basque is well studied, known for ergativity, and clearly unrelated to Indo-European. However, it is not known whether Basque is a continuation of one of the ancient populations in Europe or is a more recent arrival.

Uralic (Estonian, Finnish, Hungarian, Saami)   As for the present, in addition to Indo-European languages in Europe are found Uralic languages, also sometimes called Finno-Ugric. Their homeland is probably just north of the eastern Eurasian steppe. The story of how Hungarian came to be separated geographically from its sister languages will be told in Chapter 8. These languages all have vowel harmony and agglutinative morphology, lack grammatical gender, and are remarkable for their varying numbers of cases, with certain varieties of one of the languages, Komi, having nearly 30. Finnish and Hungarian have 15 and 21, respectively, depending on how one counts. These case endings correspond to how English uses prepositions. For example, in Finnish, the inessive case (*-ssa*) is used to express situation in time or place *Suome-ssa* 'In Finland,' the allative case (*-lle*) expresses direction or beneficiary of an action *Pane-n kirja-n pöyda-lle* 'I will put the book on the table,' the illative case (*-on*) expresses movement into something *Mene-n talo-on* 'I am going into the house,' while the translative case (*-ksi*) indicates a noun having undergone a change of state *Lumi muttu-I vede-ksi* 'The snow turned into water.'

Caucasus

Caucasian (Georgian, Chechen)   Caucasian has the oldest reconstructable protolanguage with a time-depth of 8000 years. The Caucasus Mountains are considered to be the homeland of this family. This area is what Johanna Nichols calls a *residual zone*, an area difficult for outsiders to enter and conquer, meaning that the indigenous languages there can survive and differentiate over long periods of time, often with unusual trajectories. The Georgian consonantal system, for instance, is notoriously difficult for nonnative speakers to acquire. It includes ejectives, which are voiceless consonants that include a simultaneous glottal closure. Thus, the voiceless aspirated stop [pʰ] contrasts with the voiceless ejective stop [p']. The Caucasus has also been a region of recent conflict rooted in issues of language, as we will see in Chapter 9.

North Africa, the Mideast, and Central Asia

Afro-Asiatic (Arabic, Hebrew, and Berber)   Proto-Afro-Asiatic is likely 10,000 years old. Two proposals have existed for the original homeland, one in the Middle East and the other in northeast Africa, generally the Horn of Africa. The matter has been decided in favor of Africa and is given credence by also being the place of origin of a Y-haplogroup that spread through the region. Thus, it seems that the northeastern part of the grassland that is now the Sahara Desert was the central homeland, with an eastward advance of the Semitic group into the Near East and the westward expansion of the Berber and Chadic groups. Another western expansion moved out from the center and met up with the western Niger–Congo languages, and this incursion prompted an eastward and southern expansion of the Bantu family. Because of the drying conditions in the Saharan region, Neolithic Afro-Asiatic farmers moved into river valleys and developed irrigation systems.

The people occupying the Nile developed the great Egyptian civilization. The most salient feature of the Semitic branch of the Afro-Asiatic languages is its word morphology based on the trilateral root, as mentioned in Chapter 5. The canonical example involved the root k-t-b 'to write.' By means of internal vowel alternations, the following words can be generated:

aktub	'I write'
katabtu	'I wrote'
kataba	'he wrote'
katabat	'she wrote'
kitāb	'book'
maktub	'office, desk'
maktabat	'library, bookstore'

and so forth, nearly endlessly. Note that here the prefix *ma-* means 'place (where some activity involving writing happens).'

Mongolic (Mongolian), Turkic (Turkish), Tungusic (Manchu)   The Mongolic, Turkic, and Tungusic stocks all seem to have originated in Central Asia. Because these three groups of languages share striking similarities in syntactic structure and the pronoun system, they were originally considered to be in one stock, but now a possible phylum named Altaic is proposed for them. The Altai Mountains are in the western and southwestern part of Mongolia where Russia, China, and Kazakhstan all come together, and they are so named from the Mongolian word *alt* 'gold' because of the gold deposits there.

This phylum has inspired endless debates over whether Japanese and/or Korean belong to it. In any case, the proto-speakers of Turkic, for example, being nomadic pastoralists, moved south and as far west as Turkey, along the route established as the Silk Road several thousand years later. In other words, modern-day Turkey, despite its name, is not the homeland of the Turkic stock and was originally occupied by the Indo-European Hittites. Their structural features include: case systems, little head marking, accusative alignment, simple syllable structure, front rounded vowels, no genders, simple prosodic structure (no tones, fixed stress), agglutinative morphology, and very regular verbal word formation (Nichols 2011:188).

South Asia

Dravidian (Kannad'a, Malayālam, Telugu, Tamil)   The proposed homeland for this stock is the Indus Valley in the northwest region of the Indian subcontinent, and the Harappan language and civilization identified with this region may or may not be Proto-Dravidian. This stock is another whose languages spread with the expansion of agricultural societies moving into areas occupied by hunter-gatherers. Dravidian languages are currently found now only in the southern portion of India, and the usual explanation is that speakers of Dravidian languages formerly occupied a wider area but were pushed to the south and east by the Indo-Europeans. Dravidian languages are well known for having retroflex consonants, where the tongue curves or curls itself on a point between the alveolar ridge and the hard palate. These became an areal feature of the South Asia and have been borrowed into languages of the Indic branch of the Indo-European stock.

Southeast Asia

The language stock/family map becomes particularly colorful, which is to say complicated, in this part of the world, perhaps because the land is so fertile and because there was a lot of movement and thus mixing of peoples, cultures, and languages over long periods of time. The controversial stock/phylum Austric is far from settled, and if clearer evidence for it could be found, it might include three major divisions: Austronesian, Austroasiatic, and Tai. As for the more settled categories, we have already addressed Austronesian.

Austroasiatic (Vietnamese)   The homeland for these languages seems to be the Mekong River at the place where modern-day Cambodia, Thailand, and Laos intersect. The family may well be only about 2000 years old.

Tai (Thai, Lao)   Languages in this family are distributed throughout southern China and across Southeast Asia. The family name is fraught and has been known as Tai-Kadai and as Daic; its status as an independent language family is unclear and has been linked both to the Sino-Tibetan languages and to the Austronesian. One likely homeland of this family is the present-day Guizhou province of southern China. One proposal is that proto-Daic speakers migrated back to the mainland from Formosa/Taiwan at the beginning of the Austronesian breakup. This language family, like Austroasiatic, appears to be rather recent.

Indian and Pacific Oceans

Indo-Pacific (Moni, Kutubu, Peremka)   In addition to Austronesian, already discussed, Indo-Pacific languages are found in Papua New Guinea, Melanesia, and perhaps Tasmania. Indo-Pacific may well be an areal classification, because constructing a protolanguage for these languages has proven difficult. On the other hand, population genetics now suggests that the reason for this difficulty might be that the language family is ancient and goes back perhaps as far as 40 kya. New Guinea, with its rugged terrain, counts as a residual zone, like the Caucasus Mountains. There are easily 1000 unique languages spoken in an area somewhat larger than the state of Texas.

Australia

Aboriginal Australian (Guugu Yimithirr) Today's Aboriginal Australians are descendants of the earliest humans to occupy Australia and likely represent one of the oldest continuous populations outside Africa with a time-depth of 50 kya. Because of the time-depth, there is no way to know whether all of today's 250 aboriginal languages[15] descended from one protolanguage or whether the migrating humans who settled Australia spoke languages from different families. Once again, there is much complexity and controversy surrounding how to sort out the relationships among the Australian languages. There has been so much contact between and among the languages that many shared/similar features might not have been inherited from a protolanguage but rather have diffused through them. Furthermore, it is not necessarily the case that there was only one group to move into Australia; and it is highly likely that there were repeated movements from the west and the north before sea levels began to rise some 16 kya, isolating the continent. Multiple groups moving in and mixing in complicates an already-complicated picture.

For the sake of convenience, one specialist in these languages, R.M.W. Dixon, has organized the languages into 50 groups, only some of which qualify as being low-level genetic subgroups. There is no prehistoric time of breakup as such, if one considers the continent of Australia as a homeland, which, before the arrival of the Europeans in 1788, was occupied solely by the aboriginals.

East Asia

Sino-Tibetan (Cantonese, Fujian, Mandarin, Taiwanese, Tibetan) Sino-Tibetan is one of the most important language stocks, given that it has the most speakers in the world today. The early Sino-Tibetans were a Neolithic people who lived in the central plains of what is now northern China, in the valley of the Yellow River. The time of their breakup is dated at about 6.5 kya, and the expansion was to the west and the south, with the southern movement also heading east. Those who stayed in the central plains or moved south and east became the group that has come to be known as Chinese, while those moving south and west have become known as the Tibeto-Burmans. Although there is archeological evidence dating back seven millennia, given the diversity of the modern varieties, the reconstruction of Proto-Chinese cannot date farther back than about the first millennium BCE. Proto-Sino-Tibetan was SOV. Tibeto-Burman languages have agglutinative morphology and a preference for postpostional inflectional morphology, and these features may also have been true of Proto-Sino-Tibetan. Modern varieties of Chinese, however, have little inflectional morphology and do not mark nouns for case or gender; they prefer compounding and derivational morphology.

Hmong-Mien (Hmong, Iu Mien)   Philologists now recognize the language stock known as Hmong-Mien, aka Miao-Yao, which includes languages spoken in central southern China. These languages used to be classed as Sino-Tibetan but are now understood to make a separate language family.

Paleo-Siberian   Paleo-Siberian is a term of convenience to refer to a collection of language isolates. Efforts have been made to sort out the geographic situation by identifying the family Yeniseian (Ket) whose homeland is likely the Yenisei River in central Siberia and which may not be more than 2000 years old. Chukotko-Kamchatkam (Chukchi) is another family identified as belonging to this region. Among the many other languages to be found here are Yukaghir and some varieties of Eskimo-Aleut.

North and South America

There is no homeland as such that can be posited for speakers of Native American languages. In the 1960s, philologist Joseph Greenberg proposed three waves of human movement across the Behring Straights that produced three linguistic divisions: (i) the first around 30 kya, which forms the group of General Indian and encompasses most of the languages found on the two continents; (ii) a second around 15 kya, which brought a much narrower linguistic group/stock called Na-Dené that includes the language family Athabaskan (Apache, Navajo) – Athabaskan languages are spoken in Alaska and British Columbia, and the southwestern United States; and (iii) a more recent migration, perhaps around 6 kya, to present-day Canada, bringing languages that come under the heading of the stock Eskimo-Aleut (Inuit). These are spoken from Siberia to Greenland. With the American Indian languages, as is the case for the Aboriginal Australian, Indo-Pacific, and Khoisan languages, we are out of reach of what the reconstructive method can tell us about more precise relationships among many of the Native American languages.

Nevertheless, biologists reached similar conclusions about the peopling of the Americas. Before the advent of DNA sequencing, blood typing was used to identify human groups, and it was noted early on that for indigenous populations of Central and South America, Blood Type O was found 100% of the time and nearly 100% of the time for indigenous populations within the United States. The blood-type picture changed for indigenous populations in Canada. DNA studies have reinforced the idea that the first populations to move into the New World formed a distinct group and remained in isolation because they belonged to a single Y-haplogroup, while the Na-Dené and Eskimo-Aleut belonged to a different Y-haplogroup.

Despite these coincidences with biology, Greenberg's three large groups are not universally accepted. That is to say that the subject of the historical relationships among the Native American languages is very complex indeed. Difficulties immediately arise in how to break down these three large groups into language stocks. Some of the stocks of the General Indian (if one accepts such a grouping) are relatively well defined, for instance Algonquin (Delaware, Massachusetts, Menomini) once spoken across much of the eastern seaboard of the United States and across the Mid West, and Iroquois (Wyandot, Seneca, Oneida, Cherokee) once spoken in what is Upstate New York, Quebec, and Western North Carolina and, after the Trail of Tears of the 1830s, now in Oklahoma. Another established language stock is Uto-Aztecan (Nahuatl) found in the western United States and Mexico. Proto-Uto-Aztecan dates to around 5600 years ago and seems to be a family that spread after the domestication of maize ~5 kya. However, not all the native languages identified in North America can be assigned to a clear family or stock.

The language map of South America is even more complex than the language situation in both North America and Southeast Asia. The Amazon Basin alone contains about 300 divided into 12 language stocks and some language isolates. The major language families are: Arawak, Tupí, Carib, Pano, Tucano, and Jê. The languages of this region are not easy to categorize. One specialist in these languages, Alexandra Aikenvald, has likened the Amazon to a set of Chinese boxes of linguistic areas and subareas, included within each other. For convenience, we treat the Native American languages as an areal grouping.

Models of Spread

When we began our discussion of philology and Indo-European in Chapter 3, we tried to make things as clear-cut as possible. However, the further one goes into the relationships among the branches of any language family and the further one goes back in time, the less clear-cut everything becomes. This might also be called the fun of being a philologist. The brief discussion of the Native American languages begins with the identification of the grouping General Indian, which could be called a phylum or even a macrophylum, a term we are using for a classification that has a time-depth of 15–40 kya or more.[16] Whatever the precise time-depth, they are large-scale classifications whose subgroupings do not form clear branches and subbranches. Phyla and macrophyla are hypotheses about how humans who were moving around during the period of Globalization 1.0 interacted with one another before settling down in the aforementioned fairly well-agreed-upon language stocks. The phyla and macrophyla are based on assumptions about the ways groups of people interact when they migrate and the linguistic results of those interactions. These assumptions about movement patterns and language change form the way the relationships among the languages are represented. There have been two major ways these relationships have been imagined and then represented: by means of trees and by means of waves.

Tree

The usual representation of the relationships among languages in a language family is the tree model (Figure 7.2), one of splitting and branching, as a continuous and ongoing differentiation. We have been, more or less, assuming this model in our discussion of both linguistic and population separations. Nineteenth-century philologists understood that the tree model is good for representing the splitting process that results in linguistic differentiation, say, when the Germanic tribes left the PIE homeland and began to travel west and north. A catalogue of features particular to Germanic can be made, for instance: (i) phonetic effects of Grimm's Law; (ii) a third of its vocabulary being of non-PIE origin; (iii) a unique system of strong verbs (*sing-sang-sung*)

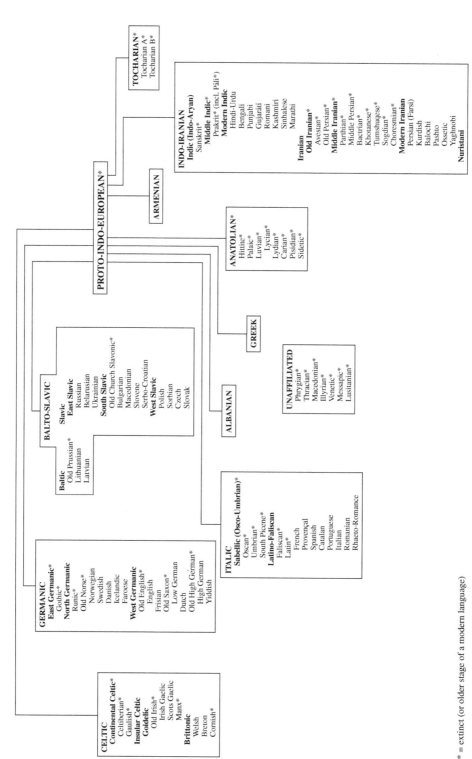

* = extinct (or older stage of a modern language)

Figure 7.2 Tree model image.

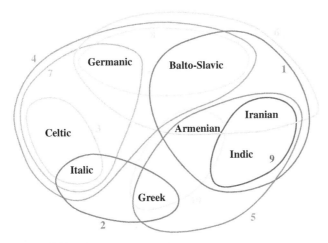

Figure 7.3 Wave model image.

and weak verbs (*walk-walked*). Incidentally, the image of the tree is the only image Darwin included in his *Origin of the Species*, and it has consolidated itself linguistically when we speak of our individual or collective *family tree*. The tree's venerability, however, is no reason to limit ourselves to it.

Wave

Nineteenth-century philologists knew that the tree model fails to represent linguistic changes that spread, like waves (Figure 7.3), over a speech-area, and various changes may extend over different parts of an area that do not coincide with the parts covered by earlier changes. Germanic and Italic, for instance, share the feature of using the perfect tense as a general past tense, while Germanic and Balto-Slavic coincide in a nasal bilabial case ending -m from *bh, a PIE voiced aspirated bilabial stop. Celtic and Italic share passive voice endings with -r#, while Greek, Armenian, and Indo-Iranian prefix #e- for past tenses. Greek and Latin have feminine nouns with masculine suffixes, that is, quite a few more than the word for 'daughter-in-law,' and so on. The tree model cannot capture these historical relationships.

The choice between the tree and the wave may well come down to aesthetic preference, whether one prefers straight lines or wavy lines, and to cognitive style, whether one is a lumper or a splitter. Of course, neither aesthetics nor style can trump careful analysis of evidence. And to repeat, the methods of linguistic reconstruction work only up to a time-depth of 10 kya. Beyond that, no graphic model is appropriate, and only statistical analyses of certain structural features can provide any possibility of linguistic relatedness, as we will see in Chapter 10.

The most important take-away from this chapter about the effects of movement is this: when a group of people who once lived together for a long period of time begins to disperse, and the people migrate away from one another, the long-term linguistic result is *isolation*. Because languages are permeable systems responsive to the ever-changing conditions of their speakers, the physical divergence of a group of people will also produce a linguistic divergence in their ways of speaking. The effects of dispersal from a homeland are apparent in new and distinct daughter languages, separated by time and space and mutual intelligibility.

Lost Tracks

As we have just seen, most of the world's languages can be grouped into families. There are, however, languages with no known historical relationship to a family, and these are called *isolates*. Korean and Japanese are sometimes classed in the phylum Altaic. However, although Korean does have similarities with other languages in the Altaic family, there is no definitive evidence whether those similarities were inherited from the protolanguage or were acquired by contact. Japanese also has similarities with Altaic languages, but it shares features with other languages in the region as well. Clearly, both of these languages are well known and well studied, but having large numbers of speakers and well-developed histories and literatures does not guarantee a language family classification.[17]

More often, a language is classed as an isolate because not enough is known about it either linguistically or historically. For instance, the Etruscan language was spoken in Italy before the Roman Empire flourished. The Etruscans handed down to the Romans the alphabet they had borrowed from the Greeks and adapted to their own use. Thousands of Etruscan inscriptions have survived. However, not enough have been deciphered to know what kind of language Etruscan was. The transcriptions petered out in the third century BCE. Another isolate is Sumerian, the oldest-known language to be preserved in written form. While its copious records written in cuneiform dating to 3300 BCE have been deciphered, there is still no way to connect it to a definite family, although Altaic and Dravidian have been suggested. Sumerian was spoken in Mesopotamia before it was replaced by Akkadian, a Semitic language in the Afro-Asiatic stock.

Two language isolates are found on the Iberian peninsula. The first is Iberian, which was spoken in southern and eastern Spain in pre-Roman times. The inscriptions that have been discovered in that language have not been successfully interpreted. However, the language was written in an alphabet with distinct Greek and Phoenician influences. The other isolate, Basque, is still spoken today in northern Spain and southwestern France, and because this language is a living isolate in Europe, it has been the subject of intense interest. One unresolved question is whether Basque is related to Iberian. An early suggestion was that Basque had similarities to languages spoken in the Caucasus. The fact that the Greeks used the term *Iberes* to refer to the people of the Caucasus gave rise to the idea that they were connected with the *Iberi* of Spain. There are linguistic features as well to tie the two, such as ergativity, which is found in both Basque and Georgian, but no lexical similarities can be found.

To try to understand to whom the Basques might be related, we turn to population genetics, and the work of Luigi Cavalli-Sforza who has mapped out the frequencies of various alleles of many genes to determine the related among populations. Because the Basques have practiced endogamy (marrying within the group) for a very long time, Cavalli-Sforza (2000:112, 121) and his team have been able to propose that the Basques are likely descended from Paleolithic and then Mesolithic people living in Europe before the arrival of Neolithic people. During the Paleolithic period, the Basques likely occupied the areas where the cave paintings have been found. These were the first, preagricultural Europeans; they were the first people to occupy present-day France 40–35 kya and probably migrated there from the southwest, although it is possible they came from the east, as well.[18] As a point of information, the Basques call their language *Euskera*.

Final Note: On Density and Diversity

We spent half of this chapter outlining the linguistic effects of humans on the move, either to hunt the game or to find fields to plant the wheat, rice, millet, or corn. We pause now to consider the reasons why humans choose not to move, why they stay where they are when they find a place they like. The fact of the matter is that languages are distributed unevenly around the world, with about half the languages of the world occupying one tenth of the world's area, namely, the area around the equator. The farther from the equator you go, the fewer languages you find and the greater the area in which each of these languages is spoken. We humans can get restless, but at the same time, we also value the principle of the least effort. If you live near the equator, you likely live in a place where you can easily meet all your subsistence needs within a small geographic area, and you are likely to be more self-sufficient and sedentary than your cousins who live in the Arctic.

Language diversity also decreases in inverse proportion to the size of the political unit encompassing a given geographical area. The landmasses of large states such as Russia, China, and the United States today are relatively less diverse linguistically than, say, the island of New Guinea, and North America is surely less linguistically diverse today than it was 500 years ago. Brazil, which is also a large state, has more diversity, since a significant portion of the country is in the tropics and includes a large part of the Amazon Basin. What we do not know is how much linguistic diversity was lost when most human populations shifted from hunting and gathering to cultivation and animal husbandry. Before the populations representing the major language families of today often expanded into areas already inhabited, there was possibly more language diversity, with more and smaller bands of hunter-gatherers speaking different languages than those that survived the expansions.

In terms of the present day, the area around the equator not only has the highest density of language diversity but also has the highest density of endangered languages. We take up the topic of the future of endangered languages in Chapter 12. In the next chapter, we turn to the topic of the conditions leading to the fact that many languages are endangered: colonization.

Language Profile: 'Olelo Hawai'i [Hawaiian (Austronesian)]

Functional overview

Hawaiian belongs to the Polynesian branch of the Austronesian languages. It was historically spoken over the hundreds of islands spread across 1500 miles, the eight largest being: Hawai'i (referred to as *The Big Island* to differentiate it from the name of the state), Kaho'olawe, Kaua'i, Lāna'i, Maui, Moloka'i, Ni'ihau, and O'ahu. These islands have been inhabited for about 3000 years. The first documented European visit was in 1778. Several decades later, namely in 1810, King Kamehameha I united the islands for the first time. Beginning in 1820, American Protestant missionaries came to Hawai'i. By 1826, they had created an alphabet for Hawaiian, and in 1839, King Kamehameha III presided over the creation of a constitution written in Hawaiian. During the nineteenth century, Hawai'i was a self-governing constitutional monarchy. In 1959, it became the fiftieth state of the United States. Hawaiian and English are the official languages.

As a result of the long contact between Hawaiians and mainland Americans and the eventual statehood of Hawai'i, common Hawaiian words such as *aloha* 'hello,' 'good-bye,' 'love,' *hula* 'dance accompanied by chant or song,' *lanai* 'porch, veranda,' *lei* 'necklace of flowers,' *luau* 'outdoor feast,' and *ukulele* 'Hawaiian guitar' have entered American English. Because of the popularity of the ancient Hawaiian sport of surfing, other words have entered American English, notably *kahuna* 'magician, sorcerer' and, by extension, any expert then specifically the leader of a group of surfers, The Big Kahuna, as well as *wahine* 'woman (in general)' and, by extension, 'female surfer.' Similarly in the local varieties of English spoken in Hawai'i, Hawaiian phrases are common. One such phrase is *p'au hana* 'it (work) is finished.' Another in widespread use is *mahalo* 'thank you.'

The Hawaiian language is not to be confused with Hawaiian Creole English, which arose at the end of the nineteenth century as a result of diverse speaking populations from the Pacific coming to work on Hawaiian pineapple plantations.

Prominent structural characteristics

Phonemic inventory Hawaiian is striking for its relatively small phonemic inventory. With eight consonants and five vowels that contrast for length, the entire inventory of 18 phonemes falls just below the threshold of 20–50 that is a worldwide norm for phonemic inventories. The consonants are: [p, k, ʔ, h, l, m, n, v/w]. The *'okina* [ʔ] 'glottal stop' (literally 'break') is represented in writing as ', and it is found in the traditional way to write the name of the state, Hawai'i [havaiʔi].[19] We saw at the beginning of Chapter 7 that another Polynesian language, Tahitian, has a glottal stop where the other languages have a medial -ng-, -g-, or -n-. So, a tendency for consonants to become glottal stops is not unusual in the Polynesian family. In Hawaiian, it is the case that the glottal stop tends to correspond to [k] in related languages. In Tuamotu, the word *tiki* 'image' is cognate with Hawaiian *ki'i*. We noted in Chapter 7 that *[t] became [k] in Hawaiian.

The glottal stop [ʔ] is phonemic in Hawaiian, as can be illustrated by the following minimal pairs:

ala 'road, awake'	*'ala* 'fragrant'
kai 'ocean'	*ka'i* 'to lead'
kiki 'to sting'	*ki'i* 'picture'

The only other consonant that merits discussion is [w], which varies geographically. On The Big Island, the variant [v] is heard, exemplified by the name of the state, noted above. On the islands of Kaua'i and Ni'ihau, the variant [w] is heard. There is also some evidence to suggest that [w]/[v] are allophones, with [v] appearing after unround vowels, for example, *iwa* 'nine' pronounced *iva*, and [w] appearing after round vowels, for example, *'auwa'i* 'ditch' pronounced as spelled.

The consonant [k] is the most common one in the language. When it comes to rendering English words in Hawaiian, [k] is often used and can substitute for 10 English consonants. For instance, the native *kika* means 'slippery.' It can, however, also be used for 'sister,' 'cider,' and 'tiger,' which might be alternatively spelled *tita*, *sida*, and *tiga*, respectively, although there is no [t], [s], [d], or [g] in the language. Similarly, the native word *kini*, meaning 'multitude,' could also be used for the English words *king*, *kin*, *zinc*, *Guinea*, *Jean*, *Jane*, and *Jennie*.

The vowels are: [i, e, a, o, u, ī, ē, ā, ō, ū]. Vowel length is phonemic, as the following minimal pairs illustrate:

kanaka 'man'   *kānaka* 'men'
kohola 'reef'   *koholā* 'whale'
hio 'to blow'   *hiō* 'to lean'
kao 'spear'   *kāō* 'crowd'

There is almost no limitation on the number of vowels that can be used together, as in the word:

hooiaioia   'certified'

and there can be entire phrases without consonants except for glottal stops (and offered here without grammatical analysis):

Ua 'ō 'ia au   'I am speared'
E uē a'e 'oe iā 'Ī'ī   'You must weep for 'Ī'ī [a person]'
E a'o a'e 'oe iāia   'You teach him'

There are no consonant clusters in Hawaiian, and all syllables end with a vowel. Given the syllable structure and the phonemic inventory, the following substitutions occur:

| San | F | ran | c | isco |
| Ka | pa | la | k | iko |

| Mer | ry | Ch | ri | st | ma | s |
| Me | li | Ka | li | ki | ma | ka |

Pronoun system The Russian–American linguist Roman Jakobson is known for having said, "Languages differ essentially in what they *must* convey and not in what they *may* convey." We have seen/will see various examples of this dictum throughout the Language Profiles at the ends of Chapters 4–12. For instance, English requires a distinction between *he* and *she*, *his* and *her*, and *him* and *her*, which many languages do not, although those languages could differentiate between a third-person male and female person in some way, if necessary.

Similarly, Hawaiian requires distinctions in the pronoun system that English does not, but English speakers could make them, by means of phrases. The distinctions are: *kā-* 'inclusive' and *mā-* 'exclusive' along with *-ua* and *-lua* 'dual' (probably historically related to *lua* 'two') and -kou 'plural, more than two' (likely historically related to *kolu* 'three'); *-lā* is third person.

Person	Singular	Dual	Plural
1 inclusive	au/wau, aʻu	kā-ua	kā-kou
1 exclusive		mā-ua	mā-kou
2	ʻoe	ʻo-lua	ʻou-kou
3	ia	lā-ua	lā-kou

This 11-way pronoun system is characteristic of Austronesian languages. So, *Ike au* is 'I know,' whereas *Ike kāua* is 'we (you and I) know,' and *Ike māua* is 'we (he and I) know.'

Hawaiian pronouns differ from English pronouns in at least three further ways:

(i)   pronouns are frequently omitted, unless there is ambiguity; the answer to the question 'Do you know?' is normally *Ike* 'Know';
(ii) in the imperative, the subject is expressed; instead of 'Go way' we find *E hele* **ʻoe** '**You** go away'
(iii) the pronoun subject of successive verbs follows the last verb rather than the first one.

ʻImi	*i*	*wahi*	*e*	*lilo*	*mai*	**ʻoia**
look	(object)	way	(intensive)	escape	hither	(subject) **he**

'He looked for a way to escape'

This pronoun system is complicated by a further distinction, namely one of alienable/inalienable possession that runs throughout the possessive pronouns (*my, your, his/her*, etc.). These are formed by adding #k- to the forms above and infixing either an *a* or an *o*. To give but one example, *kākā-kou* is 'our' (plural, inclusive, alienable), while *kōkā-kou* is 'our' (plural, inclusive, inalienable). There are over 20 forms for the possessive pronouns, whereas English has about six.

VSO *word order*   Hawaiian is VSO. We have just seen that pronouns follow verbs, which already suggests that the subject follows the verb, as it regularly does:

Ua hele	*ke kanaka*	*i Maui*
(perfective) go	the man	to Maui

'The man went to Maui.'

Ua ʻā	*ke kanaka*	*i*	*ka poi*
(perfective) eat	the man	(object)	the poi

'The man ate the poi.'

We see, furthermore, that the tense marker precedes the verb, as expected, while an indirect object will also conform to expectations of V–S–O–IO, that is, by following the direct object, as in:

Ke	*hāʻawi aku*	*nei*	*au*	*i*	*kēia*	*iāʻoe*
(present)	give away	(present)	I	(object)	this	**to you**

'I give this to you.'

Adjectives follow nouns, and word order, as opposed to any kind of adjectival marking, expresses the relationship among the terms. Thus, the word *makaʻi* can function as the noun 'goodness' or 'beauty,' or as the adjective 'good' or 'beautiful,' depending on its position:

kāna wahine maikaʻi
his wife beautiful
'his beautiful wife'

as opposed to:

kona maikaʻi wahine
her beauty womanly
'her feminine beauty'

In the order of the elements in the name of the language ʻ*Olelo Hawaiʻi*, the second element is the adjective 'Hawaiian,' and the first ʻ*olelo* can function in different contexts as the verb 'to speak, to call, to give a name.' Hawaiian has a wide range of particles to show grammatical relationships, and the ʻ*o-* marks a subject, which can also be thought of as showing slight emphasis, where to direct one's attention. If your name is Pua, you will answer the question 'What's your name?' with the answer: 'O Pua'.

Possessives   There are two kinds of possessives in Polynesian languages, sometimes distinguished by the terms *alienable* and *inalienable*. Other pairs of terms have been proposed, such as *active* and *passive* as well as *acquired* and *inherited*. In Hawaiian, possessives are marked with the postpositions *a* and *o* (*ā* and *ō* preceding syllables with long vowels and diphthongs). The postposition *a* indicates alienable, active, and acquired possession of the type:

ka lei a Pua
'the lei **of** Pua' (the one she is going to sell)

ka kiʻi a Pua
'the picture **of** Pua' (the one she took or painted)

Pua's lei and picture are not an integral part of her. She did something active to acquire them; she caused ownership. She can also do something to dispose of them, say, sell them or give them away. Most material objects take *a*.

The postposition *o* indicates inalienable, passive, and inherited possession of the type:

> *na iwi o Pua*
> 'the bones **of** Pua' (the bones in her body)

Pua did nothing active to acquire those bones. She did not cause them. She inherited them. She also cannot dispose of them. Body parts take *o*, and this feeling of inalienability extends to clothing, since it is in intimate contact with the body. Thus,

> *ka lei o Pua*
> 'the lei **of** Pua'

clearly means that this is the lei she wears. Similarly,

> *ka kiʻi a Pua*
> 'the picture **of** Pua'

means that this a photograph of her. It is (inalienably) her photograph. A few further material objects take *o*, such as one's house, canoe, land, and sometimes adzes (ax-like tools). These objects are considered important, inalienable, and likely inherited, and are things the owner will not part with. Modern things such as horses and automobiles also take *o*, likely through analogy with the canoe.

In the realm of kinship, these two kinds of possession are logical: one's generational blood relations and all ancestors are inherited, and take *o*; one's relations by marriage and all later generations are acquired, and take *a*. Thus,

> *kōna kupuna*
> 'his/her grandparent'

> *kāna keiki*
> 'his/her child'

One inherits one's grandparents. One is active in producing one's own child.

Salient cultural characteristic: Hawaiian language revival

As of 2001, native speakers of Hawaiian accounted for less than 0.1% of the population. In recent years, a Hawaiian language revival has been on the way. Although the number of native speakers today – estimated at 8000 – is still small, it is growing. The revival has been successful for a number of reasons that are particular to the history and culture of Hawaiʻi.

First, there still exist populations known as *kipuka* who live in areas bypassed by development and non-Hawaiian settlements, and who have maintained the traditional way of life, which necessarily means maintaining the use of Hawaiian in daily life. The island of Niʻihau, in particular, has retained native speakers, because it has been privately owned since 1864 and is not open to outsiders. The island of Niʻihau is the only place in the world where Hawaiian is the first language and English the foreign language.

Second, there is a 20% native population by ancestry that makes for a powerful voting bloc when it comes to deciding the use of public funds for creating and maintaining immersion schools and the necessary Hawaiian language materials to go along with those schools. The curricula of these schools are based on traditional cultural practices (chanting, fishing, taro farming, canoeing) but also include modern features, such as sports teams. Furthermore, there is another 40–50% of the population who historically came from other regions in the Pacific (as opposed to the mainland United States). This population is sympathetic to preserving island culture, one that has survived in spite of colonization and Westernization, such that there exists a strong local sense of dress, food, and customs, in short, a sense of "Hawaiian-ness."

Third, and most important in this context, is the ideology about the Hawaiian language that is in play – and it is almost the opposite of the ideology that surrounds many Native American languages on the mainland in at least two ways:

(i) There is no federally recognized Hawaiian political identity, which means there is no issue of tribal identity or unique ownership of language. Already in the nineteenth century, with diverse populations arriving on the island, there was a sense of openness, such that those incoming populations at first learned Hawaiian (while later generations shifted to English). The lack of ownership makes it easier for a language to revive in a population with diverse backgrounds, especially one that already has a sense of Hawaiian-ness. Language then serves as a strengthener of a culture that is already there, rather than as a lifeline to rescue a dying culture.

(ii) Hawaiian culture lacks the strong elder-orientation found in many Native American cultures. Although Hawaiians do respect their elders, there is less of a sense of deference to the elders' wisdom and therefore more of an openness to integrating aspects of modern life without feeling that the new – having football teams in high schools, using the latest technology – threatens traditional life. This openness has made the Hawaiian language more accessible and attractive to the younger generation (Cowell 2012).

Finally, it is good news for the Hawaiian revival that there are now radio stations that broadcast in Hawaiian as well as ʻŌiwi TV that reaches over 220,000 households.

Exercises

Exercise 1 – language families

Classify the following 30 languages according to the language families presented in this chapter. Provide at least one branch in your classification (e.g., Polish is in the Slavic branch of Indo-European). In addition, name at least one place (city, province, nation, etc.) where the language is spoken.

Afrikaans
Aymara
Cebuano
Chamorro
Chukchi
Dyirbal
Fijian
Gujarati
Hausa
Kannad'a
Khmer
Lithuanian
Luo
Malagasy
Maltese
Maninka
Miskito
Mohawk
Navajo
Oriya
Otomí
Papiamentu
Pirahā
Somali
Tajik
Tigrinya
Tok Pisin
Uyghur
Welsh
Xhosa

Exercise 2 – map making

Sketch a map depicting the full reach of Indo-European from the Indian Subcontinent in the East to the British Isles in the West. Use a different color to sketch the following branches: Albanian, Armenian, Balto-Slavic, Celtic, Germanic, Hellenic, Indo-Iranian, Italic. Label as many languages in each branch where they are spoken.

Discussion Questions

1 Discussions of the human genome are rarely found in books whose primary subject matter is language. Was its inclusion here surprising to you? What does it do for your understanding of human language to consider it in this context?
2 What is the value of historical linguistic reconstruction? What can the work of philologists tell us about historical population movements? What can the work of philologists tell us about culture?
3 Why are all models of representing historical relationships among languages necessarily imperfect ones? How does this inform your understanding about what language is?
4 Why are linguists especially interested in studying language isolates?

Notes

1 Speaking of origins, we make the following etymologic notes: *auster* is Latin for 'south wind,' and this root is found in *Australia, Austroasiatic,* and *Austronesia. Nesos* is the ancient Greek word for 'island,' *poly* is the ancient Greek word for 'many,' and *melos* is the ancient Greek word for 'dark.' Thus, Austronesia is 'south islands,' Polynesia is 'many islands,' and Melanesia is 'dark islands,' the last referring to the inhabitants' skin color. This root 'dark' is also found in *melanin, melatonin, melanoma,* etc.
2 The Human Genome Project is an international scientific effort whose first official funding came from the United States Congress in 1987. The results of the project raise issues similar to ones we raise for language, namely who has the rights to certain genes? Can they, for instance, be patented and regulated? The answers lie outside the scope of the present work.
3 The word *gene* has a Latin origin and has the same root as the word *generate*. By the sound correspondences established in Grimm's Law, *gene* is also cognate with the English words *kin* and *kind*.
4 The nucleotide variation C–G ~ T–A that the geneticist identifies as differences in the same strand is similar to the initial consonantal alternation [t] ~ [k] in Austronesian that the philologist identifies as differences in the same word. There is a long history of the importation of linguistic metaphors into the discourse on genetics, beginning with the so-called genetic code, with its long strands of ACTGs, being called *the language of life.* This practice is acceptable so long as the geneticist understands that what is being imported is a *philological* understanding of language.
5 The British, during the days of Empire, practiced what can be called *encyclopedist universalism,* which was a commitment to gathering and preserving the treasures of the world, no matter how curious. The British Museum in London with the Elgin marbles and the Rosetta stone is an example of a magnificent collection of cultural treasures. Similarly, Kew Botanical Gardens, also in London, is a living inventory of a good portion of the plants of the world, where, for instance, the genome of the *Paris japonica,* mentioned above, was sequenced.
6 Neanderthal is classed either as *Homo sapiens neanderthalus* or as a separate species of the same genus *Homo.*
7 Formosa is the historic name for Taiwan. In 1544, when Portuguese sailors came upon this place, they registered in their log the name *ilha Formosa* 'beautiful island.'

8   The coincidence can only be rough, since some cultures may practice exogamy, and depending on the factors involved in choosing a suitable partner, the genetics might or might not align up.

9   Grimm's Law is once again exemplified by the fact that *plewō comes down into English as the word *flow*.

10   A cognate set relevant for this reconstruction would be: Sanskrit *snusa*, Old English *snoru*, Old Church Slavonic *snukha*, Latin *nurus*, Greek *nuos*, and Albanian *nu*. The #sn- ~ #n alternation does, indeed, hold up in many words, for example, English *snow* and Latin *nivea*, English *sinew* and Latin *nervus*. By the way, the -u# on the Old English word is a feminine ending. See Watkins (1985) for a fuller discussion.

11   According to Jared Diamond, "Aboriginal Australia was traditionally inhabited entirely by hunter-gatherers occupying an average of 12,000 square miles per language, while neighboring New Guinea supported mostly farmers occupying only 300 square miles per language" (2012:379).

12   In the Central Highlands of Indonesian New Guinea today, the average hunter-gatherer language has 388 speakers, while the average farmer language has 18,241 speakers (Diamond 2012:379).

13   This split is the famous *centem–satem* division, that is, languages whose word for 'one hundred' begins either with [k] or with [s].

14   Some scholars propose that we are now living in the Anthropocene or "Age of Man." This is a recently coined, as-yet informal geologic period intended to mark the moment when human activities began to have significant global impacts on earth's ecosystems. Some scholars date the beginning of the Anthropocene to about 1750, that is, the beginning of the Industrial Revolution, when anthropogenic global warming is thought to have begun. Others say it began after agriculture took off 9 kya, and farmers began not only clearing forests but also carving out landscapes and waterways for paddy fields.

15   See linguist Claire Bowern's revised estimate of the number at Anggarrgoon, a website devoted to Aboriginal Australian languages.

16   Sometimes, they are called *superfamilies*, but we want to restrict the use of the term *family* in this textbook.

17   Speaking of Japan, the language Ainu, once spoken in Hokkaido, the northernmost island of Japan, is also considered an isolate.

18   A more recent study shows that when an analysis is based on a large set of what the researchers call *classical genetic markers*, it looks as if the Basques form a distinctive population. However, in a genome-wide perspective, the Basques are not particularly different from other Iberian populations (Laayouni et al. 2010).

19   The name is widespread in Polynesian languages and can be reconstructed to the Proto-Polynesian *hawaiki 'place of the gods.' In Māori mythology, for instance, *hawaiki* was the place the Māori came from before traveling to their current home (New Zealand).

References

Balter, Michael (2013a) Ancient DNA links Native Americans with Europe. *Science* 342: 409–410.

Balter, Michael (2013b) Farming's tangled European roots. *Science* 342: 181–182.

Bellwood, Peter (2001) Early agriculturalist population diasporas? Farming, language, and genes. *Annual Review of Anthropology* 30:181–207.

Brandt, Guido, Wolfgang Haak, Christina J. Adler, Christina Roth, Anna Szécsényi-Nagy, Sarah Karimnia, Sabine Möller-Rieker, Harald Meller, Robert Ganslmeier, Susanne Friederich, Veit Dresely, Nicole Nicklisch, Joseph K. Pickrell, Frank Sirocko, David Reich, Alan Cooper, Kurt W. Alt, The Genographic Consortium (2013) Ancient DNA reveals key stages in the formation of central European mitochondrial genetic diversity. *Science* 342: 257–261.

Campbell, Lyle (1998) *Historical Linguistics: An Introduction*. Cambridge, MA: The MIT Press.

Cavalli-Sforza, Luigi (2000) *Genes, Peoples, and Languages*. New York: North Point Press.

Cowell, Andrew (2012) The Hawaiian model of language revitalization: Problems of extensions to mainland America. *International Journal of the Sociology of Language* 218: 167–193.

Diamond, Jared (2012) *The World Until Yesterday: What Can We Learn from Traditional Societies?* New York: Viking Press.

Laayouni, Hafid, Francesc Calafell, and Jaume Bertranpetit (2010) A genome-wide survey does not show the genetic distinctiveness of Basques. *Human Genetics* 127: 455–458.

Nichols, Johanna (1999) The Eurasian spread zone and the Indo-European dispersal. In Blench, Roger and Mathew Spriggs (eds.), *Archaeology and Language II: Correlating Archaeological and Linguistic Hypotheses*. London: Routledge, pp. 220–266.

Nichols, Johanna (2011) Forerunners to globalization: The Eurasian steppe and its periphery. *Language Contact in Times of Globalization* 38: 177–195.

Watkins, Calvert (1985) *The American Heritage Dictionary of Indo-European Roots*. New York: Houghton-Mifflin.

Wexler, J.E., Jr (1943) *Polynesians: Explorers of the Pacific*. Washington, DC: Smithsonian Institution.

Further Reading

Elbert, Samuel and Mary Kwwena Pukui (1979) *Hawaiian Grammar*. Honolulu: University of Hawaii Press.

8

Colonial Consequences
Language Stocks and Families Remapped

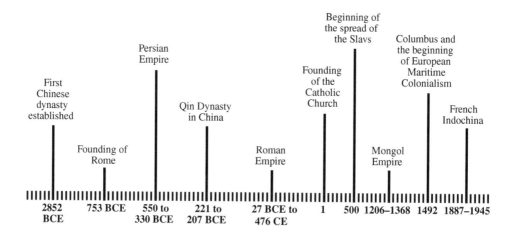

Eiffel Towers in Vietnam

Visitors to Vietnam, if they go to the mountain town of Da Lat or the beach town on Con Dao Island, might be surprised to see what looks to be a smaller version of the Eiffel Tower sprouting from the top of a building in the city center. Upon closer inspection, visitors might decide that they are indeed looking at an Eiffel Tower. They might figure that it functions as an antenna, but they might also wonder why this distinctive shape came to be on the roof of the post office. The answer is that at the end of the nineteenth century, the French created the postal system in Vietnam when it was part of the French colonial empire called *Indochine*. By the way, the main post office in Ho Chi Minh City (Sai Gon), which sports a normal-looking antenna, was designed and built by Gustave Eiffel himself. Pertinently, the Vietnamese word for

Languages in the World: How History, Culture, and Politics Shape Language, First Edition.
Julie Tetel Andresen and Phillip M. Carter.
© 2016 John Wiley & Sons, Inc. Published 2016 by John Wiley & Sons, Inc.

'post office' is *bưu điện*: *bưu* is from the French word *bureau* 'office,' and *điện* is the Vietnamese word for 'electricity.'

The French took an interest not only in the buildings they themselves built but also in those they encountered in this part of the world. The most spectacular are the temple complexes at Angkor, located in present-day Cambodia. Angkor was the ancient capital of the Khmer Empire, founded in the ninth century and abandoned in the fifteenth century to the will of the jungle. The first European to see the city was the Catholic Father Bouillevaux, who happened upon these exotic and overgrown structures in 1850. A decade later, French naturalist and explorer, Henri Mouhot, touted to the European press the beauty of this location, and Western efforts to restore the site began. The most mysterious and magical of all the temples is Ta Prohm, a veritable ruin where the sinuous roots of kapok trees, some thicker than a large man's thigh, snake around and through the temple walls. In 2001, British film director, Simon West, chose this visually startling location for the scene in *Lara Croft: Tomb Raider* where Lara encounters a mysterious girl who tells Lara where to go next. Given the partial colonization of the imagination exerted by the global movie industry, tourists today are willing to stand in line for hours on end at a particular wall in Ta Prohm in order to have their picture taken in front of this famous movie set.

The power dynamics of concern in Part II are clearly at work here in Part III. The successful expansions described in Chapter 7 involved the power of the innovation of farming, the possession of the most advanced technologies like ploughs and harnesses, the domestication of goats and yaks and horses, and the invention of conveyances such as a cart or a sled. Today, the expansive power of a culture might be the blockbuster movie. In this chapter, we foreground the movements impelled by power in the ways that certain organized political structures feel the need to expand their territory. We call these movements *colonization*. We begin with a look at the major pre-Columbian colonizers: the Chinese, the Persians, the Mongols, and the Slavs, as well as the Romans. We move on to examine the linguistic effects of another type of colonization – that which has occurred through the spread of world religions. In our review of Making Language Official in Chapter 6, we mentioned the end of post-Columbian European colonialism carried out by the British, Spanish, Dutch, French, Germans, Italians, and Portuguese, and so we do not need to review its beginnings in the present chapter. Instead, we end by taking a look at a different kind of linguistic legacy of colonialism, namely the way a variety of English has come into being in the particular eco-linguistic environment of Singapore.

Time-Depths and Terminology

In the previous chapter, we called the spreading out of a people from a homeland an *expansion*, and it is the case that many of those expansions were into already-inhabited territories. In this chapter, we explore the linguistic effects of colonialism. The word *colony* is from the Latin *colonia* 'a place for agriculture, farm, settled land.' We distinguish *expansion* from *colonialism* by defining the latter in terms of movement away from an existing established state, such as Rome, which over time acquired colonies and became an empire. We reserve the term *migration* to refer to human movements when a political border is crossed. Migrants can cross international boundaries, but they can also cross intranational boundaries, for instance when someone in the United States takes a job in another state. In ordinary speech, it is perfectly acceptable to say, for instance, that what we are calling Globalization 1.0 is a kind of first colonization of the world, and anthropologists have no hesitation saying that humans have been migrating all over the planet for a very long time. We do not insist that our terms be used in our ways outside of this book. We make the distinctions between the terms *expansion, colonization,* and *migration* here only to keep our differing time-depths straight.

Colonialism can occur by settlement, when large numbers of colonizers enter a territory and take it over en masse, or by administration, when fewer colonizers enter an area and then rule it for exploitive purposes: to send valuable natural resources or raw materials to the capital and/or to cultivate the natural resources, for example, sugar, rubber, coffee, etc., on plantations for consumption in the capital and for profit on markets around the world. As colonizers move into a territory, whether as settlers or administrators, and stay for however long they remain, their languages inevitably affect the local languages.

Let us embroider for a moment on the terminological effects of colonization on Vietnamese. The French came first as proselytizers (religious converters) and later as political and economic administrators. The French presence in Vietnam began in the seventeenth century with French Jesuit missionaries, as you may recall from Chapter 5, who established *quốc ngữ*, the transcription of Vietnamese into the Roman alphabet. In 1853, French explorers, doctors, and political administrators began to come largely in order to claim and then protect these potentially rich lands from the British and the Dutch who were already in Malay and Indonesia, respectively. In 1887, the existence of French Indochina as a political entity was established and included present-day Cambodia and Vietnam. It lasted until 1945.

The Vietnamese borrowing *bưu* is suggestive of the fact that the French set up more than just post offices and in fact established an entire bureaucracy. The presence of French loanwords in modern-day Vietnamese is light yet discernible, and the borrowings represent domains of influence and of the new. There is *ga* from French *gare* 'train station' and *ga ra* from French *garage* 'garage.' The bicycle was introduced, and now the Vietnamese have *xi clo* from French *cycle* 'cycle,' *ghi đông* from French *guidon* 'handlebar,' and *pê đan* from French *pédale* 'pedal.' There is also *vô lăng* from French *volant* 'steering wheel.' A new type of building material is called *bê tông* from French *béton* 'concrete.' A hint of French customs comes through in the half-calque/half-borrowing *tiền boa* meaning 'tip (for a service),' where *tiền* is Vietnamese for 'money,' and *boa* comes from French *boire* 'to drink,' which is found in the compound *pourboire* 'for to drink' meaning 'tip.' The French rulers have gone, but they left their footprint on the land in their buildings and their railroads and evidence of administrative and cultural effects sprinkled in the language. In Vietnam today, the colonial past is still present.

Before the arrival of the French, the Chinese dominated what is now Vietnam for a thousand years (111 BCE to 938 CE), and the effect of this domination on Vietnamese is massive and deep.[1] Entire portions of the Vietnamese vocabulary are borrowings from Chinese. The importance of Chinese on Vietnamese vocabulary is similar to that of Greek and Latin on English vocabulary. We offer here only one example out of thousands. In English, the word 'dentist' is from the Latin word for 'tooth,' namely *dens*. In Vietnamese, the word for 'dentist' is *nha sĩ*, which is a compound from Chinese borrowings *nha* 'tooth' and *sĩ* 'professional, person of highest learning.'[2] (The Vietnamese word for 'tooth' is *răng*.) The prestige of the Chinese portion of the Vietnamese vocabulary is so great that the Vietnamese people receive much etymological training throughout their school years, and they know which parts of the vocabulary are native Vietnamese and which are Chinese, in a way that English speakers do not know which part of their vocabulary is Germanic and which is French/Latin/Greek. While English speakers can put together a phrase such as *cordial greeting* with 'cordial' from Latin and 'greeting' from Germanic, the Vietnamese speaker does not. For the phrase *beautiful person*, they will choose either a Vietnamese–Vietnamese combination *người đẹp* or a Chinese–Chinese combination *mỹ nhân*.

The Middle Kingdom: Government-Encouraged Migrations

China has the longest continuous existence as a state, the longest policy of migratory colonialism, and the oldest continuous written records, some of which document those migrations. In the previous chapter, we noted that the homeland of the early Sino-Tibetans was in the valley of the Yellow River in the central plains of northern China. We noted their movements west, south, and east, with the differentiation of the population into the Tibeto-Burmans in the west and the Chinese in the south and east. When we speak of 'the Chinese,' we are speaking of the ethnic group called *Han*. They are so called in reference to the Han Dynasty (206 BCE to 220 CE). This dynasty succeeded the Qin Dynasty (221–207 BCE), which brought a number of regions under its control and became the first imperial dynasty. The name *Han* may have been preferable for this ethnic group to *Qin* because the Qin Dynasty was so short-lived. The Han Dynasty is also considered something of a Golden Age in Chinese history. Of interest is the possibility that the name *Qin* may be the etymological root of the European word *China*, although the exact etymological origin is debated. The name *Middle Kingdom* (Zhōngguó) for China refers to the original, central states in the Yellow River Valley. Beijing is not on the Yellow River, but it lies a bit north and west of where the Yellow River flows into the Pacific. The first Chinese dynasty dates as far back as 2852 BCE.

Records of government-encouraged migrations begin in the seventh century BCE, and the first ones were southward from the Wei River Valley to the lower Yangtze whose original inhabitants are identified by Chinese historians as the *bai yue* (the hundred Yue). By the third and second centuries BCE, the government records begin to include the numbers of people moved, with the first instance showing that almost two million people from the central plains moved further to the east and south, and all the way into northern Vietnam (*nam* means 'south'). Once again, the people they encountered are recorded as being the *bai yue*. The largest migration of the early period was in the second to fourth centuries CE when three million people moved from the central plains south and east to the coast. There they met the Wu and Chu peoples, both Chinese. Almost every century from the beginning of recorded Chinese history bears witness to a government-encouraged migration. In recent times, from the eighteenth to the twentieth centuries, for instance, tens of millions of people in provinces on the east coast around Beijing migrated northward to Siberia. There they met the non-Chinese Altai people. In the twentieth century people from all areas of China migrated into Inner Mongolia. And as we already saw at the beginning of Chapter 6, significant Mandarin incursions have recently taken place in the western Tibetan-speaking Quinhai Province and in the Tibetan Autonomous Region. Indeed, they have been doing so for thousands of years. A table of these impressive migrations can be found in LaPolla (2006:229).[3]

The first thing to note is that when the Chinese migrated, they rarely moved into unoccupied territory. The second thing to note is that, given the large numbers of migrating people, the indigenous populations were greatly affected, and the arrivals of Han triggered secondary migrations of the people originally inhabiting the colonized area. If the indigenous people did not go elsewhere, they were absorbed. Like the Spanish policies during the conquest of the Americas mentioned in note 6 at the end of Chapter 2, there was purposeful mixing of peoples in the colonized areas with the aim of bringing them into the Han nationality. Not surprisingly, a genetic study of the population generally known as Han shows enough geographic variation in a particular coding region of mtDNA to prompt researchers to propose new haplogroups, making the Han a far-from-homogeneous ethnic group. This genetic study was furthermore able to provide evidence for speculating that the Proto-Han made an initial move from south to north in the Paleolithic era (moving toward their homeland, in our terms) and then, after they had settled, expanded, and colonized territories from north to south, as well as east to west (Yao et al. 2002). This genetic evidence lines up not only with the prehistoric information coming from linguistic reconstructions and archeology but also with the historical records kept by the Chinese government.

Most importantly, from our point of view, the resulting mixtures of people from these migrations explain many of the features found in the current Chinese varieties, which may be as few as seven and as many as 10 or more mutually unintelligible varieties, depending on how one counts. The aboriginal *bai yue* are an important part of the linguistic story in south and southeastern China. They are non-Han, and the qualifier 'hundred' given to them by the Chinese historians suggests that those people covered by the term *yue* were of many ethnicities. Modern philologists often divide them into two groups: one that spoke Austro-Asiatic-related languages and another that spoke Tai and Hmong-Mien (known in Chinese as Miao-Yao)-related languages. In the more distant prehistoric period, the *bai yue* may have been speakers of a larger phylum, one that broke up over time and into stocks such as Hmong-Mien and putative Austric, which includes Austro-Asiatic, Austronesian, and Tai (see LaPolla 2006:233). Not surprisingly, the Chinese variety Cantonese, spoken in the south and well known in the West because it is spoken in Hong Kong, shows lexical borrowings from both Tai and Hmong-Mien. Only one syntactic construction in Cantonese will be mentioned here, namely the object–dative construction, where the direct object precedes the indirect object and is exemplified by the phrase:

ngo[5]	*bei*[2]	*cin*[2]	*keoi*[5]
'I'	'give'	'money'	'(to) him.'

Mandarin and most other Chinese varieties have the word order 'I give him money.' The preferred Cantonese word order can be found in both Tai and Mien languages. It is considered an areal feature (Matthews 2007:223–224). In Chapter 11, we will take up some of the linguistic consequences of these government-encouraged migrations.

Although very large in area, China is also relatively self-contained, with the Pacific Ocean to the east and mountains to the west. It has also been inhabited for a very long time, meaning that there has also been a long time for an organized government to form and to have been in control of the territory, as we have just seen. The other empires we want to outline in this chapter distinguish themselves from the Chinese situation in two ways. First, they are more recent, relatively speaking. Second, particular geographic conditions come into play in their expansions, and we now turn to an examination of those conditions.

Linguistic Geography: Residual Zones and Spread Zones

In Chapter 7, we mentioned in passing that places like the Caucasus and Papua New Guinea are called residual zones, and these are places where languages accumulate and survive. This term is the creation of linguist Johanna Nichols (1992) in *Linguistic Diversity in Space and Time*, where she also analyzes the language dynamics of spread zones, which are places where languages spread out and succeed one another. These two types of zones are not the only relevant ones for comparative work, but they are two important and common types of linguistic areas. They are both subcontinental in size, but their size is not what defines them. Other criteria, such as relative linguistic diversity, center/periphery, and internal stability, are the critical factors. Nichols's work is a great contribution to linguists' understanding of the languages of the world, and we summarize it here.

A **residual zone** tends to be a relatively small, sometimes even enclosed area where a higher number of languages from diverse lineages (families, stock, phyla) are spoken than in the areas surrounding it. The residual zones around the world, in addition to the Caucasus and Papua New Guinea, include: eastern Africa, northern Australia, the Pamir-Himalayan region, the Pacific coast of northern Asia (from Japan to the Behring Strait), the Pacific coast of North America, probably the southeastern United States, and presumably parts of South America. Clearly, some of these residual zones are historic; the Pacific coast of North America was once home to many Native American stocks and families, but no more.

We must also mention the Balkans. When we first brought up this language area in Chapter 3, we offered examples of structural convergences particular to the languages spoken there only in terms of examples from Romanian. Here, we return to the topic of clitics and note that the use of a proclitic to intensify meaning is found throughout the Balkans. In contemporary colloquial Bulgarian, for instance, the intensifying proclitic takes the form of *po-* and combines with nouns:

počuvik
'more of a man'

and verbs:

poubičeš
'more you like (you like more)'

(Klagstad 1963:182).

Another type of clitic is found in pronoun agreement in gender and number of the type 'I saw-her Mary.' These agreement pronouns usually occur with an accusative or dative object that is definite. Here is an example from Macedonian, a South Slavic language:

mu go	*davam*	*moliv-ot*		*na*	*momče-to*
him-it	I give	pencil-the		to	boy-the
		(definite masculine)			(definite neuter)

'I give the pencil to the boy'

The utterance begins with the clitics *mu* 'third singular, neuter dative' (which refers to the boy) and *go* 'third singular, masculine, accusative' (which refers to the pencil). These clitics set up the grammatical structure of the entire sentence, which is given particular content (boy, pencil) as the utterance unfolds. We mentioned in passing in Chapter 3 that there are limited ways humans have found to keep track of grammatical relations in a rapidly fading signal. Setting up definite objects and their relationship to one another at the beginning is one way to track slightly complex utterances.

The important point here is that clitic pronoun agreement is standard in both spoken and written Macedonian, but it is found typically only colloquially, to varying degrees, in Albanian, Bulgarian, Greek, and Romanian. It is excluded in formal contexts in these other languages because the older prestige languages did not have it, and it is therefore considered colloquial. For instance, in the translations of the Bible, Modern Greek and Bulgarian versions do not use pronoun reduplication, while Albanian and Romanian require it in some contexts (Friedman 2006:213). The usual explanation for the rise of these clitics is that the populations that spoke these languages were illiterate for so long. However, the explanation may actually lie in the fact that the rise of clitics is an effect of residual zone dynamics where many and diverse languages are spoken by multilingual populations.

In the Balkans, there is quite a lot of linguistic diversity and structural complexity in an area a little smaller than Texas. It is pertinent to note that Istanbul sits on its southeastern border. This important and attractive city drew many different people over the centuries to pillage and plunder or to ply a trade. These attempts sometimes left residual languages on the edges, namely the Balkans. The Balkans furthermore exemplify other features of the many residual zones, which can be found dotted all over the world:

(i)   Many of the languages have been there for a long time.
(ii) The populations speaking the languages do not expand; the homeland remains the homeland.

(iii) Over time, there is a net increase in the diversity of the lineages of the languages spoken there; for this reason, residual zones are also sometimes called *refugia*: languages take refuge there; however, they are not pushed into the zone but drawn into it.

(iv) Language isolates are likely to be found in these areas.

(v) There is no lingua franca for the entire area; local bilingualism or multilingualism is the means of interethnic communication.

(vi) The zones, although they are made up of languages from very different lineages, nevertheless share a standard linguistic profile of structural diversity.

This last feature of a residual zone is, perhaps, the most remarkable of all. Let us mention here one structural feature, namely clitics. These grammatical elements are sometimes called *semifree* or, even, *detached*. When they first appear in a language, they are felt as optional or as only appropriate in one speaking register, as noted above in the difference between the presence and absence of the pronoun clitics in colloquial versus formal speech in certain Balkan languages. What is interesting is that, if these clitics do attach to anything, they attach to the verbs, as in Romanian *am vazut-o pe Maria* 'I have seen-**her** (by) Mary' that is, 'I saw Mary.'

Marking of gender, number, and case on the verb, namely the head, of the sentence, instead of on the object, namely Mary, is a definite shift away from the usual Indo-European preference for marking on dependent constituents. In the Balkans, this clitic pattern is not native to any language in the zone. It could be attributed to accident or to anything else, but Nichols's educated guess is that: "The clitic pronouns are the spontaneous response to language contact, and the rise of such clitics in an otherwise dependent-marking language is to be expected in residual zones and at the peripheries of spread zones" (1992:272). Close proximity of diverse languages in a relatively small area is, thus, one of the many conditions languages catch up to. Such a condition produces the linguistic effect of speakers feeling the need to mark grammatical relations on the verb, which often comes upfront in an utterance.

A **spread zone**, by way of contrast, is a potentially larger area than a residual zone, but, more importantly, it is geographically spacious. It is also an area characterized by low genetic diversity, that is, low genetic density, which is measured by the ratio of genetic stocks to million square miles of area. To make a comparison, the residual zone of the Caucasus has six stocks and a genetic density of 16.1, while the spread zone of Europe has six stocks and a genetic density of 1.6 (Nichols 1992:233). Spread zones in the world include: the Ancient Near East, sub-Saharan Africa, the Europe in the days of the Roman Empire, the Eurasian steppe, central and northern Australia, the Great Plains of North America, Mesoamerica, and the entire Arctic region. The zones may be open, such as the Great Plains and Siberia, where people can enter from all directions, or they may be closed, when isolated by ecological barriers, for instance, the water surrounding Australia.

Spread zones have the following characteristics:

(i) Usually only one language family and possibly only one language dominate the area.

(ii)   The amount of time that it dominates is limited before another language comes along, spreads, and replaces the previously dominant language.
(iii) Languages in these areas do not stay in their original locations for long periods.
(iv)   The dominant language is dominant in terms of cultural and economic prestige and functions as a lingua franca for the entire area.
(v)   Because of this prestige, the dominant language has effects on the languages it comes in contact with.
(vi)   The profile of the dominant language spoken in the spread zone is unique to that spread zone; there is no convergence of linguistic features, such as the cliticization that seems to crop up continually in residual zones.

Like residual zones, some of the spread zones have a historic character. The Great Plains of North America, for instance, were once a spread zone just as, to their west, the Pacific coast was once a residual zone. The plains were originally covered by only a few language stocks, mainly Algonquin and Siouan. However, they lack a significant characteristic found in other spread zones. On the plains, there were no cities on the peripheries, such as there are along the southern edges of the Eurasian steppe. The lack of cities in North America could be the reason why there was *relatively* little bi- and multilingualism on the plains, because there were no settled locations where tribes/nations could meet up for trade and talk, and no centers where linguistic innovations could arise and from which the features could spread. Certainly, on the east coast, the Iroquois had what would be recognized today as towns, but they were far from the spread zone. Only Teotihuacán and Chichen Itzá, both in present-day Mexico, and then Machu Picchu in present-day Peru could be considered urban centers in pre-Columbian times.

Centers are defined not geographically but rather by the magnitude of cultural influence. London is hardly at the geographic center of Great Britain, but it has functioned historically as the linguistic center from which innovations spread. The extent of any particular linguistic spread defines the periphery.

Spreading Eurasian Empires: The Persians, Mongols, Slavs, and Romans

Nichols has devoted much research to the linguistic profile of the Eurasian steppe spread zone. This 5000-mile grassland in the center of the landmass is a closed spread zone whose east/west boundary is the Altai Mountains, which place China and Mongolia on the eastern part of the steppe and Russia and Kazakhstan on the western steppe. It is furthermore bounded on the north by Siberian forests and on the south by the Central Asian Desert, mountains, and the Gobi Desert. It begins all the way in Manchuria in northeast Asia and continues westward to the Black Sea and Moldova as well as the northern parts of Romania. It finds a tail end in Hungary. The steppe is also a relatively closed economic zone, in that steppe nomadic herding (sheep, goats, yaks) is complementary to farming-based societies found at the periphery. Although the two economic systems were dependent on one another for most of recorded history, the cities on the periphery were dominated politically by the steppe society (Nichols

2011:180). The domestication of the horse on the steppe about 3000 years ago may have given the nomads their political superiority. There is evidence that the Great Wall of China was begun 2000 years ago by Chinese farmers to keep out Mongolian horsemen from the north who needed grain.

What has happened on the steppe since the breakup of the Indo-European languages, roughly 4000 years ago, has determined the current linguistic picture for this major part of the world.

From the Persian Empire (550–330 BCE) to the Mongol Empire (1206–1368)

We begin by noting that the first steppe spread is believed to be Proto-Uralic, but it is difficult to prove definitively. The first identifiable language stock to spread over the steppe was Indo-European, and it likely spread from the western steppe. It also likely covered the steppe around the time of the Indo-European breakup about 4000 years ago. Thereafter, the succession of languages illustrates Nichols's point that the time-depths of steppe language families are shallow. The first to spread was the Iranian daughter branch of Indo-European, and Persian began to dominate in the first millennium BCE and lasted there until the early centuries CE. Replacing it came Turkic, which as a family is now about 2000 years old, and by the end of the twelfth century the steppe was Turkic speaking. Replacing the Turkic family came Mongolian whose spread was halted by medieval plagues such as the Black Death in 1348. Notice now that one of the languages in the diversity-dense Caucasus is Ossetic, an Iranian language that was drawn into this residual zone on the periphery of the steppe when Turkic began to spread. Another language found there is Karachay-Balkar, a Turkic language that ended up there when the Mongolian spread began.

When Genghis Khan united the Mongolic tribes, the dominant languages on the steppes at the time were Turkic languages, and over time more and more Turkic-speaking men were drawn into the heavily westward- (but also northward-, eastward-, and southward-) moving Mongol army. Eventually the Turkic languages found their western-most edge in eastern Europe helped along by the Ottomans; and pockets of Turkish varieties exist still today in the residual zone of the Balkans. Another language in the Balkans shows the history of the western march of Turkic, namely Bulgarian, which is a Turkic ethnonym and a Slavic language. According to Nichols (2011:183), for the societies on the Turkic–Mongolic steppe, language did not seem to be an important component of identity. Clans, and then tribes, were the important markers. Because of this sociolinguistic situation, when Proto-Hungarians joined the military, coming down from the Finno-Ugric homeland in the Uralic mountains or western Siberian forests north of the steppe, they retained their ethnic and linguistic identity for four centuries in the westward spread of Turkic–Mongolic dominance. The Proto-Hungarians came to settle on the westernmost periphery of the spread zone, namely the northern shores of the Black Sea, having survived long-range migration linguistically intact but with plenty of borrowings.

In 869, the Magyars/Hungarians were called from the Black Sea by a Germanic king who wanted their help in fighting the Slavs. Thus, the Magyars arrived in what is now known as the Hungarian steppe and absorbed whoever was already there, namely some

Germanic, Slavic, and Turkic tribes. For the next century, they generally harassed the Italians, the Germans, and the French until they were defeated and settled down; their language did not expand until the Austro-Hungarian Empire many centuries later.[4] Thus was Hungarian stranded from its Uralic sisters – Finnish, Estonian, Saami – far to the north and east, and was drawn into the residual zone of the Balkans.

Spreading languages replace nearly every language they encounter that does not make it into a residual zone. In the case of the spread of Mongolic–Turkic, Indo-European languages such as Scythian (Iranian) and Gothic (East Germanic)[5] were eliminated, along with Hunnish, which was likely Turkic, as well as eastern branches of Slavic/Russian spoken in places such as present-day Ukraine.

Nichols (2011:188) observes that the languages of inner Eurasia and especially eastern inner Eurasia share well-known structural features characteristic of the Ural-Altaic type:

   (i)   simple syllable structure;
   (ii)   vowel harmony (see Language Profile: Mongolian, Chapter 11);
   (iii) front rounded vowels;
   (iv)   no genders;
   (v)   simple prosodic structures (no tones, fixed stress);
   (vi)   agglutinative morphology;
   (vii) primarily suffixing morphology;
   (viii) case systems;
   (ix)   accusative alignment; and
   (x)   personal pronouns with [m] in the first person and a [t]-like consonant in the second.

Speakers of Indo-European languages are familiar with characteristics (vii)–(x), and (x) can be easily illustrated by English *me* and *mine* in the first person and *thou/thee/thine* in the obsolete second person. The languages of Eurasia furthermore share very regular verbal word formation in which the most basic form in the word family is intransitive, and semantic causatives are overtly derived from the corresponding noncausatives with transitizing morphology of the type: 'frighten' is 'fear' + transitiving suffix. The languages are also notably noncomplex, regular, and transparent.[6] Among the spreading steppe languages, these properties increase over time and with more easterly origin, and come to an end with Mongolian. Many of these properties are shared by languages like Tungusic and Korean at the eastern steppe periphery, thus the argument of assigning Korean to the Altaic stock.

Nichols states that residual zones the world over converge on a linguistic profile, while the languages of the spread zones are unique to each spread zone. Thus, how the languages of the Eurasian spread zone come to share this set of structural properties must be explained, and the explanation is this: there was a lack of fresh typological input into the closed Eurasian spread zone. The last spread phases on the steppe were Bulgar Turkic, Common Turkic, Mongolian, and Mongolian plus Turkic. Proto-Mongolic and Proto-Turkic were structurally very similar to begin with, and with no new languages entering the steppe, the same so-called typological package spread each time. Furthermore, the similarity of the two protolanguages for Turkic and Mongolic must owe something to contact, as they had been spoken in the same area for centuries before their spreads and had probably interacted closely throughout that time. This is a very different situation from the case of the Balkans where typologically very different languages not formerly in contact begin, over time, to produce clitics.

The discussion of the languages of the Eurasian landmass ends with the spread of the Slavs. By the fifth and certainly the sixth century CE, the Slavs occupied an area of central-eastern Europe, in the vicinity of the western Danube plain. From this relatively compact homeland, they came to occupy vast stretches of eastern Europe over the next 400 years. In the seventh and eighth centuries, they expanded to the north and east toward the Volga River, to the west toward the Alps, and to the south toward the Balkans, where they encountered people speaking a language inherited from the Romans. In this easternmost Romance territory, *invasion* is perhaps not the correct word to describe the process whereby Slavonic dispossessed Romance. It was more of a continuous infiltration. The Avars, who were kindred with the Turks, pushed a certain number of Slavs south of the Danube and into present-day Bulgaria.[7]

Slavic languages are phonetically distinctive for the array of palatalized consonants they all have, and these developed after Proto-Slavic became Common Slavonic after it broke away from PIE. Common Slavonic also tended to be conservative in terms of inflectional morphology, that is, it retained much of what was in PIE: three numbers (singular, dual, plural), three genders (masculine, feminine, neuter), and seven cases (nominative, vocative, genitive, dative, accusative, instrumental, locative). Common Slavonic had neither definite nor indefinite articles, and the modern languages today also do not. Bulgarian and Macedonian are exceptions in having articles, and their presence in these languages can be explained by areal contact in the Balkans. Similarly, the relative absence of the extensive case system of Common Slavonic in Bulgarian and Macedonian receives the same explanation.

To give examples of the Slavic case system from Polish, when *pies* 'dog' is the subject, it is in the nominative case, but to show ownership, it becomes *psa* (genitive), and to mark location it becomes *psie* (locative). Polish also marks nouns morphologically with the instrumental case to indicate 'by means of.' English speakers tend to do this with prepositions. Rather than saying 'I'm writing with a new pen,' Polish speakers say:

Piszę   nowym   długopisem
I write   new   pen
'I write with a new pen'

The case endings -*m* on 'new' and 'pen' agree and indicate 'by means of.'

The Slavic languages are also distinctive for their use of verbal **aspect** 'character/perception/view of the action' rather than **tense** 'time when.' A tense system marks the time of an event with respect to another and sorts itself into categories such as *past, present,* and *future*. The aspectual systems of the Slavic languages pair one verb used for completed actions, known as the **perfective**, with a separate verb used for an incomplete action, known as the **imperfective**. Thus, in Polish, there are two verbs for the English 'to buy': *kupić* the perfective and *kupować* the imperfective. When conjugated, the separate verbs make the aspectual distinctions. The perfective *kupiłem* means 'I bought,' while the imperfective *kupowałem* means 'I was buying.' So all

Polish verbal actions occur in pairs, which sometimes are formed through affixation, for example, *pisać/napisać* 'to write,' or are suppletive, for example, *brać/wziąć* 'to bring.' The tense/aspect system of Polish can give a sense of time that is unfamiliar to English speakers. The present tense of the imperfective *kupuję* may mean 'I buy' or 'I am buying,' while the present tense of the perfective *kupię* results in what we might call the future, since logically a completed action cannot take place in the present moment. Here the notion of tense familiar to English speakers takes a backseat to the prominence of the aspectual distinction in Polish.

Slavic specialist Alan Timberlake maps out much of the story of the Slavic homeland by means of hydronyms (names of rivers) found in and around what is known as the Ukrainian Mesopotamia, whose rivers drain southward into the Black Sea.[8] To the north, the Pripyat River, whose **etymology** is contested between being of Baltic origin and of Slavic origin, marks a zone north of which Baltic hydronyms are found and south of which Slavic hydronyms are found. So, the uncertain etymology of the Pripyat makes a kind of sense. Far to the east, the Volga, which empties into the Caspian Sea, is a Slavic hydronym meaning 'wetness, moisture' and seems to be a loan translation of the Scythian/Iranian name. On the western edge of the Ukrainian Mesopotamia, near the Dnieper River, there is a cluster of Slavic hydronyms, and it was from these population centers that the Slavs began to spread in the fifth century CE, which they did along rivers.

The Slavs went in a northerly direction, following the Dnieper and replacing Baltic populations and, further north, Finnic populations. They moved west along the Vistula into present-day southern Poland and then farther west into Bohemia by means of the Oder and Elbe Rivers. However, they did not absorb the local populations who withdrew as the invaders neared. As for their southern trajectory, there were the Dniester and Prut along the foothills of the Carpathians and then the northern shores of the Danube. Later they would be pushed into Bulgaria, as noted above. The key point is that the Slavic names for the major rivers – Dnieper, Dniester, Danube – are most likely Iranian, thereby suggesting the movement of Slavs into territories previously inhabited by Iranian people (Timberlake 2013:336–337).[9]

The arrival of the Slavs in the historic residual zone of the Caucasus has had a distinct and recently upsetting effect. Given the eventual rise of the Tsarist Empire followed by a dominant Soviet Union, Russian is now a lingua franca in the Caucasus, although historically speaking, residual zones do not have lingua francas. The large empires of the last several hundred years have altered the way residual zones have operated linguistically in the past 10,000 years. The same can be said about historic spread zones. Just as the Great Plains is no longer a spread zone today, neither is the Eurasian steppe. We will see in Chapter 9 just how dramatically Russian has affected the residual zone of the Caucauses, in specific relationship to Chechen and Georgian, both Caucasian languages, as well as to Ossetic, an Indo-European language also found in this residual zone. In short, the effect has been one of creating violence.

The Roman Empire (27 BCE to 476 CE)

We now step back in time to take account of Roman colonialism, because the Roman Empire is a story in itself. Legend has it that Rome the city-state was founded in

753 BCE. It became a Republic in 510 BCE. The linguistic consequence of the Roman Empire is found across southern, central, and eastern Europe in languages such as Catalan, French, Italian, Occitan (France), Portuguese, Spanish, Romanian, Romansch (Switzerland), and Walloon (Belgium). In the discipline of linguistics, these languages are said to belong to the Italic branch of the Indo-European languages. However, they are known popularly as the Romance languages. The term *Romance* comes from a meaning that the Latin word *Romanus* took on in 212 CE when the Emperor Caracalla decreed that all freeborn inhabitants of the Empire should thereafter be Roman citizens. The wider scope of the adjective called for a new noun. The Roman provinces had names such as Gallia, Hibernia, Hispania, and Italia; and the area to the north of the Empire where uncivilized tribes lived was called Germania. Thus, on the model of these names, the term *Romania* was coined.[10] The word is first attested in the fourth century as a comprehensive name for the whole commonwealth, which included its large Greek-speaking area. The *Romani* in the broad political sense were opposed to the *Barbari*, all who lived outside the confines of the Empire, and this latter term was a borrowing from Greek, as was pointed out in Chapter 3, which originally meant 'of unintelligible speech.'[11]

Latin first replaced Etruscan on the Italian peninsula. It later replaced Celtic in Gallia and Hispania as well as Thracian in its eastern outpost, today's Romania. The Celtic substratum influence is present in both modern French and Spanish. In French, a part of the standard counting system is vigesimal, which is based on the number 20. The French word for 'eighty' is *quatre-vingts* 'four-twenties,' and 'ninety' is *quatre-vingt-dix* 'four-twenties-ten.' This counting system is deemed to be a relic of Celtic counting practices.[12] In Modern Spanish, the borrowed word *izquierdo* 'left' is a replacement of Latin *sinister*, and it is similarly deemed to be from the Celtic substratum, although there was a hint it might come from Basque which has the word *ezke(r)* for 'left.' Philologists have concluded, however, that the Basque word is a borrowing from Celtic, because of the widespread use of cognate forms of Western Romance: Portuguese (Iberian peninsula) *esquerdo*, Catalan (Iberian peninsula) *esquerre*, Provençal (France) *esquer*, Gascon (France) *esquerr*. In the extreme east, namely Romania, the only traces of the early Thracian/Dacian substratum are found in three vocabulary items: *varză* 'cabbage,' *barză* 'stork,' and *brânză* '(feta) cheese.'

Latin was spread around the empire primarily by the army, which was originally made up of citizens but later came to enlist men from all over, who were drawn to Roman policy of granting soldiers their own land after their discharge. Today, when educated people think of Latin, they likely think of the Classical writers such as Cato, Catullus, Cicero, and Ovid. For the early writers of Latin, there was an obvious model, namely Greek, the prestige language of the day, and as the Roman Republic and then Empire developed, so did the Roman intelligentsia's interest in Greek. Written Classical Latin was thus a studied literary style and counted as H. As always, when there is an H, there is an L. In the days of the Roman Empire, L was 'country speech' known as *sermo rusticus* as opposed to H known as *sermo urbanus*. L was also called 'popular speech' *sermo plebius* or *sermo vulgaris* or just plain 'everyday speech' *sermo cotidianus, sermo usualis*. Whatever the name, it was all Latin. The Roman soldiers spoke this rustic, plebian, cotidian, and usual Latin, known by convention as Vulgar Latin. The no-fun academic name is Proto-Romance.

Because Vulgar Latin was, by definition, nonliterary speech, it was not typically written down and remains largely unattested. Nevertheless, it is easy enough to reconstruct. For instance, the Romance word for 'horse' must have come from a Vulgar Latin word much like *caballus*, because there is French *cheval*, Italian, *cavallo*, Portuguese *cavalo*, Spanish *caballo*, and Romanian *cal*. The Classical Latin word for 'horse' is *equus*, and that is what the Classical writers use. However, *caballus* makes an appearance in Horace's *Satires* in a clearly deprecatory meaning, probably something like 'nag.' So, *equus* is Classical Latin, and *caballus* is Vulgar Latin. We can also infer quite a bit about the spoken language from the comedies of Plautus, a writer who represents popular speech better than any other Latin author before the development of Christian literature. The hallmarks of colloquial Latin are:

(i)   the frequent introduction of the personal pronoun with the verb;
(ii) the use of the indicative mood where Latin would use subjunctive;
(iii) the assimilation of the neuter declension into the masculine; feminine, neuter, and masculine have remained distinct only in Romanian;
(iv) the lack of distinction between the interrogative and relative pronouns: *qui vocat?* for *quis vocat?* 'who speaks?';
(v)   a larger proportion of words that are derived – substantives expanded by suffixes or prefixes – which accounts for so much of the evolution of Romance vocabulary.

In short, what can be considered the major characteristics of today's Romance languages were already alive in spoken Latin during Classical times.

Given the crisscrossing patterns of contact, as Roman soldiers and administrators patrolled the territory, linguist John Green (1987) has pointed out it is impossible for the Romance philologist to make definitive subgroupings for these languages. Instead, he proposes three different geographic groups, based on the particular feature under review:

(i)   a North/South grouping, where French is North, and everything else is South; when looking at the phonology of these languages, French is clearly the most radically different than the Latin/Vulgar Latin base, in having lost the original final vowels and most of the final consonants; it thus stands alone in this category;
(ii) an East/West grouping, where Italian and Romanian are East, while French, Spanish, and Portuguese are West; when considering how the various languages form the plurals of nouns, the West plurals are indicated with *–s*, for example, Spanish *casa/casas* 'house/houses,' while East plurals are indicated by vocalic alternations, for example, Romanian *casa/case* 'house/houses'; and
(iii) a Center/Periphery grouping where French and Italian (and sometimes Spanish) are in the Center, while Portuguese and Romanian are on the Periphery; quite a few vocabulary items illustrate this split – to name but one, the word for 'beautiful' (masculine form given here): in Portuguese it is *formos*, in Spanish it is *hermos*, and in Romanian it is *frumos*, while in French it is *beau / bel* (before vowels) and Italian *bel*.

The Romance languages thus offer a third graphic model, beyond the tree and the wave discussed in Chapter 7, for how to represent linguistic expansions. It is the rhizome, from Greek *rhizōma* 'mass of roots.' In botany, a rhizome is the root system of plants like bamboo or bunch grasses, which have shoots that can be seen above ground but which are held together with a highly entangled set of roots. Only a rhizome can capture the tangled, intertwined sets of relationships among the Romance languages.

We have arrived at the moment when many of the world's stocks reached their geographic limits, and this was the time before the beginning of widespread literacy, world religions, and colonialism pursued on a global scale. One thousand years after the end of the Roman Empire, those speakers of Romance languages with cities on the Atlantic – the French, the Spanish, and the Portuguese – were poised to push off from those ports to sail around the world in order to claim what they could claim. This post-Columbian colonialism was to spread the tangled Romance roots all over the world.

Religions as First Nations and Missionaries as Colonizers

In the beginning, religious ideology shaped linguistic ideology. For centuries, Western European scholars tried to put Western European languages in a lineage with what they considered to be the God-given language, Hebrew. A theory of language occurs in Genesis when Adam names the animals God made. The view of language-as-inventory resides within the larger frame of a belief in an immediate, that is, nonlinguistically mediated, reality. Given that in this view there is only one reality, different languages are understood to be inventories of different labels for the same parts of the same reality. A moral issue has already stolen into the picture: Eden was monolingual; because of the sins of Babel, the world is now cursed with multilingualism. It is no wonder, then, that certain missionaries will seek to convert not only the faiths but also the languages of those to whom they are ministering, to bring all of God's children back to the word of God – or to the closest equivalent of that word on earth at the time of the ministering.

Before nation-states and their titular national languages had their twin birth in the late eighteenth century, there were religions, and religions organized the identities of the Us versus the Them: the Christians versus the Infidels, the Muslims versus the Infidels, the Protestants versus the Catholics versus the Eastern Orthodox, the Sunni versus the Shiite, the Hindu versus the Buddhists, ad infinitum.[13] Religions cohere around sacred narratives which function as origin stories, identifying those who belong in the tribe and those who do not. Thus, they preceded by hundreds and sometimes thousands of years' identification by nationality and what language a person speaks. Even today, when nation-states are supposedly secularized, it is difficult to tease apart, say, Greek, Polish, or Tibetan national identity from their religious identity as Greek Orthodox, Catholics, or Buddhists (Safran 2008:179). This is because religious identity is bound to the language of the sacred narratives, which, in turn, helped form the national identities in the first place. Two further examples: Henry VIII's authorization of an English version of the Bible, which helped to create a sense of English national identity, and Luther's German translation, which helped to foster a sense of a German nation.

No group exemplifies the religion–nation–language intersection better than the Jews. The Hebrew Bible has sometimes been called a *portable fatherland*. At the end of the nineteenth century, after almost 2000 years of Jewish diaspora and in the midst of a wave of global nation formations, the Hebrew Bible served as the authoritative reference for the claim of the Jewish nation on their ancestral homeland. When they returned to their homeland, the spoken Hebrew language revival began. Before the revival, Jews had maintained their tribal/national identity not only in their religious practice, preserved in textual Biblical Hebrew, but also in their linguistic practice: the Sephardic Jews in the Ottoman Empire spoke the Judeo-Spanish language Ladino, not Turkish, and the Ashkenazi Jews in eastern Europe spoke the Germanic language Yiddish, thereby distinguishing themselves from their Slavic-speaking neighbors. Many Jews in the United States have assimilated to English and, in the transfer, brought to American English the zest of Yiddish in words like *bupkis* 'nothing,' *goy* 'non-Jew,' *maven* 'expert,' *meshugena* 'crazy,' *mishagos* 'confusion,' *shiksa* 'non-Jewish girl,' *shtick*, *spiel*, and so forth. The Orthodox Jews in Crown Heights, Brooklyn, however, maintain their identity by continuing to speak Yiddish.

Religions, like languages, simultaneously unite (define the Us) and divide (identify the Them). In addition, religion and language share the following characteristics, as noted by Brubaker (2013): (i) individuals are born into one, the other, or both; they are sources of social, cultural, and political identification; (ii) languages that are not institutionalized are considered to be dialects, just as religions that are not institutionalized are considered to be sects or superstitions; (iii) they can be changed; a person can move to a new country and learn a new language, even forgetting the native language; a person can have a religious conversion. Religions and languages differ in that: (i) language is additive, while religion is not; a person can speak two or more languages; a person does not usually practice two or more religions; and (ii) language is unavoidable, as noted in Chapter 6, while religion is not; a person may choose not to practice a religion, but a person cannot not speak a particular language. It is the *unavoidability* of the use of a particular language in terms of the human condition that makes a particular language as precious to its speakers as breathing.

Religions, as belief systems, are vast, but they are not, point for point, coextensive with the even greater epistemological framework(s) created by and spread throughout the languages in which different religions find expression. Religions aspire, nevertheless, to universalism in a way that particular languages and then certainly nations, which have borders, do not. In the last 1400 years, Islam has conquered the hearts and minds of one billion people from West Africa to Indonesia, and the status of Classical Arabic is unparalleled. The Buddha attained enlightenment under a fig tree in India some 2500 years ago, and Buddhism spread east and west. Now Buddhist temples can be found coast to coast in the United States, and the associated terminology – *satori*, *karma*, *dharma*, *nirvana* – came along with the religion.

The Catholic Church, founded in 1 CE, is perhaps the world's oldest global organization.[14] In the post-Columbian New World, Catholic missionaries converted millions of indigenous peoples to Catholicism and shifted their languages to Spanish and French. In Indochina, the French Fathers not only romanized Vietnamese writing but also banned Chinese characters as a way to stamp out the Confucianism that had held sway in that part of the world for millennia. They began the process of transliterating the dynastic records and ancient literatures, which activity French administrators later took over. In Cambodia, for instance, these administrators were struck by what they considered the backwardness of the societies they set out to rule. Upon arriving in Phnom Penh in the 1860s, for instance, French explorers encountered the heads of executed criminals rotting under a swarm of flies atop bamboo poles, grim testimonies to the foolhardiness of anyone daring to disobey even the slightest whim of the king. The French in *Indochine* were on a *mission civilisatrice*, which meant stamping out old ways of thinking, writing, and behaving, and the most effective way was to make a clean, visual, and written break with China and the Chinese belief system of Confucianism. Above all, the French did not subscribe to the Chinese proverb: 'The wise man does not seek an empire, and the empire comes to him.' Neither did they, however, achieve full-scale language shift.

Today, English-speaking Anglicans, Protestants, Mormons, and Evangelicals make up the bulk of worldwide missions, and they are continuing the Western tradition of disrupting long-existing social, religious, and linguistic ecosystems in Papua New Guinea, Southeast Asia, Latin America and Africa. Pennycook and Makoni (2005) note that these missionaries are following British practice, established in Africa in the nineteenth century: (i) move the first converts to the new religion up in social class to become the literate proto-bourgeoisie with English as the language of upward mobility; (ii) have missionaries translate the Bible into the local languages; whether or not the missionaries demarcate one language from another in a way that corresponds to how the speakers of those languages understand their own relationships to those norms is not important; (iii) use these translations in the native populations' own languages against their own belief systems.

In the developing world today, classes in English as a second language are sometime venues of stealth religious conversion. In short, missionary work has long worked hand in glove with the colonialists who paved the way for the missionaries and then used them to civilize the native populations. We, the authors, are not against religion. We are also not against all forms of neoliberal political and economic organization. We do, however, deplore the fact that many missionaries, business people, and politicians involve themselves in linguistic ecosystems with no understanding of the language loop and no appreciation for the value of its many different and beautiful configurations.

English as an Emergent Language Family

We, the authors, call European long-distance maritime colonization *Globalization 2.0*. We now take another look at the linguistic legacy of this colonialism. Only time will tell – namely, another couple of thousand years – whether English will come to make its own language family of the same depth and diversity of, say, the Romance languages. If it does, then the origins of this new Anglo family can be explained in two words: British Empire. There are two ways to look at the impact of English in the world today: first, by cataloguing vernacular universals or, for English, angloversals, and second, by highlighting the particular influence of substrate languages of the varieties of English spoken around the world. The variety we focus on here is Singlish.

Angloversals

Szmrecsanyi and Kortmann (2008) define an angloversal as a feature that tends to recur in vernacular varieties of the globalized language English.[15] In the many varieties of English around the globe, for instance, adverbs tend to have the same morphological form as adjectives. Other tendencies include: (i) conjugation regularization or leveling of irregular verb forms. In Chapter 7, we called this process *analogy*; (ii) further leveling in the lack of subject–verb agreement: *they is, they was*, etc.; (iii) multiple negation of the type: *Ain't no cat can't get in no bin*; multiple negation has come and gone and come again in the history of English, and now it swirls around the globe; (iv) absence of copula: *She tall*; if one were to count up the languages with 'to be' (copula) and the ones without 'to be' (zero copula), the without-languages would win. Not even all Indo-European languages feel the necessity for 'to be,' the Slavonic ones, for instance. These four features reach 100% in the Americas. However, since they appear only up to perhaps 75% elsewhere in the world, Szmrecsanyi and Kortmann call them areoversals.

Substrate influences

The presence of English in Asia now looms large. Already, in 1997, an issue of the Chinese magazine known as 'Consumption Guide' published an article entitled *Zájiāo Zhōngwén* 'Hybrid Chinese.' The article points out that this hybrid language is in fashion among Chinese professionals. The language is Mandarin, but it is mixed with English, Cantonese, and Taiwanese expressions. The article notes that: "For those who frequent office buildings of foreign and Sino-foreign business, even when dealing with local professionals, if they don't understand English, they look like country bumpkins" (quoted in Zhang 2005:431–432). Knowing English brings a person into the cosmopolitan world.

The presence of English in Asia is hardly new. Beginning in the eighteenth and nineteenth centuries, a trade **pidgin**, called Chinese Pidgin English (CPE), once flourished in the port cities of China and is now extinct. A pidgin is a contact language that, by definition, has no native speakers, and the domain of its use is highly limited, either in trading transactions or on plantations. Although the exact etymology for this term is not known, one promising possibility is that the term *pidgin* came from the CPE pronunciation of the word *business*. Unsurprisingly, CPE had a strong substrate influence from Chinese, particularly Cantonese. Chinese specialist Stephen Matthews (2010:763) notes an unusual case of substrate influence in the use of *piece* as a numeral classifier in CPE, evidenced in the phrase *one piecee coolie* 'a worker.' The phrase *long time no see*, common in American English, appears to have come through CPE and is a calque of the Cantonese phrase: *hou² loi⁶ nou⁵ gin³*. The definition of a pidgin is usually contrasted with that of a **creole**, which is traditionally defined as a language whose speakers have only been exposed to a pidgin. By definition, then, a creole has native speakers. See the discussion of Haitian Creole, later in this chapter.

Turning to the many varieties of English currently spoken in this part of the world, one stands out: Singlish, which is spoken by a majority of Singaporeans as a first or second language.[16] It is also the only variety of English in Asia acquired as a primary language by its speakers, and it is interesting in the way it combines both Sinitic and Malay grammatical elements into the language. Ansaldo (2010) outlines these elements, beginning with verbless structures and topic prominence. Cantonese has the structure:

keoi⁵ hou² leng³,

and Malay has the structure:

dia banyak cantik.

They both translate word-for-word as: *S/he very pretty*. It is no wonder, then, that Standard Singlish has no copula in the presence of predicate nominals and adjectives, and accepts utterances such as *He doctor* and *He good*. Although Cantonese and Malay do not make a gender distinction in the third person singular pronoun, Singlish does.

We have already noted that Cantonese, in the Chinese family, has little inflectional morphology, as does Malay. Languages with little inflectional morphology tend to be topic prominent, that is, they put up front what the main idea of the utterance is, since they do not have inflectional morphology for the job.[17] Whatever is the main idea is put first, independent of grammatical status. Here are some Singlish examples – subject: *Today weather very hot wat* (Today's weather is very hot, as you know.); object: *Lionel met (him) already* (I have already met Lionel); or adjective: *Expensive the Durian here*. It is no surprise that both Cantonese and Malay are topic prominent as well.

When it comes to verbal marking, Singlish prefers aspect to tense. Cantonese and Malay similarly do not mark tense. In Singlish, the aspectual markers for perfective, durative, and habitual are derived from the English adverbs *already, still,* and *always*. Consider: *Oh, they go already ah?* (Oh, they have already left?), *They still give my hoping lah* (They still give me hope), and *Always seated at the cashier old lady you know* (You know, the old lady (who is) always seated at the cashier). Although it is the case that standard varieties of English do specify 'time when' (tense) of an action, the rise of aspectual distinctions, that is 'speaker's view of the character of the action,' has been occurring for the last 700 or 800 years. The progressive aspect is widespread in standard varieties of English, and an utterance such as *The house is being built* was considered unusual or even ungrammatical as recently as the eighteenth century, while the possibility of *we are being reasonable* (progressive with an adjective) did not exist until the twentieth century. Because Singlish makes little use of the progressive aspect of Standard English, it must be the case that Singlish is aligning itself with the aspectual distinctions available in the ambient languages of Cantonese and Malay.

Finally, you may have noticed several utterance final particles, such as *lah* and *wat*, which express a speaker's attitude or emotion about a situation or the speaker's belief about her interlocutor's state of mind. There are easily eight such particles in use in Singlish, all borrowed from Malay and Cantonese, and when they are borrowed from Cantonese, the complex tonal features are borrowed as well. Many more unique features of Singlish exist, in particular with respect to its vocabulary, but the few grammatical features mentioned here suffice to exemplify once again how speakers continually and creatively weave together the linguistic resources they have at hand.

Final Note: Creoles and the Case of Kreyòl Ayisyen

On the other side of the world from Vietnam, the French exercised a linguistic influence far different and greater in the New World than the one they had in Southeast Asia. In the Caribbean, the French and the Spanish were the two main contestants squabbling over who got which islands.[18] One island, Hispaniola, ended in a draw. In 1697, the Spanish took the lion's share and called it the Dominican Republic. The French took a smaller, western part and called it Haiti. Haiti is the only country founded after a successful slave revolt, which occurred in 1804, making it second only to the United States in claiming nationhood in the Western Hemisphere. Its official languages are French and Haitian French Creole, known locally as Kreyòl Ayisyen. The country's motto should be familiar to you from Chapter 4: *Liberté, Egalité, Fraternité*.

For Haitian French Creole, the **lexifier language** is French, which means that the vocabulary and structural base of Kreyòl Ayisyen come from French. However, it also has influences from West African languages, notably Wolof, Fon, and Ewe, and from the Native Caribbean language Taino. It also has Spanish and Portuguese touches. In terms of phonology, Haitian Creole is much like Standard French, in that it has the four nasal vowels exemplified in the classic phrase *un bon vin blanc* 'a good white wine,' the successive vowels being [ū] [õ] [ĩ] [ã]. It also has the fronted rounded vowel [y], but it does not have the Standard French uvular [ʀ]. Kreyòl Ayisyen also looks very different from Standard French, which spells the language *créole haïtien*. It comes as no surprise that the spelling of Haitian Creole has caused controversy for looking too English with its plentiful use of *y* and *w* and for not looking like Standard French with all its historical spellings and many silent letters.

Creoles are particularly controversial in the linguistic community. The bone of contention is over exactly how much contact the pidgin-speaking community has with the lexifying standard language as the pidgin becomes a creole. Some linguists maintain that there are strong breaks in the transmission of the lexifying language, making creole grammars nearly *de novo* creations. A strong break seems plausible, given that many of the world's recent creoles arose on coasts or islands. In Hawaii, for instance, speakers of many different languages – Malay, Japanese, Tagalog, native Hawaiian – were brought in to work on pineapple plantations more or less as slaves, and they used the language of the English-speaking owners to communicate among themselves. However, they lived apart from the English-speaking owners, and so their children who creolized the pidgin did not have extensive contact with the standard variety. It is also true that creoles such as Hawaiian Creole English and Haitian Creole French have a particular structural profile, and it is one shared by all creoles; for instance, they are all SVO. The structural profile suggests that something special happens in the transition from a pidgin to a creole. We will enlarge on the subject of the structure of creoles in Chapters 10 and 11.

Other linguists maintain that the notion of a break with the lexifying language is exaggerated, and they deny that creoles have any kind of unusual status as language qua language. They maintain that some of the features of creoles are found in the varieties spoken by the colonizers, and these features are different from those varieties spoken in the metropole, be it London, Paris, Amsterdam, Lisbon, or Madrid. We, the authors, take no position on how much contact acquiring creole speakers have with the native speakers of the lexifying language. However, we can say that there is always a strong break with the resources of the various layers of the lexifying language loop, as described in Chapter 2. Early-generation creole speakers do not have access to the links to the landscape in which the lexifying language took shape, nor do they have access to the customary cultural routines, behaviors, phraseology, and implications speakers of the lexifying language have worked out over centuries and sometimes millennia.

In any case, it can be said that when speakers turn a pidgin into a creole, the rate at which native speakers speak is naturally faster than that of the pidgin, and this speed creates phonological changes, which engender morphological changes, which in turn causes irregular forms to crop up. For instance, in Haitian Creole the definite article *-la* follows the noun: *lakay-la* 'the house' *pitit-la* 'the child.' After nasal consonants, *-la* becomes *-nã*: *nõm-nã* 'the man,' *machĩn-nã* 'the machine.' The regular phonological process of nasal assimilation creates a morphological alternation in the definite article. Such a complication is not found in the pidgin.

As a pidgin becomes a creole, the vocabulary expands to fill the expressive needs of the speakers, and its functional use extends to all areas of life. Then, inevitably, the creolized native language, like all native languages, comes to index both individual and group identity.

Language Profile: Tiếng Việt [Vietnamese (Austro-Asiatic)]

Functional overview

Vietnamese is spoken by approximately 81 million people in the Socialist Republic of Vietnam and by several million more people living outside the country. In and around Orange County California, for instance, there are more than 150,000 Vietnamese speakers. Vietnamese is in the Vietic branch of the Austro-Asiatic language family and is closely related to Mường, also spoken in Vietnam.

There are three traditionally recognized varieties of Vietnamese: North (home of the present-day capital, Hanoi), Central (home of the historic capital, Huê), and South (home of the economically vibrant Ho Chi Minh City, which is still often referred to as Saigon). Some differences are phonetic: *gì* 'what' and *giờ* 'hour, time' are pronounced [zì] and [zờ] in the North and [yì] and [yờ] in the South. Some differences are lexical: the word for 'wallet' is *ví* in the North and *bóp* in the South. Although there are some Central varieties that are considered difficult to understand, it is the case that, through education and mass media, most Vietnamese are familiar with both Northern and Southern styles of speaking.

Prominent structural characteristics

Tone versus intonation   Indo-European languages are intonation languages, which means that a vocal contour extends across an entire utterance to produce, say, a question or a statement. By way of contrast, many languages use vocal contour on individual words in order to produce different lexical meanings. These languages are called tone languages.

Vietnamese has six tones. The names for the tones name the contours: *dấu ngang* is the flat tone (*ngang* means 'horizontal'); *dấu huyền* is the falling tone (*huyền* has no special meaning, except to name the tone), *dấu ngã* is the tumbling tone (*ngã* means 'to tumble'), *dấu hỏi* is the asking tone (*hỏi* means 'to ask'), *dấu sắc* is the sharp tone (*sắc* means 'sharp'), and *dấu nặng* is the heavy tone (*nặng* means 'heavy'). In the Vietnamese alphabet, graph *đ* has the value [y], while graph *đ* has the value [d].

Vietnamese is monosyllabic, allows no consonant clusters, and has a relatively wide range of vowels. Not all syllables have a six-way tone contrast similar to: *quân* 'army soldier (archaic),' *quần* 'trousers,' *quẩn* 'to be hard-up,' *quẩn* 'to hover, to be in the way,' *quấn* 'to roll (turban, bandage),' and *quận* 'district.' However, the great majority of syllables have many tonal possibilities, for example: *dứa* 'pineapple,' *dưa* 'melon,' *dừa* 'coconut.' (Graph ư represents a high middle unrounded vowel.) Because tone is phonemic, Vietnamese speakers do not feel any special relationship among words that have the same syllable structure but a different tone, for example, the three kinds of fruit just mentioned. Nor is one felt, say, in the phrase *vòi voi* 'elephant trunk' where *vòi* is 'trunk, spout,' and *voi* is 'elephant.' These are syllabic coincidences.

Vietnamese has some evidence of tonal **sandhi**. The words *nhiều* 'many' and the number *mười* 'ten' both change to flat tone when they are in common combinations such as *bao nhieu* 'how much/many' and *hai mươi, ba mươi*, etc. 'twenty, thirty, etc.' In addition, sound change involving tone can and does occur. Currently, the phrase for 'thank you' is fluctuating between *cám ơn* and *cảm ơn*.

Classifiers Indo-European languages distinguish between count nouns and mass nouns. Words like *shirt* and *book* are called count nouns, because they can be counted: one shirt, two shirts, one book, two books, etc. Mass nouns are words like *snow* or *golf*. They cannot be counted. There is no 'one snow,' 'two snows,' 'one golf,' 'two golfs.' However, when a perspective is taken on a way to perceive snow or golf – that is, when snow or golf is viewed with respect to other potentially similar objects – the possibility arises of: one flake of snow, two flakes of snow, one round of golf, two rounds of golf. In English, the word *flake* particularizes something small and flat with an irregular boundary. Accordingly, bits of dandruff are imagined as flakes. Now what does *round* suggest? How about: "Let's give this woman a round of applause!" "Hey, bartender, I'll spring for another round of drinks for the house!"

For many Southeast and East Asian languages (Burmese, Chinese, Japanese, Korean, Malay, Thai), all nouns are considered mass nouns, and therefore all nouns, even those like *shirt* and *book* require a classifier (CL) once they are particularized. In Vietnamese, 'one shirt' is *một* 'one' *cái* (CL) *áo* 'shirt'; 'two books' is *hai* 'two' *quyển* (CL) *sách* 'book'. As in English, classifiers in Vietnamese tend to identify a set of objects by some criterion: their shape, what they are made of, how they are used, whether they are hard or soft, etc. Just as English 'piece' is a kind of default classifier for many mass nouns: piece of luggage, piece of furniture, juicy piece of gossip, etc., so the classifier *cái* in Vietnamese is general and is used with many objects: *nón* 'hat,' *bàn* 'table,' *máy may* 'sewing machine,' *thang cuốn* 'escalator,' *túi xách* 'purse,' *bảng* 'bulletin board.'

Cái can be used to make abstract nouns out of adjectives: *cái đẹp* 'beauty,' *cái ác* 'evil,' *cái tốt* 'goodness.' When *cái* is used to classify the word for *người* 'person,' as in *cái người*, it is clear the speaker has a negative opinion of that person, because the speaker has classified that person as a thing. Children overextend the boundaries of this classifier and must be corrected.

Another high-profile classifier is *con*, and it is used primarily for animals: *vịt* 'duck,' *chó* 'dog,' *mèo* 'cat,' *voi* 'elephant,' etc. The word *dao* 'knife' has curiously slipped into this category. Categories are fairly fixed, but like everything else in language, speakers determine what is what. In current Hanoi slang, one can refer to one's *xe máy* 'motorbike' with the classifier *con* (rather than the usual classifier *chiếc*), thus putting this all-important object in the light of a pony or horse. The word *sông* 'river' takes *con* as a classifier when it is seen as something that is moving and going somewhere. However, when a river is perceived from the point of view of what it is made of, namely water, then it receives the classifier *dòng*. Classifiers frame perspectives.

Expressing emotion Intonation languages can change the tonal pattern of a word in order to express a speaker's emotional or mental attitude toward a situation: "Really?" "Well, really! I never!" "I'm *really* hungry." This cannot be done in a tone language. Now, it is possible to show emotion in Vietnamese by raising one's voice in a phrase such as *Lâu quá không gặp!* ('Long time, no see!'). However, the relationships among the tones have to be preserved. Emotion can also be conveyed lexically. The English sing-song version of 'boring!' comes out in Vietnamese as *chán ngắt!* The word *chán* 'boring' alone cannot convey the extent of the emotion.

To express a speaker's attitude or emotion toward a situation, Vietnamese more often mobilizes a series of sentence enders (SE). For instance, *Thật đấy!* is the Vietnamese version of "Really!" To the word *thật* 'true' is added the SE *đấy* in order to affirm definitely that the speaker believes in what is said. Consider the following exchange between a mother and child:

Con	*lại*	*ăn*	*nữa*	*hả?*	*hả* = expresses the mother's surprise
(my) child	again	eat	more,	SE	

'Are you eating *again*?'

Con	*đói*	*mà,*	*mẹ.*	*mà* = emphasizes the child's reason
child	hungry	SE,	mother.	

'But I'm *really* hungry, Mom.'

Rhythmic balance One of the beauties of Vietnamese is heard in patterns that seek rhythmic balance. Many nouns, verbs, and adjectives in Vietnamese have two parts, such as the adjective *mệt mỏi* 'tired.' Speakers tend to use one or both parts depending on what they are qualifying. If they are speaking of their *cơ thể* 'body,' they will say *cơ thể mệt mỏi*. If they are speaking of their *tay* 'hand,' they will say *tay mỏi*. It sounds good for a two-syllable noun to be balanced by a two-syllable adjective, and a one-syllable noun by a one-syllable adjective. Many nouns have two parts that can be separated, like *tiệc tùng* 'party,' and thus it is possible to say 'fun party' two ways, either *tiệc tùng vui vẻ* or, more simply, *tiệc vui*. The possibilities run throughout the language. Take the word *đồng hồ* 'watch.' Like the word *cơ thể* 'body,' the two parts of *đồng hồ* cannot be separated. Now, take the verb *sửa chữa* 'to repair.' You can certainly speak of watch repair as *sửa đồng hồ*. It is not incorrect, but *sửa chữa đồng hồ* sounds better.

The single/double word contrast also carries meaning. The single word *bạn* means 'friend,' while the doubled *bạn bè* means 'friends in general.' A 'close friend' will be *bạn thân*, while 'close friends in general' will be *bạn bè than thiết*. The doubled version of the word carries the semantic coloring of the general case.

A Salient Cultural Characteristic: The Pronoun System

The foreigners who learn Vietnamese are often taught to use the pronoun *tôi* to refer to him or herself. This is, indeed, the easiest way to identify oneself, and *tôi* functions like the English first-person pronoun *I*. However, the Vietnamese use *tôi* only in restricted occasions, for instance, when one is giving a formal address to a large group of people. In daily life, the pronouns Vietnamese speakers use are not like those used in English that constantly shift in a conversation, where the *I* of the speaker and the *you* of the responder refer to one and the same person, only from a different point of view. Rather, Vietnamese pronoun usage reflects social roles and relationships, and the pronouns remain stable as long as one's role and the relationship with one's interlocutor(s) remain stable. When something changes in a role or a relationship, pronoun usage changes accordingly.

The sentences, above, illustrating the sentence enders *hả* and *mà* give a first idea of normal Vietnamese pronoun usage. The mother addresses her child as *con* 'child.' The child addresses himself to his mother as *con* 'child.' If the mother were to address herself in this situation, she would call herself *mẹ* 'mother.' In a family, a younger sister or brother addresses an older sister as *chị* 'older sister' and an older brother as *anh* 'older brother.' The older sister or older brother addresses younger sibling(s) as *em* (no gender distinction). One's aunt is addressed as *cô* and one's uncle as *bác*. Grandparents address their grandchildren as *cháu* 'grandchild.' The grandchild addresses their grandfather as *ông* and their grandmother as *bà*.

These basic relationships extend into all normal interactions in public life. If you are speaking with a woman you perceive to be older than yourself, you refer to her as *chị* 'older sister.' She will respond by referring to herself as *chị*. How she responds to you will depend on your relationship. If you are younger than she is, she will call you *em* ('younger sibling'). She will call herself *mẹ* 'mother' when speaking to her children. She will refer to her children as *nó* when speaking about them to someone else, which is a different pronoun than she would use when referring to a 'they,' namely *họ*, with whom she has no family relationship. When speaking with her husband, she will refer to him as *anh* 'older brother' and refer to herself as *em* 'younger sibling.' As she and her husband age, they might begin using *ông* 'grandfather' and *bà* 'grandmother' as the pronouns for one another.

The *anh/em* usage in love relationships is potentially tricky. Take the case of a young man and young woman. When they first meet, it is determined that she is two years older than he is, and so she is *chị* 'older sister,' and he is *em* 'younger sibling.' As time goes on, they decide they like one another. While they negotiate their new relationship, they call each other by their first names. When they become an item, he is now *anh* 'older brother,' and she is now *em* 'younger sibling.' After a while, they part ways, and the young woman finds a new love. One day, she and her new love run into her old love. At some point during the three-way conversation, the new love turns to the young woman and wants to know, referring here to her former love, "Why are you still calling him *anh*?"

To move within the pronoun system of Vietnamese is to experience the richness and closeness of relations that govern all aspects of private and public life. It is in this context that one can appreciate the affect behind the nickname for the revered Vietnamese leader, Ho Chi Minh, who is commonly known as *Bác Hồ*, 'Uncle Ho.'

Exercises

Exercise 1

Go to Chapter 8 on the website and listen as many times as you like to the pronunciation of the sample words illustrating the six different tones of Vietnamese.

When you feel you have a basic auditory grasp of their contours, listen as many times as you like to the well-known Vietnamese story, below, which is written out without the tones and translated. As you listen, mark each word with one of the following symbols here shown over vowel *a*: a (no mark, flat tone), à (falling), ả (asking), ã (tumbling), á (sharp), or ạ (heavy).

An Dương Vương (the title is the name of an ancient king – to get you started, all three parts of the name of this prince have flat tone)

An Dương Vương	*la vua cua nước*	*Âu Lac.*	*Nha*	*vua*	*được*	*thân*
	is king of country	Au Lac.	The	king	benefit	magician

'An Duong Vuong was the king of Au Lac. The king had the magician Kim

Kim Quy giup xây	*thanh Cô Loa,*	*gân*	*Ha Nôi*	*ngay nay.*	*Để giup*
Kim Quy help build	castle Co Loa,	near	Hanoi	those days.	In order to help

Quy's help building Co Loa castle, near Hanoi in those days. In order to help

nha vua	*bao vệ*	*đât nước*	*khoi nan*	*ngoai xâm,*	*thân*	*Kim Quy*
the king	protect	country	to be free	outsiders,	magician	Kim Quy

the king protect the country and be free of outsiders, the magician Kim Quy

trao cho	*nha vua*	*môt*	*chiêc*	*mong*	*va*	*noi:*	*"Hay sai*
give	the king	a	CL	(finger) nail	and	says:	"Ask

gave the king a fingernail and said, "Ask the

thơ gioi	*lam*	*môt chiêc*	*no*	*va*	*lây*	*mong*	*nay*	*lam thanh*
specialist	make	one CL	bow	and	use	nail	this	make

specialist(s) to make a bow and use this nail to make

lấy   no.   Với   no   ấy,   một   người lính   thương cung   có thể   giết   chết
handle bow. With bow   this, one   soldier   usually also   able   kill   dead
the bow handle. With this bow, one soldier will be able to slay thousands of

được   hang ngan   tên giặc   chỉ   băng   một   mui tên."
able   thousands   enemy   only   by   one   arrow."
enemies with only one arrow."'

Exercise 2

Chinese roots in Vietnamese   As discussed in Chapter 8, lexical items of Chinese origin
(Hán Việt) have been thoroughly woven into the Vietnamese vocabulary. Look at the
following three groups of Hán Việt compounds and determine what you think is
the best word/idea for the common element that makes these groups hang together
semantically:

a.
địa cầu = 'globe'
địa chỉ = 'address'
địa đạo = 'tunnel'
(note: Vietnamese *đạo* comes from Chinese *dao/tao* meaning 'path' or 'way')
địa điểm = 'location'
địa lý = 'geography'

What do you think the Chinese root *địa* probably means? _____

b.
ngữ căn = 'root, radical'
ngôn ngữ học = 'linguistics'
ngữ nghĩa học = 'semantics'
ngữ pháp = 'grammar'
phương ngữ = 'dialect'

What do you think the Chinese root *ngữ* probably means? _____

c.
bác sĩ = 'medical doctor'
ca sĩ = 'professional singer'
nhạc sĩ = 'professional song writer'
nha sĩ = 'dentist'
viên sĩ = 'member in an academic organization

What do you think the Chinese root sĩ probably means?_____

Determine the meanings of the following Vietnamese compounds:

  bất = 'not'; động = 'move'; sản = 'product'
  bất động sản =   _____

Hint: This compound is similar to the etymological meaning of the French word *immeuble*, which is something that does not move. Can you guess – or do you already know – what an *immeuble* is? Side note: the French word *meuble* 'furniture' denotes a thing that is movable. This distinction also works in Spanish (*inmuebles*) and borrowed into German (*Immobilien*).

điện = 'electricity'; thoại = 'speak'; di = 'move'; động = 'move'
điện thoại di động =   _____

hải = 'harbor'; sản 'product'
hải sản =   _____

máy = 'machine'
máy ảnh (ảhn = 'picture') =   _____
máy lạnh (lạnh = 'cool/cold') =   _____
máy vi tính = (vi – 'small'; tính = 'to figure') _____
thang máy (thang = 'ladder') =   _____

nhà = 'house, dwelling, abode, building, space'
nhà máy (máy = 'machine') =   _____
nhà sách (sách = 'book') =   _____
nhà thờ (thờ = 'to worship') =   _____
nhà vệ sinh (vệ sinh = 'sanitary') =   _____

núi = 'mountain'; lửa = 'fire'
núi lửa =   _____

tủ = 'closet'
tủ lạnh (lạnh = 'cool/cold') =   _____

Exercise 3 – Vietnamese classifiers

Cái and *con* are the most common classifiers in Vietnamese, but there are at least a couple dozen more that occur fairly regularly. From the descriptions of the classifiers, try and sort the following items into their proper groups.

ảnh 'picture'	đồng hồ 'watch'	táo 'apple'
bản đồ 'map'	gà 'chicken'	tạp chỉ 'magazine'
bi 'marble'	ghế 'chair'	tim 'heart'
ba lô 'backpack'	hình 'photograph'	thư 'letter'
cá 'fish'	nho 'grapes'	tối 'evening'
chiều 'afternoon'	phỏng vấn 'interview'	tranh 'painting'
chuối 'banana'	quần 'trousers'	vở 'notebook'
đảo 'island'	sách 'book'	xoài 'mango'
đá 'stone, ice'	sáng 'morning'	

bức (flat, thin, square)   _____
buổi (something occupying a relatively short   _____
period of time, up to few hours)
cái (thing)   _____
con (animal)   _____
hòn (something round and hard)   _____
quả/trái (fruit, also for something round and   _____
soft that can be held; *qua* is used in the North
and *trai* in the South)
quyển (bound paper)   _____

Discussion Questions

1   What kind of linguistic legacy did the French and the Chinese leave on the Viet-
    namese language? In general, what kinds of linguistic effects does colonialism
    instantiate in a language?
2   How does the discussion of residual and spread zones change or enhance your
    understanding of language?
3   Considering the section on spreading empires, what information was new to you?
    What is the most valuable thing you learned from reading this section?
4   How does the north/south, east/west, and center/periphery way of parsing the
    Italic branch of Indo-European square with the tree model of historical linguistics?
    What does this grouping imply about empires and movement of people?
5   Aside from the influence on writing discussed in Chapter 5, what type of influence
    has religion had on the global language scene? What do you make of this influence
    in the world today?
6   What other varieties of Global English are you familiar with? Do you think of these
    varieties as more or less intelligible with your home variety? What do you make of
    the idea that English could come to constitute its own language family at some
    point in the future? What evidence from this book supports this possibility?
7   How do pidgins differ from creoles? Have you heard these terms used in nontech-
    nical ways in popular discourse? What do they usually point to?

Notes

1   The effect of Chinese on Vietnamese is akin to the French effect on English. After centuries
    of French-speaking domination of the spheres of law and government beginning in 1066,
    English abandoned native words like *gerichte, dom*, and *synn* and adopted *justice, judgment*,
    and *crime* from French. Similarly, words such as *government, administration, court of law*,
    and, of course, *bureaucracy* are also borrowings from French.
2   Compare the German word for 'dentist' *Zahnarzt*. For the German speaker, the meaning
    of the composed word *Zahn* 'tooth' plus *Arzt* 'doctor' is transparent. For the English
    and Vietnamese speaker, the words *dentist* and *nha sĩ* are opaque. Just like the suffix *-ist*
    is found in other words for 'professional,' so *sĩ* is found in other Vietnamese words for
    professionals, such as *bác sĩ* '(medical) doctor.'

3   Journalist Tom Miller (2012) documents a kind of reverse migration, with the current movement of 200 million rural Chinese to the cities, which has fed China's economic growth.

4   When Otto the Great of Germany defeated the Hungarians in 955, he sold many of his captors into slavery. Since the Hungarians had by that time mixed with the local Slavs, Otto's victory is generally believed to be the date the word *Slav* is identified with the meaning 'slave.' It was Germanized as *sklave* and Latinized as *sclavus*. Its Venetian form was adopted into current Italian as *ciao*, '(I am your) slave.'

5   Of the Germanic languages, only North Germanic (Swedish, Norwegian, Danish, Icelandic) and West Germanic (German, Frisian, Flemish, English) survive.

6   The idea here is that the semantic transparency was an effect of widespread bilingualism and the need for ease of translation. In modern English, the relationship between semantic causatives is not always morphologically transparent, with pairs such as *sit* and *seat*, *eat* and *feed*, *fear* and *scare*. Although it is perhaps easy to see that *sit* and *seat* or *fall* and *fell* (a tree) are related, the morphological process is one of internal vowel change rather than a transitivizing suffix, and this morphological process is far from regular or productive.

7   It is simply not clear how Romanian, spoken to the north of Bulgaria, survived as a Romance language. Its last written appearance was in 587, and it did not pop up again in the historical record until the sixteenth century in religious texts written in Cyrillic.

8   The name for the original Mesopotamia, otherwise known as The Fertile Crescent, comes from the Greek [land] *meso* 'between' *potamia* 'rivers,' the two rivers in question being the Tigris and the Euphrates. By way of information, the name for the river that runs through Washington, DC namely the Potomac, is unrelated to the Greek. It comes from the Algonquin name for this river: *Patawomeck*. Hydronyms tend to be conservative. The name for the major North American river, the Mississippi, likely comes from *misi-ziibi* 'great river' Ojibwe (Algonquin). The Hudson is an exception, as it was (re)named after the explorer Henry Hudson.

9   The name *Danube* may also have a Celtic origin. The so-called Scythian ploughmen arrived in the sixth century BCE where the Danube empties into the Black Sea from its origin in the foothills to the Alps. The Celts spread into the area not long after the Scyths had left/were absorbed. At one time, the Celts controlled the area from Galați (present-day Romania), the largest port city on the Danube, to Galicia, the northwesternmost province of Spain. The place names Galați and Galicia provide evidence that the Gauls were there. Next came the Romans at the turn of the first millennium. Goths arrived from the northwest in 166 CE.

10 The name for the country in eastern Europe *România* was chosen in 1859 when Moldavia and Wallachia were united as one country, well over 1000 years after the end of the Roman Empire.

11 The name of the Berbers in North Africa comes from the Latin term. Berber is an Afro-Asiatic language. Incidentally, Caracalla was of Berber descent.

12 English has 'score,' as noted in Chapter 2. The French number *soixante-dix* 'sixty-ten' for 'seventy' is considered to be formed on the analogy of 'ninety.' Belgian French has regularized these numbers: *septante* 'seventy,' *huitante* 'eighty,' and *nonante* 'ninety,' based on the cardinal numbers of French.

13 The following discussion is generally informed by Pennycook and Makoni (2005), Safran (2008), and Brubaker (2013).

14 It is also one of the richest. In 2013, the Vatican Bank released its first-ever financial report. According to an audit done by international firm KPMG, the 2012 balance sheet of the privately held Vatican bank showed a total of €4.98 billion in assets and €769 million in equity funds. It had earnings of €86.6 million.

15   There can be any kind of -versal for a globalized language, for example, a francoversal.
16   The information and all of the Singlish examples in this section come from Umberto Ansaldo (2010).
17   We have seen that languages with lots of inflectional morphology, such as Macedonian, sometimes like to establish the grammatical relations among the elements before those elements have been introduced. Many but not all Indo-European languages tend to be subject prominent, where the subject is the element introduced first.
18   The British got Jamaica and the Virgin Islands, while the Dutch got the ABC islands of Aruba, Bonaire, and Curaçao, and split Martinique with the French.

References

Ansaldo, Umberto (2010) Contact and Asian varieties of English. In Raymond Hickey (ed.), *The Handbook of Language Contact*. Malden, MA: Wiley Blackwell, 498–517.

Brubaker, Rogers (2013) Language, religion and the politics of difference. *Nations and Nationalism* 19.1: 1–20.

Friedman, Victor (2006) Balkanizing the Balkan Sprachbund: A closer look at grammatical permeability and feature distribution. In R.M.W. Dixon and A.Y. Aikhenvald (eds.), *Grammars in Contact: A Cross Linguistic Typology*. Oxford: Oxford University Press, 205–220.

Green, John (1987) Romance languages. In Bernard Comrie (ed.), *The World's Major Languages*. New York: Oxford University Press, 203–209.

Klagstad, Harold (1963) Toward a morpho-syntactic treatment of the Balkan linguistic group. In *American Contributions to the Fifth International Congress of Slavists*. Berlin: Mouton, 176–185.

LaPolla, Randy (2006) The role of migration and language contact in the development of the Sino-Tibetan language family. In R.M.W. Dixon and A.Y. Aikhenvald (eds.), *Areal Diffusion and Genetic Inheritance*. Oxford: Oxford University Press, 225–245.

Matthews, Stephen (2007) Cantonese grammar in aerial perspective. In Alexandra Y. Aikhenvald and R.M.W. Dixon (eds.), *Grammars in Contact: A Cross-Linguistic Typology*. Oxford: Oxford University Press, 220–236.

Matthews, Stephen (2010) Language contact and Chinese. In Raymond Hickey (ed.), *Handbook of Language Contact*. Malden, MA: Wiley Blackwell, 757–769.

Miller, Tom (2012) *China's Urban Billion: The Story Behind the Biggest Migration in Human History*. London: Zed Books.

Nichols, Johanna (1992) *Linguistic Diversity in Space and Time*. Chicago: The University of Chicago Press.

Nichols, Johanna (2011) Forerunners to globalization: The Eurasian steppe and its periphery. *Language Contact in Times of Globalization* 38: 177–195.

Pennycook, Alastair and Sinfree Makoni (2005) The modern mission: The language effects of Christianity. *Journal of Language, Identity and Education* 4.2: 137–155.

Safran, William (2008) Language, ethnicity and religion: a complex and persistent linkage. *Nations and Nationalism* 14.1: 171–190.

Szmrecsanyi, Benedikt and Bernd Kortmann (2008) Vernacular universals and angloversals in a typological perspective. In Markku Filppula, Juhani Klemola, and Heli Paulasto (eds.), *Vernacular Universals and Language Contact*. London: Routledge, 33–55.

Timberlake, Alan (2013) Culture and the spread of Slavic. In Balthasar Bickel, Lenore Grenoble, David Peterson and Alan Timberlake (eds.), *Language Typology and Historical Contingency: In Honor of Johanna Nichols*. Amsterdam: John Benjamins, 331–356.

Yao, Yong-Gang, Qing-Peng Kong, Hans-Jürgen Bandelt, Toomas Kivisild and Ya-Ping Zhang (2002) Phylogeographic differentiation of mitochrondrial DNA in Han Chinese. *American Journal of Human Genetics* 70: 635–651.

Zhang, Qing (2005) A Chinese yuppie in Beijing: Phonological variation and the construction of a new professional identity. *Language in Society* 34: 431–466.

Further Reading

Greenberg, Joseph (1963) *The Languages of Africa*. Bloomington: Indiana University Press.

Greenberg, Joseph (1987) *Language in the Americas*. Stanford, CA: Stanford University Press.

Krishnamurti, Bhadriraju (2003) *The Dravidian Languages*. Cambridge: Cambridge University Press.

Ladefoged, Peter and Ian Maddieson (1996) *The Sounds of the World's Languages*. Oxford: Blackwell.

Osborne, Milton (1975) *River Road to China: The Mekong River Expedition 1866–1873*. New York: Liveright.

9

Postcolonial Complications
Violent Outcomes

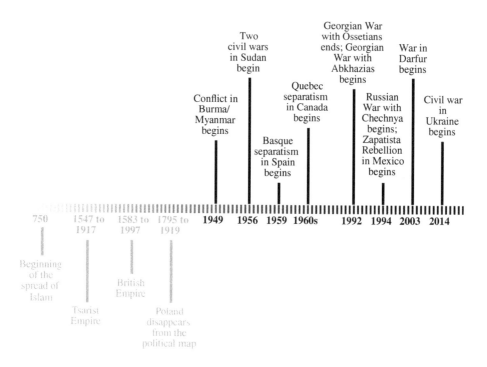

Tamil Tigers Create New Terrorist Techniques

In the Indian Ocean off the south coast of India is the island nation of Sri Lanka. The majority population is the Sinhalese, an ethnogroup who tend to be Buddhists and who speak Sinhala, an Indo-European language. They share the island with the

Languages in the World: How History, Culture, and Politics Shape Language, First Edition.
Julie Tetel Andresen and Phillip M. Carter.
© 2016 John Wiley & Sons, Inc. Published 2016 by John Wiley & Sons, Inc.

minority Tamils, who tend to be Hindu. Their language, Tamil, is Dravidian. In the 1980s, the people of Sri Lanka began to suffer the experience of terrorist bombings in their capital city, Colombo, and surrounding countryside, perpetrated by Tamil Tiger separatists who wanted their own state. Earlier in that decade, one Tamil Tiger, Shankar Rajee (pseudonym), on a trip to London met up with Palestinian militants, traveled with them to Beirut, and imported from the Palestinian Liberation Organization the practice of terrorist bombings. In return, here is what Rajee *exported* to the Middle East: the wearable detonation device known as the suicide belt, suicide bombing itself, the use of women in suicide attacks, and the idea of tying together terrorists and financiers into an international network of militant uprisings (Meadows 2010).

What could have been the impetus behind Rajee's desperate need to create the techniques of modern terrorism? The answer is: issues surrounding language and its social-psychological cousin, religion, that swirled into the vacuum created when the British colonialists left Ceylon in 1948.[1] Suddenly the island became an independent nation and eventually renamed itself The Republic of Sri Lanka. One of the seemingly simple, natural, and yet most disastrous moves the new government made was the passage of the Sinhala Only Act in 1956,[2] which ended the status of English as the official language and barred Tamil from the schools and government institutions. Overnight, more than a million Tamils became officially illiterate, and all of them were now at a severe disadvantage in obtaining jobs in the civil service. Violence broke out in Tamil communities, which in turn provoked a Sinhalese backlash.

Over the next 15 years, more language laws and other pro-Sinhalese reforms were enacted, and government troops were regularly deployed in agitated Tamil communities. By the 1970s, interest in a separate Tamil nation evolved into a bona fide separatist movement with militant leanings. In 1975, the group Liberation Tigers of Tamil Eelam ('homeland') was formed to fight for Tamil freedom in Sri Lanka. The group came to be known as the Tamil Tigers, and their violence eventually escalated into outright terrorism, which continued nearly unabated for the next two decades. Finally, in 2002, the war-fatigued nation decided upon a ceasefire agreement between the Tamil Tigers and the Sinhalese-led government. The issue of Tamil separatism came to an end.

The Tamils are one of the sad epilogues to the intertwined stories of the eighteenth-century nation-state and post-Columbian European colonialism. When Europeans left their colonies during the twentieth century, interethnic conflicts not in play prior to the colonial era often split along linguistic lines as former colonies struggled to establish themselves as nation-states. The logic used to construct the state became the same logic used to challenge it, and separatist movements began to arise all around the world, always splitting along linguistic lines. They continue to do so, because the one nation, one language ideology gives any ethnogroup the sense of a right to their own nation, to their own political border. Among the many things that move, then, in these postcolonial times are national borders, as do money and weapons, and with them, people. When money and weapons are in the hands of a militant minority ethnogroup, guerilla and/or terrorist tactics become the order of the day, as we saw for Sri Lanka. When they are in the hands of a militant majority ethnogroup and/or recognized government, an unfortunate trend of mass murder can be traced around the world.

The term *final solution* was used by the Nazis during World War II to refer to the eradication of the Jews from Nazi Germany either by expulsion or by extermination. During the Yugoslav wars of the 1990s, the term *ethnic cleansing* entered international discourse. Unfortunately, mass murders have not been confined to Nazi Germany and the former Yugoslavia. The International Criminal Court in The Hague can and does prosecute individuals for genocide and crimes against humanity.

In this chapter, we review postcolonial separatist movements around the world, all with profiles of violence and all tethered to issues of language.

What's in a Name? Burma/Myanmar

In 1989, the military dictatorship in power in the Southeast Asian country then known as Burma established a language committee charged with regularizing the spelling of Burmese place names in English. The committee's primary work was to replace or modify the often haphazard spellings given to Burmese cities by the British authorities in the nineteenth-century colonial period, bringing those English spellings closer in line with actual Burmese pronunciations. Accordingly, the English name for the capital Rangoon was changed to Yangon. The committee finished its work by recommending one final change: the renaming of the country from Burma to Myanmar. The diverse ethnolinguistic minority groups in the country reacted with anger, and the event became another moment of volatility in what is the world's longest running armed geopolitical conflict, now in its seventh decade.

Burmese is the language spoken by the Burmans, the largest ethnic group in the country. Like many languages of Southeast Asia (see Map 9.1), Burmese marks strict lexical and grammatical distinctions between registers, which are styles of language used for specific purposes. It is therefore not unusual that in Burmese, two names for the country exist: *Myanma*, used in the written literary register, and *Bama*, used in the colloquial spoken register. The two names for the country have existed alongside one another for several centuries. The government's language committee argued that *Myanma* was the official name of the country in written Burmese, and therefore recommended the English name Myanmar.[3] The military dictatorship, ever suspicious of the colloquial varieties of Burmese in which *Bama* was the preferred country name, agreed. For their part, ethnic minority groups, which number more than 100 in Burma, argued that both terms were ultimately of Burmese origin and were therefore exclusionary to other language groups, and they were therefore opposed.

Among the most vocal opponents of the name change were an ethnogroup known as the Karens. In reality, *Karen* is a cover term for a variety of loosely related ethnic groups numbering more than four million in Burma, nine million in the region. The Karen peoples speak a number of related languages, sometimes referred to collectively as *the Karen languages*, which include Pa'O, Red Karen (Karenni), and S'gaw Karen. Though linguists agree that Karen languages are part of the Tibeto-Burman branch of Sino-Tibetan, there is not yet agreement about whether the so-called Karen languages form their own subbranch. The fact that the Karen languages are not

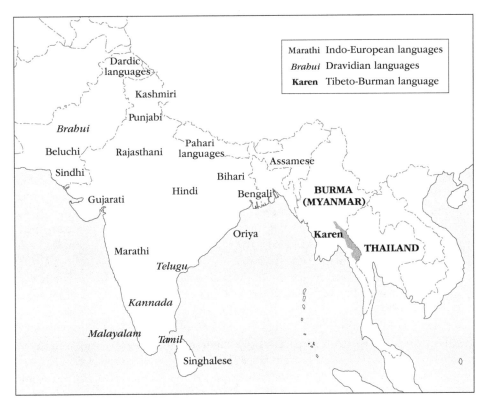

Map 9.1   Languages of South Asia (Dravidian languages italicized), Tibeto-Burman language bolded.

mutually intelligible has contributed to the underestimation of the Karen population within Burma. From the perspective of the Karen people, this underestimation contributes to their marginalization within Burmese society.

The Karens have been engaged in continuous armed conflict with the Burmans since 1949. The nature of the violence, however, cannot be reduced to Karen versus Burman, Karenni language versus Burmese language, or other such posings. The violence is instead triangulated against two more sets of related conditions: the nature of colonial intervention by the British from 1824 to 1948, and the postcolonial conditions established by the hasty British exit from the region.

In the midnineteenth century, the British Empire was at a high tide with colonies stretching from Hong Kong to Bombay. By midcentury, the fertile Irrawaddy Delta in Southeast Asia was still unclaimed by Europeans, and the British wanted it for rice production. They had already set up colonies in the interior of Burma, where they controlled the production of timber, oil wells, and mines. In 1852, they also seized control of the Irrawaddy. The draining of the delta for paddy land sent some people out of the region. Others, who wanted to work the paddies, came into the region. Burma was being transformed from the outside, and people began to scatter, disrupting long-term settlement patterns.

In the midst of this movement, colonial administrators began to play favorites with local groups, the two factors leading to British favoritism being willingness to convert to Christianity and willingness to learn English. In British Burma, it was the Karens, who already felt dominated by the Burmans, who collaborated most closely with the British. The British encouraged Karen groups to convert to Christianity, and many did. The Burmans, who felt marginalized, displaced, and exploited by the British, accused the Karens of sympathizing with Imperialists. The Burman and Karen groups were already at odds, and the preconditions for postcolonial violence were thus already in place during the colonial era.

Throughout the 100-year period of British rule, the Karens developed a keen sense of national consciousness, led at first by those who converted to Christianity. Language was an important theme in Karen nationalism, and the first Karen-language newspaper was printed in 1841. By 1928, with the British still in power, calls were issued for a state uniting the various Karen-speaking groups. In 1942, when the Japanese occupied British Burma as a part of World War II, the Burmans sided with the Japanese, while the Karens sided immediately with the British.

When the British left the region in 1948, the colonial structure immediately collapsed, and the Karens lost their ties to power. While many other ethnic groups agreed to join the independent Burma that emerged in the postcolonial period, the Karens disagreed, instead forming the Karen National Union. They took up arms and for a time even took control of large parts of the country, although eventually their control waned, and they were relegated further and further to the border with Thailand. By the 1990s, the Burman government had labeled the Karens *terrorists*, and some Karen groups did in fact take up guerilla tactics as they watched their influence wane. Others, as many as 100,000, crossed the border to seek refuge in Thailand, thus illustrating a common story for many ethnogroups in the postcolonial era: violence begets emigration.

Today, the Karen question in Burma is still unanswered, and Burma is one of the most militarized countries in the world. The Karen National Union remains suspicious of the central government, whom they perceive as wanting to Burmanize ethnic minority groups. Therefore, the maintenance of Karen ethnic identity is seen as a strategy for ongoing self-government. Language is of course everywhere at issue and at stake. While the Burmese language is the medium of instruction in most schools, the Karens advocate that their languages should be the medium of instruction in Karen-majority areas of the country, an issue we saw in Chapter 6 and the curricular status of Tibetan in Western and the Autonomous Region of Tibet.

The history of violence in Burma over the past seven decades sadly shows that one effect of colonialism in the postcolonial era is often violence and that this violence causes people to move, thereby dislocating and dispersing ethnic groups and their languages. This history also highlights the role of language in ethnic identity. For many ethnogroups, certainly the Karens, language and ethnic identity are worth fighting for. Conflict over the country's name – Burma or Myanmar – is not superficial political wrangling among differing political parties. Rather, it is deeply symbolic of the larger tensions at play involving language, ethnic identity, and national sovereignty in the postcolonial era.

Modern Sudan: The Clash of Two Colonialisms

Ancient Nubia was the region along the Nile River in present-day Egypt and Sudan. It was originally inhabited by the Noba people, also known as the Kushites, who created a flourishing civilization and who spoke Old Nubian, a now-extinct Nilo-Saharan language. Around 1500 BCE, the ancient Egyptians, who spoke Old Egyptian, a now-extinct Afro-Asiatic language, moved south into the Nubian region and colonized the Nubians, making them subjects of the Pharaoh. Egyptian rule lasted about 500 years until the Kushites reasserted control, and the Kingdom of Kush was established. Two points can now be made. First, events surrounding the movements and expansions of peoples explored in Chapters 7 and 8 likely played themselves out much like the story here; however, the details for the rest of the world are lost to us in the absence of written documents, except for the case of China whose records are as old as Egypt's. Second, the pattern of colonialism and conflict is particularly old in this fertile region of the world.

Religion now enters the picture with the introduction of Christianity and Islam into the region during the first millennium CE. Christianity entered North Africa through contact with the Roman Empire. The Copts, an ancient ethnogroup who spoke Old Egyptian, were among the first in the region to adopt Christianity, and they spread the religion southward. The language Old Nubian is known today through several hundred pages of Christian religious documents kept by the Copts and written in the Coptic alphabet.[4] By the sixth century, much of southern Nubia, that is, present-day Sudan, had been Christianized.

A short century later, the Islamicization of North Africa began as Muslim Arabs moved west from the Arabian peninsula to conquer northern Nubia, which also brought language shift, such that Egyptians today speak (modern) Arabic. The Arabic language and Islamic religion also began to trickle into various Christian kingdoms in southern Nubia, called by the Arabs *Bilad al-Sudan* 'Land of Black People'. The movement of Arabs into Nubia created two important and long-lasting conditions. The spread of Islam over several centuries first facilitated the spread of Arabic throughout the northern part of modern-day Sudan and second instantiated a longstanding but loosely recognized north/south division split along ethnic, religious, and linguistic lines. The northern region was established as ethnically Arab, religiously Muslim, and linguistically Arabic speaking. The southern region was ethnically Black African, religiously Christian, and linguistically diverse.

Next up came British colonialism. Between 1899 and 1956, the British controlled modern-day Sudan through their colonial territory in Egypt. During this period, known as Anglo-Egyptian Sudan, British administrators promoted policies that directly troubled the north/south split. First, after World War I, the British folded the Sultanate of Darfur, an independently functioning Nile Valley territory to the west, into Sudan. Second, they exacerbated differences within Sudan, transforming what was once a loose north/south division into two clearly distinct cultural and linguistic regions: north and south.

The stage was now set for modern state of Sudan to be plagued with not one but two geopolitical conflicts, both involving the Arabic-speaking majority in the centrally located capital, Khartoum. The majority were in conflict, on the one hand, with the Fur-speaking minority in the western region of Darfur and, on the other, with the mostly English-speaking region in the south, now known as the independent Republic of South Sudan.

Conflict in Darfur

The name *Darfur* is the Arabic for 'realm of the Fur,' given to the region between Sudan, Chad, and Central African Republic. The Fur are an ethnogroup who speak a Nilo-Saharan language, also called Fur. In the second half of the twentieth century, the conflict in the region spun out into a bewildering number of cascading conflicts characterized by three types of movement: (i) the movement of a border, (ii) the mass movements of people within and across borders, and (iii) the movement of money and arms into the region.

When the British drew independent, precolonial Darfur within the border of the newly formed state of Sudan, they also pushed Sudan into geopolitical conflicts with neighboring Chad and Libya, because these two states had longstanding conflicts with the Sultanate of Darfur. Second, the border between Darfur and Chad was historically porous and easily negotiated. Darfuri camel herders easily moved west over the border into Chad for greener pastures, where rainfall was greater. However, beginning in the 1980s, the ethnic conflict in Chad, left in the wake of French colonialism, resulted in a reversal of this historical movement, as several hundred thousand Chadian refugees, mostly nomadic Arabs, moved east over the border into Darfur (Sudan). The new arrivals into Darfur taxed the local ecosystem and increased local hostilities. The Fur people are farmers and not nomadic, and they differentiate between *Kain-Solonga* (Fur for 'our Arabs'), or Sudanese Arab nomads who traditionally move north and south within Darfur, from the Chadians who move east and west. By the 1990s, over half a million people were moving about Darfur, escaping various conflicts from north, south, east, and west. Tensions simmered between Arab-speaking nomads and the sedentary Fur.

The movement of weaponry into Sudan and Darfur from the east and west only added to the volatility. At the beginning of the 1980s, United States President Ronald Reagan began to supply arms to Darfur in order to create an alliance against Muammar al-Gaddafi's Libya. By the end of the 1980s, it was the case that "though short of water, Darfur was awash in guns," as historian Mahmood Mamdani so trenchantly put it (2009:222). The climax came in 2003 when the Fur and their allies, who were speakers of the Nilo-Saharan languages Beria and Masalit, took up arms against the central Sudanese government. This government, in turn, responded by arming poor, nomadic Arab tribes in Darfur known as the *Janjaweed*, whose name is an interesting compound comprising the Arabic words for 'man,' 'gun,' and 'horse.' The *Janjaweed* are accused of ethnic cleansing of indigenous groups in Darfur, including the Fur. This war set in motion yet another reversal: the movement of some 200,000 Darfuris back across the border into eastern Chad. The events of 2003 started the armed conflict known as the War in Darfur, which, at the time of writing, is still unresolved.

In sum, Darfur illustrates two general points. First, the movement of ethnogroups from one location to another often begets geopolitical conflict, just as geopolitical conflict often begets the movement of ethnogroups. Second, language and cultural differences are often perceived to be the causes of geopolitical conflict in the postcolonial era. However, geopolitical conflicts also create new situations of language contact as speakers flee violence, move into exile, and sometimes return home. Violent conflict thus keeps people moving, which alters the layout of the linguistic map.

Conflict in South Sudan

Under British rule, the northern and southern regions of Sudan were administered separately. The British grouped southern Sudan with its other colonies in East Africa, Uganda and Kenya among them, and administered the north as a unit with Egypt, in part on the basis of linguistic affinity, because both northern Sudan and Egypt are Arabic-speaking. As was often the case, colonial powers played favorites in their African colonies, and in Sudan, the British favored the south. The favoritism was based on the fact that Christianity was already widespread in the south. The use of English was actively encouraged in the south.

Following pressure from the north to integrate both regions, Britain finally capitulated in 1946, and both regions were thereafter administered together. Arabic was made the official language, and the balance of power quickly shifted to Arabic-speaking Khartoum. After 55 years of British rule, Sudan was given its independence in 1956, but the southerners, who were privileged under British rule, quickly perceived that the north was imposing Arabic and Islam on them. The first of two civil wars soon broke out, which collectively killed over two million people and displaced five million more. A peace agreement was reached in 2005, and in 2011, following a referendum, the South was granted independence and became the Republic of South Sudan with the capital city of Juba.

While Darfur continues as a region of Sudan, South Sudan was successful in arguing for a separate state, in part, on the basis of language difference. English, a prized artifact of British colonialism, was made the official language of South Sudan, and some 60 regional languages have been recognized as national languages. These belong mostly in the central and eastern Sudanic branches of Nilo-Saharan languages, as well as some Niger–Congo languages such as Ngbaka and Sere. In South Sudan, Arabic has not been named an official language and has not been given official recognition by the new government. After generations of educating students in Arabic, schools throughout South Sudan have now switched the medium of instruction to English.

Despite the state solution and attendant language policies promoting English, conflict continues in South Sudan. Millions of Arabic-speaking refugees from the north have sought refuge in the south, and the presence of traders from Kenya and Uganda have added to the linguistic diversity of South Sudan, where 150 tribal languages are already spoken. The ongoing fluctuations of diverse populations make uniting the country through English an uphill battle and engender further division and conflict. Although language issues are not necessarily the driving force behind conflict in the region, they are tightly interwoven with the political, historical, religious, and economic issues that have led to volatility in Sudan and South Sudan.

The Caucasian Quasi-States: Two Types of Conflict

The Caucasus is a complicated region with an even more complicated history. From Ancient Persia to Byzantium, from the Ottoman Empire to the Soviet Union, the Caucasus region has fallen under the reach of powerful empires since antiquity. Caucasian cultures have thus developed through a historical–political dialectic with their colonizers. Similarly, the languages of the Caucasus have also always been spoken alongside one imperial language or another, be it Persian, Arabic, Turkish, or Russian. As one of the world's residual zones, the Caucasus also has a complex linguistic profile.

In the twentieth century, the most important external force operating in the region was the Soviet Union. Although the Caucasus was already in the orbit of Russian culture during the Tsarist Empire, it was formally folded into the USSR beginning in the 1920s. This arrangement lasted until the dissolution of the Soviet Union in 1990, when 15 Soviet republics from Eastern Europe to Central Asia were given their independence. Three of these states were in the Caucasus region: Armenia, Azerbaijan, and Georgia. Armenian, Azerbaijani, and Georgian were quickly named as the titular official languages of the new states, respectively.

For the nation-states that emerged out of the former Soviet Union, the transition from Soviet republics to independent nations was a surprisingly peaceful one. However, the development of independent nations and their attendant post-Soviet nationalisms took place alongside a remarkable number of violent conflicts involving contested regions within the Caucasus. Some of these regions fell within the borders of new nation-states – most notably the now independent nation of Georgia – while others remained within the post-Soviet Russian Federation. In both cases, the contested regions are considered to be the historical homelands of indigenous ethnogroups of the Caucasus.

Here, we focus on three of these regions: Abkhazia, Chechnya, and South Ossetia. We consider them to be 'quasi-states' because they:

(i)   have declared their independence from other nations;
(ii) operate their own regional governments;
(iii) have well-developed nationalisms with wide local support;
(iv) have well-defined political agendas, including language policies; but
(v)   are not formally recognized by most or any of the international community as independent nations.

These three quasi-nations illustrate two types of postcolonial conflict: first, conflict between the former colonial power and a previously colonized ethnogroup; and second, conflict among ethnogroups previously colonized by the same power. As an example of the first type, Chechens have been in direct conflict with Russia since the end of the Soviet Union. As an example of the second type, Abkhazians and Ossetians have been in conflict with Georgia, which was once also subjugated to Soviet interests.

In postcolonial situations, groups who previously shared a common enemy can turn violent toward each other.

First type: Chechen conflict with Russia

In the late 1930s, ethnic Chechens began to organize a guerrilla movement in the Northern Caucasian Mountains. The movement was designed to culminate in an armed insurgency that would deliver Chechnya from the newly formed Soviet Union. The insurgency began as planned in 1941, but following the destruction of entire Chechen villages by Soviet air raids, Chechen rebels turned to coalition building, seeking the support and participation of other Caucasian ethnic groups in the region. Their ranks swelled. Some 5000 men, mostly Chechens and Ingush, joined the insurgency. Despite broad support throughout the Caucasus for the insurgency, rebels were unable to withstand Soviet attacks. By 1943, with World War II raging on, Chechnya found itself still squarely with Soviet borders, its bold insurgency defeated.

The Soviet solution to the Chechen problem following the insurgency was massive ethnic cleansing. In 1942, half a million Chechen and Ingush people – virtually the entire population – were forcibly resettled from their homes in the Caucasus to regions such as Siberia and Kazakh (present-day Kazakhstan). Thousands who did not leave were executed. Thousands who did leave did not survive. Some rebels kept the movement going by escaping into the depths of the mountains. Others formed new rebel groups in exile. Neither of these was successful in changing the political fate of Chechnya, or the exilic situation of Chechen people who were, in some estimates, reduced in number by 50%.[5]

Soviet policies toward ethnogroups began to shift in the post-Stalin era, and in 1956, Chechens were invited to return to Chechnya from exile. When they arrived, they found the homeland they had left was no longer theirs. Russian speakers had occupied their homes. Their books, historical records, and other documents, recorded in Chechen, had been burned. Chechen towns had been renamed in Russian. Postexile Chechnya was, in effect, bereft of the Chechen language. The Russification of Chechen places during the exile period presaged a long phase of strict pro-Russian policies within Chechnya during the postexile period, which lasted until the fall of the Soviet Union. By the midtwentieth century, the Chechen people had repopulated Chechen lands, but the Chechen language and culture were still at risk of falling into extinction, given the assimilatory pressures imposed by Soviet leaders.

Russian-initiated assimilatory pressures on Chechens may have in fact resulted in the opposite effect: a heightened sense of ethnic, linguistic, and eventually national Chechen identity. A 1989 census of the Russian Federation found that the Chechen region had the highest proportion of speakers who considered the local language, Chechen, to be their native language and the primary language of daily communication. Therefore, the major pieces of modern nationalism, strong ethnic group identity and distinctive language among them, were already in place when the first post-Soviet independent states began to appear on the map in 1991. Chechnya followed suit, announcing its independence as the Chechen Republic of Ichkeria to the world in 1991. Thousands of non-Chechens fled the Caucasus.

Neither Russia nor the West recognized the declaration of Chechnya, which continued to operate as a quasi-state within Russian borders in the first years of the 1990s. Russia, fearing the very disintegration of the Russian state following the disintegration of the Soviet Union, developed a hardline with Chechnya. By the end of 1994, Russians sent tanks into the streets of Grozny, the Chechen capital, in an operation they believed would last a matter of days. The First Chechen War, as it was later named, lasted for two years. In the end, Grozny was leveled, 100,000 people were killed, and four times as many were displaced. Russian troops left defeated and embarrassed. Russia had failed to convince the world that Chechnya was a bona fide part of its federation. The quasi-state status of Chechnya continued.

The violence did not subside after the war, and stable conditions did not last long. A number of terrorist attacks around Russia in the late 1990s were blamed on Chechen terrorists. These attacks provided the rational for a second invasion in Grozny. This time the Russian military was better prepared, and Grozny was brought fully under Russian control. However, military conflicts between colonial power and the colonized are rarely final. In 2010, the Moscow metro was bombed, and in 2011, the Moscow airport. These terrorist-style attacks have been linked to Chechen militants.

Second type: Abkhazian and South Ossetian conflict within Georgia

Since 1922, the region of the Caucasus known as Ossetia has been divided in half, yielding two political regions known as North and South Ossetia. The northern region has long been associated with Russian and is today formally a republic within the Russian Federation. The people in North Ossetia speak Russian, a Slavic language, and Ossetic, in the Eastern Iranian language of the Indo-European stock. The status of the southern region is contested but associated with Georgia by most of the West. The people in South Ossetia speak Russian, Georgian, and Ossetic. Georgian is a Caucasian language, and the Caucasus is considered the homeland of the Caucasian languages.

During the start of the Soviet era, South Ossetia was administered by the regional Georgian government based in the capital, Tbilisi. During this era, relations among Ossetians and Georgians were strong. The Ossetic language was permitted, widely spoken, and even used as the medium of instruction in Ossetian schools. By the late 1980s, Soviet politics under President Mikhail Gorbachev shifted toward an approach known as *glasnost*, or political transparency. As Communist Party censorship waned with glasnost policies, calls for independence movements increased, sweeping through the Soviet Union's republics.

Both Georgia and South Ossetia developed nationalistic ambitions during this period, and in the race for greater autonomy, tensions began to emerge between ethnic Georgians and ethnic Ossetians. In 1989, just as South Ossetia was seeking greater regional autonomy, the Georgians, in their own bold act of nationalism, established the Georgian language throughout Georgian territory, including in South Ossetia. The Ossetians responded by declaring independence. At the critical juncture of sociopolitical change in the Caucasus region, language was once again the lynchpin issue.

War erupted almost immediately. Georgians entered the Ossetian regional capital, known to Ossetians as Tskhinvali and to Georgians as Samachablo. On both sides, schools were demolished, and homes were burned. By the end of 1992, when the war officially ended, more than 1000 people had been killed, many through forms of violence unsanctioned by international law. Roughly half of South Ossetia fell under control of a pro-Russian, Russian-backed government, which was set up after the war. Tens of thousands of Ossetians fled the region, some south into Georgia proper, some north into North Ossetia, and others elsewhere into the Caucasus region. These movements did nothing to settle the conflicts in the region.

In 1992, as one war ended in Georgia, another began. This time the conflict was in the breakaway province of Abkhazia, which found itself within Georgia's new borders after 1991. Abkhazians are an ethnogroup indigenous to the Caucasian Mountain region. Most people speak Abkhaz, a Caucasian language. A minority of Abkhazians speak a South Caucasian language known as Mingrelian. Multilingualism in the region is high, and most Abkhazians also speak Georgian.

Abkhazia declared independence from Georgia in 1992. This was seen as a threat to Georgia's own status as a tenuously independent nation. The Georgian military entered Abkhazia and easily pushed back the mostly unarmed Abkhaz nationalists, taking control of the Abkhaz capital, Sokhumi. The separatists connected with a broader network of ethnogroups in the Caucasus, who supported Abkhaz separatism. Among them were the Ossetians and Chechens. One year later, better trained and better armed, Abkhaz separatist groups returned to take their capital from the Georgians. With the help of militant sympathizers from Russia and the greater Caucasus, more than 200,000 ethnic Georgians were forcibly moved out of Abkhazia. Then came a brutal, two-week-long attack on Georgian civilians living in Sokhumi. Women were raped, whole families were murdered in broad daylight, and people were indiscriminately tortured. The Sokhumi Massacre, as it is now known, formed a part of a broader ethnic cleansing of Georgians from Abkhazia.

Meanwhile, in South Ossetia, fighting between ethnic Ossetians and Georgians occurred in fits and starts for about 15 years following the 1992–1993 war. As the specter of the Russian-backed government in South Ossetia became increasingly a thorn in the side to the Westward-looking Georgian government, the political stakes grew higher. In 2008, the long-simmering tensions reached a boil. Ethnic Georgians and Ossetians accused each other of shelling their villages. Georgia then launched a full strike in Ossetian Tskhinvali, sparking a war that was technically between Georgia and Russia, who had already stationed troops in the region. Fighting followed for five days. The Ossetians claim the attack was unprovoked. The Georgians claim they were provoked by the mounting presence of the Russian military.

In 2008, as Georgia was embroiled in war with Russia over South Ossetia, Abkhazia also entered the fray. Russian troops entered Abkhazia, helping push out the Georgian military presence that remained after the end of the 1993 Abkhaz War. When the 2008 war between Georgia and Russia ended, both Abkhazia and South Ossetia once again proclaimed their independence, which has only been recognized by Russia and a handful of its allies. Georgia considers Abkhazia and South Ossetia to fall within its borders. Because the majority of the world happens to agree with Georgia and does not recognize Abkhazia and South Ossetia, since 2008, both regions have operated as quasi-states with a great deal of autonomy, but without international borders. The conflict thus remains unresolved.

The languages of the conflict were those of the quasi-states (Abkhaz, Chechen, Mingrelian, Ossetic), a post-Soviet independent nation (Georgian) and the preindependence imperial power (Russian). English has also played a role. During the 2008 war with Russia over South Ossetia and Abkhazia, the Georgian president was Mikheil Saakashvili. He spent formative years abroad, including in the United States, where he attended Columbia Law School in New York City and acquired a native-like command of English. During the 2008 war, Saakashvili conducted live television interviews with North American networks in English, which helped him frame the conflict as fundamentally about Russian aggression and to win support with international audiences. In postcolonial conflict, winning the support of your enemy's historical antagonists is an important symbolic move. The globalization and high value placed on speaking English – an issue we take up in Chapter 2 – helped make this possible for Georgia.

Poland's Shifting Borders

Tourists to the Ukrainian city of L'viv (Polish: Lwów) will find the menus at the restaurants in the city center printed in English, German, Hebrew, Russian, and Ukrainian, but not in Polish. The almost total absence of the Polish language in this city is surprising not only because L'viv is only a three-hour bus ride from Przemsyl, the nearest Polish border city, but also because L'viv was a Polish city beginning in the fourteenth century and is considered by the Poles to be one of Poland's greatest cities. However, today L'viv is in Ukraine, and one is more likely to hear English on the streets than Polish. The Polish past has been erased.

During the past 1500 years, the Polish borders have expanded and contracted with the ebbs and flows of changing economic, political, and military conditions. At the height of the Polish–Lithuanian Empire in the Middle Ages, Poland's territory expanded some 400,000 square miles. In 1795, at a time when the modern nations were emerging in Western Europe, Poland disappeared from the political map for well over a century, as it was divided by three empires: Austrian, Prussian, and Russian. Polish intellectuals helped maintain the language in exile. In the twentieth century, Poland was reborn at the end of World War I. The Second Polish Republic, as it was known, ended with dual invasions in 1939: Germany from the West, and Russia from the East. This marked the start of World War II, the culmination of which resulted in the territory of modern Poland.

Two developments took place at the end of World War II that shaped the linguistic landscape of Central-Eastern Europe. First, the borders of Poland, Ukraine, and Germany were redrawn, and Poland became a satellite of the Soviet Union. Poland's borders shifted significantly westward, losing eastern territories annexed by Russia, and gaining German-speaking territories to the west, including the city of Gdańsk (German: Danzig). Significant numbers of Poles suddenly found themselves in Ukraine, Belarus, and Lithuania, while Germans found themselves in communist Poland. Second, the Soviet government wanted to create homogeneous ethnic states throughout Eastern Europe through both ethnic cleansing and population redistribution. A Soviet-initiated resettlement agreement in 1944 oversaw the movement of

Poles and Jews westward out of what was now western Ukraine into Poland, while Ukrainians and Lemkos, a Slavic people like the Ukrainians, were sent eastward out of communist Poland into Ukraine. Similar forced movements at the behest of Josef Stalin took place between Poland and Belarus and Poland and Lithuania. In 1945, Germans were forcibly removed from western Poland.

These population movements had at least two effects on language in the region. The first relates to the distribution of languages in Central-Eastern Europe, such that people were moved to fit the ideology in which languages and nations align with perfect congruency. The linguistic diversity of prewar Poland, which included the language varieties of Poles, Germans, Jews, Ukrainians, and Lemkos, among others, was thus obliterated in order to create a postwar Poland that is 97% Polish, nearly perfectly homogeneous in ethnic and linguistic terms. That is, the language diversity that reflected over 1000 years or more of movement of people and languages in and about this region was reformulated to create language silos corresponding to national borders.

In what became western Ukraine, a campaign of de-Polinization sought to erase Polish language and culture. The Polish city of Lwów became the Ukrainian city of L'viv. In the region shared by Ukrainians and Poles known as Galicia, multilingualism had been the norm for centuries, as Ukrainians and Poles mixed freely with Yiddish-speaking Jews. Post-World War II policies all but ended this multilingualism: the Galician Jews were eliminated by the Holocaust, thus eliminating Yiddish, while the number of Polish speakers in the region dwindled from 1.8 million (prewar) to 150,000 after Galicia became a part of Ukraine. The multilingualism characterizing Galicia for several hundred years ended with the shifting of territories and bodies after the end of World War II.

In what became western Poland, a campaign of de-Germanization took place, which included not only the banning of German-language instruction and German books, but also the removal of German inscriptions from towns, shops, churches, and homes. The German cities of Breslau and Stettin were transformed into the Polish cities of Wrocław and Szczecin. Some three million Germans were also forcibly moved westward into the new German territory and out of the new Polish territory. In a twist of fate, speakers of Silesian – a Slavic language similar to Czech and Polish with heavy German influence – suddenly found themselves to be living in Poland, after centuries of living under German influence. In sum, once again, the movement of Poland's borders westward and subsequent ethnic cleansings and movement of people throughout the region resulted in linguistically homogeneous regions where multilingualism once prevailed.

The second, related effect of the post-World War II movement of borders on language was the dispersal and disappearance of countless Slavic varieties from what was once a clear Slavic dialect chain between Ukraine and Poland. Although linguists classify Polish as a Western Slavic language and place Ukrainian in the Eastern Slavic branch, the languages once seamlessly blended into each other in the rural villages along the historical borders. After the war, ethnic Poles who found themselves in western Ukraine were sent to cities such as Gdańsk in northern and western Poland where they were needed to fill the void of the Germans who were forced west. The rural varieties of Polish, influenced from centuries of contact with Ukrainian and other Slavic varieties, would not have been well received in the north and mostly disappeared. Language varieties such as Rusyn (also known as Ruthenian) and Lemko, which are sometimes considered to be varieties of Ukrainian and sometimes as distinct languages, were dispersed from their homeland and largely consolidated into the larger groups into which their speakers moved.

Terrorism on the Iberian Peninsula: Basque and the ETA

The Basque language survived the rise and fall of the Roman Empire in Iberia and centuries of Spanish rule before confronting the biggest threat to their language in nearly 2000 years: General Francisco Franco. In the years of his oppressive dictatorship (1936–1975), Franco's aggressive federalization efforts included the marginalization of Spain's regional languages and cultures. Laws were passed curtailing the use of languages other than Castilian, and those individuals caught breaking the language laws were fined or imprisoned. More importantly, Franco devised an ideological campaign that changed the way many Spaniards thought of Iberian languages. The federal government began referring to languages such as Catalan and Galician as *dialects*, thus assigning them an inferior status. Government media was set up in such a way that serious news stories were covered in Castilian (Spanish), while frivolous stories were covered in the non-Castilian languages. The ideological campaign was successful in casting these languages as inferior to Castilian in the minds of many Spaniards. All of the regional languages, including Basque, suffered setbacks.

In 1959, eager to promote Basque language and culture in light of Franco's restrictions, a group of young Basque speakers formed a loose coalition. They called themselves *Euskadi Ta Askatasuna* (ETA), Basque Homeland and Freedom. Although they began with noble intentions, the ETA, as they are known in Spain and abroad, quickly turned to violence of the kind the Tamil Tigers would later perpetrate. In 1961, they attempted to derail several trains carrying Franco supporters into San Sebastián, an important Basque city. In 1967, they began robbing banks, and by 1968, they claimed their first casualty in a shootout between ETA and the *Guardia Civil*. Some 800 deaths have been attributed to ETA since then. As ETA's interest shifted from preserving Basque language to advocating for an independent Basque state, they transitioned quickly into a paramilitary group recognized as a terrorist organization by most of the world.

The postdictatorship Constitution of 1978 references Spain's internal multilingualism and was printed in five versions: Castilian, Catalan, Basque, Galician, and Valencian.[6] The Constitution also called for the protection of the regional languages, and greater autonomy for Spain's various linguistic regions,[7] including the Basque Autonomous Community, commonly known as the Basque Country (*el País Vasco*) and the Chartered Community of Navarre, where Basque is most widely spoken.[8] Despite these constitutional provisions, ETA's efforts continued for several decades, ending after a so-called permanent ceasefire was finally signed in 2012. ETA finally declared an end to its fight with the Spanish government and with it an end to its efforts to define an independent Basque nation. Although the violent conflict seems to have ended, interest in the preservation of the Basque language has not. From the time of Franco's death in 1975, *Ikostolak* – public and private schools in which Basque is the language of instruction – became popular throughout the Basque Country, and they remain so today.

Québécois Consciousness and the Turbulent 1960s

In the late 1950s, a linguist and social psychologist by the name of Wallace Lambert conducted an experiment designed to study the ways in which Anglophones and Francophones perceived French and English. He asked two groups of study participants – Québécois and Anglos – to listen to the voices of two speakers, one reading a text in French (a Francophone), the other a translation in English (an Anglophone). He then asked participants to rank the two speakers on a numerical scale for a variety of personality characteristics, including beauty, height, intelligence, dependability, religiosity, and self-confidence.

What he found was stunning. Instead of each group favoring their own language, Lambert found language perceptions to be driven by social status, irrespective of the primary language affiliation of the person taking the study. Thus, the Anglo participants favored the English voice for almost all characteristics, including intelligence and beauty, but only favored the French voice for one: sense of humor. Not only did the Québécois participants agree with the Anglos in ranking the English speaker higher than the French speaker for a majority of the characteristics, but they actually rated the English speaker higher on intelligence than the Anglos rated themselves. Furthermore, the only characteristics the Québécois attributed to the French speaker were religiosity and kindness.

What is even more remarkable about Lambert's study is that the voices used – that of the Anglophone and the Francophone – actually belonged to the same speaker, a bilingual who read each of the passages. This means that the differences in the ratings between the "two" speakers could not then be attributed to differences in text, voice, level of education, age, gender, or any other factor besides the perceived difference between French and English. Therefore, at the time the study was conducted, it could be concluded that in the minds of the Québécois, English speakers were smarter, more beautiful, taller, more self-confident, and more reliable than French speakers. It was no surprise that the Anglos felt so strongly about themselves; after all, they were the group with social and political power. It was, however, surprising for many to learn that the Québécois had so strongly and thoroughly internalized the negative attributes associated with French. While the Occitan minority in France experienced *vergonha* in the eighteenth century on account of their social and linguistic standing vis-à-vis the French, in the twentieth century, Canada's French-speaking minority experienced *vergonha* on account of their standing vis-à-vis Canadian Anglophones.

Lambert's study contributed to the Québécois consciousness raising efforts at the time, which took place against the backdrop of cultural and economic development known as la Révolution tranquille 'the Quiet Revolution.' During this period, the idea of Quebec nationalism became popular, and debates about language frequently resulted in heated protests. In 1969, in a visit to Montreal, French president Charles de Gaulle pronounced, "*Vive le Québec libre!*" 'Long live free Quebec!', thus stirring nationalistic ambitions. The same year, some 10,000 French-speaking students protested at McGill University, shouting "*McGill aux québécois, McGill français*" 'McGill for the Québécois, French McGill.' They argued that the university, located in French-speaking Montreal, should be bilingual.[9]

Against the backdrop of the Quiet Revolution, a more violent campaign for Quebec sovereignty was being waged. The *Front de libération de Québec* was a Quebec nationalist group that bombed nearly 100 sites during the 1960s. They commonly targeted elite, English-speaking neighborhoods. In 1970, violence captured the attention of the whole of Canada, when the FLQ kidnapped two members of government, who were taken at gunpoint from their own homes. The FLQ kidnappers demanded that French- and English-language broadcast media read aloud the full copy of the FLQ Manifesto, which critiques the economic, political, and language conditions of Quebec. It ends with the following passage:

> In the four corners of Quebec, may those who have been contemptuously called 'lousy French' and alcoholics start fighting vigorously against the enemies of liberty and justice and put out of commission all the professional swindlers and robbers, the bankers, the businessmen, the judges, and the sold-out politicians!!!
> Long live free Quebec!
> Long live our imprisoned political comrades!
> Long live the Quebec revolution!
> Long live the Front de libération du Québec!

In the face of these inflamed actions, passions, and rhetoric, the citizens feared mass violence would sweep Quebec. The national government responded by temporarily putting in place the War Measures Act, which gave the government wartime powers in searching and detaining individuals. The crisis escalated further when it was announced that the second kidnap victim had been killed in captivity. Finally, after more than 60 days in captivity, the first kidnap victim was released, and the kidnappers were given safe passage to Cuba. The event came to be known as the October Crisis.

Quebec in the 1970s saw rapid yet less violent political change, which further shifted power from the Anglophone minority to the Francophone majority in Quebec. These changes increased the visibility of French in the province. The *Parti Québécois* emerged on the political scene and by the end of the decade had won enough seats in the *Assemblée Nationale du Québec* to propose a referendum on the issue of sovereignty. The referendum took place in 1980 and was defeated by 60% of the electorate. Fifteen years later, in 1995, a second referendum came up for a vote and once again was defeated, this time by a razor-thin majority. While a solid majority of Francophones voted for secession, over 90% of the Anglophone minority voted against it. Joining them were Mohawk and Cree populations, who wanted their nations to remain a part of Canada.

Although the referenda for sovereignty failed, the French-speaking majority in Quebec have been successful in passing legislation to protect the French language, and shifting the balance of power in their favor.

The Zapatista Uprising and Indigenous Languages in Chiapas

In Mexico on New Year's Day, 1994, 3000 members of the newly formed Zapatista Army of National Liberation (EZLN)[10] descended from the jungles in the southern state of Chiapas[11] onto the streets of San Cristóbal de las Casas, an important Spanish colonial town. Dressed in black vests and brandishing a mix of ancient weapons and modern assault rifles, they stormed the town hall of San Cristóbal, burning land deeds, and eventually seizing control of the town, along with five other municipalities in the state. The Mexican government promptly issued a military counteroffensive, and intense fighting ensued for 11 consecutive days.

Between 145 and 1000 people were killed in the rebellion, depending on which side you ask. Although an exact death toll is unknown, what is clear is that the Zapatista Uprising, as the 1994 event in Chiapas has since been named, was successful in disrupting the status quo. First, it sparked a wave of protest and rebellion in Mexico that resulted in greater autonomy for indigenous groups. It also happened to disrupt the Mexican political system, precisely as the federal government was poised to implement policies designed to thrust Mexico – its indigenous communities and all – fully into the global economy. Seeing the writing on the policy wall, the Zapatista Uprising was designed to push back against the people, forms of government, epistemological frameworks, languages, and other forces of assimilation pulling southern Mexico further into the modern, postcolonial nation-state.

For seven consecutive decades beginning in the early twentieth century, Mexico was ruled by a single political party, the Institutional Revolutionary Party, or PRI, as it is known in Mexico. In Chiapas, *campesinos* 'farmers' and peasants, usually indigenous Maya, and speakers of Tzeltal and Tzotzil, were long forced by elite land owners, usually Spanish-speaking *mestizos*, to cast ballots for PRI candidates in national elections. Locally, PRI influence was evident throughout Chiapas, where they kept a stranglehold on local media, schools, and civic organizations. Spanish was the language of the nation-state, and it was likewise the language of the political infrastructure in Chiapas.

In response to these conditions, the Zapatista Army began to take shape in the 1980s. In the beginning, the movement comprised mostly nonindigenous *mestizos* interested in advocating for land reforms, which were guaranteed in the Mexican Constitution of 1917 but mostly ignored by the PRI. Over time and with the help of the Roman Catholic Church, which was also at odds with the PRI, they began organizing in indigenous communities, helping locals learn how to speak up for their own interests, and speak out against the abuses of the nonindigenous political machinery. As the movement gained momentum, the state – led by the PRI – responded with tactics of fear and intimidation in Maya communities. The communities pressed back, as indigenous men joined the Zapatista guerillas in the jungles of Chiapas, this time ready to take up arms.

As the movement became an army, a non-Maya, Spanish-speaking *mestizo* man known to the world by his nom de guerre *Subcomandante Marcos* emerged as the figurehead for the EZLN. Rumored to be a university professor, Marcos provided the Zapatistas with the anticapitalist energy and focus on social and economic justice that provided the ideological basis for the uprising of 1994, which, in the Zapatista view, was considered war on Mexico. Marcos planned the rebellion to take place on the eve of the start of NAFTA, the North American Free Trade Agreement, an accord that created the world's largest trade bloc between Canada, Mexico, and the United States. The signing of NAFTA happened also to be a signature policy issue for the PRI. For the Zapatistas, however, NAFTA was considered a death sentence, as poor farmers would no longer be able to compete with the commercial farms in the United States. Although NAFTA did move forward, the uprising of 1994 took its toll on the Mexican government. The Zapatistas managed to retain control of indigenous land in Chiapas, and in 2000, PRI was voted out of office for the first time in seven decades.

As violent clashes between *campesinos*, Zapatistas, Mexican military, and paramilitary groups continued for more than a decade after the uprising officially ended, Chiapas became one of the most militarized regions in the Americas. The violence did not deter the Zapatistas from practicing self-government, and by 2003, they initiated *Juntas del Buen Gobierno*, a community-based, cooperative political system in which pre-Columbian forms of governance are observed. In this cooperative political system there are no parties, and community members serve as officeholders on a rotational basis. Most of the languages of Chiapas belong to the Western Maya language group. These include Ch'ol, Chontal, Chuj, Jacaltec, Kanjobal, Motozinlec, Tojolabal, Tzeltal, and Tzotzil. A few non-Mayan languages such as Zoque, a Mixe-Zoquean language, are also spoken in the region. Just as the indigenous cultures of Chiapas have been influenced from colonial influence – Tzotzils are mostly protestant Christians, while Tzeltals are mostly Roman Catholic – the languages have also been influenced from the history of sustained contact with Spanish. Spanish loanwords are easy to identify in Tzotzil – *bino* (*vino* 'wine'), *martoma* (*mayordomo* 'custodian'), and *rominko* (*domingo* 'Sunday') among others. The /r/ sound in 'rominko' did not exist in either Ch'ol or Tzotzil prior to contact with Spanish, but entered both languages through Spanish loanwords, and has since spread to some native words. The colonial Tzotzil word *kelem 'young man' became *kerem* 'boy' in modern Tzotzil. Structural modifications such as these are normal linguistic consequences of language contact and cannot readily be undone, even with the types of strong political intervention that put parts of Chiapas under Zapatista control.

In the Zapatista strongholds of Chiapas where the uprising of 1994 took place, language maintenance is high. Some communities have been successful in stopping or even reversing the cross-generational language shift to Spanish that has been under way since at least the early nineteenth century when Spanish was promoted as the language of Mexico as set forth in Chapter 6. Some Maya languages – Ch'ol, Tojolabal, Tzeltal, and Tzotzil among them – are even considered to be thriving. The vitality of these languages is due to the Zapatista educational system, in which indigenous languages are the medium of instruction but also inform the whole of the curriculum, which is rooted in the Maya tradition of communal living. Because Chiapas is home to nearly 15% of Mexico's total indigenous population and more than 50 distinctive language groups, the focus on local language and culture in Zapatista schools makes sense. The fate of all of these languages is nevertheless at stake, since the issue of land rights remains far from settled.

In 2012, a communiqué issued by the EZLN reached the international press. It read, "Did you hear that? It is the sound of your world crumbling. It is the sound of ours resurging." On that day, 50,000 Zapatistas – mostly from Tzeltal, Tzotzil, and Ch'ol indigenous communities – returned to the streets of San Cristóbal de las Casas. This time, wielding no weapons, they marched in silence, black balaclavas (ski masks) covering their faces in the style of Subcomandante Marcos. The march coincided with two significant events in the intertwined cultural and political life of the Maya and the Zapatistas: the end of the creation cycle in traditional Maya scripture and the fifteenth anniversary of the Acetal Massacre of 1997 in which 45 unarmed indigenous people were slain by a paramilitary group while attending a prayer meeting.

In the 2000s, with PRI out of power, the Zapatistas shifted their focus to the cultivation of civic life in the autonomous regions and the preservation of traditional indigenous culture. This emphasis is now in question, since after more than a decade on the sidelines, PRI – the Zapatistas' primary political antagonists – returned to power in 2012. However, the 2012 march through the streets of San Cristóbal may have also been a signal that, 20 years following the original uprising, the Zapatistas still hold sway in Chiapas.

Final Note: The Parsley Massacre in the Dominican Republic

The island of Hispaniola, located dead center in the Caribbean Sea, is divided between the western third, which is occupied by the Kreyòl-and-French-speaking nation of Haiti, and the east two-thirds, which is occupied by the Spanish-speaking Dominican Republic. The two countries are separated by the Massacre River, so named for a bloody struggle between the French and the Spanish during the colonial era. The violent colonial past was matched by an equally violent event in the twentieth century, the infamous Parsley Massacre of 1937.

From 1930 to 1961, the Dominican Republic was ruled by the dictator Rafael Trujillo, known in Spanish as *El Jefe* 'The Boss.' He promoted a cult of personality that, among other things, involved renaming Santo Domingo, the capital city, Ciudad Trujillo 'Trujillo City.' Trujillo's story is bound with the race–nation–language triad described in Chapter 4. There is evidence that Trujillo used powder and whitening creams to lighten his face in order to appear more European. Trujillo also initiated a so-called open-door immigration policy, in which certain groups, namely the Japanese, Spanish, and Jews, were allowed to seek citizenship in the Dominican Republic. It seems his goal was to lighten the population. He had an equal desire to rid the Dominican Republic of dark-skinned Haitians.

In 1937, as Haitians were leaving the Dominican Republic en masse, Trijullo called in the military to attack the border region and to kill as many exiting Haitians as possible. However, since it was not possible to discern a Haitian from a Dominican on the spot based on apperance alone, a linguistic test was devised. The test exploited the articulatory difference in the pronuncation of [r] between Kreyòl and Spanish. The [r] of Spanish is an alveolar trill, at the beginning of a word like *rojo* 'red' and where a double-r appears in orthography, in a word like *perro* 'dog.' Elsewhere, it is an alveolar tap [ɾ]. In contrast, the sound in Kreyòl is pronounced as a uvular trill [ʀ]. The chosen word for the linguistic test was *perejil* 'parsley.' On the basis of whether your place of articulation of [r] was the alveolar ridge, or about five centimeters back in the oral cavity at the uvula, you either lived or died. Those who pronounced the word with the Spanish tap were free to go. Those who pronounced it with the uvular trill were killed on the spot. Over the course of a few days, 10,000–30,000 Haitians died. The massacre is known in Spanish as *el corte* and in Kreyòl as *kuoto-a* 'the cutting.' We will say it: there is nothing new under the sun.

Trujillo's Parsley Massacre was not the first of its kind. In Biblical times, the Hebrew word *shibboleth* 'ear of corn' was used by the Gileadites to distinguish the Ephraimites whose language variety did not have phoneme /ʃ/. After the Ephraimites lost a battle to the Gileadites, they went to the River Jordan to return home. As a linguistic test to cross the river, the Gileadites had them say the word for 'ear of corn,' and 42,000 of them were killed when they replied, "Sibboleth."

Neither were the language silos created in Eastern Europe at the end of World War II an innovation. In the midnineteenth century, the United States government established similar silos, called Indian Reservations, west of the Mississippi. These reservations were set up on the basis of language difference, partitioning the Cherokee (Iroquois) from the Creek (Muskogean) from the Catawba (Sioux) with delineated boundaries like those separating France from Spain and Germany. In pre-Columbian times, the area of what is now modern-day north Georgia was settled by speakers of Cherokee, Creek, and Catawba who encountered one another frequently.

No one can unscramble an egg. Nor can one reverse the effects of history. Neither do we want to say that pre-World War II Europe or the pre-Columbian Americas were Eden. What we do want to say is that now, going forward, language diversity is not a problem, and it does not need to be resolved, through attempts either to segregate language communities against their will or to eradicate languages deemed undesirable or unnecessary by those in positions of power.

Language Profile: Tamil (Dravidian)

Functional overview

Most speakers of Tamil live in Tamil Nadu, a state on the east coast of India that extends south abutting the Bay of Bengal all the way to the southern tip of the subcontinent, where it meets the Indian Ocean. Tamil Nadu is roughly the size of New York State, but has more than three times the number of people. Most of them, some 60 million, speak Tamil. The language is also spoken by about 4 million people in the northeastern part of the island nation of Sri Lanka, which lies due south of Tamil Nadu, and by a few million others in Malaysia, Singapore, and parts of East Africa. The largest concentration of Tamil speakers is in Chennai (formerly Madras), the capital of Tamil Nadu. Tamil is a language in the Tamil branch of the Dravidian language family.

Speakers of Tamil are invested in beliefs about the antiquity of their language and consider Classical (Old) Tamil to be the most pure form of the language. Contemporary speech varieties vary according to caste (sociolects) and region (varieties). Caste differences in speech are highly recognizable. The varieties spoken by Tamil Brahmins, for example, are known as *Braahmik* and are considered to be highly

Sanskritized. The variety spoken in the central part of Tamil Nadu is said to have changed the least from Classical Tamil. The style of this variety spoken by educated non-brahmins in this region is the basis of contemporary Popular Standard Tamil. The Sri Lankan varieties are less influenced by Sanskrit but have borrowings from Portuguese, Dutch, and English. Sri Lankan Tamil and Tamil of Tamil Nadu are sometimes considered mutually unintelligible, and the Sri Lankan varieties are sometimes said to be more similar to Malayalam, another Dravidian language. The remarkable diversity of the Tamil-speaking regions is further complicated by the diglossic situation we describe at the end of this profile.

Prominent structural characteristics

Retroflex consonants In most varieties of English, the word 'pop' begins with the bilabial stop /p/, 'throw' with the interdental fricative /θ/, 'take' with the alveolar stop /t/, 'chocolate' with the alveo-palatal affricate /tʃ/, 'yes' with the palatal approximate /j/, and 'good' with the velar stop /g/. In making these consonant articulations, ordered here from the front of the mouth to the back, English skips entirely over the part of the oral cavity between the alveolar ridge and the hard palate known as the postalveolar region. This is the place of articulation for retroflex consonants, which are only found in some 20% of the world's languages but which are especially prominent in the languages of South Asia.

Retroflex consonants are formed when the tip of the tongue curls back and makes some type of contact with the postalveolar region. The type of contact depends on the manner of articulation. In Tamil, there are four retroflex consonants with different manners of articulation:

(i)   voiceless retroflex stop /ʈ/, as in [eʈʈɯ] 'eight';
(ii) voiced retroflex nasal /ɳ/, as in [aɳal] 'neck';
(iii) voiced retroflex lateral approximant /ɭ/, as in [puɭi] 'tamarind';
(iv) voiced retroflex approximant /ɻ/, as in [ʋeɻi] 'way.'

Approximant consonants are like fricatives in that the articulators approach each other very closely, but unlike fricatives, no turbulent noise is produced. The retroflex approximate /ɻ/ can be heard in the pronunciation of the name of the language, 'Tamil,' as [t̪ɐmiɻ]. Retroflex articulations often color neighboring vowels, giving them an r-sounding quality in perception.

In terms of phonology, the Tamil retroflex consonants are contrastive, and minimal pairs are found with consonants of the same manner of articulation and different places of articulation. The retroflex nasal /ɳ/, for example, can contrast with the alveolar nasal /n/, creating meaning distinctions in pairs such as *maɳa* 'frangrance' and *mana* 'mind.' The retroflex lateral approximate contrasts with the alveolar lateral, yielding minimal pairs such as *puli* 'tiger' and *puɭi* 'tamarind.'

Contrastive vowel length If you are an English speaker, you may greet an old friend with a form of the salutation 'hey' in which the vowel is elongated several times the usual length (heeeey). Or to emphatically disagree with an interlocutor, you may likewise elongate the /o/ in 'no' (noooo) to emphasize your position. Although you do nuance the meaning of the words 'hey' and 'no' when you do this, you do not fundamentally change their meaning; 'no' in effect still means 'no.' This is because English does not make use of differences in vowel length to make lexical or grammatical contrasts.

An important characteristic of Tamil phonology is that, in contrast to English, vowel length is used to make phonological meaning contrasts. For each of the five vowel sounds /a, e, i, o, u/, there are phonologically contrastive long variants /aː, eː, iː, oː, uː/. The duration of the long vowels is roughly double that of the short vowels, though the duration varies depending on phonetic environment.

Each of the the 10 vowels is represented in writing with a unique letter.

	Short	Long
i	இ	ஈ
e	எ	ஏ
a	அ	ஆ
o	ஒ	ஓ
u	உ	ஊ

Lexical minimal pairs illustrate the difference between short and long vowels, for example:

Short		Long	
pal	'tooth'	*paal*	'milk'
vidi	'fate'	*viidi*	'street'
todu	'touch'	*toodu*	'earring'
mudi	'hair'	*muudi*	'lid'

'Caste' noun classes As we mentioned in Chapter 2, some languages group nouns into categories based on what appear to be the natural characteristics that they name. These categories are called noun classes. In many languages of Europe, Africa, and Australia, nouns are classed according to grammatical gender. Grammatical gender is found in about one-fourth of the world's languages, and among them, the masculine/feminine/neuter system of classification found in languages such as German and Polish is especially common. In noun class languages, the classes codetermine, along with case, number, and person, the type of morphology a noun will receive. Adjectives, verbs, and other grammatical elements are also affected in the sense that they must be in grammatical agreement, or morphological symmetry, with the noun.

In Tamil, nouns are classed first into one of two semantic 'superclasses,' known as 'rational' and 'irrational,' or 'high caste' and 'low caste.' The rational class aggregates all *uyarthinai* 'humans,' *thevar* 'gods,' *naragar* 'the devil,' and other mythical beings. Everything else (abstract nouns, animals, and objects) is grouped together in the irrational class. Grammatical gender, in combination with number, only emerges in the form of subclasses within the superclasses. The rational class comprises masculine singular, feminine singular, and a plural category that does not distinguish gender. The irrational class comprises subclasses that only distinguish number – singular and plural – and in this respect, irrational nouns can be said to be neuter.

The semantic noun classes in Tamil have morphological and syntactic consequences. First, the classes determine the morphological endings for some of Tamil's 10 cases. The rational feminine noun *penn* 'girl' has a morphology that resembles the irrational noun *maram* 'tree' in certain cases (ACC – *penn-ai, marath-ai*; DAT – *penn-ukku, marath-ukku*), but for some cases, the endings are distinct (LOC – *penn-idam, marath-il*; ABL – *penn-idamirunthu, marath-ilirunthu*). In terms of syntax, two nouns of the same super class can combine in the same noun phrase, while a rational and irrational noun cannot. 'Men and women have perished' is a possible utterance because the noun phrase subject comprises two nouns of the same rational class. 'Men and tigers have perished' is not possible, since men (rational) and tigers (irrational) come from distinct super classes. In Tamil, this idea is expressed by repeating the predicate, as in 'men have perished and tigers have perished' (Dixon 1982, 170).

Inclusive/exclusive pronouns In the languages of Europe, subject personal pronouns slot into a familiar pronominal paradigm in which unique forms represent first, second, and third persons in singular and plural number. The Italian pronouns (singular – *io, tu, lui/lei*; plural – *noi, voi, Loro*) is fairly typical of these languages. Each unique subject pronoun (e.g., *noi*) cooccurs with a unique set of verbal morphology (e.g., *mangiamo*) in the various verbal tenses. Of note is that Italian, like English and the other languages of Europe, subsumes two senses of the first person plural into a single grammatical form, namely, *noi* or 'we.' The form may mean 'we, you and I' or 'we, I and others but not you.' This means that on occasion, speakers may find themselves in conversations in which it is unclear whether or not the addressee is included as a part of the subject.

In Tamil, these two senses correspond to separate and distinct subject personal pronouns. These forms are known as inclusive, when the addressee is included in the meaning, and exclusive, when the addressee is not included in the meaning. The first-person plural-inclusive is *naam* 'we' (you and I) and the first-person plural-exclusive is *naangal* 'we' (I and others but not you). In some languages that make this distinction, inclusive and exclusive forms cooccur with separate verbal morphology. This is not the case in Tamil, as verbs occurring with both *naam* and *naangal* take the same endings.

Beyond their function in the morphosyntax of Tamil, the inclusive/exclusive distinction also plays an important pragmatic role (Brown and Levinson 1987:203). The inclusive subject pronoun *naam* and the corresponding object and possessive pronouns are used in positive expressions of politeness. In Tamil culture, it is considered rude to refer to 'my mother,' 'my family,' or 'my car.' Instead, inclusive possessives are used to convey a sense of shared ownership. A polite invitation to dinner may invite the addressee to dinner at our (inclusive) home.

Vaanka, namma viiTTlee caappiTalaam.
Come, our-INCL house we eat.
'Come, let's eat at our house.'

A salient cultural characteristic: Tamil 'H' and 'L' diasystems

As early as the third century BCE, Tamil scholars produced a remarkably sweeping description of the ancient Tamil language, including grammar and phonology, orthography, and the major literary works of the day. This work is known as the *Tolkāppiyam*, which is derived from the Tamil words *Tonmai* 'ancient' and *Kappiam* 'literature.' The notions of 'language' and 'literature' have therefore been tightly intertwined with one another in the Tamil linguistic imaginary since antiquity, and today the *Tolkāppiyam* is still considered an important authority on the language.

The Classical literary language, known as *Centamil*, is highly revered in contemporary Tamil culture, and for centuries it has been formally studied by students in schools. No one speaks *Centamil* as a first-language variety. Instead, children learn one of the caste- and regional varieties described earlier in this profile. These varieties are known in general as *Koduntamil*. The functional alternation between these two types of language has created a situation of diglossia similar to that involving Arabic described in Chapter 3. In Tamil Nadu, *Centamil* is the H (high) variety, and *Koduntamil* is the L (low) variety.

In all diglossic situations, the H (high) and L (low) varieties are arranged in complementary distribution, such that in situations where H is used, L is not, and vice versa. H emerges in the formal domains of religion, education, and media, while L is relegated to informal domains, such as in talk between friends. What makes the Tamil diglossic situation unique is that H and L constitute distinct diasystems, or systems of related but distinct language varieties (Britto 1986). In Tamil, the language varieties constituting the H and L diasystems differ in terms of phonology, morphology, and lexicon. The social context and degree of formality determine which variety or varieties within the H or L diasystem continuum will be used. In formal education and religious situations, *Centamil*, the highest of the H varieties, is most commonly spoken. In news media such as television, radio, and newspapers, Popular Standard Tamil is used. This variety is less formal than *Centamil* but still falls within the H diasystem.

The social and pragmatic meanings attached to all H and L varieties are easily understood by Tamil speakers. When a politician begins a speech with formal greetings in one of the H varieties, it is clear that the intent is to establish status, credibility, and authority. When the politician switches to an L variety, listeners appreciate the social meaning: solidarity, warmth, and familiarity. This type of diglossia – constituted by H and L diasystems – has been in place in the Tamil-speaking world for centuries. Full participation in Tamil life requires the ability to command various H and L codes as well as knowledge of the unspoken pragmatic rules for knowing when, where, and how to move between them.

Exercises

Exercise 1 – map making

Moving borders are not inconsequential for speakers and their languages. Perhaps no nation has experienced more border shifts than Poland. Some of these, and their effects on Polish, German, Ukrainian, Lemko, and Ruthenian, were described in this chapter. Make a map (or a series of maps) depicting Poland's shifting borders in the following years: 992 (Mieszko I unites Polish tribes), 1569 (Polish–Lithuanian Commonwealth), 1795 (third partition of Poland), 1918 (recreation of Polish state), 1939 (World War II partition), and 1945 (postwar period).

Exercise 2 – spotlight on South Sudan

At the time of the printing of this book, the most recent group to successfully argue for a separate state was the South Sudanese, as described in this chapter. Besides English and Arabic, what are the other major languages of South Sudan? Who speaks them? Describe the linguistic, religious, and cultural practices of these groups. Prepare your findings in the form of a short report or presentation.

Exercise 3 – you decide

The conflicts in South Ossetia and Abkhazia remain unresolved, as set forth in this chapter. As we have seen, language issues are at the fore of the conflict. You have once again been appointed as a special commissioner to the United Nations, and your charge is to inform your colleagues about the language situation in the Caucasus, focusing specifically on Georgia and these breakaway regions. Based on your findings, what do you recommend about the status of South Ossetia and Abkhazia?

Exercise 4 – linguistic perception

Using your university library catalogue, read the Lambert et al. (1960) paper published in *Journal of Abnormal and Social Psychology* mentioned earlier in this chapter. First, write a one-paragraph summary of the study that describes the methods, the participants, the study findings, and the major conclusions. Then, imagine that the experiment was to be run in your community comparing languages such as Punjabi and English if you live in London, Cantonese, and Mandarin if you live in Hong Kong, and Xhosa and Afrikaans if you live in Cape Town. What do you hypothesize about how study participants might perceive these languages if they believed they were listening to different speakers? Use the same variables used by Lambert (intelligence, beauty, etc.). What is the basis for your hypotheses?

Discussion Questions

1 The authors write that "the logic used to construct the state became the same logic used to challenge it." Use examples from the chapter to illustrate what this means. What other geopolitical conflicts, historical or present, can also be used to illustrate this point?

2 What kinds of power dynamics has European colonialism left in its wake? How do these dynamics play out among different ethnogroups inhabiting the same postcolonial context?

3   What do the authors mean by the term *quasi-state*? How does this term challenge your understanding of the form of political organization we have referred to in this text as the nation-state? Does the term *quasi-state* make you adjust your understanding of language in any way? How?

4   The authors decided to include this chapter on language violence and geopolitics in the section of this book focusing on movement, rather than the more obvious section on power. What kinds of movements are caused by language-related geopolitical conflict, and what kinds of movement result in geopolitical conflict? What other situations are you aware of that have resulted in movements of people and language that have resulted in some type of conflict?

5   Tsar Nicolas II (1868–1918) is reported to have said, "There is no Ukrainian language, just illiterate peasants speaking Little Russian." This expression – Little Russian – reappeared during the 2014 geopolitical conflict between Russian and Ukraine over the Crimean Peninsula. What do you make of this usage? What is its rhetorical effect?

6   What do you make of the violence waged by groups such as ETA, the Tamil Tigers, and the *Front de libération de Québec* on behalf of linguistic freedom and political independence? Can you think of any other, nonviolent tactics these groups could have used? Would they have been effective?

7   Do you imagine that the Zapatista political intervention in the Chiapas region of Mexico will continue to be a successful one? What conditions would promote continued peace and maintenance of indigenous languages? Under what conditions might violence return?

8   The race–nation–language triad discussed in Chapter 4 once again comes into play in the context of the Dominican Republic's Parsley Massacre. How does this triad play out in other national contexts you are familiar with? Is violence always involved?

Notes

1   The state of Israel also came into being in 1948. The Palestinian Liberation Organization was founded in 1964. The first Palestinian suicide attack was in 1989.

2   The Sinhala Only Act was rescinded in 1987, and Tamil became an official language along with Sinhala, but by then the damage had been done (Kanaganayakam 2009).

3   The final [r] was added to account for the tone on the final syllable in *Myanma*. The committee based the English pronunciation on the so-called 'r-less' varieties, such as those spoken in England, in which the final [r] is vocalized, approximating the Burmese pronunciation. The rhotic pronunciation in American English yields a markedly different pronunciation of the country.

4   See footnote 8 in Chapter 5.

5   In 2004, the European Union voted to classify the forced removal of Chechens to Siberia a case of genocide.

6   The Valencian version of the Constitution was exactly identical to the Catalan one. The insistence by Valencians that the Constitution be printed in putative Valencian was an indication that the region may seek regional autonomy for itself in the future. As we have

seen before, the claims to linguistic difference do not always require linguistic differences to exist.

7 In 2014, the government of Catalonia held a nonbinding public vote on the issue of regional independence. Eighty percent of those who cast a vote did so in favor of full independence. The federal government in Madrid does not acknowledge the vote, and therefore the status of Catalonia's statehood remains unresolved.

8 Note that Basque is spoken in the French department of the Pyrénées Atlantiques, just north of the Spanish Basque Country.

9 Today, about 18% of McGill students are Québécois, and students are allowed to submit work in French or English, though the medium of instruction remains English.

10 The Zapatistas are named for Emiliano Zapata, who is known for his advocacy of peasant land rights and as an influential figure in the Mexican Revolution, which began in 1910.

11 Chiapas state is named for the indigenous Chiapa people, who have mostly been assimilated into the broader mestizo ethnicity.

References

Britto, Francis (1986) *Diglossia: A Study of the Theory, with Reference to Tamil*. Washington, DC: Georgetown University Press.

Brown, Penelope and Stephen Levinson (1987) *Politeness: Some Universals in Language Usage*. Cambridge: Cambridge University Press.

Dixon, R.M (1982) *Where Have All the Adjectives Gone?* Berlin: Walter de Gruyter & Co.

Kanaganayakam, Chelva (2009) *Things Fall Apart* from a Sri Lankan perspective. *Postcolonial Text* 5: 1–11.

Lambert, W.E., R.C. Hodgson, R.C. Gardner, and S. Fillenbaum (1960) Evaluational reactions to spoken language. *Journal of Abnormal and Social Psychology* 60: 44–51.

Mamdani, Mahmood (2009) *Saviors and Survivors: Darfur, Politics, and the War on Terror*. New York: Random House.

Meadows, Mark (2010) *Tea Time with Terrorists: A Motorcycle Journey into the Heart of Sri Lanka's Civil War*. New York: Skull Press.

Further Reading

Britto, Francis (1991) Tamil diglossia: An interpretation. *Southwest Journal of Linguistic: Studies in Diglossia* 10: 60–84.

Crassweller, Robert (1966) *D. Trujillo: The Life and Times of a Caribbean Dictator*. New York: Macmillan.

Ferguson, Charles (1959) Diglossia. *Word* 15: 325–340.

Kamusella, Tomasz (2013) The Silesian language in the early 21st community on the roller-coaster of politics. *Die Welt der Slaven* 58: 1–35.

Lapidus, Gail W. (1998) Contested sovereignty: The tragedy of Chechnya. *International Security* 5: 201–250.

Linek, Bernard (2001) De-Germanization and re-Polinization in Upper Silesia, 1945–1950. In Philipp Ther and Ana Sijak (eds.), *Redrawing Nations: Ethnic Cleansing in East-Central Europe, 1944–1948*. Lanham, MD: Rowman and Littlefield.

Schiffman, Harold (1980) The Tamil Liquids. *Proceedings of the Sixth Annual Meeting of the Berkeley Linguistics Society*, 100–110.

Schiffman, Harold (1996) *Linguistic Culture and Language Policy.* London: Routledge.
Schiffman, Harold (1999) *A Reference Grammar of Spoken Tamil.* Cambridge: Cambridge University Press.
Ther, Philipp (2001) A century of forced migration: The origins and consequences of "ethnic cleansing." In Philipp Ther and Ana Siljak (eds.), *Redrawing Nations: Ethnic Cleansing in East-Central Europe, 1944–1948.* Lanham, MD: Rowman and Littlefield, 43–72.

Part IV
Effects of Time

Introductory Note: On Time

Because languages are sociohistorical products, the effects of time have been operating throughout this book, and they have been operating at various scales. In Part
II, we concentrated on the recent history of the last 200 years to examine the power
dynamics involved in the political ideology of the monolingual state. We also looked
back at the beginnings of recorded history by outlining the steps toward writing that
began about the fourth millennium BCE in Egypt and around the third millennium
BCE in China. In Part III, we stepped farther back in time, namely 10,000 years, to
identify the homelands of the current language stocks of the world, and we tracked
the subsequent movement of peoples from those homelands. We then outlined some
of the consequences of colonialism, with particular attention to the span of the last
3000 years. In Part IV, we now put time at issue and foreground its effects in order
to discuss the following:

(i)   Deep time. Language is not an ornament on the human condition, like the
      star placed on the Christmas tree when the lights go on. Language is rather a
      fundamental part of our biology, and as such it has been woven into our bodies
      over a very, very long period of time. Just as a basic knowledge of genetics is
      necessary for any student of the languages of the world, so is knowledge of
      basic evolution. In Chapter 10, we outline some of the ways the looping of
      the language loop through human communities has remade parts of human
      biology. We are interested to see how the instantiation and development of the
      language loop has made us the particular kind of primate we are. Our grandest
      timescale is the last six million years, when humans split from chimps, but our
      more particular focus is on the last 150,000 years when our earliest ancestors

Languages in the World: How History, Culture, and Politics Shape Language, First Edition.
Julie Tetel Andresen and Phillip M. Carter.
© 2016 John Wiley & Sons, Inc. Published 2016 by John Wiley & Sons, Inc.

were living in Africa. We will also consider the kinds of structural properties we can attribute to language at a time-depth up to 40,000 years, by which time all continents were inhabited by humans.

(ii) Recorded history. In Chapter 8, we saw how the written records of the succession of Chinese dynasties kept from the seventh century BCE to the present helped us understand the spread of the ethnic Han into new territories and their colonization of those territories. In Chapters 3 and 7, we engaged with the ways philologists have used written records for the retrospective activity of reconstructing protolanguages whose contexts are necessarily lost to us in prehistory. In Chapter 11, we now take another look at written records, this time in order to have a more fine-grained understanding of how languages change when the historical, social, and political contexts of those changes are better known and available for study. We choose one of the many language stories presented in Chapters 3–9 and present the specifics of the ways these languages have attempted to catch up to the conditions imposed upon them.

(iii) The future. At the end of Chapter 7, we mentioned that the highest density of language diversity is around the equator. We also noted that the highest number of endangered languages is found in that same area. There is no doubt that the creation and expansion of nation-states with concomitant colonialism in the last 500 years have contributed to the endangerment of languages spoken today by smaller groups organized in more traditional societies. Languages not found around the equator, such as Irish and Basque, have also faced challenges for survival, crowded as they are by large national languages, and ones with international presence, no less. In Chapter 12, we review some of the reasons for language death, and we examine factors that lead to partial or complete language revival. We end by looking at some of the responses of contemporary speakers of endangered languages toward the endangered state of their languages, and we discuss what they are and are not willing to do to ensure that their languages survive to the next generation.

One of the conditions language is always catching up to are the attitudes about particular varieties of language created by certain conditions. Attitudes about language are as subject to change as every other aspect of language. In our daily lives, we, the authors, try to always practice what we call *generous listening*. This practice keeps our ears open to the beauty of all linguistic varieties around us.

10

The Remote Past
Language Becomes Embodied

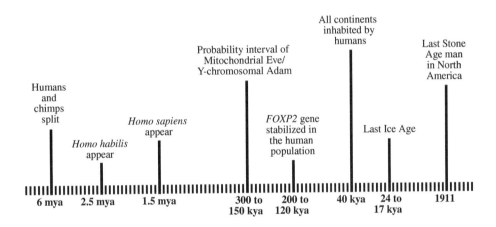

Look There!

We have defined language as an orienting behavior that orients the orientee within his or her cognitive domain. When we think about deep time and the coevolution of the human brain and language, we speculate that the first linguistic orientation was likely that *of* orientation: the way that one person's verbalization, no doubt accompanied by a gesture and a touch, turned another person's attention and bodily movements in a particular direction. *Look this way, not that way;* or: *Follow me;* or: *The good game is over there.* We could also call this orientation *pointing the way.* Linguistic pointing is known by the term **deixis**, from the Greek adjective *deiktikos* meaning 'pointing.'

Deixis indicates the position of people, objects, and events with respect to a particular point of reference. Deictic categories include personal pronouns (*I, you, he,*

Languages in the World: How History, Culture, and Politics Shape Language, First Edition.
Julie Tetel Andresen and Phillip M. Carter.
© 2016 John Wiley & Sons, Inc. Published 2016 by John Wiley & Sons, Inc.

she, etc.), demonstrative pronouns (*this, that*), spatial adverbs (*here, there*), and temporal adverbs (*today, tomorrow, yesterday*). How a language divides up the semantic space of the personal pronouns, for instance, can sometimes place this language in a long lineage of languages making similar distinctions. Whether or not a language has a deictic category, say, that of tense, can be similarly indicative of lineage inclusion or exclusion.[1] When it comes to the languages of the world, aspect is a more frequently occurring distinction than is tense. It also seems to be the case that children master aspect before tense in languages that have both categories (Andrews 2012:222). Possible measures of what counts as basic in language might be categories that most languages have and/or what children around the world are likely to pick up on more readily. The presence or absence of such a basic and widespread category as aspect may or may not be indicative of lineage inclusion or exclusion.

In this chapter, we are interested in getting down to the basics, to the bottom of things linguistic. That is, we will do so in so far as we can for such a complex sociocultural product as language, which has only left traces of itself since recorded history. We will investigate what psycholinguists, evolutionary biologists, population geneticists, and deep-time historical linguists are able to tell us about linguistic states of affairs in the great blank space stretching from the chimp–human lineage split about six million years ago up until 40 kya when the lineages that eventually split into stocks were taking shape. We will paint what we can of the picture of how *Homo sapiens sapiens* are also *Homo loquens*.

Seeking Linguistic Bedrock

We opened Chapter 2 with a discussion of the differing frames of reference to describe spatial relations on the horizontal plane, and we chose this particular topic to orient you from the beginning to the differing orienting possibilities afforded through different languages. We return to the topic here in order to observe that, while many species have excellent navigating skills (bats, migratory birds, bees), humans cannot be counted among them, and neither can our primate cousins who tend to be a sedentary lot. Humans have long had to rely on language and culture – and increasingly accurate navigational technology – to get from Point A to Point Z.

Languages with absolute frames of reference induce in their speakers a kind of knock-on GPS. However, what the exact coordinates are, how fully they are specified, and whether or not they line up with the Western polar system of north, south, east, and west can vary greatly from language to language. We know from Chapter 7 that the Austronesians were excellent navigators.[2] The Austronesian language Balinese has an absolute frame of reference, but instead of four points, it has only two: one axis is determined by the monsoons and thus operates as a fixed and abstract axis, and the other axis is determined by a location of the central mountain on the island, such that one's relationship to it continually changes as one travels around the island (Levinson 2003:49, Wassman and Dasen 1998). As always, linguistic structures both support and are supported by cultural practices. In Bali, the absolute system is important in daily life and discourse, and there is evidence that Balinese children as young as four years old retain certain memories in terms of the absolute system (Levinson 2003:312).[3]

The relative frame of reference, on the other hand, is viewer-centered, and the planes of the body serve as the coordinates with an up and a down, a front and a back, and a left and a right. So, the utterance *The man is to the left of the house* entails a viewer with a perspective on the situation that tells us the location of the man with respect to the house but gives us no information about the house itself. For those of us who live our lives through a language with a relative frame of reference, we think it entirely natural to use the planes of our body to orient ourselves and our fellows in our environments. However, many ethnogroups get along just fine in the world without ever distinguishing between left and right.

How do these frames of reference arise? Where do they come from? Body parts are often the sources for the names of different parts of objects, say, the foot of a mountain or the leg of a table. As we have just said, basic body parts are: the front, the back, and the sides. When terms become grammaticalized, they can then serve as generalized references. The utterance *The man is in front of the house* specifies the location of a man with respect to a facet of the house, a facet that is intrinsic to it, namely the front door. As with all things linguistic, such a seemingly and supposedly natural idea as *front* can have widely different interpretations across languages and cultures. In English, *front* refers to how one uses an object (front of the TV, front of the book, front of the car, etc.). In Tzeltal, spoken in Mexico, such a term for an object has nothing to do with how someone uses it but is rather based on the object's own facets. And other languages assign fronts to things English speakers do not. In Chamus, a Nilo-Saharan language, trees have fronts according to the direction they lean. From a linguistic point of view, the intrinsic frame of reference is basic. Only once we humans began to cognize the world through language could we imagine ourselves as one of the objects in the universe and create a frame of reference relative to ourselves in terms of left and right. However, the key point is that it is not necessary to create a relative frame of reference, if the ethnogroup is doing just fine with the intrinsic frame of reference. As Stephen Levinson in *Space in Language and Cognition* puts it: "The intrinsic frame of reference is close to linguistic bedrock, in that it is near universal ... [and] children appear to acquire it earlier than other systems" (2003:81).

We begin with the human body in order to open up onto the deep-time story of how we humans have come to orient ourselves and others in our respective cognitive domains.

The Primate Body and Human Adaptations to Language

Although good navigational skills are not part of the order Primates, we primates are very good at social cognition, and we have eye, hand, and even foot preferences. Our foot preferences come from the arboreal existence of our ancestors. Living in trees in the primate past (and which some primates still do) has at least two consequences of note in the primate present: (i) to this day, primates tend to have one leg shorter than the other; and (ii) our primate ancestors had a preference for standing in trees while holding on to a branch with the right hand, leaving the left hand free for foraging. Thus it is in modern primates that the right hemisphere is specialized for, among other things, spatial cognition and survival-related risks such as emergencies, while the left

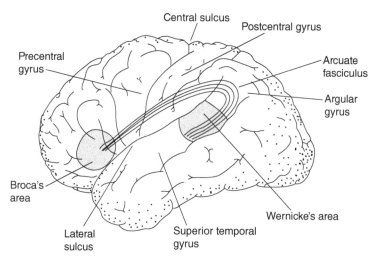

Figure 10.1 The brain.

hemisphere is specialized for, among other things, routine behaviors. Keep in mind that the two hemispheres of the brain are in contralateral relationship to the two sides of the body, such that the left hemisphere mediates the right side of the body, while the right hemisphere mediates the left.

We will compare the human body with the nonhuman primate body by means of a scan from head to foot.

The primate brain

The primate brain (Figure 10.1) is three brains in one, beginning with the so-called reptilian brain. The structures of the reptilian brain include the spinal cord, the cerebellum, the medulla, and the pons. These structures control the body's vital functions such as balance, body temperature, breathing, fight or flight, heart rate, and hunger. On top of the reptilian brain sits the so-called mammalian brain. Its structures include the limbic system and the basal ganglia, and these structures mediate memories of good and bad experiences, emotion, and value judgments. The so-called primate brain is wrapped around the mammalian brain, and its structures include the cerebrum, or white matter, and the neo-cortex, or gray matter. If the thin cortical rim were peeled off and flattened out (*cortex* means 'bark'), the neo-cortex of the monkey brain would have enough to cover a postcard, apes could cover one sheet of paper, and humans could cover four sheets of paper.

In nonhuman primates, the cortical area mediating vocalization is in the limbic association cortex, an area that has an intermediate position between the functions of the limbic system and the cerebral cortex. Because nonhuman primate vocalizations (and their conspecifics' responses to them) are largely involuntary responses to stimuli, often predators, it makes sense that the limbic system handles this function. In humans, by way of contrast, the language-production area has moved into the prefrontal neo-cortex. It is furthermore found in the left hemisphere of most people, with some exceptions for a subsection of left-handers who have this area in their right hemisphere and an even smaller percentage of people who have this area distributed in both hemispheres. This location also makes sense because, for humans, language is a routine behavior.

The language-production center in humans is known as *Broca's area*, and it is named after the nineteenth-century neurologist who discovered the relationship of this brain region to language production. People with damage to this area owing to accident, stroke, or tumor have difficulty producing speech. They can understand what is being said to them, and they know what they want to say, but they simply cannot get it out. Broca's area is adjacent to the motor cortex, which location goes a long way to explaining its relationship to speech production. When dealing with language and the brain and damage, everything depends on location, location, location: where the lesions occur and how extensive they are will determine the type of disability and the possibilities of recovery. For instance, a lesion in one part of the brain can cause the loss of color vision, although the person can still name colors, while a lesion in another part of the brain will cause the person to lose the ability to name colors, although they can still separate colors into categories. What is clear, however, is that everything is connected and that Broca's area is not the be-all and end-all of speech production. Evolutionary biologist Philip Lieberman notes that, "Aphasia – permanent loss of language – never occurs in the absence of subcortical damage; it occurs only after damage to the basal ganglia and pathways to them, leaving Broca's area intact" (2013).

Another language area in humans is known as *Wernicke's area*. People with damage to this area cannot understand what is being said to them. They cannot answer a simple question, and whatever they do say makes no sense at all, although they say it perfectly grammatically and with no production difficulties. Just as Broca's is called a *production disorder*, so Wernicke's is called a *reception disorder*. The speech these people produce is fluent nonsense. Wernicke's area is near primary auditory cortex, and it is possible that the person so afflicted can neither hear nor understand what is being said, nor can this individual monitor his or her own speech. There is another area near the auditory cortex not far from Wernicke's called Heschel's, and lesions to this area produce word deafness. The person can still hear environmental noises, but the person has lost the ability to hear language. They may well retain the ability to speak, read, and write.

Two points need to be made. First, we do not want to say that language is *in* these areas any more than we want to say that walking is in the legs; rather, Broca's, Wernicke's, and Heschel's are areas where certain modalities of interactions converge in order to synthesize a behavior. If there is a disruption in the area, the behavior cannot be synthesized, and thus the behavior cannot be produced well or at all. Although there are important localizations in the brain for certain language behaviors, we think of language as a whole-brain activity such that damage to almost any area of the brain can have undesirable linguistic effects. For instance, there is a structure in the basal ganglia called the putamen, which aids mammals in the movement of limbs. In a multilingual human, damage to the putamen may impede this person's ability to stay on track in one language or another. Furthermore, damage to the cerebellum, which is in the reptilian brain, can cause speaking, listening, reading, and writing deficits and dysfluencies.

Second, areas such as Broca's, Wernicke's, and Heschel's are not necessarily devoted exclusively to language production and reception, and damage to these areas will cause other motor disorders, such as palsies, and other kinds of cognitive disabilities. Because there are so many noninvasive brain-imaging technologies available today, it is no longer necessary to determine the particulars of brain function through the study of how and when it malfunctions. It has been shown, for instance, that Broca's area is involved in such nonlinguistic tasks as searching for a target hidden within a complex geometric pattern, solving math problems, holding information in working memory, and perhaps supporting musical abilities.

Ears

When a physical object is set into vibration, a sound wave is produced. Plucking a guitar string, tapping a piano key, striking a tuning fork, and vibrating the vocal folds in the human larynx all produce sound waves, which propagate through a physical medium. For human language, the typical medium is air. The waves move from the sound source, namely the vocal tract, when air molecules compress together and spread apart. The human ear is adapted to frequencies of human speech, and so articulation and acoustics are therefore two sides of the same coin.

We perceive speech when a sound wave reaches our eardrum and is processed by the part of the cerebral cortex known as the auditory cortex. Part of what we perceive is pitch. We perceive a sound to be high pitched or low pitched depending on the rate at which the physical object – our vocal folds, for example – vibrate. This rate of vibration is known as the fundamental frequency and is measured in Hertz (Hz), or cycles per second. Different voiced sounds (vowels and voiced consonants) are produced when the sound wave is filtered by the human vocal tract. When we say that [a] is a different sound from [i], it is not only because the former is made by retracting the tongue body while opening the mouth, and the latter is made by advancing and raising the tongue body while keeping the lips spread, but also because these articulatory movements filter the acoustic sound wave being emitted by the vocal folds. The shape the vocal tract assumes when articulating [a] creates a unique filter that amplifies certain components of the sound wave while dampening others, resulting in particular sound waves that we perceive as speech.

Linguistic tones, in a language like Tibetan or Vietnamese, are identifiable levels or movements of pitch that occur when speakers vary the frequency of a vowel. Humans are capable of perceiving sounds within the range of 20 Hz to 20 kHz, although most human voices use a pitch range of between 80 Hz and 250 Hz.

Mouth

The lower part of the nonhuman primate face has none of the mobility and coordination of the human mouth, jaw, and tongue. In the area around the mouth, humans have around 100 muscles. When we are speaking, these muscles respond to one of three commands every couple of milliseconds: relax, contract, or maintain tension. This is a complex physical feat. The complexity of speech production is compounded by our ability to anticipate upcoming sounds and the lip gestures required to articulate them. Take the words *constrict* and *construe*. In the first word, when we pronounce the vowel of the second syllable, our lips are not rounded. In the latter word, when we pronounce the vowel of the second syllable, our lips are rounded. Now, say these two words out loud, but stop yourself a split second before completing the first syllable. You will notice that just as you are forming the consonant cluster *str-* your mouth has already anticipated the lip shape for the upcoming vowel.[4] No nonhuman primate can do this. In the 1970s, when researchers began to study the possibility of teaching human language to chimps, they had to construct boards with lexigrams the chimps could manipulate with their hands in order to make requests or to answer questions.

Larynx

In comparison with all other animals, the human larynx, which houses the vocal folds, commonly called 'vocal chords,' is low in the throat. This lowered position increases the possibility of choking but enhances humans' ability to produce speech by creating more space for the vocal tract. Human babies are born with the larynx relatively high in the throat. It lowers slowly, and at around three months, the larynx is low enough for the baby to begin to babble. By the end of the first year of life, the larynx has settled into position. Babbling is a very important activity, because it creates connections between the larynx and the prefrontal cortex, and all babies babble, even deaf babies babble, because it is an activity of a normally maturing body. If a baby does not babble, it is a sign that the child will have severe cognitive deficits. Studies have shown that the sounds of babbling babies vary with the ambient language, so that babies in French-speaking environments babble slightly differently than babies in English-speaking environments.

In humans, the larynx is the point of contact between the viscera and the prefrontal cortex. The relationship between viscera and the skeleton in speech is the inverse of the relationship between the viscera and the skeleton in nonhuman primate vocalizations. In the latter, the relationship is more like that when humans are laughing or crying: the skeleton is stable, while the viscera are in motion, and the breath is being panted in or out. In the former, namely speech, the skeleton is mobile, the viscera are stable, and the breath is flowing across the places of articulation, for example, larynx, velum, palate, teeth, and lips. In this context, it is pertinent to note that babies only babble when they are calm. When they are upset, we know what they do: they cry. Speech, by way of contrast to crying, is a routine behavior of a relaxed nervous system, which is why it is so difficult to speak while crying.

Lungs and diaphragm

Human respiration is different than nonhuman primate respiration in that humans have cortical control of the diaphragm. We manage the air pressure in our lungs by the length of what we have to say, and we time our breathing accordingly. Evolutionary biologist Terrence Deacon speculates that the human adaptation of respiration to speech was two million years in the making.

Hands

We primates are a touchy-feely bunch. It is difficult for us to keep our hands to ourselves and off other things and other people. Although we humans no longer pick nits off our best friends' skins, we understand the grooming behaviors of our cousins. Evolutionary psychologists Louise Barrett and Robin Dunbar believe language started as a kind of grooming behavior at a distance. Indeed, when two people are no longer on speaking terms, it is akin to being off one another's grooming list or, in more modern terms, defriended from social media. There is some truth to the idea that the kinds of partnerships nonhuman primates create through actual touch humans now do with language. With spoken language, human hands are now free to do other things, namely gesture communicatively, which nonhuman primates do not do.

When speaking of communicative hand gestures, we do not mean the kind when you twirl your forefinger around your temple to signal 'crazy' or when you put your thumb up to signal 'good, okay.' These gestures are culturally conventional and conscious, and they are called *emblems*. By way of contrast, the gestures of the speech–gesture circuit are idiosyncratic, manufactured on the fly, imagistic, and largely unconscious. This circuit is, furthermore, an integrated whole. People who suffer from Broca's impairment not only have disrupted speech but also have halting, stutter-like gestures while attempting to speak. The gestures of people who suffer from Wernicke's impairment are like their speech in that they are fluid but 'all over the place.'

The strange case of IW[5] confirms the integrity of the speech–gesture circuit. At age 19, IW lost all sense of touch and proprioception below the neck. This meant he lost all motor control that depends on bodily feedback. For instance, when we walk, we receive proprioceptive feedback from the soles of our feet, and this feedback keeps us on track and moving forward. IW slowly relearned to walk and eat, and do everything else, not by regaining his lost proprioception and spatial position sense but by using cognition and vision. Of interest here is that fact that his ability to gesture when speaking was not lost, while instrumental gesture was. That is, he cannot pick up a brick if he cannot see his hands. However, he can and does gesture while speaking, even if he cannot see his hands.

Feet

When we said that language is not in any particular area of the brain any more than walking is in the legs, we did not make the comparison at random. Walking, like language, involves motor control, and Philip Lieberman, quoted above, argues that motor control was the preadaptive basis of human syntactic ability, that there is a syntax of walking just as there is a syntax of talking. Putting one foot in front of the next, putting one word after the next, does require motor control. In the case of humans, this sequencing activity begins when the baby starts to crawl, which marks an important stage in the organization of the nervous system. There is evidence to suggest that a baby who skips the crawling stage and immediately walks upright is at some risk of developing different kinds of language disorders, dyslexia for instance.

Whatever the relationship of walking to speaking, it is the case that the first members of our genus *Homo*, namely *Homo habilis*, appeared about 2.5 mya, made crude stone tools, and walked upright out onto the African savannah. A couple of million years later, *Homo sapiens* arrived on the scene with the cranial volume, but not the skull, of modern humans. It was not until about 100–200 kya that skulls of modern humans could be found in southern and eastern Africa. We believe that, by this time, humans had fully developed language, such that these modern humans were now cognizing the world in a way markedly different from that of their nonhuman primate counterparts.

Nevertheless, language is not coextensive with the whole of human cognition. Take, for instance, the semantic congruity effect. When asked to compare two large animals, such as a cow and an elephant, adult humans are much quicker to respond when the question is, "Which is larger?" rather than "Which is smaller?" When asked to compare two small animals, such as an ant and a rat, they are much quicker to respond when the question is, "Which is smaller?" rather than "Which is larger?" It has been shown that there is a similar semantic congruity effect that appears when monkeys are asked to make numerical judgments. It thus seems to be that this effect is a consequence of the comparison process in primate cognition rather than of any linguistic or symbolic ability, in the latter case, whether or not the primate in question possesses symbols to represent numbers. In humans, the semantic congruity effect appears through our language, but it is not caused by our language. It is part of our primate heritage. Thus, human cognition is sometimes labeled *hybrid*, because it is primate cognition with a distinct linguistic twist.

Evolution in Four Dimensions

Charles Darwin's *The Origin of Species* got the evolutionary ball rolling in 1859 (Darwin [1859] 1968). However, it was not until the midtwentieth century when the study of evolution was allied to the genetics developed in the wake of Darwin's contemporary, Gregor Mendel, that the scientific discipline came fully into existence. It is called the neo-Darwinian synthesis. Since its inception, the discipline has been very genecentric, perhaps appropriately so given the complexities of the genetic structure of any population a researcher chooses to investigate. In recent decades, however, scientists interested in genetics and evolution have expanded their search for explanations of how certain organisms are – and have come to be – the way they are, and so now in addition to studying genes, scientists also consider epigenetic networks, behavior, and, in the case of humans, symbolic systems. In other words, there is a second neo-Darwinian synthesis afoot.

Speaking of genetics, it is important to note that the term *genetic code* is a misnomer. In the early days of the neo-Darwinian synthesis, the term was borrowed from information theory. It was used to describe the relationship between the genotype and the phenotype, and the term suggested that all information necessary to produce an organism was 'in' the genes, thus making the phenotype a 'read out' of that coded information. In the first step of the transition from genotype to phenotype, the idea of a code is apt, in that a gene is transcribed to RNA and then used in the production of a protein. After this genetic moment, however, all the rest is **epigenesis**, that is, development, and the term *code* no longer applies. It is sometimes the case that the presence of one particular gene links directly to a phenotypic result. For instance, the presence of the gene for the neurodegenerative disorder Huntington's disease means that the person carrying it has 100% chance of acquiring the disease. Mostly, however, phenotypic results are caused by networks of genes, and individual genes may participate in a wide array of phenotypic results.

Evolutionary biologists used to speak of evolution in terms of changes in gene frequencies, as if all of evolution was driven by genetic change. More recently, evolutionary biologists have taken a renewed interest in the encounter of the organism and the environment, which involves a reappreciation of the importance of behavior. Now, evolutionary biologists are more likely to talk in terms of organisms inheriting both genes and environments, and to think of evolution in terms of developmental systems with longitudinal stability. One of the stabilities to have entered the developmental system of the human way of living is the presence of language. Just as when inorganic matter was transformed into organic matter, and a new sphere came into existence, namely the biosphere, so the creation of language has brought a new sphere into the world. Some call it the *noosphere*, from the Greek word *noûs*, which corresponds to the Latin word *intellectus*. We humans now mediate a great deal of our social world, our cognitive world, and our environment through language. We talk about things, we talk through things, and we try to come to understandings of things.

Sometimes, we get our understandings wrong. In Chapter 4, we eliminated the term *race* from our account of the languages of the world because it was incoherent in practice. Now, we explain how the term is incoherent biologically. In evolutionary discourse, two kinds of traits are talked about: connected traits and mosaic traits. A connected trait is a trait you cannot change without affecting a great deal else in the organism. Having two lungs is a connected trait, because lung number is influenced by the genes and by the developmental system giving rise to a bilateral organism. It is also a hugely old trait in the animal kingdom. A mosaic trait is one that can evolve independently of any other trait with little or no effect on the rest of the organism. One such mosaic trait is skin color, and there is evidence, based on changes in one particular gene, that Europeans lightened up rather recently, say, 12 to 6 kya. In fact, it turns out that over time, the same (or similar enough) population can go from light to dark to light again, depending on the circumstances.

Mosaic traits are often what are called *anthropometric traits*. These include skin color, nose length, eye shape, and hair type, which are under strong selection by climate. Lighter skin is necessary at higher latitudes where there is less sun, and people living in those latitudes need to absorb more sun in order to produce Vitamin D. These higher latitudes are also colder, and a longer nose allows the air to warm up a bit before reaching the lungs. The epicanthic fold at the eye also provides an extra bit of protection from the cold. Straight hair keeps warmth on the head, while kinky hair keeps sweat off the head. These traits vary with latitude. By way of contrast, as population geneticist Luigi Cavalli-Sforza notes, "genes [rather than anthropometric traits] are considerably more useful as markers of human evolutionary history, especially migration. They vary more with longitude" (2000:65). For the purposes of our discussion about race, the genetic shuffle, which gives rise to these anthropometric traits, simply does not line up into categories with characteristics useful to biologists. Races are gerrymandered results of variable attitudes attached to visible characteristics.

The Genetic Story

Modern genetics is fascinating, and learning about genetics is like blowing open a door on what makes us human. The effort of the preceding section was not to downgrade genetics, but only to assign it its proper place in the second neo-Darwinian synthesis. In order to tell our story, we need all the genetic information we can get.

We start by identifying a woman named mitochondrial Eve who lived about 190 kya (with a probability interval of 300 to 150 kya) and who is the mother of our species. The name is provocative, and we hasten to add that she was not the only woman alive at the time. Rather, she is the woman from whom all current human mitochondria descend. Her lineage is the one to have made it through whatever bottlenecks early modern humans passed through before leaving Africa. A **bottleneck** occurs when a population's size is reduced for at least one generation, which also thereby reduces genetic variation.[6] Our hearty Eve is complemented by Y-chromosomal Adam and, no, it is not likely they knew one another. The age of Y-chromosomal Adam is difficult to pinpoint, and a suggested range is that of mitochondrial Eve.

One of the most important genetic changes to be introduced into the human genome involves the *FOXP2* gene found in a region of 50–100 genes on chromosome 7. In 2001, a group of geneticists at Oxford University and the Institute of Child Health in London showed that mutations in this gene cause a wide range of language disabilities based on a family known as KE, a number of whose member exhibit severe disruptions to grammar and to speech production. That is, they have trouble controlling the fine muscular movements in the lower half of their face. *FOXP2* is found in all mammals for which a complete genome has been sequenced. In mice, it seems to serve some role in vocalization.

A team of researchers at the Max Planck Institute for Evolutionary Anthropology in Leipzig, Germany sequenced the *FOXP2* genes of a chimpanzee, gorilla, orangutan, rhesus macaque, and mouse, and then compared them with the human sequence. They discovered that there have been only three changes in the gene's protein sequence of 715 amino acids in the past 70 million years, that is, since the last common ancestor of humans and mice. Two of these changes have occurred in the last six million years, namely after the human and chimp lineages split. The team estimated that the *FOXP2* gene became what we might call fixed in the human population – that is, all humans could be determined to harbor the last amino acid substitution – between 200 and 120 kya.

Note that this gene is not *for* speech production or grammar. The *FOXP2* gene codes for a type of regulatory protein, known as a transcription factor, which is involved in modulating the expression of other genes, that is, it participates in whether other genes are turned on or off. The protein produced by *FOXP2* belongs to a subclass of transcription factors known as forkhead proteins, and many members of the forkhead family are known to be key regulators of embryogenesis. Of note is the fact that *FOXP2* seems to be important in regulating key pathways in the developing lung, heart, and gut, such that to call it a language gene makes no more sense than calling it a lung gene. Many forkheads are, furthermore, critical for the normal patterning of the central nervous system, and there is evidence to suggest that *FOXP2* has effects in subcortical structures that participate in the human reiterative ability in domains as different as syntax and dancing. Clearly, bodily changes are allied to genetic changes. As we have just seen, one of these changes in humans, minute in size, has had large consequences. The amino acid substitution of *FOXP2* has helped to make human language a connected trait from the soles of our feet to the tops of our heads.

The first split in the human lineage is between Africans and non-Africans who are descended from the East Africans who spread out over the world and inhabited all continents by 40 kya. When Cavalli-Sforza sampled 2000 populations worldwide, which clustered into 42 groups on the basis of 110 genes, he found that the six African populations he sampled differed more from one another and then the rest of the world than any of the other 36, with the people the most genetically removed being the people of Central Africa represented by the Aka, Efé, and Mbuti. Of interest is the fact that every population is made of genotypes originating in more than one continent, and that includes the Berbers, one seventh of the African population, whose genome has a Eurasian character. Cavalli-Sforza speculates that either today's Berbers are descendants of a group with a branch who settled in Europe or yesterday's Berbers were a mix of North Africans, Europeans, and people from the Middle East. He notes, "The two hypotheses are not mutually exclusive and might both be true" (2000:88).

Because humans have been in Africa for such a long time, it has been difficult to determine the language stocks with their relatively shallow time-depth of 10,000 years from the macrofamilies with their far greater time-depths.[7] In the 1950s and 1960s, historical linguist Joseph Greenberg made a four-way classification for African languages: Afro-Asiatic, Niger–Congo, Nilo-Saharan, and Khoisan. He made these classifications using differing criteria for classification and knowing they had differing time-depths, and he put all languages with **click consonants** into Khoisan despite the fact that the languages were very different in other respects. Please see the Language Profile for !Xóõ, this chapter, for a discussion of clicks.

Ethnogroups speaking languages classed in the putative Khoisan stock/ phylum tend to be relatively small populations of hunter-gatherers, with the groups quite isolated one from the others and surrounded by languages from different stocks. Many of the original hunter-gatherers in Tanzania, for instance, have been absorbed or displaced over the last 4000 years by successive migrations into the territory of herders and cultivators speaking Afro-Asiatic languages (Cushitic family), pastoralists speaking Nilo-Saharan languages (Nilotic family), and agriculturalists speaking Niger–Congo languages (Bantu family). In order to get a sense of the potential relatedness of the click languages, Tishkoff et al. (2007:2191) compared mtDNA and Y-chromosomal variation between click-speaking populations found in Tanzania and those found in Namibia and Botswana. They discovered that these populations diverged on the order of 55–35 kya, and they speculated that among the factors contributing to their isolation could be the long dry period in southern Africa at the height of the last glaciation about 24–17 kya. They make the assumption that click phonemes arose only once and speculate that: "click phonemes arose on the order of tens of thousands of years ago in sub-Saharan Africa" (Tishkoff et al. 2007:2193). The designation of Khoisan as a phylum seems reasonable.

Although Greenberg's classifications have become traditional in many accounts, we update the picture for present-day Africa through Nichols's linguistic geographic work. In addition to Afro-Asiatic, which is the only proven stock, she proposes the following areas: (i) Macro-Sudan (centered on Greenberg's Niger–Congo), whose languages have features such as vowel harmony, complex tone systems, and SOV order; (ii) Kalahari Basin (based on Greenberg's Khoisan) whose languages have clicks and head-marking; (iii) Chad-Ethiopia which is disproportionately Afro-Asiatic; (iv) the

Berber spread zone in the Sahara, now undergoing shift in the face of Arabic; and (v) the Bantu spread zone now engulfing the Kalahari Basin (Nichols 2010:363–364).

Once we leave Africa, we can trace the trail of the Y-chromosome through the work of Rootsi et al. (2007) in an article whose title tells it all: "A counter-clockwise northern route of the Y-chromosome haplogroup N from Southeast Asia towards Europe." The NO haplogroup has two branches: N and O. The O branch includes the vast majority of men in East and Southeast Asia, as well as those in Oceania, and it looks to be about 30 kya old. The N branch is newer and postulated to begin a spread northward and then westward perhaps around 17–12 kya. Given that this branch is currently present in Siberia but absent in Native Americans, the N branch must have split after eastern Paleosiberians moved into the Americas. However, it could also be the case that the genes of the Paleosiberian men with the N-innovation did not make it into the Native American pool by one of two ways. Either these men did not produce offspring who survived long enough to reproduce, in which case the lack of the N-innovation in the Americas is a result of a lack of genetic fitness; or these men all happened to die by accident, say, by falling off ice floes in Berengia, the vast ice age land bridge, as they made their way to the New World. In the case of accident, the lack of the N-innovation in the American population would be called **drift**. In either case, the N-innovation did not make it into the Americas.

However, the Q-group did, and this group is widespread in the oldest populations to inhabit North and South America. When a small group inhabits a new space and then multiplies over time, the genetic profile of the larger, downstream population reflects a founder's effect of the original settlers. Another way of describing the founder's effect is by saying that those lucky few who are first at bat significantly determine how the rest of the game is played. As for the N-innovation-carrying men who produced offspring who produced offspring,[8] their haplogroup is found most at high latitudes, and it spans the Far East to Eastern Europe. The biological evidence is thus consistent with the linguistic evidence for language families and stocks, their homelands, and their westward spreads across the Eurasian steppe outlined in Chapters 7 and 8.

At the same time, there is no equal mtDNA story. The mtDNA haplogroups characteristic to Southeast Asian populations occur in, for instance, Baltic-speaking countries with a total frequency of less than 1%. These contrasting stories give us a picture of a world with men on the move and women largely stationary. However, when it comes to the genes, Cavalli-Sforza (2000:82) points out that Y chromosome mutations are highly clustered geographically, which suggests that men move very little genetically. For genetic mobility, what counts is where people settle for marriage, and in most traditional societies around the world, it is the women who change residences more often than men, making women more genetically mobile. Of related interest, in the click languages study cited above, male–female migration patterns were complementary. There was higher female migration from hunter-gatherer groups into nearby pastoralist or agricultural groups, while there was higher male migration from pastoralist or agricultural groups into hunter-gatherer groups (Tishkoff et al. 2007:2192).

A recent archeologic find gives a fascinating new glimpse into the picture in the northern part of Eurasia before the start of the counterclockwise northern and western tour of the N haplogroup. The genome of a Siberian boy who lived 24 kya has now been sequenced. His Y chromosome belongs to haplogroup R, and his mtDNA belongs to haplogroup U. These haplogroups are found exclusively in people living in Europe and regions of Asia west of the Altai mountains, and so it is not terribly surprising to think he belonged to a lineage of people who either later moved west or came from the west. What is a surprise is that a portion of the boy's genome is shared only by today's Native Americans and no other groups. A further surprise is that the boy's genome shows no connection to modern East Asians. Because DNA studies strongly suggest that Native Americans are related to modern East Asians – perhaps Siberians, Chinese, or Japanese – it is a puzzle to think the boy could be related to Native Americans and not also to East Asians. However, there is no doubt that the boy's genome represents ancient Native American roots. It has also cleared up a previous puzzle: why the 9 kya Kennewick man (Columbia River, Kennewick, Washington) had some European-like features. Until this boy's bones were investigated, Kennewick man was considered to be an anomaly, and the common idea was that any of the Eurasian features found in Native American genes were a result of postcolonial mixing. Now, it seems that Native Americans have very deep genetic roots with Europeans (Balter 2013a, 2013b).[9]

We take a final look at the kind of light DNA can shed on linguistics in the intriguing hypothesis advanced by Dediu and Ladd (2007). This hypothesis involves a possible relationship between the distribution of tone languages in the world, namely those in sub-Saharan Africa as well as Southeast and East Asia, and the presence or absence of certain alleles on two brain-development genes, *ASPM* and *Microcephalin* (*MCPH*). Both *ASPM* and *MCPH* help determine the size of the brain and skull by being involved in cell-cycle regulation, such that if there are deleterious mutations to these genes, not enough cells will divide in the right way, and the brain and skull will not grow to proper proportions. Both of these genes have a pair of favorable mutations that are called *derived* (*D*), such that now, in addition to *ASPM* and *MCPH*, there are the variants *ASPM-D* and *MCPH-D*. In other words, both genes now have two haplogroups, and their ages are estimated at 5.8 kya (14.1–0.5 kya) and 37 kya (60–14 kya), respectively.

Both haplogroups show signs for positive selection and geographic distribution. Taking a geographic survey of the world, *ASPM-D* has high frequencies in Central and Western Asia, Europe, and North Africa, and very low frequencies in Asia, Europe, and the Americas. It has moderate frequency in North and East Africa, and Southeast Asia. It is very rare in Central, Western, and South sub-Saharan Africa. For its part, *MCPH-D*, being older, coincides with the introduction of anatomically modern humans into Europe about 40 kya (see Map 10.1), as well as the shift in the archeological record indicative of modern human behavior, such as art and the use of symbolism. This variant is widely distributed across the world, but not very frequent in Africa (Evans et al. 2005). Returning to *ASPM-D*, it has shown strong positive selection in primates leading to *Homo sapiens*, especially in the past six million years in which *ASPM* acquired one advantageous amino acid change every 350,00 years. Thus, its role in human-brain evolution seems clear. The recent appearance of the new allele *ASPM-D* suggests that it is continuing to evolve in modern humans (Mekel-Bobrov et al. 2005).

Furthermore, *ASPM-D*, in particular, shows signs of accelerated evolution in humans, with approximately two favorable mutations per million years. In the areas of the world where the new alleles (*D*-variants) are relatively rare, tone languages are common, and both historical and geographic factors can be ruled out to explain this

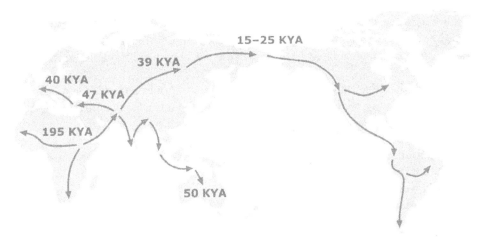

Map 10.1   Expansion of human species (http://www.sanger.ac.uk/research/projects/human evolution/). Reproduced by permission of Genome Research Limited.

negative correlation with tone and the population frequency of *ASPM-D* and *MCPH-D*. Although Dediu and Ladd acknowledge that the effects on the *D*-variants on brain structure remain largely speculative, it is nevertheless possible that the variants introduce a biasing effect with respect to the cognitive capacities involved in processing phonological structures. Dediu and Ladd (2007:10944) do not doubt that all normal children learn the languages of the community in which they are raised, but it is nevertheless worth imagining that cognitive biases in a population of language learners could influence the direction of change such that "extremely small biases at the individual level can be amplified by th[e] process of cultural transmission and become manifest at the population level."

Whether or not Dediu and Ladd's hypothesis will survive further scrutiny is not at issue. Rather, we introduce it in order to underscore a point we would like to make in this book, namely that students of linguistics can and should be expected to have a decent grasp of linguistic geography, language family structural characteristics, typological and areal features, as well as population genetics in order to evaluate the kinds of information and hypotheses they are apt to encounter in their research. They also need a good idea about social and political linguistic effects, as well. However, for the time-depth of this chapter, the sociopolitical effects are unknown and unreconstructable, if we even wished to use a term like *political* to refer to events in a time before identifiable political structures with administrative hierarchies existed.

Grammatical Categories and Deep-Time Linguistics

We turn to Johanna Nichols, once again, in our attempt to establish relationships among languages at a time-depth greater than 10,000 years where the graphic model such of the tree with its branches, the wave with its isogloss bundles, or the rhizome with its tangles cannot capture the possible relationships. Only statistical approaches and knowledge of favored and disfavored structural patterns can help fill in the blanks of the dispersals of languages and the encounters of speaking groups. Rather than establishing individual etymologies and comparing particular grammatical structures, deep-time historical linguistics depends on typological information as the best guide to what linguistic structure may have been like at the beginning of human movements around the world.

A hardly exhaustive list of the relevant structural categories includes the following. First is the inclusive/exclusive pronoun distinction. As was noted in Chapter 7, Austronesian languages have both we-inclusive and we-exclusive first-person plural pronouns. This feature is not found in the languages of Europe. It is, however, widespread in Australia and the southern and eastern New World, the latter languages descending from the earliest colonizers. Those who came into the New World later settled in the north and west, and the occurrence of this inclusive/exclusive in North America is statistically that of the Pacific coast of Asia.

Second is the numeral classifiers. Mentioned in Chapter 2 is the fact that some languages distinguish between mass nouns and count nouns, while others treat all nouns only as mass nouns. As it turns out, noun classifier languages are strongly areal in distribution. They are concentrated in Southeast Asia, including the western Pacific, and coastal western America. The distribution of this feature is what Nichols says "can be reduced to a single circum-Pacific hotbed" (1992:133).

Third is the presence or absence of alienable versus inalienable possession, discussed in the Language Profile for Hawaiian in Chapter 7. Diegueño, indigenous to California, makes a distinction between *ʔ-schwataɬ* 'my mother' (inalienable 'my' *ʔ*) and *ʔ-schwanʸ-schwawa* 'my house' (alienable 'my' *ʔ-schwanʸ*). Such a distinction is widespread in Native American languages.

Fourth is whether sentences align to the accusative type, where Subjects and Agents line up and Objects are distinct, or to the ergative type, where Subjects and Objects line up, and Agents are distinct. To remind you, the alignment distinction turns on the difference between transitive verbs and intransitive verbs. Transitive verbs are ones that can take an object: 'She bought the pig.' Intransitive verbs are ones that cannot take an object: 'John fell.' Thus, an accusative type language is one in which the nominative case lines up with the Subject, and the accusative case lines up with the Object, no matter what kind of verb is used. The accusative type is the one readers of this book are likely most familiar with. The ergative type is found in languages like the language isolate Basque and the Caucasian language Georgian.

The ergative type is also found in Dyirbal, an Aboriginal Australian language, where the Subject of an intransitive verb (here: *to return*) is in the absolute case:

> *yabu*   *banaga-nʸu*
> 'mother'   'returned'
> absolutive case/zero morpheme   nonfuture
> 'the mother returned.'

The Subject of a transitive verb (here: *to see*) is in the ergative case:

> *numa*   *yabu-ngu*   *bura-n*
> 'father'   'mother'   'see'
> absolutive case/zero morpheme   ergative/morpheme ngu   nonfuture
> 'the mother saw the father.'

Note, first, that 'father' is the Object of a transitive verb and is in the absolute case just like the Subject of an intransitive verb and, second, that normal word order puts the Object first, making the order OSV.

Specialist in Aboriginal Australian languages, R.M.W. Dixon explains the logic of ergativity to be one of marking true agency. In the case of a sentence like 'John fell,' *John* is in the nominative case in transitive languages. In an ergative language, *John* is in the absolute case, because he is not seen as the agent of the action. He is treated grammatically as no different than the object of a transitive action done by someone else; he is an object not in control of the action. When it comes to John being the agent of an action, as in 'John killed the snake,' then John is marked for ergativity (Dixon 1994:214). Despite the logic that governs ergativity, the overwhelming global pattern is for accusative alignment. Languages with ergative constructions tend to cluster geographically.

Fifth is head marking versus dependent marking; we had our first look at this structural feature at the end of Chapter 1 in the discussion of the grammatical category of possession. The distinction belongs to Johanna Nichols, and she has increased typological understanding by showing how the preference for one or the other kind of marking runs throughout the whole grammar. In the simplest definition of the terms, the head determines the possibility of the occurrence of the dependent. For instance, we can talk about a house without referring to the person who owns it, so the house is head, and the potential possessor is dependent. On page 17 we saw in the pairs of phrases from English, Spanish, and Hungarian that English and Spanish put the grammatical marking on the possessor, while Hungarian puts it on the thing possessed, the head. Furthermore, we can talk about a house without specifying what color it is. So, the house is still the head, and now the adjective is the dependent. The Indo-European languages retaining gender classes, which is all of them except Afrikaans, Bengali, English, and Persian, mark the lexical properties of the head noun on the dependent adjective. A head-marked example comes from Shuswap, spoken in British Columbia:

wist   *t-citx*
'high'   'house'

where the word *wist* 'high' bears no marking, while the *t-* clitic on *citx* 'house' marks the particular case of the noun. A dependent-marked example comes from Russian:

zelen-yj   *dom*
'green'   'house'

where the *yj* suffix on the adjective *zelen* 'green' indicates the lexical properties of the house, which is singular and masculine, as well as its syntactic properties, namely that it is nominative (subject); the global preference is for head marking.

Just as the basic word-order patterns of a language harmonize with the word-order patterns of smaller units, so head-marking and dependent-marking preferences harmonize with basic word-order patterns. Nichols observes that head-marking morphology favors verb-initial order, while dependent-marking morphology disfavors it, and there seems to be a cognitive–communicative reason. When the verb comes first, as it does in head-marking languages, the grammatical relations, which are marked on the verb, are established at the outset. When the nouns come first in a language having at least some dependent-marked morphology, then the grammatical relations, which are marked on the noun, are established at the outset. Nichols concludes, "Establishing grammatical relations at the beginning must be communicatively efficacious, in that it streamlines the hearer's processing" (1986:82). When it comes to determining who did what to whom, dependent-marking languages distribute all the grammatical information onto the *who*, the *what*, and the *whom*, as we are familiar with from the Indo-European case system, and these are the dependents. Head-marking languages will put this information on the *did*, namely the verb (head) in a combination that might look like this: *the man, the woman, the book, it-to-her-he-gave.*

Perhaps what is most remarkable about the head/dependent-marking distinction is its stability and conservatism of morphological marking type. Even in a geographical area where there is intensive linguistic convergence such as in a residual zone, the languages gathered there may massively borrow lexical items one from the others, the phonologies of the languages may come to share many properties, and grammatical realignments may occur (including ergativity and word-order type). Plus there might be near-identity of material culture and folklore. However, in the Caucasus, for instance, the strongly head-marking Northwest Caucasian languages and the strongly dependent-marking Northeast and North Central Caucasian languages have never given up their long-term marking type (Nichols 1986:98). Thus, the preference for marking type may be one of the oldest diagnostic criteria for establishing long lineages.

From the geographic distribution of the aforementioned five structural features, we can come to a plausible conclusion that there was a west-to-east movement out of Africa and into the Near East and from there to the tropical Pacific. Northward expansion, including colonization of the New World, occurred later (Nichols 1992:259). After that, there was a counterclockwise movement from Southeast Asia north and to the west, such that all language stocks found in Western Europe today – Indo-European, Uralic, and Turkic – originated east of the Urals. As for the case of Basque, it is not known whether it is a sole surviving remnant also from the east of a pre-Indo-European spread across the Eurasian steppe or whether it is a continuant of an indigenous Cro-Magnon language. All that is known is that Latin did not completely wipe out Basque, but it did succeed in reducing it to its own stock (Nichols 1992:236).

The accumulation of large databases such as the *World Atlas of Language Structure* (Oxford, first published in 2005) has permitted historical linguists to compare structural features in order to determine the statistical regularities that suggest lineage affiliations. This database has been put to inventive use in a recent article that lines up structural features of hunter-gatherer languages and contrasts them with those of languages spoken by agriculturalists. Apart from predictable differences in vocabulary developed as part of the agricultural lifestyle, unexpected typological differences emerge, the most significant being that, among languages spoken by hunter-gatherers, there is a strong tendency not to have a dominant order of major sentence constituents, and if there is one, it is *not* SVO. It is also the case that hunter-gatherer languages prefer small vowel inventories. Finally, with regard the tripartite lexicalization of *finger–hand–arm*, it is very uncommon worldwide that no division is made among the three body parts, and it is very common worldwide that a three-way division is made. Hunter-gatherer languages, however, prefer to distinguish *hand* from *arm* but not *hand* from *finger*. The speculation is that hunter-gatherer societies make little use of rings, thereby making the differentiation of the fingers from the hand less salient (Cysouw and Comrie 2013).

Complexity and the Arrow of Time

Paleontologist Simon Conway Morris (2011) has said, "Once there were bacteria, now there is New York" as a way to sum up the obvious increase in complexity since the origin of life on this planet. Researchers in a range of contemporary sciences – from physics to biology to economics to linguistics – have circled around the topic of complexity and tried to understand the seemingly general phenomenon that highly unstable, dynamics systems – such as the cosmos, living beings, cultures, and languages – become more complex over time and that the complexity is irreversible. When dealing with stable and undynamic systems, the concept of complexity is not problematic. If one is counting and comparing the number of parts in various objects, then one can confidently say that a computer is more complex than an abacus. Transferring this quantitative understanding to the realm of biology, one measure of complexity might reasonably be the degree of hierarchy found in various organisms as they develop over time: prokaryotic cells without nuclei came first; they were followed by eukaryotic cells with nuclei; it took more time to develop complex multicellular organisms and then even more time for certain organisms to organize themselves into even more complex colonies. The historical trajectory of this biological nestedness is a clear case of an increase in complexity over time.

Turning to matters of language, we have some ideological clearing to do before we can move forward. In the case of the topic of complexity, a twofold clearing is in order. The first clearing came around the turn of the twentieth century when anthropologically oriented linguists, in particular those studying Native American languages, worked to break the old association between linguistic complexity and technological complexity. Previous generations of European and American intellectuals had subscribed to a tripartite cultural and linguistic global hierarchy with so-called Barbarians at the bottom, Savages in the middle, and Civilized People at the top. The civilized people were, of course, those who had the most technologically advanced materials, namely all those things listed in the Final Note in Chapter 2 that the English and Spanish brought with them to the New World. Franz Boas, Edward Sapir, and Leonard Bloomfield were among the early twentieth-century linguistic anthropologists to show that Native American languages were every bit as evolved as European languages in terms of expressive power and structural complexity. Other linguists came to the same understandings of indigenous languages in Australia, Africa, and other technologically undeveloped places. In fact, it was noted that some so-called primitive peoples spoke languages with amazingly intricate structures.

A truism took hold in linguistics that all languages were equal in terms of complexity. Call this *equilibrium linguistics*, and it entails a view that the same degree of complexity will be found in all languages in terms of their states at any given time and in their states over time. In comparing two languages at their present states, Hawaiian and

English, we observe that Hawaiian has a phonemic inventory of 18, while English has double that number at 36. The supposed phonemic simplicity of Hawaiian is, however, offset by its 11-way personal pronoun system, which is more complex than the mere five of Standard English. Thus, in their current states, it can be said that Hawaiian and English are equally complex, although their complexities are found in different places.

When comparing states of the same language at two different times, a similar equilibrium of complexity is supposedly at work. Old English had an amount of inflectional morphology that Modern English speakers find completely baffling, exemplified by lines 4 and 5 of *Beowulf*:

Oft	*Scyld Scefing*	*sceaðena*	*ðreatum*
adv	subject	gen. pl.	dat. pl.
Often	Scyld Scefing	enemies'	troops

monegum	*mægðum*	*meodsetla*	*ofteah.*
dat. pl.	dat. pl.	gen. obj.	V
from	many groups	meadbenches	took away

The indirect objects of the main verb *ofteah* 'took away' are in the dative plural case. The object of a transitive verb would normally be in the accusative case. However, in this case, it is in the genitive, which makes *ofteah* a verb of the genitive of depriving. What? The Modern English speaker wonders: Why all the unnecessary morphological complexity to say something as simple as *Often Scyld Schefing took away many enemies' mead benches?*[10] On the other hand, Old English had only two tenses, present and past, while Modern English has a greatly expanded verbal system. Old English speakers would be perplexed how to understand (and by the need for!) the verbal sequences in an utterance such as *She will have already completed her homework before I even begin to start mine.* The inflectional complexity of Old English is gone, but the tense/aspect complexity of the Modern English verb system is in full swing. It would seem that in the passage of time, English has had neither a net gain nor a net loss of complexity.

The second ideological clearing has just now begun at the start of the twenty-first century, and it was creolist John McWhorter who shot the first salvo across the bow of equilibrium linguistics with his article entitled "The world's simplest grammars are creole grammars" (2001). We said above that unstable, dynamic systems seem to increase in complexity over time and that the complexity is irreversible. Creoles present an interesting case in that they are language loop reboots. We said at the end of Chapter 8 that whatever the relative exposure to the standard lexifying language that a generation of children creolizing a pidgin had, there is necessarily a strong break with the standard lexifying language loop as a whole, in that languages are coral reef accumulations of habits of mind and cultural practices. In our terms, we would say that McWhorter is right to say that it takes time for a language to loop in and around itself, and the ways that language does so are what we call *linguistic structure*. So, a language just starting down its path will likely have fewer loops, a looser weave so to speak, than a language that has been on the road for millennia. Creoles offer cases of what happens when the arrow of time is interrupted, and the complexity of the lexifying language is reversed in the born-again creole.

McWhorter's study of 19 English-, French-, Dutch-, and Portuguese-based creoles show that they all share a similar grammatical profile, and none of them have features found widely distributed in languages with long histories such as the ones listed in the above subsection and which McWhorter identifies as:

> ... ergativity, grammaticalized evidential marking, inalienable possessive marking, switch-reference marking, inverse marking, obviative marking, 'dummy' verbs, syntactic asymmetries between matrix and subordinate clauses, grammaticalized subjunctive marking, verb-second, clitic movement, any pragmatically neutral word order but SVO, noun class or grammatical gender marking (analytic or affixal), or lexically contrastive or morphosyntactic tone beyond a few isolated cases. (2001:163)

Since none of these more elaborated features are strictly necessary for communication, they can be seen as what happens over time when the language keeps looping around itself. McWhorter calls these loops "baroque accretions" and the "weight of 'ornament' that encrusts older languages." The oldest of the creoles in use today are not very old. They are the Portuguese-based creoles of Cape Verde, spoken on an island in the middle of the Atlantic Ocean, and Guinea-Bissau, spoken on the west coast of Africa, both of which date back only to the late fifteenth century. The French and Dutch Caribbean creoles trace back to the late seventeenth and eighteenth centuries, while the English creoles of the Pacific go back to the eighteenth century. Hawaiian Creole English emerged only toward the end of the nineteenth century. In the terms of this book, young creoles have not yet confronted as many conditions to catch up to as have older languages.

McWhorter defines complexity in quantitative terms. A phonemic inventory is more complex the more members it has. A tonal system is more complex the more tones it has. A syntax is more complex when it has more asymmetries (e.g., German is SVO in main clauses, SOV in subordinate clauses, and requires SV inversion after an initial adverb; cf. English *Never have I seen such a mess*) and/or more overt or grammaticalized expressions for more semantic and/or pragmatic distinctions than another language. He makes no claims that these complexities come with more difficulty of production or processing, since he assumes that human cognition is capable of processing great degrees of what he calls *overspecification*. Linguists have long recognized that the phonemic inventories of smaller, isolated languages tend to two extremes: either very many or very few. The ones with very many phonemes have complex phonologies by definition, while the ones with very few phonemes exhibit their complexity in word length, as in the case of the name of Queen Lili'uokalani born Lydia Lili'u Loloku Walania Wewehi Kamaka'eha, last monarch of Hawaii. McWhorter wants to extend the study of relative complexity into all parts of the language, understanding that the label *complexity* has no qualitative value.

At work here is the perhaps surprising factor of second-language learners. In languages with many phonemes, the phonetic space is crowded from the point of view of second-language learners and is therefore difficult to acquire. In languages with few phonemes, words tend to become long, which puts a load on working memory for second-language learners. Languages with significant numbers of second-language learners tend to have 20–50 phonemes, and English is exactly in the middle of that range. What is at issue here is primarily the consonant inventory, with 26 of the 39 Standard English phonemes being consonants.[11]

Second-language learners also play a role in the structure of languages that have spread across an area by means of language shift. These languages also tend to be less complex in McWhorter's terms and therefore also more regular and transparent. When it came to the Altaic languages that successively spread across the Eurasian steppe, Nichols notes that they were well designed not just for translatability with other languages they were in contact with but also for second-language learners (Nichols 2010:191). So, among the many conditions to which languages are always catching up is: whether they are spoken by small, isolated communities, in which case the linguistic structures can become elaborated over time and not particularly transparent to potential second-language learners; or whether they are spoken by larger groups in contact with other groups and second-language learners, in which case they may become structurally more regular. Their lexicons will derive, for instance, 'teach' from 'learn' and 'show' from 'see' and 'drop' from 'fall' with the same morphological process, such as the English causative -en found in 'blacken' and 'lighten,' but which is inconsistently applied, as the teach/learn, show/see, drop/fall suppletives show.[12]

Structural complexity does not correspond to conceptual complexity. In English, one can say *I am in the poorhouse* meaning 'I don't have a lot of money'. One can also say *I am house poor* meaning 'I have a large mortgage and associated monthly expenses I can hardly keep up with'. These two phrases would be counted as structurally less complex than the corresponding ways they could be expressed in any of the Romance languages, for instance. The two phrases are, however, not conceptually less complex in English, and understanding them requires quite a lot of inference and cultural knowledge. David Gil, one of the editors of *Language Complexity as an Evolving Variable*, contributes a chapter in his volume entitled "How much grammar does it take to sail a boat?" He is a specialist in Indonesian, and he offers examples of four different colloquial varieties of this language, all of which exhibit the structurally noncomplex features of:

(i)   no word-internal morphological structure;
(ii) no distinct syntactic categories; and
(iii) no distinct construction-specific rules of semantic interpretation.

He notes that: "Speakers of these different varieties range from westernized and upwardly mobile office workers in high-rise buildings in Jakarta, through shopkeepers and rice-farmers across the archipelago, all the way to New Guinea highlanders in penis gourds and grass skirts" (Gil 2009:28). His point is a fine inversion of the old technological complexity–linguistic complexity association. And on our most complex technology to date, namely our smart phones, the motto for our texting practices could be: keep it simple.

Final Note: The Last Stone Age Man in North America

When the Spanish made their first settlements in California in 1769, some 250,000 Native Americans lived there. From what is available in the historical records, these peoples can be grouped into 21 known nationalities, or small nations, which can be further separated into subnationalities, tribes, and tribelets to come to a total of 250 distinct groups. The concentration of languages associated with these groups in this area can be divided into six major phyla, and their number is the reason historic California is considered a residual zone. The relationships among the tribes, at least to outside observers, were described as one of intimate separatism. The arrival of the Europeans did not cause them to band together against the invaders, nor were they particularly interested in assimilating to the new and dominant culture. The California Gold Rush of 1848 marked the beginning of the end for many tribes, and the 1860s and 1870s were the years when the clashes – meaning massacres – between the Indians and the Whites reached a climax.

During this period, one tribe of hunter-gatherers, the Yahi in northern California, was reduced to a small group of people, which included a boy born around 1860. Forty-one years later, in 1911, this boy had grown into a man and was the sole survivor of his tribe.[13] Emaciated and without any clothing except a covered-wagon canvas he wore around his shoulders, he was discovered by Whites living in Oroville, California who took him to the sheriff. After attempts to speak with him in a variety of languages failed, Professor Thomas Waterman of the University of California was brought to town. Waterman was a student of Franz Boas, and he specialized in Native American languages. After some investigation, he came to understand that this man spoke a variety of the Yana language. He was called Ishi after the word for 'man' in his language. The name *Yana* means 'person, human being,' and over and over in English the tribal names for California Indians come from the answer to the European question "Who are you?" which prompts the usual Indian answer, "I am a person." What else to answer? To the Native American, the question is a rude one, if not rudely meant. It was not the usual custom in Indian society to bandy one's name about, and certainly not to a stranger.

Ishi lasted five more years among the Whites, who treated him well, but he succumbed to tuberculosis 1914 and died of it in 1916. During his time among the Whites, he provided as much information as he could about his culture and language. He made a map of Yana territory with villages and trails, and heads of salmon runs. He demonstrated how he made his bows out of juniper wood and arrowheads out of stone. He was Edward Sapir's informant for a Yana grammar and Yana folk tales and lore. Like many Native American languages, Ishi's variety of Yana was polysynthetic and had male and female language, that is, separate forms for verb endings, pronouns, and demonstrative pronouns used by the men and the women.[14]

The point of this story is that the last Stone Age man in North America spoke a fully elaborated language, and he brought it forward into a world that knew steam engines, telephones, automobiles, and airplanes. Whatever might have been the beginnings of language 100+ kya, anything resembling a primitive language became elaborated tens of thousands of years before the first Americans crossed the Behring Straits.

Language Profile: !Xóõ [Taa (Khoisan)]

Functional overview

The vast, dry savannah that stretches across a wide swath of Southern Africa is known as the Kalahari Desert. The large lowland part of the desert that covers most of present-day Botswana and a large part of neighboring Namibia is known as the Kalahari Basin. It is the historical homeland of a linguistic and cultural Sprachbund, comprising the pre-European and pre-Bantu people of Africa. Linguists have traditionally referred to these people as Khoisan. Most of the languages in the Sprachbund are endangered; the most widely spoken is Khoekhoe, which has about 250,000 speakers. Most of the languages are historically unwritten, though orthographies have been devised, largely for the purpose of making bilingual dictionaries.

The southernmost part of the Kalahari Basin, located in the south and west of Botswana and the eastern part of Namibia, is home to speakers of the Taa language. The Taa, historically hunter-gatherers, are today experiencing pressure by national governments to abandon their nomadic lifestyles and settle on permanent farms outside of the desert. As this change happens, the number of Taa speakers is dwindling. In Botswana and Namibia, Taa is of low prestige, and many speakers are switching to European, Bantu, or other languages. This trend applies to Khoisan languages in general. There are between 3000 and 4000 Taa speakers in Botswana, and no more than a few hundred more in Namibia. Speakers of Taa come from a variety of ethnic groups, collectively known as San. Taa language varieties are in the Tuu branch of the Khoisan language family. Some linguists have called the validity of Khoisan as a singe language family into question, as there is some evidence that the languages of the Kalahari Basin are not all genetically related.

The Taa language can more accurately be described as a great dialect chain running east to west from Botswana to Namibia. Adjacent varieties are mostly mutually intelligible with one another, but varieties separated by great distances are not. The two major varieties are West !Xoon, spoken in Namibia, and those known as 'N|ohan, spoken on the border region, and East !Xoon spoken in Botswana. The established boundaries are being erased, as Taa speakers from across regions come into contact with one another on account of resettlement by national governments and patterns of assimilation.

Prominent structural characteristics

Click consonants   If you learned English as a child, you likely learned to imitate the clip-clop sound that a horse makes when it walks along a hard surface by varying the pitch as you made a clicking noise with your tongue. If you were naughty, your caretaker may have made a similar sound that English speakers have decided to spell *tsk-tsk*. These sounds are known as click consonants, and unlike in English, they are phonemic in all the languages of the Khoisan family and many Bantu languages spoken in sub-Saharan Africa.

Unlike the other consonants we have described thus far, clicks are not made by expelling air from the lungs. Instead, they are formed when the tongue creates two points of contact within the oral cavity, creating a pocket of air that, when released, creates a loud clicking noise. The anterior point of contact may be bilabial /⊙/, dental /|/, lateral /‖/, alveolar /!/, or palatal /ǂ/. The posterior point of contact, which is not customarily transcribed phonetically, is either the uvula or the pharynx.

In Taa language varieties, the precise number of clicks is debated, but a fair esti-mate is between 80 and 120, though the number varies from variety to variety. Click consonants are extremely frequent in Taa; well over half of all Taa words begin with a click, and some 70% of all words contain a click (Traill 1994). The Taa click inventory includes all of the anterior places of articulation described above. The following exam-ples illustrate each of the five basic click anterior places of articulation in word-initial, prevocalic position:

bilabial	⊙oɑ	eye
dental	ǀàa	move away
lateral	ǁáɑ	camelthorn tree
alveolar	ǃā:	to wait for
palatal	ǂabá	peg

We have said that there are more than 80 click consonants in Taa. This number is based on the fact that each of the five basic clicks can be coarticulated with a preceding or following consonant. Each combination yields what is in effect a unique click sound. The following examples show each click in the context of a preceding voiced velar stop and illustrate how unique clicks are created with coarticulation:

C+bilablial	g⊙hòō	sour berry
C+dental	gǀhâ:	stale meat
C+lateral	gǁhàā	bone arrow
C+alveolar	gǃhàā	thorn
C+palatal	gǂxˀā:	sneeze

Ejective consonants   With the exception of the click consonants we have just seen, all of the other speech sounds we have examined in this book involve what phoneticians call a pulmonic airstream mechanism, which means the air comes from the lungs. We have seen that in describing the speech sounds of the world, voicing, place of artic-ulation, and manner of articulation vary, yielding consonant sounds from the voiced bilabial stop [b] found in many languages from Armenian to Zapotec, to the voice-less pharyngeal fricative /ħ/ of Arabic and Somali. As different as these sounds are from one another, they are all produced with air that ascends from the lungs. Most of the sounds in the languages of the world are produced with the pulmonic airstream mechanism.

In addition to clicks, speakers of Taa produce a number of sounds in which the airstream begins at the glottis rather than at the lungs. These sounds are known as ejectives. To produce an ejective consonant, the glottis is raised, and the oral articula-tion – the tongue tip and the alveolar ridge, for example – is tightly held. This causes air pressure to build up greatly in the mouth. When the oral articulation is released, an audible burst can be heard. All ejective consonants are voiceless, and all of them are obstruents, which are a class of consonants with a constricted airflow (stops, fricatives, and affricates).

The varieties of Taa differ in the number of ejective consonants they produce, but the following four or five are fairly common: /p'/, /t'/, /ts'/, /k'/, /q'/. The ejective /ts'/ is released as an affricate; all others are released as stops.

t'qàa   thigh muscle
d͡ts'qàa   to be very wet

Ejectives can occur with other consonants, as illustrated above, but they also very commonly occur in clusters with clicks. These clusters, which begin with a click and transition to an ejective, are known as ejective-contour clicks. They are common in Taa languages and are characteristic of Khoisan languages in general. The following examples illustrate velar (/k'/) and uvular (/q'/) ejectives in ejective-contour clicks:

|q'ɔ́n   small
‖k'qâà   grass
!k'gá: to spread out
!q'ama   species of grass
g≠k'qàna   tobacco

Aspiration   When producing the word 'pat,' most speakers of English, depending on where in the world they are from, articulate the word as [pʰæt], with a small puff of air after the [p]. The same speakers are unlikely to produce the same puff of air when they articulate the word 'spat' as [spæt]. This is because these sounds – [p] and [pʰ] are in complementary distribution with one another in English. [pʰ] occurs at the beginning of words, [p] in other environments.

The puff of air that occurs with 'pat' is known as aspiration, a topic we introduced in the context of Grimm's Law in Chapter 3. Aspiration occurs on voiceless consonants, which are produced with the vocal folds in the open position, when the vocal folds remain open after the release of the consonant. Because the vocal folds are in vibration during the production of voiced sounds, they typically close at the release of the consonant, and aspiration does not occur.

In Taa language varieties, aspirated voiceless stops /pʰ, tʰ, kʰ, qʰ/ occur in words such as *pʰālìtʃè* 'maize meal,' *tʰāli* 'skin for carrying child,' and *g≠qʰèē* 'breast milk.' In concert with the voiced and voiceless unaspirated, these consonants form part of what Maddieson (2011) estimates may be the largest consonant inventory in the world, namely 122. The large number of consonants is driven by the large number of click consonants, which may also be aspirated, such as in the following words listed from the front of the mouth to the back:

ŋʘʰái   ask
ŋ|ʰābe   hunting bow
ŋ‖ʰábe   to deviate
ŋ!ʰāŋkâ   backwards
ŋ≠ʰàā   ahead

At least some of the aspirated consonants listed here create meaningful phonological contrasts with their unaspirated pairs. In the following minimal pair, the meaning difference between 'stick' and 'carry with a strap' is contrasted by the presence or absence of aspiration on the lateral click /‖/.

ŋ‖ʰáa   carry with a strap over the shoulder
ŋ‖áa   stick

A salient cultural characteristic: Khoisan onomastics

Khoisan-speaking groups were traditionally nomadic hunter-gatherers who roamed the Kalahari Desert in search of game, berries, fruit, and roots. The nomadism of the people affected not only how the language diverged into separate languages and varieties, but also the ways speakers named themselves and their languages. The study of the origin and use of naming practices is a field known as onomastics.

The language that we have called Taa has many other names depending on whom you ask. !Xoon is one of the two major dialect groups, and its speakers refer to their language as *!Xóõ, !xõ, !kɔ̃ː, !kõ, Khong*, or one of many other linguonyms, or language names. Speakers in the 'Nǀohan group refer to their language as *Ngǀuǁen, Nguen, Nǀhuǁéi, ŋǀuǁẽin, ŋǀuǁẽi*, or *ŋǀuǁen*. The naming is of course not haphazard but rather reflects the fact that Taa is actually a dialect chain running from central Botswana in the east to central Namibia in the west. The name of the language family itself, Khoisan, derives from the ethnonyms of two of the largest groups who speak Kohisan languages, namely, the Khoe and the San.

The names that Khoisan-speaking groups have used to refer to themselves also gives us a sense of Khoisan cultures. The Khoe and the San have traditionally referred to themselves with terms that mean 'people' or 'human.' In !Xóõ and other Taa languages, the word *taa* means 'human,' and in fact most Taa speakers refer to their common language as *Taa-ǂaan*, where *ǂaan* means 'language.' Linguists have used the word *tuu* as the name of the subgroup of Khoisan languages into which Taa falls, but in general Khoisan, *tuu* simply means 'people.' The !Kung are another traditional San hunter-gatherer society who live in the Kalahari. They speak a language also called !Kung, but refer to themselves as *Ju'hoansi*, meaning 'people.' Khoikhoi is the name used by another San group to refer to themselves. *Khoi* means 'people,' and *khoikhoi* means something like 'the real people.' This naming practice is not incidental, but instead reflects the cultural belief that the indigenous people of the Kalahari are 'the people' who promote peace with the self, others, and the environment (Chebanne 2010:88).

The beliefs of outsiders about Khoisan people and their languages are also reflected in the names they have given them. The Khoikhoi, who speak a language of the same name, were once called Hottentots by the Dutch, who believed *hot, en*, and *tot* to be common words in Khoikhoi language. Outside of Africa, the San are known as Bushmen, a term that entered English in the late eighteenth century from the Afrikaans term *boschjesman* 'man of the bush.' While some San find this term to be derogatory, some others have embraced it. Today, the Botswana government uses the English name Remote Area Dwellers to refer to all nomadic Khoisan groups. This technical term does not acknowledge the language and culture of the Khoisan groups and is a part of a program of resettlement in which nomadic peoples are encouraged to give up their nomadic folkways and become pastoralists.

Exercises

Exercise 1 – absolute frame of reference

Chances are you speak a language with a relative frame of reference rather than an absolute one. As such, you speak, think, and orient yourself in terms of up and down, left and right. As an experiment, try and spend an afternoon, or at least a couple of hours, living with an absolute system. Use the Sun or the compass on your smart phone to help you track north, south, east, and west. As you go about your afternoon, keep a log of your movements – *I walked northwest from the Gold Garage to the Student Center. I ordered a smoothie, and placed my books on the table to the south of me. A stranger asked for directions to the library; I told her to head due west from the library...*" At the end of your afternoon, reflect on your movements. Was it hard to adjust? Did you find yourself slipping into relative language and frames of mind?

Exercise 2 – acoustics

In this chapter, we discussed pitch and vowel quality. Linguists can measure both of these instrumentally, and so can you. For this exercise, you will need to download the free phonetics software, known as PRAAT, on your computer. Then, using the voice memo on your smart phone or some other recording device, you will record your own voice at a variety of pitches in order to discover the relationship between pitch and vowel quality. Start with the vowel [a] – record it at three separate pitches: low, medium, and high. Then, do the same thing for the vowels [u] and [i]. Next, open each of your recordings in PRAAT. Place the cursor over the middle of each vowel. Click the tab that says "Formant Listing" and write down the first two formants (F1 and F2) – these are the vowel qualities. Then, click on the tab that says "Pitch listing." Write down the number. Do this for each of the vowels you recorded in each of the pitches. Then, write your observations – do you think pitch affects vowel quality?

Discussion Questions

1   What is the most interesting thing you learned about the primate brain from reading this chapter? How does this inform your perspectives on language?
2   In this chapter, the authors write that by 100–200 kya, humans were "now cognizing the world in a way markedly different from that of their nonhuman primate counterparts." Thinking back on Chapter 2, what does it mean to "cognize the world?"
3   What does it mean to speak of human cognition as "hybrid" cognition? Is this a new expression for you?
4   We have noted that race is not a biologically meaningful category, but we know from Chapter 4 that it is nevertheless socially very powerful. How do you explain

the disconnect between what is known scientifically and the ways in which we have organized society around race?

5 What do you make of the discussion of structural complexity toward the end of this chapter? What was the main point? Why do you think people are drawn to questions about the complexity of language?

6 What is the takeaway message from the story about Ishi in the final note?

Notes

1 As noted in Chapter 8, the modern Slavic languages do not have tense; they have aspect. The absence of tense in Slavic does not exclude it from the Indo-European stock. Rather, Slavic aspect is a historical development from the PIE tense system.

2 The Austronesians knew that the presence of smaller birds in the sky indicated the proximity of land, and they followed the migratory paths of larger birds to sail between islands. In addition, they used the clues of coconut shells, turtles, and twigs to signal the nearby presence of land (Pereltsvaig 2012:159).

3 Levinson goes on to note that in Bali, there is a greater variability in spatial frames in older children. Once they go to school and start speaking Indonesian, they become acquainted with the relative system of Indonesian.

4 Some speakers of American English may have some lip rounding in anticipation of the 'r' [ɹ]. For those speakers, we predict that there will be less lip rounding in the case of *constrict*.

5 The identities of persons whose case histories appear in published research are kept private by the use of their initials only.

6 Neanderthal and Denisovan mtDNA belong in the homo lineage, but not in the modern human one.

7 The difficulties of sorting out the language stocks in Africa caused by the great span of time humans have been there are matched by the difficulties of assigning clear language stocks in Southeast Asia because this fertile area with lots of coastline has been conducive to human crisscrossing in the last 10,000 years.

8 The traditional notion of genetic fitness is defined when one's genes are secured in the pool when one's children reproduce.

9 The Native American Graves Protection and Repatriation Act of 1990 stipulates that human remains affiliated with tribes must be returned to those tribes for reburial, which is reasonable. However, the sometimes-ambiguous conditions of the act hamper the work of paleopathologists and bioarcheologists in the United States.

10 Germanic warrior traditions involved the camaraderie of beer drinking. Taking away the enemies' mead benches was equivalent to conquering them.

11 Hunter-gatherer societies are necessarily small, given the method of food acquisition. We have also said that their languages favor small vowel inventories. Because the relationship between the size of the population and the size of phonemic inventory relates to *consonants*, it remains to be investigated whether the size of vowel inventories varies by size of nonhunter-gathered communities (Cysouw and Comrie 2013:389).

12 See also footnote 6, Chapter 8.

13 See Theodora Kroeber (1961) for a fuller account of Ishi. Several television and film accounts also exist, for instance the 1992 documentary *Ishi: The Last Yahi* by Jed Riffe.

14 The existence of male and female speech is not unusual in traditional societies. Avoidance speech or what is sometimes called *mother-in-law speech* is found in Aboriginal Australian, Austronesian, and Native American languages.

References

Andrews, Edna (2012) Markedness. In Robert I. Binnick (ed.), *Tense and Aspect*. Oxford: Oxford University Press, 212–236.

Balter, Michael (2013a) Ancient DNA links Native Americans with Europe. *Science* 342: 409–410.

Balter, Michael (2013b) Farming's tangled European roots. *Science* 342: 181–182.

Cavalli-Sforza, Luigi (2000) *Genes, Peoples, and Languages*. New York: North Point Press.

Chebanne, Andy (2010) The Khoisan in Botswana: Can multicultural discourses redeem them? *Journal of Multicultural Discourses* 5: 87–105.

Cysouw, Michael and Bernard Comrie (2013) Some observations on typological features of hunter-gatherer languages. In Balthasar Bickel, Lenore A. Grenoble, David A. Peterson, and Alan Timberlake (eds.), *Language Typology and Historical Contingency: In Honor of Johanna Nichols*. Amsterdam: John Benjamins Publishing Company, 383–394.

Darwin, Charles (1968 [1859]) *The Origin of Species by Means of Natural Selection or the Preservation of Favoured Races in the Struggle for Life, Edited and with an Introduction by J.W. Burrow*. London: Penguin Books.

Dediu, Dan and D. Robert Ladd (2007) Linguistic tone is related to the population frequency of the adaptive haplogroups of two brain size genes, ASPM and Microcephalin. *Proceedings of the National Academy of Sciences* 104.26: 10944–10949.

Dixon, Robert M.W. (1994) *Ergativity*. Cambridge: Cambridge University Press.

Evans, Patrick D., Sandra L. Gilbert, Nitzan Mekel-Bobrov, Eric J. Vallender, Jeffrey R. Anderson, Leila M. Vaez-Azizi, Sarah A. Tishkoff, Richard R. Hudson, and Bruce T. Lahn (2005) Microcephalin, a gene regulating brain size, continues to evolve adaptively in humans. *Science* 309: 1717–1720.

Gil, David (2009) How much grammar does it take to sail a boat? In Geoffrey Sampson, David Gil, and Peter Trudgill (eds.), *Language Complexity as an Evolving Variable*. Oxford: University of Oxford Press, 19–33.

Kroeber, Theodora (1961) *Ishi in Two Worlds: A Biography of the Last Wild Indian in North America*. Berkeley: University of California Press.

Levinson, Stephen (2003) *Space in Language and Cognition: Explorations in Cognitive Diversity*. New York: Cambridge University Press.

Lieberman, Philip (2013) Synapses, language, and being human. *Science* 342:944–945.

Maddieson, Ian (2011, September 24) Consonant inventories. In Matthew S. Dryer and Martin Haspelmath (eds.), *The World Atlas of Language Structures Online*. Retrieved from Max Planck Digital Library. http://wals.info/chapter/1.

McWhorter, John (2001) The world's simplest grammars are Creole grammars. *Linguistic Typology* 5.2: 125–166.

Mekel-Bobrov, Nitzan, Sandra L. Gilbert, Patrick D. Evans, Eric J. Vallender, Jeffrey R. Anderson, Richard R. Hudson, Sarah A. Tishkoff, and Bruce T. Lahn (2005) Ongoing adaptive evolution of ASPM, a brain size determinant in *Homo sapiens*. *Science* 309: 1720–1722.

Morris, Simon Conway (2011) Complexity: The ultimate frontier. *EMBO Reports* 12: 481–482.

Nichols, Johanna (1986) Head-marking and dependent-marking grammar. *Language* 62.1: 56–119.

Nichols, Johanna (1992) *Linguistic Diversity in Space and Time*. Chicago: The University of Chicago Press.

Nichols, Johanna (2010) Macrofamilies, macroareas, and contact. In Raymond Hickey (ed.), *The Handbook of Language Contact*. Oxford: Wiley-Blackwell, 359–375.

Pereltsvaig, Asya (2012) *Languages of the World: An Introduction*. Cambridge: Cambridge University Press.

Rootsi, Siiri, Lev A. Zhivotovsky, Marian Baldovic Caron, Manfred Kayser, Ildus A Kutuev, Rita Khusainova, Marina A. Bermisheva, Marina Gubina, Sardana A. Fedorova, Anne-Mai Ilumäe, Elza K. Khusnutdinova, Mikhail I. Voevoda, Ludmila P. Osipova, Mark Stoneking, Alice A. Lin, Vladimir Ferak, Jüri Parik, Toomas Kivisild, Peter A. Underhill, and Richard Villems (2007) A counter-clockwise northern route of the Y-chromosome haplogroup N from Southeast Asia towards Europe. *European Journal of Human Genetics* 15: 204–211.

Tishkoff, Sarah, Mary Katherine Gonder, Brenna M. Henn, Holly Mortensen, Alec Knight, Christopher Gignoux, Neil Fernandopulle, Godfrey Lema, Thomas B. Nyambo, Uma Ramakrishnan, Floyd A. Reed, and Joanna L. Mountain (2007) History of click-speaking populations of Africa inferred from mtDNA and Y chromosome genetic variation. *Molecular Biology and Evolution* 20.10: 2180–2195.

Traill, Anthony (1994) *A !Xóõ dictionary. Quellen zur Khoisan-Forschung 9*. Cologne, Germany: Rüdiger Köppe.

Wassman, J. and P. Dasen (1998) Balinese spatial orientation. *Journal of the Royal Anthropological Institute* 4: 689–711.

Further Reading

Andresen, Julie Tetel (2013) *Linguistics and Evolution. A Developmental Approach*. Cambridge: Cambridge University Press.

Barrett, Louise, Robin Dunbar, and John Lycett (2002) *Human Evolutionary Psychology*. Princeton, NJ: Princeton University Press.

Deacon, Terrance (1997) *The Symbolic Species: The Co-Evolution of Language and the Brain*. New York: W.W. Norton.

Lieberman, Phillip (1984) *The Biology and Evolution of Language*. Cambridge, MA: Harvard University Press.

Lieberman, Phillip (1991) *Uniquely Human: The Evolution of Speech, Thought, and Selfless Behavior*. Cambridge, MA: Harvard University Press.

Lieberman, Phillip (2000) *Human Language and Our Reptilian Brain: The Subcortical Bases of Speech, Syntax, and Thought*. Cambridge, MA: Harvard University Press.

Lieberman, Phillip (2006) *Toward an Evolutionary Biology of Language*. Cambridge, MA: Harvard University Press.

Maturana, Humberto and Francisco Varela (1980 [1972]) *Autopoiesis and Cognition: The Realization of the Living*. Dordrecht, Netherlands: D. Reidel Publishing.

Maturana, Humberto and Francisco Varela (1992 [1987]) *The Tree of Knowledge: The Biological Roots of Human Understanding, Revised Edition*, translated by Robert Paolucci. Boston: Shambhala.

Oyama, Susan (1985) *The Ontogeny of Information: Developmental Systems and Evolution*. Cambridge: Cambridge University Press.

Oyama, Susan (2000) *Evolution's Eye: A Systems View of the Biology–Culture Divide*. Durham, NC: Duke University Press.

Traill, Anthony (1985) *Phonetic and Phonological Studies of !Xóõ Bushman*. Hamburg, Germany: Helmut Buske.

UCLA Phonetics Lab Archive. !xoo. http://archive.phonetics.ucla.edu/Language/NMN/nmn.html.

11

The Recorded Past
'Catching Up to Conditions' Made Visible

Mongolian Horses

In the early thirteenth century, Genghis Khan united a variety of Mongolia's nomadic tribes. Because of the Mongolians' exceptional skill as horsemen, Genghis Khan was able to conquer many of his neighbors. In 1204, he subdued the Uyghur people in what is now Xinjiang, a western province of China. There, he captured a scribe named Tata-tyngaak and commanded him to adapt the Uyghur alphabet[1] to write Mongolian. The Mongols were such fierce horsemen they were able to conquer their neighbors in all directions (Map 11.1), such that by the time of Genghis Khan's grandson, Kubla Khan, the Mongolian Empire had spread west across the Eurasian steppe, as we saw in Chapter 8. In 1271, Kubla Khan established the Yuan Dynasty, the first foreign dynasty to rule all of China, which lasted almost another 100 years. Still today, the horse is important in Mongolia, and not only because they outnumber the people there by an order of four to one.

Horses and horse culture are woven into the Mongolian language and thus exemplify the kind of ethnosyntax described in Chapter 2. The typical way to say 'Welcome' in Mongolian is *tavtai morilno oo!* Another, older way to say it is *morilooroi*, literally 'come by horse please.' Certainly, no one says this any more, because a Mongolian is now likely to arrive at a friend's house by car, bus, or other modern means. However, the word *mor* 'horse' is still found in the usual phrase *tavtai morilno oo!* It is furthermore a gentle welcome, *tavtai* meaning 'peaceful' [arrival by horse]. The unremarkable word *bracelet* in Mongolian also reveals an equestrian connection. In English, the word was borrowed from French, and in French, the association is with *bras* 'arm,' the location on the body where the bracelet is placed. In Mongolian, *bogoivč* 'bracelet' is also associated with a body location, namely *bogoi* 'wrist.' However, both of these words derive from the verb *bogoidax* 'to lasso.' A bracelet is thus the action of

Languages in the World: How History, Culture, and Politics Shape Language, First Edition.
Julie Tetel Andresen and Phillip M. Carter.
© 2016 John Wiley & Sons, Inc. Published 2016 by John Wiley & Sons, Inc.

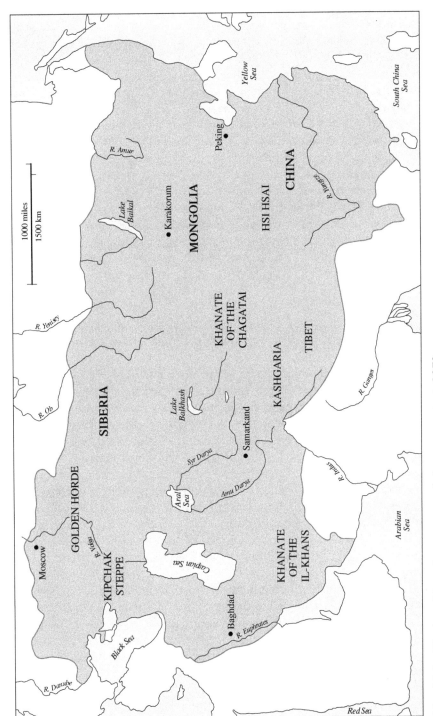

Map 11.1   The later Mongol conquests at their greatest extent: 1270.

encircling the wrist with a rope. The Mongolians are never far, linguistically speaking, from their horses.

Why are horses relevant at the outset of Chapter 11? Because in this chapter, we endeavor to explain what we can of the specific ways languages catch up to conditions when we have historical records of them. We know what we know of the history of Mongolian because there are 800 years of recorded history. The Mongolian script is, furthermore, written vertically top to bottom and has the rhythmic curves it does because Genghis Khan wanted to make sure his scribes could write it while riding their horses. Now, there's a technological innovation to keep an empire up and running. In this chapter, we want to exploit the records produced by such technological innovations, including those of today's digital archives, in order to look more closely at how languages change over time. In Chapters 3 and 7, we outlined the principles and methods of historical reconstructions that give us a picture of languages before recorded history. Here, in Chapter 11, we examine what we can of language and language change when we have written and/or digital records at our disposal.

We now put the linguistic flesh on the bones of the various stories we have been telling throughout Chapters 3–9. Because the time period of Chapter 10 lies far outside written history, we cannot reconstruct any linguistic specifics for that chapter. We take each chapter in turn.

Chapter 3: The Invariable Word in English

In the discussion of morphological typology, we noted English speakers' preference for the invariable word. This preference shows a particularly complex and delayed way in which language is always catching up to conditions. Old English, a West Germanic language, had rich inflectional morphology with five syntactic cases: nominative, genitive, dative, accusative, and instrumental. As a result of the Danish invasions of England in the eighth and ninth centuries, the case system of Old English started to weaken as speakers of a North Germanic language, Old Norse, began to interact with the West Germanic speakers of Old English. Because the two languages' case (systems) did not fully agree, speakers became understandably confused. Often the oldest records of a Western European language are in the form of translations of Latin texts. However, Old English has unusually ample written records that are not translations of Latin texts, and so examples of the breakdown of the case system can be found in records of the ordinary language.

One example will suffice: the ninth-century manuscript known as *Oðere's Voyage* describes an account of a voyage into the North Sea by a man named Oðere. In the midst of the description, the following prepositional phrase stands out: *on ðæm oðeram ðrim dagas* 'on the third day.' The first three words *ðæm oðeram ðrim* are in the dative plural case marked by a final -*m*, since they are in a phrase that begins with the preposition *on*. However, the head of that prepositional phrase, namely *dagas* 'days,' is not in the dative case but rather in the nominative. The so-called correct dative form would have been *dagum*, but evidently the writer of this account did not feel that *dagum* sounded right, despite the fact that the three preceding words had the final -*m* ending of the dative plural. Something about the noun *dagas* in this speaker's mind could be separated and made distinct from the preceding adjectives modifying it. The breakdown of the case system took hundreds of years with thousands of speakers making millions of linguistic decisions moving in the same direction as the writer of Oðere's voyage.

The arrival of Norman French in England with William the Conqueror in the eleventh century took a further toll on Old English inflectional morphology, this time in the gender system. Old English had three genders: masculine, feminine, and neuter. By the time Norman French arrived in England, the PIE three-way gender system in French had decreased to two: masculine and feminine. Norman French for 'the flower' was *la flour*, a feminine noun. It so happened that Old English for 'the flower' was *ðæt bled*, a neuter noun. What were speakers to do in the face of such a clash? We know the answer. They replaced *bled* with *flour* and discarded the gender distinction. Incidentally, the Old Norse word for 'flower' was *blom*, and English speakers borrowed that word as well. It has survived as *blossom*. The point is: the confusions and choices ensued until the eventual collapse of both the case and gender systems.

Hundreds of years later, speakers are still trying to level out the remaining differences in the case system of the pronouns, with the relative and interrogative pronoun *who/whom* distinction gone the way of the dodo easily 100 years ago or more, although it is still sometimes taught in classrooms. Eventually the current competition between *between you and me* and *between you and I* will sort itself out and no doubt in relation to which way the other pronouns go. Perhaps the leveling will be complete, and subject and object pronouns will have one form for all speakers. Or perhaps English will become diglossic with stable and salient H and L versions, with H reserving for itself the prestige of pronoun distinctions, and L the language of the home and/or the hoi polloi.

Whatever may happen to the pronouns, English speakers are still left with what might be called the historical wreckage, to speak here very metaphorically, of the synthetic Indo-European past. In Chapter 3, we compared English typologically to Chinese, the latter typing very nicely as an analytic language with little morphologic variation in its forms. In Chinese, the word 'three' is *san*, and the word 'ten' is *shí*, and they combine without morphological change in combinations to make both 'thirteen' and 'thirty.' English, by way of contrast, has not one but three forms of the concept 'ten': *ten*, *-teen*, and *-ty* and two forms of the concept 'three': *three* and *thir-*. English also retains pairs of words that hide the workings of a polysynthetic morphology, which means that it is difficult to separate out the different parts of the word-formation process, as in the relationship between *young* and *youth*, *foul* and *filth*, *broad* with *breadth*, *whole* or *hale* with *health*. Speakers do what they can with the materials at hand and the need to get through their day, and the languages they speak are fascinating refractions of imperfectly applied processes that nevertheless always seek some kind of grammatical equilibrium.

Chapter 4: The Shift to Head-Marking in French

You will remember from Chapter 4 that during the French Revolution, Abbé Grégoire was determined to annihilate all forms of language in the newly forming nation-state that were not *Île de la Cité* French. Two hundred years later, it is clear that he made an impact in reducing language variety in France. However, he did not succeed in wiping all non-Parisian forms of the language off the map. In any case, he was never going to be able to stop any, much less all, varieties of French from changing.

There is evidence that colloquial modern French is becoming a VSO language, given the quantity of utterances like:

> *il*   *est*   *joli*   *ce coin*
> it   is   lovely   this corner
> 'this area is lovely.'

Such an utterance is a statement, and the subject *ce coin* comes after the verb. The (formerly) subject pronoun *il* 'he/it' is now functioning less like a subject pronoun and more like an agreement prefix. The transforming of both subject and object pronouns into clitics in French is occurring throughout informal speech. Although it is perfectly grammatical to say:

> *je*   *connais*   *cet*   *homme*
> I   know   this   man

it is more normal to say:

> *je*   **le**   *connais*   *cet*   *homme*
> I   him   know   this   man

where **le** is now an object pronoun. The point is that languages can and do change their word-order preferences over time. In the last 2000 years, the SOV preference of Latin has transformed into the SVO preference of spoken French, which is further transforming into a VSO language.

With regard to this shift to head-marking in progress in the grammar of French:

- it is a hallmark of the spoken language;
- it is pervasive and not limited only to subjects and objects but is also found in the genitive-type: *il **en** a marre Paul **des études*** 'he (genitive *en*) has enough Paul of studies'/'Paul is tired of his studies';
- the change is more widespread in the southern half of France and so is presumably the place where the shift originated; and
- the grammatical information about the subject *ce coin* 'this corner,' which has not yet appeared, has already been signaled by the (soon-to-be former) pronoun *il*, which is migrating in spoken French toward becoming a clitic associated with the verb.

Now, notice one more thing: the order of the first three or four words – *il est joli, je le connais, il en a marre* – stays the same, as they are in standard/formal French. The syntax remains; the interpretation of the elements changes. These are good examples of an adage well known to historical linguists: yesterday's syntax is tomorrow's morphology.

The question can now be asked: Is this head-marking shift related to other developments in the language? The answer given by Stephen Matthews, author of the article "French in Flux" (1989), is Yes. The reinterpretation of the pronoun *il* as a new clitic is related to other grammatical evidence that pronouns are generally being reinterpreted throughout the language. As mentioned in Chapter 8, French is the Romance language with the most radical phonology, that is, the most distant from Latin, with significant loss of endings both on nouns showing gender and verbs showing person. Given the erosion of the endings on verbs, personal pronouns have long been necessary to indicate who or what is doing something. With the exception of the second person plural/polite *vous* 'you' form, there is no audible difference in the overwhelming majority of verbs for the other persons. There is a visible written difference, but in French (as in English), writing preserves what were phonetic differences hundreds of years ago. Thus, today, the colloquial conjugation of *parler* 'to speak' is:

	Singular	Plural
First person	je parle [paʀl]	
Second person	tu parles [paʀl]	vous parlez [paʀle]
Third person (he/she)	il/elle parle [paʀl]	ils/elles parlent [paʀl]

As you see, all forms of the verb are pronounced [paʀl] except for *vous parlez* 'you (plural/polite) speak,' which is [paʀle]. The form of the first person plural has been left blank, because leveling of endings on verbs has continued to now include a strong tendency for the first person plural *nous* 'we' to be doubled by the indefinite pronoun *on* 'one.' In the phrase *nous on parle* 'we/one speaks,' the verb form is again [paʀl] and is opposed to the more formal/standard *nous parlons* where the form of the verb is [paʀlõ].

The point here is that although the personal pronouns operated for hundreds of years simply as personal pronouns, they now seem to be functioning overall as clitic markers. The once purely emphatic statement *moi je parle* '**I'm** speaking' was made by adding the stressed pronoun *moi* to the phrase. Now, however, the *je* seems to function as part of the verb as an agreement marker, and the *moi* is now there to indicate who is doing the speaking in a nonemphatic way. Further evidence that the personal pronouns have morphed into clitics can be seen in the fact that they cannot now be used deictically. When pointing to someone in English, it is perfectly natural to say: "She's French." However, in French, you now have to say, "*Elle, elle est française.*" This doubling is redundant only if the second *elle* were actually (still functioning in the speaker's mind as) a pronoun. Finally, in the varieties where the head-marking shift is strongest, these (former) pronouns no longer undergo subject–verb inversion in questions of the standard sort:

Où	*est*	*mon*	*livre?*	*Où*	*est-il?*
Where	is	my	book?	Where	is-it?

The more normal spoken way to say this now is:

Où	il	est	mon	livre?
Where	it	is	my	book?

Three points can now be made, all relevant to this chapter as a whole:

- When a grammatical change is taking place in a particular language, it does not do so all at once. Rather, changes occur item by item. For French, the changes in the pronouns may well have begun with the first person *moi je parle*, since it is the prototypical deictic expression, and then extended easily to the other persons *toi tu parles, lui il parle*, and *eux ils parlent*; what is interesting is to see how there has been parallel cliticization throughout the language.
- What looks like doubling or even redundancy in *moi je parle*, where the 'I' is marked twice (once with *moi*, a second time with *je*), is actually common cross-linguistically as a language shifts from dependent- to head-marking.
- These new structures, these reinterpretations, often arise when a grammatical structure first used for a certain effect becomes so widespread that it loses its effect and becomes the norm.

It seems to be the case in French that these newer structures arose and are still most common in affective utterances, ones that have a stronger emotional pull on the speaker than other utterances. Matthews (1989:196) offers a host of examples:

Je	l'aime	moi	Marie
I	her-love	me	Mary

'I **love** Mary'

and

il	est	joli	ce	coin
it	is	pretty	this	corner

'This area is **lovely**'

as well as

je	m'en	fiche	moi	de ce boulot
I	me-genitive	don't care	me	of this job

'I don't give **a damn** about this job,'

along with other expressions of admiration, disapproval, annoyance, frustration, delight, and so forth.

Although the French language has not been affected by the series of invasions that so dramatically reformed English, it is the case that French, just like every other language, has its share of variants, because it has its share of speakers and speech communities. Out of these communities come the forms that are in play and available for other speakers to either adopt or reject. It could very well be that the strong sense of standardized French in the north is (one of) the condition(s) the speakers in the south are pressing off and away from.

Chapter 5: Writing and e-Arabic

A written language is a conservative language. Once something is put down in writing, it takes on a certain force, which the phrase *written in stone*, referring to the Ten Commandments, strongly conveys. We saw in Chapter 8 that in the Balkan languages, translations of the Bible tend not to have clitic pronoun agreement, because the older prestige languages did not have it, and these agreements are considered colloquial. We have just said that French and English spellings are historical and reflect pronunciations of the time when spelling became standardized for these two languages. Generation after generation of English-speaking children are taught to wrench their spellings to match early fifteenth-century pronunciations, thereby causing a visual disconnect between written and twenty-first-century spoken English the world over. Once upon a time, the word *knight* really was pronounced [knixt], but not lately.

That was then. Now there's texting. The use of *u* for *you*, *ur* for *your* and *you're*, and *r* for *are* is so widespread in texting as to have become standard. This diglossic spelling situation is not new but rather a continuation of what might be called *advertising English* where *light* becomes *lite*, *night* becomes *nite*, *snow* becomes *sno*, and *grow* becomes *gro*. And comedy clubs do not play for *laughs*, they play for *laffs*. What the future of these visual doublets is is anyone's guess. Ours is that H and L versions of written English will become more pronounced, and prestige will accrue to those who know the traditional spellings. Recall from the discussion of diglossia in Chapter 3 that uses of H and L varieties depend on the situation. Well-educated speakers know when to speak and write H, as well as when to speak and write L.

Nowhere is the spelling revolution more dramatic than in Arabic-speaking countries, which are the countries for which the terms H and L were originally invented. The prestige of Qur'ānic Arabic, aka Classical Arabic and/or Modern Standard Arabic (MSA), has been so great that local, colloquial forms of Arabic were not deemed worthy of writing down. The innovations of texting and tweeting have ushered a sweeping change into the Arabic-writing world. As we noted at the end of Chapter 5, access to the Internet is no longer a luxury but rather a modern need. Mobile technologies have not only provided access to large sections of the population that were poorer and less educated but also made it possible for those people to communicate through their colloquial forms of Arabic. Those who do not command MSA and/or French, the colonial legacy language in many places in North Africa, are no longer completely disenfranchised. Mobile technologies do not solve all inequalities, but they do create openings for people who previously had few before.

In the case of Arabic, which is traditionally written in the Arabic script, a visual transformation is discernible, for now previously unwritten colloquial forms of Arabic are being written in a script other than Arabic. The Roman alphabet is the obvious choice, and the transliteration from Arabic to Roman is also known as ASCII-ization, which has produced a creative and visually interesting phenomenon. Arabic texters have worked out how to represent letters in the Arabic alphabet that do not exist in the Latin alphabet, and they do this sometimes by means of numbers. Here are a few examples: the letter ح [ħ] is represented by 7, as in *7abibti* 'my darling.' The letter خ [x] is 7', as in *7'ali* 'my maternal uncle.' The letter ع [pharyngeal glottal] is rendered by 3, as in *3rabi* 'Arab,' while غ [ʀ] is 3', as in *3'areeb* 'strange.' The letter ص [ṣ] is seen as 9, as in *9iyam* 'fasting,' while ض [ḍ] is 9', as in *9'araba* 'hit.' The letter ط [ṭ] is rendered by 6, as in *6ayib* 'nice.' Then there is ء [ʔ], which is represented almost logically, one could say, by the number 2, as in *2lam* 'pain.' We are back in the days of boustrophedon 'as the ox ploughs,' where texters flip the direction of the numbers, when necessary, to produce a symbol that most closely resembles the Arabic letter. These number touches give the script a nice and modern Arabic look while at the same time giving the written L colloquial varieties the H prestige of the Roman alphabet.

Why and how did these new orthographic conventions arise? In a survey of female university students conducted in the United Arab Emirates (Palfreyman and al Khalil 2003), the students cited as the main reasons for using this romanized script the ease of typing in such a format, the privacy it provides, since their parents and/or teachers cannot read this script, as well as the intrinsic interest of writing an unusual script. One student wrote that the script functions as an in-group code, "kind of a funky language for teenzz to use," thus making it the orthographic equivalent of slang. The survey respondents also reported they had learned this script before entering university, and they had learned it mostly interacting with relatives, especially relatives living abroad, and acquaintances online. Although there are now webpages devoted to this script, its dissemination seems to have occurred not through particular web-sites but rather more informally, through one-on-one or group chat interactions. Like most linguistic innovations, it is difficult to pinpoint the originators. When asked who the students thought had created the system, their answers were "I don't know," "Arabs living abroad," and/or groups with whom they could identify, such as "young people," or "chatters." The domain of use of this script is so far confined to personal communications and URLs, but it has also been used in a fast-food advertisement on posters in Dubai (Palfreyman and al Khalil 2003). It will be fascinating to see if it emerges into more mainstream arenas to compete with the standard English-to-Arabic transliteration system already in use throughout the Middle East, for instance, in airports and on road signs and other public venues.

Beyond the visual changes to traditionally written Arabic come some of the expected changes to the language through borrowings and calques of computer terminology, mostly from English. As usual, speakers borrow words and adapt them to their own phonologies. Arabic does not have either [v] or [p], so a word such as *device* is pronounced (and then written in either Roman and Arabic script) *dīfāys*, and *virus* becomes *fayrūs*, while *Skype* becomes *skāyb*. Otherwise, Arabic is able to accommo-date new cyber terminology with little difficulty, such as *email, flash drive, chat, site,* among others, plus variations of *web* that come out as either *wāb* or *wīb*. Again, as usual, e-Arabic uses a lot of calques and half-calques from English where such things as *secure chat, motherboard, desktop, and electronic mail* are rendered /tšat maħmī/, /al-lawħa al-umm/, /saṭh al-maktab/, and /barīd iliktrūnī/, respectively.

Much has been made of the role played by social media in the Egyptian Revolution of January, 2011. In the summer of 2010, a Facebook page was created by a man named Wael Ghonim. This page became the virtual town square that would eventually sound the call for an uprising on January 25 in Cairo's physical Tahrir Square (ASCII-ized: Meedaan al Ta7reer). On the assigned day, the turnout on Tahrir Square was higher than anyone had imagined and led to a nationwide media campaign condemning the protests. It also led to Ghonim's arrest by the Egyptian State Security on January 27. What happened the next day was most unexpected. In his memoir, Ghonim writes:

> Then, the Egyptian regime committed a fatal mistake. On the morning of Jan28, all communication in the country was cut off. All three cellular operators, Internet services, and short messaging services ceased to work. Little did the regime know that this was the single largest promotional effort possible for the revolution. Every citizen who had not heard of the uprising now realized that a major challenge to the regime must be under way. Huge numbers of people decided to take to the streets, some for no other reason than just to find out what was happening. (2012:212)

A lot of commentary does not seem necessary here. People like to be connected and stay connected: 100 kya, we sat around the campfire, telling the day's stories; today, we gather around the glow of our phone screens. Those with the power to deliberately cut the connection often do not have the power to control the consequences.

Chapter 6: Mongolian Cases

As we said at the beginning of this chapter, Mongolian has an 800-year history of written records starting in the thirteenth century with Genghis Khan. This period is sometimes called Middle Mongolian and runs from the thirteenth to the sixteenth centuries. It contrasts with Proto/Old/Ancient Mongolian, which refers to the time up through the twelfth century. The Modern Mongolian period begins in the seventeenth century with the conversion of the Mongolian people to Buddhism. The earliest literary work in Mongolian is *The Secret History of the Mongols* (circa 1240), likely originally written in the Mongolian version of the Uyghir script but whose only surviving copies are in Chinese characters. The long history of written Mongolian now serves various purposes: it can provide evidence for or against a relationship between Mongolic languages and languages from other stocks; and it can allow people in the present a perspective from which to observe language change in progress. We focus here on three of the eight Mongolian cases: accusative, genitive, and directive, and discover what they can tell us about both historical relatedness among languages and language change. (See Language Profile, this chapter, for the full list of cases.)

Accusative

In this book we have classed Altaic as a phylum that includes three language stocks: Turkic, Tungusic, and Mongolic. The question of whether or not Korean and Japanese belong here has not been settled. Everyone agrees that Turkic, Tungusic, and Mongolic are SOV and have postposed agglutinative morphology with similar grammatical functions as well as vowel harmony. What is at issue is whether these features are a result of: (i) shared inheritance from a proto-language; (ii) typology (certain features in language tend to hang together, and the cluster found in the purported Altaic phylum can be found in other places in the world); or (iii) contact, given that the speakers of the various languages have lived in the same part of the world for centuries.

The accusative case, which indicates the direct object, has played a role as scholars have attempted to establish a phylum for Altaic. There is an intriguing similarity between the Old Turkic accusative ending *-(i)g and the Modern Mongolian accusative ending *-iik* (spelled *-iig* but pronounced with a final [k]). What does the historical record of Mongolian tell us? It turns out that the appearance of the Mongolian -g# does not make an appearance in North Mongolian manuscripts until the end of the sixteenth century and in other varieties until the middle of the seventeenth century. Furthermore, the Proto-Mongolian accusative case suffix appears to be *-i/ji. The appearance of the -g# in Modern Mongolian can be explained by the fact that in the development of the language, the genitive and the accusative endings started to merge, and certain varieties of Mongolian overcame the convergence by lengthening the accusative ending to *-jigi*, which became over time *-iik*.[2]

The point here is that *-g of the Old Turkic accusative and the -k (spelled -g) of the Modern Mongolian accusative are a coincidence and not a sign of shared inheritance. Some scholars are nevertheless willing to say that the vowel *-i* in the Proto-Turkic and Proto-Mongolian accusative is inherited from Proto-Altaic.

Genitive

Another case perhaps determinative of whether or not there is a justifiable phylum Altaic is the genitive, and this is the case indicating possession. There is a strong and widespread use of the suffix *-in* and/or variations of such an ending always involving a nasal to indicate possession in Mongolic, Turkic, and Tungusic languages. It has been suggested that this so-called original [n] is found in Austroasiatic and Austronesian languages as well and also used in ways to suggest possession. It is even found in the Russian genitive case form *-un*, which is used almost exclusively with proper names and kinship terms, meaning that this ending has a non-Slavonic origin (Solntseva and Solntsev).

The widespread nature of this consonant and its associated meaning is surely not one of coincidence, as is the -g# in Old Turkic and Modern Mongolian. It is rather more an indication of an areal feature, one that is very old in this long-inhabited part of the world. That is to say that its distribution in the world's languages argues against a particular association with Altaic, as such. At the same time the appearance of this genitive in the three candidate language families for Altaic does not rule out that they shared the inheritance of it from a common proto-language, say, Proto-Altaic.

As was said in Chapters 3 and 7, in order to establish a family or a stock, the philologist must find *massive* lexical and grammatical similarities. Yes, there are lexical and grammatical similarities among the so-called Altaic languages, but they are not massive. They seem to have come to exist through contact and diffusion, common enough processes the world over. The term *Altaic* is nevertheless justifiable in the sense that we use it in this textbook to capture the effects of this long-term contact.

Directive

Scholars of Mongolian have noticed that since the early 1990s, a new case is coming into existence, and it seems to be developing out of the directive case.[3] The directive is the case that has historically indicated direction toward something, such as a person, place, or thing. It is marked with the unbound postposed morpheme *roo* or *ruu*, depending on the demands of vowel harmony (see Language Profile, this chapter). For instance, going 'toward me' is *nad roo*, while going 'toward (the town of) Erdenet' is *Erdenet ruu*. The new case has the bound morpheme ending *-eer* and could therefore be confused with one of the forms of the instrumental case, but apparently it is not. Before the early 1990s, one could say:

bi	*delguur*	*ruu*	*yavcan*
I	store	to/toward	went

'I went to the store'

and

bi	*Romin*	*roo*	*yavcan*
I	Romania	to/toward	went

'I went to Romania.'

Now, however, one can also say:

bi	*delguureer*	*yavcan*
I	store-toward/around	went

'I went around shopping/I shopped around'

and

bi	*Romineer*	*yavcan*
I	Romania	toward/around went

'I traveled around Romania'

The explanation for this new form is the following: only since the end of Socialism in the early 1990s did people have freedom to travel and a sense that one could 'go around' rather than just 'toward' something. This new feeling required an expansion of the unidirectional sense of *roo/ruu* to produce the multidirectional suffix *-eer*. Here is a very neat example of the way a language catches up to conditions. A change in political regime effected a change in behavior of the people formerly living under that regime, which also triggered a linguistic change to express that change in behavior. The development of *-eer* is still in progress.

Chapter 7: Reformulating Hawaiian Identity

Instead of using written records in order to look back and reconstruct some features of historical change in Hawaiian, here we use the written records of Hawaiian, along with newer technology, to look forward and account for the Hawaiian language revival, mentioned at the end of the Language Profile in Chapter 7. The very existence of the written records is one of the reasons the current language revival has a foothold. Surely they are important because they are valuable documents of the language, but they are even more important for what they represent: a time when Hawaiians were independent and self-governing. Thus, the records represent a tradition of longstanding and widespread literacy in the native population, and this tradition is alive today, given that native Hawaiians are better educated (in English) and better integrated into the American Middle Class than are most other Native American populations on the mainland (Cowell 2012). The Hawaiian language revival is, furthermore, taking place in a context that is less about reviving the language as a principal goal and more about reformulating and strengthening a Hawaiian identity that is already in place.

According to the records of the Hawaiian Historical Society, the first printing press arrived in Hawai'i with Protestant missionaries in 1822. In the presence of those who had brought the press, the Maui Chief Ke'eeaumoku did the honors: he put his hand to the lever, pushed down, and brought into existence the first page printed in Hawaiian and English. It was for a speller to be used in the schools organized by the missionaries. The chief is reported to have said *makai* 'good,' recognizing the importance of this moment. Indeed, in short order, Hawaiian was transcribed into the Latin alphabet, and over the course of the nineteenth century, both materials printed in Hawaiian and literacy rates in the native population increased. In particular, newspapers were printed in abundance. At the time, the first language of all native Hawaiians was Hawaiian.

In "The Hawaiian model of language revitalization: problems of extension to mainland America" (Cowell 2012), linguist Andrew Cowell describes the importance of the nineteenth-century records. First, as we have just said, these records anchor a tradition of literacy in the native population.[4] Second, they were written by native speakers and thus reflect what was important to them. The documents record Hawaiian resistance to colonization, for instance, along with traditional oral poetry. There is, furthermore, a clear sense in the documents that part of their function was to record and save the language, to provide materials for future generations. Here we remind you that, as mentioned in Chapter 5, the decision taken almost 2000 years ago to write the Mishnah, the first documentation of the oral tradition of Judaism, was inspired by a (correct) perception that soon there would no speakers of Hebrew left. Similarly, although the Hawaiian language was alive, and literacy was spreading, nineteenth-century Hawaiians (also correctly) feared for the future of their language. Just as the long tradition of written Hebrew provided leverage to revive it as a spoken language, so can the tradition of written Hawaiian help in its revival.

The beginning of the end of the language the Hawaiians feared occurred in 1893 when American soldiers overthrew what would be the last Hawaiian monarch, Queen Lili'uokalani. The Hawaiian language was almost immediately prohibited in schools across the archipelago, as monolingual English instruction replaced monolingual

Hawaiian instruction. Hawaiian children were punished for speaking the language, and teachers were fired for encouraging or allowing it in class. The numbers of Hawaiian speakers fell precipitously. By the 1980s, when the ban on Hawaiian in schools was officially overturned, there were only about 1000 native speakers of Hawaiian left in Hawaii, and about half were over the age of 70. Hawaiian was on the brink of loss less than a century after it was banned in schools.

Although an impassioned language revitalization movement got going in the 1980s with the introduction of immersion preschools known as *Pūnana Leo*, the scope of the efforts was limited, in part, by the physical distance imposed by the islands themselves. The dispersal of speakers enrolled in immersion classes across many islands made out-of-class engagement with the language nearly impossible. Moreover, Hawaiian was figured culturally as the language that connected students to their past, while English was the language of the future. By the dawn of the twenty-first century, young Hawaiians watched television in English, texted in English, blogged in English, and participated in social media such as Twitter and Facebook in English. English was the language of the digital age in Hawaii and the preferred language of the youth.

The same technology that once seemed to remove Hawaiian youth further and further from the Hawaiian language is now being recruited to revitalize it. Scholars, language activists, and educators are using digital technology to revolutionize the revitalization movement in four respects:

- to preserve existing written forms of the language;
- to make the language available in new platforms for communication;
- to cheaply develop new materials in the language; and
- to make the language available and easy to use in a variety of new technologies.

In 2002, Apple launched a Hawaiian language version of its Macintosh operating system, Kauakukalahale. In that same year, the first column in a major newspaper to be written in Hawaiian was published and became available online, and over 100,000 Hawaiian language documents were digitized and stored electronically in Ulukau, the Hawaiian Language Digital Project. The rise of self-publishing and the availability of affordable printing products have meant that authentic Hawaiian teaching materials can be produced locally, providing immersion classes with up-to-date resources. And students enrolled in those classes can now communicate synchronously via email, chat, discussion boards, and other forums with Hawaiian language immersion students outside their classes and across the archipelago. In addition, the establishment of the *Kōmike Kua'ōlelo* 'Hawaiian Lexicon Committee' has helped in the revival efforts by overseeing the development of new vocabulary that did not occur naturally after the push for English in the schools and daily life began a century ago.

Perhaps most important in the revitalization effort is the sense of Hawaiian-ness and language ideology already in place on the islands. As mentioned in the Language Profile for Chapter 7, native Hawaiians did not have in the past, nor do they have in the present, feelings of exclusivity toward Hawaiian identity and the Hawaiian language. Neither was there ever the idea in circulation that if one did not speak Hawaiian, one could not be Hawaiian. Cowell describes this general cultural sense as one of "expansive inclusivity." Thus, among all populations living in Hawaii, there is widespread understanding of, support for, and participation in such traditional Hawaiian activities as surfing, pig hunting, hula, traditional fishing, luaus, wearing leis and aloha clothing, and the rest. This expansive inclusivity has made it easier, rather than more difficult, to recruit interest in reviving the Hawaiian language, since the language becomes one more resource to strengthen prevailing cultural values. In the terms of this book, the Hawaiian language has many activities and artifacts into which it can now loop itself. The language is not bearing all the responsibility of reviving the culture.

Cowell points out that the historical and contemporary cultural situation in Hawaii is quite different than for most mainland Native American cultures in that, despite the skyscrapers on Waikīkī Beach, traditional Hawaiian culture permeates the general culture, and the language has remained present in the place names, Mauna Loa, Mauna Kea, and Honolulu – just to name a few. Native American Arapaho speakers from the Wind River Reservation, Wyoming who came to Hawaii to visit the immersion schools were struck by this cultural presence. One of them noted that the Hawaiians' "life is all around"; that is, dispersed in the general culture the way Arapaho culture in Wyoming is not. Still, it takes committed language activists to revive a language, and in Hawaii these are the native Hawaiians. They now benefit from their ancestors' openness to others. They also find creative ways to blend the new with the old. Cowell reports on a high school football team that calls its plays traditional voyaging terminology. In recent years, football practices on the islands have become increasingly "Polynesian."

Among the conditions language is always catching up to are the technological means of reproducing the language and disseminating it along with long-existing attitudes that can be recruited for new purposes.

Chapter 8: Varieties of Chinese – Yesterday and Today

The last 3000 years of Chinese government-encouraged migrations of the Han people were outlined at the beginning of Chapter 8. Because the Han migrated into already-inhabited areas, language contact was inevitable. Because the prestige of the Han culture was so great, Chinese became the donor language, and language shift was invariably to Chinese. We saw in Chapter 5 the importance of Chinese logograms in the early writing systems of Korean, Vietnamese, and Malay, and their continuing influence in Japanese. Here, in Chapter 11, we note the kinds of historic substratal influences the migrating Han encountered leading to the many, not-mutually intelligible varieties of Chinese. Next, we look at what variationist sociolinguists[5] are able to tell us about two contemporary varieties of Chinese.

Varieties of Chinese: yesterday

Overall, it can be said that, although the Chinese varieties from north to south do not precisely constitute a dialect chain, they do exhibit a continuum of features that reflect the features of the languages of the various peoples they encountered. Those who came to rule also left their linguistic marks. In the middle of the last millennium, the Yuan dynasty rulers spoke Mongolian, while the rulers who came both before and after the Yuan, such as the Manchus, spoke Tungusic languages. In northern varieties of Chinese, more Altaic (Turkic, Mongolic, Tungusic) features are found, such as fewer tones, more SOV sentences, and less complex classifier systems. For instance, Mandarin, spoken in the north, has only four tones, which is considered on the low end. Following the end of the Qing Dynasty at the beginning of the twentieth century, the Manchu-speaking population in the north shifted to Mandarin. They brought with them the distinction between inclusive/exclusive 'we,' namely *zánmen* and *wǒmen*, respectively, where other, more southern varieties of Chinese have only *wǒmen*. It can also happen that, in the north, Altaic case endings have been borrowed along with SOV order, which represents a typological change of Chinese from isolating SVO to agglutinating SOV (Matthews 2010:761).

As one moves south, Chinese varieties have more tones, more SVO constructions, and more complex classifier systems. For instance, Cantonese, spoken in the south, has six tones (or nine, always depending on how one counts), while southern Min varieties such as Hokkien and Chaozhou have seven to eight. Among the many structural features in Cantonese that can be attributed to contact with languages to the south is the position of the adverb. In Cantonese, the adverb follows the verb, whereas in Mandarin, the adverb precedes the verb. Compare the following:

Cantonese:

ngo^5   *zau^2*   *sin^1*
'I'   'go'   **'first'**

and Thai:

phon   *pai*   *koon*
'I'   'go'   **'first'**

as well as Cantonese:

zung^6   *jau^5*   *seoi^2-zam^6*   *tim^1*
'still'   'have'   'water-flood'   **'too'**
'There was flooding **too**'

and Thai:

ko   *naam-thuam*   *duay*
'also'   'water-flood'   **'too'**
'There was flooding **too**'

(Matthews 2007:229). Just as there has been a kind of Altaicization in the north, so there has been Taicization in the south. The features that result have been several thousand years in the making, and historical linguists show us the cases where the changes have been established.

Varieties of Chinese: today

Beijing Variationist sociolinguists tell us of changes in progress, and we review here two studies, one of contemporary Beijing speech and one of contemporary Taiwanese Mandarin. The first study by sociolinguist Qing Zhang (2005) bears an attention-getting title: "A Chinese yuppie in Beijing: Phonological variation and the construction of a new professional identity." The Chinese word for 'yuppies' is, by the way, *yǎpíshì* and includes, in addition to the English meaning of the word, connotations of global orientation, trendiness, and sophistication. Part of this global orientation involves Western pop music, particularly American pop, Hollywood movies, and TV serials. Particularly big hits are *Friends* and *The Big Bang Theory*, which show independent young adults living together rather than with their parents, in addition to more recent series such as *Criminal Minds*, *Homeland*, and *House of Cards*. However, the bulk of the global orientation is toward cultural production in varieties of Chinese beyond the mainland border, namely movies and music made in Hong Kong and Taiwan, which are jointly referred to in Mandarin as *Gǎngtái*.

In her study, Zhang investigates four phonetic variables found in Beijing speech, only three of which we will mention here:

- the rhotacizing of final syllables called *érhuà*, which involves the addition of a sub-syllabic -r [ɹ] to the final;
- the change of the retroflex[6] initials /ʂ/, /tʂ/, and /tʂʰ/ called *ruòhuà*, which 'softens' or 'makes sonorous' consonants so that they sound more like [ɹ]; and
- the realization of a neutral tone, as a full tone is a weakly stressed syllable.

The first two variables, both involving [ɹ], are highly characteristic of Beijing speech, so much so that Beijing locals have the phrase *jīngqiāngr jīngdiàor* – note the final **rs** – that means 'Beijing tune.' Beijing speech is equated with heavy-r speech, and people outside of Beijing notice it and are apt to comment on it. Because of the national importance of Beijing and a rich tradition of writing in Beijing vernaculars, this heavy-r speech comes with its own cultural persona for Beijingers, namely that of the *jīng yóuzi* 'Beijing smooth operator.'

The third variable involving tone is not found in Beijing speech at all but is associated with *Gǎngtái* pop music stars and business people. Zhang (2005:444) dubs it "the cosmopolitan variable" because it is identified as both nonlocal and nonmainland. The variable can commonly be heard in telephone interactions with professionals in foreign business. They are likely to say *xiānshēng* 'mister' and *xiǎojiě* 'miss' using the full tone in the second syllable of both address terms, while Beijingers would normally use a neutral tone, as in *xiānsheng* and *xiǎojie*.

So now what are young, upwardly mobile professionals to do, linguistically speaking? They will want to capture some of the 'smooth operator' coolness for themselves by adopting the [ɹ] Beijing style, but not too heavily to be mistaken for a strict local, and they will be interested in exploiting the full tone variants for the cosmopolitan touch. Indeed, Zhang found that young professionals working in foreign-owned companies in Beijing employed both these linguistic resources to create a new cosmopolitan version of Mandarin, while young professionals working in state-owned companies favored the use of local features only.

Taiwan   The study of variation in contemporary Taiwanese Mandarin also provides understanding into how and why people choose to speak the way they do. The official language of Taiwan is Mandarin and was declared so in 1946 after the KMT[7] government of the Republic of China took control of the island. An aggressive ideological and language teaching campaign ensued and was coupled with suppression of local Chinese varieties including Hoklo (=Taiwanese, a Hokkien variety of the Min Nan branch of Sinitic) as well as aboriginal languages from the Austronesian language family. By the late 1980s, the KMT regime had succeeded in establishing Mandarin as the prestige variety and the ideology that speaking Standard Mandarin was a sign of loyalty to the Republic and the regime. However, the Mandarin spoken in Taiwan today is not the Beijing-based standard taught in elementary schools. Taiwanese Mandarin (TM) has regional features. For instance, it participates in the general southern pattern, also found in Cantonese, of using the verb 'say' as a complementizer. A translated TM sentence such as 'she with me talk **say** not available' has the grammatical effect of: 'she told me **that** she wasn't free' where 'say' functions as 'that.' However, large-scale language contact accompanying the intensive spread of Mandarin has also produced a set of local features that form the new TM variety.

Owing to continued reinforcement of the Beijing standard in Taiwan through education and the media and no effort to standardize TM as such, several unofficially sanctioned local TM features are in considerable variation. They are of particular interest to the sociolinguist, because they have become resources for individuals speaking the variety to position themselves in relation to socially available identity categories and the ideologies surrounding them. Sociolinguist Dominika Baran's (2014) variationist study brings us inside the dynamic world of two variables in particular, namely the de-retroflection of [ʂ] and a labial glide deletion where [wo] becomes [o]. Both of these features have a high degree of salience as stigmatized variants, and speakers use them or avoid them for various effects. TM speakers are aware of the retroflex feature and even have a name for it: *juǎnshé*, literally 'curled tongue.' They use this term to describe Standard Mandarin, and we have just seen that Beijing Mandarin is, indeed, known for its r-heaviness.

Baran conducted fieldwork in a high school outside of Taipei, the capital. In this high school, the students are placed into one of three tracks, based on entrance exam scores: (i) college preparatory; (ii) office administration and computer technology; and (iii) electronics and car mechanics, a track that school administrators say is made up of 'troublemakers.' A first categorization is predictable: girls will use the features of TM less than boys, because both TM and Hoklo (the source of the variations) are associated with masculinity, since they are perceived as lacking in refinement. Furthermore, it turns out that Taiwanese speakers in general find de-retroflection relatively acceptable, and this is because it is a symbol of local pride. The glide deletion is more stigmatized, partly because it is associated with the south and is perceived as unsophisticated and backward.

In sum, students in the college prep track have a lower degree of de-retroflection and glide deletion, while the students in the electronic and car mechanic group have a higher degree of these TM features. A higher degree of glide deletion signals a local orientation and is a resource for performing masculinity, while those students with higher professional aspirations show a higher degree of conforming to the features of Standard Mandarin, which include the retroflexed [ʂ] and the presence of the glide. When asked to reflect on their linguistic choices, some students were explicit that their choice of using the TM features were in direct challenge to the idea that TM was unrefined and insisted that speaking TM was the best variety to choose when establishing friendship and intimacy. The main idea here is that students actively use these features to challenge dominant ideologies and the rigid institutional structures that dictate how the school treats them and what it expects of their futures (Baran 2014).

It may strike some readers that much ideological weight is being said to hang from the slender threads of heavy-r speech, full tones, de-retroflection, and a vowel cluster. This is, however, the point of much of current variationism, namely that speakers create, detect, and act upon the speech variables (in these two cases, phonetic) available to them. To take an example of a phonetic variable very close to home for the authors of this book, namely the American college campus, for some years now the mid round back vowel [o] has had a slightly fronted variant, resembling a French or German [œ], especially before a nasal, making *phone* [fon] into [fœn]. The variant is found in the speech of young women, and one can hear it at Duke University. It is correlated with higher education and then, likely, socioeconomic class.

A recent study of the speech of sorority girls at neighboring University of North Carolina-Chapel Hill showed a higher presence of this fronted vowel when the girls were talking among themselves, which is not surprising. What is of interest, however, is that the vowel showed up in individual interviews more often when informants were speaking of sorority matters, suggesting that the vowel is indexing a sense of identity. At this point, unlike the feature *juǎnshé* 'curled tongue' in TM speakers' consciousness, the fronted round vowel variants in American English seem to fall below the threshold of awareness and are unnamed by those who use it. Only linguists interested in such matters have taken note of it.

Chapter 9: Juba Arabic Pidgin, Nubi, and Other African Creoles

Postcolonial consequences in Africa have not always necessarily been violent. However, they have always been *linguistic*. After the seventh century, the Arabs spread Islam to this part of the world. Beginning in the sixteenth century, European colonizers came to the continent. In this section, we look more closely at the processes of pidginization and creolization, first in terms of Arabic and next in terms of English.

An Arabic-based pidgin and creole

In the Sudan, diverse language groups in various socioeconomic and political forms – traders and merchants, nomads, herders, refugees, colonialists, militiamen – have been on the move for millennia. At the end of the nineteenth century and since the Egyptian military campaigns, a pidginized variety of Arabic has been spoken in what is now South Sudan. It likely arose in the military camps (Versteegh 1984:117), and it is variably known as Mongallese, Bimbashi Arabic, or Juba Arabic, this last in reference to the linguistically diverse city of Juba, also located in South Sudan, where it was spoken. Pidgin Juba Arabic eventually became the creolized variety known as (Ki-)Nubi.

In Sudan, the prestige variety of Arabic is based on the speech of Khartoum, the capital. Patterns of movement bringing speakers of Khartoum Arabic into contact with Juba Arabic speakers in the South likely resulted in two related developments. First, as is common with creole languages, speakers of Juba Arabic could adjust their speech along what linguists refer to as the creole continuum, which encompasses the range of varieties between the most creole form, the basilect, and the form closest to the standard form, the acrolect. An exchange in a Juba market may occur in a basilectal form, while a person from Juba speaking with someone who lives in Khartoum may speak with an acrolectal form. Second, as more and more speakers of Juba Arabic spent time on the acrolectal side of the continuum in Khartoum, the next generations of Pidgin Juba speakers made it a native language, Nubi, which over time seems to be decreolizing, that is, losing its creole features and developing features associated with standardized national varieties.

Nubi is the best known of the Arabic creoles. In terms of phonological features alone, it is almost unrecognizable as a variety of Arabic:[8]

- There has been a loss of distinction between the emphatic and nonemphatic consonants, as well as the merger or disappearance of most velars and pharygeals;[9] there has also occurred the loss of final consonants (somewhat like the loss of final consonants in French) of the type: *bayt* 'house' > *bée* and *ṣandūq* 'box' > *sondú*.
- The definite article *al-* has been reinterpreted as part of the (indefinite) word, and thus: *al-'aẓm* 'the bone' > *láádum* 'bone'; *al-fíl* 'the elephant' > *lifíli*, 'elephant'; *an-nās* 'the people' > *áánas* 'people'; the reinterpretation of morpheme boundaries is common in pidginized and creolized varieties, and even in noncreolized varieties such as Spanish, which borrowed the definite article *al-* from Arabic as part of the indefinite word, as in *alfombra* 'pillow,' *almacen* 'store,' *almuerzo* 'lunch,' *arroz* 'rice,' etc.
- Nubi has developed a pluralizer for collective nouns, from the Classical *nās* 'people,' as in *nas-babá* 'the group of father, fathers as a whole' and *nas-yalá* 'the group of children, children as a whole.'
- The comparative may be expressed by means of a form of the Classical *min*, such as *rági dé kebír **min** íta* (man that old **than** you) 'that man is older than you,' or *kél dé kebír **fút(u)** búra* (dog that big **pass** cat) 'a dog is bigger than a cat,' where the de-verbal particle *fútu* 'to pass' is used for comparative purposes; again, such a construction is common in the world's creoles – for instance, Kreyòl Ayisyen, discussed in the final note of Chapter 8, has the construction *li lèd **pase** u* (she ugly **pass** you) 'she is uglier than you.'
- The probable ancestors of Juba Arabic and then Nubi are likely some form of a Sudanese or Egyptian colloquial, which has aspectual prefixes attached to beginnings of verb forms. These were mostly lost when the pidgin came into being and had to be rebuilt, again as preverbal markers. For instance, in Juba Arabic, the marker *bə* is found to indicate present/future: *ána bə rówa fi súg* 'I will go to the market.' What is interesting to consider are the ways that Nubi has now expanded what was a rather simple, perhaps four-way tense/aspect distinction into 10 or more possibilities, which include, among others, nonpunctual, future progressive, past progressive, and counterfactual.

Here, we mull over some of the points made at the end of Chapter 10 and note that complexity tends to arise over time in highly unstable, dynamic systems such as language, and as is the case from the development of Juba Pidgin into Nubi. An analogy can be made to card games. If a group of beginners takes up a new game with one another, they are likely not only to become more skillful at that game but also to elaborate it in certain ways and/or to create new, more complicated games. They do not necessarily have to, of course. Some of us still get pleasure out of playing Go Fish.

English-based pidgins and creoles

The dual realities of Africa's inherent multilingualism and its history of colonialism mean that a large number of the world's creole languages are located on this continent. As a result of European colonialism, English-based creoles are present in Sierra Leone (Krio), Liberia (Kreyol) and Nigeria (Pidgin); Portuguese-based creoles are found in Cape Verde (Cape Verdean Creole) and Guinea-Bissau (Guinea-Bissau Creole); and a French-based creole exists in Seychelles (Seychellois Creole). Throughout West Africa can be found West African Pidgin English (WAPE), which is a dialect chain made up of both pidgins and now creoles. WAPE has been around long enough for some features to have become stabilized.

The Nigerian variety, for instance, has several well-developed structural features. First, it has an intensifier particle, a low-tone *o*, used thus:

mek una kom   o
'help'   'please'

It also has the particle *na*, which has developed three uses, first as a rhematizer:

na   di kasava   wi plant
'it was' 'the cassava' [that] 'we planted/were planting'

second as a focus marker:

i bi   na grup   we pipul dzoin
'it is' 'a group' [that] 'people joined'

and third as a copula (be):

mi papa   na   fara
'my father' 'is' [a] 'farmer'
mi family   na   katolik
'my family' 'is' 'Catholic.'

Finally, it has postpositional *dem* as a plural marker:

di   pikin-dem
'the' 'children'
dis   woman-dem
'these' 'women.'

Like all pidgins and creoles, Nigerian Pidgin builds vocabulary through reduplication (doubling of syllables), which is necessary because pidgins tend to reduce consonant clusters. Thus, *was* is 'wash,' while *waswas* is 'wasp,' and *san* is 'sun,' while *sansan* is 'sand.' Creoles were once stigmatized for the liberal use of reduplication for vocabulary enhancement and grammatical structures, because it was deemed so-called baby talk.

While it is true that baby talk is made up of reduplication forms such as *mama, papa, wawa,* and so forth, it is also the case that the process is found in languages around the world for various purposes:

- In English, it is used for intensification in phrases such as 'that's a big big dog' and 'he's a boy boy.'
- In French, it has an 'as such' meaning: *ce n'est pas mon métier métier* 'it isn't my job/profession as such, it isn't really my job/profession.'
- PIE leveraged reduplication to make some past tenses, whose remnants can be found in the Latin forms *do-dedi-datus* 'I give' 'I gave' and 'given.'
- In Yélîdnye, an Indo-Pacific language spoken in Papua New Guinea, *kpêdekpêde* 'black' reduplicates a nominal root denoting a tree species, *kpaapíkpaapî* 'white' reduplicates the nominal root denoting a pure white cockatoo, and *mtyemtye* 'red' reduplicates a nominal root denoting a startling crimson parrot; in Walpiri, an Australian language, *walyawalya* from *walya* 'earth' denotes deep browns, reddish browns, lighter (yellowish) browns and oranges, yellowish salmons, pinkish purples, and other light purples, that is, just about the range of colors the earth takes on in the central Australian desert; in addition, Kuku-Yalanji, another Australian language, has the color term *ngala-ngala* from *ngala* 'blood,' denoting a red that does not include yellow. All of these color terms could be thought of as instances of the 'as such' example from French.

Final Note: Language Change in Progress

In Chapter 3, we introduced the work of nineteenth-century philologists who believed that language change could be studied only after the dust had settled, so to speak, when the results of any change could be captured by a rule of the type: PIE *$*p$* becomes *f* in Germanic. The study of language change was thus focused on dead languages, ones that had left their traces in recorded history and that served the purposes of reconstructing prehistory. Here at the end of Chapter 11, we look at the work of sociolinguist William Labov who, beginning in the 1960s, challenged the conventional philological wisdom by turning his attention to living language. Armed now with new ways to record and analyze language by means of tape recorders and voice imaging technology, Labov took the study of language change out of the library and into the world. He made it possible to study language change *in progress.*

Labov determined that the study of language change also needed to be undertaken in the social context. As we have shown in various places throughout this book, linguistic structure is always bound to social structure. Now, we add the piece that two (or more) forms of the 'same word' or 'same construction' count as linguistic variables, and these variables can and do vary by social structure. Linguists who study the relationship between social and linguistic variables are known as variationists. In his landmark variationist study, *The Social Stratification of (r) in New York City Department Stores* (Labov 1966), Labov was interested in the r-variable, because the speech of New Yorkers has traditionally alternated between being r-full, where the [r] is pronounced, and r-less, where it sounds more like a vowel. He asked salespeople in three different stores – Saks, Macy's, and S. Klein – a question for which the response would necessarily be *fourth floor*, thus eliciting the r-variable. He found that the presence or absence of [r] was stratified, based on the social position of the store in which the question was asked. Employees at the store with the highest-status clientele, namely Saks, exhibited the (more prestigious) r-full pronunciation in *fourth floor* most often, while employees at the store with the lowest status clientele, S. Klein, exhibited the (less prestigious) r-less pronunciations most often.[10] Labov showed that the presence or absence of [r] varied with the socioeconomic class of the speaking context.

Now, 50 years later, it can be shown that the r-less variant is fading. The question then becomes: Why? The shift toward r-fullness in the speech of more New Yorkers today may be due to influxes of people coming to the city speaking r-full varieties of English. Or it may be due to the fact that the New York City r-less variant has become further stigmatized through associations with working-class speech and identity. The point is: speakers – consciously, semiconsciously, or unconsciously – either play up or play down their use of particular variables for social effect and in certain cases that has an important role in language change in progress.

Labov – and many sociolinguists working with him – has spent many years studying a chain shift in progress involving the six vowels in *bat, bit, bet, but, bought*, and *bot* (as in 'robot') that has been called "the Northern Cities Shift." The shifting vowels are concentrated around cities around the Great Lakes such as Syracuse, Rochester, Buffalo, Cleveland, Detroit, Chicago, Milwaukee, and Green Bay. Evidence of the shift can be found as far east as Rhode Island and even, in the case of some vowels, as far south as Indianapolis and St. Louis. Examples of the shift can be heard in the way speakers in the northern cities pronounce the word *block*, which sounds like the way people in other parts of the country pronounce *black*. Furthermore, the word *buses* now sounds like *bosses*, while *desk* now sounds like *dusk*. When one vowel changes, it can trigger a **chain shift**, so that all other vowels must now also jockey for position and move into new spaces.[11]

The fact that a chain shift is afoot is not in doubt. How or why it is happening is not as clear. Labov speculates that the change may have started in the early nineteenth century when workers speaking different varieties of English were brought together to build the Erie Canal. Rapid linguistic change is an expected result of such a sudden mixing. Given that these six particular vowels in English have been stable for a thousand years, this relatively rapid vowel shift counts as one of the many ways that language is always catching up to conditions. So does the gradual loss of the r-less variant in New York City speech. Language change is at all times a contingent process, where historical events and speakers' interpretations of the linguistic results are ever at work.

Language Profile: монгол хзл [Mongolian (Mongolic)]

Functional overview

Mongolian is spoken by about 2,800,000 people who live primarily within Mongolia, with a smaller portion of speakers inhabiting parts of northern China. In Mongolia, about half the population live in the capital city Ulaan Baatar (улаан баатар means 'red hero'). The other half live in the geographically diverse countryside consisting of mountains, steppe, and the Gobi Desert, all of which span an area almost the size of Alaska; and now you know at least one word in Mongolian: гоби (*gobi*), which means 'desert.' The most widespread ethnicity is the халх (khalkha), which name also applies to the official language known as Khalkha Mongolian.

Several Monogolic languages are spoken on Russia's southern border with Mongolia. In Inner Mongolia, now an autonomous region in China, the Mongolic variety Daur is spoken. Within Mongolia, there are also other groups of Mongolic speakers. One can be found around Lake Khuvsgul in the north, namely the Buriat who speak a language of the same name. Around that lake can also be found the Dukha (also known as Tsaatan) who are reindeer herders who live in teepees and whose lives revolve around reindeer and their migration routes. Their language is Turkic. Mongolians are traditionally nomadic. They are known for living in portable yurts, which can be erected by a couple of people in a couple of hours, depending on the weather. Incidentally, the word 'yurt' is Russian; the Mongolian word is гэр (*ger*) 'house.'[12] Mongolians are also known for the art of throat singing, хөөмий (*khөөmii*).

The most famous Mongolian is Genghis Khan [1162?–1227; чингис (*chingghis*) 'great' and хаан (*khaan*) 'king']. His unification of various nomadic tribes and the subsequent spread of the Mongol Empire in all directions led Mongolian to become a Eurasian steppe spread zone language for several centuries. Genghis Khan also adopted the Uyghur alphabet for Mongolian from a Turkic language spoken in what is now western China. In recent years, this old script, known as монгол бичиг (*mongol bichik*) 'Mongolian script,' has become a symbol of national unity and pride. It is seen today on buildings, on the currency, and in newspapers, and it is taught to children throughout their school years.

Mongolia was a socialist state from 1921 to 1990. In 1942, the Mongolian language was transliterated into Cyrillic. Two new letters were added that made it different from the Cyrillic used to write Russian, namely ө [œ] and ʏ [u]. These two vowels are necessary, because they are phonemic in Mongolian and essential to the process of vowel harmony.

Prominent structural characteristics

Vowel harmony On the first day of Mongolian language class, your teacher will likely give you the following commands:

уншаарай (*onshaarai*)	'read please'
хэлээрэй (*kheleerei*)	'say please'
сонсоорой (*sonsooroi*)	'listen please'
өгөөрэй (*өgөөrөi*)	'give please.'

Note that the bold endings, which make the polite form of the commands, have four different vocalic possibilities. The vowel of the ending is determined by the vowel in the root word. The basic division is between what, in Mongolian, are called female vowels, namely и [i], ө [œ], э [e], ү [u], and male vowels, namely у [o], o [ɔ], a [a], and я [ya]. In phonetic terms, this distinction amounts to one, more or less, between front vowels and back vowels. Any root with a male (back) vowel will trigger the ending -аарай, as in уншаарай, гараарай (*garaarai*) 'go out please.' Any root with a female (front) vowel will trigger the ending – ээрэй, as in хэлээрэй, бичээрэй (*bicheerei*) 'write please.' Note further that back round midvowel o [ɔ] and front round midvowel ө [œ] trigger full identity of the vowels: сонсоорой versus өгөөрөй. We saw an example of full identity in the opening story of Chapter 11: морилоорой (moril**ooro**i) 'come by horse please' = 'welcome.'

When vowels are being matched for frontness or backness and/or roundedness, this phenomenon is called *vowel harmony*. In other words, front vowels harmonize with front vowels, back vowels with back, while the 'birds' of the rounded midvowel 'feather' harmonize together. This phonetic feature gives Mongolian a soothing sound, especially in such phrases as сайхан амраарай (*saikhan amrarai*) 'pleasant rest please,' which is said at the end of the day or workweek, or уучлаарай (*oochlaarai*) 'excuse please,' which often comes up.

Many languages, such as Finnish and Hungarian, exhibit vowel harmony, as well as languages from the Turkic and Tungusic families. In Mongolian, vowel harmony is completely consistent. If the answer to the question 'Where are you from?' is France, the answer is: Францаас (Frantsaas). If it is Mongolia, the answer is: Монголоос (Mongoloos). If a morphological ending to make something into a noun is formed from a verb with a female vowel such as сэтгэх (*setgekh*) 'to find something new,' we have the word сэтгүүл (set**guul**) 'magazine.' If a male vowel is involved, such as the verb сурах (*sorakh*) 'to study,' the noun comes out as сургууль (*sorgool*) 'school.' Note that the -Vx ending to make the infinitive follows the principles of vowel harmony: сэтгэх (*setgekh*) versus сурах (*sorakh*).

Another audible feature of Mongolian is its wide array of consonant clusters. For instance, the cluster -mtl- is found in the word амтлагч (*amtlagch* pronounced amtlakhch) 'spice' and -vts- found in word хувцас (khovtsas) 'clothing.' The female name Eternal Flower Мөнхцэцэг (*mønkh* 'eternal' *tsetsek* 'flower') has the medial consonant cluster -n-kh-ts-. The clusters start piling up when verbs are conjugated and nouns declined.

The case system   Mongolian is a regular SOV language with agglutinative morphology that is suffixing. It has no noun classes, and adjectives precede nouns. There is a singular/plural distinction: for instance, зочин (*zochin*) 'guest' and зочид (*zochid*) 'guests' and хүү (*khyy*) 'son' and хүүдүүд (*khyydyyd*) 'children.' The singular/plural distinction, however, is not relevant when one counts: нэг ном (*nik nom*) 'one book,' хоёр ном (*khoer nom*) 'two books,' etc., where ном (*nom*) 'book' does not change. The definite/indefinite distinction appears only when a noun is made particular.

There are eight cases. First, the nominative in Mongolian is the same as in Indo-European languages and indicates the subject of a sentence. At all times, the case endings preserve vowel harmony. Of interest in the case system are the following points.

Second, the genitive shows possession, just as does English *-'s*, as in *Jane's coat*, in Mongolian: Жаргалын пальто (*Jargaliin palto* 'Jarwal's coat'). If English did not have so many borrowed words, a place where you would go to get books and to get medicine could very well be called *books' place* and *medicine's place*, respectively. This is exactly the case in Mongolian: номын сан (*nomiin san* 'book-gen. place') 'library' and эмийн сан (*emiin san* 'medicine-gen. place') 'pharmacy.'[13]

Third, the dative, generally case ending -д/-т (*-d/-t*), is used inflectionally to indicate the indirect object or 'place where.' The phrase *to go home* is: гэртээ харих (*gertee kharikh*), where the -т- on *ger* 'house' is the dative. Харих (*kharikh*) means 'to go,' and the -ээ# (*-ee*) is reflexive: 'one is going to one's own house.' The -t# on the Russian word 'yurt' may be the Mongolian dative ending, since the phrase 'to go home' is a commonly heard one.

Fourth, the accusative marks the direct object, but only when the object is specific. In the phrase *I am reading the/a book*, the direct object ном (*nom*) 'book' has no ending. However, if the phrase is *I am reading this book*, ном takes the accusative ending -ийг (*-iik*): тэр номыг (*ter nomiik*) 'this book.' When put into the accusative case, the consonant cluster in the girl's name Eternal Flower Мөнхцэцэгийг (*Mönkhtstsgiik*) extends to -n-kh-ts-ts-g- because the two э [i] vowels are elided to put the phonetic stress on the ending -ийг (*-iik*). The name is still spelled with the two э [i] vowels. Note: when the voiced velar stop г [g] comes at the end of the word, it is pronounced as a voiceless velar stop [k]. This phonetic phenomenon is called **final** devoicing, sometimes known by the German term *Auslautsverhärtung*, since it is characteristic of German phonology.

Fifth, the commitative ending -тай (*-tai*) has the function of the English preposition 'with.' If I am going *with Jargal*, it is Жаргалтай (*Jargaltai*). If I'm going *with Dorj*, it is Доржтой (*Dorjtoi*).

Sixth, the ablative ending - aac (*-aas*) can mean movement away from a place, such as coming from the capital, Ulaan Baatar: Улаан Баатраас (*Olaan Baatraas*). Or it can govern the case of certain verbs. 'To ask' асуух (*asookh*) your багш (*bagk* pronounced *bakhsh*) 'teacher' a question is: багшаасаа асуух (*bakhshaasaa asookh*) 'to ask (from) (your) teacher (a question).'

Seventh, the instrumental -aap (*-aar*) is 'by means of.' Simply put, one eats сэрээгээр (*sereegeer*) 'by means of a fork' or савхаар (*savkhaar*) 'by means of chopsticks.'

Eighth, the independent directive morpheme руу (*roo*) is the opposite of the ablative and means movement toward a place. I can go *toward Jargal*: Жаргал руу (*Jargal roo*) or *toward Beijing*: Бээжин рүү (*Beijing ruu*).

Shared states of information   When an English-speaker hears a piece of new information or receives information contrary to expectation, he might say, "Oh." This seemingly throwaway syllable does useful communicative work. It gives the utterer a moment to register whatever the news is. It lets his/her speaking partner know that the information he/she has imparted is, in fact, news. Different languages have different ways of orienting their users toward their own states of information and those of their interlocutors.

In Mongolian, if a person has already asked a question and received an answer, and now needs to be reminded of that answer, the person asks the question again using the sentence ender билээ (*bilee*). In English, one might ask: "What's your name, again?" or "*What's* your name?" to emphasize that one realizes one has already asked. However, English does not have a necessary grammatical marker for such a situation.

The different ways the verb байх (*baikh*) 'to be' is used show how speakers orient themselves and others to the conditions of a particular situation. Let's say I need John for some reason, but he is not in my visual field. To ask someone where he is, I say:

Жон   хаана   байна вэ?
John   khaan   wen
John   where   is
Where is John?

If John is not in my visual field, and I want to know about his location with no specific need of him, I ask:

Жон   хаана   байгаа вэ?
John   khaan   baigaa
John   where   is
Where is John?

If I want to ask about John's location, say, where he is living, I ask:

Жон   хаана   байдаг вэ?
John   khaan   baidgoo
John   where   is
Where is John (on a nonmoving basis)?

In addition, there is a tense called the *unknown past*. It has the endings жээ (*jee*) and чээ (*chee*), and indicates that the person using the form is just learning of an event. This past tense is often used in the media, because reporters and broadcasters are often just learning about the events they are reporting on. The tense can also be used for actions that happened other than planned. But mostly it expresses an action that happened in the past but the speaker is just now learning of it.

If you go to bed at night and it snows, when you wake up and look out the window, you are likely to say:

цас   оржээ
tsas   orjee
now   opened
It snowed (and I just found out).

You could also say: цас орсон байна (*tsas orcon ben*) 'it snowed (and I just found out).'

Ethnosyntax To extend what was said in the opening to this chapter and the importance of horses in the Mongolian language and culture, it is only natural that horses are woven into common phrases. There is the expected:

бэлгийн	морины	шүдийг	үздэггүй
belgiin	*morini*	*shudiik*	*uzdeg-gui*
gen	gen	acc	
gift	horse's	teeth	look-not

Don't look a gift horse in the mouth.

There is also:

уур	хүнийг	зовооно,	уул	морийг	зовооно
oor	*khuniik*	*zovoono,*	*ool*	*moriik*	*zovoono*
	acc			acc	
steam/anger	person	pains,	mountain	horse	pains

Anger pains the person, like a mountain pains a horse = Don't get angry

as well as:

хүн	болох	багаасаа,	хүлэг	болох	унаганаасаа
khun	*bolokh*	*bagaasaa,*	*khulek*	*bolokh*	*ohaganaasaa*
		abl			abl
person	becomes	childhood-from,	steed	becomes	foal-from

A person becomes from childhood, as a (good) horse comes from a foal = Well begun is half-done.

In addition, the orientations established during the time when nomadic culture was the norm have remained. The door of a *ger* always faces south. So, when one gets up in the morning and steps outside, the Sun in the east is to one's left. Therefore, the word зүүн (*zuun*) means both 'east' and 'left.' Similarly, the word баруун (*baroon*) means both 'west' and 'right.' Even in the city, Mongolians give directions based on a southward-facing orientation. Furthermore, there is a modern word for 'door,' namely хаалга (*khaalga* pronounced *khaalak*). However, if you arrange to meet someone outside the door of, say, a restaurant, you use the expression with the word for the door to a *ger*, үүд (*uud*): үүдэнд уулзья (*uudend oolzii*) 'door-at let's meet.' The -энд (-end) is the dative case.

Salient cultural characteristic: borrowing and naming

Mongolian is not a borrowing language, like English. Although Mongolia has been surrounded by powerful countries and cultures for thousands of years, it has taken relatively little from them, linguistically speaking. To the east, south, and west is China. From the end of the seventeenth century until 1921, Mongolia was ruled by the Manchu-led Qing Dynasty. In Mongolian, there are the borrowed Chinese words гуанз (gwanz) 'cafeteria,' цонх (tsonkh) 'window/glass,' and the nearly universally borrowed word цай (tsai) 'tea,' along with other words here and there. During the twentieth century, Mongolia had a mostly cordial relationship with Russia, her neighbor to the north, and borrowings from that language include, among others: билет (*bilyet*) 'ticket,' кино (*kino*) 'cinema,' and ломбард (*lombard*) 'pawn shop.' The borrowings include Western-style articles of clothing or objects, such as a VCR (приставка *pristavka*), introduced into Mongolia by the Russians.

On the whole, however, semantic fields in Mongolian are more likely to be built up out of its own resources. For instance, the morpheme эм (*em*) produces a wide array of related words: эм (*em*) 'medicine, drug,' эмч (*emch*) 'doctor,' эмийн сан (*emiin san*) 'pharmacy,' эмийн санч (*emiin sanch*) 'pharmacist,' эмнэлэг (*emnelek* pronounced *emlek*) 'hospital,' and so forth.

In one area, however, Mongolians have borrowed, and that is naming practices through the influence of Tibetan Buddhism, which began in the seventeenth century. As an example of reverse influence, the name for the Tibetan spiritual leader, the Dalai Lama, comes from Mongolian Далайлам (*Dalailam*) 'ocean/universal monk.' In Mongolian, the man's name Дорж (*Dorj*) is from Tibetan and means 'bold.' It corresponds directly to the Mongolian male name with the same meaning Бат (*Bat*). The names Даваа (*Davaa*), Мягмар (Myagmar), Лхагва (Lkhagva), Пүрэв (Purev), Баасан (*Baasan*), Бямба (Byamba), and Ням (Nyam) are also from Tibetan and mean 'Monday,' 'Tuesday,' 'Wednesday,' 'Thursday,' 'Friday,' 'Saturday,' and 'Sunday,' respectively. The name means the person born on that day and can be combined with both men's and women's names to form a compound name. Mongolians often do not name their children themselves, but rather leave that important activity to the monks.

Traditionally, Mongolians use their clan name in front of their first name. A Mongolian's clan name serves the role of preventing intermarriage. Because the Mongolian population is fairly small, marriage between people within the same clan name is prohibited. A person's clan or father's name is rarely used in spoken language. To address one's teacher, for instance, one uses her first name and says: Алта багш аа! (*Alta bakhsh aa*) 'Hello there, Teacher Alta.'

Exercises

Exercise 1 – history of English

The grammar, lexicon, and phonology of Modern English have been shaped by many nonlinguistic conditions, including those described in the first part of this chapter. Make a timeline of the major events in the history of the English language that have affected the development of the grammar. Begin in 449 CE and continue to the present, drawing an arrowhead at the end of your line rather than a point in order to imply that the interweaving of nonlinguistic events and English grammar will continue into the future. Where possible, annotate your timeline with the linguistic effects of the historical moments you track.

Exercise 2 – language variation in China

Read the Zhang (2005) study mentioned in the section on Chinese in this chapter. First, describe the methods – how did she collect her data? How were the data analyzed? Then, summarize the findings, paying attention to the political and economic conditions that give rise to the types of identities Zhang studied. Be sure your essay addresses the question about how language variation is used to create or contest identity formations.

Exercise 3 – creole languages

All language varieties emerge from the conditions in which they are embedded – that has been the major point of this book. In this regard, creole languages are precisely no different from the so-called noncreole languages. Nevertheless, because creole languages are all born of language contact situations in which two speech communities differ in social power, creole languages do tend to develop in similar ways. In this chapter, we have discussed some creole languages spoken in Africa. For this exercise, turn your attention to the Americas (North, Central, and South America, as well as the Caribbean). Make a list of at least five creole languages spoken there, providing the location, parent languages, and number of speakers for each. For one of them, write an abbreviated language profile, along the lines of the profiles presented at the end of the chapters in this book. The bulk of your profile should be on the structural features of the language you are profiling.

Exercise 4 – chain shifts in American English

In our final note, we mention one vocalic chain shift currently taking place in the English in the United States: the Northern Cities Shift. There is also a Southern Cities Shift afoot. For this exercise, you will make a sketch of that shift, as well as a second shift taking place in the United States, called "the Southern Shift." On two separate sheets of paper, sketch the vowels of American English according to tongue position (front, mid, back and high, central, low). On the first, use arrows to indicate the direction of the movement of the vowels involved in the Northern Cities Shift. Add words to indicate pronunciation. On the second, use arrows to indicate the direction of the movement of the vowels involved in the Southern Cities Shift. What do you notice about the direction of the vowels in questions? Based on what you have read and drawn, are pronunciations in the United States South and Northern Cities becoming more or less similar?

Discussion Questions

1 As we have illustrated in this chapter, what becomes historical language change only follows from language variation at a particular point in time. For many people, language change in the long historical view is okay, even something to romanticize, but the language variation that leads to it is rarely considered in positive terms. That is, many people have no problem accepting the language differences between

Beowulf, Chaucer, and Shakespeare, but shudder at the language variation that will lead to tomorrow's language change. Why do you suppose this is the case?

2   What kinds of spelling practices do you have in different electronic media, texting, email, social media, etc.? Do your spelling conventions differ across platforms? Do they change depending on your interlocutor? What other factors influence your spelling decisions?

3   If you send text messages in languages other than English, what kinds of spelling conventions do you use? What kinds of texting abbreviations are common in the languages in which you text?

4   Do you think technology will be successful in revitalizing Hawaiian? What are the limitations, and what are the possibilities?

5   This chapter mentions several studies that indicate that speakers actively use the social meanings associated with language variation to take particular stances in discourse or to create particular identities. Are you aware of this process at work in your own life, or going on around you? What are the social meanings of particular pronunciations in the language varieties spoken in your speech community?

Notes

1   Uyghur is a Turkic language, and its alphabet is based on the Arabic alphabet.

2   Why the syllable *-gi* was chosen to lengthen the ending is another story. One explanation is that epenthetic [g] is always used in Mongolian to break up a string of four vowels that occur when a case ending beginning with a long vowel is added to a noun ending with a long vowel. The [g] is the go-to 'empty' consonant of choice in Mongolian. Many languages have such a consonant to break things up, for example, the epenthetic [t] in French as in *aime-t-il?*

3   Personal communication with teachers at Prime Bridge School, Ulaan Baatar, Mongolia.

4   As Cowell points out, the only other Native American population to have a history of literacy are the Cherokee.

5   Variationism is defined and described in the Final Note to this chapter. It is most closely associated with the sociolinguist who pioneered the approach, William Labov.

6   A retroflex consonant is articulated by curling the tip of the tongue back behind the teeth to touch the palate.

7   KMT = Kuomintang, literally 'Chinese National People's Party.'

8   All examples are from Versteegh (1984:120–124).

9   See Language Profile: Arabic in Chapter 5, for an explanation of these terms.

10 Variable features vary both throughout groups and in the speech of an individual. That is, if a feature is considered variable (*-ing* versus *-in'* in English), no one speaker will use either one or the other of the forms 100% of the time. Variationists work with statistics and the social meanings of the frequencies.

11 Meanwhile, a second chain shift is under way in the South, in which the vowels are going in the opposite direction, such that *bed* sounds like *bay-uhd*, and *kid* sounds like *kee-uhd*.

12 The Mongolian word for 'family' is гэр бүл (*ger bʏl*), that is, 'house+all members.'

13 Whether the -ii- of the ending -iin is spelled -ий- or -ы- depends on the root vowel, with front vowels taking -ий- and back vowels taking -ы-. The pronunciation is the same.

References

Baran, Dominika (2014) Linguistic practice and identity work: Variation in Taiwan Mandarin at a Taipei County high school. *Journal of Sociolinguistics* 18: 32–59.

Cowell, Andrew (2012) The Hawaiian model of language revitalization: Problems of extension to mainland America. *International Journal of the Sociology of Language* 218: 167–193.

Ghonim, Wael (2012) *Revolution 2.0: The Power of the People is Greater than the People in Power.* Boston: Houghton Mifflin Harcourt.

Labov, William (1966) *The Social Stratification of (r) in New York City Department Stores.* Washington, DC: Center for Applied Linguistics.

Matthews, Stephen (1989) French in flux: Typological shift and sociolinguistic variation. In Thomas J. Walsh (ed.), *Synchronic and Diachronic Approaches to Linguistic Variation and Change. Georgetown University Roundtable '88.* Washington, DC: Georgetown University Press, 188–203.

Matthews, Stephen (2007) Cantonese grammar in aerial perspective. In Alexandra Y. Aikhenvald and R.M.W. Dixon (eds.), *Grammars in Contact: A Cross-Linguistic Typology.* Oxford: Oxford University Press, 220–236.

Matthews, Stephen (2010) Language contact and Chinese. In Raymond Hickey (ed.), *Handbook of Language Contact.* Malden, MA: Wiley Blackwell, 757–769.

Palfreyman, David and Muhamed al Khalil (2003) A funky message for teenzz to use: Representing Gulf Arabic in instant messaging. *Computer-Mediated Communication* 9: 1.

Solntseva, V. Nina and M. Vadim Solntsev (1995) Genitive case in Altaic languages and in some languages of Southeast Asia. *Mon-Khmer Studies* 25: 255–272.

Versteegh, Kees (1984) *Pidginization and Creolization: The Case of Arabic.* Amsterdam: John Benjamins.

Zhang, Qing (2005) A Chinese yuppie in Beijing: Phonological variation and the construction of a new professional identity. *Language in Society* 34: 431–466.

Further Reading

Bassiouney, Reem (2009) *Arabic Sociolinguistics.* Edinburgh: Edinburgh University Press.

Gruntov, Ilya (1998) *The Accusative Case in Mongolian Languages: A Diachronic Approach.* Moscow: Russian State University for Humanities.

Hassleblatt, Cornelius (2011) Language at the literal and figurative levels. In Cornelius Hassleblatt, Peter Houtzagers, and Remco Van Pareren (eds.), *Language Contact in Times of Globalization.* Amsterdam: Rodopi, 61–76.

Labov, William (1972) *Sociolinguistic Patterns.* Philadelphia: University of Pennsylvania Press.

Miller, Catherine (2007) Do they speak the same language? Language use in Juba local courts. In Everhard Ditters and Harald Motzki (eds.), *Approaches to Arabic Linguistics.* Leiden, Netherlands: Koninklijke Brill.

Thomas J. Walsh (1988) *Synchronic and Diachronic Approaches to Linguistic Variation and Change.* Washington, DC: Georgetown University Press, 188–203.

Tosco, Mauro (1995) A pidgin verbal system: The case of Juba Arabic. *Anthropological Linguistics* 37: 423–454.

Weinreich, Uriel (1953) *Languages in Contact: Findings and Problems.* New York: Publications of the Linguistic Circle of New York.

12

The Imagined Future

Globalization and the Fate of Endangered Languages

Gold in the Mayan Highlands

For thousands of years, the K'iche' people have revered the golden kernels belonging to a plant known as *maize*. Their sacred stories tell of the first humans who were fashioned from the bread made from these kernels and who were given the gift of language. More recently, a new and very different kind of gold is present in the highlands. It is the multinational Goldcorp, Inc., which is based in Canada and operates mines throughout North and South America. Goldcorp is publically traded on the New York Stock Exchange. It has been given a license by the Guatemalan government to mine gold, silver, nickel, and other minerals from 23 square kilometers of K'iche' land.

A 20-hour drive northwest from Guatemala City through the Mayan regions of the lush Western Highlands leads to a town named Sipacapa. Most of the drive is on unpaved roads, winding through tropical vegetation – bananas, coffee, and cacao at lower altitudes, and the golden maize at the foggy higher altitudes. For the Sipacapa – who speak the K'iche' language called Sipakapense – the land is sacred, and they are fighting to protect it. Mayan communities in Guatemala have long protested mining on their land. In December, 2013, with the help of local *campesinos*, the Sipacapa set up two blockades on the Pan-American Highway, a vital thoroughfare connecting Guatemala with Mexico and the rest of the Americas. These blockades were specifically to stop Goldcorp, Inc.

At the same time, the Sipacapa fight to save their homeland from exploitation, they also fight to save their language from extinction. The two struggles are not unrelated. Sipakapense, like other K'iche' languages – Achi, Kaqchikel, and Tz'utujil among them – is intimately intertwined with the local ecosystem, with the hills, the dense fog that caps them, and the golden maize from which humankind was given life. Even the name of the language – K'iche' ('many trees' < *k'i* 'many,' *che'* 'tree') – reflects this fact. Like most Mayan languages in Guatemala and Mexico, Sipakapense

Languages in the World: How History, Culture, and Politics Shape Language, First Edition.
Julie Tetel Andresen and Phillip M. Carter.
© 2016 John Wiley & Sons, Inc. Published 2016 by John Wiley & Sons, Inc.

is endangered. Knowing what to do about it, however, is no easier than knowing how to stop a multinational mining corporation with a federal mining license.

In this chapter, we look at the various ways languages around the world are endangered in light of present global economic conditions, and we highlight some of the measures being taken to preserve them.

Beyond the Nation-State: The Globalized New Economy

To answer one of our guiding questions, Why does the current map of the linguistic world look the way it does?, we devoted Chapter 4 to considering the effects of the nation-state in shaping national and language borders. To answer another one of our guiding questions, How did it get to be that way?, we dug down into multiple historical layers: (i) in Chapter 10, the deep-time of the first dispersal of humans around the globe in the last 100,000 years; (ii) in Chapter 7, the near-prehistory expansion of the language stocks as people moved away from their homelands; and (iii) in Chapter 8, the historical colonizations that led to the pre-Columbian extents of most language families.

We now pose a new question: How is the current map of the linguistic world changing? Here, in Chapter 12, we turn our attention to a set of emergent economic and social forces operating beyond the borders of the nation-state, known by the popular cover term *globalization*. Globalization is not disconnected from the state formation and colonialism that preceded it. Indeed, globalization is possible only because of these earlier types of consolidation. It was surely furthered by the collapse of the Soviet Union in 1990, which opened vast areas of the world previously closed to capital markets. The more recent liberalization of economic conditions in China has opened the gates of the last dam stopping the powerful flow of money around the world. And now we have planted both feet firmly back in the dynamics of Part II: The Effects of Power, although we never really left them.

At present, the economic and political forces of globalization appear to be transforming global relations in ways that seem to eclipse the conditions that gave rise to them. In other words, although the world has been globalizing since at least the end of the fifteenth century, there is something new and remarkably different about today's globalization. British sociologist Anthony Giddens, early on in the process, identified globalization to be "the intensification of worldwide social relations which link distant localities in such a way that local happenings are shaped by events occurring many miles away and vice versa" (1990:64). Twenty years later, Belgian sociolinguistic J.M.E. Blommaert reaffirms that globalization is "new in intensity, scope, and scale" (2010:1).

Because globalization is ongoing, and no definitive theoretic perspective on it can yet exist, our speculation on the future of the linguistic map reformed by globalization will be undertaken in terms of the theoretical economic models of the immediate past. Economic theory during the twentieth century was dominated by two influential thinkers: the Englishman John Maynard Keynes in the first half of the century and the American Milton Friedman during the second half. Keynes is credited with influencing national economic policies that moved the West out of the Great Depression, past the economic devastation of World War II, and into a period of economic expansion lasting through the 1970s. Keynesian economics is rooted in the notion of the mixed economy, one fueled predominately by a private sector tempered by the intervention of the State, when necessary. Government policy was necessary, in Keynes's view, because an unregulated private sector could lead to macroeconomic turbulence. Keynes was instrumental in setting up the World Bank, a United Nations institution designed to provide loans to the developing world, and the International Monetary Fund (IMF), which was designed to facilitate a system of international payment among countries after World War II. Keynesian economics held sway in the West until the elections of Margaret Thatcher in the United Kingdom and Ronald Reagan in the United States.

Beginning in the 1980s, government policies turned toward the thinking of the Chicago School of Economics, led by Milton Friedman who articulated a strong view of free markets with little intervention from the State. Friedman's neoliberalism, guided by the principle of the free market, dramatically reshaped the global economic scene. The three pillars of neoliberalism – free trade of goods and services, free circulation of capital, and freedom of investment – required the elimination of trade barriers and the liberalization of restrictions on international investment. Free trade agreements, such as the North American Free Trade Association (1994), and economic and monetary unions, such as the European Union (2000), are noteworthy examples. The result has been the integration of labor markets, the end of truly national economies, and the rise of what sociolinguist Monica Heller (2011) recognizes as the globalized new economy.

As neoliberal policies were enacted in domestic markets, the global market expanded, with several important consequences:

(i) decreased regulation has increased the power of multinational corporations and has resulted in greater mobility of capital, labor, and production sites; off-shoring (moving labor or operations to another country for cost advantages) and outsourcing (contracting a third party, often in another country to do work more cheaply) have become common business terms;

(ii) the role of the State in the economy has diminished; industries that were once public – from the airlines to electricity to telecommunications – have been privatized; and

(iii) as privatization shifted more power to the private sector, corporations have been given greater freedom and have amassed more power and wealth.

This last point is crucial. In 2012, Apple, Inc., maker of the popular iPods, iPads, and computers had a market value of US$460 billion, more than the entire gross domestic product of Sweden. Private corporations hold more sway than ever before and can make decisions more deftly than democratic states ever could. These decisions may well involve issues of language. To give but one example, in 2013 Tokyo-based Bridgestone Corporation, the world's largest maker of tires, announced it had adopted an official language: it is not Japanese, but English.

The globalized new economy has required increased coordination from a central source. The IMF and the World Bank – which began with much smaller aims – have stepped in to assume this role. These two institutions now perform surveillance on national economies and set global economic guidelines. At present, 188 countries are members of the IMF. Increased economic coordination requires a certain amount of linguistic coordination. The official language of the IMF and the World Bank is English, with conferences held with simultaneous translation into Arabic, Chinese, French, Russian, and Spanish. The official languages of the World Trade Organization are English, French, and Spanish.

The effects of globalization are stark and pervasive. They can be seen, first, in the global circulation of cultural forms such as hip hop, which was created in the South Bronx in the 1970s and now flourishes in places like Mongolia and Malaysia. The effects have produced linguistic superdiversity in urban centers around the globe, such as New York, London, and Shanghai. Most importantly for this chapter, they have liberalized national markets, thereby mobilizing the individuals in those markets, with attendant effects on the language(s) they speak.

Money Talks: What Language Does It Speak?

For India's newest state, Telangana, which was once a part of Andhra-Pradesh, the answer is: the Telanganese variety of Telugu, a Dravidian language, spoken there. Since the midtwentieth century, India's states have been created largely along linguistic lines, and so the Telanganans argued that their variety of Telugu was distinct enough to warrant a new state. Whether or not it is, is another story. Nevertheless, in 2013 they got their state, most likely on economic grounds: the city of Hyderabad, an affluent technology hub, is located there. Here is a version of the Golden Rule: those with the gold, rule. Clearly, the Telanganans have benefitted from the globalized new economy and Hyderabad's importance in it.

To India's north lies Nepal, a small landlocked country, with a very different relationship to the global liberalization of national markets. The Nepalese are the majority ethnic group, and they speak Nepali. What sets Nepal apart from its neighbors in South Asia – India, Myanmar, and Bhutan – is that it never fell under European colonial rule. As a result, the monarchy it established when the Nepalese Kingdom was formally declared in 1768 remained in place until 1990, when the country underwent its first democratic revolution. The colonial languages that impacted the rest of Asia – English, French, and Portuguese – therefore never had a significant impact on Nepal, whose closed economy and political system provided an unintended buffer around the Nepali language and the other 100 or so indigenous languages of the Kingdom.

In the 1990s, Nepal underwent a democratic revolution. For the first time, the country opened its doors to foreign investment and implemented economic liberalization policies that reformed the previously closed economy and promoted privatization. Nepal joined the World Bank and the World Trade Organization. Multinational corporations based in both the East and the West poured in almost overnight. These developments in finance, trade, and investment opened the door to the world's emerging international lingua franca of business: English. After centuries of avoiding the encroachment of English taking place all around it, Nepal invited English in when it opened its doors to foreign investment. While colonialism took English to India, China, Malaysia, and Myanmar, the new globalized economy took it to Nepal.

Industries previously blocked or limited from operating in Nepal were introduced and expanded during the 1990s and 2000s. The tourist industry expanded particularly rapidly. Curious tourists the world over flocked to Nepal to witness the untouched beauty of the Himalayas, take a peek at Nepalese culture, and participate in so-called eco-tours. Because virtually no one outside of Nepal speaks Nepali, business catering to international tourists quickly adopted English as the industry language. English is now seen and heard throughout the capital city of Kathmandu, from the Internet cafes where tourists check their email to the restaurants where they eat, the hotels and hostels where they sleep, and the tour shops where they register for mountain hikes. Even in rural Nepal, where local languages other than Nepali are spoken, locals use English to sell souvenirs and traditional wares to tourists. For Nepalese seeking employment in the booming tourist industry, knowledge of English bestows an undeniable economic advantage.

English, Nepali, the local languages, and other international languages that enter the country through business and tourism can now be understood as being in competition with one another in Nepal. The French sociologist Pierre Bourdieu has named this type of competition the **linguistic marketplace**. In his view, different language varieties accrue different market values in accordance with their perceived socio-economic value and the prestige of the social groups who speak them. Linguistic marketplaces are inherently unequal in two ways. First, within a given linguistic market, speakers hold differing amounts of linguistic capital, a type of cultural asset that affords social and economic benefits along the lines of economic capital (money). Just as economic capital provides access to social status and social mobility, so too does linguistic capital. It provides access to work, positions of prestige, and positive social evaluations. Second, not all language varieties are accorded the same value within the market. The language varieties associated with groups in power are positively valued, while those associated with powerless groups are not. Success in a given linguistic marketplace means having access to the power languages. In Nepal, this means that the aspirations of the emerging middle class are tied to English.

Although speakers are clamoring to learn English throughout much of the developing world, the effects of global markets on language are as unpredictable as the markets themselves. In Nepal, we observe several interesting effects of the globalized new economy on the language scene. First, the international labor market has pulled Nepalese citizens from Nepal. As a result, Nepali is now spoken in Nepalese emigrant communities in parts of the world such as the Mideast and Asia. This means that there are fewer young adult speakers of Nepali at home and therefore fewer people to actively transmit the language to children, the next generation of speakers who would otherwise keep the language going.

Second, Nepalese are aware of the threats that the globalized new economy poses to their language and culture, and they perceive the most acute threat to be toward the local languages rather than to Nepali. Therefore, more and more people report positive identification with indigenous ethnicities and the local languages, as opposed to Nepali. Census takers in 1991 found that the number of Nepalese reporting Nepali as their primary language decreased for the first time. The reason for the decrease in reporting owed not to an actual significant decrease in Nepali speakers but rather to an increase in people claiming an indigenous language.

The situation in Nepal forces us to resist facile simplifications about the relationship between the globalized new economy and language. Economic forces beyond the control of the individual invited English into the country, and this invitation will surely have a displacing effect on Nepal's languages. In this sense, we see economic policies now disrupting the local linguistic ecosystem in the ways that colonialism and religious missionaries did in other parts of the world. In fact, some people say globalization is colonialism by another name. At the same time, Nepalese are clamoring to learn English for its attachments to material and symbolic forms of capital. They want to be linked to the rest of the world as much as everybody else does.

When the Language Loop Unravels

We spent the first half of Chapter 2 describing the ways language loops in several directions at once, namely around: (i) cognitive domains, (ii) landscape, (iii) cultural contexts, (iv) itself, and (v) discourses and ideologies. If even one of these loops gets disrupted, the entire fabric of the language can start to unravel. For instance, loss of a landscape or an ecosystem can endanger the speakers and their languages as much as it can other flora and fauna living there. So can a belief system, if a group decides their language is no longer worthy of passing down to the next generation. It can also happen that population movements alter the cultural context in which a language is spoken, and speakers shift from one language to another. In this section, we describe examples of the three types of language loss just described, and they have been labeled (i) sudden death, (ii) radical death, and (iii) gradual language shift in multilingual settings (Campbell & Muntzel 1989).

Sudden death: the Pawala of Tasmania

To the south of Australia, the island of Tasmania was once home to the Palawa people and their language. For nearly 40 millennia, the Palawa people developed mostly in isolation from Aboriginal Australia and the rest of the world. The Palawa language likely formed a dialect chain running across the Tasmanian island. The varieties spoken on the northern, western, and eastern extremes of the island were more than likely mutually unintelligible. Palawa culture was integrated with and embedded in the ecosystem of Tasmania. Coastal regions provided shellfish and crustaceans for consumption. Coastal plains and dense inland forests provided opportunities for foraging and hunting. Clans stayed mostly in their own regions of the island but moved about for food according to the seasons. Palawa life and language were thus linked with landscape, rhythms of movement, and cultural practices, which had been worked out over the millennia in a way one could say was well knit.

In 1803, the British arrived to build their colonies, and the Palawa ecosystem was thrown into immediate chaos. Free settlers and farmers were encouraged by the colonial government to take up permanent residence on Palawa land. Key hunting grounds became privately held farmland, and well-developed hunting routes and techniques were disrupted. In the realm of hunting, the Palawa now competed with the British, who hunted not only for sustenance, but also for furs and other resources. The

Palawa's primary dietary protein source quickly evaporated. And Palawa immune systems were unprepared for European disease. In 1829, an outbreak of influenza wiped out much of the Palawa population in the south and west of the island. Tuberculosis, syphilis, and other venereal diseases took their toll, as did conflict with free settlers and escaped penal colony convicts.

When the British arrived, there were as many as 5000 Palawa people living in Tasmania. After three decades of colonialism, some 95% of the Palawa had died or been killed; their population in 1833 had been reduced to 300. The last speaker of any Tasmanian language variety died in 1905. Although it took about a century to completely eradicate the Palawa language, it was functionally gone by 1843 when 99% of the speakers had died or been killed. Today, Tasmania is Australia's most English-speaking state (Australian Bureau of Statistics 1999).

Radical death: the indigenous languages of El Salvador

In the 1920s, El Salvador was characterized by remarkable socioeconomic inequality. More than 90% of its private land was owned by a handful of powerful families, who were also heavily involved with the government. Coffee was a cash crop, and those who worked the coffee plantations were usually indigenous and always poor. The onset of the Great Depression and the corresponding collapse of the price of coffee made tense sociopolitical conditions between the classes worse. By the start of the next decade, the country was breaking under the weight of its own inequality. In 1932, indigenous groups – most notably the Pipil – joined forces with Communist political rebels to fight back.

At first, the indigenous uprising was successful. Towns were seized, and the political system was disrupted. The elite took note, and the Salvadoran military responded with force. Those assumed to be guilty of participation in the uprising were taken from their homes and killed by government soldiers. Indigenous physical appearance and indigenous dress were taken by the military as prima facie signs of culpability. Though only 100 people were killed in the popular uprising, the military response that followed it resulted in the death of some 25,000 people, mostly indigenous speakers of languages such as Cacaopera, Lenca, and Pipil.

Under these negative conditions, two ethnic communities – the Cacaopera and the Lenca – immediately abandoned their languages in favor of Spanish as a part of their survival efforts. Because they believed that speaking Cacaopera and Lenca in public linked them to indigenous identities, thus making them vulnerable to police and military intimidation, they simply stopped speaking those languages. And parents, believing that knowing the ethnic languages would be detrimental to their children's physical safety in the future, opted not to transmit their languages to their children. With this disruption in transmission, Cacaopera and Lenca made a rapid disappearance, called *radical* because it was in response to severe political oppression.

When linguists went to investigate the languages of El Salvador in the 1970s, they found a few people who could recollect certain words and phrases of Cacaopera and one speaker of Lenca. Pipil fared better than Lenca and Cacaopera on account of its larger number of speakers. Nevertheless, Pipil speakers were gradually abandoning their language in favor of Spanish.

Language shift and attrition: the influence of Swahili in Tanzania

When the British took control of Tanzania from Germany at the end of World War I, they made three decisions that would affect the vitality of more than 100 languages in the region for decades to come. First, they established English as the official language of the country and promoted its use in the domains of science and higher education, and in the upper levels of government. Second, they promoted the use of the widely spoken local Bantu language, Swahili, in lower levels of government and primary education. Finally, recognizing the administrative value of a widely understood lingua franca, they promoted the standardization of Swahili.

When the British selected English as the official language of Tanzania, they also provided the Tanzanian independence movement with a convenient foil. English was the language of the colonizers, and if colonialism should go, so should its language. Therefore, when the Tanganyika African National Union was formed in 1954, it rallied people for independence through the use of Swahili. When independence was achieved 10 years later, Swahili was the obvious choice for Tanzania's official language. Since independence, Swahili has become a powerful symbol in Tanzania's ongoing nation-building efforts. The fact that Swahili had undergone standardization and was already widely in use in the state domains of government administration and education meant that it was poised to spread quickly and deeply throughout the country. It is therefore the case that today the biggest threat to the indigenous languages of Tanzania is not from English but from another indigenous language, namely Swahili.

In the outskirts of the remote Kilosa District, many hours from the bustling Swahili-speaking cities of Dar es Salaam and Dodoma, a single narrow road leads to a series of villages high up in the mountains. Together, the villages are known as the Vidunda Ward, home to the Vidunda ethnic group. The Vidunda people speak a Bantu language of the same name. The only speakers of the language are those born in the Ward and a very few number of people from other ethnic groups who relocate there from neighboring wards. The Vidunda population is small and shrinking: there are some 10,000 people today, down from twice as many in the late 1960s. The fact that there are virtually no second language speakers combined with a dwindling population and the perceived economic value of Swahili has left Vidunda prone to cross-generational language shift, the gradual displacement of one language by another.

In Vidunda Ward, the shift to Swahili is well under way. Swahili is used rather than Vidunda for selling agricultural products in cities outside the ward, as well as in contact with government agencies, including those that enter the community, such as health organizations. Swahili is now the compulsory language of instruction in the schools, as mandated by the federal government of Tanzania. In Vidunda Ward, language shift to Swahili is complete in almost all formal domains, and formal language encounters in other domains are almost always in Swahili. The young are the most likely to use Swahili in the widest array of social domains. Matengo is a Bantu language related to Vidunda, which is also spoken in Tanzania. Although, with 160,000 speakers, Matengo is more robust numerically than Vidunda, the same types of conditions promoting language shift in the Vidunda Ward are also at work in Matengo communities.

If the current economic, political, and cultural conditions in Tanzania remain stable, it is likely that cross-generational language shift to Swahili will continue to affect ethnic communities throughout the country, and mother-tongue languages will continue to disappear. Nevertheless, what will happen to Vidunda, Matengo, and more than 100 other ethnic languages in Tanzania is impossible to predict. The futures and fates of languages cannot be predicted in advance because languages are bound to human conditions, which are inherently unpredictable.

Language Hotspots

We said at the end of Chapter 7 that the area around the equator not only has the highest density of language diversity but also has the highest density of endangered languages. The historical conditions of the past 500 years – European colonialism, the rise of the nation-state, and the spread of compulsory education, among others – facilitated a first acceleration in the loss of languages in the world (Map 12.1). It also set the stage for the globalization that has led to a hyperacceleration of language attrition. Currently, about 25 languages disappear from use every year, roughly one language every two weeks. At this rate, more than 50% of the languages spoken in the world today will have fallen from use by 2100. Should the rate of attrition accelerate even further, as many as 90% of the world languages could be lost somewhere around the twenty-second century. It is possible to imagine that in 2115, the projected population of 11 billion people may speak somewhere between 500 and 1000 languages.[1]

In his book *The Last Speakers: The Quest to Save the World's Most Endangered Languages* (2010), linguist K. David Harrison gives the term language hotspot to identify the regions with the greatest linguistic diversity, the greatest language endangerment, and the least documented languages. These language hotspots understandably coincide with the biodiversity hotspots described by biologists, such that species and ecosystems, languages, and the cultural knowledge linking languages to ecosystems are

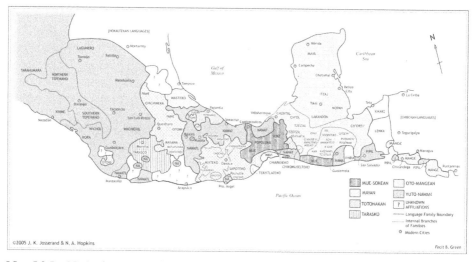

Map 12.1 Native languages of Mesoamerica, approximate distributions at European contact, circa 1500. A patchwork of Mayan, Yuto-Nahua, and Oto-Manguean languages.

simultaneously at risk for extinction. The triple extinction of ecosystem, language, and culture is completely consistent with the conditions that unravel the language loop.

The top five language hotspots are:

(i)   Northern Australia;
(ii)   Highland South America;
(iii) Northwest Pacific, North America;
(iv)   Siberia, Russia; and
(v)   Oklahoma, United States.

Other highly endangered regions with great linguistic diversity are Eastern Melanesia (especially Papua New Guinea), West Africa, Greater South Asia, and Southern South America. Here, we focus on two of the top five language hotspots: Australia and Siberia.

Northern Australia   William Brady is an elder in the Night Owl clan of the Gugu-Yaway people. He is also an expert hunter and knows his part of the outback better than almost anyone. When Harrison and his colleagues made a trip to Northern Australia, they met with Brady, who describes his language as including whistles and animal sounds. These exist so that hunters can speak to the animals. If they cannot speak to them, they are not good hunters. For Brady, there is a language of the bush, and if you do not speak it, you had better not go into it. Brady has long appreciated what many linguists have only fairly recently theorized as ethnosyntax: languages exist in an intricate web within the ecosystems where they are spoken. The Gugu-Yaway language is thus continuous with the bush, the species that inhabit it, and the cultural practices (hunting) that developed through living in it.

Gugu-Yaway is one of a hundred or more languages at risk for extinction in Australia, the top-ranking language hotspot in the world, owing to its great language diversity and great extinction risk. Others are Nangikurrunggurr 'Language of the swamp people', Ngengiwumerri 'Language of the sun and cloud people', Kalaw Kawaw Ya, Nigarakudi, Kulkalgowya, Magati Ke, and dozens more, each embedded in the ecosystem where it is grounded. For example, Harrison explains that the Nangikurrunggurr use what are called *calendar plants* as cues for gathering food. The bark of the gum tree, for instance, lets locals know when the sharks in the river are fat and may be hunted. This is namely when the bark peels easily from the trunk. Locals know to gather crocodile eggs along the riverbanks when the kapok tree blooms, and its seed-pods release fluff into the air. This is the type of specialized knowledge that disappears when languages are lost.

Siberia   The Tofalaria is a region in Eastern Siberia, Russia. Touching Central Asia, Tofalaria is one of the most remote parts of all of Russia. The region is home to the Tofa people, who speak a language of the same name. The Tofa live off the animals and vegetation provided by the Siberian forests, and from the milk of their most important animal, the reindeer. The Tofa are traditionally reindeer herders and even ride domesticated reindeer to do their hunting. The language has words for concepts such as 'smelling like reindeer milk' and 'three-year-old male uncastrated rideable reindeer.'

For the past 400 years or so, Russian has been encroaching on the languages of Siberia, which come from diverse language families. Tofa children today mostly speak Russian. As the language fades from one generation to the next, so does the intimate knowledge it encodes about the local ecosystem. With the exception of languages like Buryat and Yakut, most of the other languages of Siberia – about three dozen – are facing the same fate as Tofa, namely language shift to Russian. It is possible to imagine that within the next 100 years, this language hotspot will cease to exist as such, and Russian will be the only language of Siberia.

Rethinking Endangerment

Today more than 90% of the word's languages have less than one million speakers, and 50% of the world's languages have less than 10,000 speakers. Without intervention to change course, not only will the languages of today's hotspots become extinct, but today's linguistic safe zones will become tomorrow's language hotspots.

However, the probability of a language's survival does not come down to the number of speakers alone. A language with 50,000 speakers is in one sense worse off than a language with twice as many speakers, but we cannot predict with complete certainty which language will disappear first. This depends – like so many language questions – on the sociohistorical conditions in which the language is embedded, including the forces supporting the maintenance of the language, and the pressures operating against it. A critical factor in language survival or death is perception, that is, how the speakers understand the value of their language. Thus, a language with 50,000 speakers may be more 'healthy' than the language with twice as many speakers if the speakers perceive it to be worthy of transmission and actually do so.

Linguist Louis-Jean Calvet has devised a gravitational model of language to help us rethink language endangerment. In his view, the worldwide 'galaxy of languages' is made up of a number of language constellations, each comprising a central language and a number of peripheral ones. Within a given constellation, the central language exerts a gravitational pull on the peripheral languages; speakers are either obligated to learn the central language (by law or through compulsory education) or seek to do so on their own volition. The peripheral languages are therefore linked to the central one through bilingual speakers. The central languages of different constellations may or may not be linked to one another by bilingual speakers but may be linked to a supracentral language. The supracentral languages may or may not be linked to one another through the speech of bilinguals, but will be linked to a hypercentral language, what Calvet calls "the keystone of the linguistic gravitational system" (2006:60).

Taken together, the world's languages constitute a complete gravitational system, and can be grouped into four distinct levels according to the weight of their gravitational pull:

- Level 4 (peripheral). The vast majority of the world's languages, some 4000–5000, comprise level 4. These are the so-called peripheral languages, which include all of the languages of the current language hotspots, and many others. Speakers of level 4 languages may be monolingual, bilingual in another peripheral language, or bilingual in a higher-status language.

- Level 3 (central). The peripheral languages in level 4 cohere around 100–200 central languages. In Africa, these languages include Wolof and Bambara, in South America, Quechua, and Czech and Armenian in Europe. First-language speakers of these languages tend also to be bilingual in a level 2 language.
- Level 2 (supercentral). The supercentral languages are the most widely spoken languages in the world today. They include Arabic, Chinese, French, Hindi, Malay, Portuguese, Russian, Spanish, and Swahili. Those who speak a supercentral language as their first language are unlikely to acquire either a central or peripheral language. They may be monolinguals in their first language, are very frequently bilinguals in another supercentral language, or may acquire the level 1 language.
- Level 1 (hypercentral). There is currently one language in this category, namely, English. Those speakers who have English as their only first language tend to be monolinguals.

Two observations about bilingualism characterize this system. First, although many speakers are native multilinguals in that they acquired two or more languages as children, those speakers who acquire a second language at school or as an adult will tend to acquire a language from the level immediately higher than their own. For example, in the case of the West African nation of Senegal, a child who speaks Diola (level 4) in the home may first acquire Wolof (level 3), the language of the largest ethnic group and the most spoken language in Senegal. When the child goes to school, she will be required to learn French (level 2), which she must speak with great facility if she is to study at a Senegalese university. Depending on her social status, profession, and other socio-economic opportunities, she may acquire English (level 1) later on. Our second observation is that bilingual acquisition within a given constellation is unidirectional. That is, a first-language speaker of Diola may well be motivated to learn Wolof, but it is extremely unlikely that a first-language speaker of Wolof will be motivated to learn Diola. It is even less likely that a French monolingual will learn Diola.

Over time, the gravitational pull of central, supercentral, and hypercentral languages shifts speakers from periphery to center. This movement alone does not pose a threat to the peripheral languages as such, since a peripheral language can be maintained alongside a central one, a central language alongside a supercentral one, and so on. However, moves from one level to the next very frequently are accompanied by language attrition and disruptions in transmission. When the Diola speaker learns Wolof, she may decide only to transmit Wolof to her children. This situation is what poses the greatest threat to the 4000–5000 peripheral languages. Not only do very few people learn peripheral languages as second languages, but first-language speakers often give them up as they are pulled to the center.

Those peripheral languages located within the so-called language hotspots are those clearly most at risk for extinction, followed by the peripheral languages elsewhere. However, if we think into the future, it is possible to imagine the gradual displacement of the central languages as well. The major languages of Southern Europe, Central Europe, Eastern Europe, and Scandinavia are important national languages, which also serve as the vehicular language of education in the nations where they are spoken. But from Sweden to Denmark, Poland to Czech Republic, the young and the educated are increasingly multilingual, often in a supercentral language such as French, Russian, or Spanish, and very often in English as well. While the central languages are not in immediate danger of loss, the ubiquity and economic potency of the hypercentral language of English have many people and governments worried.

We will consider the possible fate of only one European language, level 3 Swedish. Although Sweden has language minority groups, 95% of Swedes speak Swedish, which is also spoken in parts of Finland and is mutually intelligible with the other North Germanic languages, Norwegian and Danish. For several centuries, it has also been the primary language of local and federal government. It is also the primary vehicular language of education. In these respects, Swedish is a so-called healthy national language with 9 million speakers, giving it a relatively high number of speakers worldwide, a very high proportion of use within Sweden, and the support of social structures of education and government. When we consider these factors, Swedish is a very healthy language, especially when compared with the peripheral languages found in the hotspots.

There are signs, however, that some Swedes perceive Swedish to be threatened. The perceived threat comes from Sweden's de facto second language, which is none of Sweden's neighboring languages (German, Danish, Finnish, or Norwegian), but rather English. Fully 89% of Sweden's population say they speak English well enough to have at least a basic conversation, almost as many people who claim to speak Swedish. And their use of English is not sporadic – 39% of all Swedes say they use English on a daily basis, while another 20% say they use it frequently but not daily. This means that almost three-fifths of all Swedes use English on a very regular basis, and almost nine-tenths are able to do so with great facility. This facility comes from the fact that all Swedish schoolchildren are required to study English, and proficiency in English is required for entrance into Swedish universities. A great deal of television and radio programming is available in English, which reinforces school-based acquisition. English is now fully integrated into Swedish culture, government, and civic life.

From its days as a great European power in the seventeenth century, through to the rise of the modern Swedish nation, Swedes never felt the need to declare an official language. The language of government and civic life has always been Swedish, and therefore any law proclaiming the same would have been redundant. However, in 2005, with the forces of globalization evermore present and English more widespread than ever, a bill was proposed to name Swedish the official language of the state. The bill narrowly failed. Three years later, a similar bill was proposed, and this time it passed, designating Swedish the main language of Sweden for the first time in Swedish history. One the one hand, the law simply describes what is an empirical reality – Swedish is the main language of the state. On the other hand, the very passing of the law implies that there is a perceived need for it.

Technology to the Rescue

Languages that have been spoken for thousands of years can be lost remarkably quickly – sometimes in as little as a generation – when the local ecologies in which they are embedded get disrupted, and their speakers are displaced or intimidated. The reversal of language attrition, namely language revitalization, is unfortunately much harder to achieve, either for practical reasons, for instance, there are few remaining speakers, or for issues of social power, for instance, these speakers lack access to needed resources and support. While language attrition is very often easy to initiate and easy to achieve, revitalization is difficult to initiate and difficult to achieve. Hebrew is, of course, the most spectacular success story with zero native speakers a century and a half ago and over five million today. We mentioned the revitalization effort for Hawaiian, now with 8000 speakers, in the Language Profile to Chapter 7 and again in Chapter 11, and it considered something of a success story. So is the revitalization of another Austronesian language, Māori, with 60,000 speakers now, a rebound from near-extinction through dedicated revitalization efforts.

Strategies for revitalizing native languages depend on the wishes of the community and the vitality of the language. If the language is relatively healthy but not used in schools, communities can develop two-way dual-language immersion programs to promote bilingualism. If, on the other hand, the language is spoken only by a few elderly speakers, communities may pair elders with young adults to teach the language through conversation. All preservation efforts – whether they involve linguists, community activists, or only the speakers themselves – must take into account the entire language loop; that is, what is relevant and important to the speakers. Harrison (2010) cautions that some preservation efforts, such as writing dictionaries, grammars, and recordings, have the value of museum artifacts rather than of living language.

Nevertheless, we, the authors, see the value of the use of technology in producing native-language scripts in the digital era and in pedagogical strategies in native communities. The most successful revitalization efforts have always been those that help a language adapt to new conditions, and the new conditions now are digital. A notable exception are the Amish, who have been successful at maintaining Pennsylvania Dutch by opting out of globalization altogether and maintaining the historical conditions in which their language is supported.

The Hawaiians we saw in Chapter 11 are not the only language community to use modern technology in the pursuit of language revitalization. Young speakers of Shoshone developed a monolingual Shoshone video game titled *Enee* 'fear' to teach Shoshone language in an entertaining way. A Cherokee language app can be downloaded onto smartphones and other digital devices from the online iTunes store. The Māori stream videos of fluent speakers on their websites and have created a digital repository of Māori poetry (Ka'ai et al. 2013). While these technologies cannot by themselves reverse the attrition of indigenous languages, they can increase community access to endangered languages while at the same time making the languages seem relevant in the digital age.

A powerful resource for endangered languages is the Unicode Consortium, mentioned in passing in Chapter 5. The question of whether or not to develop writing systems for indigenous languages is an important one in many community language revitalization efforts. Some indigenous communities with unwritten languages believe language to be sacred only in oral form and choose not to develop writing systems for revitalization. Others are eager to record their languages and promote them with new technologies. However, the development of a script may not be enough. In the digital age, languages also need fonts.

Unicode is a universal catalogue for all of the characters in all of the world's writing systems that have fonts to be used in all modern software. When a script is encoded in Unicode, speakers of languages using those scripts have access to the breadth of knowledge via the Internet, ease of communication via email, and immediate online commercial transactions that characterize written language in the digital age. Speakers of languages with scripts not included in Unicode are left out of these technological advances or must participate using another language or script. If the speakers are involved in revitalization efforts, inclusion in Unicode facilitates native-language education, such that materials can be typed, and therefore literacy in the target language. Thus, the encoding of scripts for indigenous and minority languages is essential for those language communities wishing to use their languages digitally.

The process, however, is not easy. All additions to the Unicode catalogue require a written proposal, a step that assumes those requesting encoding for their languages are bilinguals or have outside assistance. Because a given script may vary from variety to variety, significant time and financial expense may be required to standardize the script before requesting Unicode encoding. These factors may deter indigenous language communities from requesting that their language's script be encoded. Approximately 100 scripts used by indigenous communities in Africa, the Americas, and Asia remain unencoded, not including those scripts that have not yet been devised for previously unwritten languages. The Script Encoding Initiative, hosted by the University of California, Berkeley, seeks to help language communities prepare the formal proposals required to request Unicode encoding.

In the West African nations of Guinea, Ivory Coast, and Mali, speakers of languages such as Bambara, Dyula, and Maninka write their languages using an alphabet known as N'ko. The script was developed in 1949 in order to give African languages a script suited to their linguistic features, rather than European ones. Originally used to write only Maninka, the script became so valuable that it was recruited for use in other languages in the region. It short, N'ko was a twentieth-century success story suited to twentieth-century technology.

Sixty years following the introduction of the N'ko in West Africa, the digital age arrived, and with it, new forms of written communication. Email, blogs, Facebook, Twitter, and other forms of social media emerged as important platforms for written language. But with no official computer typeface, or font, speakers of languages that use the N'ko alphabet were blocked from participating in the digital revolution using their mother tongues. A lack of access to global technology is a factor that facilitates language attrition, while a sign of linguistic vitality in the twenty-first century is whether or not a language can by typed in its own script.

The younger generation in the country of Georgia, for instance, has made an alphabet choice. Facebook became popular in Georgia around 2008. For the first two or three years, posting was carried out in the Latin alphabet. But, then, around 2011, young Georgians decided they wanted to write in the Georgian alphabet, and now Facebook postings among Georgians are in their own script.

The Microsoft Local Language Program is another powerful resource for endangered languages. It is designed to introduce technology into the developing world in a way that respects local languages, including developing fonts for languages with unique scripts. In the 2000s, the program teamed up with linguists and language organizers in Africa to develop a font suited to a wide range of languages in Africa. The font is called Ebrima and is suitable for all languages written with the N'ko scripts, including Bambara, Dyula, and Maninka. In the years since Ebrima was introduced, more literature has been published in Maninka, including weekly and monthly period-icals. This suggests that more people may want to consume the news in written form in their first language.

Not all language communities have responded to Microsoft's language initiatives so favorably. As Harrison (2010) points out, the ethnic group in Chile known as the Mapuche were angered when Microsoft translated Windows into their language Mapudungun. A community leader wrote this open response: "The appropriation of our language as fundamental part of our culture by researchers, linguists and public officials constitutes violation of our inherent and inalienable right to our cultural her-itage." This reminds us that revitalization efforts – such language communities choose to engage in them – are only successful in so far as they work within the community's orientation to language.

Anishinaabemowin Revitalization in Wisconsin

The Algonquian language family once stretched continuously from present-day North Carolina north through central Canada and west to present-day Montana. Its lan-guages – Cree, Massachusset, Menonimi, and many others – were as distinctive from one another as the cultural groups who spoke them. Many of the languages were lost to the effects of European colonialism, but many others have managed to survive, if tenuously. One of the surviving languages is Ojibwe (Anishinaabemowin), which is still spoken by about 55,000 people as a series of mostly mutually intelligible varieties throughout the Ojibwe homeland, the Great Lakes region of Canada and the United States.

Like most Native American languages, Ojibwe is considered extremely endangered. The number of speakers is considered relatively high for a Native American language, but the speakers are spread out across a great swath of territory, from the Dako-tas, northern Michigan, Wisconsin, and Minnesota in the United States, to as far east as Quebec in Canada. As the language has dwindled in number in the United States, efforts to revitalize it have become a top priority in many communities. On the Leech Lake Reservation in Minnesota, the Niigaane Ojibwemowin Immersion School opened its doors to Ojibwe children for the first time in 2003. From kindergarten to the sixth grade, children receive Ojibwe-language instruction in all curricular areas. The goal is to produce the next generation of Ojibwe speakers in the community. Simi-lar efforts are being made in Ojibwe communities throughout the Great Lakes region.

Margaret Noodin is a professor, poet, and scholar of Native American studies living and working in the state of Wisconsin. She is also a leader in the efforts to revitalize Anishinaabemowin, the local name for Ojibwe. We invited Professor Noodin to tell the story of the Anishinaabemowin language in her words. She sent us the following poem, written in Ojibwe and with an English translation:

Gabe-agindamwag.	Eternal Counting.
Niizhiwag, biimiskobizowaad	As a pair, they rotate
Gizhibaawaashiwaad	turning in the wind,
didibaabizowaad, giizhigo-maadagewaad	spinning, swimming in the sky
Giizis, Dibiki-giizis, ganjiwebinidizo.	Sun, Moon, pushing one another.

Gabe-agindamwaad.	Eternal Counting.
Agwaayaashkaa,	The tide comes in,
Animaashkaa,	the tide goes out,
Ezhi-ombishkaaying kina,	the way we all rise,
ezhi-naanzhiodetaaying.	The way we are all lowered by our hearts.

We also asked Professor Noodin to describe the hopes, challenges, pleasures, and fears of the Anishinaabemowin revitalization effort. This is what she told us:

In Milwaukee, Wisconsin, I walk into Anishinaabemowin language class and talk with brilliant, hard-working students who represent both the near and distant future. They are the long shadows of their ancestors' past as the people lived through evolution, migration and colonization. Some days we count by twos or tens just to prove we can push our minds to play outside English. Then, we talk of seasons and stories and pretend to be people of the past or animals who speak, always playing with words, description, and conjugation. We talk of the way we build sentences from the center, the way our lives and our earth expand with ancient and unstoppable centrifugal force. Then, I walk out, we all leave, and I can't see whether or not we've made a difference at all. Like the Sun and the Moon and the tides of my poetry, the forces that control our lives and our language are not visible at the micro level. I can't see if that hour has become a part of memory, if our laughter or frustration will ripple forward into our lives, if the Anishinaabe way of speaking will be pulled into the next generation … or not.

At home I sing with my daughters and friends. We call ourselves Miskwaasining Nagamojig, the Swamp Singers, because the Anishinaabe are people of the great lakes and great forests and vast networks of rivers and swamps that make up the places between. For centuries, the women in Anishinaabe communities have been especially attentive to the water. There are words for smooth or choppy water, words for deep and dangerous water and words for the bright beautiful stuff of life we all need to survive. The language carries the echo of *nibii* 'water' in *niibiish* 'the leaf'. It carries an understanding of the waved and rhythmic way we submerge our consciousness in *nibaa* 'to sleep' and the way we disintegrate back into the cycle of life in *nibo* the word for 'death.' This is the way every language weaves its epistemology into language, layering ideas and perspectives with sound and syntax. This is the way we arrange meaning in patterns of communication that lead to lyric ceremonies, celebrations of shared experience, songs of meeting by the water, singing with the water. We sing in Anishinaabemowin because we want to save these words and ways of knowing, ways of helping one another heal, stand strong, bear pain, forgive, and let go. When used regularly by real people as a living language, any language can be the tissue that builds the bones of identity. In one of our songs we say,

Shkaakaamikwe g'gikenmaanaa	Mother Earth we know her
G'gikenmaagonaan pii nagamoyaang	She knows us when we sing

There are many lessons in these words. Shkaakaamikwe literally implies a feminine ability to renew, neither the word for 'mother' *gashe* nor 'earth' *aki* are in the name, but the reciprocal relationship is clear. Further evidence of the relationship is the verb form that shows two animate beings knowing and hearing one another.

To share songs like this one and stores related to it, to reach beyond the places we can touch and see, we created a website, an address in the ether, commonly referred to as the cloud. The site[2] is a commons that connects us like the great inland seas that surround us. We post words and sounds in Michigan and Wisconsin for cousins in Ontario and Minnesota. We reach across two big nations, the United States and Canada, as if they did not exist and sometimes we hear from faraway friends who are working with their own languages in Ireland, Wales, China, New Zealand or Siberia. Over 3500 connect with us via the internet, and we consider all the files to be open archives for the future.

Our work with language is to gather the data, respond to the tides, stay on the paths that keep us suspended. Our words are an orbit we'd like to think we maintain, but perhaps it is the cycle of exchange that actually maintains us.

We thank Professor Noodin for sharing her story.

What Is Choice?

In the future, speakers across the world will increasingly be faced with a decision that many of our readers may find impossible to imagine: the decision to trade in the language of the home for a language of prestige. As hyperacceleration of the world's languages continues apace, this decision will be faced not only by a small minority groups pressured into acquiescing to larger regional languages – speakers of Karen pressured to learn Burmese, for example – but also for speakers of large regional languages, who will feel pressure to learn the globalizing languages – speakers of Burmese who experience the urgency of Mandarin or English. Neither politicians, who may wish for speakers to give up minority languages, nor linguists, who may wish for speakers to keep them, can decide. The decision quite simply belongs to the speakers who are faced with making language decisions for themselves, their families, and their communities.

Except in the cases of sudden and radical death, outlined above, the statistics we have provided throughout this chapter about language loss are the result of decisions made by speakers to either abandon their mother tongue or not pass it down to their children, or both. The future of the world's languages is therefore a future based in hundreds of millions of individual decisions. But what does it mean to make a choice about something so fundamental to identity as language?

First, the decision to abandon a language is often made in the context of harmful language ideologies that are rooted in the interests of those in positions of political, economic, and cultural power. That is, ideologies that articulate the value of majority languages while demoting the value of minority languages exist because powerful individuals, groups, and institutions benefit from them.

Second, harmful ideologies about language tend to be linked to other ideological formations having to do with race, class, tribe, region, and nation, which further promote inequality and consolidate power for those who already have it, while relegating to the margins those speakers who already reside there. In other words, speakers of minority language varieties often experience multiple forms of oppression at the same time. The decision to abandon a marginal language for an ostensibly more prestigious one may be perceived as the most feasible way of avoiding broad social stigma.

Third, language decisions are often presented to speakers as false dichotomies: give up X to acquire Y. Acquiring Swahili does not actually *require* the loss of Vidunda, for example, though this may well be the impression children get from attending schools in which Swahili is the only language of instruction.

Fourth, choices about language are often presented with false guarantees: give up the home language, and success will follow. It may well be the case that English will give a speaker more linguistic capital than Nepali in the linguistic marketplace, but then again it may not. Acquiring Swahili may well improve the economic conditions of those in Vidunda Ward, but then it also might not.

Language is always catching up to the conditions that set it in motion in the first place. As a result of the last 100,000+ years, language has constantly looped itself not only around an individual's neuronal pathways but equally significantly around the speakers in a community, the landscapes they live in, and the educational and political structures they create. Sound inventories increase or decrease and/or might change character, shifting from nontonal to tonal. Lexical items know nothing of linguistic borders. Particular syntactic structures may arise out of the pressures of multilingual residual zones. Belief systems spread through religions and economies. In the end, individual and individual communities have always had a choice about what language(s) they speak and how they speak, whether they knew it or not.

Final Note: Our Advocacies

We urge speakers to empower themselves with information in order to make the best choices concerning the survival of their language(s). We appreciate that while not all speakers are eager to rescue their imperiled languages from extinction, we believe language death nevertheless to be a global problem deserving of political, intellectual, and humanitarian attention. In writing this book, one of the things that struck us most powerfully was the magnitude of this problem, both in terms of the rate of disappearance of the world's languages and in terms of the burden of language death, which disproportionally falls on the shoulders of those who speak minority languages.

For others of us not speaking an endangered language, we advocate additive multilingualism or bidialectalism, depending on where you live. We acknowledge that dignity is tied to identity, and identity is tied to language. Therefore, no matter what language or language variety you speak, you should never have to feel *vergonha*, that is, the feeling of shame for speaking a socially stigmatized language variety, or the feeling of shame of having given up the home language due to social pressure to do so. We cannot tell leaders and policy makers around the world what decisions to make about language matters in their countries or regions, but we can ask them to become informed about some of the basic working of language, what we are calling *the language loop*, and of language communities and their gifts, needs, and interests.

Above all, at the end of this book, we want to state that linguistic diversity is not a problem to be managed. It is a fact of life to be celebrated.

Language Profile: K'iche' [Quiché (Mayan)]

Functional overview

Quiché belongs to the Eastern Branch of the Mayan language family. Classical Quiché is the name given to the historical variety of the language that was spoken throughout

Central Guatemala at the time of the Spanish conquest in the sixteenth century. This variety was preserved in a number of historical texts, including the Mayan creation story, which we describe at the end of this profile. The number of speakers of Quiché today is uncertain, but linguists estimate the figure to be between one and two million speakers, who live mostly in Guatemala's central highlands and around the cities of Chichicastenango and Quetzaltenango. Most of these speakers are bilingual in Spanish, but there may be as many as 300,000 monolingual speakers of the language. Quiché is the most widely spoken of Guatemala's approximately 23 indigenous languages, making it the second most spoken language in the country following Spanish. The modern language is written with one of a number of spelling conventions that make use of an adapted Latin alphabet. Though literacy remains low in Quiché, the language is increasingly used in local schools throughout Central Guatemala. Quiché has been recognized with 20 other Mayan languages as a national minority language, giving it some recognition but no official language status. Spanish remains the only official language of Guatemala.

The Quiché-speaking region of Central Guatemala comprises five distinctive regions: north, south, east, west, and central. The central variety, spoken in the heavily Mayan Quetzaltenango Department, is the variety of Quiché used most often in formal education and the media. For the most part, the various regional varieties are mutually intelligible and differ from one another primarily in terms of their vocalic systems. These differences represent historical change from Classical Quiché. For example, the western variety known as Nahualá spoken in the Sololá Department is considered by linguists to be linguistically conservative for preserving sounds from the classical variety that have been lost in other Quiché varieties. One such feature is the historical distinction between long (/aː, eː, iː, oː, uː/) and short /a, e, i, o, u/) vowels, which has not been maintained elsewhere.

Prominent structural characteristics

Consonant inventory: ejectives and implosives   In the language profile from Chapter 10 (!Xóõ), we saw that while most sounds in the world's languages are produced using air from the lungs (the so-called *pulmonic airstream mechanism*), some languages use sounds that rely on airstream sources originating in other parts of the vocal tract. One example of this are the ejective consonants first introduced at the end of Chapter 2. These consonants rely on an airstream originating at the glottis rather than the lungs. Ejective consonants are very common in Quiché, and in fact the first sound of the name of the language *K'iche'* begins with the ejective /k'/. When speakers pronounce the name of their language, several things happen in quick succession. First, the glottis raises from its default position. At the same time, the back of the tongue raises and makes a tight constriction with the velum. As a consequence of this configuration, air pressure builds up, causing an audible burst upon its release.

All spoken varieties of Quiché have ejective consonants, as well as their voiceless stop and voiceless affricate equivalents. That is, the inventory of voiceless stops and affricates /t, ts, tʃ, k, q/ corresponds one to one to the inventory of ejectives /t', ts', tʃ', k', q'/. For example, *ixoq* 'woman' ends with the voiceless uvular stop /q/, while loq' ends with the voiceless uvular ejective /q'/.

In our list of stop and ejective consonants above, we purposefully left out the voiceless stop /p/, which occurs in words such as *paxik'* 'acorn.' There is nothing remarkable about /p/ as such; however, its glotallized counterpart in Quiché is not the expected ejective /p'/ but rather /ɓ/, a voiced bilabial implosive. Implosive consonants differ from ejectives in a couple of ways. First, they have a mixed airstream mechanism: pulmonic egressive (air ascends from lungs) and glottalic ingressive (air flows into the vocal tract through the nose or mouth). That is, as the glottis moves downward, air simultaneously rises from the lungs. Second, rather than releasing an audible puff of air, implosives are released by drawing air inward. When speakers of Quiché pronounce words containing the implosive, such as *kixkab'* [kiʃ-kaɓ] 'earthquake,' outsiders sometimes perceive them to be 'inhaling' or 'swallowing' the 'b' sound.

Some varieties of Quiché also have a voiceless bilabial implosive, which is produced with the vocal folds closed. This is an extremely rare sound in the world's languages. Voiced implosives are considered an areal feature in the languages of sub-Saharan Africa.

Verb morphology We have seen several times that languages might have either: accusative alignment, in which the subjects of transitive and intransitive verbs are seen as separate from the objects of transitive verbs; or ergative alignment, where the object of the transitive verb is grouped with the subject of an intranstive verb, and these are seen as distinct from the subject of a transitive verb. In the language profiles on Kurdish (Chapter 4) and Tibetan (Chapter 9), we have seen how ergative systems work in specific detail. In this profile, we revisit ergativity one last time in order, first, to note that many of the world's ergative languages are found in the indigenous languages of the Americas and, second, to illustrate how ergativity works in the broader context of Quiché verbal morphology.

All Mayan languages demonstrate ergativity, including Ch'ol, Mam, Q'anjob'al, Tzotzil, Tzeltal, and of course Quiché. As in other Mayan languages, ergativity in Quiché is expressed morphologically with verbal markers. Ergative morphemes on the verb stem mark subjects of transitive verbs, while absolutive morphemes mark the subjects of intransitive verbs. These morphemes coordinate with other verbal morphologies expressing aspect and mood. Given that all of this grammatical information is provided morphologically on verbs, we can note that Quiché is thus an inflectionally rich language. The following template (Pye 2001) shows the structure of Quiché verbs and the order in which inflections are applied to the stem.

aspect + Absolutive (+ movement) + (Ergative) + stem (+derivation) (+termination)

We will work through certain of these inflections in order from left to right, beginning with aspect. In modern Quiché, all inflected verbs are marked for one of four aspects, as follows:

- k – incompletive
- x – completive
- ch – imperative or irrealis
- Ø (unmarked) – perfective

Thus, in the verb *kawaʔik* (S/he is eating), the aspect marker *k* indicates that the act of eating is in progress.

Should the verb be intransitive, the next morpheme to appear in the sequence is the absolutive marker, which varies in form depending on grammatical number (first – *in*, second – *at*, third – Ø, unmarked). If the verb should be marked for ergativity, the ergative morpheme comes next in the sequence. In this case, the form not only varies by grammatical number but also is conditioned by the following phonetic environment, with different forms appearing before vowels and consonants, as follows:

Person	prevocalic	preconsonantal
1	inw	in
2	aw	a
3	r	u

Termination (TERM) affixes follow ergative morphemes in the inflectional sequence and are used to mark the transitive/intransitive dimension of the verb. The following two examples illustrate the primary verbal morphemes in Quiché verbs:

kawaʔik

k	-	Ø	-	waʔ	-	ik
ASP		3A		eat		TERM

'S/he is eating it.'

xintijoh

x	-	Ø	-	in	-	tij	-	oh
ASP		3A		1E		eat		TERM

'I ate it.'

In the first example, the aspect prefix *k* indicates that the action is ongoing, while in the second example the prefix *x* indicates that the action is completed. The termination suffixes *ik* and *oh* coordinate the transitivity of the verbs. We will see how these suffixes work in more detail in the next section on *antipassives*.

Antipassives   In English, if we want to emphasize *who* is responsible for a particular action in a sentence, we use the active voice. 'Juan won the spelling bee,' 'Marta ate the cake,' and 'Keisha finished the report' illustrate this type of construction. The noun phrases 'the spelling bee,' 'the cake,' and 'the report,' are direct objects in the examples above but can be promoted to the role of grammatical subjects in a type of construction known as the passive voice. This construction allows speakers of English to emphasize *what* received the action rather than *who* performed the actoin. The subject of the active voice (Juan, Marta, and Keisha) may appear in prepositional phrases or not appear at all, again depending on what a speaker wishes to emphasize. For example, 'Juan won the spelling bee' can be reformulated as 'The spelling bee was won (by Juan),' while the other sentences can be reformulated as 'the cake was eaten (by Marta),' and 'the report was finished (by Keisha).' Writing teachers in the United States are renowned for telling students to avoid the passive voice at all costs – the

active voice supposedly makes for more lively reading – but in truth both constructions have their place and depend on the needs of the writer or speaker.

Quiché has active and passive constructions similar to those in English. But because
Quiché syntax is ergative in nature, it also has a type of construction known as antipassive in which the object of the transitive verb (the spelling bee, the cake, the report,
from the earlier examples) is deleted rather than the subject. Antipassive constructions
are found in ergative languages including Basque, the Australian Aboriginal language
Dyirbal, the Native American language Salish, and various Austronesian languages,
in addition to Quiché and other Mayan languages. Like passives, antipassives are also
about perspective taking; they allow speakers to emphasize the transitive subject.

The following example (Pye and Quixtan Poz 1988) illustrates a Quiché transitive
verb in the active voice. The aspect marker 'k' marks the verb as incomplete (INCOM),
and the verbal marker 'oh' marks the verb as transitive.

k	-	at	-	inw	-	il	-	oh
INCOM		2A		1E		see		TRANS

'I see you'

In the active sentence, the second person singular pronoun 'you' appears in the
absolutive case, and the first person singular pronoun 'I' appears in the ergative case. In
the following examples illustrating the Quiché antipassive, the suffixes /ow/ and /n/
(ANT – antipassive) are added to make the transitive sentence intransitive. As such, the
transitive object does not appear, and the subject now appears in the absolutive case
rather than the ergative case, in keeping with the arrangements of ergative grammar.

k	-	in	-	tzuku	-	n	-	ik
INCOM		1A		look (for)		ANT		INTRANS

'I look for'

k	-	at	-	ch'ay	-	ow	-	ik
INCOM		2A		hit		ANT		TERM

'You hit.'

These sentences sound odd to English speakers, who expect grammatical complements
with transitive verbs, but to speakers of Quiché, these constructions are an ordinary
part of the language.

A salient cultural characteristic: the *Popul Vuh*

According to Quiché tradition, the world, in the beginning, was an empty, motionless,
and silent expanse of sky and sea. But then came "the word," as it is recorded, and
"like a lightning bolt it ripped through the sky, penetrated the waters, and fertilized
the minds of the Earth-Water Deities." The earth emerged from the sea; plant and
animal life proliferated. The golden kernels belonging to a plant known as *maize* were
ground into a thick dough, out of which the first humans – four men followed by
four women – were shaped and given life. The Heavens blew mist into the eyes of

the men in order to limit their sight to the earth, not the heavens. This way, earth's people were oriented to their land and to their communities. The first humans were also given the gift of language – K'iche' – which permitted them to understand and connect with one another as they connected with the earth.

This creation myth is the first story recorded in the *Popul Vuh* 'Book of the Community', the sacred book of cultural narratives belonging to the Quiché people. The book itself is significant for three reasons. First, it gives us a sense of the time-depth of Quiché oral culture: engravings discovered by archeologists in Central Guatemala depicting creation stories from the *Popul Vuh* date to at least 300 BCE. This means that the Quiché people have been telling their stories in the Quiché language for well over two millennia. Second, it illustrates the relationship between writing systems and religion. When the Spanish arrived in the early sixteenth century, they burned their way through the Native Americas, but they also left behind the Latin alphabet. Mayan authors were thus able to record the *Popul Vuh* in a modern script between 1554 and 1558. In the eighteenth century, a parish priest presiding in Chichicastenango translated the Quiché version into Spanish. Finally, the *Popul Vuh* shows that in the Quiché account of the world, human life has been divinely bound to language and to the earth from the very beginning. The three are inextricably linked, as illustrated in the following verses from the *Popol Vuh*, presented first in Quiché, followed by a translation in English.

Kate q'ut xkikoh pa tzih utzakik, Ubitik
Qanabe chuch, Qahav.
Xa q'ana hal, Zaqi hal utiyohil.
Xa 'echa raqan, Uq'ab vinaq.

And so then they put into words the creation, the shaping
Of our first mother and father.
Only yellow corn And white corn were their bodies.
Only food were the legs, and arms of man. – *Popol Vuh*

Exercises

Exercise 1 – language shift

In 1978, sociolinguist Susan Gal wrote an influential paper titled 'Peasant men can't get wives: Language change and sex roles in a bilingual community' in the journal *Language in Society*. In the paper, she outlined the shift from Hungarian to German in a bilingual community in Austria. She found that women are further along in the shift to German than men, and she attributed this finding to conditions that are economic in nature. Read the paper carefully. Then, write a summary that addresses the following questions: What are the economic conditions promoting language shift in the community? How is gender implicated in these conditions? How is the situation described by Gal similar or different to the situation of language shift in Tanzania described in this chapter?

Exercise 2 – you investigate

We have seen that perceptions about language are important in influencing a speaker's decision to maintain a heritage language or shift to an incoming language. Design a survey that queries attitudes toward the maintenance of indigenous, minority, or immigrant languages in the community, state, province, or country where you live. Ask survey respondents about the issues you think are most important. You may include a general question gauging support for language maintenance efforts in general, another asking about the use of minority languages as the medium of instruction in schools, and an other about the use of tax dollars to pay for language maintenance efforts. Your questionnaire should ask a minimum of 12 questions, and no more than 30. Tailor your questions to your community as much as possible. Finally, tabulate your results and present your findings by representing your data visually.

Exercise 3 – writing unwritten indigenous languages

An important step in preserving indigenous languages is to write them down. Use the Internet to find one of the several thousand unwritten languages that has been described by linguists. First, read about the structure of the language. Then, imagine that you were working with the speech community to devise a writing system. Describe what kind of writing system you will use (logogram, abjad, alphabet, syllabary) and state if you will invent a new script or borrow/adapt a current one. Refer to the information given in Chapter 5 about choosing a writing system. Besides you and the community members, what other individuals, groups, or institutions have an interest in the script you develop? Describe the cultural, economic, and political issues that are at stake. Write a report or make and give an oral presentation on your recommendation.

Exercise 4 – you decide

From the language hotspots described in this chapter to speech communities around the world, language shift is a problem of global proportions. Keeping in mind that a speech community's decision to shift to another language is a complicated one that cannot be dictated from the outside, brainstorm ways to challenge the problem of language shift in your community. The first step will be to consult the speakers of the language in question, if you are not one yourself. Beyond that, be creative. How will you fund your efforts? How will you promote your efforts in the community? From whom will you seek support? Who is your audience? What messages about language maintenance, language shift, and language diversity do you intend to promote?

Exercise 5 – language hotspots

Choose one of the hotspots not covered in this book. Make three lists: (i) languages spoken in your chosen hotspot; (ii) cultural practices of the speakers of those languages and/or specialized cultural knowledge; and (iii) endangered flora and fauna in the same hotspot. For each language you list, provide the estimated number of speakers in the most recent year for which information has been published. You likely will not find the same amount of information for each list. That is okay. The second list may be especially sparse depending on how much anthropological work has been done on the groups in question. The point is for you to appreciate the triple threat of extinction: biodiversity, languages, and local knowledge.

Exercise 6 – your advocacies

This book ends with a list of the authors' advocacies. Having read the book in its entirety, write a statement outlining your own advocacies. Make your advocacy statement as realistic as possible, keeping in mind the realities of the new global economy, the pressures of language policy, the pressures of so-called soft power, and so forth. The authors implement their advocacies through their writing, teaching, and by donating the royalties from the sale of this book to the endangered language fund. Explain how you will implement your advocacies.

Discussion Questions

1   Consider the terms presented in this chapter having to do with the new global economy: neoliberalism, offshoring, and outsourcing. What do these terms have to do with language? That is, what effects do they, and the new global economy in general, have on language or on specific languages?

2   What kinds of effects do you imagine that the privatization of public markets has on the types of language policies discussed in Chapter 6? Is the state relevant anymore in setting language policy? Has the power shifted completely to the private sector?

3   What do you make of Nepal's decision to invite English into the country when it liberalized its economy? What do you imagine the effect will be on Nepali? What about the other languages of Nepal?

4   Does globalization necessarily pose a threat to linguistic diversity? In what ways can the forces of globalization be recruited to promote linguistic diversity?

5   The most common form of language death is cross-generational language shift, and it is under way in speech communities around the world. How does it proceed? What pressures condition an individual's choice to maintain a heritage language or shift to another language? Have you personally experienced pressure to give up or adopt a language?

6   Some people have said that knowledge of crocodile eggs and reindeer milk is not relevant in today's world, and that the loss of the languages that encode that knowledge is therefore not a problem. Keeping in mind that this is a complex issue, and no speaker should be told what to do with his/her language, what do you make of this idea? Can you imagine ways in which balancing both old and new is feasible?

7   If you are reading this book in the language in which it was written (English), you are a speaker of a level 1 language, in Calvet's terms. If English is your first language, have you made efforts to learn a language on level 3, 2, or 1? Why or why not? What factors led to you learning or not learning a language on another

level? If English is not your first language, what factors conditioned your learning it? What ideologies, discourses, and attitudes convinced you that learning English was worth your time? That is, have you experienced the gravitational pull of English?

8   What are the advantages and disadvantages of English as a global lingua franca? Now, we can ask one last time: What should the role of the state be in passing language laws, in light of the expansion of English? Consider the case of Sweden presented here to start your discussion.

9   What do you make of the decision by the Mapuche to reject a Mapudungun translation of Microsoft Windows? Imagine yourself as the Mapuche – what kinds of positions, stances, and histories may have led to this decision?

10 What do you think of Professor Noodin's Anishinaabemowin (Ojibwe) poem? What do you notice about the Anishinaabemowin words? What about the content? Did you try and read the Anishinaabemowin words out loud? Why or why not?

11 What was your reaction to Professor Noodin's reflections on Ojibwe revitalization efforts? She writes about laughter and frustration – what do those affects and postures refer to?

12 Do you agree or disagree with the advocacies the authors set forth at the end of the book? What things would you amend, add, or remove?

13 Now that you have finished reading the entire book, how do you think your view of language has changed? What is the most important thing you have learned from reading this book and thinking about its content? What do you think you will take away with you?

Notes

1   New languages are of course entering the world scene as others die, which makes such estimations very tricky. But under the current conditions, existing languages are disappearing at a rate faster than that at which new languages come into existence. So, while the declining number of languages is somewhat offset by new languages, the estimated figure for 2015 remains nevertheless much lower than the estimate for the current number of languages spoken.

2   See www.ojibwe.net.

References

Australian Bureau of Statistics (1999) *Demography – Australia*. Canberra: ABS.

Blommaert, Jan (2010) *The Sociolinguistics of Globalization*. Cambridge: Cambridge University Press.

Calvet, Louis-Jean (2006) *Towards an Ecology of World Languages*. Malden, MA: Polity Press.

Campbell, Lyle and Martha Muntzel (1989) The structural consequences of language death. In Nancy Dorian (ed.), *Investigating Obsolescence: Studies in Language Contraction and Death*. Cambridge: Cambridge University Press.

Giddens, Anthony (1990) *The Consequences of Modernity*. Stanford, CA: Stanford University Press.

Harrison, K. David (2010) *The Last Speakers: The Quest to Save the World's Most Endangered Languages*. Washington, DC: National Geographic Society.

Heller, Monica (2011) *Paths to Post-Nationalism: A Critical Ethnography of Language and Identity*. Oxford: Oxford University Press.

Ka'ai, Tania, John Moorfield, and Muiris Ó Laoire (2013) New technologies and pedagogy in language revitalization: The case of Te Reo Māori. In Mari C. Jones and Sarah Ogilvie (eds.), *Keeping Languages Alive: Documentation, Pedagogy, and Revitalization*. Cambridge: Cambridge University Press, 115–127.

Pye, Clifton (2001) The acquisition of finiteness in K'iche' Maya. In *BUCLD 25: Proceedings of the 25th Annual Boston University Conference on Language Development*. Somerville, MA: Cascadilla Press, 645–656.

Pye, Clifton and Pedro Quixtan Poz (1988) Precocious passives (and antipassives) in Quiché Mayan. In *Papers and Reports on Child Language Development*, Stanford, CA, 27.71–80.

Glossary

Absolute (spatial frame of reference) – system referring to the location of objects in space with respect to one another on the horizontal plane defined in relation to arbitrary fixed bearings, for example, cardinal directions, up/down hill, upriver/downriver.

Accusative alignment – where the subjects of both transitive and intransitive verbs are in the nominative (subject) case, while the object of a transitive verb is in the accusative (object) case; contrasts with ergative alignment.

Agglutinative morphology – a word-formation process where morphemes are affixed to roots with no significant phonological changes to the root and where the morphemes are readily identifiable and easily segmented.

Allele – alternate form of a gene or a group of genes in close proximity on a chromosome.

Analytic morphology – one meaning per morpheme where all morphemes are free, that is, considered separate words.

Aspect – a verbal distinction that indicates the manner in which an action or event takes place, particularly with respect to its duration in time; see **Tense**.

Bottleneck – when a population's size is reduced for at least one generation, which has the effect of reducing the variation in the subsequent gene pool of a given population.

Calque – word or phrase expression formed by the literal translation of each element comprising the word/phrase/expression from another language, for example, 'quick silver' as a direct translation from the Latin *argentum vivum,* in the sense of *quick,* meaning 'alive.'

Chain shift – a process in phonology of interrelated sound changes in which sounds, often vowels, move and replace one another in orderly succession.

Chromosome – an organized structure of DNA found in cells, specifically in the nucleus.

Languages in the World: How History, Culture, and Politics Shape Language, First Edition.
Julie Tetel Andresen and Phillip M. Carter.
© 2016 John Wiley & Sons, Inc. Published 2016 by John Wiley & Sons, Inc.

Click consonants – consonants produced when air is drawn into the lungs rather than out of the lungs commonly present in Southern African languages.

Clitic – a morpheme that is unable to stand alone as an independent form for phonological reasons but has the syntactic characteristics of a word.

Contour tone – changes in pitch within a single syllable to describe a voice that may rise, fall, fall–rise, stay flat, or break in the middle of a word, or any other kind of vocal sliding.

Creole – traditionally defined as a language with native speakers whose sole input is a pidgin.

Deixis – the position of people, objects, and events with respect to a particular point of reference; categories include personal pronouns, demonstrative pronouns, spatial adverbs, and temporal adverbs.

Dependent – when one syntactic category depends on the presence of another; in the phrase *the red house*, 'red' is the dependent, meaning that its presence is dependent on the presence of *house*, whereas *house* could stand alone; see **Head**.

Dialect chain – a group of geographically contiguous language varieties where Variety A is mutually intelligible with Variety B, B and C are mutually intelligible, C and D are mutually intelligible, A and C are somewhat mutually intelligible, but A and D are not.

Diglossia – a social situation where power (high status = H) and solidarity (low status = L) languages exist side by side and are two forms of the same (or similar enough) language but with sharply distinct domains of use; H may be used in school, government, and so on, while L may be used at home or more casual settings.

Discourse – characteristic ways of talking about and understanding both conscious and unconscious ideas, attitudes, thoughts, ideologies, and accepted sets of beliefs, all of which affect behaviors and have consequences.

Drift – when an otherwise viable (adapted) organism does not reproduce, owing to chance and/or accident.

Ejective – a stop consonant produced with a double closure of the vocal tract, one forward and one back, where the back closure is maintained until after the forward closure is released.

Epigenesis – the development of an organism; all that occurs after the genetic moment of the DNA being transcribed to produce a protein.

Ergative alignment – where the subjects of transitive verbs are in a particular case known as the ergative, while the subjects of intransitive verbs and objects of transitive verbs are in what is called the absolutive case; contrasts with accusative alignment.

Ethnogroup – a group identifiable by an assemblage of markers including dress, diet, belief systems, rites and rituals, kinship organization, common ancestral or social history, and language; replaces the incoherent concept of race.

Ethnosyntax – the relationship between the grammar of a language and the culture/behavior of its speakers; can be called *cross-cultural pragmatics*.

Etymology – the original meaning of the root of a word; the etymology of the word *etymology* is from the Greek word *etymon* 'true'; linguists no longer think that the so-called true meaning of a word is the meaning the root might have had hundreds or thousands of years ago.

Family – a group of languages exhibiting historical relatedness at a time-depth of 2500–4000 years.

Fusional morphology – many meanings per morpheme; in Spanish, the ending on the verb *hablo* 'I speak' means three things at once: first person, singular, present tense.

Gene – basic unity of molecular inheritance; physically, the particular sequence of a combination of four organic molecules; functionally, the unit that codes for a particular protein.

Genome – the entirety of an organism's basic physical hereditary material.

Genotype – an individual's genetic makeup.

Grammarian – a person who is devoted to maintaining prescriptive rules.

Haplogroup – a group of similar haplotypes that share a common ancestor having the same single nucleotide; commonly referred to as deep ancestry.

Haplotype – a collection of specific alleles in a cluster of tightly linked genes on a chromosome that are likely to be inherited together.

Head – when one syntactic category determines the presence or absence of another; in the phrase *the red house*, 'house' is the head, because it is required for something to be attributed to it, namely its redness; see **Dependent**.

Ideogram – a culturally conventional word-picture of a thing, action, and concept rather than specific sequences of sounds, for example, 'thumbs up' may express "Good job."

Ideology – a set of unquestioned, inherited beliefs that represents the interests of particular individuals, groups, or institutions.

Imperfective – an aspectual distinction denoting incomplete actions common in Slavic languages.

Intonation language – a language where changes in the tonal contour of an entire utterance affect interpretation of that utterance as a statement, question, expression of surprise, and so on.

Intrinsic (spatial frame of reference) – system referring to the location of objects in space with respect to one another on the horizontal place defined in relationship to a part intrinsic to a particular object, say, in relationship to its side, front, or back.

Isolate – a language with no known language relative; the single example of a language stock.

Isolating morphology – one morpheme, one word; in English, the phrase *I see the boy* counts as four morphemes and four words; see **Polysynthetic morphology**.

Lexifier language – language providing the majority of the vocabulary and structural base of a creole or pidgin language.

Lineage – a cover term for any language grouping of any age.

Linguistic marketplace – a term coined by French sociologist, Pierre Bourdieu, referring to the market values different languages have in accord with the perceived socioeconomic status and the prestige of the social groups who speak them.

Linguistic reconstruction – retrospective activity whereby historical records of a language are compared in order to hypothesize what the protolanguage might have been like.

Logogram – an abstract symbol uniformly interpreted as particular sequences of sounds.

Manner of articulation – interactions of the articulators (tongue, teeth, palate, velum) when making a speech sound; the kinds of closures and interactions that produce stops, fricatives, affricates, trills, etc.

Marking – typically prefixes, infixes, or suffixes that show grammatical relationships.

Morpheme – the smallest meaningful component part of a word; the word *unbuckle* is composed of two morphemes, *un-* (a bound morpheme) and *buckle* (a free morpheme).

MtDNA – mitochondrial DNA, found outside the nucleus in a cellular organelle called the mitochondrion; it does not recombine, and it is passed from the mother to all offspring.

Nation – an imagined community that aligns with a sociopolitical structure and that also presupposes a willingness on the part of the members of the community to cohere culturally; often comes with a belief that the nation should be monolingual.

Natural class – class of sounds that share one or more common features, such as voiceless stops in English, which include [b, d, g].

Ontogeny – the individual development of an organism; see **Phylogeny**.

Perfective – an aspectual distinction denoting completed actions common in Slavic languages.

Phenotype – the particular set of characteristics of an organism, many of which are observable; see **Genotype**.

Philology – the practice of taking language out of context in order to study it; traditionally understood as the study of language and its development, and, more specifically, the study of European languages for the purpose of reconstructing their history.

Phoneme – the smallest unit of sounds that can make a meaning contrast; [b] and [p] are both phonemes in English because the words *bit* and *pit* have a meaning contrast.

Phylogeny – the historical development of a species; see **Ontogeny**.

Phylum – a language group with a possible relationship that dates back 15,000–40,000 years or more.

Pidgin – a contact language with no native speakers whose domain of use is highly limited, usually only to trading transactions or on places of enforced labor, such as plantations.

Places of articulation – the points of contact at which the airstream is modified, and an obstruction occurs in the vocal tract to produce phones; these include bilabial, alveolar, palatal, and velar, among others.

Polysynthetic morphology – many morphemes, one word; also called *synthetic* or *incorporating*; see **Isolating morphology**.

Pragmatics – the study of how context affects the interpretation of meaning.

Prosody – rhythm, prominence, or intonation, often used to separate parts of a sentence, emphasize selected elements, or communicate other important information.

Protolanguage – a common ancestor language to a family or a stock; Latin, more specifically Vulgar Latin, is the protolanguage of the Romance languages; the reconstruction language known as Proto-Indo-European is the protolanguage of the Indo-European stock.

Race – a socially constructed and biologically incoherent category that has structured and continues to structure our society by attempting to categorize human groups in terms of a combination of variable factors such as national affiliation/origin, physical characteristics, ethnicity, and so on.

Radical – a semantic marker in Chinese writing, which provides clues about the logogram's meaning.

Reconstruction – a process in comparative linguistics that puts together a picture of a protolanguage from examining the changes that have taken place among related languages to have developed from that proposed protolanguage.

Relative (frame of reference) – system referring to the location of objects in space with respect to one another on the horizontal place expressed in terms of how the viewer perceives the object in relationship to him-/herself.

Residual zone – a relatively small sometimes even enclosed area where a high number of languages from diverse lineages are spoken; see **Spread zone**.

Sandhi – a phonological process that occurs at a word or morpheme boundary.

Spread zone – a geographically spacious area where a low number of languages from few diverse lineages are spoken; see **Residual zone**.

State – the bureaucratic operation that assures the functioning of a nation in terms of laws, police force, educational system, border patrol, and so on.

Stock – a group of languages related at a time-depth of 5000–10,000 years; Indo-European is a language stock.

Tense – the verbal category that marks 'time when'; often includes a present, past, and a future; see **Aspect**.

Tone language – a language in which pitch differences alone signal differences in meaning.

Variety – a version of a language associated with a particular region or social group typically characterized by phonological, syntactic, and/or lexical differences; a neutral term; preferable to the term *dialect*, which often has an associated stigma.

Y-DNA – Y-chromosome passed along solely in the patrilineal line from father to son.

Subject Index

Page numbers referring to figures are in *italics*.

abjad writing, 102
Abkhazia, 238, 241–242
Ablaut, 117
Aboriginal Australians, 22–23, 28, 164
absolute frames of reference, *27*, 262–263,
    288
academies, 127–129, 137
Accademia della Crusca, 127
accusative alignment, 34–35, 86, 180, 208,
    276
accusative case, 301–302
Adams, John, 128
adverbs, 216, 217, 262
African Americans, 79, 143, 314
agglutinative morphology, 52, 170, 178,
    181, 208, 302, 316, 353
agriculture, 175
Ainu people, 80–81
Alexander III of Russia, 68
alleles, 163
alliteration, 30
alphabets, 102–103
    Cyrillic, 110–111
    genealogy, *122*
    Greek, 103–105
    Roman, 103–105, 106, 109, 123,
        299–300

Altai Mountains, 206
alveolar trill, 14
Amazon Basin, 6, 183
America, 36
    see also Mesoamerica; United States
American Airlines, 9–10
analogy, 171–172, 216
analytic morphology, 52
Anatolian steppes theory, 175
Anderson, Benedict, 74
Anglican Church, 108
angloversals, 216
Angola, 139
animal communication, 23–24
anthropometric traits, 270
antipassives, 345–346
aphasia, 265
Apple Corporation, 305, 326
Arabic script, 106, 108–109, 114, 299–300
areal classification, 48–51
areoversals, 216
Arjia Rinpoche, 126
Arnaz, Desi, 17
ASCII-ization, 299–300
aspect, 209, 217, 344
aspiration, 286
ASPM gene, 274–275

Languages in the World: How History, Culture, and Politics Shape Language, First Edition.
Julie Tetel Andresen and Phillip M. Carter.
© 2016 John Wiley & Sons, Inc. Published 2016 by John Wiley & Sons, Inc.

Assad, Bashar al-, 85
assigned identities, 77
Atatürk, Mustafa Kemal, 109, 128
auditory cortex, 266
Austin, Stephen, 4, 155
Australia, 145, 181, 333
Austro-Hungarian Empire, 68
Avars, 209
Azerbaijan, 114, 128
Aztecs, 96

babies, 267
Bactria-Sogdiana, 175–176
bai yue, 201
Bali, 262, 289
Balkans, 203–204
Bangladesh, 136
Baran, Dominika, 309
Bar-Kokhba Revolt, 107
baroque accretions, 281
Barrett, Louise, 268
basal ganglia, 265
Basque people, 186–187
Basque separatism, 244–245
Beauzée, Nicolas, 71
Bedouin, 119
bees, 23
Beggar Prince, The, 19
Belgium, 132
Bellwoor, Peter, 175
Beowulf, 280
biasing effect, 275
Bible, 107–108, 112–113, 204
    book of Genesis, 213
Big Bang Theory, 308
Bildung, 73
bilingualism, 8–9, 142–143, 227
    see also multilingualism
Blommaert, Jan, 113, 325
blood typing, 182
Bloomfield, Leonard, 279
Boas, Franz, 279, 283
Bolsheviks, 110–111
bonobos, 25
Bopp, Franz, 42, 43
borrowings, 170–171
bottleneck, 271, 353

boustrophedon, 103
Brady, William, 333
brain, *264*
Brazil, 81–82, 84
    ethnic Japanese in, 81
BRCA, 162, 163
Bridgestone Corporation, 326
British Empire, 233, 235–236
    see also United Kingdom
British Museum, 195
British Raj, 136–137
Brittany, 6
Broca's area, 265
Brussels, 132
Buddhism, 151–152, 214, 320
Burkina Faso, 131
Burma, 232–234
Burmans, 233–234
Bush, George H.W., 66
Bushmen, 287–288

Cacaopera, 330
calendar plants, 333
California, 16, 282–283
    Gold Rush, 283
calques, 16, 200, 216, 353
Calvet, Louis-Jean, 334
Cambodia, 215
Campbell, Lyle, 177
Canada, 144–145, 245–246
Cape Verde, 281
Caribbean, 56
cases
    accusative, 301–302
    directive, 303–304
caste nouns, 252–253
Catalonia, 140
catastrophism, 12
Catherine the Great, 127
Catholicism, 106, 214–215
Caucasus, 178–179, 278
Cavalli-Sforza, Luigi, 78, 186–187, 270,
    272
Central Asia, 179
central languages, 335
cerebellum, 265
Chad, 236

chain shift, 314, 321
Chaucer, Geoffrey, 130
Chechnya, 238, 239–240
Chennai, 250
Cherokee people, 36–37, 104–105, 109, 250
Cheshirization, 148
Chiapas, 247
Chicago School, 326
Chichen Itza, 206
children, 262
Chile, 339
China, 97, 101–102, 108, 111–112, 131, 201–203
    government-encouraged migrations, 201–203
    historical dialects, 306–307
    language control, 145
    Tibet and, 125–126
    women in, 113
Chinese script, 97, 104
choice, 341–342
chromosomes, 162, *163*
Churchill, Winston, 66
Chu-Sung, 97
citizenship, 79–80
classification, areal, 48–51
classifiers, 31–32, 220, 225–226
click consonants, 272, 284–285
clitic pronouns, 50, 88–89, 203–205, 209, 296–298, 354
Coahuila, 4
code switching, 8, 18–19
coffee, 330
cognates, 45–46, 172–173
cognition, 23, 26–28
cognitive domains, 8
colonialism, 138–139, 200, 215, 235–236
    see also postcolonial states
colonization, 199
complexity, 279–282
compromise pattern, 131
Confucianism, 214, 215
connected traits, 270
consonants, 13–14
    click, 272, 284–285
    clusters, 316–317

ejective, 34, 285–286
    loss, 46
Consumption Guide, 216
contingency, 36
contour tones, 49, 354
coordinations, 26
copula verbs, 149–150
count nouns, 31
Cowell, Andrew, 304
creoles, 216, 218–219, 280–281, 310–313, 321
    see also pidgin languages
Croatia, 53, 63
Cubans, 10
cuneiform script, 95, 97
Cyrillic alphabet, 96, 110–111, 315

Dalai Lama, 126, 147, 320
dancing, 29
Darfur, 235, 236–237
Darwin, Charles, 12, 185, 269
databases, 278
de Gaulle, Charles, 246
de Landa, Diego, 96
dead reckoning, 22, 26–27, 30
Dediu, Dan, 275
deep time, 259–260
deixis, 261–262
Denisovians, 164–165
Department of Motor Vehicles, 146
dependent marking, 277
dependent noun, 17, 55
derived gene, 274
Devanāgari, 96, 103, 123
Devy, Ganesh, 57–58
dialect chains, 7, 11, 75, 76, 284, 287, 306, 309, 329
dictionaries, 13, 75, 117, 337
diglossia, 56, 118–119, 254, 299, 354
diphthongs, 44, 191
directive case, 303–304
discourses, 32–33
dissimilation, 46
Dixon, R.M.W., 181, 277
DNA, 164, 182, 270–274
dollar sign, 100
Domergue, Urbain, 72

dominant language pattern, 132, 136–139
Dominican Republic, 249–250
drift, 273, 354
Dryden, John, 130
Dubar, Robin, 268
Duke University, 160, 310

ears, 266
East India Company, 40
East Timor, 138
Ebrima, 338–339
education, 139–143
Egyptian Revolution, 301
Egyptian script, 100
Egyptians, 95–96
ejectives, 34, 178, 285–286, 343–344, 354
El Salvador, 330
Elizabeth II, 130
emblems, 268
emoji, 123
emotion, 221
empires, 110
Encephalitozoon intestinalis, 162
Encyclopédie, 91
encyclopedist universalism, 195
endangerment, 334–335
    revitalization, 336–339
endearments, 16
Enee, 337
Enfield, Nick, 29
England, 56
English for the Children, 141–142
English as a Second Language (ESL),
    142–144
Enlightenment, 70
epigenesis, 269, 354
epistemology, 69–71
equality, 32
equilibrium linguistics, 279
ergative alignment, 35, 86–87, 148–149,
    276, 344–346, 354
Eritrea, 139
Estonia, 144
ethnic cleansing, 232, 239
ethnic identity, 77–78
ethnogroups, 79, 129, 135, 160, 178,
    230–232, 237–240, 354

Ethnologue, 107
ethnosyntax, 29, 292, 319, 333, 354
etymology, 50, 98, 195, 210
Eurasian steppe spread zone, 206–207
European Union, 326
Euskadi Ta Askatasuna (ETA), 244
evolution, 279
exclusive pronouns, 253–254, 276
expansion, 175, 199
    rhizome model, 213

Facebook, 338
families of languages, 168
Farruko, 15
feet, 268–269
Fishman, Joshua, 142
forkhead proteins, 271
Formosa, 173
FOXP2 gene, 271
frames of reference, 22–23, 26–28, *27*, 34,
    262–263
    absolute, *27*, 262–263, 288
    relative, *27*, 263
France, 72–73, 76, 76–78
    Brittany, 6
Francia, José Gaspard Rodriguez de, 134
Franco, Francisco, 244
Franklin, Benjamin, 74–75
Freedom Fries, 145
French Revolution, 72–73
Friedman, Milton, 325
Friends, 308
Front de libération de Québec (FLQ), 246
functional classification, 55–57
fundamental frequency, 266
fusional morphology, 53

Gaddafi, Muammar al-, 236
Gal, Susan, 347
Galicia, 243
Gandhi, Indira, 137
Gandhi, Mohandas, 136
Gangtai, 308
gender systems, 14–15
generous listening, 260
genes, 162
genetic classification, 46–48

genetic code, 269

genetics, 162–166, 176, 269–270, 270–275
 mutations, 274
 see also DNA; genotype

Genghis Khan, 109, 207, 292, 294, 301, 315

genitive case, 302–303

genocide, 232, 239

genome, 162

genotype, 163, 269, 272, 355

Georges-Picot, François, 65

Georgia, 240–241, 338

German Romanticism, 73–74

Germany, 73–74, 79–80

germination, 46

Ghonim, Wael, 301

Giddens, Anthony, 325

Gil, David, 282

Gimbutas, 176

globalization, 113, 325–327
 1.0 (human global colonization), 164, 183, 200
 2.0 (imperial maritime expansion), 215
 Nepal, 327–328

Goldcorp, Inc., 324

Gorbachev, Mikhail, 240–242

Goths (subculture), 63

grammar
 convergence, 48, 50
 dialects, 83
 ergativity, 35, 86–87, 148–149, 276, 344–346, 354
 mixed languages, 12, 16
 prescriptive, 42–44
 word-order typologies, 53–55

grammarians, 33, 42–43, 64, 71–72, 112, 117, 130, 355

Graubünden, 133

Great Migration, 9–10

Great Plains, 206

Great Schism, 105

Greek alphabet, 103–105

Green, John, 212

Greenberg, Joseph, 53, 182, 272

Grégoire, Abbé Henri, 72, 295–296

Grimm, Jacob, 42, 43, 73, 117

Grimm's law, 42, 45, 58–59, 183

group identity, 7

Group Keepers of the Basque Language, 128

Guatemala, 324–325, 343

Gugu-Yaway people, 333

Guinea, 338

Guinea-Bissau, 281

Gutenberg, Johannes, 92

H languages, 56, 254

Hadden, Alfred Cort, 164

Haiti, 71

hamza, 116–117

Han Chinese, 201

Han Dynasty, 101

hands, 267–268

Hangzhou Bay, 173

haplogroup, 164, 177, 179, 182, 202, 273–274

haplotypes, 164, 355

Harlem, 9–10

Harrison, K. David, 332

Hawaii, 188, 218, 281, 304–306

head marking, 205, 277–278, 295–299

head nouns, 17, 55

Hebrew Bible, 107

Heller, Monica, 326

Henry VIII of England, 108, 112, 213

Herder, Johann Gottfried, 73, 79

Heschel's area, 265

high language, 115–116, 299

Hindu law, 41

hiragana, 104

Hispaniola, 218, 249–250

Hittites, 174

Ho Chi Minh, 223

Hokey-Pokey, 30

Homo habilis, 268–269

homonyms, 100

honorifics, 28–29

Horace, 212

horses, 292–294

howling, 23

Human Genome Project, 162, 195

human leucocyte antigen (HLA), 165

Humboldt, Wilhelm von, 73

Huntington's disease, 269–270

hydronyms, 210, 227
hypercentral languages, 335

I Love Lucy, 17
identity, 76–78
   Hawaiian, 304–306
ideograms, 100, 355
ideology, 33, 57, 66, 69, 72–74, 127, 355
   Japan, 80–82
   see also religion
immigration to United States, 9–10
imperative mood, 87
imperfective, 209–210, 355
implosives, 343–344
inclusive pronouns, 253–254, 276
India, 56, 57–58, 327–329
   minority language support, 140–141
   official languages, 136–137
   Tamil separatism, 145
   Three Language formula, 140–141
Indian Reservations, 250
indicative mood, 87
indigenous languages, 133–135
Indochina, 214–215
Indonesia, 135, 138, 262–263
inflectional morphology, 14, 15, 181, 209, 217, 228, 244
insanity, 63
Institutional Revolutionary Party, 247
International Monetary Fund (IMF), 326
Internet, 112, 338
intonation languages, 49, 219–220
intrinsic frames of reference, *27*
Inuit, 159
Iraq, 66, 85, 86
Irrawaddy Delta, 233–234
Ishi, 283
Islam, 89, 106, 108–109, 214
Islamic State of Iraq and Syria (ISIS), 85
isolates, 45, 80, 178, 183, 186–187, 205, 276
isolating morphology, 53, 307, 355
Israel, 107, 145–146, 256
Istanbul, 204
Italy, 75
Ivory Coast, 338
IW, 268

Jabal an-Nur, 94–95
Jahilliyyah, 119
Jakarta, 282
Janjaweed, 236
Japan, 80–81, 84, 113, 127
Jefferson, Thomas, 71, 74, 128
Jobs, Steven, 105
Johnson, Samuel, 128
Jolie, Angelina, 162
Jones, William, 40–41
Joseph II (Holy Roman Emperor), 68
Journal de la langue française, 72
Judaism, 106, 214
Juntas del Buen Gobierno, 248
jus sanguinis, 79

Kalahari Basin, 48
Kalahari Desert, 283–284
Kamechamha I, 188
Kamechamha III, 188
kanji, 104
Kanzi, 25
Karachay-Balkar, 207
Karens, 232–233
katakana, 110
Kauakukalahale, 305
Ke'eeaumoku, 304
Kennedy, John F., 79
Kennewick Man, 274
Keynes, John Maynard, 325–326
Khoc, 287
Khoikhoi, 287
Khoisan people, 177
Kiarabu, 106
Kibbee, Douglas, 129
K'iche' people, 324
Kilosa District, 331
kipuka, 193
Kirkuk, 86
kora, 151
Koran, 55–56, 94–95
Korea, 145
Kubla Khan, 292
Kurdí Petí, 89
Kurdish people, 84–90
Kurgan theory, 174–175

Kurmanji, 86
Kuwait, 66

Labov, William, 313–314
Ladd, D. Robert, 275
Lambert, Wallace, 245–246
language
  definitions, 4–6, 9
  major and minor types, 33–35
  number of, 6–9
  organic conception, 70
  origins, 9–13
  political conception, 70
  referential function, 24–25
  typologies *see* typologies
language academies, 127–129, 137
language extinction, 332, 334–335
language families, 44
language hotspots, 332–334
language inspectors, 144–145
language isolates, 45
language loop, 23–26, 37
language socialization, 78
language stocks, 145, 168, 177, *184*
  Australia, 181
  Caucasus, 178–179
  Central Asia, 179–180
  East Asia, 181–182
  Europe, 178
  Indian and Pacific Oceans, 180–181
  Middle East, 179
  North Africa, 179
  North and South America, 182–183
  South Asia, 180
  Southeast Asia, 180
Laos, 29
larynx, 267–268
Last of the Mohicans, 36
Latin alphabet, 114, 122
Latvia, 144
law, 41, 129–130
Lawrence, T.E., 66
Lemkos, 243
Lenca, 330
Leopold II of Belgium, 91
Levinson, Stephen, 263
lexifier language, 218, 355

Lhakar Movement, 147
libel, 10
liberty cabbage, 145–146
Libya, 139
Lieberman, Philip, 265, 268
Lili'uokalani, 281, 304–305
lineage, 213, 262, 355
lingua francas, 69
linguistic marketplace, 328, 342, 355
linguistic reconstruction, 43–44, 168–174
  regularity of sound change, 44–45, 170
linguistic standardization
  language academies, 127–129
  national consciousness and, 71–74
linguistic structure, 280
linguistics, 42–43
loan words, 13–15, 89–90, 127–128, 171
logograms, 100, 101–106, 108, 110–111,
  113, 355
Los Angeles County, 146
Louis XIV of France, 71
low language, 299
Lowth, Robert, 43
Lumbee people, 82–83
lungs, 267–268

Macintosh operating system, 305
Magyars, 207–208
major and minor languages, 33–35
majority languages, 141–143
Mali, 338
mammalian brain, 264
Mandela, Nelson, 139, 155
mantras, 151
Mao Zedong, 102, 111–112, 128–129
Māori, 161, 337
Mapuche, 339
Marcos, Subcomandante, 247
Marido en Alquiler, 18
marking, 14, 205, 217, 277–278, 281, 355
mass nouns, 31, 220
Matthews, Stephen, 216, 297
Mayan people, 96
McWhorter, John, 280–281
Melanesia, 180
Mendel, Gregor, 269
Mesoamerica, 48, 96, 123

Mesopotamia, 227
messenger stick, 97
Mexicans, 18
Mexico, 5, 18, 30, 71, 263
    Coahuila y Tejas, 3–4
    Constitution, 134
    Zapatista Uprising, 247–249
Miami, 10, 16
Microcephalia gene, 274
Microsoft Local Language Program,
    338–339
Middle East, *67*, 175, 179
migration, 9–10, 199–200
minority languages
    promotion of, 140
    support for, 140–141
Mishnah, 304
Miskwaasining Nagamojig, 340
missionaries, 106–107, 214–215
mitochondrial Eve, 271
Modern Family, 17
Mongolia, 143, 292, *293*, 315
Mongolian script, 315
mood, 87–88
morphemes, 14–15, 52–53
    boundary, 311
    inflectional, 15
    plural, 32
morphology, 51–52, 344–345
    agglutinative, 52, 170, 178, 181, 208,
        302, 316, 353
    analytic, 52
    fusional, 53
    inflectional, 14, 15, 181, 209, 217, 228,
        244
    isolating, 53, 307, 355
    polysynthetic, 53, 283, 295, 296
    see also syntax
Morris, Simon Conway, 279
mosaic traits, 270
mouth, 266–267
movement, 159–160
mtDNA, 164, 202, 273–274
Muhammad, 94–95, 112
Müller, Friedrich Max, 12
multilingual states, 132–133
    postcolonial, 133–135

multilingualism, 50, 127, 335
    postcolonial, 312
        compromise pattern, 133–135
        dominant language pattern, 136–139
        neutral language pattern, 135–136
    Spain, 244
    United States, 142–143, 154
    see also bilingualism
mutual intelligibility, 6–7
Myanmar, 232–234

Nakasone Yasuhiro, 80
nation states, 69–71
    linguistic standardization, 75–76
    multilingual, 132–133
    national consciousness, 71–75
nationalism, 73–74, 76
Native American Graves Protection and
    Repatriation Act (1990), 289
Native Americans, 36–37, 82–84, 104–105,
    250, 283, 306, 339–341
natural class, 167, 355
Navajo people, 37
navigation, 25
Neanderthals, 164–165
Nehru, Jawaharlal, 137
neoliberalism, 326
Neolithic culture, 165
Nepal, 327–329
Netherlands, 132
neutral languages pattern, 132, 135–136
New York City, 8, 314–315
Nicholas I of Russia, 110
Nichols, Johanna, 175, 203, 206, 275–276,
    277
Niger-Congo, 177
Niigane Ojibwemowin Immersion School,
    339
Nikkeijin, 81
nomadic herding, 206
nominative–accusative languages, 147–148
Noodin, Margaret, 339–340
noosphere, 270
Norman Conquest, 38
North Africa, 179
North American Free Trade Agreement
    (NAFTA), 18, 326

North Atlantic Treaty Organization
  (NATO), 109
North Carolina, 82–84, 104–105
North Korea, 145
nouns
  caste, 252–253
  count, 31
  dependent, 17, 55
  head, 17, 55
  mass, 31
  pluralization, 16–17
Nubia, 235
nucleotides, 162
numeral classifiers, 31–32, 276
Nüshu, 113

Oakland Unified School District, 143
Obama, Barack, 71
object writing, 97–100
object–dative construction, 202
oblique case, 86–87
October Crisis, 246
Oðere, 294–295
official languages, 55–57, 131–139
Okinawans, 80
one-drop rule, 78–79
onomastics, 287–288
onomatopoeia, 24
ontogeny, 5, 23, 355
opportunity, 32
organic conception of language, 70
Ossetia, 240–241
Otto the Great of Germany, 227
Ottoman Empire, 66, 69

Paine, Thomas, 74
Pakistan, 135–136
palatization, 46
Palawa, 329–330
Palestinian Liberation Organization (PLO),
  256
paper, 102
Papua New Guinea, 6, 180
Paraguay, 56, 71, 133
Paris, 76–77
Paris japonica, 162
Parsley Massacre, 249–250

past tense, unknown, 318
perfective, 52, 83, 190–191, 209
peripheral languages, 334
Persian Empire, 207
Persian Gulf War, 66
Persian script, 106
personality, 8
Peru, 71
petroglyphs/petrograms, 99
pharynx, 116
phenotype, 163, 269, 356
Philippines, 137
philology, 40–42, 162, 173, 356
  wave representation, 185–186
phonemes, 14, 188–189
  number of and complexity, 281–282
  trading, 48–49
phonetic influence, 48–49
phoneticization, 99, 100
phonetics, 13–14
phonology, 14
phyla, 45
phylogeny, 5, 23, 356
Pickering, John, 91
pictographs, 98–99
pidgin languages, 216, 310–311
  see also creoles
pinyin, 112
Pipil, 330
places of articulation, 251, 267, 285,
  356
Plautus, 212
plurals, broken, 118
pogroms, 107
Poland, 242–244
police, 146
political conception of language, 70
political power, 108–111
Polynesia, 161–162, 165–166
polysynthetic morphology, 53, 283, 295,
  296
Poplack, Shana, 20
Popul Vih, 346–347
Portugal, 127
postcolonial states
  compromise pattern, 133–135
  dominant language pattern, 136–139

postcolonial states (*Continued*)
  neutral language pattern, 133–135
  see also colonialism
power, 56, 63–64
power languages, 56, 254
PRAAT, 288
pragmatics, 30–31, 356
prescriptivism, 129–131
primates, 25, 263–264, 274
print capitalism, 74–75
production disorders, 265
prokaryotes, 279
promising, 10
pronouns, 222–223
  demonstrative, 262
  inclusive/exclusive, 253–254, 276
  personal, 296–297
pronunciation, 44–45
prosody, 14, 356
protolanguages, 44, 159, 162, 169–170,
    171–172, 178, 208
Psychological Science, 122
Puerto Rican communities, 8
pulp fiction, 102
Pūnana Leo, 305
Pure Tamil movement, 145
purification, 89–90
Puritans, 38
putamen, 265
Putin, Vladimir, 111

Qing Dynasty, 319–320
quasi-states, 238–239
Quebec, 144–145, 245–246
Queen's English, 130, 153
Quiet Revolution, 245–246
quinceañera, 30
Quinhai Province, 125–126
quippa camayocuna, 98
Qur'an, 55–56, 94–95

Rabbit-Proof Fence, 22
race, 78–79, 270
  incoherence of term, 270
  Japan, 80–81
radicals, 101, 152, 357
Rajee, Shankar, 231

Rangoon, 232
Reagan, Ronald, 236, 326
Real Academia Española, 153
reality, 70
rebus, 99
received pronunciation, 130
reception classes, 140
reception disorders, 265
reconstruction (linguistic), 43–44, 168–174
reflexive verbs, 15
refugia *see* residual zones
relative frames of reference, *27*, 263
religion, 105–108, 112–113, 167–168, 320
  as nation, 213–215
  see also missionaries
Renfrew, Colin, 175
reptilian brain, 264
residual zones, 178–179, 203–210, 278,
    342
respiration, 267–268
retroflex consonants, 251
rhizome model, 213, 275
rhythmic balance, 221–222
rivers, 210
RNA, 269
rock drawings, 99
Roman alphabet, 103–105, 106, 109, 123,
    299–300
Roman Empire, 211–212
Roman numerals, 123
Romania, 110
romanji, 104
Romanov dynasty, 68–69
Romanticism, 70, 73–74
Royal Asiatic Society of Bengal, 41
runes, 96
Russia, 68–69, 110–111, 114
  Chechen conflict, 239–240
  Siberian language hotspot, 333–334
  see also Soviet Union
Russian Academy, 127–128

Sackashvili, Mikheil, 242
Sagard-Théodat, Gabriel, 107
San Cristóbal de las Casas, 249
San people, 287
Santa Ana, Otto, 142

Santiago, Bill, 16
Sapir, Edward, 9, 279
Script Encoding Initiative, 338
scripts
    Arabic, 106, 108–109, 114, 299–300
    Chinese, 97, 104
    cuneiform, 95, 97
    Cyrillic, 96, 110–111, 315
    Egyptian, 100
    Persian, 315
    Roman, 103–105, 106, 109, 123,
        299–300
    Uyghir, 315
Scythian ploughmen, 227
Sears, Richard, 124
second-language learners, 281–282
Secret History of the Mongols, The, 301
Sejong, 109
Se-quo-ya, 104–105, 109
Sheridan, Thomas, 43
Sibawayh, 117
Siberia, 333–334
sign languages, 1, 4, 6, 47, 146
SIL International, 107
Singapore, 216
Sino-Tibetans, 181–182
Sipacapa, 324
Sixteen Candles, 30
skeleton, 267
skin colour, 270
slander, 10
slang, 18, 120, 143, 160
slavery, 64, 81, 112–113
Slavic people, 209–210
Slovakia, 144
Snow White and the Seven Dwarfs, 19
social media, 301
*Social Stratification of (r) in New York City
    Department Stores, The,* 314
socialization, 78
solidarity languages, 55–56
Somalia, 139
sound symbolism, 20
South Africa, 139
South Asia, *233*
South Korea, 145
South Ossettia, 238, 240, 241

South Sudan, 237–238, 310–312
Southeast Asia, 180
Soviet Union, 110–111, 238–239
    collapse, 325
    see also Russia
Spain, 127, 140, 244–245
    see also Catalonia
Spanglish, 4
Spanish Armada, 36
spatial adverbs, 262
spatial frames of reference, 22
speech acts, 10
Sprachbund, 50
spread
    rhizome model, 213, 275
    tree models, 183–184
    wave models, 185–186
spread zones, 205–206, 208, 210, 273, 310
Sri Lanka, 230–231, 250
Stalin, Josef, 111, 114
standardization, 71–74, 127–129
steppe society, 207
Stewart, Jon, 21
stock (language), 168
subjunctive mood, 87–88
Sudan, 177, 235–238, 310–312
supercentral languages, 335
Sweden, 336
Swift, Jonathan, 128, 130
Switzerland, 56, 132–133
Sykes, Sir Mark, 65–66
Sykes–Picot agreement, 65–66
syllabaries, 103–104
syllable signs, 100
symbolic resources, 70
syntax, 16, 253, 268, 346
    cross-linguistic influence, 50
    see also ethnosyntax; morphology
Syria, 86

taboo replacement, 173
Taco Bell, 20
Tahrir Square, 301
Taipei, 309
Taiwan, 173, 308–309
tally, 97
Tamil Nadu, 58, 145, 250

Tamil Tigers, 231
Tanganyika African National Union, 331
Tanzania, 272, 331–332
Tasmania, 180, 329–330
Tejas, 4
Telangana, 327
Telemundo, 18
telenovela, 18, 21
television, 17–18
tense, 150–152, 209, 357
  aspect and, 262
  markers, 191
  past, 171, 185
  present, 210
Teotihuacan, 206
terms of address, 16
Texas, 4, 16
texting, 299
Thatcher, Margaret, 326
Thomas, George, 145
Thonmi Sambhota, 152
Thoth, 96
Tibet, 125–127, 131, 146–147
Tibetan Buddhist Canon, 152
Timberlake, Alan, 210
Timor-Leste, 138
Tocharians, 174
Tofalaria, 333–334
tone languages, 49, 220
tonogenesis, 148
Toribio, Jacqueline Almeida, 19
tourism, 328
Trail of Tears, 36–37
Treasures of the Azerbaijani Language, 114
Trujillo, Rafael, 249–250
Ts'ang-Chieh, 97
tunings, 24–25
Turkey, 85, 108–109, 114
  Language Commission, 128
Tuvan, 28
typologies, 51–55
  head/dependent, 55
  morphological, 51–53
  word order, 53–55

Ueda Kazutoshi, 80
Ukrainians, 243

Ulaan Batar, 315
Unicode Consortium, 105, 114, 123,
  337–338
uniformitarianism, 12
United Arab Emirates, 300
United Kingdom, 72, 146
  see also British Empire
United States, 64, 145–146
  African Americans, 79, 143, 314
  educational system, 141–142, 142–143
  immigration, 79
  Indian Reservations, 250
  multilingualism, 142–143, 154
  national languages, 131–132
  Native Americans, 36–37, 82–84,
    104–105, 250, 283, 306, 339–341
  presidency, 71–72
  race politics, 78–79
  see also America; California; North
    Carolina
unknown past tense, 318
Uyghir script, 315
Uyghur, 292
Uzhhorod, 160

variationism, 313–314, 322
variety (of a language), 6–7, 8, 9
Vatican Bank, 227
Vaugelas, Claude Favre de, 129
velar stop, 34
Venezuela, 71
verbs
  conjugation, 14–15
  copula, 149
  morphology, 344–345
  suffixes, 15
  volitional, 150–151
Vergara, Sofia, 17
vergonha, 73, 75–76
vervet monkeys, 25
Vidunda Ward, 331, 342
Vietnam, 106, 198–199, 219–220
viscera, 267
vocal tract, 266
Voice of America Radio, 66
Volga, 210
volitional verbs, 150–151

Volk, 73
vowels, 13–14

Walkabout, 22–23, 26
wampum belts, 97–98
war, 10
War Measures Act, 246
Washington, George, 75
Waterman, Thomas, 283
Weinreich, Max, 20
Wernicke's area, 265
Whitney, William Dwight, 12
Whorf, Benjamin Lee, 48–51
William the Conqueror, 38, 295
Wisconsin, 339–341
Wolf, Friedrich August, 42
Wolfram, Walt, 13
wolves, 23
women, 113
Wong-Fillmore, Lily, 142
word order typologies, 53–55
word play, 99–100
World Atlas of Language Structure,
    278
World Bank, 326–327
World Trade Organization, 327
World War II, 242
written language, 56, 260
    abjad, 102
    alphabets, 102–103
    electronic, 299–301
    object writing, 97–100

origins, 95–97
political power and, 108–111
religion and, 105–108
scripts
    Arabic, 106, 108–109, 114, 299–300
    Chinese, 97, 104
    cuneiform, 95, 97
    Cyrillic, 96, 110–111, 315
    Egyptian, 100
    Persian, 315
    Roman, 103–105, 106, 109, 123,
        299–300
    Uyghir, 315
    syllabary, 103–104
    Tibet, 152
    writing materials, 102
    writing systems, 100–105, 337–338

Xinhua News Agency, 145
Xinjiang, 174

Y chromosome, 164, 273–274
Yahi people, 283
Yangon, 232
Y-chromosomal Adam, 271
Yupik, 28
yuppies, 308

Zentella, Ana Celia, 142–143
Zhang, Qing, 307–308
Zionism, 107, 110
    see also Israel

Language Index

Abkhaz, 13, 241–242
Achi, 324
African American English, 52, 64
Afrikaans, 139, 155n5, 194, 255, 277, 287
Ainu, 80, 127, 196n17
Akkadian, 95, 186
Albanian, 50, 173, 194, 196n10, 204
Alsatian, 72
American Sign Language (ASL), 4, 24, 47, 146
Apache, 182
Arabic, xx, 8, 51, 54, 56, 69, 77, 85, 89–90, 92, 95, 98, 102, 114–121, 124n8, 128, 136, 145, 146, 179, 214, 235–238, 254, 255, 273, 285, 299–301, 310, 311, 322n9, 327, 335
Arapaho, 306
Armenian, 68, 146, 185, 194, 238, 285, 335
Assyrian, 98
Asuri, 85
Austro-German, 68
Aymara, 133, 194
Azerbaijani, 114, 118, 123n6, 128, 238

Bahasa Indonesian (BI), 110, 135, 138, 165
Balinese, 135, 262

Bambara, 335, 338
Basque, 35, 45, 59, 72, 90, 128, 178, 186–187, 196n18, 211, 244, 257n8, 260, 276, 278, 346
Belarusian, 105
Bengali, 58, 135, 136, 277
Berber, 69, 106, 179, 227n11, 272
Beria, 236
Biblical Hebrew, 102, 107, 128, 214
Bimbashi Arabic, 310
Breton, 6, 72, 90
British Sign Language, 47
Bulgarian, 50, 59, 96, 105, 203–204, 207, 209
Buriat, 315
Burmese, 49, 220, 232–234, 256n3, 341

Cacaopera, 330
Cantonese, 7, 49, 64, 108, 142, 181, 202–203, 216–217, 255, 307, 309
Cape Verdean Creole, 281, 312
Catalan, 7, 72, 140, 211, 244, 256n6
Catawba, 250
Cebuano, 137, 194
Chamorro, 194
Chamus, 263
Chaozhou, 307
Chechen, 178, 210, 239, 242

Languages in the World: How History, Culture, and Politics Shape Language, First Edition.
Julie Tetel Andresen and Phillip M. Carter.
© 2016 John Wiley & Sons, Inc. Published 2016 by John Wiley & Sons, Inc.

Cherokee, 54, 71, 92n6, 104–105, 109, 124n11, 183, 250, 322n4, 337
Chinese, 7, 32, 49, 51, 52, 53, 98, 101–102, 127–128, 145, 171, 200–201, 306–308, 319–320
Chinese Pidgin English, 216
Ch'ol, 248, 344
Chontal, 284
Chuj, 284
Chukchi, 182, 194
Coptic, 124n8, 235
Corsican, 72
Creek, 250
Croatian, 7, 50, 63, 68, 105
Czech, 7, 76, 105, 243, 335

Danish, 7, 51, 227n5, 336
Delaware, 182
Digueño, 296
Diola, 335
Dutch, 7, 8, 37, 56, 59, 132, 135, 153, 155n5, 251, 281
Dyirbal, 194, 276, 346
Dyula, 131, 338

Efik, 96
English, xviii, 1ff, 13ff, 24, 29ff, 36ff, 37, 38n2, 38n3, 41ff, 54, 56, 59, 60n10, 87, 89, 97–98, 104, 117, 127, 128, 130, 131, 137, 138, 139, 141–143, 145, 153, 155n7, 171–172, 216, 226, 227n5, 234, 237, 245, 255, 257n9, 280, 281, 313, 314, 320, 321, 322n10, 322n11, 336, 341
Estonian, 45, 59, 144, 154, 178, 208
Etruscan, 122, 178, 186, 211

Farsi, 106, 146
Fijian, 98, 194
Filipino, 137
Finnish, 45, 49, 59, 68, 98, 178, 208, 316, 336
Flemish, 7, 72, 132, 227n5
Formosan, 165
French, xviii, 7, 8, 15, 16, 29, 44–46, 49, 51, 54, 56, 58, 59, 68, 69, 71, 72–73, 75, 76ff, 88, 110, 118–120, 124n13, 127–128, 129–133, 144–145, 153, 167,

171, 199, 200, 211, 212, 214, 218, 225, 226n1, 227n12, 245–246, 249, 257n9, 267, 281, 292, 295–299, 310–313, 322n2, 327, 335
French Canadian, 245–246
French Sign Language, 47
Frisian, 227n5
Fujian, 181
Fula, 131
Fur, 236

Galician, 244
Gascon, 211
Georgian, 54, 69, 178, 186, 210, 238, 240–241, 276, 338
German, xviii, 7, 24, 44, 49, 53, 55, 56, 59, 68, 76, 96, 97, 117, 132–133, 153, 171–172, 213, 225, 226n2, 227n5, 242, 243, 255, 281, 310, 317, 336, 347
Gothic, 98, 208
Greek, 41, 42, 44, 45, 50, 51, 56, 57, 69, 98, 102–103, 105, 122, 163, 164, 168, 172, 174, 185, 186, 195n1, 196n10, 201, 204, 211, 213, 227n8, 261, 270, 271, 354
Guaraní, 56, 133–134
Gugu-Yaway, 333
Guinea-Bissau Creole, 281, 312
Gujarati, 136, 194
Gullah, 9
Guugu Yimithirr, 22, 26, 34, 38, 181

Haitian Creole, 216, 218–219
Hausa, 34, 54, 194
Hawaiian, xx, 54, 115, 162, 166–168, 170, 187–194, 279–280, 304–306, 337
Hawaiian Creole English, 218, 281
Hebrew, 43, 57, 95, 102, 106, 107–108, 128, 179, 213, 214, 242, 304, 337
Hindi, 7, 48, 56, 58, 96, 106, 124n12, 136, 137, 140–141, 147, 355
Hinglish, 124n12
Hittite, 174
Hmong, 29, 124n12, 182
Hokkien, 307
Hoklo, 309

Hungarian, 17, 45, 50, 60n8, 68, 69, 76, 144, 178, 208, 277, 316, 347
Hunnish, 208

Iberian, 186
Icelandic, 227n5
Igbo, 96
Ilokano, 49, 137
Inuit, 182
Irish, 79, 96, 260
Italian, 7, 16, 44, 46, 49, 56, 59, 68, 75, 110, 127, 133, 138–139, 153, 171, 211–212, 227n4, 253
Iu Mien, 182

Jacaltec, 248
Jamamadi, 54
Japanese, 28, 32, 37, 45, 49, 54, 55, 80–81, 84, 104, 108, 142, 145, 179, 186, 218, 220, 301, 306, 326
Javanese, 135
Juba Arabic, 310, 312

Kalaw Kawaw Ya, 333
Kamba, 37
Kanjobal, 248
Kannad'a, 48, 123n4, 180, 194
Kaqchikel, 324
Karachy-Balkar, 207
Karen(ni), 232, 341
Ket, 182
Khmer, 49, 194
Khoi, 177
Ki'che', xx, 34, 35, 324–325, 342–347
Kikongo, 82
Kimbundu, 82
Komi, 178
Korean, 28, 32, 45, 47, 49, 54, 108, 109, 111, 127, 142, 145, 179, 186, 208, 220, 301, 306
Kreyol, 312
Kreyòl, 56, 249–250
Krio, 312
Kuku-Yalanji, 383
Kulkalgowya, 333
Kurdish, xx, 35, 69, 85–90, 344
Kurmanji, 85, 86
Kutubu, 181

Ladino, 214
Lao, 7, 29, 180
Latin, 41, 44, 46, 56, 57, 58, 68, 69, 75, 76, 91n2, 95, 98, 110, 124n4, 170, 172, 195n1, 195n3, 196n10, 199, 201, 211–212, 270, 227n4, 227n11, 278, 296, 297, 313
Latvian, 68, 144
Lemko, 244, 255
Lenca, 330
Lithuanian, 194
Lumbee English, 83
Luo, 194

Maasai, 37
Macedonian, 50, 96, 204, 209, 228n28
Magati Ke, 333
Malagasy, 54, 170, 194
Malay, 32, 49, 135, 165, 217, 218, 220, 306, 335
Malayālam, 123n4, 180
Maltese, 194
Mam, 344
Manchu, 179, 306
Mandarin, 7, 64, 108, 125, 126, 142, 147, 165, 181, 203, 216, 255, 307, 308, 309, 341
Maninka, 194, 338, 339
Māori, 162, 168, 196n19, 337
Mapudungun, 339, 350
Marathi, 48, 58, 96, 136
Martha's Vineyard Sign Language, 47
Masalit, 236
Massachusetts, 182
Matengo, 331–332
Mayan, 96, 106, 134, 248
Menonimi, 182
Migrelian, 241–242
Miskito, 194
Mixtec, 134
Mohawk, 194
Mongallese, 310
Mongolian, xviii, xx, 54, 96, 108, 109, 140, 143, 179, 208, 292, 294, 301–303, 315–320, 322n2, 322n12, 322n13
Moni, 181
Motozinlec, 248

Nahualá, 343
Nahuatl, 183
Nangikurrunggurr, 333
Navajo, 182, 194
Ndebele, 139
Nepali, 96, 327–329, 342, 349
Ngbaka, 237
Ngengiwumerri, 333
Nigarakudi, 333
N'ko, 338
Nootka, 53
Norman French, 295
Norwegian, 7, 49, 60n9, 96, 227n5, 336

Occitan, 72, 73, 90, 211, 245
Ojibwe, 227n8, 339–341, 350
Okinawan, 80, 127
Old Bulgarian, 96
Old Church Slavonic, 96, 196n10
Old Egyptian, 235
Old English, 16, 30, 49, 54, 60n10, 96,
    112, 171, 196n10, 226n1, 280, 294–295
Old Norse, 98, 171, 294–295
Old Nubian, 235
Old Persian, 41
Old Phoenician, 103
Oneida, 183
Oriya, 136, 194
Ossetic, 207, 240
Otomí, 194

Palawa, 329–330
Pampango, 137
Pa'O, 232
Papiamentu, 194
Pennsylvania Dutch, 337
Peremka, 181
Persian, 40, 69, 89, 90, 106, 118, 124n16,
    146, 207, 238, 277
Pidgin, 312
Pilipino, 137
Pipil, 330
Pirahã, 194
Polish, xviii, 7, 24, 53, 59, 98, 105, 110,
    129, 146, 209–210, 242, 252, 255
Portuguese, xviii, 7, 44, 46, 48, 49, 81, 82,
    110, 138, 139, 211–212

Powhatan, 71, 91n6
Provençal, 211
Punjabi, 136, 255
Putonghua, 125, 131, 152

Q'anjob'al, 344
Quechua, 8, 123n6, 133
Quiché *see* K'iche'

Roma, 50, 60n7
Romanian, xviii, 16, 30, 32, 44, 46, 49, 50,
    59, 69, 88, 110, 203, 204, 205,
    211–212, 227n7
Romansch, 133, 211
Rotokas, 13
Russian, xvii, 7, 59, 60n9, 68, 96, 98, 105,
    107, 110–111, 127, 144, 154, 238, 240,
    242, 277, 320, 335
Rusyn, 244
Ruthenian, 244, 255

Saami, 208
Salish, 346
Samoan, 98, 162, 167–168
Samoyed, 45
San, 177
Sanskrit, 41, 44, 57–58, 136, 141, 145,
    196n10, 251
Scottish, 51
Scythian, 208
Sedang, 13
Seneca, 183
Serbian, 7, 50, 63, 105–106
Sere, 237
Seychellois Creole, 312
S'gaw Karen, 232
Shoshone, 337
Shuswap, 277
Silesian, 243
Singlish, 215, 216–217
Sinhala, 115, 230–231, 256n2
Sipacapense, 324
Slovak, 7, 68, 76, 105, 144
Slovenian, 105
Somali, 69, 139, 194, 285
Sorani, 85, 86, 89
Sotho, 139

Spanglish, 1, 8, 11, 13ff, 50, 153
Spanish, xviii, 1ff, 13ff, 36, 44, 46, 49, 51, 56, 58, 59, 71, 75, 79, 106, 110, 120, 127–128, 133–134, 137, 139, 140, 142, 146, 153, 154n2, 155n4, 167, 211–212, 214, 225, 247ff, 277, 279, 311, 327, 330, 335, 336, 343, 347
Squamish, 54
Sumerian, 95, 186
Swahili, xviii, 52, 106, 110, 120, 170, 177, 331, 335, 341
Swazi, 139
Swedish, 7, 49, 59, 227n5, 336
Switzerdeutsch (Swiss German), 59, 133
Syriac, 85
Syrian, 98

Tagalog, 49, 137, 170–171, 218
Tahitian, 162, 167–168, 188
Taiwanese, 7, 181, 216
Taiwanese Mandarin, 165, 307–310
Tajik, 48, 106, 124n16, 194
Tamil, xx, 8, 48, 58, 115, 137, 141, 145, 180, 231, 250–254, 256n2
Tatar, 68, 91n3, 111
Telanganese, 327
Telugu, 123n4, 180, 327
Tetum, 138
Thai, 7, 49, 180, 220, 307
Tibetan, xx, 35, 49, 54, 115, 125–126, 131, 146–153, 181, 202, 234, 266, 320, 344
Tigrinya, 194
Tocharian, 174
Tofa, 333–334
Tojolabal, 248
Tok Pisin, 194
Tongan, 162, 168
Tsaatan, 315
Tsonga, 139
Tswana, 139
Turkish, 8, 50, 52, 69, 89, 109, 111, 118, 120, 128, 146, 170, 179, 207, 214, 238

Turkmen, 85
Tuvan, 28
Tzeltal, 134, 247, 248, 263, 344
Tzotzil, 247, 248–249, 344
Tz'utujil, 324

Ukrainian, 7, 68, 69, 96, 105, 242–243, 244, 255, 256
Urarina, 54
Urdu, 7, 48, 106, 118, 135, 136
Uyghur, 194, 315, 322n1

Valencian, 244, 256n6
Venda, 139
Viduna, 331–332, 341
Vietnamese, xviii, xx, 24, 31–32, 49, 54, 106, 108, 114, 171, 148, 180, 198–199, 200–201, 214, 219–226, 266, 306
Visayan, 137

Walloon, 211
Walpiri, 313
Welsh, 48, 54, 146, 194
West African Pidgin English, 312–313
Wolof, 177, 218, 335
Wyandot, 107, 124n13, 183

Xhosa, 139, 155n6, 194, 255
!Xóõ, xx, 13, 124n17, 272, 283–288

Yana, 283
Yélîdnye, 313
Yeniseian, 182
Yiddish, 106, 214, 243
Yoruba, 82, 177
Yucatec, 134
Yupik, 28

Zapotec, 134, 285
Zoque, 248
Zulu, 139, 177

CPSIA information can be obtained
at www.ICGtesting.com
Printed in the USA
JSHW042240160222
23000JS00002B/6